Marketing Strategy Masterclass

The 100 questions you need to answer to create your own winning marketing strategy

For Jack

This book is much more Jack's than he will ever believe.

Far more than just 'being his turn'; to see focus and determination in one so young has served, more than once, to keep me working on what has turned out to be a very long project indeed.

Thank you Jack

Marketing Strategy Masterclass

The 100 questions you need to answer to create your own winning marketing strategy

Including the new 'SCORPIO' model of Market Strategy

First Edition

Paul Fifield

AMSTERDAM • BOSTON • HEIDELBERG • LONDON • NEW YORK • OXFORD
PARIS • SAN DIEGO • SAN FRANCISCO • SYDNEY • TOKYO
Butterworth-Heinemann is an imprint of Elsevier

Butterworth-Heinemann is an imprint of Elsevier

Linacre House, Jordan Hill, Oxford OX2 8DP, UK
30 Corporate Drive, Suite 400, Burlington, MA 01803, USA

First edition 2008

British Library Cataloguing-in-Publication Data
A catalogue record for this book is available from the British Library

Library of Congress Cataloging-in-Publication Data
A catalog record for this book is available from the Library of Congress

ISBN: 978-0-7506-8631-0

For information on all Butterworth-Heinemann publications visit our website at elsevierdirect.com

Typeset by Charon Tec Ltd., A Macmillan Company

Printed and bound in Hungary

08 09 10 11 12 10 9 8 7 6 5 4 3 2 1

Contents
(short form)

Contents

Preface

> 'When China wakes it will shake the world'
>
> *Napolean Bonaparte*
> *Emperor of the French*

I have wanted to write this book for a very long time – but events and circumstances always prevented me from doing so.

This is a different book from my normal publications – it is much more of a 'how to' version than normal, and unashamedly so.

Rather than try to write a learned tome, I have tried to write a book that:

- Makes sense to the medium-sized business that books, that universities and professional institutes (mentioning no names) singularly fail to serve. Good or 'professional' marketing is absolutely *not* the sole preserve of the Unilevers and Proctor & Gambles of this world, and must be spread wider.
- Has a beginning, a middle (muddle?) and an end, that can be followed by the busy practitioner.
- Is true to the *REAL* nature of marketing, not what marketing seems to have become in those larger organisations – advertising and promotion.
- Will (I hope) prove the inspiration for all those UK and European organisations determined to survive and flourish against 'unfair' price competition from China, India and other developing countries – *price is absolutely not* the only game in town!

Ultimately then, this book is about do-it-yourself (DIY) Marketing Strategy. I have worried long and hard over the 100 questions and, although they are not perfect they are, as far as I can make them for this edition, the best process for developing your own marketing strategy that I can devise.

Finally, why the title? Marketing Strategy Masterclass – apart from the question of perceived value (see Chapter 11), Marketing Strategy is just too important to be consigned to 'dummies' – only 'masters' need apply.

Avid readers will notice a small overlap with the 'sister publication' 'Marketing Strategy, 3rd edition', published in 2007. The two volumes cover the same content but in very different ways, for different audiences.

I wish you a very profitable time using this book.

Paul Fifield
Winchester
October, 2007

Introduction

> 'Ideas are far more powerful than guns. We don't let our people have guns, why should we let them have ideas?'
>
> *Joseph Stalin (1878–1953), General Secretary of the Communist Party of the Soviet Union's Central Committee 1922–1953*

This book is not necessarily intended to be a 'good read' although I believe it has its moments. This book is intended, first and foremost, to be a step-by-step guide to help you to develop a marketing strategy for your business. In other words, a simple plan that will help you build a 'safer' business. By *safer* I mean building a business that is not focused primarily on the product or service that you provide but on the customers who pay you to 'hire' your product or service to do a job that they believe needs doing.

As Joseph Stalin recognised, *ideas* are far more powerful than guns. Ideas of how to create new, customer-pleasing offerings will always be more powerful than cutting prices. This book is about helping you to create those ideas.

This book is aimed, above all, at 'marketing' practitioners, no matter the title under which they operate, these are the people who have to plan and implement customer solutions for a profit. In other words, every business owner or manager who stands or falls according to whether their customers decide to buy the product or service offered.

With such an audience in mind I have decided to break down the strategy approach into a three-step process:

- Part One will look at the preparatory analysis that is essential to the development of any robust, practical marketing strategy
- Part Two looks in more depth at the specific question of how to develop and plan marketing strategy using the SCORPIO approach
- Part Three considers how your business might co-ordinate the SCORPIO elements to best effect
- Part Four separates marketing strategy from marketing tactics and considers how strategy is implemented.

The approach of this book

Having been lulled into a sense of security so far by (I hope) everything seeming to make some sense, we arrive at the diagram. The good news is

A flow chart for evolving marketing strategy

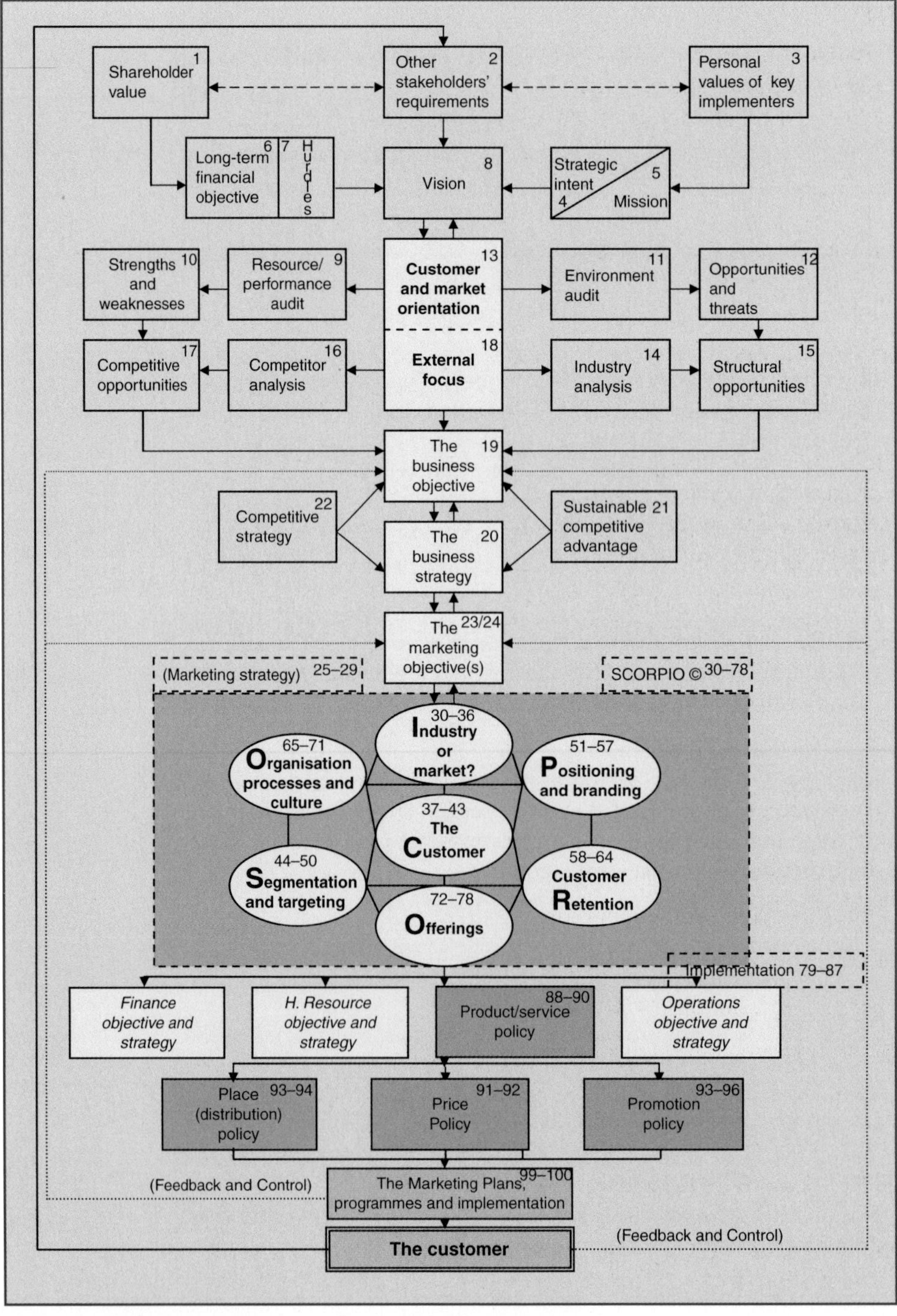

that the whole strategic process can be represented in one flow chart; the bad news is that it is more than a little complicated and we will need the whole of the rest of the book to go through it! A firm believer in the need to get all the pain out of the way at the outset so that we can fully enjoy the recuperation, I have laid out the full plan in all its malevolence in the flowchart.

Assuming that your eyes are still focusing, a few points should be made at this stage:

- This chart is intended to show the *approximate relationships* between the various aspects, analyses and decisions that go to make up the business and market strategy formulation process.
- The arrows are intended to show one *possible* route for logical thought through the process.
  - However, as we shall see later, this is one, but not the only route
  - The numbers in the boxes relate to the 100 questions that form the basis of this book.
- Since every organisation faces different competitive and market conditions, then no single strategic process can possibly be proposed to suit all needs.
  - This chart should *not* be viewed as a blueprint.
- Practitioners should feel perfectly free to adapt and amend the diagram to meet their own needs.
  - Certainly some sections might be jumped and others emphasised to meet specific requirements.
- Before you skip or downgrade a stage in the process, make sure that you fully understand what it is you are leaving out!
- We will use this chart as a guide through the book – I have constructed the series of 100 questions based on this diagram.

MARGIN NOTES

In the same way that an ant may eat an elephant (a spoonful at a time), we will have to break the complete diagram down to bite-size pieces, before we can hope to put any of this into practice. To do this it is probably easier to see the whole diagram as a composite of the usual steps in strategy development. The four key stages are:

- Part One: Preparing for the marketing strategy
- Part Two: Developing the marketing strategy (SCORPIO)
- Part Three: Co-ordinating SCORPIO
- Part Four: Implementation, from strategy to tactics

■ Part One: Preparing for the marketing strategy

Before we can hope to develop even the most rudimentary strategic decisions, a degree of analysis is required. Working with customers may be more art than science but working on gut feeling is not the same thing as working by the seat of the pants. We should never forget that the quality of gut feeling or intuition improves with the amount of painstaking research that goes before. The groundwork preparation stage can be put into three steps.

- Understand the internal business drivers:
  - There are essential forces alive in every organisation that cannot just be ignored.
  - The owners and key managers of the organisation are human beings and they have needs, wants and demands that your organisation must satisfy.
  - You must understand these important forces as many of them can run directly counter to the needs of the customer.
  - It will be your delicate task to manage these often opposing demands so as to satisfy as many people as possible inside the organisation while creating unbeatable value for the customer.
  - Easy!

The internal business drivers

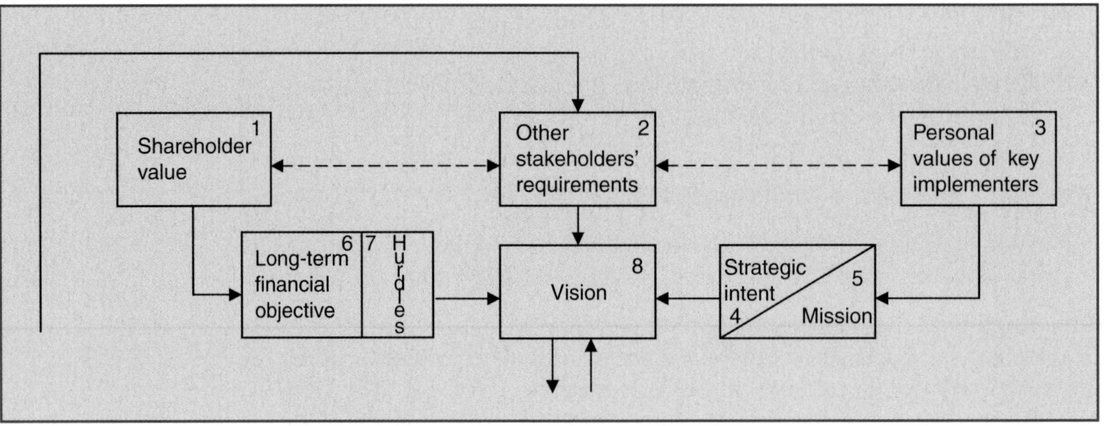

- Understand the external environment:
  - No modern organisation, regardless of size, can pursue its goals in disregard of the business environment within which it operates.
  - We will look at what can be learned from the environment.
  - Have you ever wondered why, when the same facts exist to be uncovered by all, some organisations are successful in the marketplace while others are not?
  - The secret normally lies, not in the quality of the information itself, but rather in the way that it is perceived and interpreted.
  - Customer and market orientation is the key – one that is obvious to smaller companies but somehow less obvious as organisations get bigger.

The external environment

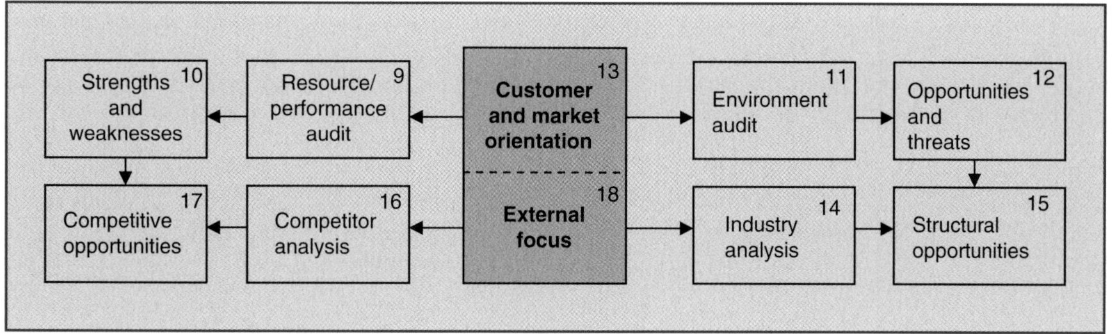

- Understand (or develop) the business strategy:
  - The whole area of business strategy experienced something of a hype during the 1980s and 1990s, mostly produced by the thoughts and writings of Harvard's Michael Porter and imitators.
  - While Porter's books adorn countless thousands of influential bookshelves, developing business strategy now seems to be no easier than it ever was.

The business strategy

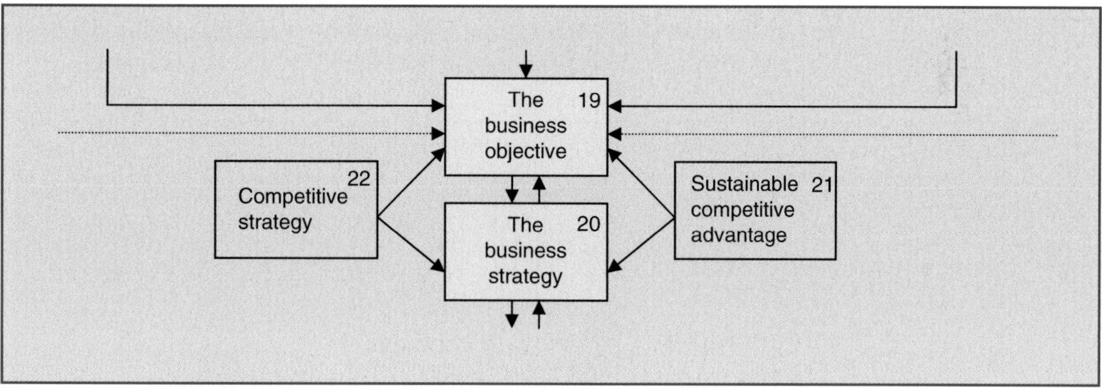

■ Part Two: Developing the marketing strategy (SCORPIO)

This, the main part of this book, covers the various elements of marketing strategy. I have been careful to separate marketing strategy from marketing tactics and have concentrated on the critical influence of the market on the organisation's activity.

MARGIN NOTES

The SCORPIO model of marketing strategy has been many years in the making, working with real practitioners in real businesses facing real problems. Many of the headings in this part will be familiar to you although how they fit together may not. Nobody wants to play the role of guinea pig when dealing with strategic issues, practitioners want solutions that work; that have worked before, that will produce the results.

As a testimonial for the approach, I can quote the case of a recent client who sent the SCORPIO model that we had been working with for six months to an academic friend for his opinion. The blistering email reply was 'But is all the stuff we've seen before, there's nothing new here at all'. Exactly. I couldn't have put it better myself.

■ Part Three: Co-ordinating your marketing strategy

Now that you have all the elements of your marketing strategy in place, what are you going to do with them? You will need to organise the components into:

- The minimum (backbone) strategy that allows you to compete in your chosen market
- The defensive strategy so that, when you win all the new business, you don't lose it all just as easily
- The offensive strategy so that you (and everyone else in the organisation) knows exactly how to win the right (not just any) business.

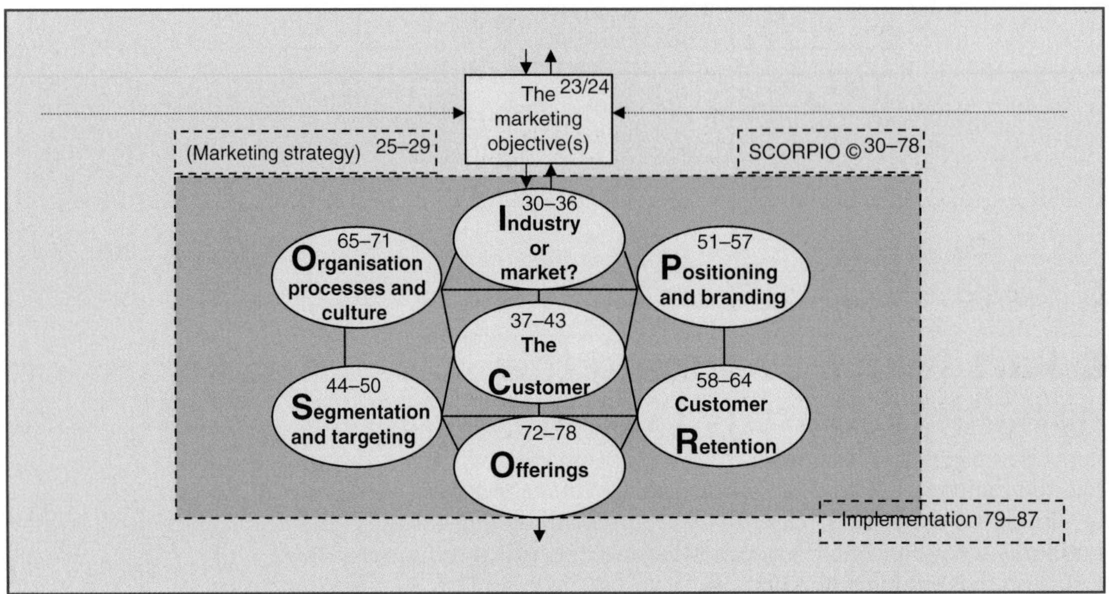

■ Part Four: Implementation, from strategy to tactics

The final section deals with the subject area that is probably most familiar to day-to-day practitioners. I shall not deal with the area of marketing tactics in any depth – this job has been very successfully accomplished in a number of other publications and you, like me, probably have your favourites.

The main aim of this part is to demonstrate the relationship between marketing strategy and tactics. More importantly, we will look at the whole area of strategic implementation, an area far too often ignored by strategic writing.

This section will look at sometimes invisible barriers to the implementation of marketing strategy and what can be done about them. It will also look at using 'the system' to help support and implement sometimes radical ideas that marketing strategy represents.

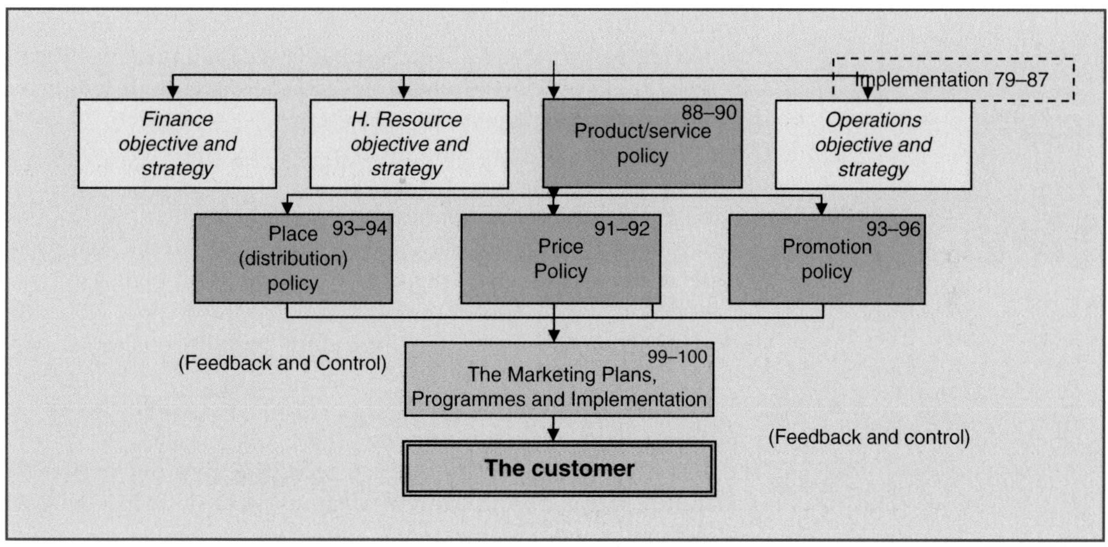

■ Getting started

Just before we jump into the detail, there are one or two 'definitions' that we need to agree. This is important, not to be pedantic but to make sure that we are all talking about the same thing later on. The key questions we need to answer are:

- What is marketing?
- What is strategy?
- What is marketing strategy?

MARGIN NOTES

Definitions of marketing are all over the place but enormous confusion still persist about exactly what marketing is, and is meant to be, all about. The concept is not new, it is not difficult to understand, it is not difficult to explain to the troops and our customers love it. Why then does it seem almost impossible to implement?

The headings are:

- Marketing is all about the market, and about customers.
- Originally, marketing was intended to be the co-ordinating activity designed to identify, anticipate and focus the rest of the organisation on customer needs.
- Today, too many organisations (and marketers themselves) think that marketing is about producing the advertising, the website and the brochures.
  - We need to be clear here, 'marketing' is *not* the same thing as 'marketing communications and services'.
  - However, this misapprehension is so widespread that the word 'marketing' has effectively been hijacked to mean communications – often the business development function has grown to take over the more important aspects of marketing.
  - Marketing is about *much* more than marketing communications.
- Marketing and sales are different things
  - Sales is about ensuring the customer buys what the company happens to make – everything starts with the product or service.
  - Marketing is about ensuring that the company makes what the customer wants to buy – everything starts with the customer.
- Marketing is an 'attitude of mind' that should permeate the entire organisation.
  - It states quite categorically that we recognise that our existence, and future survival and growth, depends on our ability to give our customers what they want.
  - Internal considerations must be subservient to the wider needs of the marketplace.
  - In other words, 'the customer is king'.
- Marketing is a way of organising the business so that the customer gets treated like a king.
  - If we accept that the organisation exists and will continue to exist only as long as it continues to satisfy the needs of its customers, we must ensure that the organisation has a structure that will enable it to deliver.
  - If an organisation is to survive in today's ever more fast-changing environment, it must make itself more responsive to its customers.

- Typically this will mean
  - Shorter chains of communication and command and fewer 'levels' or 'grades'
  - Fewer people employed in 'staff', 'headquarters' and other non-customer related functions and
  - An overall structure and business design that reflects the different needs of the people who buy from the organisation rather than technical specialisations of the people who work inside it.

- Marketing is a range of activities used by the marketing department to meet marketing, marketing and business objectives.
  - Centred mainly on the concept of the marketing mix (traditionally accepted as including product, price, place and promotion), this is the technical 'how to' of the discipline.

- Marketing is the producer of profits for the whole organisation.
  - Profits are generated by markets.
  - Profits are not generated by products, by efficiency, by management or even by diligent workforces.
  - It is only the customer's willingness to pay the right (premium) price for the right product or service, which keeps anyone in business.
  - Marketing, as the primary interface between the organisation and the markets that it serves, is then the primary producer of the organisation's profit stream.

MARGIN NOTES

Peter Drucker on marketing:

'Only marketing and innovation produce profits for an organisation, and all other areas should be regarded as costs'

It is in the area of profit that we meet what is probably the most critical role of marketing. In almost every organisation there is likely to be conflict between the customer's need for value and the organisation's need for profit and efficiency.

It is the role of marketing to search for and strike the elusive (and changing) balance between these two demands. We also need to ask ourselves:

- Given that there is more than one way of satisfying customer demand, which route is the most efficient from the organisation's cost point of view?

- How can we best balance customer need for value against the organisation's need for profits?

Profit is a function of the price that the customer is willing to pay and the cost of production and sale. Successful and effective marketing (if measured in profit terms) must pay attention to both these areas. Marketing is definitely *not* about satisfying customers at any price. Marketing is about satisfying customers *at a profit*.

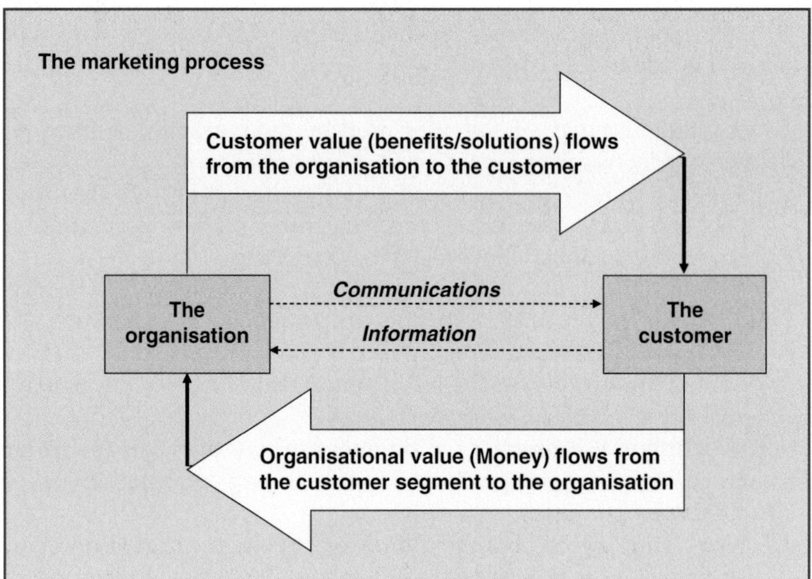

MARGIN NOTES

I'm glad that's clear …

What is strategy?

The word 'strategy' has become one of the most common and badly used words in business writing. Everywhere we look we see terms such as:

- Business strategy
- Corporate strategy
- Marketing strategy
- Strategic marketing
- Product strategy
- Pricing strategy
- Advertising strategy
- Internet/Online strategy and even
- Discount strategy.

The word strategy is almost synonymous with 'important'. Overworking the word in this way helps nobody. It simply serves to confuse.

There will be ample opportunity for you to complicate the issues later on, but for the moment I offer you a simple (but accurate) definition of these important terms:

Objective	Strategy	Tactics
'The goal, aim to which all the resources of the business are directed'	*'The means of achieving the objective'*	*'Manoeuvres on the field of battle'*
This means that objectives are about things we want to achieve – *not* about how we should achieve them.	This means that strategies are concerned with *how* we achieve the objectives, and action.	Tactics are driven by(in order): **1** The strategy **2** The realities of the battleground/marketplace
Objectives should always start with the word 'To …'	Strategies should always start with the word 'By …'	A big, important tactics does *not* become a strategy

And, the strategy 'headlines':

- Strategy is longer term;
  - Since strategy is about marshalling the gross resources of the organisation to match the needs of the marketplace and achieve the business objective, this cannot be a short-term activity.
- Strategy is not changed every Friday;
  - Constant change produces uncertainty, confusion, misdirection and wastage – not results.
- Strategy is not another word for important tactics
- Strategy is not top management's secret
  - Top management can decide the strategy on their own (it is normally safer by far that they involve others in the process too) but they cannot implement it alone.
- Strategy is not just a public relations exercise
  - It must be capable of implementation.
- Strategy is based on analysis and understanding, not straws in the wind
  - We will need to understand why things are happening as well as just knowing what is happening.
- Strategy is essential to an organisation's survival
  - If you don't know where you are going, then any road will take you there.

MARGIN NOTES

What is marketing strategy?

The major problem for the practitioner, who would actually like to do something about the organisation's marketing strategy, is where to start. There are too many conflicting definitions and we are left with burning questions:

- What is marketing strategy?
- What is included in marketing strategy?
- Where does marketing strategy start and finish?

Ultimately, marketing is about winning customer preference.

- Given that different customers will have different preferences (in different situations – see Chapter 7 Market Segmentation), each organisation will have to respond according to its own particular organisational and market circumstances.
- Marketing strategy then will mean different things to different organisations. It will fulfil different needs both within the organisation and in the marketplace.
- Organisations differ in a number of important respects
    - The variety and nature of markets served
    - The variety and complexity of products and/or services offered
    - The diverse nature of technology and operating processes used
    - The 'sophistication' of existing planning and forecasting procedures
    - The characteristics and capabilities of the individuals involved in the strategy formulation and implementation processes
    - The 'norms and values' of the business environment within which the organisation must operate
    - The nature of competitors
    - The 'thirst' in the organisation for growth and advancement and
    - The nature and demands of the stakeholders and so on …

MARGIN NOTES

So, what is marketing strategy? As with most things, this is best answered by asking, what does marketing strategy do?

> Marketing strategy is the process by which the organisation aligns itself with the market it has decided to serve.

In this way marketing strategy translates the business objective and strategy into market terms and marketing activity.

The marketing strategy 'headlines' are:

- Process:
  - Marketing strategy is a management process.
  - In other words it is 'A set of actions or steps towards achieving a particular end' (Oxford.com).
  - It is not (and should not be confused with) a good idea, a great idea, a plan or a wish.
  - Marketing strategy involves understanding what we are trying to do, more about marketing objectives later, and then identifying all the little steps and activities that together will make it happen – and then, making sure it happens.
  - Yes, it is a surprise to a lot of people!

- Organisation:
  - Means everyone in the organisation.
  - It doesn't mean just marketing, or sales, or even operations, let alone accounts – it means all of them working together.

- Align:
  - Alignment is the key word in the sentence.
  - The organisation only exists (let alone flourishes) as long as it delivers what customers want.
  - It is difficult enough to work out what customers want now and might want in the future – when they often don't know themselves.
  - You can at least reduce the odds by aligning yourself to your customers (rather than to your products, technology or industry) so that you are well placed to pick up the slightest cue.
  - And remember customers need different things at different times, for different reasons and will change their mind – for no reason at all.

- Market:
  - So exactly which customers do you wish to align to? *Everyone* is not a good answer.

- Serve:
  - Yes, serve – you are not in the driving seat, the customer is.

MARGIN NOTES

■ Working with the book

With a business audience in mind I have decided to break down the strategy approach according to what seems logical from a practitioner's point of view. Readers approaching the subject from a more academic point of view, perhaps after a course of marketing at a university or business school, may find parts of the process unusual. If so, the companion book 'Marketing Strategy' 3rd edition (Butterworth Heinemann, 2007) will be a more useful read.

Consequently, I have opted for the 'bullet list' approach that you are told not to use in proper books – but it does make understanding easier. So be ready for:

- Bullets
- Input
- Some answers to questions I am always asked
- Questions you must focus on
- Checklists to measure your progress.

The 100 Questions:

MARGIN NOTES

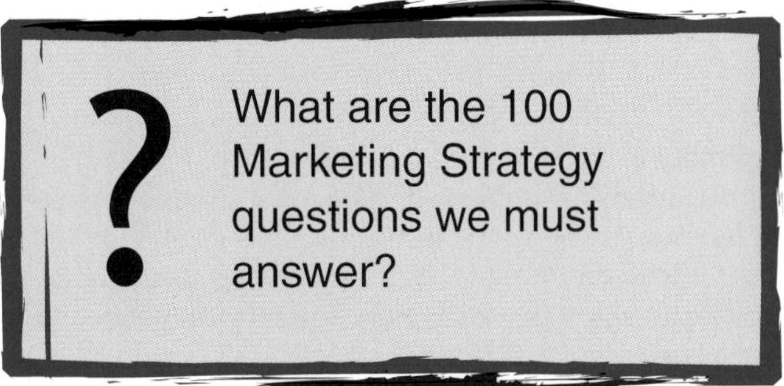

?
What are the 100 Marketing Strategy questions we must answer?

A practical book for a practitioner audience needs to be driven by considered action, not just thinking. To that end, I have structured the entire book around a series of 100 questions that you will need to answer if you hope to create a workable marketing strategy for your organisation. The questions drive all of the chapters and sections of the book and are also included in their own section in the appendix, where they can be used as a checklist.

All the questions *must* be asked, although not every question will need to be answered – different organisations will have different priorities.

To make the approach of this book as practical and as accessible as possible for everybody, whether from a traditional educational route or completely ignorant of the popular 'theories' that dominate today's marketing teaching, the book will follow the four-step approach to strategy:

- Part One: Preparing for the market strategy
  - Before you can hope to develop even the most rudimentary strategic decisions, a degree of analysis is required.

- Marketing may be more art than science but working on gut feeling is not the same thing as working by the seat of the pants.
- We need to:
  - Understand the internal business drivers
    - Customers are important, more important than they are treated in most organisations, true – but the customer is not all.
    - There are essential forces alive in every organisation that cannot just be ignored.
  - Understand the external environment
    - No man (or organisation) is an island – clichéd but true.
    - No 21st century organisation, regardless of size and market power, can pursue its goals in disregard of the business environment within which it operates.
  - Understand (or develop) the business strategy
    - While Harvard's Michael Porter's books adorn countless thousands of influential bookshelves, developing business strategy now seems to be no easier than it ever was.
  - Develop the marketing objectives
    - So exactly what are you planning to do over the next few years?
    - Wait and see what turns up?
    - Wait and see what the market throws at you?
    - Or, take some control …?

- Part Two: Developing the marketing strategy (SCORPIO)
  - This, the main part of the book, covers the various elements of market strategy.
  - I have been careful to separate marketing strategy from tactics, a common fault in too many businesses, and have concentrated on the critical influence of the market on the organisation's activity.
  - This section looks at:
    - **S**: Segmentation and targeting – what are the segments in the marketplace and which ones should we own?
    - **C**: The Customer – who are our customers and what do they want from us?
    - **O**: Offerings – what is our unique offer to the customer?
    - **R**: Retention – what are we doing to plan that our customers come back to us?
    - **P**: Positioning and branding – how are we 'unique' and what brand values do we support?
    - **I**: Industry or market thinking – do we describe our business in industry terms or in customer terms?
    - **O**: Organisation – what do we do to ensure we have the organisation structure and processes that will support a customer approach?

MARGIN NOTES

- Part Three: Co-ordination SCORPIO
  - Backbone strategy
  - Defensive strategy
  - Offensive strategy

- Part Four: From market strategy to tactics
  - The main aim of this part is to demonstrate the relationship between market strategy and tactics and the whole area of strategic implementation.
  - Finally, we will look at the minimum list of marketing issues that you must control if you want the organisation to implement anything close to what you intended.

Enjoy

MARGIN NOTES

PART I

Preparing for the marketing strategy

> 'Chance favours only the prepared mind'
>
> *Louis Pasteur (1822–1895), French chemist*

This is where we start asking the questions …

Over the years, I have found that having the right question is normally much more effective than trying to come up with an answer that will work in every organisation or business in every market – answers like that just do not exist.

Questions, on the other hand, can stimulate thinking in ways that can defy standard 'industry' logic and 'conventional wisdom' – both enemies to good marketing/customer strategy.

The format for the rest of the book is simple; I pose the question, and then I try to explain what issues, data and concepts you ought to bear in mind when looking for an answer that works for your organisation. Of course, not every question will be relevant to your specific organisation, market target customers or product/service. *But*, before you jump over a question that 'isn't relevant', make sure that you aren't just falling into the trap of 'group think' and conforming to industry and technical/professional unthinking 'truths'. Customers like clearly different offerings and to create these you just might have to spend some time on those irrelevant questions.

Finally, even in a book of this size I can't be definitive, nor can I cover all eventualities and all types of market and organisation – but I can try!

CHAPTER 1

The internal business drivers

> 'Drive thy business, let not that drive thee.'
>
> *Benjamin Franklin (1706–1790), American Statesman, Scientist, Philosopher, Printer, Writer and Inventor*

Marketing and business strategy, if they are to be practical, must be based on an assessment of reality not on hopes or wishful thinking. The successful practitioner/operator/manager is one whose plans work in the only arena that counts – the marketplace. Plans that are based on hopes, inaccurate analysis, or worse, no analysis at all cannot expect to withstand the onslaught of determined competition.

MARGIN NOTES

The common thread that binds all these business drivers together is *people*. Apart from the (all-important) customer, there are other people who also have demands on the business. Like customers, these people expect their needs to be met. Failure to do so may not mean the failure of the enterprise but will certainly mean the failure of the marketing strategy.

So, who are these other people?

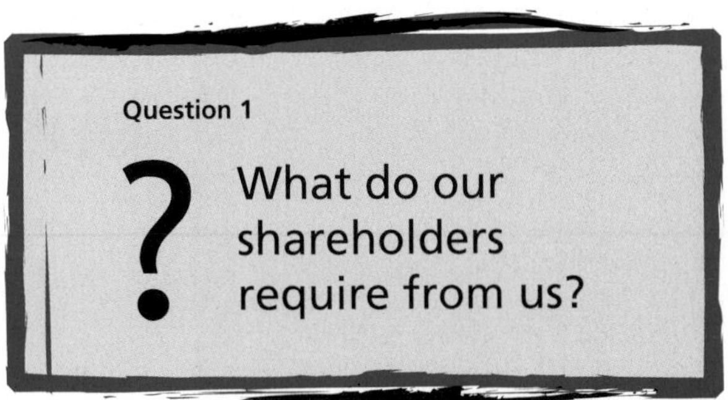

Question 1
?
What do our shareholders require from us?

Shareholders are the people who own the business or organisation:

- In *theory*, the relationship here is very simple.
  - The investors in the organisation invest in anticipation of a return on their capital; they are, *in fact and in deed,* the owners of the business.
  - As owners the investors employ the board to manage the business on their behalf and, should the returns not meet their expectations, the investors (as owners) have the power to remove part or all of the board and replace it with other directors.

- In *practice*, the relationship is far more complicated; there are investors and investors.
  - In a publicly quoted company the stockholders may be institutions such as insurance companies or pension funds, there may be private individuals and there may also be other publicly quoted companies holding stock.
  - Also, stockholders may be primarily national or international in character. It also follows that different investors may have different needs.
  - Some may be investing for the long term, some for the short term. Some may require no income – seeking a long-term increase in the capital value of their stockholding, others may be far less interested in capital growth but more concerned to secure a regular income stream from the investment, normally in the form of dividends.
  - Yet others may require a mixture of both capital growth and income.
  - The organisation might also be a smaller part of a larger organisation – in this instance there is but one owner.
  - In the case of the private company the director or directors may also be the owners, and then the returns required may be for a steady or rising income stream over the longer-term or for shorter-term capital accumulation.

- The past 10 years has also shown that (at least some) investors are willing to exercise their legal rights and take directors to task.
  - There have been some lively annual general meetings where small shareholders have taken the 'fat cat' directors to task over salaries and incentive schemes that seem to pay out even when sales and profits are in decline.
  - Large institutional investors are also flexing their muscles more and are becoming important players in underperforming organisations when it comes time to re-elect directors or even deal with potential take-over bids.
  - In each case, it is the board's strategy that is being assessed, not the directors themselves.

- Apart from the share or stock capital there is also long-term debt financing normally provided by major institutions such as banks and, more recently, venture capital (VC) companies.
  - The various banks are also the products of their own internal organisational culture as well as the national culture from which the organisation operates.
  - The different banks' views will also differ as to what is long and what is short term.
  - Venture capitalists work on a different basis and exist (unlike the banks) to invest in 'risk'.

MARGIN NOTES

  - The dot.com escapade showed the power (if not the wisdom) of the VCs and their willingness to take on all types of 'risk'.
  - Nowadays VCs (the ones that survived the dot.com bust) are a little more careful but still often expect only one investment in five to pay off – which explains why they can look for 35% per annum return on all their investments.

Action

- The marketing strategy needs to produce the 'right' value for the organisation.
- You will need to understand the makeup of the ownership structure of the organisation as precisely as possible.
- You, or the person responsibility for the strategy, will only be allowed freedom to direct as long as the investor is getting what he or she wants/expects.
- Such expectations may include:
  - A return on capital invested
  - Employment
  - Global market share
  - Environmental/social returns, etc.
- And all these are likely to change with political climates and changes in government (or government policy) over time.

MARGIN NOTES

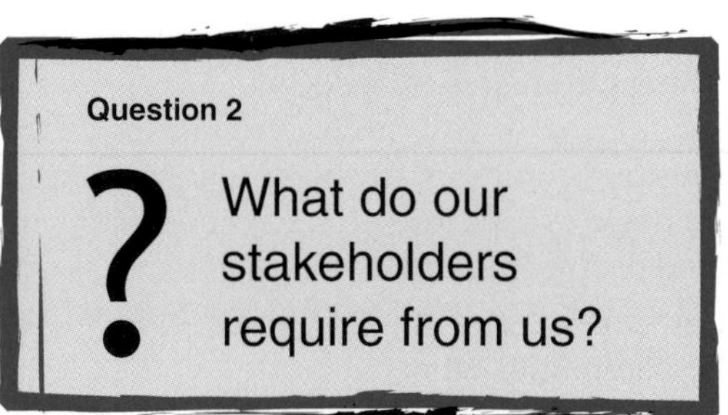

Question 2
?
What do our stakeholders require from us?

Shareholders are not the only people you have to satisfy, because they are not the only group that believes they have a 'stake' in your business.

Apart from the shareholders and the implementers/key management team, there are others who have needs and expectations and who will, rightly, expect a degree of service and satisfaction from the organisation.

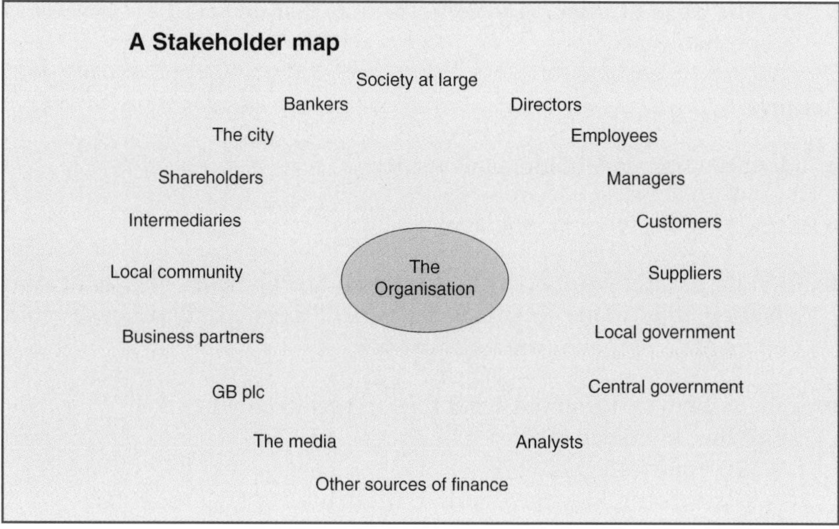

MARGIN NOTES

The RSA (Royal Society of Arts, London) research discovered that UK society generally no longer 'defers' to business activity and organisations need to actively maintain public confidence in company operations and business contact if they are to continue to enjoy a 'licence to operate'. The RSA concluded that, in the future, successful organisations will 'value reciprocal relationships and work actively to build them with customers, suppliers and other key stakeholders through a partnership approach and, by focusing on, and learning from, all those who contribute to the business, will be best able to improve returns to shareholders'.

The idea that business needs (or at least cannot avoid) adversarial relationships with stakeholders if they are to make a profit is seriously outdated. These 'yesterday' organisations still firmly believe that shareholders would have to be the losers if employees, suppliers, customers or the country were made more important.

Profits come from satisfied customers who come back. Satisfied customers are created by companies who:

- Understand their customers.
- Build alliances with their staff, communities and suppliers to deliver superior Customer Value.
- These companies are created by investors/stakeholders who take a long-term interest in what the organisation is trying to achieve – as a way of maximising long-term financial returns.
  - The stakeholder concept term is not just a 'good thing'. It is a highly 'profitable thing'.

- The days of viewing stakeholders as just innocent bystanders is probably gone.

Action

- Identify your stakeholders (all of them).
- Even the ones who are not 'active'.
- Identify exactly what you get from your stakeholders and what contribution they make to satisfying your customers (like how would you manage of they turned against you).
- Talk to them and find out what they expect from you:
  - What do they want?
  - What must they have?
  - What would they be surprised/delighted of they received?
- Carry out a cost/benefit analysis of what more you could give them – and what you would get for it.

MARGIN NOTES

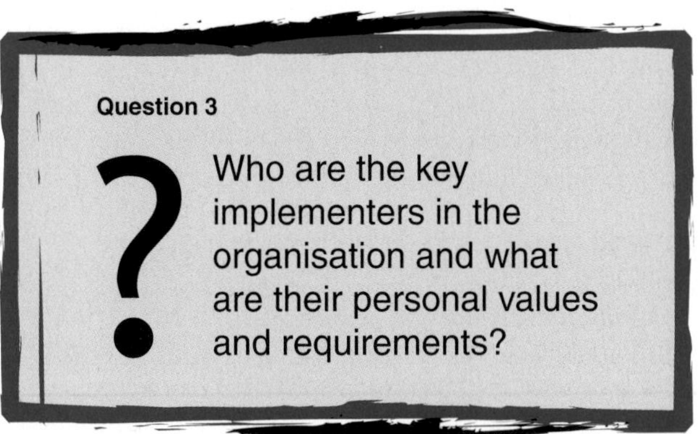

Question 3
?
Who are the key implementers in the organisation and what are their personal values and requirements?

The term 'key implementers' refers to that select group or body in an organisation who actually make the decisions and who are central to what the organisation does. It may or may not include the board in its entirety. It may mean the board, it may mean the board plus a number of very senior managers, it may just mean the owner/managing director and a special friend or colleague, or it may mean the chairman and part of the board. It may include the owner/chairman's wife/children/family. In any event these are the people who really count:

- The key implementers, individually or probably as a group, will have a very clear idea of what type of organisation they wish to work for, what type of organisation they wish to create, the types of products and services they wish to market, the types of customers they wish to serve and the types of businesses they wish to be in.

- At the same time they will also have a very clear idea of what businesses and activities they and their organisation will *not* be involved in.
  - It is, if you like, a kind of moral and ethical 'personal ambition blueprint' against which all possible strategic alternatives will be assessed.
  - If a possible strategy contravenes the personal values of this group it will of course be countered with non-emotional arguments based on good business practice – but it will be countered, and strongly and then rejected.
  - Some organisations (and key implementers) would rather die than change what they are and what they believe in – this is human nature and we should accept it.

Human nature is just like that. And there's no way that we are going to change human nature. The most profitable route for you and the organisation is not to beat them but to join them. A strong market influence within the key implementers can do nothing but good.

MARGIN NOTES

Action

- The lesson is clear – even when the strategy and the strategic approach seem to be 'by the book', you must talk to and understand the key implementers and the social system to which they belong.
- Implementation is more important than the plans. Implementation has to fit what the organisation is.
- The first thing to do is to start sharing your experience and insights with others.
  - Show how marketing is just really common sense, it's not black magic nor does it have to be a threat to any of the longer established functions in the organisation.
  - Try to demonstrate that customers are important to the vision thing.
  - If the key implementers hold fast to a vision that's great. If customers could share that vision just imagine what we could do together.

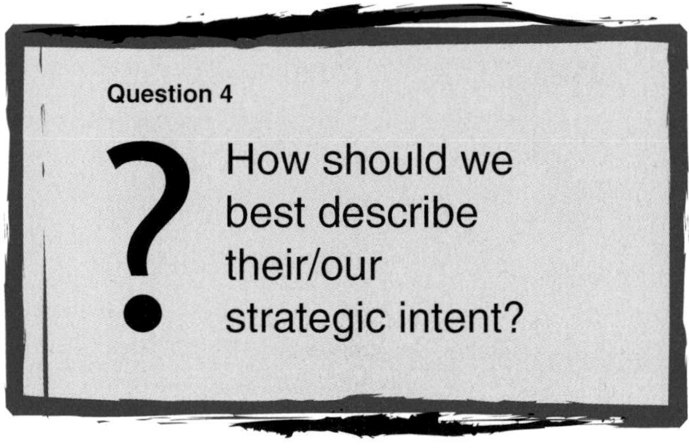

Question 4
?
How should we best describe their/our strategic intent?

Two professors (Hamel and Prahaled) spoke about what they called 'Strategic Intent' in a 1989 edition of The Harvard Business Review. They argued (before the Japanese bubble burst) that Western companies focus on trimming their ambitions to match resources and, as a result, search only for advantages they can sustain. By contrast, Japanese companies leverage resources by accelerating the pace of organisational learning and try to attain seemingly impossible goals.

- The idea is simple.
- Don't be resources driven.
- Be market/customer driven and work out what you want to do.
  - And then find the resources to do it.

For good or for bad, this concept of strategic intent has been watered down, hijacked and generally messed around with so that nowadays it really means that a company exhibits strategic intent when it relentlessly pursues a certain long-term strategic objective and concentrates its strategic actions on achieving that objective. Put the words strategic intent into Google and see how many brave and stirring (if unbelievable) statements appear.

MARGIN NOTES

Action

- Find out what appears to me the driving concept behind your company/business (remember it might not be written down).
- Ask people what it is that drives them and their thinking (remember that they might not tell the whole truth, especially of it is a Western or UK company and most of the managers are male and the motivation is emotional).
- Don't just believe what you hear or read – understand what you see.
- Go back to the history of the organisation.
- Understand how you can use the strategic intent to fuel your marketing strategy

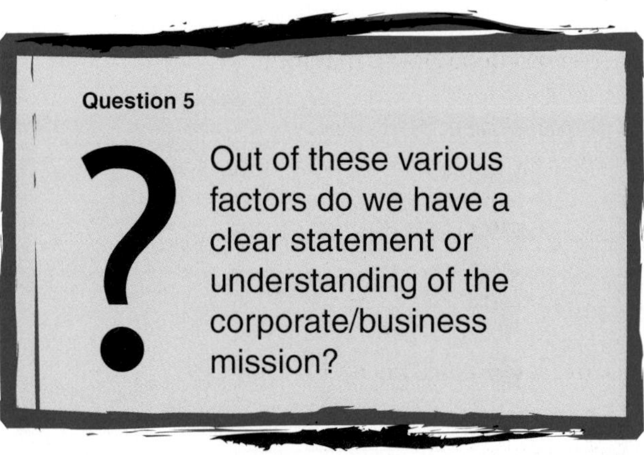

Question 5
?
Out of these various factors do we have a clear statement or understanding of the corporate/business mission?

What seems to drive the organisation? Mission (statements) can give us another clue as can the leadership style of the organisation. The mission should bring together the apparently diverse groups that we have discussed above and give overall direction.

- But what is a mission (statement)?
  - At its simplest level, the mission is a statement of the core values of the organisation and as such is a framework within which staff and individual business units, divisions or activities prepare their plans.
  - It should be constructed in such a way that it satisfies and can be subscribed to by the most important groups of people who have expectations from the organisation.
  - It is not the same thing as a business objective.
  - Missions are non-specific and are difficult to achieve cleanly on their own.
  - A business objective, by contrast, should be both measurable and achievable and is normally expressed in quantitative terms.

- A more important question is what does the mission statement actually do?
  - This will influence its content.
  - Above all else, the mission statement should do as its name implies, it should give the organisation a clear mission or purpose.
  - It should give all people connected with the organisation a clear sense of where the organisation is headed.
  - If the mission statement is sufficiently motivating, then everybody should share a sense of direction, opportunities, significance and ultimately, achievement.

MARGIN NOTES

Action

- Search the paperwork for recent mission statements and other declarations of purpose.

- Match these with behaviours that are:
  - Overt
  - Rewarded by the organisation
  - Rewarded by the market (customers).

- Are you going in the right direction?

- Is your strategy right for the market?

- Is your strategy going to meet any resistance?

- What are you going to do about it?

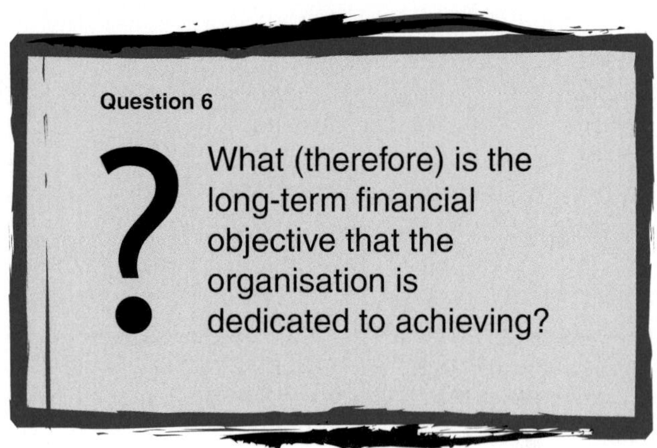

Question 6
?
What (therefore) is the long-term financial objective that the organisation is dedicated to achieving?

MARGIN NOTES

It all seems to come down to money in the end doesn't it?

By the long-term financial objective we don't mean all the annual, quarterly or monthly financial targets that abound in any sizeable organisation and act primarily as control systems against planned targets.

- The long-term financial objective is that requirement placed on the organisation, specifically on the board of directors, by the individuals and institutions who have invested in the organisation in the expectation of a financial return.
  - Not being too delicate, this is what you have to achieve if everybody is to keep their jobs.
  - In short, the financial objective is a *hurdle* to be overcome.

- By translating business performance into numbers we have a convenient means by which the investors/owners, who have no day-to-day involvement in the running of the organisation, may understand how their appointed managers have performed over the past period.
  - While it also gives us a fairly good indication of what we must achieve in future periods, it provides absolutely no indication at all of how to achieve these future results or how to run the business.

- The long-term financial objective acts extremely well – as a financial objective.
  - Being a narrow measure it cannot be used as a surrogate business objective as it lacks the breadth to be an efficient driver of the business, and the people in it.
  - There is more (much more) to running a successful business and developing a competitive marketing strategy than the long-term financial objective, but more of that later.

Action

- We must understand who the investors in the organisation are.
- What do they want.
- How (not whether) can we deliver what they want – then, if we are lucky, we are all left a degree of liberty to run the business.

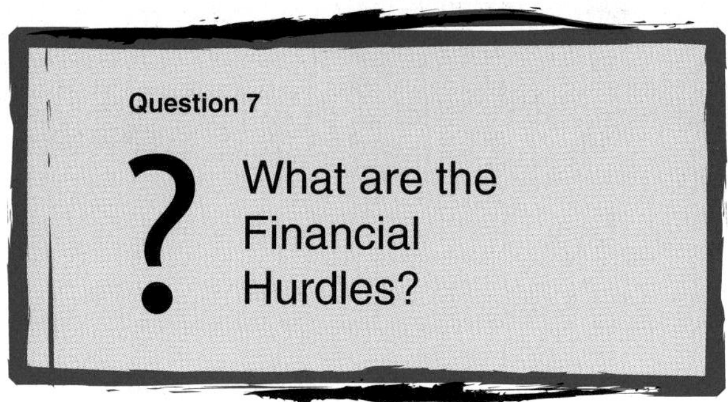
Question 7
?
What are the Financial Hurdles?

MARGIN NOTES

Well, it all comes down to money …

Every organisation has one or more 'financial imperatives' that it must satisfy to remain in business. These are not the same as objectives. These 'hurdles' just need to be seen, measured and *jumped*. They should *not* guide the destiny of the organisation.

- Yes, I know – and the Finance Director shouts a lot and everybody else does seem to accept that x% increase in return on investment (ROI) is a normal 'business objective' but that does not make it right.
- Financial targets are just hurdles that we have to jump – but that changes nothing.
  - To make more money, we need to focus, not on money but on the business/customer purpose that makes it possible.
- The use of the word 'hurdle' is deliberate.
  - You remember the hurdles race at school or the Olympics? Well, you must also remember who the winner is.
  - The first one over the end line wins.
    - The hurdles are just things in the way that you have to jump over to get to the winning post.
    - There are no prizes for how neatly the hurdles are jumped, or how high, or how fast or even how many are touched or knocked down.
    - All this is irrelevant.
    - So it is with financial hurdles.

First, agree the Financial *Hurdles*

Every organisation has one or more 'financial imperatives' that it must satisfy to remain in business. These are not the same as objectives. These 'hurdles' just need to be seen, measured and jumped. They should *NOT* guide the destiny of the organisation

Our financial hurdles are:

1. ....
2. ....
3. ....
4. ....

MARGIN NOTES

- All you have to do is to make sure that the minimum financial returns demanded by the shareholders are achieved.
  - Generally (there are some exceptions such as environmental or green shareholder requirements) shareholders are not concerned *how* you jump over the hurdles just that you jump them.
- Shareholders establish the nature and shape of the hurdles, but
  - customers determine where the winning line is.

In the marketing strategy process it is important that we identify – clearly – the financial hurdles that the organisation must jump. We identify them, we list them, we ensure that we do not forget them; we ensure that we jump them. But we *do not allow the hurdles to dictate our customer/market actions.*

The vision and business objective will give us the direction that will enable us to jump the hurdles.

Action

- Identify all the financial hurdles.
- Identify all the non-financial hurdles that will have a financial effect.
- Identify the exact height of each hurdle. (How high do we have to jump?)
- Make sure that your marketing strategy and everyone associated with it understands that:
  - The hurdles must be jumped.

- The hurdles need not be exceeded.
- Jumping the hurdles is not enough to win the race.

More definitions, more words and more uncertainty: visions, missions, objectives, where will it end?

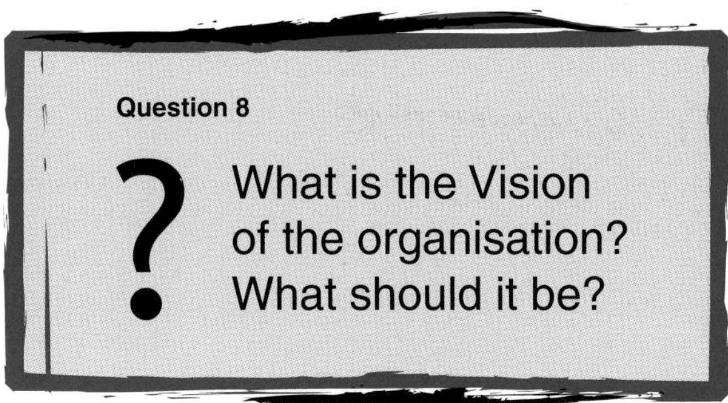

Question 8
?
What is the Vision
of the organisation?
What should it be?

MARGIN NOTES

Definitions vary but for our purposes:

- Mission is a statement of the organisation/business values (how it likes to do business).
  - Nice but arguably not essential.
- Vision is a clear(ish) idea of what the organisation/business is going to be in x years time.
  - Important if you want to enthuse people to follow you.
- Objective is a precise (quantified) definition of what the organisation will achieve by a certain date (depending on the measures chosen).
  - Important for investors and bank managers but even quantified measures have been known to change over time.
- Strategy explains how the objective will be achieved.

Visions are a good thing. They allow emotion to enter business and give leaders some currency. They also flesh out the story underneath/behind the boring numbers and give everybody something exciting to belong to. We are human after all.

But, importantly, the Vision is about much more than the numbers – because business is about much more than the numbers.

The never-ending debate is all about the purpose of business and the measures of success, and it gets confusing. Two great business writers Levitt (Harvard) and Drucker said that:

> The Purpose of Business:
>
> *'To Create, and keep a customer'*

Which is blindingly obvious really; the more customers we create and the longer we manage to keep them, the better and bigger the business gets. So everybody should be focused on creating and keeping customers, and their jobs defined in these terms – if only.

- Unfortunately, the picture gets confused when we consider the measure of success – and (possibly the most) important measure of how well an organisation achieves this is profitability.
  - Financial measures then are a measure of *success* – not the *purpose* of the organisation.
  - In fact, people in most (especially larger) organisations appear to be focused on generating profits, and their jobs defined in these terms.
  - This is madness, since few people have any direct effect on profits or any idea what they should be doing to influence them.

MARGIN NOTES

- Profits are not only important; they are vital for survival.
  - But, the pursuit of short-term profits for their own sake can destroy an otherwise successful business.

- Visions are a powerful way of breaking out of the 'any-good-business-objective-must-be-in-financial-terms' dead end.
  - A lot has been written about 'the vision thing' in recent years, some good and some laughable.
  - The personal values of the key implementers, once combined, create the vision driving the organisation and so what has been called the 'strategic intent' behind the group.
  - This vision, sometimes written, more often than not implicit and mutually understood, needs to be clarified and defined before taking the process any further.
  - The vision is often central to the organisation's success.
  - The Vision is not the same as an objective since it is not normally quantified.
  - Rather it is a picture of what the future of the organisation looks like.
  - Vision enables the organisation to set a broad strategic direction and leaves the details of its implementation to be worked out later.
  - In the absence of a clear vision (articulated or not) the organisation will probably be in trouble and without some light to guide it the organisation will flounder aimlessly.
  - Having said this, organisations without a vision are really quite rare.
  - The vision may be unclear, ragged around the edges, or even rather too emotional for senior managers to admit to – but it is normally there.
  - It is often better to dig deep to find what makes people come into work in the mornings than to go through the (often pointless) exercise of trying to create a vision from scratch, what people are happy to put down on paper may not be what they are really willing to fight for.

MARGIN NOTES

Action

- Talk with others in the organisation/business.
  - Putting together the vision statement can be quite a lengthy process of discussion within the organisation. Indeed, practical experience has shown me that when visions simply emerge like a brand new car model from behind the locked doors of the senior management group, they do not tend to be anywhere near as effective as if discussions have been carried out with the staff and the other stakeholders that affect the organisation.
- Resign yourself to a lengthy period of discussion – with all sorts of 'interested' parties.
- Produce a multitude of views, feelings and beliefs from all sectors.
- This will generate a mission statement that runs to not one but maybe two or more closely typed pages.
- Précis, précis and précis again – a good vision must be easily communicated, so it needs to be short.

■ The strategic questions (1–8)

If you have been following the process so far, you will be able to answer some of the questions already – here are the first 8.

Before you happily jump a question and tick the 'Not important' box – make sure that you really are not confusing 'Not important' with 'Too difficult'.

And, don't think you can come back to these difficult questions later – if you don't sort out this mess first, your marketing strategy won't be built on sound foundations.

No.	Strategic question	Our strategic answer	Importance	✓
	Part One – Preparing for the Marketing Strategy			
	Internal business Drivers			
1	What do our shareholders require from us?		Must have	
			Nice to have	
			Not important	

2	What do our stakeholders require from us?		Must have	
			Nice to have	
			Not important	
3	Who are the key implementers in the organisation and what are their personal values and requirements?	1	Must have	
		2	Nice to have	
		3	Not important	
4	How should we best describe their/our strategic intent?		Must have	
			Nice to have	
			Not important	
5	Out of these various factors do we have a clear statement or understanding of the corporate/business mission?		Must have	
			Nice to have	
			Not important	
6	What (therefore) is the long-term financial objective that the organisation is dedicated to achieving?		Must have	
			Nice to have	
			Not important	
7	What are the Financial Hurdles?	1	Must have	
		2	Nice to have	
		3	Not important	
		4		
8	What is the Vision of the organisation? What should it be?		Must have	
			Nice to have	
			Not important	

CHAPTER 2

The external environment

> 'Life is what happens to you
> while you're making other plans'
>
> *John Lennon, (1940–1980),*
> *English songwriter, singer,*
> *author and political activist*
> *and one of the founders of The Beatles*

In the previous chapter we tried to uncover the most important internal drivers of the business. If the organisation has a mission statement or a clearly articulated vision this will help us focus our attention on the more important aspects of the external environment, which we must assess next.

MARGIN NOTES

Attempting to lay any sort of plans for the future without first gathering some (at least enough) information is not only foolish; it is also complacent and arrogant. Knowing that information must be gathered is one thing, knowing how much and what to gather is quite another.

The questions to guide you through this particular maze are:

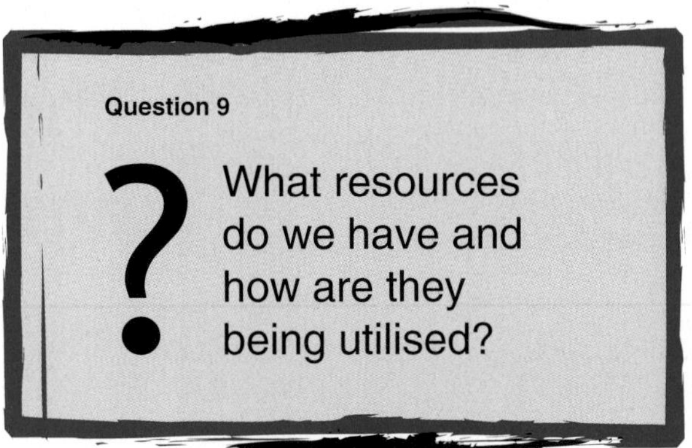

Question 9
?
What resources do we have and how are they being utilised?

A resource audit is another of those grand titles, which just disguises a very simple question – what are the capabilities of the organisation?

A practical strategy is one that is achievable. (Did I really write that?).

An organisation or business just cannot achieve its vision without the resources and the capability to achieve those objectives. This does not mean that your vision must be solely driven by the resources available; we can convert and/or acquire additional resources (given the time) and a sufficiently compelling story but even so we need to be reasonable.

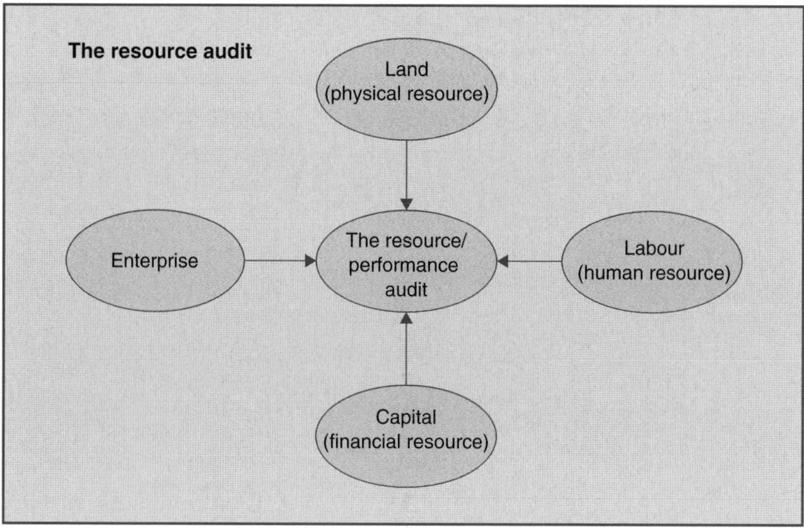

MARGIN NOTES

The resource audit is simply a way for you to assess what resources are available to you (and your strategy/vision) now. This is important because the audit should show you:

- Resources currently being utilised productively
- Resources missing (needed for vision)
- Resources currently being utilised unproductively (very common since organisations tend to lag behind market changes; we go on doing things and producing products and services too long after the customers have moved on to something new).

The easiest approach for the organisation to break down its resources under the four traditional headings – land, labour, capital and enterprise – and see what it's got.

You need to know exactly what the organisation or business can deliver to the marketplace and precisely what delivery levels would be impractical, at least in the short to medium term. In the medium to longer term constraints may be overcome by building up resources or by buying in additional resource. Strategic alliances to support key strengths might also be considered.

- Land (physical resource)
  - Under this heading you should consider resources such as:
    - Production facilities and capacity
    - For products:
      - Factories
      - Locations

        - Output capacities
        - Flexibility of production lines
        - Methodologies
        - Age of the plant
        - Recent levels of investment
    - For Services:
        - Office space
        - Flexibility of space use
        - Number of retail or other outlets
        - Access points for customers
        - Delivery trucks
        - Rolling stock
        - Mechanised plant and equipment

- Labour (human resource)
    - Labour is another simplified term that we use to cover all forms of human resource open to the organisation. We are concerned with:
        - Manual labour
        - Mental labour (knowledge workers)
        - Flexibility of the human resource to meet the new challenges
        - Industrial relations
        - Training and management development
        - Skills base
        - Internal communications
        - Organisation:
            - Structure
            - Design
            - Culture
            - Morale
    - There are also specific questions that the organisation should be asking about its top and middle management capabilities:
        - How good are they?
        - How responsive is management to change?
        - How competitive in nature?
        - How independent?
        - How needing of guidance/control?

- Capital (financial resource)
    - This category refers to the financial muscle called for in a market strategy.
        - Whether the strategy eventually calls for consolidation, redirection, head-to-head competition or the erection of barriers to entry to your marketplace, the costs are already high and are getting higher.
        - Financial strength is no guarantee of long-term survival, but it helps.
        - Naturally, the eventual strategy for the organisation must be formulated within the confines of the finances that the organisation either has or is able to access.

MARGIN NOTES

- Enterprise
  - This last category covers the whole area of creativity and business acumen needed to survive in competitive marketplaces.
    - Enterprise is the collection of ideas, new thoughts and drive required by an organisation if it is going to continue to grow, change and flourish in the years ahead.
    - Marketing does not have the monopoly.
    - The behaviour of individuals (including the level of enterprise) inside an organisation is very largely dictated by the organisation structure and culture.
    - The structure of the organisation, its processes, reporting systems, reward systems, implicit and explicit culture and its communications all serve to spell out to people what behaviours are valued and will guarantee progress within the system.
    - We will look more closely at this problem, and what can be done about it, in Chapter 10.

MARGIN NOTES

Action

- Review and assess all elements objectively

- Assess in terms of current position, relative to competition and future vision

- Assemble overall audit from all four elements – all four elements are required if the organisation is to have a future. We can all think of good examples of failures where:
  - Organisations that have been flush with money but have had no good ideas.
  - Young thrusting organisations full of new ideas and revolutionary thoughts but with little or no capital to back them up.
  - Creative Western organisations that generate ideas, which in the absence of sufficient *patient* capital, have gone to the Far East where they have been successfully modified and marketed.

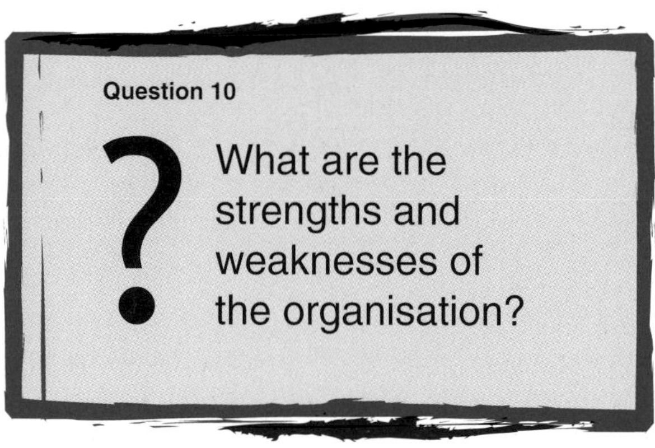

Question 10
?
What are the strengths and weaknesses of the organisation?

Falling straight out of the resource audit, you should now be in a situation to identify your particular strengths and weaknesses.

The idea being, of course, that your eventual marketing strategy will be one that:

- Exploits the organisation's strengths
- Protects its weak nesses.

I know it seems obvious to play it this way round but you would me amazed at the number of otherwise quite rational practitioners who:

- Did not like the strengths that the market said they had.
- Believed they had strengths – that the market did not see or believe.
- Insisted that they had no weaknesses at all.
- Would only produce plans for doing what they had always done/ what they had told the parent company they would do.
- Incentivised the sales force to sell more of what customers wanted least and lost them most money.

MARGIN NOTES

SWOT analysis (1)

(Internal/Controllable)	(External/Uncontrollable)
Strengths	Opportunities
1	1
2	2
3	3
4	4
5	5
6	6
Weaknesses	Threats
1	1
2	2
3	3
4	4
5	5
6	6

It is, of course, inevitable that an organisation will start looking at its strengths and weaknesses through internally focused eyes; that is essentially what the resource audit is all about. Nevertheless, you need to realise that *a strength is only a genuine strength if your target customers say it is!*

This is not always an easy idea to grasp, shut away as most managers are from paying customers.

First, the SWOT basics, just so we all know what we are talking about and we can carry out the same thinking:

- Strengths and Weaknesses are:
    - Internal issues and are therefore
    - Controllable
    - You are supposed to be able to do something about these.
- Opportunities and Threats are:
    - External and therefore
    - Beyond your control
    - You have to work with what you have got here, at least in the short term.
- Strengths are real strengths only if your target customers believe you have them.
- Weaknesses are real weaknesses only if your target customers believe you have them.
- You should not attempt to list every single issue under each heading, just the (±6) most important ones.
- Every time I do this with a company, the weaknesses list is at least twice as long as the strengths list:
    - This is nonsense, stop beating yourself up!
- The objective is *not* to list all the most important issues under each heading and then put the analysis away in a desk drawer.
- The objective is to *do something* with the results of the analysis.

MARGIN NOTES

The organisation's beliefs must be tested in the marketplace to find out, clearly, whether the customers agree.

- If your customers don't agree, all is not lost, at least for the flexible company.
    - The choice now is to either:
        - Build on the strengths that the customers believe we have (even if we don't believe it – yet), or
        - Attempt to change the customers' beliefs about the strengths and convince them that we have different strengths from what they understand.
    - Much depends obviously on what the beliefs are but you should remember that:
        - Customers believe what they believe.
        - Customers beliefs and attitudes are not formed or changed overnight.

- Customers will not change what they believe just because you say so, they may want to experience the difference for themselves.
- Customers may not be attracted to what you want them to believe about your offering.
- This is starting to sound expensive.

When you help to put together the strengths and weaknesses analysis for your organisation you should remember one thing – it pays to be honest – no matter whose feelings you might hurt. Your organisation/business may not be able to deal with an honest assessment of its strengths and weaknesses but a simple re-statement of company conventional wisdom will do no good at all. Restrict circulation of the analysis to preserve morale if you must – but be honest with yourself.

MARGIN NOTES

Action

So, what should you be doing with the analysis? First you need to:

- Dry run the exercise to see if you have enough data/information to make it worthwhile.
  - Ask people inside what they think.
  - Especially ask everybody who interacts with your customers what they believe the customers would say are your strengths and weaknesses.
  - Ask your suppliers and your intermediaries or channel partners what they think.

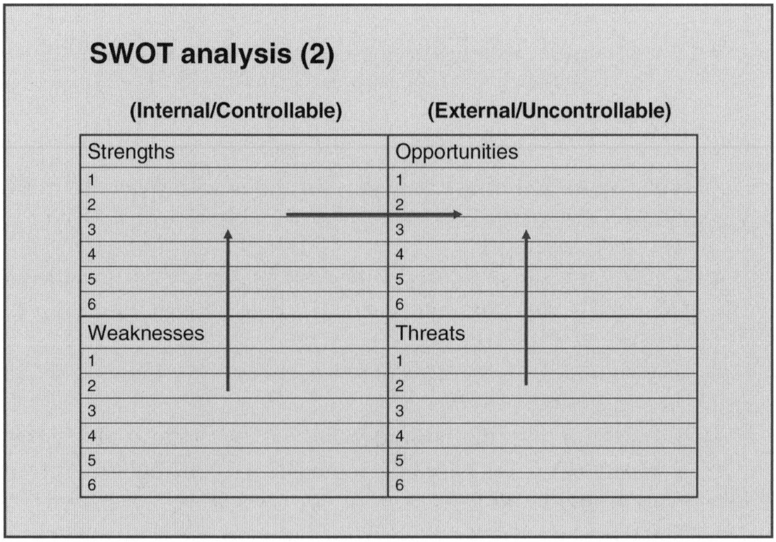

SWOT analysis (2)

(Internal/Controllable)	(External/Uncontrollable)
Strengths	Opportunities
1	1
2	2
3	3
4	4
5	5
6	6
Weaknesses	Threats
1	1
2	2
3	3
4	4
5	5
6	6

- If it's looking thin, try finding a little money and getting a specialist market researcher to ask your customers for you – you must know what they think of you.

- You can also consult industry/market 'experts' and see what they think are the threats/opportunities for everyone – use external information if you trust its source.

- Then, take it one step further – use 'convergence arrows':

This is a quick way of giving initial direction as well as assessing the final marketing strategy. Three arrows are inserted into the SWOT diagram. These arrows show the three (really powerful but annoying) questions you should ask yourself to work out what your marketing strategy and plans needs to be doing for you:

- Weaknesses → Strengths:
  - What can you do (or plan to do) to turn weaknesses into strengths?
    - The traditional skill here is to turn a 'limited' offer into a 'specialist' one.
    - One of the oldest examples must be Avis car rental, who could (at the time) not challenge the power of the market leader (Hertz) so made a strength out of the fact that being 'Number Two' meant that they had to try harder so would give better service.
    - More recent example would be Green and Blacks chocolate – its taste is too bitter for children so it is positioned as an adult treat.

- Threats → Opportunities:
  - What can you do (or plan to do) to turn a threat into an opportunity?
    - For example, EU legislation on recycling has shown how the fastest movers can make their offerings different from slower competitors.
    - External 'threats' such as legislation, de-regulation, Internet and technology and fashion have helped many organisations change by presenting *big* shifts in market conditions that they can respond to.
    - Often it is the small but relentless changes that provide most danger because the managers just don't see them until it's too late.

- Strengths → Opportunities:
  - What can you do (or plan to do) to focus your strengths on to the opportunities?
    - You thought that this would happen automatically, well, it won't.
    - Once you have agreed them focus the strengths where they will do most good.
    - There is no point directing weaknesses at opportunities or even strengths at threats. But you would be amazed …

MARGIN NOTES

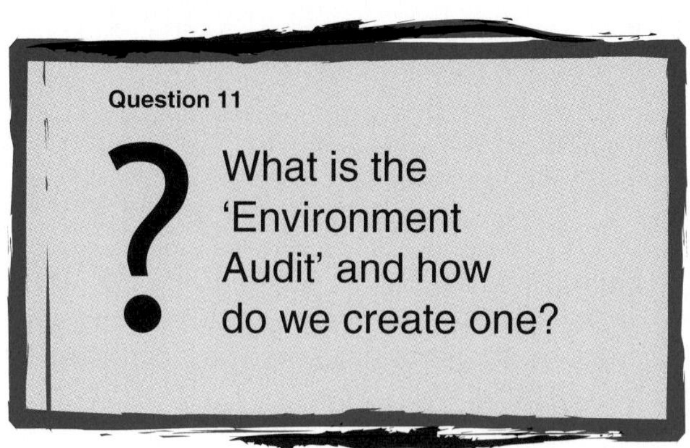

Question 11
?
What is the 'Environment Audit' and how do we create one?

MARGIN NOTES

Auditing the environment in which the organisation must operate is arguably *the most important* and most significant data gathering activity that any organisation, business, firm, service or even government department, can undertake.

The past decade has provided a number of changes for all types of organisation – globalisation of business and competition, the increasing sophistication of customers and the explosion of 'choice' (more about that later) – means that a single organisation can no longer control a market and dictate terms like they used to. Apart from governments, nationalised industries and pseudo-privatised monopolies such as railways and utilities, competition has forced all organisations and businesses to pay more attention to customer needs than before.

The 1980s saw the beginning of a shift in power away from the producer towards the customer, ignited by the work of Ralph Nader and others. In the 1990s this trend accelerated, driven by early globalisation. The late 1990s saw a brief displacement as the dot.com era suggested that new rules of economics had been discovered and sales revenue and profits were no longer measures of business success. This stage passed with the dot.com collapse and the early 2000s continued what organisations 'thought' customers wanted; lower and lower prices at the expense of differentiation, quality and service. Currently, some astute organisations appear to be veering away as the cliff edge comes into view, but a lot of lemming organisations are still heading for the great 'let's give it away and have the whole market' graveyard. The environment controls us all; we need to understand the rules of the game.

If you don't understand the environment in which you have to operate, how can you or your organisation possibly hope to establish its special market position enjoy the long term profits that come from successful marketing?

But, the term 'environment' means too many different things? The traditional environment definition is the 'PEST' analysis – taken from the original:

- Political
- Economic

- Sociological
- Technological

framework. I have enlarged this structure over recent years as more aspects of the environment start to have a direct impact on organisations and need to be taken into account for any practical strategy. Originally I added:

- Customer/Market
- Competition

To focus the analysis on the more important but more 'micro' issues in the environment. More recently I have added two new dimensions to my PEST analysis:

- International
- Environmental

MARGIN NOTES

The 'PEST' analysis

Political	Economic
1	1
2	2
3	3
4	4
5	5
Sociological	**Technological**
1	1
2	2
3	3
4	4
5	5
Customer/Market	**Competition**
1	1
2	2
3	3
4	4
5	5
International	**Environmental**
1	1
2	2
3	3
4	4
5	5

The 'PEST' analysis is not particularly clever or advanced but it does the job.

Although these classifications are obvious, they are not absolute and some degree of overlap is quite normal. The questions you need to think through for each heading are:

- Political Factors:
  - Under the political heading we are concerned with the motives and the actions of governments and the way that, via legislation,

regulation and the legal/political system, they impact on business.

- Our first efforts must be directed at trying to understand exactly what effects these measures have on how we run our business.
  - Try, for example, to imagine what we would be doing differently if these rules and regulations did not exist.
- Secondly, we need to try and grasp the reasoning behind the legislative and legal regulation.
  - What is the political ideology that forms the basis of the regulation?
  - It is only by understanding why governments and regulators act the way they do that we will have any chance of anticipating the most likely future changes in legislation.
  - If we can predict future moves then we can plan for them.
- A 'quick' checklist for your political assessment might include:
  - Role of government, regulator or participator
  - Political ideology
  - Political motivations
  - Rate of change of political direction
  - Political stability over time
  - Political attitudes to:
    - Competition
    - Social responsibility
    - Environmental matters
    - Customer protection
  - Legislative effects on:
    - Organisational structure
    - Organisational behaviour
    - Employment
    - Salaries and payment levels
    - Employment conditions (health and safety, etc.)
    - Profits (taxation/repatriation, etc.)
    - Permitted markets
    - Product policy
    - Pricing policy
    - Distribution policy
    - Promotional policy

MARGIN NOTES

- Economic Factors
  - Under this heading we should be considering issues such as the current and likely future economic issues that will affect how we run and plan our organisation's business.
  - Taxation can appear under the economic heading as well as the political heading.
  - A 'quick' checklist for your economic assessment might include:
    - Gross domestic product (GDP):
      - Per head

    - Social/private
    - Distribution
    - Regional disparity
  - Government policy:
    - Fiscal
    - Monetary
  - Industrial:
    - Structure
    - Growth
    - Labour rates
  - Income:
    - Current
    - Growth
    - Distribution
    - Relation with population groups
  - Wealth:
    - Distribution
    - Effect on buying power
  - Employment:
    - Structure
    - Full-time/part-time
    - Male/female
    - Regional disparity

MARGIN NOTES

- Sociological Factors
  - This aspect of the environment is probably the most difficult to understand, quantify and predict, dealing as it does with people and human behaviour.
    - Unfortunately, it can be the most devastating to our business fortunes if we are unlucky enough to get it wrong.
    - Basically we are dealing with people's motivations, needs, wants and perceptions and, more broadly, how society or culture is changing over time.
  - A 'quick' checklist for your sociological assessment might include:
    - Cultural/sub-cultural groups:
      - Characteristics
      - Growth/decline
    - Demographics:
      - Socioeconomic groupings
      - Home ownership
      - Geography
      - Family structure and influence
      - Family life stages
      - Usage patterns
    - Natural segments:
      - Characteristics
      - Differentiators
      - Growth/decline/change

- Psychographics:
  - Preferences
  - Benefits
  - Attitudes and belief systems
- Social trends:
  - Changes in personal value systems
  - Changes in the structure of society
  - Changes in moral and ethical positions
  - Changes in belief systems
  - Changes in attitudes (to (for example) NGOs, genetics, etc.)

MARGIN NOTES

- Technological Factors
  - A 'quick' checklist for your technological assessment might include:
    - Rate of technological change:
      - Organisation's ability to keep up
      - Customer acceptance
    - Research and development:
      - Cost of investment
      - Matching customer needs
      - Control
    - Production technology:
      - Costs versus savings
      - Internal skill base
    - Protection of technology:
      - Patents
      - Copyrights
      - Impact on investment
    - Universal availability of technology:
      - The rat race to technological edge
      - Product differentiation possibilities

- International Factors
  - The number of organisations which have no international markets, no international suppliers for various components or raw materials and no international competition in the domestic market are becoming fewer and fewer every year.
  - A 'quick' checklist for your international assessment might include:
    - International 'Political' issues
      - Growth of China and India
      - EU and regional policies
    - International 'Economic' issues
      - Outsourcing?
      - Growth of China and India
      - Fairtrade
    - International 'Sociological' issues
      - Social and Culture – beware, the big one
    - International 'Technological' issues
      - International movement of IP

  - International 'Environmental' issues
    - Global warming
    - Environmental pressure groups
  - International 'Customer/Market' issues
    - Culture
  - International 'Competitive' issues
  - These, for each market addressed, or from which we receive competition

- Environmental Factors
  - Environmental and ecological awareness too has entered the mainstream.
  - A 'quick' checklist for your environmental assessment might include:
    - Sustainability
      - Global warming
      - Political football?
      - Carbon exchange
      - A 'Fad', a 'Trend' or a 'Bubble'?
      - Where next? – which way you bet on this one could seriously affect your future
    - Fairtrade
    - Pirating
    - Alternative technology
    - Customer willingness to pay a premium

- Customer/Market Factors
  - See below and also Chapter 6

- Competition Factors
  - See below

MARGIN NOTES

Action

Keeping up with changes in the environment (sometimes called environmental scanning) is not an option – you live off the environment, you must understand it.

You have no choice but to:

- Understand the environment in which you have chosen to play
  - What does 'external' mean for your business?
  - What business are you in? So, what should you measure?
  - What changes are 'blips'?
  - What changes are structural? – it is not going back

- Be prepared for the future
  - Change is the order of the day in the business environment

- Make the exercise a regular activity
  - The environment audit is not an exercise that can be completed and then forgotten.

- It is not an exercise that can be safely carried out on an annual basis – there is too much important change.
- Create a tracking mechanism that will show up the most important changes as they occur.

- For each change noted
  - What is the effect on you and your organisation/business?
  - What must you do about it?

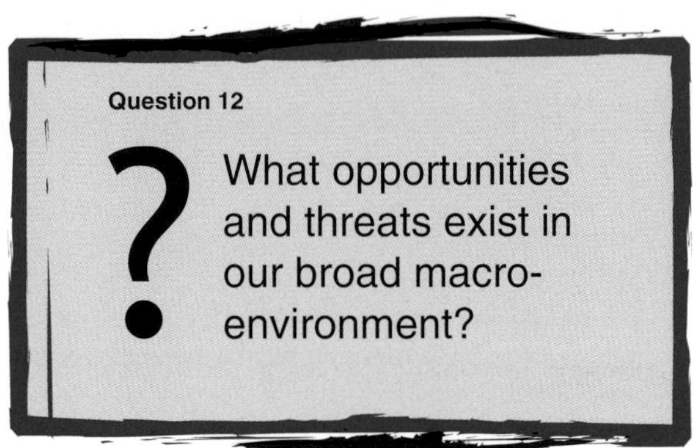

Question 12
?
What opportunities and threats exist in our broad macro-environment?

MARGIN NOTES

Having done our best to make sense of what is going on in the wider business environment, we need to turn this information into action.

You will need to:

- Search through the environment for the business opportunities that appear to be open to us.
  - It takes time to develop new products and new services and to develop and open new markets.
  - If we are given a hint from the environment audit that new market possibilities are likely to open, then we should plan our time accordingly and be ready when the market appears.
  - Arriving six to nine months late (even consistently), along with the all the other late arrivals, is hardly the best way to win a positive market reputation.

- Identify the threats that may appear in the business environment, especially those that might seriously hinder our development and continued prosperity.
  - In my experience, the list of threats is twice or three times longer than that of opportunities.
    - I must admit I am never quite sure whether this is because the environment really is tough out there or because a pessimistic nature is a prerequisite for the modern manager.
    - Be this as it may.

- The important thing is not just to identify the threats, but to be able to do something about them.
  - As long as they are spotted early enough most threats can either be neutralised or avoided by the organisation – or even, if you are very good, turned into opportunities.

- It's not just tomorrow's threats and opportunities that can be unearthed by a solid environment audit.
  - If your organisation is about to start an audit for the first time you are likely to discover an interesting collection of threats and opportunities sitting right underneath you now – you just did not know they were there!
  - Foregoing opportunities is one thing, not knowing about a threat until a few years of declining profits makes it too late to do anything about it, is quite another.

MARGIN NOTES

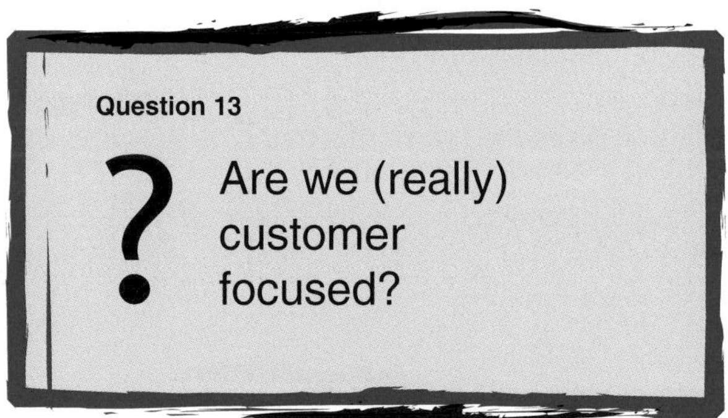
Question 13
?
Are we (really) customer focused?

We will deal with the whole question of customer orientation and organisational culture in much more detail in Chapter 6. For the moment though, we will consider this question from the data gathering perspective.

Even the two great bestselling strategy books of the last Century, Porter's '*Competitive Strategy*' and '*Competitive Advantage*' (New York Free Press, 1983 and 1990), both require (although this is not explicitly stated) that the organisation be market/customer oriented for the proposed strategic approach to work. Porter's whole approach is based on the importance of looking outward to the environment and the competitive marketplace rather than basing our future on purely internal considerations.

This attitude reflects the approach of most companies – we all manage to speak a good line, but when it comes down to the wire …

A driving organisational culture and state of mind that is focuses inward rather than outward at the customer, not only chooses to uncover the wrong data from the environment, but is also most likely to misinterpret the data which is collected.

Action
You need to:

- Understand what it (really) means to be outward looking and customer focused
  - Customer focused organisations are not easy to find but see if you can find one outside your industry
  - Study how it operates
  - Study how it treats customers (it won't just give them what they want every time – it does not work like that)
  - Study how it deals with staff/internal issues
  - Study how it represents customers inside the organisation.

- See of you can translate these activities into what it would mean for your organisation

- Calculate how different you are – how inward looking are you really?

- Identify the natural bias this internal focus has on the:
  - Data deemed necessary
  - Data collected
  - Information translated from this data.

- Draw up and implement plans to collect data and information to counteract this bias and to interpret the environment from a customer perspective.

MARGIN NOTES

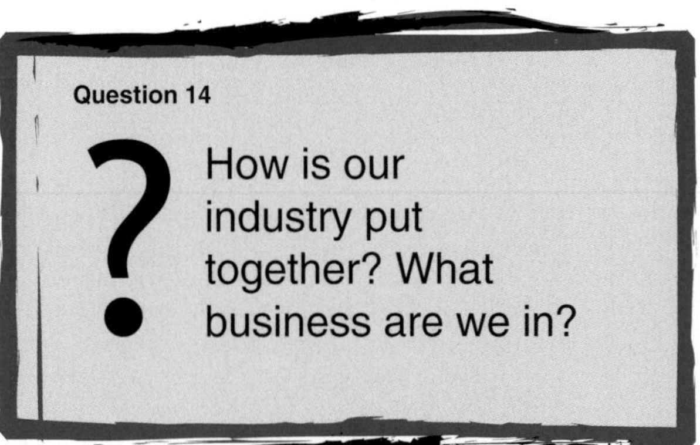

Question 14
?
How is our industry put together? What business are we in?

You are on a journey. The industry you are part of, is also on a journey. You can decide to accept the route that everybody else is travelling or you can decide to break out. In any event, knowing where the group is travelling will give you some choice.

There are a number of (sometimes quite complicated) analyses to assess your industry's position. I think these are interesting but too complicated to explain to others in the organisation – so can alienate the marketing strategy ('too academic') rather than help involve people in the future. I prefer to use a simpler (less complicated but less accurate) but more easily recognised model, the Product Life Cycle. Trust me, in this business, simpler is better.

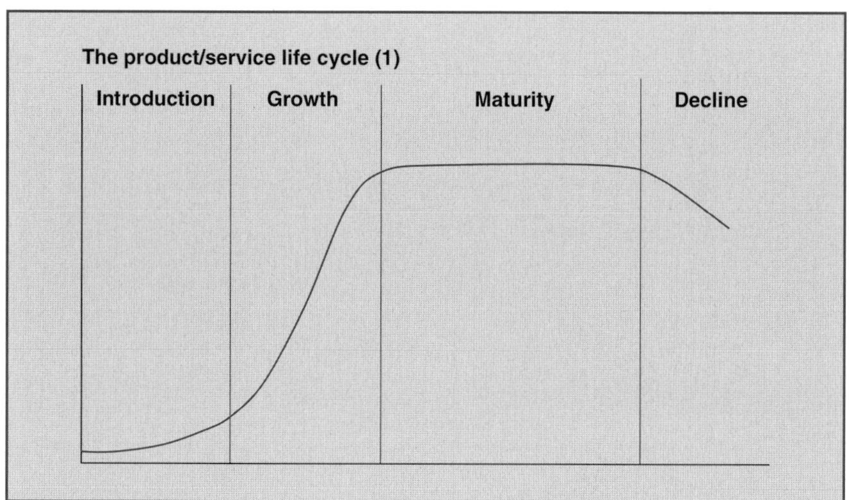

MARGIN NOTES

A brief recap – as I am sure you know, the life cycle can be applied to a product, service, product category or brand. On the other hand, while it can be a useful 'concept' it is less useful as a 'model' because it is not always easy to tell exactly where you are on the curve – until you have passed the point. But it is still useful for explaining what the future *might* look like.

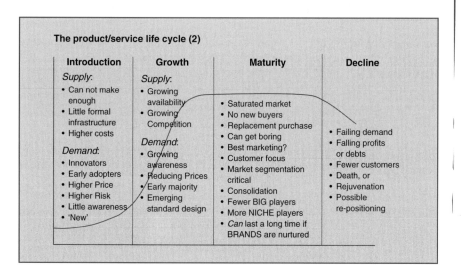

The product/service life cycle (2)

Introduction

Supply:
- Can not make enough
- Little formal infrastructure
- Higher costs

Demand:
- Innovators
- Early adopters
- Higher Price
- Higher Risk
- Little awareness
- 'New'

Growth

Supply:
- Growing availability
- Growing Competition

Demand:
- Growing awareness
- Reducing Prices
- Early majority
- Emerging standard design

Maturity

- Saturated market
- No new buyers
- Replacement purchase
- Can get boring
- Best marketing?
- Customer focus
- Market segmentation critical
- Consolidation
- Fewer BIG players
- More NICHE players
- *Can* last a long time if BRANDS are nurtured

Decline

- Failing demand
- Falling profits or debts
- Fewer customers
- Death, or
- Rejuvenation
- Possible re-positioning

There are four recognised stages to the life cycle as the product or service or category proceeds from introduction through growth into maturity and eventually into decline and death. How long the cycle lasts depends on the market and the organisations involved. Again, the stages are well documented in most marketing texts.

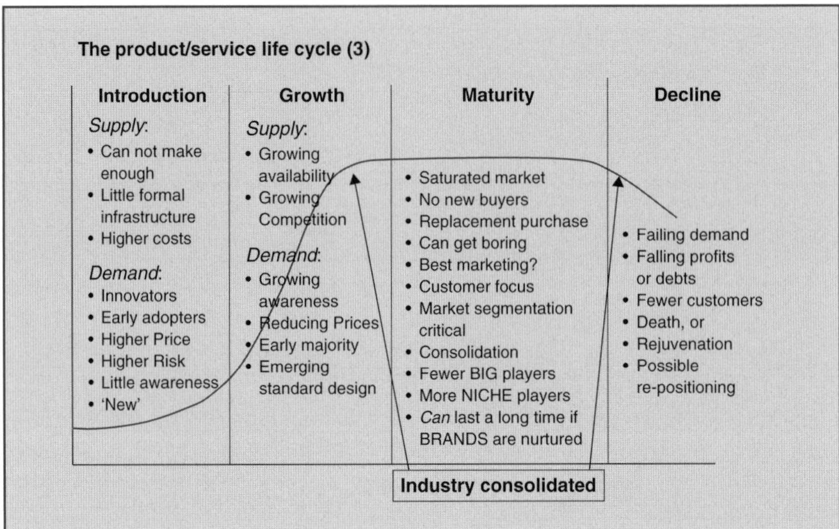

MARGIN NOTES

However, we know more about the PLC than is usually explained in the introductory texts. There are two points at which the industry consolidates or suffers a 'shake-out' of firms. Naturally consolidation occurs when the entire industry starts to decline but an earlier (and more widespread) shakeout occurs before this.

At the point between the rapid growth stage and the maturity stage is the most dangerous *for the majority* of organisations in an industry. Let's think why.

- The business starts slowly, and then takes off.
- Growing industries/markets are a special environment and they can support a wide range of organisations, all trying to carve out market share at the same time.
  - Because the whole market is growing many companies can prosper as they offer very different product/service solutions and do so at very different levels of efficiency and profitability.
  - At this stage, sales is definitely the name of the game.
  - Margins always seem to be under pressure but nobody really suffers very badly, there is always enough profit for sizeable sales commissions and recruitment of new sales people.
  - It is a time for new ideas and new technology and new markets and new stars in the business world.

- Then comes the 'downfall' – the market becomes saturated.
  - Every customer who wants a telephone, car, washing machine, mobile telephone, online game, mp3 player – now owns one.
  - The market (and sales) stops growing.
  - Customers only buy to replace existing product or service.
  - All of a sudden, the business is not growing at the heady 25 or 30% per year – it might even be contracting.

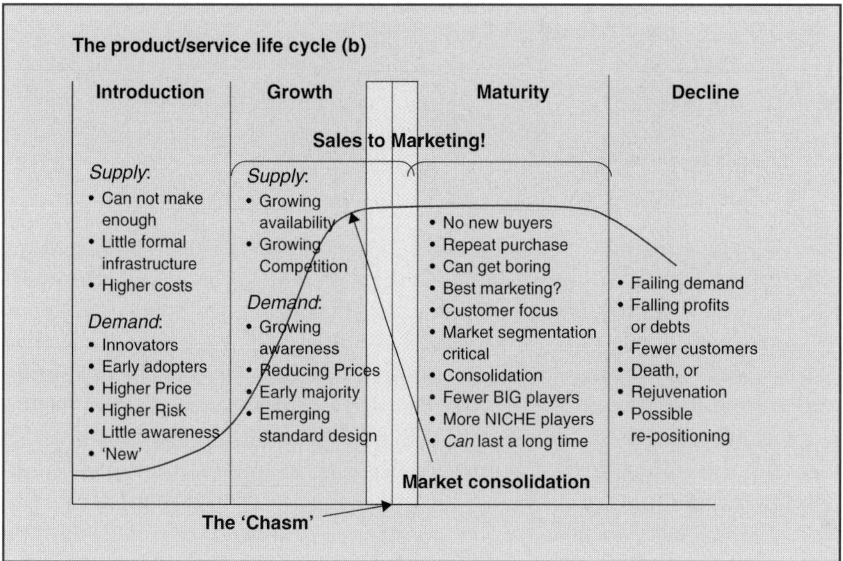

MARGIN NOTES

- Market maturity is not so much a difficult time – it is a different time from the stage that went before it:
  - In the rapid growth period, the successful organisation will focus on:
    - Managing the product or service
    - Managing the sales operation
    - Managing the business growth
  - In the mature stage, the entire emphasis shifts from internal to external, *from product to customer* – the successful organisation will focus on:
    - Managing the insight and knowledge of customer needs
    - Managing the focus on the most appropriate market segments
    - Managing the product or service differentiation
    - Managing and caring for the brands
    - Managing the realignment of the organisation and its activities to the constantly migrating needs of the customers.

The fact is, the skills required by the organisation to succeed in maturity are *so different* from the skills required to succeed in the growth stage that very few organisations manage the change. According to Markides and

Geroski ('*Creating new radical markets – The myth of first mover advantage*', Market Leader, Spring 2004) the car and tyre businesses show what happens everywhere – according to their research:

- Car business:
  - More than 70 firms rushed to enter the car business in the first 15 years of existence.
  - More than 1,000 firms populated the industry at one time or another.
  - By the late 1950s there were only 7 left.

- Tyre business:
  - There were more than 274 competitors in the market for tyres in the early 1920s.
  - 50 years later no more than 23 survived.

MARGIN NOTES

The following table shows what typical types of business and market activity will be associated with the different stages of the life cycle. This analysis is not new although I have updated it for this book. You can see how the necessary skills simply scale up between Introduction and Growth stages, and between Maturity and Decline stages. At the same time, there is an unavoidable 'chasm' between the skills needed in Growth and in Maturity. It is no wonder that so few organisations manage the transition.

Action
The questions for you and your organisation then are quite straightforward:

- Where do you think you (and your industry) are on the Product Life Cycle?
- If you are in the Growth stage, how long (this is the difficult one) do you think you have before the market moves to Maturity?
- Do you have the skills to succeed in Maturity?
- Can you learn or acquire the skills you need?
- How much resistance will you face from senior management in the organisation?
- Do the answers above suggest that you are working for one of the (few) survivors or one of the (many) impending casualties?

The PLC and Marketing Activity

	Introduction	Growth	Maturity	Decline
Characteristics Sales	Low sales	Rapidly rising	Peak/static sales	Declining sales
Costs	High cost per customer	Average cost per customer	Lower cost per customer	Low cost per customer
Profits	Negative	Rising	High	Declining
Competitors	Few	Growing number	Declining rapidly	Declining to final few
Marketing Objectives				
	Create awareness and trial	Maximise market share and hold	Maximise profits while defend selected market segments	Reduce expenditure, milk the brand or rejuvenate
Marketing Strategy Segmentation/Targeting	Anyone who will listen	'Mass market'	Key to success, identify and differentiate	Focus on final segments
Customer	Innovators	Early adopters	Middle majority	Laggards
Offerings	New and basic	Better product, standard emerging	Differentiation of product and support services	Focused offering to remaining customers
Retention	Less important than initial sales	Sales growth key in growing business	Key activity by targeted segment	Decide when to abandon
Position/Brand	Establish awareness	Establish position as key player	Establish brand as *unique* within smaller field	Focus brand on final specialisation or rejuvenate

(*Continued*)

The PLC and Marketing Activity (*continued*)

	Introduction	Growth	Maturity	Decline
Industry or Market?	New offer may not have industry definition	Industry definition for growth phase	Market definition essential for survival	Focused application definition
Organisation	Small, entrepreneurial Start-up	Structured sales organisation	Structured market and customer focused organisation	Smaller focused specialist organisation
Marketing Tactics				
Product	Basic product that early adopters will help perfect	Finished offer range with service and warranty	Differentiate, brand and focus on targeted segments only	Phase out weak items and focus on final versions
Price	Cost-plus large margin	Reduce price to penetrate market	Increase price to differentiate offer from competitors	Cut price or increase price further to specialise
Place/Distribution	Build selective distribution	Build intensive distribution	Build intensive and segment – focused distribution	Go selective: phase out unprofitable outlets
Promotion	Build product/ service awareness and promote trial	Build awareness and interest in mass market	Stress brand differences and benefits to targeted segments	Reduce to level needed to retain hard-core loyalists

Additional activity

Here are some additional questions that we will answer, in more detail, in Chapter 5:

- How do you define the industry you are part of?
- Is this really the business you are in?
- Is Harley Davidson in the motorcycle business?
- Does Starbucks sell coffee or a place to meet your friends and work colleagues?
- Is the 'coffee business' at the same stage of the PLC as the 'meeting friends and colleagues business'?

Intrigued? – I hope so

MARGIN NOTES

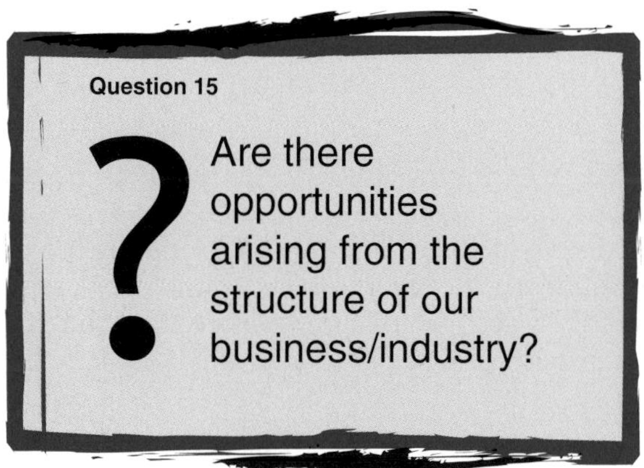

Question 15
?
Are there opportunities arising from the structure of our business/industry?

Industries will vary from one to another as the strengths of the five competitive forces (see below) will differ. The reason for this is largely because of the different marketing–economic and production–technical characteristics which underlie each different industry. These important characteristics are known as the industry structure.

Your organisation has the power, through the business and marketing strategies that it chooses, to influence the structure of the industry within which it operates. One way of understanding structural opportunities, is to look at Porter's 5 Forces Model, which describes five distinct competitive forces that Porter says will collectively determine the profitability of any industry. A few examples may serve to illustrate the point.

- Industry competition:
  - Competing organisations can group together to mount collaborative generic advertising and promotional campaigns with the aim of expanding the total market size.

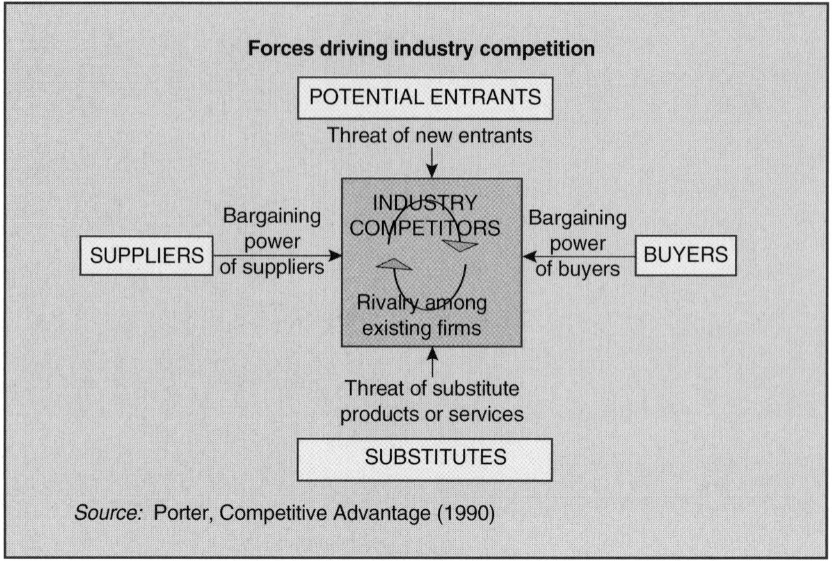

Source: Porter, Competitive Advantage (1990)

MARGIN NOTES

- Increased market size obviously reduces the intensity of direct competition since there is a larger market to fight over.
- On the down side there is the question of a larger market acting as a magnet for outside organisations unless entry barriers are high.
- Collaboration such as this has been used in Europe in industries such as insurance, shock absorbers and beef.

- New entrants:
  - Can be combated by building significant (and durable) entry barriers.
  - Marketing barriers in terms of brand loyalty and product differentiation can be very effective but tend to take time to construct; and are also quite investment hungry.
  - Other methods include lobbying government for protection of the industry, perhaps through;
    - Increased specialisation, or
    - Driving down the unit cost of production to a level which inhibits new entrants.
  - Beware, technical barriers are often at the mercy of technical leapfrogs – which overnight can make a very expensive barrier obsolete.
- Substitution:
  - Here it pays big dividends to keep in very close contact with your customers.
  - Change may not be possible if too many people in your organisation would rather die than change – a surprisingly popular competitive response I have found!
  - Substitutes need not necessarily be a threat to the industry or our position – especially if we are the organisation marketing the substitute.

- Supplier power:
  - There are two ways of dealing with the problem.
    - Attempt to negate the power of certain suppliers by locating alternative sources of supply.
    - Take advantage of the possibly concentrated supply situation by integrating backwards into the supply end of the industry.
- Buyer power:
  - This falls into two broad categories.
    - The concentrated power that comes from either a small number of buyers or a smaller number of very large volume buyers;
      - You can either further concentrate the purchase activity of the industry to create equal strength to the buyers.
      - Or broaden the product or service scope to encourage new buyers into the industry and thereby reduce the power of the primary buyers.
    - The second category of buyer power, price sensitivity, and the most obvious solution is to build strength on brand awareness, product differentiation and loyalty in the marketplace.
      - This is a high cost, long-term solution but should deliver better prices, margins and so, profits.
      - Major packaged goods producers such as Heinz and Kellogg's use this approach successfully.
      - As do B2B organisations such as JCB, Accenture and Rolls Royce engines.

MARGIN NOTES

Action
What opportunities does your industry structure offer you? Too many players, in all sorts of markets and industries, forget that they are *not* there to fight the competition, but to serve the *customer* better – the two are not the same.

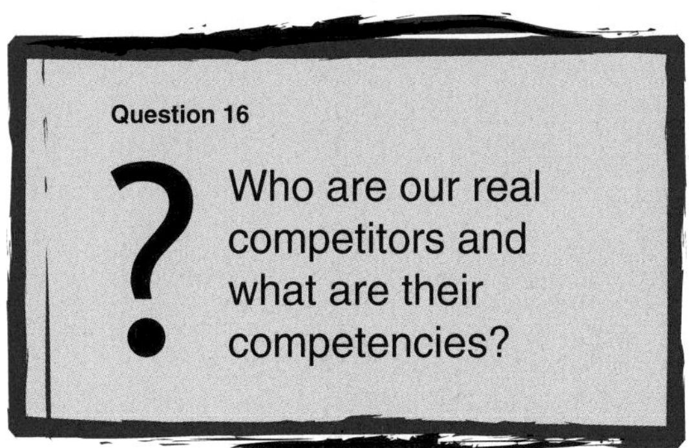

Question 16
?
Who are our real competitors and what are their competencies?

We all agree that we need to understand our competitors better than we do at the moment, but let's try and understand why it is so important to uncover what our competitors are trying to do in the marketplace.

- Regardless of what your organisation/business produces, as soon as you make an offering to the market what's the first thing the customer is going to do? Compare!

- As much as we would like to believe that our customer is a rational, decision-making being; potential buyers are simply not used to making decisions in a vacuum.
- In order to judge the benefits of your offering and the claims that you make, their first step is always going to be to compare your offering to an alternative offering made by an organisation they *believe* to be a competitor.
- We all know this is what happens, so why ignore it?
- We also know that if we don't compare well, we don't sell very much.

MARGIN NOTES

- Competitor analysis is obviously a 'good thing', but where to start?
  - Most organisations have a database (of sorts) on (who they think are the) competitors and their capabilities and activities.
  - Although this information is often gathered in an ad hoc manner from meetings, customers, intermediaries and the sales force, it is, of course, the systematic process carried out over a longer period of time that tends to develop a better understanding of our competitors' ambitions and capabilities.

- But beware. If you focus only on your direct competitors in mind then you have left yourself and your organisation open and vulnerable.
  - In the previous section we looked at the 'five forces' of competition.
  - Levitt said that '*Customers just need to get things done. When people find themselves needing to get a job done, they essentially hire products to do that job for them*'.
  - And there are always different ways of getting a job done, including not doing it at all.

- You must ensure that you have looked at the competitors from the customers' perspective.
  - When Cadbury finds that its sales of chocolate to teenage girls in the UK are falling – because they are spending their limited financial resources on mobile phone top-up cards instead, then it has a marketing challenge on its hands.
  - One that would not have shown up by looking at other chocolate producers alone.

Action

You have two separate tasks here:

- First; the *what?*; this data is easier to collect and concerns what the competitor is currently doing and what (in our opinion) it is able to do:
  - What is the competitor's current strategy?
  - How is the competitor currently competing with our organisation?
  - You can collect this data from:
    - Published material such as annual reports, press commentaries
    - Responses from customers

- Second; the *why?*; this is more useful to developing an understanding of our competitors, and their capabilities:
  - What are the future goals of the competitor and of its management?
  - What are the assumptions that the competitor and its management hold about themselves and the industry in which they operate?
  - You can collect this insight from:
    - Some published material such as analysts assessments and annual reports
    - Responses from intermediaries/channel partners

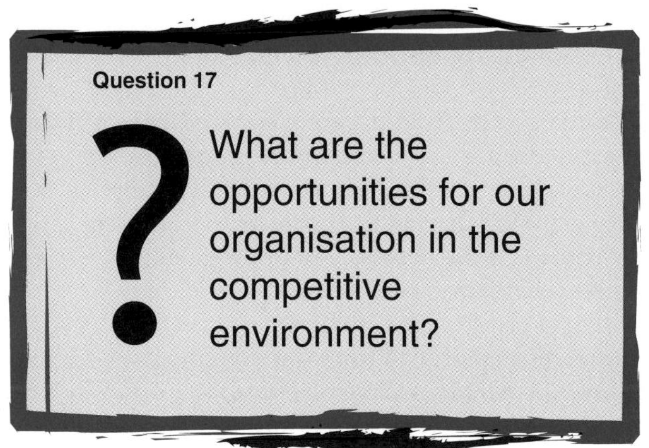

Question 17
?
What are the opportunities for our organisation in the competitive environment?

MARGIN NOTES

There is no point collecting data and information unless you intend doing something with it.

The primary aim for any organisation must be to win and to keep profitable customers. Straightforward, bloody, head-to-head feuds should not be the aim of the organisation. While competition itself *may* bring certain benefits to the customer, for the organisation it is an extremely wasteful and expensive exercise. An understanding of any likely retali-ation should permit us to sift through different strategic alternatives and to choose those activities that will produce the maximum return.

Action
You need to ask yourself some questions:

- First, our own situation:
  - What are our own internal capabilities?
  - What are the main trends in the broad macro environment in which we operate?
  - What are the structural opportunities that exist within the five competitive force framework of the industry?

- Next, the competition:
  - Who are our competitors? Direct (national and international) and substitutional?

- Which competitors seem satisfied and comfortable with their current situation?
- Which competitors?
- Which Market segments are our different competitors most concerned with?
  - Where they see their future and the types of market they would like to penetrate?
- Where are particular competitors vulnerable?
- Are there identifiable gaps in the market – things that nobody is doing?
- Is there a market in the gap – are there unserved customer needs?
- Which activities of ours might provoke the strongest competitive response?
  - This can come from different competitors for different reasons (large, expanding competitors might resent your ambitions while slow, comfortable competitors may fight viciously to protect what market they control.
- What would be the best way of approaching these opportunities? Where is the balance between:
  - Using our particular strengths.
  - Reaping most return from our activities.
  - Minimising competitive response.

MARGIN NOTES

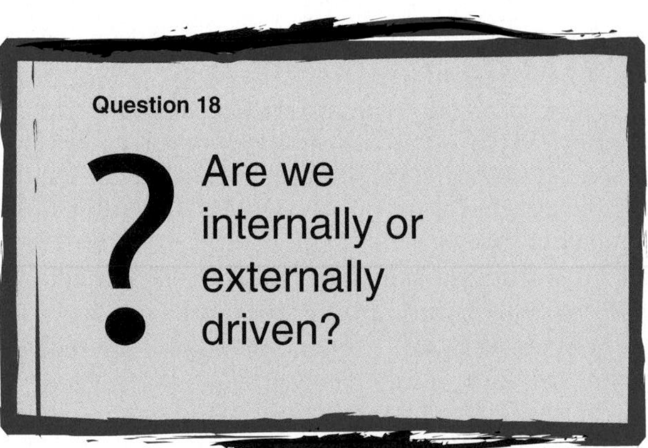

Question 18
?
Are we internally or externally driven?

I, and others, have written long and hard about the need to be focused on external events rather than internal issues. It seems patently obvious to me that all the important things are outside the business:

- Customers
- Competitors
- Political, Economic, Sociological and Technological trends that affect both of these If only because they all drive revenues.

But talking about it does not make it happen and the majority of organisations would rather spend their time and efforts on those important internal issues that they know so well.

Recent UK and European emphasis on 'compliance', 'health and safety' and 'risk management' have simply added to the problem with the constant threat of customer and/or government litigation. Now it almost makes good business and financial sense to spend valuable time and money *not* making mistakes. Customers, as always, will simply take the opposite, self-interested, view and wander off when the risk averse organisations fail to deliver the new products and services they crave.

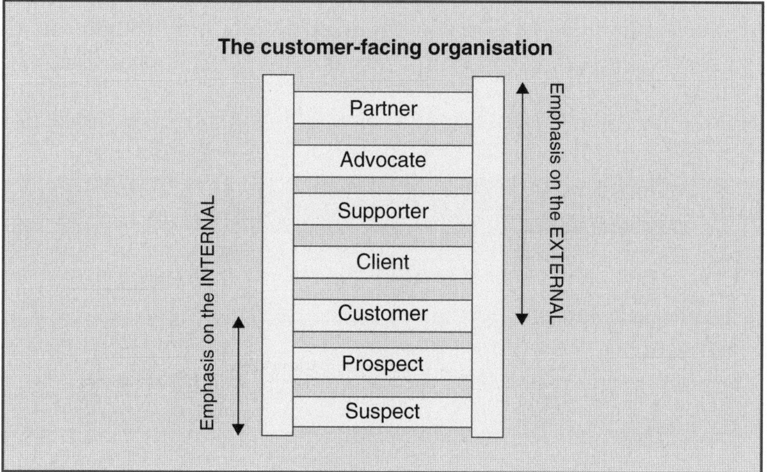

MARGIN NOTES

Ultimately, nothing matters apart from customers (sorry, but it's difficult to put that less forcefully) so I use a very simple measure to tell me whether an organisation is predominantly internally or externally focused. It all depends on how they see their customers. If they deal with them as if they are partners, advocates, supporters or clients, then they understand the importance of customers – the external view will dominate to a greater or lesser degree.

If the organisation looks upon customers as numbers, the anonymous mass that exist to soak up the product of the factories or service systems, then the internal view will dominate.

Action
I have tried everything.

Every organisation is different, but it seems to me that there is a very strong correlation at least between internal focus on the one hand and company size, complexity and the existence of a 'professional management' cadre on the other. I wonder if the two might be linked.

■ The strategic questions (9–18)

Here are the next 9 questions for you – they get more important, but they don't get any easier.

This is the section where you are most likely to start confusing 'Not important' with 'Too difficult' in the ✓ column. Just because it might involve data from outside the organisation/business does not mean it's either too difficult or not worth the effort. If it's 'Must have' and you don't know, then you just have to find out – it's not that difficult really.

No.	Strategic question	Our strategic answer	Importance	✓
	External business drivers			
9	What resources do we have and how are they being utilized?		Must have	
			Nice to have	
			Not important	
10	What are the strengths and weaknesses of the organisation?		Must have	
			Nice to have	
			Not important	
11	What is the 'Environment Audit' and how do we create one?		Must have	
			Nice to have	
			Not important	
12	What opportunities and threats exist in our broad macro environment?		Must have	
			Nice to have	
			Not important	
13	Are we (really) customer focused?		Must have	
			Nice to have	
			Not important	
14	How is our industry put together? What business are we in?		Must have	
			Nice to have	
			Not important	

15	Are there opportunities arising from the structure of our business/industry?		Must have	
			Nice to have	
			Not important	
16	Who are our real competitors and what are their competencies?		Must have	
			Nice to have	
			Not important	
17	What are the opportunities for our organisation in the competitive environment?		Must have	
			Nice to have	
			Not important	
18	Are we internally or externally driven?		Must have	
			Nice to have	
			Not important	

CHAPTER 3

The business strategy

> 'Strategy without tactics is the slowest route to victory. Tactics without strategy is the noise before defeat.'
>
> *'Sun Tzu (c. 544 BC – 496 BC), the author of The Art of War, a book on military strategy*

We need to spend a little time looking at business or corporate strategy, because it drives marketing strategy. Lest there be any confusion, business/corporate strategy and marketing strategy are *not* the same thing.

But, this is *not* a book on corporate strategy – that is a debate we can usefully avoid. The whole 'industry' was started by Ansoff in an article called ('Strategies for Diversification', Harvard Business Review 1957), popularised by Porter (in the 1980s), widened by Mintzberg (in the 1990s) and now you have to beat off the strategy gurus with a large stick.

Before we can begin to discuss marketing strategy proper we need certain minimum data on which to build our plans. To develop the marketing strategy we need:

- To agree the business/corporate *objective.*
  - The organisation needs a clear objective in order to be able to set its own (marketing) objective(s).
  - If a clear overall objective for the organisation is not specifically stated, some sort of hypothesis will have to be made.
- To agree the business/corporate *strategy.*
  - How the organisation intends to achieve the agreed business/corporate objective.

MARGIN NOTES

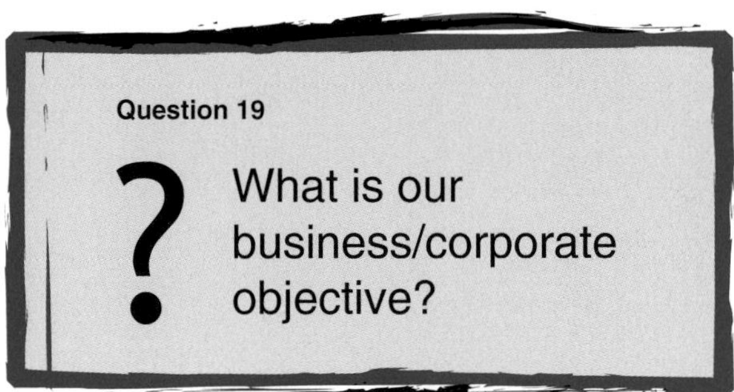

Question 19
?
What is our business/corporate objective?

First, the 'headlines':

- The Business Objective is defined as:
  - The goal or the aim to which all activities of the organisation are directed
  - An objective should always begin with the word 'To ...'

Not necessarily an area you will want to get into, unless you are managing as well as marketing director (and why not?) in which case you will need more guidance from a more specialist text. For the rest of us, the reasoning is simple; if the organisation does not have a single, clear, concise business objective then it is more than likely that activities will be directed in a number of different (and possibly conflicting) directions with the net result that the organisation is seriously wasting resource (money, time and management effort). How do you hope to develop a coherent – and focused – marketing strategy in such an environment?

Tick the boxes as you go …

The '12 rules of engagement' for setting the business/corporate *objective* are:		
No.	**Rule**	✓
1	The business objective is not the same as the financial objective(hurdle) – see chapter 1 ● The business objective is about codifying the purpose of the organisation ● The financial hurdle (some call it the objective) is about measuring how successful the organisation has been	
2	If the senior management is too hidebound to separate finance and business, you are going to have to come up with a 'hypothesis' of the business objective that meets the needs of all the stakeholders and jumps the financial hurdles	
3	You need a single objective. Multiple objectives are easier to agree but only lead to conflict	
4	The business objective should be no longer than one (short) sentence – so it needs to be understood	
5	The first word of the objective is 'To …'	
6	The business objective should be achievable, not wishful thinking.	
7	The objective should be quantifiable in some form	
8	There has to be some time limit on the achievement of the objective	
9	There must be some form of quantifiable success criteria	
10	The business objective must be consistent with both the internal capabilities of the organisation and with the desires of the key implementers and their personal vision of the future	
11	The objective must be consistent with the external environment and the opportunities and constraints that we have identified	
12	The business objective must be both understandable and capable of communication throughout the organisation	

Action

The only guidance I can give you here is to take your time and make sure you do as thorough a job as you can. While you seem to wasting inordinate amounts of time on pointless discussions, remember that this is an investment, not a cost. Time invested in agreeing the objective, especially in recruiting the hearts and minds of others in the objective, will be paid back many times over later in the process.

The right objective will give the company wings; the wrong one will doom it to being an also-ran in a commodity market.

Given all the pointers above, you must (specifically, not generally) decide the following:

- What business you want to be in (see Chapter 5)
- What market(s) or segment(s) you intend to target and do business in (see Chapter 7)
- What constitutes 'success'
- The date by which you will have achieved the objective
- The business/corporate objective: 'To be ... by (date)' see below for some examples:
  - The natural choice (for the business you have decided you are in)
  - The first choice (for specified customers or benefits)
  - The benchmark provider of (whatever benefits you offer)
  - The thought leader (good for the leader who isn't the biggest)
  - The most (add your preferred differentiation)
  - The M&S/BMW/BA (add your own benchmark company) of the xzz business.

MARGIN NOTES

Question 20

? What is our business/corporate strategy?

More 'headlines':

- Business strategy is defined as:
  - The one route which is both necessary and sufficient to achieve the business objective
  - A strategy should always begin with the word 'By …'

The '6 rules of engagement' for setting the business/corporate *strategy* are:

No.	Rule	✓
1	The strategy must be driven by the objective that it seeks to implement	
2	One strategy is better than lots of different strategies that will conflict and compete	
3	The first word of your strategy is 'By …'	
4	The best strategy is one that is *necessary* to achieve the objective. If its not necessary (to achieve the objective), we should not do it	
5	The strategy also needs to be *sufficient*, of itself, to achieve the objective	
6	The strategy needs to be *different* from the competition if you desire more than average returns from the sector	

Tick the boxes as you go …

For any given objective there is normally a series of alternative strategies, which may be seen as being viable ways of achieving the objective.

- To take a perhaps over-simplistic example let us assume that your objective is to get from your home in London to a meeting in Brussels.
  - There are obviously a number of alternative strategies for achieving this objective:
    - You could drive from London to Dover; you could then pick up the ferry or rail tunnel from Dover to Calais and drive through France to Belgium to Brussels.
    - You could take the Dover to Calais or Ostend ferries and drive down from there.
    - You might decide to get on a train at London, travel through the Channel Tunnel rail link direct to Brussels.

    - You might decide to fly so you travel from London through to Heathrow; Heathrow to Zaventem and from there to Brussels centre which may involve the use of trains or taxis.
    - Centre to centre helicopters may be an option for the select few.

- Whichever route you choose your preferred strategy will probably be based on other aspects such as the time available, the relative desire for other stops en route, the convenience and timing of the schedules and so on.
  - Your objective is clear (to arrive in an agreed place at an agreed time for a meeting), but there appear to be strategic options:
    - 'By air' –
      - is insufficient given that neither airport is in the right place
    - 'By Sea' –
      - is insufficient for similar reasons
    - 'By rail, sea and air' –
      - includes at least one mode that in unnecessary
    - 'By train and taxi' –
      - could be both necessary and sufficient if the timetables suit meeting times
    - 'By train and taxi, on way to my holiday' –
      - could be necessary and sufficient –
      - and different if this is how you wish to stand out
    - 'By personal jet and chauffeur' –
      - is also necessary and sufficient and different and gets you remembered another way
    - 'By Ryanair from London to Brussels/Charleroi' (not knowing that it is 60 km from Brussels) –
      - is also necessary and sufficient and different and gets you remembered another way!

MARGIN NOTES

Action

Work on your own agreed business objective and draw out all the possibilities before you start to decide:

- What are you trying to achieve?

- What steps are 'necessary'?

- What steps are 'sufficient'?

- What steps are 'different' and would support your unique market position?

- What steps are 'really ordinary' and would threaten your unique market position n if you employed them?

- Which step combinations are, at the same time *necessary, sufficient* and *different*?

- Have you allowed for changes in market conditions?
  - What would happen to your plans if some basic assumptions changed?
  - Have you built in flexibly?

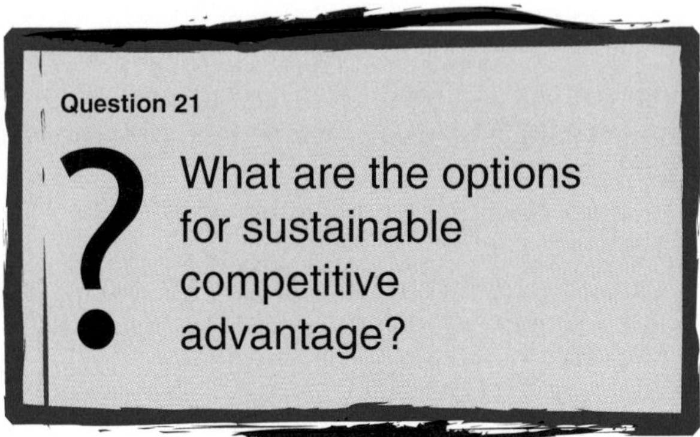

Question 21
?
What are the options for sustainable competitive advantage?

MARGIN NOTES

We have all heard of the term Sustainable Competitive Advantage, although few have ploughed through the economics texts that describe it in technical detail. The concept of sustainable competitive advantage is not a new idea. It can be found in the early origins of economics, basic marketing – and in everyday common sense.

The 'headlines' are:

- If an organisation is able to do something better (customer perception) than its competitors it will make better profits.

- If an organisation is only as good as everybody else it will only make standard profits.

- If an organisation is worse than its competitors at what it does it will make inferior profits.

Nothing too controversial there.

The aim of competitive strategy is to find ways of *avoiding* competition and making superior profits. So, the search must be for ways of achieving some form of *advantage* over our competitors which will enable us to make better than average profits. Also, the advantage itself must be *sustainable* over the long term to generate reasonable and consistent profit flows.

- Identifying (and then selecting the most appropriate) competitive advantage is not as easy as it would appear to be at first glance.

- In the marketing texts of the 1960s and 1970s we would read a lot about the same thing but then it was called a USP (unique selling proposition); although at the time the concept was applied mainly to product features rather than organisations.

- Many textbooks still attempt to reproduce lists of areas of sustainable advantage that the organisation might wish to consider; these used to cover SWOT, industry analysis, structure, environment and all sorts.

- Over the years though, the lengths of the lists have all shortened.
  - With the widespread application of knowledge and technology, there are few areas that can now offer any long-term advantage.

- Having said this, a short-term advantage may still be worth having – but it will have to be replaced eventually.
  - When we look at today's competitive markets it becomes obvious that genuine long-term sustainability is rare.

- The debate was moved into a new area by Hamel and Prahalad who coined the term Core competencies (which are those capabilities that are critical to an organisation achieving competitive advantage), but we will look closer at this idea in Chapter 10.

MARGIN NOTES

However, to start the ball rolling, we can turn again to Porter, who suggests there are three *generic* strategic alternatives open to the organisation. There is, in fact, a fourth, which, although it is not to be recommended, does appear to be very popular with too many organisations. According to Porter, the organisation which decides and then consistently follows one of these three prime strategic strategies successfully, will achieve good profits and above average returns on its investment.

Porter's generic strategies

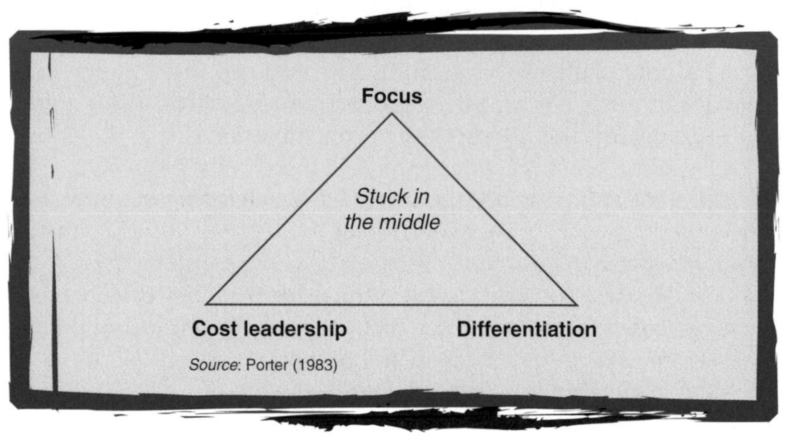

Source: Porter (1983)

Porter describes three generic strategies:

- Differentiation
  - The organisation will be operating throughout the complete market rather than addressing one or two specific segments of the marketplace.
  - The organisation will probably be marketing a fairly *wide range* of products and/or services.
  - The company and its products will have to be differentiated in some way from the competitive offerings.
  - The product or service must in some way be 'unique' in the customers' perception.
  - Differentiation is really all about creating brand identity and loyalty.
    - The power of a well-known brand helps avoid price competition and offers scope for relatively higher margins
  - To be a practical strategy, the difference between the organisation's product or service and the competitors' offers must be sustainable and believable over the longer term.
  - Any given marketplace will only be able to support as many clearly differentiated positions as the target customers deem credible.
    - The number is difficult to predict and will depend, among other things, on the sophistication of the market and how much investment has been made by the main players in explaining the different positions.
  - Buyers, both industrial and consumer, are 'free spirits' (like cats) and perceptions of what constitutes a credible and differentiated position will differ from person to person and change over time.
    - You must carefully monitor the situation and adjust your market position over time if it is to endure.
  - Costs (investment) for the differentiating organisation are likely to be higher because of the costs of developing and maintaining a 'unique' market position.
  - Much of the cost will be associated with promotion and marketing support although products and services may require additional investment too.
  - The potential rewards from a differentiated strategy are significant but it is not a route to be recommended for those organisations driven only by short-term considerations.
  - Over time, costs will have to be kept close to the industry average – differentiation can't be used to disguise inefficiency.

MARGIN NOTES

- Cost leadership
  - The organisation will do everything in its power to drive its cost base down to the point at which it is able to produce products or services at a lower cost than any of its competitors.
  - Cost leadership is an absolute term.
    - By driving to be the lowest cost provider it means that there can only be one in any market.

- This means that, in a price war, the lowest cost provider will be the last organisation making (any) profits.
- Lowest cost does not have to mean lowest price.
  - There is nothing to stop the lowest cost provider marketing at a price that is similar (or even above) its competitors.
- To achieve overall cost leadership the organisation must dedicate itself to leading edge (for the market) cost reduction activities.
- The cost leadership position can be investment intensive, especially in information and production technology – it costs money to drive costs down
- There are potential dangers in this approach:
  - Cost inflation can erode the advantage over time.
  - Technology doesn't progress smoothly but advances by (leapfrog) jumps.
    - You could be displaced.
  - Internal focus might be the biggest single danger in the cost leadership strategy.
    - Low cost cannot be achieved at the cost of customer benefits.

MARGIN NOTES

- Focus
  - The organisation concentrates its effort, not across the entire market as in the case of the differentiation and cost leadership, but on one or more specific segments of the marketplace.
  - The organisation will need to develop a credible position in the marketplace because customers will have to see even more uniqueness from the focused organisation.
  - Customers must understand the reason for its specialisation in a segment.
  - A focus strategy can be a powerful way of building barriers to competition in a small (but profitable) part of the total marketplace.
  - A true niche player will be exploiting a segment that is too small for the larger companies to attack.
  - Success will come from the organisation's ability to tune its efforts to its particular customers' needs.
  - The organisation will be more precise than the differentiated organisation since it has fewer customers in its target market.
  - The organisation can defy comparison with competitors and should not be forced to operate on prices that are determined by others.
  - The organisation will dedicate itself to the needs and wants of the specific target customer base – to the exclusion of non-targeted segments.
  - The product/service range will probably be quite narrow (range), but also deeper (specialisation), to offer greater choice to a restricted part of the marketplace.
  - Finally, the risks:
    - A structural shift in the marketplace could cause the mass emigration of customers to new markets.

  - How do we define the segment into which we are going to focus our attention in the first place? (see Chapter 7).
  - As we grow the segment (and the revenues/profits that flow from it) it might become vulnerable to attack from the larger organisations.
  - As the segment grows we could become prey to even more focused organisations who stake a claim to one particular part of our target segment.
  - With success can come greed and the need to grow takes the focused organisation into areas that reduce its (perceived) specialised position.

- Stuck in the middle
  - This approach was not explained by Porter
  - It is too popular in too many organisations
  - It is the result of not following through on any one of the three strategies described above.
  - The organisation achieves its stuck-in-the-middle position by:
    - Being reasonably successful for a number of years and not recognising any need to develop a clear and distinct long-term strategy.
    - Apathy reigns, competition increases and revenues and profits start to decline.
    - When things get uncomfortable, someone says 'We should concentrate on what we are good at, let's drive for a specialist position and let's hike the prices'.
      - The focus strategy is on the agenda
    - The organisation pursues this for almost a year without seeing any significant return on the bottom line.
    - Somebody (else) says, 'What we ought to do is to spend some money on advertising. Broaden the scope, let's get some more people involved in this marketplace and let's get out and push the name, push the products and widen the appeal'.
      - The differentiation strategy is on the agenda
    - Almost a year later sales have increased somewhat but profits are largely unchanged.
    - Then somebody (else) says 'It's all become a bit slack around here, what we ought to do is to start planning some cuts to control the costs and improve the profits'.
      - The low cost strategy is in the agenda.
    - After almost a year the superficial economies are all used up and cost cutting, to be taken any further, will start to eat into the core of the business.
    - Somebody (else) then says 'What we should do is focus a bit more on what we do really well and dump all this additional activity, it does nothing but confuse everybody'.
      - The 'focus' strategy is on the agenda again

MARGIN NOTES

- This 'fictitious' organisation is one that is completely dominated by short-term considerations and lacks/sees no value in a long-term strategic view.
- The problem is not that it does not try various strategic approaches but rather that it perseveres with none of them.
- It is stuck in the middle of the process: never managing to break out of what is a vicious circle leading ultimately only to its own demise.
  - Being 'stuck in the middle' means that there is no clear differentiation between the players.
  - Where there is no differentiation, price competition follows.

Action
Your biggest problem will be avoiding the stuck-in-the-middle approach, because:

- There is safety in numbers.
- Too many organisations are trying doggedly to maintain the 'all-things-to-all-men' approach to the marketplace.
- They find it difficult to compete against clearly and credibly positioned competition.
- They find it difficult to maintain a customer and market orientation because the nature of the customers that they think they are serving changes on too regular a basis.
- As the profit situation steadily deteriorates over time they inevitably become prey to shorter and shorter time constraints and end up driven by either short-term sales cultures or short-term finance requirements.
- They are, at least, doing something – everybody knows they are paid to do, not just to think!

The only solution for your organisation if it is in this situation is to:

- Attract or develop a particularly strong management team capable of forcing the organisation through the pain barrier.
- You must assess the market opportunities and drive for one or other of the strategic routes.
- Undertaking a rational *analysis* of the marketplace and the opportunities and threats that confront the organisation must be followed by a *decision* on the best strategic route for the future.

MARGIN NOTES

- A *relentless drive* for that position is the only thing that will break the vicious circle.

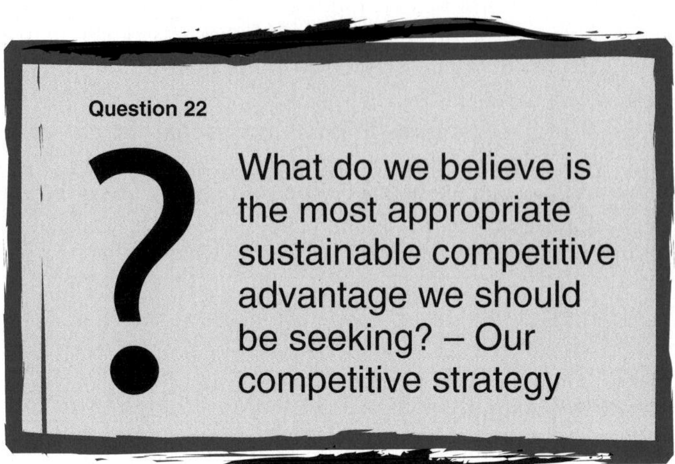

Question 22
?
What do we believe is the most appropriate sustainable competitive advantage we should be seeking? – Our competitive strategy

MARGIN NOTES

Much of the different work on Porter's original ideas has little or no application value to the practicing manager but there are points of light out there, specifically some work by Treacy and Wiersema (*'The Disciplines of the Market Leaders'*, Harper Collins 1997) which has been built on by Peter Doyle (*'Value-based Marketing: Marketing Strategies for Corporate Growth and Shareholder Value'*, John Wiley 2000) and these add some useful ideas for us that want to apply them.

Treacy and Wiersema looked at the Porter's generic strategies model and came up with some nice, simple ideas. They looked at the problem and concluded that:

- Strategy is about resource allocation.
  - In other words, it is about how you decide to spend/invest your money, which is always limited.
- You can decide to spend it on:
  - Being the same as everybody else (Porter's idea of 'stuck-in-the-middle')
  - Being different from the competition (a very good idea)
- If you have decided that you (really) want to be different, you can decide to invest you money on one of:
  - Product Leadership (producing better or the best product)

- Management Efficiency (being the most efficient operator)
- Customer Intimacy (getting closer or closest to your customers)

Working on the options above, Treacy and Wiersema then looked at the idea of 'excellence' in relation to spending/investing the money and suggest that, from a customer perspective, only 'Excellent' and 'Adequate' really exist – How true!

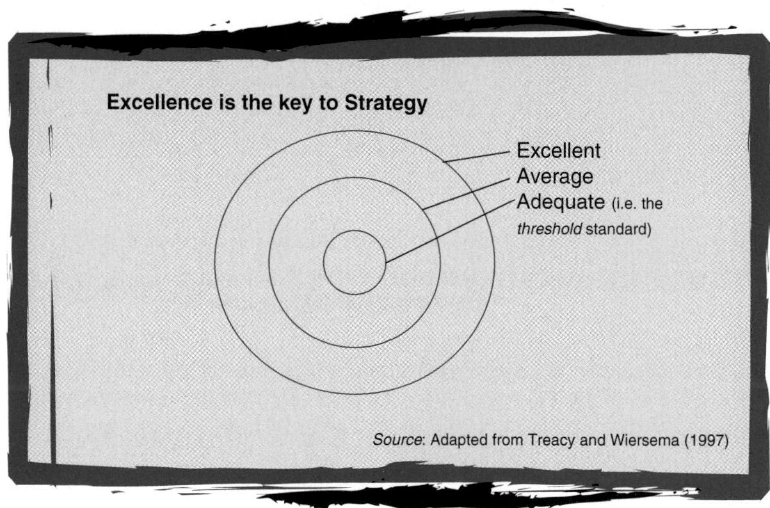

Source: Adapted from Treacy and Wiersema (1997)

MARGIN NOTES

In other words:

- Customers notice;
  - If an offering is 'excellent' because it stands out from the competing offerings.

- Customers notice;
  - If an offering falls below what is the minimum acceptable standard (the threshold standard) because it falls below what the customer expects it to do (benefits) for them, it is not 'fit for purpose'.

- Customers don't notice;
  - If the offering falls anywhere between these two points, it is just another (undifferentiated) player in the competitive melee.

- 'Average' is not a customer concept;
  - It is produced by the industry and is the 'industry standard' produced through inward looking benchmarking activities.

MARGIN NOTES

This is perhaps easier to see if we overlay the three ways of spending/investing money in the organisation:

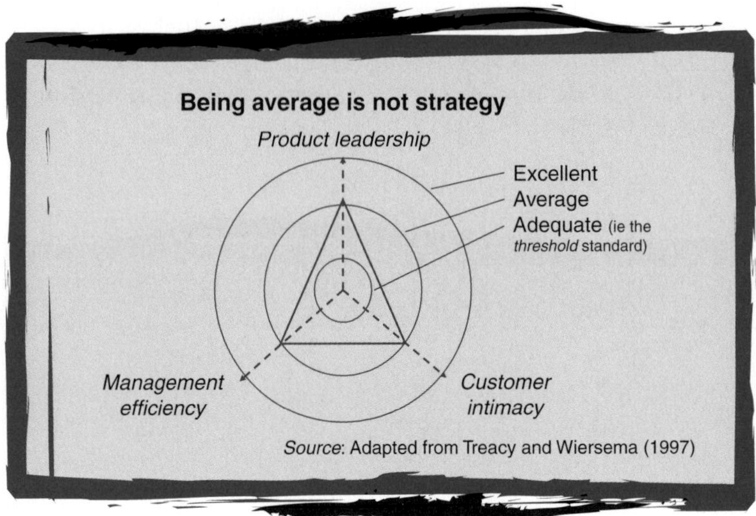

Source: Adapted from Treacy and Wiersema (1997)

Treacy and Wiersema suggest that most organisations prefer to work, invest and spend to be 'Average' on all three dimensions, fearing that to fall below the *industry standard* on any single dimension would be to make the organisation vulnerable.

This is of course internally focused nonsense. Customers are the key to our business survival and growth and what they say should always take precedence. Money (and other resources) are always limited and need to be spent carefully, wisely and with a view to creating a customer-based sustainable competitive advantage.

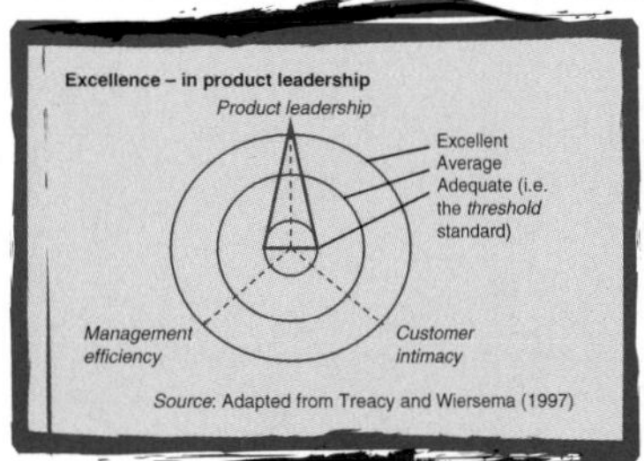

Source: Adapted from Treacy and Wiersema (1997)

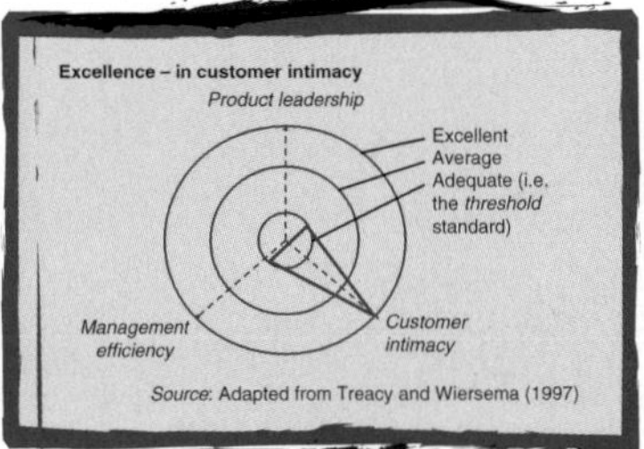

Source: Adapted from Treacy and Wiersema (1997)

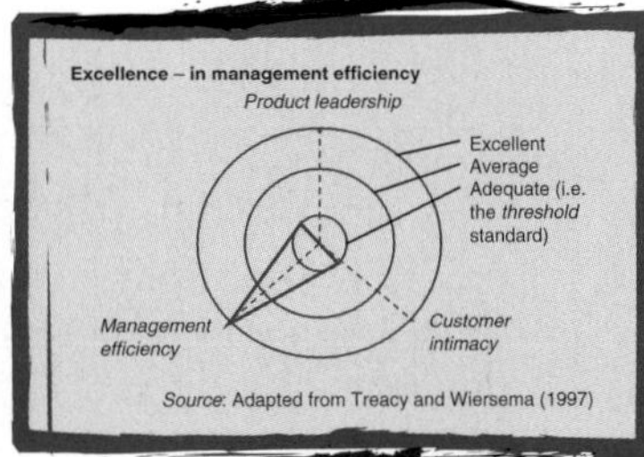

Source: Adapted from Treacy and Wiersema (1997)

As shown in the above figures the idea is to spend/invest enough to create a competitive advantage by being 'excellent' in one of the three key internal areas, either:

- By creating the best product/service:
  - Means producing what the customers sees as the best product or service (it meets their needs best) and then making sure that

the back up service and support is 'good enough' not to be an issue.

- By being the most efficient organisation:
    - Means being the best at systems, distribution and processes, while making sure that the product/service is OK, and that you are close enough to customers to meet their needs

- By being closest to the customer (intimacy):
    - Means knowing the customer better than anybody else and delivering solutions that customers really value.
    - All the time ensuring that you don't let anybody down and the product/service works and the service/distribution and management processes all work too.
    - In the B2B situation, this alternative is more popular than many organisations would be prepared to admit – in the world of professional direct sales forces, relationships, repeat business and profits are less due to 'excellent products' than excellent relationships between individuals.

MARGIN NOTES

They suggest you do this (resources always being limited) by diverting resource away from those two areas that you have decided *not* to compete in. Diverting the resources will make you fall below the industry defined 'Average' but customers won't notice this – as long as you ensure that you don't fall below the 'Adequate' level.

Action

Treacy and Wiersema conclude that, to win in bland, commodity-driven markets, you must:

- Pick a market to dominate:
    - Do NOT dabble or aggregate markets.
    - Not always popular with sales teams who think that every sale is a good sale and don't understand the value of specialisation.

- Decide a single factor for competition:
    - Do NOT try to be good at everything.
    - Again, unpopular.
    - Remember that to get something, you will have to give something up.

- Focus resources to that end:
    - Do NOT allow history and politics to direct resources.
    - Business is about where you decide to invest resources for tomorrow's returns.
    - Yesterday is another world.

All in all, excellent advice – but you might have a few problems.

Practical strategy is the name of the game – and I do it for a living. All the logic of the Treacy and Wiersema approach is so sensible, obvious and unavoidable – which means that;

- It won't be argued against in any sensible strategy meeting or process – which also means that
- It probably won't be followed.

No matter the agreement in the groups or the consensus on the awayday, when managers get back to real jobs they will consider it just so much group hysteria. They just won't reduce expenditure back to threshold levels. Somehow it will seem just too difficult and they will feel an all-encompassing need to protect their organisation from such dangerous madness. How could anyone allow their business to be exposed in such a way? What would happen if the competition found out?

MARGIN NOTES

Believe me, this will definitely be a step too far. And of course, if your managers don't reduce their expenditure in the areas where you (all) have decided you won't seek excellence, then:

- You will not have the resources available to invest in becoming excellent in the area you have chosen.
- You will not be excellent or even different.
    - You will be exactly the same as your competitors, 'average'.
- You will not find additional resources for the 'madness'.
    - So the organisation will have to fight the same old fires with the same (reducing) resources.
- You will only have price to compete on, because you will be 'ordinary'.
    - If you aren't the lowest cost producer – but how could you be without the resources to invest in driving down costs – you will eventually lose the price war.
- You will remember that Paul Fifield said that strategy was fun, he didn't say it was easy.

The area of sustainable competitive advantage is critical for the overall long-run success of your organisation/company. It's important because it gives you the opportunity of imposing your will on the marketplace, of choosing how you are going to compete – and on what grounds.

If your organisation can get its sustainable competitive advantage right then you will be taking control of your own destiny. You won't be forced just to react to competition. You won't always be on the defensive reacting to what other organisations are doing.

■ The strategic questions (19–22)

Here are the next 4 questions for you – they get more difficult, we are starting to move into some decision-making.

Every time we make a decision we also close some opportunities down – that's difficult. Make sure that when you put the ✓ in the 'Not important' column, it is not just another way of describing what one of my clients used to call the 'too hard basket'.

No.	Strategic question	Our strategic answer	Importance	✓
	The business strategy			
19	What is our business/ corporate objective?		Must have	
			Nice to have	
			Not important	
20	What is our business/ corporate strategy?		Must have	
			Nice to have	
			Not important	
21	What are the options for sustainable competitive advantage?		Must have	
			Nice to have	
			Not important	
22	What do we believe is the most appropriate sustainable competitive advantage we should be seeking? – Our competitive strategy		Must have	
			Nice to have	
			Not important	

CHAPTER 4

The marketing objectives

> 'In order to change the world, you have to get your head together first'
>
> *Jimi Hendrix (1942–1970),*
> *American guitarist, singer and songwriter*

Setting marketing (or market) objectives is never an easy business. But it is more important that most organisations ever imagine. Why?

- There is a big difference between *corporate* or *business* objectives and *marketing* objectives.
- Corporate/business objectives are defined as 'the goal or the aim to which all the resources of the organisation are directed.'
- Marketing objectives do not focus on the overall 'goal or aim' for the organisation
  - Marketing objectives must focus on: 'Taking the business/corporate objective and translating it into terms that can be actioned by the organisation.'
- Normally this means translating the business/corporate objective into terms of products/services and markets (the product/market match).
- In this review of your marketing objectives we will look at:
  - The planning period
    - What is a reasonable time scale for your market objective(s)?
  - What makes a good market objective?
    - There is a wide choice – what works – and what doesn't?
  - Using market objectives
    - What do you do with them once you have got them?
- The planning period depends on your organisation.
  - Typically I would always suggest a planning period of 3–5 years for business/corporate objectives and 18–24 months for marketing/market objectives.
  - You cannot make them longer if you are in a slower changing business with longer lead times.
  - You can make them shorter if you are *really* in a fast changing business – but not just because you *think* you are in a fast-moving business.
- Before you work on quarterly targets for everything (yes, such nonsense does exist) ask yourself whether customers' needs and wants really change that fast.

MARGIN NOTES

- Some fashion markets (such as toy crazes among primary (elementary) school children and fashion accessories in secondary (high) schools) really do come and go that fast but mainly organisations confuse customer needs (what they want) with technology advances (what we can do).
- The two are not the same.

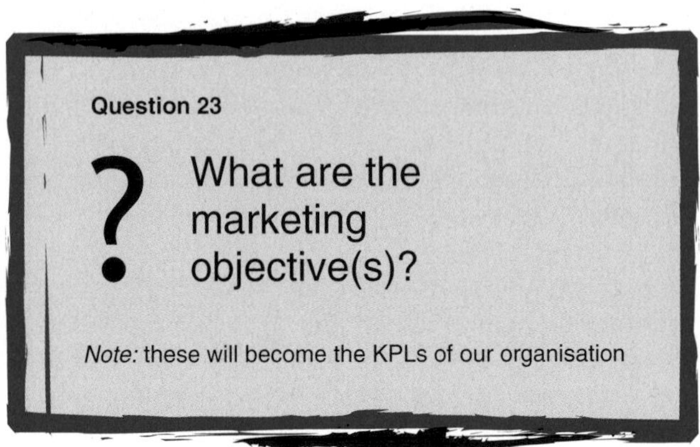

Question 23
?
What are the marketing objective(s)?
Note: these will become the KPLs of our organisation

MARGIN NOTES

You really are spoiled for choice. Here is a list of some of the ones that I tend to use, but the list is not exhaustive and others (if they are customer driven) may be added.

- The marketing objectives need to be chosen carefully.
  - There is no hard-and-fast rule but I tend to work on selecting between four (better) and six (maximum) objectives, which, taken together, *will create behaviours in the organisation that we believe will achieve the business/corporate objective.*
  - It is not a question of any individual marketing objectives; it is a question of the combined effect of all the objectives selected.
  - For example, selecting apparently conflicting objectives such as:
    - Market/segment position
    - Product development
    - Profitability and
    - Innovation
  - ... will promote a marketing plan (and KPIs, see below) that drive the organisation towards:
    - A branded position
    - In selected market segments
    - That require innovative solutions
    - But that also improve profitability and avoids buying market share.
- With apparently 'conflicting' objectives, such as these you can point implementers towards the right, selected market opportunities (that will achieve the organisation's unique business objective) rather than just any objective like '*grow*'.

  - In the example above, the implementers will be targeted (and probably bonused) in a way that forces them to think carefully about the business they should be seeking.
  - As long as rewards are only linked to achieving all objectives, not on an objective-by-objective basis, you should be successful.

- The two rules are:
  - First, start with the business objective and strategy
  - Second, decide what combination of market objectives will achieve it.

Some components for your own original combination might include:

- What 'position' do you want/need to own?
  - Market/segment position:
    - Is there a particular market or market segment where we need to achieve a particular (unique) market position?
    - Which market or segment?
    - What is the required brand/position?
    - What are the intended brand-building activities?
    - How will this help achieve the business/corporate objective?
  - Do you need to position yourself within a particular segment?
    - Market/segment share:
      - Is there a particular market or segment where we need to support our presence?
      - Which market or segment?
      - What are the 'growth' objectives?
      - What are the 'maintenance' objectives?

- Are there some segments where we need to stop investing and start extracting profits?
  - Market/segment harvesting:
    - Is there a particular market or segment where we need to limit our support activities and withdraw cash?
    - Which market or segment?
    - What are the 'harvesting' objectives?
    - What are the timescales?

- Are there some segments you must be a part of, or even dominate?
  - Market/segment entering:
    - Is there a particular market or segment that we need to enter?
    - Which market or segment?
    - What are the objectives?
    - What are the timescales?

- Are there some segments you should get out of?
  - Market/segment exiting:
    - Is there a particular market or segment that we need to exit?
    - Which market or segment(s)?

MARGIN NOTES

    - What are the likely effects on existing customers?
    - What are the exiting objectives and timescales?

- Is there a (or more) segment that you need to penetrate? The time for playing has passed …
  - Market/segment penetration:
    - Is there a particular market or segment where we need to increase our presence?
    - Which market or segment?
    - Why?
    - What are the penetration objectives?
    - What are the timescales?

- Maybe there is a segment (or two) that we need to take control of, and develop from the front? Sometimes leaving things to the market just is not enough …
  - Market/segment development:
  - Is there a particular market or segment where we need to develop ahead of normal market growth rates?
  - Which market or segment?
  - What are the development objectives and timescales?

- New product development (NPD) cannot be ignored. What new products and services do you have to develop? Sometimes you cannot leave everything to others.
  - Product development:
  - Are there particular products and/or services that need to be developed?
  - Why? – What are the identified areas of customer need that these are to be based on? (not on simple technological advancement)
  - Are (if so which?) product/service development objectives supporting moves to modify the product/service portfolio to better meet customer needs or reposition the organisation of brand?

- Not an easy option, but if there is nothing else, maybe it is time to look at new products/services in new markets! Make sure all your other options are exhausted first.
  - Diversification:
  - Is there a need to diversify (product/services and markets or segments) that we are not in?
  - Product or market diversification?
  - Which product/service areas are diversification prospects?
  - Which markets or segments are diversification prospects?
  - Note that this is not a low-risk objective

- Lots of people think it is all about growing, not everybody though. If you are in the 'we-must-grow' groups you absolutely must think through what type of growth you want to invest in.

MARGIN NOTES

- Growth (after Doyle):
  - Do we need to set market objectives for growth?
  - If so:
    - Specify clearly growth terms for the objective
    - Specify also the type of Growth that you are setting as the objective, as explained by Doyle:
      - Radical (example; by acquisition)
      - Rational (example; new technology)
      - Robust (example; slow and steady)

- Innovation – a good thing, but often misunderstood. You should always be on the lookout for new ways of improving customer satisfaction, but not just new ways of doing things – even if it reduces some small cost.
  - Innovation:
    - Are we sure that we mean new answers to existing problems and not new problems?
    - Which customers? Some customers want innovation. Some want new and better without knowing that things are changing.
    - Are we positioning innovation carefully and linking this objective with others that will reduce the most dangerous effects of undirected innovation drives?

- Another good thing, but not always recognised by customers. Be careful that you don't end up 'trading off' productivity benefits against customer costs.
  - Productivity:
    - Use this as another balancing objective. Productivity is typically an internal, efficiency issue but it can be important. More productive competition can still be beaten if our offer is more 'effective' but the difference cannot be too great.
    - Choose this objective to blend with and balance other, more customer-focused objectives.

- Revenue is vanity, but important nevertheless.
  - Sales revenue:
    - As a market objective, sales revenue needs to be chosen with care.
    - Sales revenue should only be combined with customer-driven objectives.
    - Revenue objectives are particularly useful during the rapid growth stage of development when, combined with market/segment share; it can form a good basis for successful transition into the maturity stage.

- Profit is sanity, so don't incentivise revenue without a profit override

MARGIN NOTES

- Profitability and/or margins:
  - If sales revenue (turnover) is 'vanity'; then profitability is 'sanity.
  - Profitability is a requirement for survival and growth.
  - Use as a specific market objective if you need to enforce premium prices on an organisation that may be used to seeking volume (the 'mass market') at any price.

- And, cash is still king.
  - Cash flow:
    - Cash flow is still the biggest reason for company failure – not a particularly customer-focused item but an important one.
    - A difficult objective to have on its own but very important if combined with strong, customer-focused objectives when it can help the organisation to identify market opportunities that are also good for cash flow.

MARGIN NOTES

- Some bubbles burst, others become mainstream. While it is happening it is all real, and customers want more and more.
  - Public responsibility:
    - At the moment a lot of organisations are focusing on their 'corporate and social responsibilities' (CSR). Whether this is a long term activity or the latest in a long line of management 'fads' will be revealed in time.
    - Other issues may include sustainability/environmental/carbon issues.
    - Nevertheless there may be specific objectives to be applied here that relate to governmental tax/incentives issues.
    - These should not be confused with market objectives concerned with your brand (see Market/segment position above) which are about your organisation's 'uniqueness' and you may have decided to differentiate by public/environmental issues.

- You may have very specific objectives that refer to your organisation of industry
  - Other measures:
    - These objectives may be specific to your particular business or industry, or even to your unique market position.
    - *Before you dive for this option though, ensure that you are not just taking the easy option.*

There is absolutely no point in deciding on your marketing objectives unless you use them – what the world does not need is more pointless bureaucratic rituals.

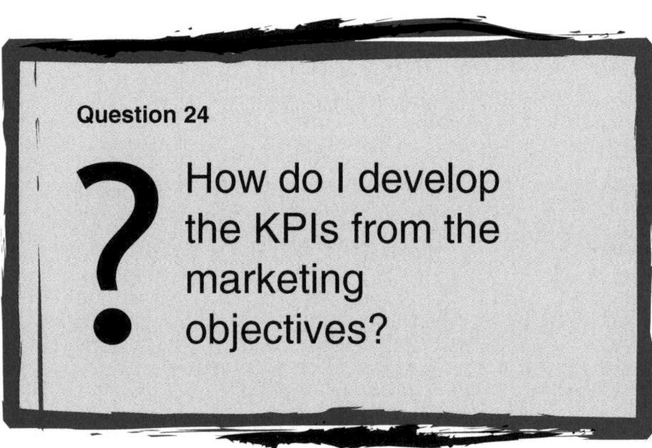

Question 24
?
How do I develop the KPIs from the marketing objectives?

Apart from using market objectives to drive the marketing strategy and plans (more of that later) there are two other key areas where your hard work will be rewarded:

MARGIN NOTES

- Resource allocation:
  - Resources are finite, every company has the same problem; this is how competitive organisations work.
  - In my experience, this is not really a problem; the real issue is normally not insufficient resource, but resource misallocation.
  - Resources are often allocated to what was important yesterday, not today and certainly not tomorrow.
    - Managers tend to be much quicker at asking for money to develop new products/services or new markets, but slower at cutting off support from products/services or markets that are in decline.
  - You can use the marketing objectives to rectify the position. I use the time-honoured (but still effective) traffic light method.
  - Your marketing objectives should allow you to agree:
    - [RED Activities]
      - What activities and projects must stop now because they do not support the objectives.
    - [AMBER Activities]
      - What activities should be put on hold pending more information that will decide whether they support the objectives or not.
    - [GREEN Activities]
    - What activities and projects must be supported/accelerated now, because they support the objectives

You will be surprised how much this exercise can focus internal attention on agreeing what the right market objectives should be. What might have appeared to some to be an academic exercise suddenly has the potential to reduce the size and importance of internal empires. If you are kind,

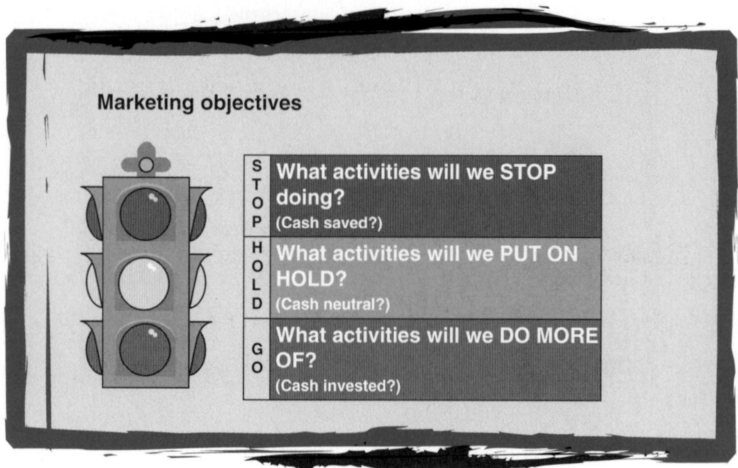

Marketing objectives
S T O P What activities will we STOP doing?
(Cash saved?)
H O L D What activities will we PUT ON HOLD?
(Cash neutral?)
G O What activities will we DO MORE OF?
(Cash invested?)

MARGIN NOTES

you might even warn people that the selection of particular objectives has certain effects. You will gain their attention – and their involvement.

- Organisational behaviour (market focus):
  - If you are to achieve the business objective, the marketing objectives must be achieved.
  - The only way to guarantee this outcome is to ensure that the *market objectives become the organisation's Key Performance Indicators* (KPIs).
  - Most organisations have KPIs and many managers wonder where these KPIs come from. A very good question that you should ask people.

- This is the way it is *meant* to work, if your organisation is to remain focused on its customers:
  - *Customers* provide all the money.
  - *Customers* will continue to pay the organisation money as long as it delivers what they want and value.
  - *Customers'* needs, wants and values change over time.
  - *Everyone* in the organisation needs to work together to satisfy the customer, everything else is an additional overhead/burden on those working for the customer.
  - *Marketing* should be the coordinating function that focuses the resources and effort of the organisation on the one thing that will ensure survival and growth – *the customer*.
    - Marketing services departments are not the same thing.
  - *Market objectives* are derived from a detailed assessment of the market/customer opportunities and threats and encapsulate the very best chance the organisation has of commercial success.
  - *The market* is highly competitive and everyone is fighting for *the customers'* attention and business.
    - To be successful, our organisation has to focus all its resources and efforts (as single-mindedly as possible) on achieving the

market/customer objectives (and so achieving the business objective).

- *We do this* by using the (agreed) market objectives as the KPIs for the whole organisation.

MARGIN NOTES

Marketing objectives become 'KPI's

	Marketing objectives	Key performance indicator	Detail
1			
2			
3			
4			
5			

Marketing objectives become KPI's an example

	Marketing objectives	Key performance indicator	Detail
1	**Market/segment position**	• Awareness and preference measures • Brand value movement	Preference changes by segment to appraisals Create brand equity monitoring tool
2	**Profitability**	• Percentage margin (gross) to x% • Profitability growth by y% • Returns of faulty product to z% • Analysis of products/sectors/ markets over whole life cycle	
3	**Product development**	• Consumer needs (research?) driven • Product life cycle analysis	
4	**Innovation**	• At least one on-objective new idea implemented per year giving £1million incremental revenue • Non product (service-based) innovation	Focus NPD and bonus to revenue Bind NPD and Market research activities

MARGIN NOTES

As the diagrams show:

- You take the four/five (or if you insist, a maximum of six) market objectives and turn these into KPIs.
  - Choose more than this and you end up with an organisation run by targets, without any understanding of the reasons behind the targets.

- This process should not involve changing the nature or content of the marketing objectives, just modifying the odd word so that it can easily be used and communicated internally.

- The KPIs can then be broken down into more detailed sub-objectives for transfer internally.
  - But they must retain the customer focus from the market objectives that generated them.

- The more people understand that they work and thrive only at the pleasure of customers, the better the organisation will function.

- In a detailed process, the KPIs would eventually translate into personal objectives and form the main part of appraisal systems.

- But don't expect to achieve this without a fight.

■ The strategic questions (23–24)

Here are the next two questions for you. More decisions I'm afraid, but this time not just difficult, absolutely critical. If you get this stage right, you don't just get good marketing objectives, you start to do the REAL marketing job, you start to get the whole of the rest of the organisation focused on the customer.

Take your time. Each marketing objective *must* do two things for you:

- It must focus the marketing and the entire 'executive' arm of the business on doing the 'right things.'

- It must be capable of being translated into KPIs that make sense to people in disciplines outside marketing.

I am always tempted at this point to remove the 'Nice to have' and the 'Not important' from the ✓ boxes. Nothing (so far) has been this important, at least in creating a customer-led organisation. But, we all have to allow for some self-determination, and I suppose 'death wish' too …

No.	Strategic question	Our strategic answer	Importance	✓
	The marketing objectives			
23	What are the marketing objective(s)? (*Note*: these will become the KPIs of our organisation)	1	Must have	
		2	Nice to have	
		3	Not important	
		4		
		5		
24	How do I develop the KPIs from the marketing objectives?		Must have	
			Nice to have	
			Not important	

PART II

Developing the marketing strategy

> 'Never let an inventor run a company. You can never get him to stop tinkering and bring something to market.'
>
> *E F Schumacher (1911–1977), British statistician and economist and Chief Economic Advisor to the UK National Coal Board*

MARGIN NOTES

You will probably have noticed that this section (and most of this book) is wrapped around a 'model' or 'concept' called SCORPIO. On the one hand, it makes this book unique in that, so far, there is no accepted model or concept that explains exactly what marketing strategy is all about – or even what is included in marketing strategy, and what is in either business/corporate strategy or marketing tactics.

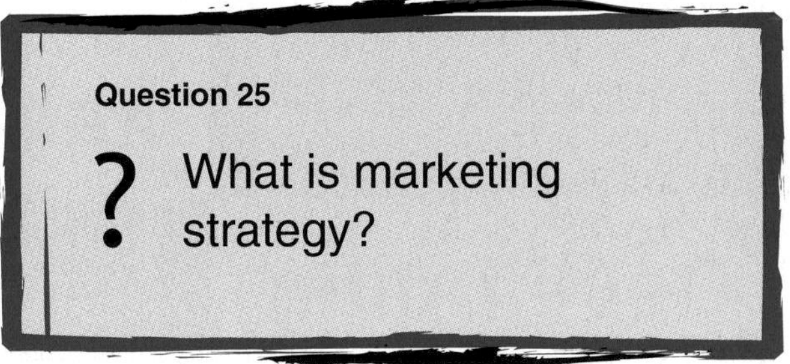
Question 25
?
What is marketing strategy?

In the introduction, we learned that 'Marketing strategy is the process by which the organisation aligns itself with the market it has decided to serve'. There we also learned a lot about what it is and what it does.

In this way marketing strategy translates the business objective and strategy into market terms and marketing activity.

In practical terms, your marketing strategy is the process by which you engage with everyone in the organisation and you focus their activities and outputs on your target customers' current and likely future needs and wants.

Just so that you know that the SCORPIO idea did not arise out of thin air – or even academic research, let me take you through the process of discovery that I went through.

- I have been working in the area of marketing and marketing strategy for many years now, sometimes teaching, sometimes (as little as possible) setting and marking examinations – but mostly working with

organisations and helping them develop their customer and market-based strategies for future growth and prosperity.
  - The most recent 20 or so large organisations I worked with since I wrote the 2nd edition of 'Marketing Strategy' have been the main catalyst for the SCORPIO idea/concept/model/acronym.
    - The idea comes out of developing real strategies for real companies – and we know *it works*!

- First – who is getting all the airtime?
  - There are two main *prima donnas* out there,
    - Business/Corporate Strategy and
    - Marketing Tactics.

- Business/Corporate Strategy has been an important topic for years since the great military strategists (probably starting with Sun Tzu in 500BC) who captured the public and business imagination after the Second World War.
  - The pace picked up then with many important writers and really took off when Harvard's Michael Porter started to write books in the early 1980s.

- Marketing, as it is normally understood, really got going in the 1960s after the publication of Theodore Levitt's important article 'Marketing Myopia' (Harvard Business Review August 1960).
  - Although there has been much 'too-ing and fro-ing' about the numbers of Ps in the true marketing mix and whether 'relationship marketing' is different from 'emarketing', and whether anybody cares, all the writing has been about the day-to-day activities that constitute marketing activity.
  - Now we see such an obsession with one of the Ps – *Promotion* (marketing communications) – that not much else gets a mention.

MARGIN NOTES

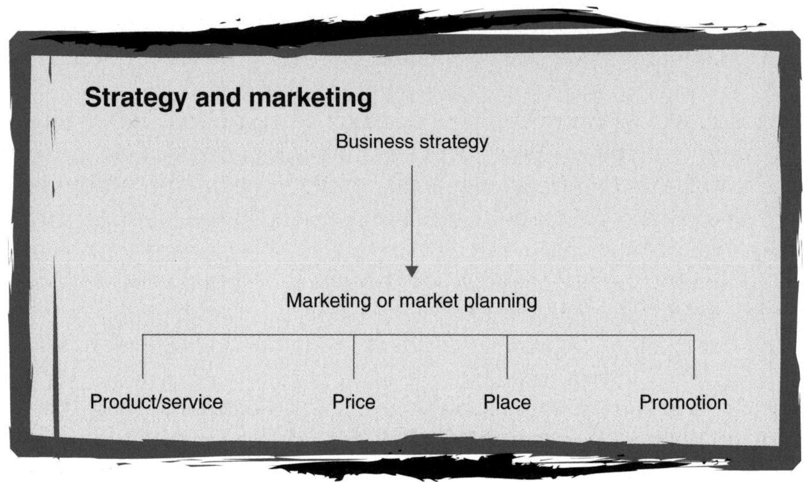

- For the hard-pressed practitioner, there is, at best, an uncomfortable handshake between these two bodies of knowledge.
  - My concern has always been, not what they cover but what seems to be missing from either area.
  - To take just one example, where is the *brand* covered in either of these two specialisms?
    - If we look at the marketing tactics first we will expect to find the brand somewhere but no (it does not begin with P so it is at a disadvantage straight away) it just does not seem to figure in the list.

MARGIN NOTES

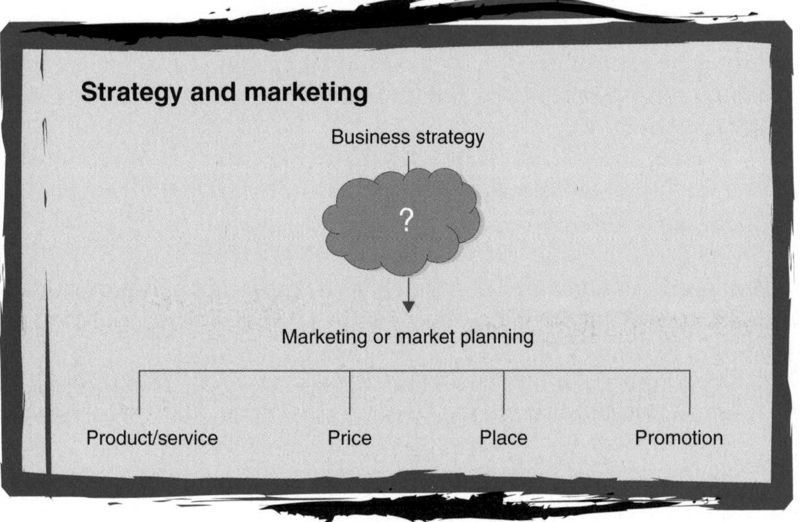

- If you look carefully at the books you will find elements of brand tucked away under:
  - The product heading
  - You'll find some elements under pricing in the sort of vague hope that brand might generate a premium pricing
  - You will find something in the area of distribution and, of course
  - You will find elements of brand under anything to do with promotion – but, of course, everything seems to have been hammered into the promotion element at some point by somebody.
- Looking for some guidance on branding issues in the business/corporate strategy area is just as challenging.
  - Does brand appear as a primary method of differentiation in Porter's generic strategies? – No.
  - Is it picked up under the financials as probably the most successful method of acquiring wealth? – No.

- The best you can say about brand is that you might (if you are very lucky, and very, very good) be able to re-assemble all the various, dismembered components of brand to create something useful for your own marketing strategy.
  - The problem with this situation is that marketing plans and strategies just are not put together with this level of rigour.
  - Secondly, elements such as brand are just too important to be dealt with at the individual component level.
  - The brand, and other elements (as we shall see soon) need to be analysed, assessed, presented and developed *as a whole* rather than as a component tucked away/lost in four or five different elements of the marketing mix and the corporate strategy process.

- Once you get to the point of realising that there is something important missing in the books and articles, it is a relatively easy step to identify exactly what is missing.
  - *All the elements of what has to be marketing strategy are missing.*

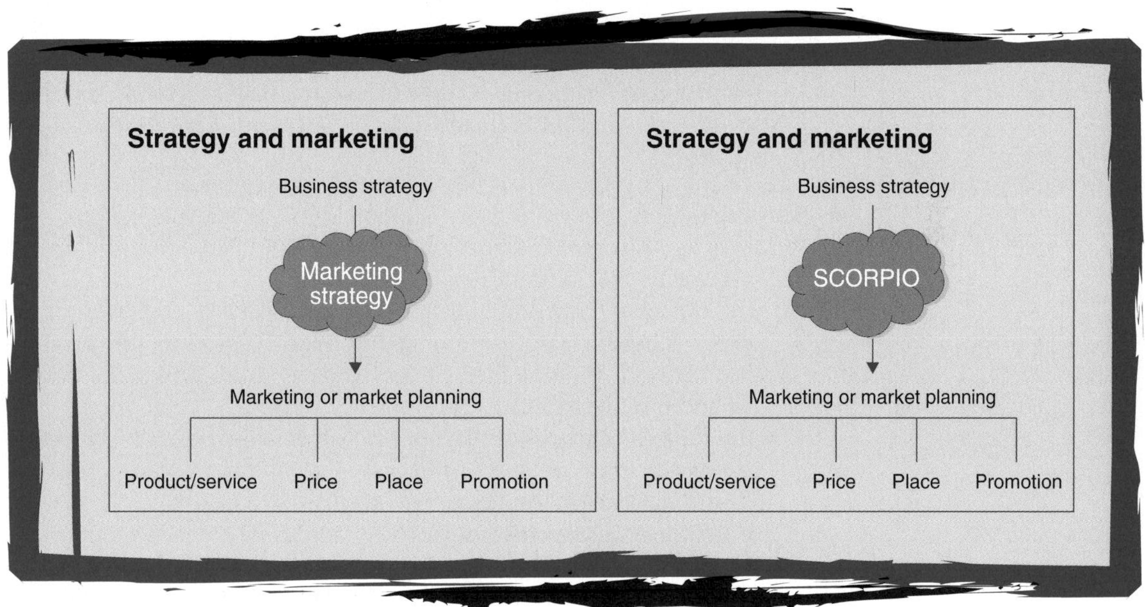

I have spent much of the past 10 years trying to put these different elements into a simple structure and in some easy-to-deal-with format that would serve me (and my clients) as a day-to-day guide for assessing and developing real-life marketing strategy.

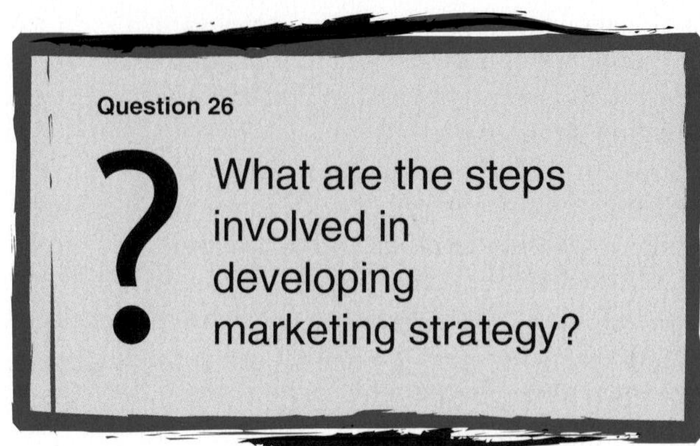

Question 26
?
What are the steps involved in developing marketing strategy?

The rest of this book is dedicated to taking you through the elements of marketing strategy so that you can manage them for yourself, as a very brief overview the SCORPIO components are:

MARGIN NOTES

- Segmentation and Targeting:
  - This is one of the critical areas of modern marketing, which is just missed completely in the skirmishing between the corporate strategy specialists, large organisational marketers and business school academics.
  - In today's complex and rapidly changing markets it has to be evident that the 'mass market' is an idea whose day has (definitely) gone.
  - If the mass market is dead then the segment must be the key to success.

- The Customer:
  - Imagine this, the customer does not formally appear anywhere in 'takeaway' marketing theory.
  - The business/corporate strategy people all (sort of) *imply* a customer focused organisation rather than a product or production focused one but then never go far enough down the line to explain exactly what this means.
  - The fabled 'marketing mix', on the other hand, merrily proceeds to identify four or seven interacting elements of things that we should be *doing to* the customer.
    - But who is the customer?
    - Where do we find any worthwhile discussion about who the customer is, what the customer wants, what the customer needs or how we should be anticipating these needs for products and/or service development?
    - This is simply nonsense – customers are much too important to deal with in component parts.

- Organisation – Processes and Culture:
  - Don't say this has no place in market or corporate strategy discussion but belongs with the HR people, this is exactly my point.

- Even if we are faced with a superb business/corporate strategy, brilliantly executed marketing tactics and an ingenious and customer focused market strategy between the two, nothing will ever happen unless the people in the organisation want to do it.
- This has to be part of the job, abdicate it and you can kiss goodbye to the idea of satisfied customers.

- Retention (Customer):
  - Fredrick Reichheld's book ('The Loyalty Effect: The Hidden Force Behind Growth, Profits, and Lasting Value', Reichheld & Teal, Harvard Business School Press; 2001) demonstrated that it is far more profitable to retain an existing customer than go to all the expense of acquiring a new one.
  - But little has really changed in most organisations – why?
  - Because retention is a strategic issue rather than tactical one and it needs to be developed and structured into the very psyche of the organisation if it is to succeed.

- Positioning and Branding:
  - We have already spoken about branding and how it is one of the most important missing links between corporate strategy and marketing tactics.
  - But, to this needs to be added the concept of positioning which is simply far too important to be left to the promotional element of the marketing mix.

- Industry or Market?:
  - This issue picks up the whole (and unpopular) question of what business (Industry) your organisation acts as if it is in.
  - And what business (Markets) your organisation ought to be in.
  - The question was first posed by Levitt in 'Marketing Myopia' in 1960.
  - The answer, and the ensuing debate, is critical if you are to be successful in breaking out of the product/production obsession that kills most organisations.
  - Despite being more than 40 years old, the answer (and the debate) is nowhere to be found in either business/corporate strategy or marketing tactics.

- Offerings:
  - Not to be confused with the product under the Ps, the 'offering' forms the link between the discussion at corporate level about differentiation and value chains – and the debate at marketing tactics level about products and services.
  - Ultimately the organisation will be as successful as its offering is perceived by its target market – no less, no more.

MARGIN NOTES

In diagrammatic form, we have:

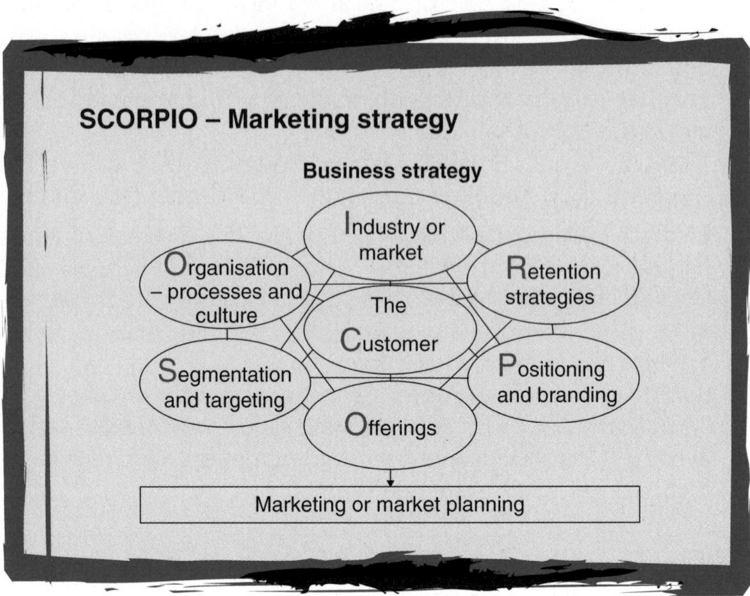

MARGIN NOTES

Before we look at these seven SCORPIO elements of marketing strategy, there are seven (just coincidence – really!) rules to the marketing strategy game.

- All of the seven elements are interrelated:
  - That is to say that you cannot make decisions or progress in one of the seven element areas without affecting decisions in the other. Therefore,

- You will need to work on all of the seven elements at the same time:
  - Rather than work on one element and attempt to complete it before starting on the others.

- Not all of the seven elements will carry equal importance:
  - At least for your business.
  - The nature, structure, size and competitive situation of the organisation will determine which of the elements have most importance at any point in time. However,

- None of the elements can be omitted from the strategy:
  - Every time I work with SCORPIO I find that the balance between the elements is different.
  - On the two occasions when I thought I had found a situation where one or more of the elements was not relevant, I actually found that I had missed something important in the analysis.

- There is no pre-ordained order to the process:
  - I tend to use the sequence that I have used in this book, starting with Industry and Market and finishing with Offerings, but you need not necessarily follow this process order.
  - Feel empowered to move as you find most comfortable.

- The process is 'iterative':
  - You will need to move from one section of the diagram to another as you build (or even craft) a market strategy that makes sense.
  - As you grow your understanding of one area, you will inevitably affect decisions made in another.

- The process grows and develops over time:
  - Like the famous marketing mix.
  - Don't expect to arrive at a 'SCORPIO Moment' where everything falls into place and the 'answer' is revealed.
  - The right answer (if such a thing exists) depends on the market and there, we know, rules change daily.

Apart from these rules, there are no rules …

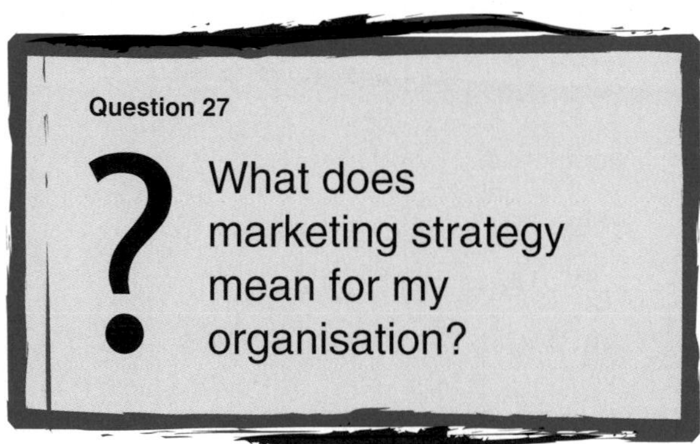

Question 27
?
What does marketing strategy mean for my organisation?

MARGIN NOTES

Given that customers needs and wants change over time, it does not really matter whether you call it marketing strategy or something different, unless your organisation has a *process* that enables it to (re)align its activities to meet customers' current and likely future needs and wants – it will be left behind by the competition.

When you look at it so simply, marketing strategy really is the difference between *continued* success and failure. For most organisations however, it is about wasting valuable resources by making products and services that don't exactly meet customers' needs – but meet what we think our customers should need …

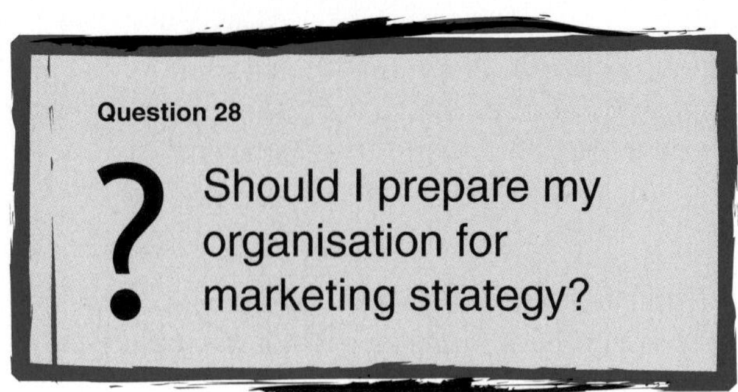

Question 28
?
Should I prepare my organisation for marketing strategy?

Yes.

The marketing strategy process is not another once-every-year-ritual; it is a continual process of learning how to closer to customers who keep changing their minds through an impossible-to-predict process.

MARGIN NOTES

Almost regardless of what the strategy turns out to be, there will almost certainly be some *change* about. And people don't much like change. If they are not to resist the change, they need to be prepared and know what the change is likely to be, and the reasons for it.

More of this in Chapter 10.

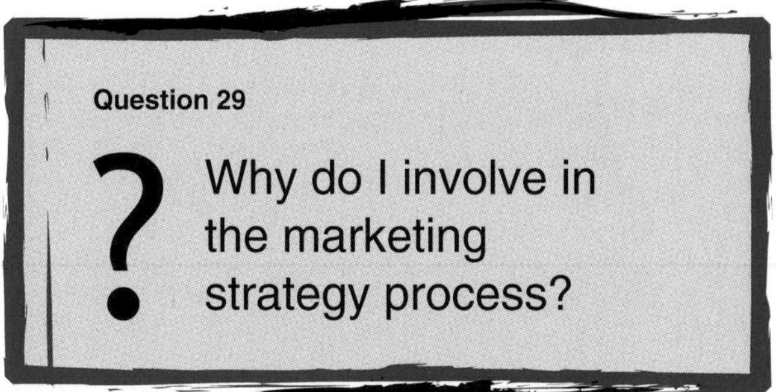

Everyone.

I am always asked if I am serious about that answer. And I always am. If there is anybody in the organisation who thinks that the customers' needs and wants have nothing to do with them, why are they there? If they are on the payroll, the customers are paying their wages.

If not everyone realises that the customer is paying their wages, that is another matter entirely. But we still need to involve them in the process, or outsource them.

More of this in Chapter 10 as well.

Finally, SCORPIO also evolves over time:

If there are any changes to the SCORPIO model you will find these on

- www.elsevier.com
- www.fifield.co.uk/scorpio

MARGIN NOTES

CHAPTER 5

Industry or Market?

> 'Boxing is just show business with blood'
>
> *Frank Bruno (1961),*
> *British former heavyweight champion boxer*

We begin our journey to create the most competitive marketing strategy that your business/organisation has ever implemented; we start with what might be the most difficult question of them all. What business are you in?

MARGIN NOTES

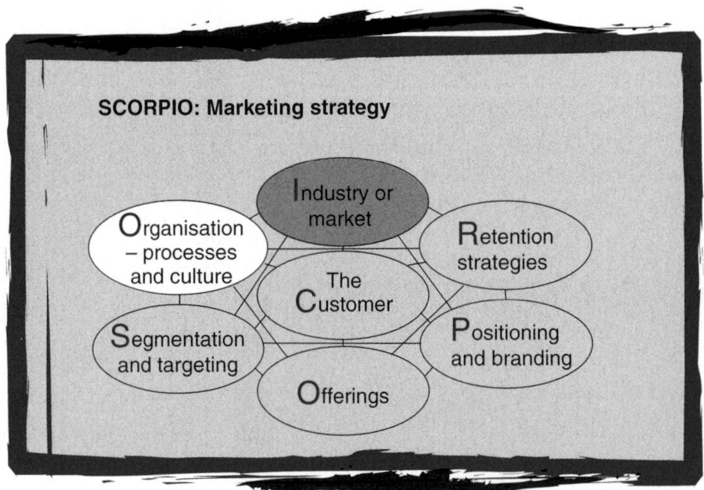

The whole question of what business you are in – and what business you ought to be in or want to be in has been a great debate since Theodore Levitt first raised the issue in his seminal article 'Marketing Myopia'

Traditionally there are two ways in which 'your business' might be described and defined by the organisation:

- The *products and services* sold, the technology that it will use to produce products and services or the industry the organisation is in.
- The *customer needs* that the organisation will satisfy.

Just to be difficult (and not take a consumer product like shampoo or soup) let's take a medium-sized organisation operating internationally, which makes fire hose. This company could define the business that it is in a number of different ways – in each defined 'business' it would seek different opportunities, for example:

- Industry or technology thinking:
  - If the organisation defines its business as hose technology this would then naturally send the organisation seeking opportunities in a variety of markets where there was a need for this type of technology.
  - This might include garden hoses or using the hose technology to reline gas and oil pipelines as an alternative to pipe replacement.

- Market or customer thinking:
  - Depending on how the organisation defines its customers and their needs, it could define itself as being in:
    - The 'fire business' and meeting the needs of people in that group.
      - In this case if the organisation wishes to expand it might start looking at alternative products and services to deliver to the fire industry as a whole, such as extinguishers and fire blankets.
  - Alternatively the organisation could define itself as being in:
    - The 'electronic fire detection and safety business'.
      - This might lead it to investigate sprinkler systems or escape products.
  - Another alternative could be:
    - The 'fluid transfer business'.
      - It would then, should it wish to expand, be seeking opportunities in which perhaps the fire industry would remain a large but just one segment within a market needing to transfer various fluids from one point to another.
      - Examples might include:
        - Entering the pipeline business or
        - Managing a fleet of airport tankers for flight refuelling.

MARGIN NOTES

See what I mean?

If you don't have a clear understanding of what you do, you might even be growing in all sorts of business areas at the same time. You might call it opportunism; your customers might call it too confusing.

- How your organisation sees itself will affect the way you see your markets and, most importantly, the way you sees your future.
  - The 'art' in the process should also be evident – there is more than one way that you can define your business.
  - Giving the consumer goods an even break, lets imagine the advantage for Kellogg's of not being obsessed with 'cereals' because it would lose business to non-cereal competition, but where should it see its future?

- Business definitions such as:
  - 'Breakfast cereals'
  - 'Breakfast'
  - 'Morning goods'
  - 'First meal of the day'
  - 'Snacks'
  - 'Nutrition'
  - 'Children's health'.
- Will all offer very different competitors, opportunities and threats to the organisation? Which is the best way forward?

Why is your business definition important?

MARGIN NOTES

- Every time that I have worked with organisations and tried to wrestle with this difficult question, I have always found that a business definition which is based on customer needs will have a much stronger effect on the organisation (and is more easily communicated to the marketplace) than traditional definitions based on industry or technology.

- This is the point made by Levitt who argues that the business should always be viewed as something that delivers customer satisfactions not something that simply produces goods or services.
  - He then goes on to make the classic argument in his article '*Marketing Myopia*' that had the US railroads defined their business in terms of customer/market needs (that they were people and goods movers) rather than in production/industry terms (that they were in the business of running a railroad), they might today be running the airlines …

- Obviously there is a world of difference between being able to identify a need and the ability to deliver a sound product or service to meet that need.
  - Nevertheless, there is much to be said for focusing on customer needs and allowing them to direct the future of the business rather than just getting better and better at producing things that customers don't want!

- Another reason for preferring the business definition to be based on customer/market needs is that it is the only base that will fully support the cultural change in the organisation from a production to a market orientation.
  - Also, as we will see, it helps to define more clearly the competition facing the organisation as well as potential areas for real and profitable growth.

- Finally, before we get into the detail of the subject, it needs to be said that the majority of organisations do *not* view their business from a

customer/market perspective, preferring the traditional technology/industry definition that everybody has been brought up with.
  - This is understandable (if dangerous) since people spend most of their day inside the company looking at products, services and technology rather than facing outwards towards the customer.
  - Some organisations really would prefer to die than to change. I have worked for two.
  - Somebody has calculated that the 'half-life' of a modern organisation is around about 40 years – and the relatively early demise of most organisations can be laid at the door of the technology/industry focus that drives them.
  - You are more likely to find a customer-based definition of business driving the organisations that have been around for longer – while basic customer needs such as personal mobility; communication; nutrition; and the need for status and individualism all tend to be relatively stable over the longer period, the products and services which people buy to satisfy these needs have changed quite dramatically over just the past 20–30 years – as have the technology bases used to produce these goods.

- Organisations that have been around for a while tend only to have achieved this through switching their technology focus on a reasonably regular basis.
  - Take for example the case of IBM, which traces its origins back to tabulating and time recording machines at the end of the 19th century.
    - IBM moved to electric counting machines in the 1920s.
    - To transistorised mainframe computers in the 1950s.
    - To the personal computer in the 1980s.
    - To integrated business solutions in the 1990s.
    - Then migrated into business services in the new millennium.
  - Even if IBM is not your first choice for a customer focused organisation, remember that it can track its history back well over 100 years.
  - Remember also that the death roll of organisations that were once great in computing and IT is long – and is growing daily.

MARGIN NOTES

To recap, the reasons why you should be very concerned about getting your business definition right are:

- It defines your real competition
- It defines your customers' needs
- It defines your potential for growth
- It defines your strategic threats and opportunities
- *It can kill you early if you* don't *get it right.*

MARGIN NOTES

The way we work now (and for all the SCORPIO elements) is to break the central question down into a number of bite-sized chunks, and then offer some answers. Starting with the vexed question of should we be driven by Industry or market thinking, the following seven (coincidence again) questions should help you work out the answer for your organisation:

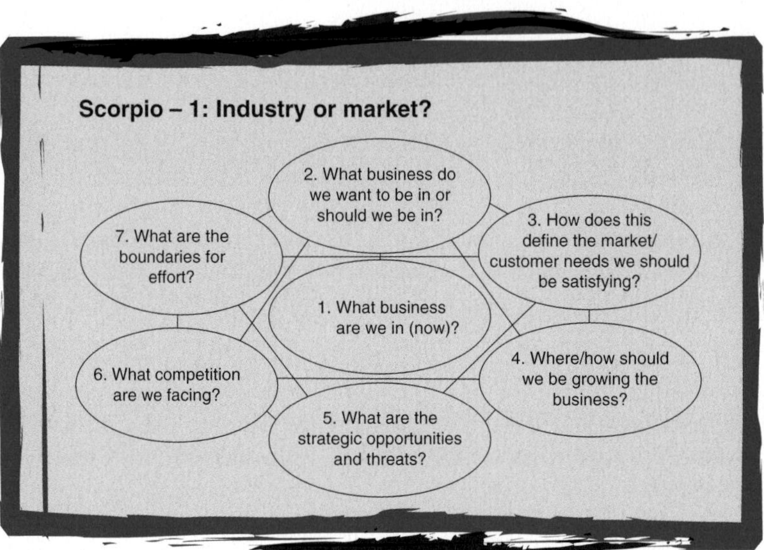

As we work through this section, you should try to remember Levitt's description of *your* marketing process:

> *'Customers just need to get things done. When people find themselves needing to get a job done, they essentially hire products to do that job for them'.*

Ah!

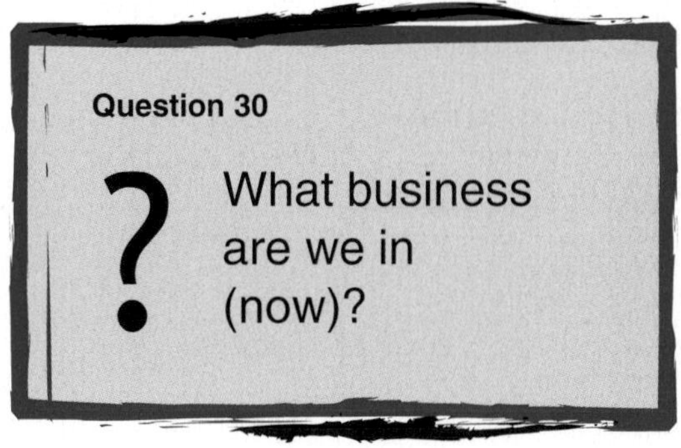

Question 30
?
What business are we in (now)?

In my experience, the questions:

- 'What business we are currently in?'
- 'What business we want (or maybe better put) do we need to be in, in the future?'

Are separate questions and need to be asked separately.

The first question – What business are we currently in? – needs to be answered with some honesty.

- If you truly believe that your organisation is market and customer oriented, and that its primary concerns are with identifying and satisfying customer needs, then you need not worry about answering this first section …
  - If (and I have to say that this relates to practically every company I have ever worked with) you feel that you have market aspirations but your organisation is primarily dominated by production/ technical and industry factors then you should ask yourself what business you are really in now – this drives the whole culture and thinking in your organisation.

- Before you pile in and make yourself unpopular, take a moment to look at things in a slightly more analytical way.
  - We need to ponder the question of 'Value Migration'.
    - We will look at this phenomenon later, but here it might help you understand how your organisation thinks and sees its world.
    - You cannot hope to change things unless you understand why things are as they are.
  - The value in a market is a function of what customers perceive to be valuable to them (solutions to problems they believe they have) and so, what they will be willing to pay.
    - Unfortunately for organisations (who would like stability), customer value (what customers see as valuable/useful to them) changes over time.
    - To some extent, this change is driven by organisations and product/service improvements and to some degree driven by customer needs, taste and fashion etc.

- One easy way to understand this is through an example; let's take the case of the motorcar over the past 50 years.
  - As soon as Henry Ford had managed to bring the car within the reach of the common person (like you and me), having a car was all that mattered and any colour was a fine colour.
  - After a while of driving around in this wonderful invention, that was the same as everybody else's wonderful invention, the value in the market shifted (migrated) from just having a car to get

MARGIN NOTES

around; towards design, fashion and styling – and being *different* from everyone else.
        - The 1950s saw an explosion of different designs, styling, colouring and annual developments in fashion.
    - In the 1960s perceived customer value migrated again and customers were willing to pay more for reliability and economy with the arrival of the Japanese cars in many world markets.
    - The 1980s and 1990s saw a gradual shift away from reliability per se (all cars were now seen as reliable and so this was no longer a differentiator) and the value migrated (back) to style as well as fuel economy.
    - Now value is migrating again, this time to more environmental issues such as fuel economy and emissions.

- Similar migrations of customer value will have happened in your markets as well.
    - Remember, it is likely that your organisation was well positioned against customer value in the past; it was successful after all.
    - But things move on and value migrates in a market – if you don't keep up you lose out.

- A final word of warning; it is only the *people* in your organisation that get things done and deliver benefits to customers, and so make profits.
    - Change as fundamental as the definition of what business we are in, if it is carried out effectively, can (probably will) change the entire stance of your organisation including which parts of the organisation are seen as the most valuable for the future.
    - But – organisations are only collections of people – people sometimes act in irrational ways.
        - People generally seem to dislike change, not only do people not like change, they can actively resist change.
        - Sometimes they are right to resist change and sometimes they will kill the organisation by resisting.
        - There is in the nature of people such a strong tendency to keep with the past, to keep with what is known (even if that is *proved* to have no future customer value), that some (especially senior) managers would rather see their organisation die than make the (necessary) changes.

Ah well …

MARGIN NOTES

Frequently asked questions in marketing strategy

For the next seven chapters, while we are discussing the SCORPIO elements of your marketing strategy, I have moved from the 'Action Point' approach we started in Part one, marketing strategy is more complicated than that.

Rather than be prescriptive (I have no idea what drives your organisation, nor do I know from a distance which particular business definition or market position would be best for you) I will offer you some (my) answers to the types of questions that I have been asked over the years.

You shouldn't expect these answers to be *exactly* right for you and your organisation, because your marketing strategy:

- Is about being *different* from everybody else
- Is about remaining *relevant* to your customers as their needs and wants change
- Will be *unique* to your organisation
- Cannot be created or developed by following a *standard process* or blueprint that has been successful for somebody else
- Will not be revealed by following others.

Here is the first set of FAQ's, about what business you are in now:

1 Industry or market?		
1.1 What business are we in (now)?		
1.1.1	Is the definition product or technology based?	Here you have to put aside the aspirations you may feel for your business and deal only in fact. Do you make and sell laptop computers, televisions, chocolate bars or kettles. Or are you in the 'business efficiency' business, the 'entertainment' business; the 'nutrition' business or in the 'household chores' business? At this point there is no reason for any self-delusion; and if you work in Yellow Pages or Thomson Directories there is absolutely no point in you being the only one to believe that you are in the information business if everybody else in the organisation believes that they are in the business of printing and distributing directories.
1.1.2	Do we understand where the current definition came from?	It always makes sense to understand the history of an organisation. People's perception of their current business will normally be driven by their past, the history of the organisation, past success (a tricky one to deal with this, especially if not everybody has recognised the current decline) and the tradition of the current leaders of the business. If you need to change people's perception of what business they are in it is useful to understand what drives this perception. This gives you some idea of how difficult it might be to change things – as well as which 'open doors' could be pushed.

1.1.3	Understanding past and future value (migration)	Do you understand where you were successful in capturing value in the past and do you understand where the value is migrating to in the future? How well do you think you are positioned to capture the future value in the market?
1.1.4	What are the likely effects of staying with the current definition?	If you need to change your business definition (and, of course, this is by no means certain yet) you will undoubtedly meet some resistance. There is always resistance to change. Human beings are just built that way so don't complain, accept it and deal with it. One way of dealing with resistance to change is to calculate the likely effects of staying as we are with no change. If the organisation continues to focus on product, technology or production processes in the belief that this will form the basis of a winning and competitive strategy for the future what do you see as the likely effects of this?
1.1.5	Does our current marketing make sense to the customer?	Every organisation communicates what it believes to be important to its customer base. I can always see when there are communication problems when an organisation tells me it needs to *educate* the customer base before they can hope to sell anything. I am not saying that education is necessarily wrong but I have still to find customers who don't really understand what their own problems are. Maybe it is less about educating the customer to understand our technology and more about educating our organisation to be able to translate what its technology does into terms the customer can easily understand (benefits). If customers in your industry need to be *educated* then maybe your marketing is not making enough sense to them – and your customer base is vulnerable.
1.1.6	How does it affect our planning and marketing?	Dramatically, will be the answer although you may not see this straight away. For now, just think about how business definitions have affected the way different organisations have planned over the last 20 to 30 years. Ford makes cars, BMW is in the driving business – can you see how their planning has been affected by these definitions? IBM is in business services, Sony is in entertainment – can you see how this has affected their plans and how they compete in the home computing area?
1.1.7	Who in the organisation is most attached to the current definition?	Those managers, functions and departments that are most closely related to the current definition of business will inevitably see themselves as 'under threat' – for their positions as well as their status within the organisation. Tread carefully.

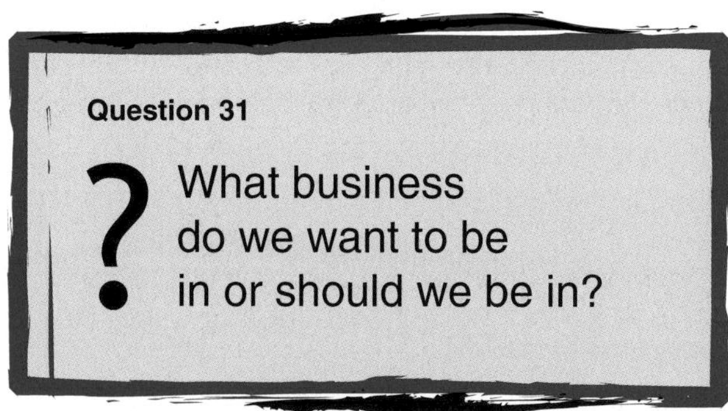

Question 31
?
What business
do we want to be
in or should we be in?

The question of what business your organisation wants (or needs) to be in, is one which is fraught with difficulties and problems.

Not only is any move away from the traditional 'industry-based' definition of business seen as 'flaky', 'irrelevant', or even worse 'Californian', it is often seen as just dangerous and misleading especially if the organisation is under competitive pressure. In this environment of cynicism and hostility, you are well advised to tread very carefully indeed.

The ideal business decision is not something you should come to lightly nor is it something you should do in isolation of the rest of the organisation and particularly the senior management team. It is something you should do carefully and slowly, testing the concepts and ideas with the target marketplace as you go.

The best way to proceed here (I have always found) is to look at some examples of organisations who have applied (to a greater or lesser extent) this approach and who appear to have implemented it successfully.

MARGIN NOTES

Industry or market? 1

Industry definition	Company	Market definition
	Harley Davidson	
	Swatch	
	Black & Decker	
	Amtrak	
	Sony	
	Jaguar	
	Rolex	
	A Busch	
	Revlon	
	RAC	
	Nestle	
	Starbucks	
	Louis Vuitton	
	Google	

Here is a selection of examples (based on data in the public domain), they are not particularly new but they tend to be both well known and also (importantly) tend to be quite successful in getting the message across.

Industry or market? 2

Industry definition	Company	Market definition
Motor Cycles	Harley Davidson	
Watches	Swatch	
Electric Motors	Black & Decker	
Railroads	Amtrak	
Electronics	Sony	
Cars	Jaguar	
Watches	Rolex	
Beer	A Busch	
Cosmetics	Revlon	
Breakdown services	RAC	
Food	Nestle	
Coffee Shops	Starbucks	
Luggage	Louis Vuitton	
Search Engine	Google	

MARGIN NOTES

I have listed these organisations together with what might be viewed as their typical industry or technology/product definition – in other words defining the organisations by the products or services that they produce. So for example Harley Davidson obviously makes motorbikes, Swatch makes watches and Black & Decker produces products with electric motors in them.

While most (if not all) of these companies are household names, they have also looked quite carefully at defining the business that they are in and have publicly commented on the effects that this definition has on their day-to-day operations.

If we then look at some of the business definitions that these organisations have made for themselves (I make no comment as to whether these are the 'right' business definitions) we can see some interesting scenarios start to take shape.

- To take Harley Davidson as an example:
  - In the 1970s Harley Davidson was doing quite badly as a classic motorcycle manufacturer in the United States, under threat from the Japanese imports as were other domestic producers at that time.

Industry or market? 3

Industry definition	Company	Market definition
Motor Cycles	Harley Davidson	Big Boys' Toys
Watches	Swatch	Fashion Accessories
Electric Motors	Black & Decker	DIY (Do-It-Yourself)
Railroads	Amtrak	Transport (people & goods)
Electronics	Sony	Entertainment
Cars	Jaguar	Status
Watches	Rolex	Jewellery
Beer	A Busch	Friendship
Cosmetics	Revlon	'Hope'
Breakdown services	RAC	Managing customers' journeys
Food	Nestle	Nutrition
Coffee Shops	Starbucks	The 3rd Place(between home & work)
Luggage	Louis Vuitton	The Art of Travelling
Search Engine	Google	Organising the world's information

MARGIN NOTES

- When it was trying to work out how to respond to the Japanese threat it started (innovatively) by talking to its existing customers and it found a number of interesting pieces of information:
  - The average buyer of a new Harley Davidson was over 50 years old.
  - The buyers were predominantly male.
  - Before the purchase of the new Harley, they had compared this, not to other motorcycle products, but to quite different categories such as:
    - A home swimming pool or
    - A European vacation.

- This insight caused Harley Davidson to reconsider its position and to start thinking about the benefits which were flowing from the purchase of a new Harley Davidson motorbike.
  - Their new business definition (Big Boys' Toys) has led them into many new market areas with a completely different marketing mix from classic (now, non-competitive) motorcycle producers.
    - They now make the majority of their profit from accessories rather than the motorbikes.
    - The product is to be found on display, not in out of town low rise motorcycle outlets but next to *other* fashion retailers such as Armani and Versace on the premier fashion streets of most major cities in the world.

The other examples are similar in that they demonstrate how a new (market/customer focused) business definition can often lead to both innovative marketing solutions and powerful and profitable market positions for the organisation and the brand.

- Swatch makes fashion accessories that happen to tell the time rather than watches.
- Black & Decker is a major player in the DIY (Do-it-yourself) business with products such as the Workmate which do not include an electric motor at all.
- Amtrak (US Railroads) is from Theodore Levitt's original work in 1960 and has already been cited.
- Sony says it is in the entertainment business rather than electronics and this is the definition that led to the acquisition of film studios and music labels.
- Jaguar sells status rather than ordinary motorcars.
- Rolex finds it much easier to sell jewellery pieces at prices far above those that would be commanded by simple (or even ornate) 'watches'.
- Busch, the makers of Budweiser and other beers, considers that it is in the friendship business rather than simply brewing beer.
- Charles Revson stated (in far less politically correct times) that in the factory he made cosmetics while in the drugstore he sold 'hope'.
    - Today, female (and male) cosmetics are obviously priced towards the hope that they offer rather than the raw materials that they contain.
- The Royal Automobile Club (RAC) always saw itself as more than a breakdown service – that was the role of its more mass-market oriented competitor, the Automobile Association (AA).
- Nestlé has broadened its portfolio in a careful and considered way, always, it hopes, in areas of nutrition rather than sweets, chocolate and candy – differentiation is everything.
- Starbucks say that it is the third place (between home and work) which explains why its coffee shops are full with people making telephone calls having meetings outside of the traditional office and work places.
- Louis Vuitton has always made great (and expensive) luggage and has learned how to deal with cheap, Far East competition.
    - The Economist (September 2006) reported that Vuitton's new flagship store in Paris recently opened an art gallery on the seventh floor called the 'Espace Culturel Louis Vuitton'.

MARGIN NOTES

  - It also reported that some 3,000–5,000 visitors come every day, the large majority of whom are tourists and that it is one of the most-visited landmarks in Paris – right behind the Eiffel Tower and Notre Dame cathedral.
  - Louis Vuitton is the LVMH group's most successful brand and in 2007 accounted for about one-quarter of its €14 billion ($17 billion) annual sales and about one-third of its profits ...

- Google – enough said I think ...

Working out your own definition of the business you want to be in is not going to be easy, do not assume you can rattle it off in a few hours. We all understand the technical/industry definition and have lived with it for years. We may be ready to move to a new definition but most other people in the organisation will not, so tread carefully.

For B2B markets, definitions can be more technical or scientific as long as the target market understands clearly what the definition means to them (benefits received) – and what offerings would fall within this definition and which ones would definitely fall outside.

Services are relatively new to marketing too and will have similar problems. There is no point in settling for an impossibly wide definition such as 'peace of mind' instead of 'insurance' – it is simply too big to get your arms round and, far from giving the dominant sales force 'room to move' it provides too much room to create a profitable *focused* differentiation.

No, we could be talking days or even weeks of exploration here.

- Get some people together whose opinions others in the organisation trust.

- Work through the concept, liberally sprinkled with examples such as those above, that people can relate to easily.

- Start by trying to understand exactly what benefits your existing customers are paying for (market research comes in handy if you have any) but if not, remember that Levitt said '*A product is what a product does*'.

- Try to define the business (what you do every day) in terms of these (and related) customer benefits.
  - Be patient, people who have been working with the product (or service) for years will just have forgotten that they *produce* solely that others might *consume*.

- Identify alternative sources of the benefit, from your and from other industries.
  - This identifies substitute competition (see Chapter 2).

MARGIN NOTES

- Then, you should take some time *trying on* the new business definitions, rather like a new coat.
  - For those of you waiting for a more scientific approach – I can only apologise.
- A big and important hint.
  - The more people you can involve in the process, the slower the decision making ***but*** the easier the internal marketing of the new business definition and the change process.

The next FAQs, about what business you should be in are:

1 Industry or market?		
1.2 What business do we want to be in or should we be in?		
1.2.1	Will the customer understand it?	Remembering (of course) that the customer is the source of all revenues and profits, it is important that whatever definition you use is one that the customer ultimately understands. This is not to say that the words you use to define your business are necessarily the ones that will appear in any form of advertising or promotion – these can always be crafted later on by specialists in advertising agencies and so forth. Rather it is important that we pick a market definition that the customer understands and the customer can easily grasp the types of product and service offerings that we will be making.
1.2.2	What does the 'SWOT' analysis tell us about the business definition?	You will remember from our previous discussion that the SWOT analyses need to be constructed from the customer's rather than the organisation's perspective. This means that the key headings of 'strengths' and 'weaknesses' will be assessed and analysed from the customers' and prospects' perceptions and we will start to understand the different strengths and weaknesses which the market believes we have. With a little further analysis, the strengths and weaknesses feedback may start to give us some clues as to the business that our customers and prospects already consider us to be in. You may even decide to swim with the flow ...
1.2.3	Is there a gap in the market – and a market in the gap?	Typically when I take clients down this route of re-assessing the nature and the definition of the business that they are in, it does not take long before managers see opportunities that they had not previously seen when they were looking at the market through more product focused eyes. However, we need to offer a word of caution. Identifying potential gaps in a marketplace, no matter that that marketplace has only been newly described and defined by you/your manager/the organisation, does not necessarily mean that there is a profitable opportunity for you. So before you plunge in head – first it might be worthwhile either to do a little market research or even a little test marketing to find out whether you have spotted a gap or a mirage.

1.2.4	Where is the 'value' in the market and can we extract it?	The critical question of customer value is dealt with at some length in Chapter 11. To précis the argument contained there, we are saying that value is driven by the perception of customers and value can be described as the benefits and/or solutions that customers desire and are willing to pay for. Probably the first thing to do when looking at a redefined business is to try and understand where the customer value is. In the case of Harley Davidson, the typical 'motorbike values' of speed and versatility do not necessarily operate in the big boys toys business where classic designs, accessories and sound take centre stage. The second part of this question focuses on the ability to develop products and/or services that will attract the attention of the (new) market and attract the premium prices that these deserve.
1.2.5	Is there room to differentiate and grow?	Differentiation is critical to any form of robust market strategy (see Chapter 8). We need to ask ourselves whether there is enough potential for differentiation and growth to make this business definition a workable one for our organisation.
1.2.6	Will the staff and other stakeholders understand the business definition?	Not only does the customer have to understand the definition, and find it believable, it is also important that the people in the organisation (who have to deliver the promises) can also understand the definition and play their part in satisfying customers. Also, there will be a range of other stakeholders including business partners whose allegiance, support and cooperation you will need to make the new business definition a reality Often, organisations dealing with diverse (B2C and B2B) markets that rely heavily on intermediaries and distributors, see changing the business definition a problem. Not a problem necessarily, just change – differently defined businesses have different distribution systems and partners – don't get locked into partnerships that belong to the past and not the future
1.2.7	Can we do it? Do we (really) want to do it?	This is an important question but you don't have to share it with other people in the organisation if you don't want to! Business is a people process and not a scientific one. it is important that you are able to look beyond the rhetoric inside the organisation and to identify when there is real appetite for or resistance to change. If the key people in the organisation don't really understand the options or don't really intend to change to the extent that would make the new business definition operable you have three alternatives: **1** Push on with the analysis and redefinition regardless but it will never carry through to effective operation. **2** Recalibrate your business definition down to one that the key opinion leaders inside the organisation can deal with and is as stretching as the organisation can bear, develop this definition and drive the organisation on. **3** Find a new job.

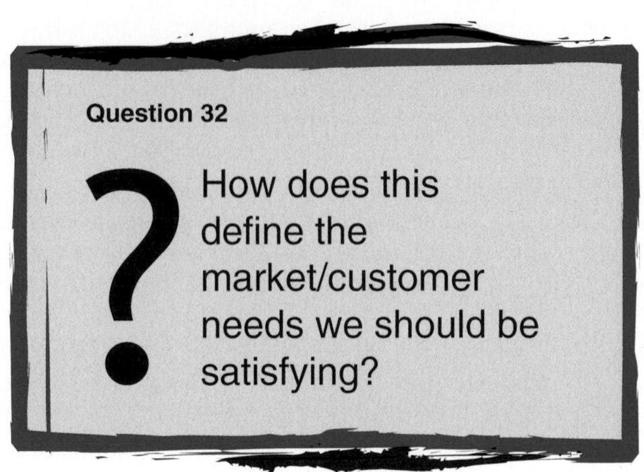

MARGIN NOTES

Now all the process starts to get tricky, we are entering real marketing territory.

Just to recap on the basic points for those of you who may have lost sight of what we are trying to do; real marketing is not about selling products or clever packaging and even neat advertising. It is about:

- Identifying customer needs and wants.
- Designing products and services that meet these needs and wants.
- Delivering benefits or providing solutions.
- Distributing these products and services to them in the most efficient manner available.

How we define the particular market that we will be addressing is critical for our organisation and our scope as well as our competition. The business definition clarifies exactly the particular needs, wants, desires and motivations of our customer that we should be satisfying – and those that we should not. This distinction becomes apparent when we look at some of the companies in the tables above, it is clear that Rolex's definition of being in the jewellery business starts to define a particular market and a set of customer needs. An obsession with watches and the minutiae of the product is unlikely to reveal the market need for a £10,000 (€$15,000) piece of jewellery that also happens to tell the time!

Finally, it is important to note that if the new definition of the business does not clearly define the market customer needs we should be satisfying then maybe it is not the right definition. You can achieve a lot with experience and insight but independent research can sometimes add a previously unimagined dimension to the discussion.

Next, the first in a series of boxes from Rolls Royce. I asked them to comment on their progress against the SCORPIO model and their comments are reproduced in each of the seven sections.

Rolls-Royce

Rolls-Royce plc is a global business providing power systems for use on land, at sea and in the air. The Group has a balanced business portfolio with market leading positions in the civil and defence aerospace, marine and energy markets.

The Marine business within Rolls-Royce is focused on the provision of power, propulsion and motion control solutions to commercial and naval customers worldwide.

These systems are critical to the safe and effective operation of ships at sea and typically represent a significant proportion of both building and operating costs.

Our objective is to add value for our customers through the supply and support of efficient, reliable, cost effective, safe and environmentally responsible power, propulsion and motion control solutions.

Some examples of where our capability is applied to beneficial effect include:

- Development of innovative ship designs with integrated power and propulsion systems that increase cargo carrying capacity and extend operational range.
- Optimised hull and propulsion system designs that reduce drag and resistance with consequent improvement in fuel efficiency and reduction in emissions.
- Reduction of power and propulsion system noise and vibration to improve passenger comfort on cruise ships, ferries and luxury yachts.

MARGIN NOTES

The FAQs are:

1 Industry or market?		
1.3 How does this define the market/customer needs we should be satisfying?		
1.3.1	Does it help us understand the customer better?	One of the (many) reasons for undertaking this exercise and redefining the business is that it should give us a better understanding of the customer, his or her needs, the way our customers lead their lives and how our products and service fits into their lives. If your revised definition of the business does not do this then maybe you have not found the right definition.

1.3.2	How does it add to current knowledge?	The majority or organisations that I visit know far more about the products or service that they provide than the customers who purchase the offering. This is not only an unwelcome state of affairs it is competitively dangerous. The new definition should give us a greater understanding of the customer needs and add to existing knowledge about the product or service. *Note*: We are *not* talking about supplanting your no doubt leading technical knowledge, all we want to do is to ensure that your knowledge about your customers needs and wants is *as good*.
1.3.3	Does it clearly aid differentiation?	Let's be up front here. If it does not help you differentiate your offer then it is not serving the purpose. Differentiation is the name of the game (Chapter 8) and the market definition that makes it easier for us to differentiate our products and services from the competition is what we are all looking for. If it does not do this then you need to try another definition.
1.3.4	Does it clearly identify needs we should *not* be satisfying?	Customers will always attempt to understand your product or service offer in terms of what they believe it does – and what they believe it does not do. Buyers (B2C and B2B) will always seek to compare your offer with a competitor's. If we know this is what they are going to do, we need to make it easy for them. The definition should help you decide what benefits you do not offer.
1.3.5	How far does it take us from our product/ technology competencies?	Answers such as 'not very far' and 'a long way' could both be acceptable depending on your organisation's circumstances. As little movement away from technical competencies of the organisation as possible has got to be a good thing. This means that a large number of people in the organisation can go on (at least for the moment) doing what they have always done, all the changes are restricted to 'unimportant' areas such as presentation, packaging and promotion. Once people in the organisation get used to the idea of what is happening and why, they will be more open to the changes required.
1.3.6	Can we satisfy the needs identified?	The answer here has got to be 'Yes, but' Redefining the business in such a way that you are incapable of meeting and satisfying any of the needs would be foolish. On the other hand, expecting to be able to satisfy all the new needs from day 1 is equally foolish. What we need to know is whether we have a reasonable chance of satisfying enough needs to keep the business moving and we have the ability to grow into or acquire skills necessary to meet more of the needs in future years.
1.3.7	Do we have the people and culture to make it happen?	Ah a people question again! (see Chapter 10) Now before you rush to say no it is going to be doom, disaster and the people in the back office will kill the organisation; remember that every business thinks its own organisation is incompetent and the grass is always greener ...

You need to take a dispassionate view of this question but you need to take a view. The question is how flexible is the organisation? Is there enough movement within the culture in order to make the shift to a market-based definition practical in the short to medium term? One would hope that by the time the long term arrives you have demonstrated the validity of the approach and there are enough wins to create more converts to the cause.

The problem though is the early years. If you really think that your people and/or the culture are not up to the change you might be best advised to go back and look at a less adventurous definition to work with.

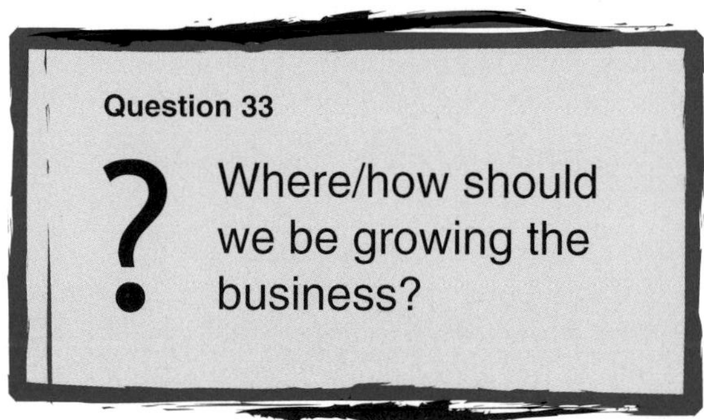

Question 33
?
Where/how should we be growing the business?

MARGIN NOTES

This is the next question to define whether or not we have discovered the most appropriate new definition for the business; does it give you some idea about how you are going to grow the business in the future? Growth is a big and difficult area and too many books and commentators deal with the concept 'growth' without really defining exactly what they mean – so you need to be careful. To help you in this area there are one or two pointers that you need to think about.

- Growth does not necessarily means sales growth or volume growth:
  - Although this is the definition that most sales people will employ without thinking about it.
  - The company that grows its sales can go bankrupt if profit growth does not keep pace.

- We cannot just give the sales team a hard time:
  - A number of so called marketing objectives can also lead to a similar situation.
  - The idea of growing market share has also been known to kill organisations because using (or throwing away) profits in order to buy market share does not seem to make very much sense at all.
  - Again, the profit/margin argument has to be answered.

- How much growth is the right growth?
  - There is a difficult one!

- It all largely depends upon the growth and/or the status of the market that you have defined you want to be in.
- How fast is the market growing, are you going to be growing over or under that speed?
- Are you measuring this in volume terms, value terms, market share terms or other terms?
- Regardless of how or where the market is growing it is generally accepted that every organisation needs to grow year on year by at least somewhere between 2% or 3% just to avoid stagnation.

- Non-financial growth.
  - This does exist.
  - There are many ways that an organisation can grow and some of these do not include financial measures.
  - You need to be looking at how the organisation is developing as a business – and as a culture, is it a learning, adapting and evolving organisation or is it a static organisation that is losing touch with its marketplace?

MARGIN NOTES

- We also need to think about direction of growth.
  - Many organisations are simply given a set figure of absolute or percentage growth from 'on high' that must be achieved.
  - 'Don't talk to me about market conditions; we have shareholders who expect a return regardless'.
  - So, the financial hurdles get higher every year.

Previously you would have worried about how to hit the numbers. It used to be easy to see where the cuts could be made; you could see the costs clearly. Spotting where extra sales could come from was more difficult, everywhere you looked you were fighting the same competitors every day.

Changing the business definition should change much of this. Depending on how you redefine the business you want to be in, you should see many more business opportunities that you saw before. Previously, you saw product opportunities and sales objectives – but you were never sure if there was a wiling market ready to buy. Now you should see the world differently, market opportunities – your concern now should be can you make a product or service that will meet the needs?

Deciding where to grow the business now becomes a strategic question; your job should not be 'how do we grow?', but 'where should we be growing?' Take back control.

Successful organisations all tend to start by being strongly customer driven and using a benefits-based definition of the business they are in. In a competitive environment it is the only way to succeed against entrenched competitors. Over time, internal focus tends to move away from customers to processes, systems and 'professional management'.

Established organisations do have a choice however, rather than simply succumbing to the new entrants in their turn, they can decide to redefine their business and regain their customer focus. Corporate 'renewal' is never easy although some may prefer it to a steady, if stately decline.

The FAQs are:

1 Industry or market?		
1.4 Where/how should we be growing the business?		
1.4.1	Do the growth prospects excite the organisation, management and staff?	With the redefinition of the business, we should expect to see greater opportunities for growth. As the organisation learns to look beyond its traditional industry/product boundaries, market (customer) opportunities appear rapidly. However, these opportunities need to be exciting in financial terms but also for the people who work in and for the organisation. Exciting prospects engage your people and encourage them to see change as new and exciting rather than bad, dangerous and scary.
1.4.2	Does it show potential areas of significant market growth (gap)?	Depending on your chosen business definition, is your target market growing, declining or static – and in what terms (turnover or profit)? Obviously not all markets can be growing, that rather defies the laws of physics, but you do have a choice about which markets you want to play in – and there is no rule that says you can only profit in dynamic youthful markets.
1.4.3	Are the growth areas 'innovative'?	A lot has been talked about 'innovation'. The books, magazines and popular press are rife with 'innovative ideas' and some even go on to define exactly what innovation means. I will not pursue this topic too deeply here (see Chapter 11) beyond saying that innovation needs, of course, to be customer driven and ideally needs to be delivering the marketplace with new solutions rather than new problems! Most of the serious texts on innovation include redefining the business you are in as one of the key ways that an organisation can improve its innovation activity. Understanding how the market works in customer perception rather than product feature terms is the first step in identifying new or latent customer problems for which you can develop innovative and creative solutions.
1.4.4	Are the growth areas profitable?	Deceptively simple but a big question. Marketing should be about profits and if the new market opportunities are not profitable why are you looking at them? Fortunately, in most cases, customer benefits tend to be more profitable than product features.
1.4.5	Are the growth areas 'logical' to the customer?	A product features-driven business will plot its growth in technical feature terms – it is what it understands and it assumes that customers follow the same logic.

		Customer benefits-driven businesses will plot their growth into areas that customers find logical, even if this means straying outside what it believes is its core technology. So successful can this approach be that Harley Davidson reputedly makes more profits out of 'accessories' than it does out of motorbikes.
1.4.6	Are there sufficient growth prospects for at least 3–5 years?	This one really goes without saying. If you are going to shift the focus of the organisation this will inevitably cause some upheaval especially when people realise that it is not just another advertising slogan and that they may actually have to start behaving differently. Achieving the shift is not going to be a short term activity so it is important that you can see some life in the new business definition and that it will sustain the organisation over the planning period and beyond.
1.4.7	How different is the route from that planned before?	This is the tricky part. Not easy to do accurately, but the 'planners' in the organisation will insist. You will need to find a convincing way of demonstrating the route you see into the newly defined business, the different activities and process involved and the expected outputs from the change. Everybody knows that such predictions are impossible but with a spread sheet nothing should be beyond your powers.... Then, depending upon the culture and willingness (or desperation) to change, the organisation might be prepared to shift the planning focus from the old to the new immediately, or to look at a 2–3 year period of 'dual planning' that allows both to run side by side. A change of this magnitude (if you do it properly) will involve many people and could prove fatal to a number of sacred cows so don't rush it. Moving sales from industry verticals to benefit segments and finance from product profitability analysis to customer lifetime profitability analysis are just two of the big challenges. There is a lot to be done and maybe the best way to eat an elephant is, as the ant knows, a spoonful at a time!

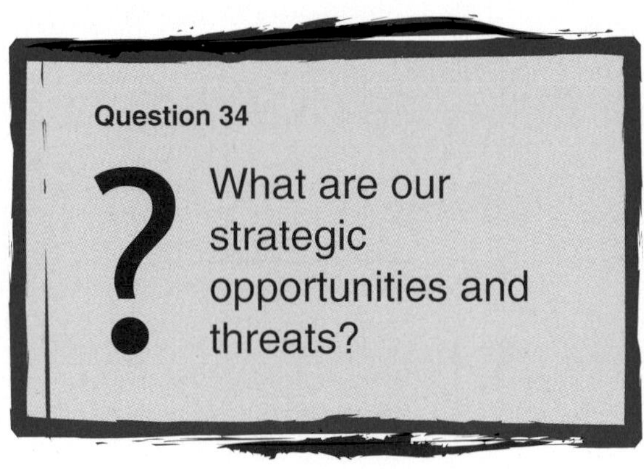

Question 34
?
What are our strategic opportunities and threats?

If your 'new' business definition has held up this far then it is time to start doing some basic analysis. What we need to do next is identify the key numbers that will eventually feed into the plans and the planning process.

We should start, at the beginning, with an understanding of the external environment – of the business described by the *new* definition. We know that most organisations produce standard 'PEST' and 'SWOT' analyses as a type of marketing and planning 'habit', and then do nothing with them. It is like many activities in modern business, we do them because we have always done them, but we cannot remember why …

Our first task then, is to brush off and re-focus these two analyses to find out whether they give any more insight into the needs/wants of the target marketplace and what our ultimate market objectives should be.

MARGIN NOTES

Starting with the PEST analysis; typically we don't look for too many major changes in the PEST analysis because the newly defined business will not (or should not) be too far away from the one in which the organisation is currently working. However some of the impacts of the external environment can be more or less severe within different business/market definitions. For example, with Harley Davidson, we can imagine that moving from trying to sell 'motorbikes' to selling 'big boys toys' means that with a market age of 53+ (the average age for a new Harley Davidson owner) things like the current (and likely continuing) pensions crisis could be a more significant effect on this group than some markets that are driven by the younger generations.

With the SWOT analysis we may be expecting a greater degree of change. A proper SWOT analysis (although these are still too rare) should take strengths and weaknesses (the internal and controllable elements) as they are seen by *customers* and prospects, not just as seen by the people inside the organisation. Opportunities and threats (the external and uncontrollable elements) will be dictated by the terms of the business in which we want to operate. Here we have more work to do. Strengths and weaknesses will now need to be assessed from the perspective of your *new* target market (for example; big boys (Harley Davidson), fashion seekers(Swatch), DIY enthusiasts(Black & Decker) and travellers(Amtrak)).

The model described by Hamel and Prahaled helps us understand this difference. In their original 1994 article, they suggested that *latent* needs and wants contained most of the unexploited opportunities and the unidentified threats for the business. This is because organisations tend to

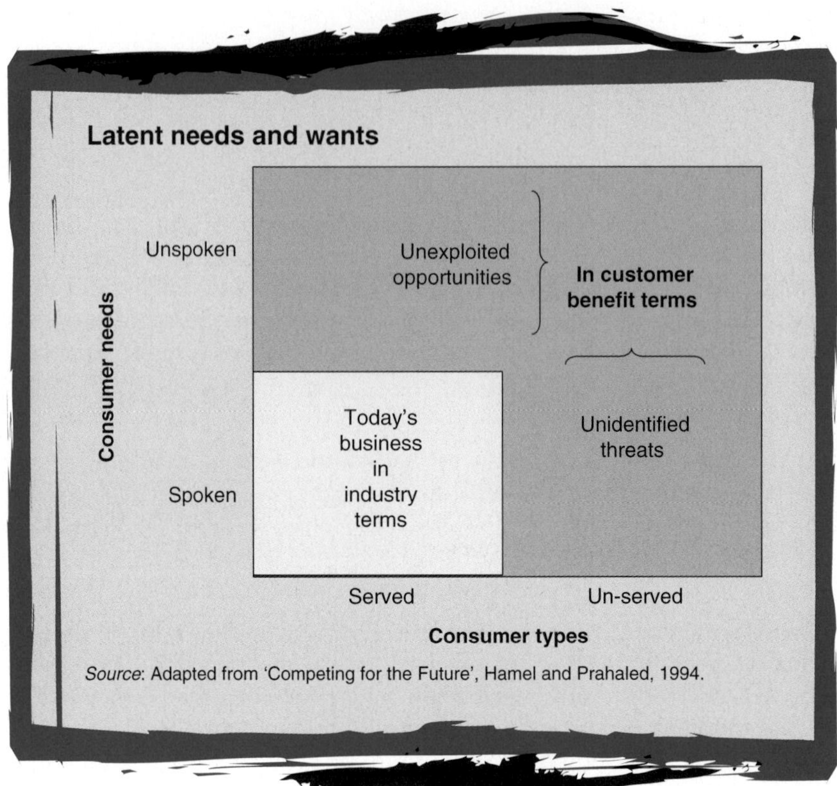

Source: Adapted from 'Competing for the Future', Hamel and Prahaled, 1994.

MARGIN NOTES

talk to existing customers about issues, concerns and needs they can articulate. This focus on 'today's business' can make us blind to the needs of potential customers (not currently served) and to needs/wants that they are not (yet) able to articulate.

In the same way, the organisation that moves from its technical/product business definition (making motorbikes) suddenly sees different opportunities and threats as it starts to look at the world through a different 'lens'. Just knowing that we are concerned with customer needs (big boys' toys) means that we talk to different people and we talk to them in a different way. We ask different questions and we are ready to hear different answers. We understand different issues so we see different possibilities. The possibilities, to succeed or to fail, have always been there, but have been hidden from us up until now.

To finish this section on a literary note, Marcel Proust said: '*The real voyage of discovery consists, not in seeking new landscapes, but in having new eyes*'.

The FAQs are:

1 Industry or market?		
1.5 What are our strategic opportunities and threats?		
1.5.1	Does our 'PEST' analysis change in the new market definition?	Pull out and dust off your old copy of the PEST analysis; you know, the one that you update every year from what you have retained from listening to the television news every night. If you look at this analysis dispassionately, you will probably find the 'conventional wisdom' that comes from the 'industry' and is never questioned. Your question now is, are they still such important drivers to your newly defined business? Do your 'new eyes' show you any environmental issues to which members of the 'old industry definition' remain blind?
1.5.2	SWOT – what are the new opportunities?	One of the main reasons for refocusing the business from an industry to a market definition is the identification of new business opportunities. What are these opportunities? Where are they? How big are they? How do we get into them? We need to put numbers against the opportunities.
1.5.3	SWOT – what are the new threats?	Just as there is no such thing as a free lunch there is also no such thing as a new opportunity without new threats! Don't assume they are not there and certainly don't assume, just because you may be one of the first movers in your industry to shift emphasis, that you will not be meeting competitors from different industries in the new redefined market.
1.5.4	SWOT – what are the new weaknesses?	As with any proper SWOT analysis, the strengths and weaknesses need to be seen from the customer's perspective. We will have weaknesses as long as our target customers believe we are not skilled or willing to deal with needs or wants that they consider to be important. Having redefined the business it is almost sure that the new definition includes some customers we have not previously included in our target market. So it is unlikely that we would have canvassed their views and opinions on our organisation, our brand, our position and our image as well as the ability of our products to meet their particular needs.
1.5.5	SWOT – what are the new strengths?	We also need to find out what our new strengths are perceived to be in this new market. Be sure to assess all these new strengths, not just the ones that you or people in your organisation believe they can deliver.
1.5.6	SWOT – how do the 'new' and 'old' compare?	Advanced analysis here! Put the old SWOT next to the new SWOT and spot the differences. This analysis will stand you in good stead when it comes to answering difficult questions from colleagues reluctant to change.

1.5.7	What actions result from this analysis?	So what are you going to do about it? 1 Identify the current marketing and sales activities which appear to be getting in the way of creating a reasonable and credible position in the newly defined market (shooting itself in the foot) 2 Stop these activities 3 Identify the easiest areas of growth in the newly defined business 4 Achieve some 'quick wins' fast 5 Demonstrate to the rest of the organisation that the crazy guys may have a point and recruit converts

MARGIN NOTES

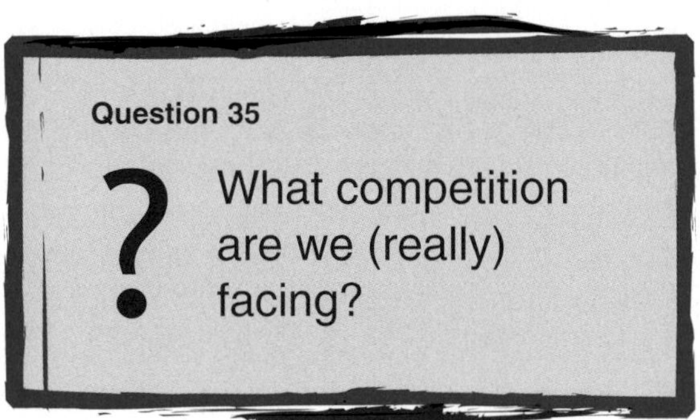

Question 35
?
What competition are we (really) facing?

Review the new definition of the business that you have chosen.

As you move from an industry to a market-driven definition of the business you are in, it is fairly sure that you will leave a lot of your (former) industry competition behind you. It is equally sure that, as you move, you will encounter new competition from different industries. Again, Harley Davidson loses its direct competition with other motorbike manufacturers but starts to pick up competition from holiday companies, swimming pool makers and producers of conservatories! Equally, Sony loses some direct competitors who just make electronic products but then faces new competition from other forms of entertainment such as live shows, gambling, older technology books and magazines and newer technology iPods.

On the one hand, it might be attractive to move into a position where you're no longer competing with the people and organisations you have historically met (and benchmarked) time and time again. On the other hand, you would be well advised to assess the new competition quite carefully. For example, a manufacturer of small electrical domestic appliances (such as kettles and irons) who redefines its business as being in 'household tasks/chores' might suddenly come face to face with the cleaning giants such as Unilever and Johnson & Johnson. Moving from a 'small pond' to compete in a 'bigger pond' means that there might be more opportunities for growth but you also meet bigger fish.

This is perhaps a good opportunity to dust off the old 'Porter's Five Forces' diagram (see Chapter 2) and apply it with some degree of vigour. The 'Five Forces' process looks at the five key forces of competition that work on any organisation. The central box in the diagram considers the normal and day-to-day rivalry that exists between organisations in the *same industry*. This is fierce, hand-to-hand competition but it is not always the most dangerous. As you move from industry to market-defined business then the other boxes start to take on a new life and also a new importance. For example:

- Buyer power
  - You will need to assess the new market that you want to move in and understand whether they are;
    - Small in number or
    - Concentrated in a particular area of geography or interest or
    - Likely to purchase a significant portion of your output.
  - In any of these cases they will have some degree of power over the products, the product ranges and the prices that you charge.
  - Remember that concentration and the amount that they buy may refer to the channel as well as the number of customers, a highly concentrated distribution system (such as Supermarkets) gives you a certain problem.
  - If, on the other hand, buyers are many and different and your product/ service/ brand is sought after, you have more power over the situation and they are less of a competitive threat
- Supplier Power
  - If you have powerful suppliers (they are very few, concentrated or could integrate forward and take over your business) then you have less bargaining power.
  - Weaker suppliers (many competitors and options for you to buy) provides you with a stronger position
- New Entrants
  - Any assessment previously carried out into potential new entrants into the market will be outdated by your new business definition.
  - You need to assess how easy it would be for entrants to enter this newly defined market.
  - It will be easier if there is a common technology required to deliver products, services and solutions, little brand franchise and easy access to distribution channels.
  - You have more protection from new entrants if you have some intellectual capital which others cannot acquire or there is some form of restriction over distribution channels

MARGIN NOTES

- Substitutes
  - The threat of substitutes will also be different in the new business.
  - A substitute is an alternative method/process/purchase that will allow the customer to achieve (almost) the same end as if they had purchased a solution from your organisation.
  - In Levitt's terms, they can hire another product/ service and get the same job done (but differently).
  - A new business/market needs different motivations so you will be under different substitute threat.

To some extent, the resistors of change (who can always be heard to cite 'better the devil you know than the devil you don't') have a fair point here. In the industry-defined business you (and everybody else) understood the competition, what people were able to do, what they were willing to do and how much you could threaten them without suffering retaliation. In the new business, the rules have changed. You will have new competition, many of whom are unknown quantities and the rules of the competitive game may have changed. It is important that you align carefully the boundaries of your new business so that you only take on the level of competition which you are willing (and able) to deal with.

The FAQs are:

1. Industry or market?		
1.6 What competition are we (really) facing?		
1.6.1	Who are the competitors in the 'new space'?	You need to list and identify all of the new players who appear to be active in the market that you are planning to enter: • Who are they? • What are their strengths, weaknesses, market positions? • What is their parent company if any? • How long have they been working in the market? • What is the industry from which they have come? Don't guess, ask the customers, they will tell you who is in and who is out
1.6.2	Does Porter's Five Forces analysis show new threats?	What threats does your analysis of the Five Forces model identify? Can you satisfactorily protect yourself against these threats – or can you avoid them? Are the threats too dangerous to allow you to continue with your new business definition or will you have to amend it in some way?
1.6.3	Do we understand the new and potential competition?	Do you have a workable understanding of the new competition and do you understand what it is likely to do when it realises that you have turned your focus from an industry to a market perspective. When you declare yourself a player in the new market, how is the competition likely to respond?

1.6.4	What business do new/ potential competitors believe they are in?	How do you believe your new competitors define the business they are in? Have they defined it in exactly the same way as you? Are they working in their own (different) definition of an industry and happening to be working next to you almost by accident? Remember that you will only encounter direct competition from those organisations who have defined their business roughly the same way as yours. This does not mean that competition from other people who have defined their business slightly differently is going to be less troublesome. In fact competition coming *from the side* can be more surprising and more difficult to predict.
1.6.5	How does 'substitute competition' in the new business affect us?	The fact that we are looking at a different business/market means that the substitutes will be different from an industry/product-defined business. As the customers are different so the needs, wants and benefits demanded are different – so the substitutes for delivering those different benefits will be different as well. The problem is, if we have no experience of what the substitutes are we may not see the real competition in time to prepare.
1.6.6	What are the competitors' plans and ambitions in our market?	It is always better to face the competition prepared. As soon as we have identified the most important new competitors it is important to try and understand their ambitions are for the future, their preferred method of operation and their plans – as far as these can be determined. Fore-warned is fore-armed, and it is not as difficult as you might imagine.
1.6.7	How do we build competitive response into our plans?	Competitive response modelling is not an 'option'; it is the only professional way to go. Surprise is *not* a good or profitable approach.

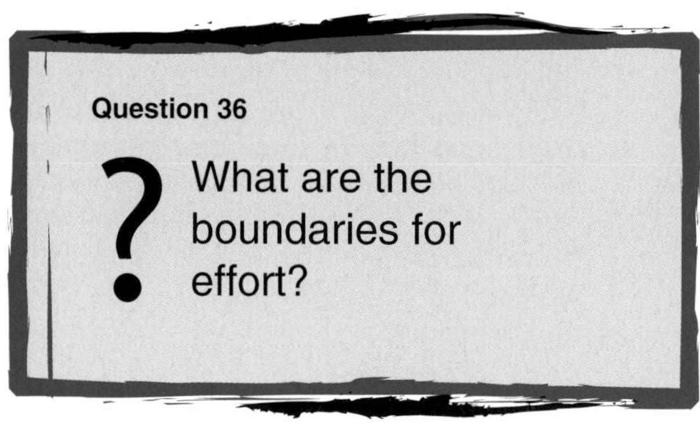

Question 36
?
What are the boundaries for effort?

If you have got to this point with only insignificant or cosmetic changes to your new business definition it could be that you have found the most appropriate route for future development. In which case you now need to start planning the actual activities that the new business definition implies you should be undertaking.

Any good marketing organisation knows that its activities and plans are driven, not by its products or services, but by the markets and customers it wishes to serve. The more you focus on defining your business around the customers who (you hope) will buy your products and services, the better chance you have of understanding what they need from you and what you have to provide in order to grow the business. The more you are able to move to a market/customer-driven understanding the more you will be able to put the industry requirements into the background.

MARGIN NOTES

The other side of the coin says that no matter how fast, nimble and good you are, resources will always be limited – the pot is never bottomless. In which case, we need to know where to place our limited investments (time money and ingenuity) for maximum return. Again, the customers will tell us if only we can imagine and formulate the right questions.

Enter the trusty traffic lights (see Chapter 4).

- The right business definition should be able to tell us where we should devote our time and resources (the GO/green area) – and where our attention will be wasted (the STOP/red area).
  - The customers (if approached correctly) will tell you where they see most (customer) value (customer value has many definitions; I use the definition of 'the perfect solution to my problem', see Chapter 11).
  - In investment terms, the organisation should seek to invest in areas of highest perceived customer value because there will be found the highest prices and greatest potential for loyalty/retention.

- The STOP/red areas will include activities that are seen by customers as delivering no (customer) value.
  - Beware here.
  - Some activities are really wasteful in customer terms and can be stopped, but – some of these 'wasteful areas' may be viewed internally as important to the organisation – so only stop these carefully.
  - Some areas may be important in providing service to customers but they are not seen in that light, (imagine for example doctors' receptionists or hospital casualty administration), in these cases the activities cannot be dropped but they need to be re-packaged, represented or reformulated so that they are seen positively by the customers.

So what do you do next?

The FAQs are:

1 Industry or market?		
1.7 What are the boundaries for effort?		
1.7.1	What should we be doing *more* of?	More focused definition of the business and understanding of particular customer needs should start to highlight areas where we could add customer value at relatively low cost. Where are the first (easy win) activities that will gain us traction in the new market?
1.7.2	What should we be doing *less* of?	There are two things that readily spring to mind: **1** We need to stop doing things that cost the organisation money but also seem to add little or no customer value. **2** We need to stop doing things which, while perhaps adding some value in our mind, appear to be stopping the customer from buying from us (negative value).
1.7.3	Where are the 'quick wins' in the market?	As we move from an industry to a market-defined business we absolutely need quick wins; for two reasons: **1** You need to be demonstrating to everybody else in the organisation that there is mileage to be made from the new definition. People tend to take to change slowly but faster (and with slightly fewer saboteurs) if they can see that there are returns in doing things in a different way. **2** Quick wins demonstrate to the marketplace that you are taking the market and customer needs seriously.
1.7.4	What are the skills and/or knowledge gaps that must be filled?	Chapter 6 spends some time on this issue, but for now the key aspects are: **1** Knowledge of customer needs, wants and motivations is about competitive advantage – it is so much more than just a 'cost'. **2** Until you have moved from the industry to the customer-defined business, you don't know what you don't know – a competitive disaster waiting to happen. **3** Once you know what you don't know, you can start to find out – if you discover what you don't know before the others (and find out) you are at a competitive advantage, use it.
1.7.5	How should we reallocate marketing investments?	Here the answer should be slowly and carefully. We don't want to frighten too many of our colleagues and partners. A more pragmatic approach is to use the quick wins to focus attention on the way that money and investment have been allocated in the past. As soon as you are able to get people's attention and their acceptance that there are different ways of allocating resources then the battle is almost won.
1.7.6	What are the implications for strategy and planning?	Ultimately we will need a completely new strategy and set of plans because the market (as we understood it) has changed. If the new and old plans could be run in parallel for a couple of years, people could get used to the new ways of working. Also we need to say a word or two about the plans themselves. Ideally, we would leave the planning process as open and fluid as possible.

		As we learn more about the nature, composition and dynamics of the business we are in, we will need to be flexible in how we create/ implement plans to identify and extract value from the market. Planning formats and processes that have been developed over time to meet the needs of the industry-driven business may not be as useful in the new business.
1.7.7	What are the implications for the organisation and its people?	This can be summed up in one word – scary. We will be looking at how we deal with this organisational change later in Chapter 10. For the moment, you just need to be aware that change is definitely not seen as a good thing for most people – even if it is necessary for the organisation's survival. If you don't want a critical mass of people trying to resist change (even if it will mean the death of the organisation) then you must tread carefully.

■ The Strategic Questions (25–36)

MARGIN NOTES

In this first part of the SCORPIO marketing strategy discussion, we have looked at the all-important question of 'what business are we in?' Levitt attempted to answer the question in 1960, and I have been trying to do the same with organisations for a very long time.

The question is deceptively simple, the logic is unavoidable, but the solution can be elusive. Some organisations manage the change and others do not. Of course, not all organisations survive to an old age …

We have looked at some of the issues involved in deciding how to redefine the business and what the best definition might be. As always, there are no hard-and-fast rules since every organisation is just a collection of people – and people need much more than hard logic to persuade them to do something different.

Deciding what business the organisation needs or wants to be in is obviously a business strategy question – but it is a key market strategy issue too and deserves its place in the SCORPIO model. The business definition, we shall see, determines directly:

- Which customers we need to attract
- Which market we segment (very important)
- The competitive position and brand decisions which are relative to the competition
- The offerings
- The most appropriate methods of retention
- The most effective organisational processes to operate in the business

Here are the next questions for you. More decisions I'm afraid, but this time maybe not *final*. The SCORPIO process is an iterative one, that is to say you make some decisions and find out that you may have to *re-make* them again later in the light of other decisions made elsewhere in the SCORPIO model. Decide but be prepared to re-decide again later.

Likewise, the question of how important are the decisions, is also a relative question. Tick the relevant boxes now and see whether you need to change the importance levels after you have worked other SCORPIO areas.

No.	Strategic question	Our strategic answer	Importance	✓
	Part Two – Developing the marketing strategy			
25	What is marketing strategy?		Must have	
			Nice to have	
			Not important	
26	What are the steps involved in developing marketing strategy?		Must have	
			Nice to have	
			Not important	
27	What does marketing strategy mean for my organisation?		Must have	
			Nice to have	
			Not important	
28	Should I prepare my organisation for marketing strategy?		Must have	
			Nice to have	
			Not important	
29	Who do I involve in the marketing strategy process?		Must have	
			Nice to have	
			Not important	
	Industry or market?			
30	What business are we in?		Must have	
			Nice to have	
			Not important	
31	What business do we want to be in or should we be in?		Must have	
			Nice to have	
			Not important	
32	How does this define the market/customer needs we should be satisfying?		Must have	
			Nice to have	
			Not important	

33	Where/how should we be growing the business?		Must have	
			Nice to have	
			Not important	
34	What are our strategic opportunities and threats?		Must have	
			Nice to have	
			Not important	
35	What competition are we (really) facing?		Must have	
			Nice to have	
			Not important	
36	What are the boundaries for effort?		Must have	
			Nice to have	
			Not important	

CHAPTER 6

The customer

> 'It is not the employer who pays the wages. Employers only handle the money. It is the customer who pays the wages.'
>
> *Henry Ford (1863–1947), American industrialist and pioneer of the assembly-line production method*

The customer is the name of the game.

MARGIN NOTES

Customers produce all the organisation's revenues and profits and are the only reason for an organisation's continued existence. At the very least the organisation intent on survival will need to know:

- Who its customers are and
- What they want.

If you and your organisation want more than simple survival, you will need to know much more if you are to compete successfully in rapidly internationalising and commoditising markets.

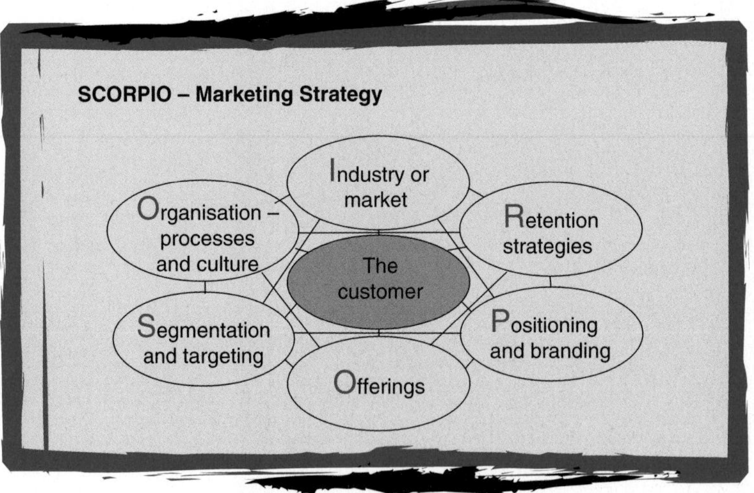

Although *knowing* may itself be a tall order – often customers don't really *know* what they want, they just want – and need. But, before we go any further, I need to explain quite carefully that there is a difference between *knowing* what your customers (and prospects) really want from you and:

- You *assuming* you know (better than they do) what they want
- You *knowing* what they *ought to* want
- You *guessing* who they are and what they mig.ht want
- You *hoping* that they are going to want what you have decided to make
- You *not caring* who they are or what they want because you have sales targets to make and you will always find somewhere to unload the stuff

Knowing exactly what your customers (and prospects) want is not easy – it is impossible – but you can reduce some of the risk if you talk to them. I don't want to get too technical, too early but asking customers (rather than guessing) is called Market Research.

There is no reason to start re-checking your meagre budgets – it needn't be either difficult or expensive. It is probably going to be better than guessing whatever you do. So let's deal with the issues of research – up front.

MARGIN NOTES

■ Market research

Before we start it is probably worth dealing with one or two definitions.

- Market research or marketing research:
  - Although nowadays these two terms tend to be used synonymously, I think it is useful that we understand where these words originally came from.
  - Market research
    - Officially applies to research into markets, in other words their size, composition, buyer's needs and wants and so forth.
  - Marketing research
    - Covers research into the organisation's marketing activities and its ability to address its markets.
- Data or information:
  - This is a pair of terms that also tend to be used interchangeably but here it causes problems in understanding.
    - Data can be defined as 'things which are known or granted from which inferences may be drawn'
      - they are essentially the raw material of market research.

        - Information is best defined as 'that which reduces uncertainty in the receiver'.
    - If you are struggling to understand a word of what I have just said then you have just received a whole chunk (is that a technical term?) of data. I will try and turn this data into information with an example.
        - Imagine that you are at a party (yes I know, you have no time to go to parties but bear with me) you are being introduced to someone new by a mutual friend.
        - During the process your name is given, this is data, but since you knew your name already it has reduced no uncertainty on your part.
        - The person you are being introduced to is named to you and this can be considered as information because it has now reduced some uncertainty about this new introduction.
    - The distinction between data and information is an important one because the development of a marketing strategy is not aided by the accumulation of random data on markets or on market or marketing activity.
        - It is only by the careful acquisition of practical and relevant information that areas of doubt and uncertainty can be reduced and effective plans made for the future.
    - Of course, information is much more difficult to acquire than data.
        - While data is the raw material of the market researcher the marketing practitioner should only be interested in acquiring relevant and usable information.

MARGIN NOTES

- Product research or market research:
    - Market research implies research into the workings of the market.
        - Who are today's and tomorrow's prospective customers?
        - What are their likely needs?
        - What will they buy?
        - What selection will they choose from?
        - How much will they pay?
    - Unfortunately, most organisations' strategic research budgets do not appear to be spent answering these types of questions.
        - The majority of 'market research' spend (at least in my experience) seems to be dedicated to 'product research' projects.
    - Product research normally involves batteries of questions asking respondents for their thoughts and attitudes on existing products, new product concepts and possible modifications.
        - Often hundreds and thousands of pounds, euros and dollars are spent assessing customers reactions to likely changes in price, colour or design – and promotional and communication changes.
        - All of this is useful data, certainly for practical day-to-day tactical marketing, but it rarely helps the development of a

robust marketing strategy – this requires information on customers rather than products.

- We need to know
  - How our customers lead their lives
  - How they run their businesses
  - How they regard their families
  - What they do in their leisure time and
  - What problems they believe they have.
- Armed with this insight we can then begin to do the proper marketing job and blend packaging design and modify our product service so it meets the needs that they have, or are likely to have, rather than the needs we think they ought to have.
- Real market research is not easy. Maybe that's why its not common. Interestingly enough, the reasons for not conducting this type of market research clearly demonstrate some of the problems facing marketing today:
  - 'We have never done it.'
  - 'Qualitative research is all a bit touchy-feely.'
  - 'How do you find out what the customers themselves don't know they want?'
  - 'This organisation works on numbers – not loose concepts or ideas.'
  - 'The market research agencies we use just don't do that sort of thing.'
  - 'Sorry, the finance people just wouldn't buy it.'
  - 'The product managers hold the research budget and they have their product targets to meet this year thank you.'
  - 'There's no budget for that sort of thing, every pound/dollar we spend has to be set-off against an existing profit centre.'

MARGIN NOTES

■ The market research process

In its simplest form any market research project can be broken down into five distinct stages. It matters little the size of the project, the complexity of the project or even the importance of a project to your organisation's long-term goals, these five stages should always be followed if the money involved is to be an investment rather than just a cost:

- Define the problem and the research objectives:
  - Any market research project which does not have clearly defined objectives at the outset is likely to run out of control very fast.
  - It is essential that the people commissioning the research (you?), the people using the research (you and others in your organisation) and the people carrying out the research have a very clear

understanding of what everybody is trying to do and how the results will eventually be used.
    - Research will be more effective (and cost efficient) if it is directed at filling in identified gaps in market or customer information.
    - Simple curiosity is never enough to justify any form of market research project.

- Develop the research plan:
    - We don't need to get complicated and technical, we only need to understand a minimum of the jargon to make sure that the researchers will be delivering what is needed at the end of the project.
    - Running through the principle points:
        - Data sources
        - There are two main sources of data open to the researcher, primary and secondary data.
            - Primary data
                - It is original data collected directly by the organisation (or its agency).
                - Primary data is more relevant to the problem in hand but it does tend to cost more money to collect.
            - Secondary data
                - Is data that already exists somewhere else. It may exist in the form of:
                    - Government statistics
                    - Data produced by private organisations
                    - Internal data that already exist inside your organisation but may just not be in the right form for analysis at the moment.
                - Secondary data ought always to be the starting point of any data collection given that it is normally cheaper to collect.
        - Collecting primary data
            - There are two types of data to be considered.
            - These come under the headings of qualitative and quantitative data.
                - Qualitative research
                    - Will normally precede quantitative in a project, since it is concerned with the behaviour of organisations, competitors, markets and customers and is mostly concerned with asking why people act in a certain way as well as what people want.
                    - Qualitative data is important because it will help identify the questions that need to be asked in any broader quantitative stage.
                - Quantitative research
                    - It is a broader scope of research where we try and find out exactly how many people have a particular problem and might value a particular solution.

MARGIN NOTES

        - Quantitative research is often about putting numbers on to qualitative issues.
    - Research instruments
        - This includes some indication of the research instruments to be used in the collection of the data.
        - For example
            - Questionnaires (for quantitative data collection)
            - Discussion guides (for qualitative research).
        - It may also include some information on sampling techniques and contact methods by which data will be collected from respondents.

- Collect the data
    - Data collection is the next and probably the most expensive phase in the research project.
    - This is the point at which the fieldwork is carried out.

- Analyse the data
    - Once the data has been collected, depending on the nature of the research, it should describe the nature and process of the statistical methods to be used.

- Present the findings:
    - This is the stage of the research project where the results of the fieldwork and/or analysis are presented back to you (the commissioner and/or the proposed user of the research).
    - This is the point at which you will be very happy that you decided to invest some serious time in developing and agreeing a market research objective which ties into the strategic problem at hand.
    - A good research presentation should be light on process methodology and statistical analysis and should concentrate much more on the implications of the findings for the problem that originated the research.

MARGIN NOTES

What can market research do?

Maybe this final section ought to be called 'what can't market research do?' since nowadays market research has become a major tool in the armoury of the market facing organisation. It goes too far when managers will not move a muscle without a market research project to back-up any activity.

The 'headlines' are:

- Market research is definitely not an alternative to management decision making.

- No market research, no matter how deep, complicated and detailed, can ever be seen as a substitute to creative decision making by professional managers (that's you!).
- At its very best, market research might be able to remove some doubt and clarify some options or alternatives.
- It may even be seen as a tool which can improve the quality of decisions – but it is not, of itself, a decision-making mechanism.

- Market research, in common with a number of scientific and pseudo-scientific management tools, can suffer from the widespread complaint of 'spurious accuracy'.
  - Market research results can never be completely accurate since they are dealing with human nature.
  - They are dealing with a small sample of a dynamic marketplace which has been 'grossed up' to give total market results.
  - There will always be a form of inherent bias in market research results.
  - This error should be plainly and clearly understood by everyone reading research results.

- Last, market research is not an end in itself.
  - It is simply a means by which some risk can be removed from marketing activity.
  - Ultimately, only the business decision counts, not the market research itself.

MARGIN NOTES

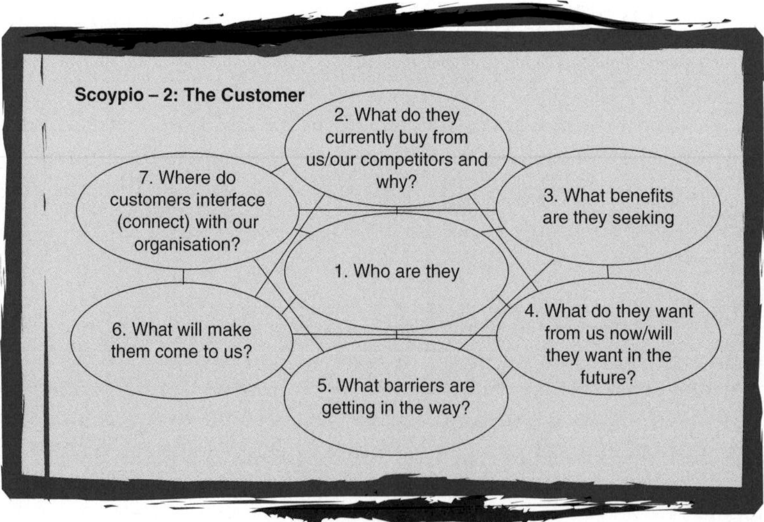
Scoypio – 2: The Customer
1. Who are they
2. What do they currently buy from us/our competitors and why?
3. What benefits are they seeking
4. What do they want from us now/will they want in the future?
5. What barriers are getting in the way?
6. What will make them come to us?
7. Where do customers interface (connect) with our organisation?

Marketing strategy doesn't need market research as much as it desperately needs some good answers. Practical marketing strategy has to be based on reasonably well understood customer needs, wants and motivations if it is to provide longer-term solutions that customers will want to buy. The better we understand our customers and their needs the better the quality of the marketing strategy will be and the better the bottom line will look. Unfortunately, all that glitters is not gold – and some 'market research' documents are not what they might appear.

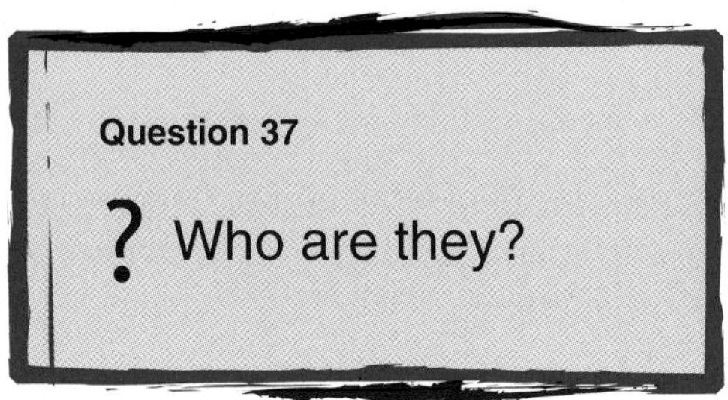
Question 37
? Who are they?

MARGIN NOTES

A wise organisation knows its own customers.

A good way to think about your customers is like an *asset*. In fact, your customers are probably the biggest single asset your company owns. Like any asset, the job is:

- To identify it
- To maintain it and
- To maximise returns from it.

Stage one, is to know where your assets are. In market terms – know your customers.

Customers are human beings (even business (B2B) buyers) – much more complicated than serial numbers or barcodes. In this section we will look at how we can get to know our customer base and who and where the invaluable data is held.

The Marketing Information System (MkIS) is a good place to start, but we look at that more closely in Chapter 9.

Before we look at some of the FAQs in this area, a few words about what many customers expect you to know about them …

- The past 10 years has witnessed an unparalleled growth of information technology (the customer knows this because you have forced them to present their information in computer-friendly formats, more than once) as well as the number of attempts to try and bring all this data together into one central point where it might be analysed and finally understood.

- However, despite the enormous advances in data mining, database management and processing capability *the single view* of the customer is as elusive now as it has always been.

- Despite the millions spent on this particular holy grail, few (especially large) organisations have yet to reach the point where they are able to bring together the customer data that *their customers think they ought to be able to use.*

- Most customers (not that anybody bothers to ask them), especially those who are being told they should be looking for a 'relationship' (see Chapter 9) with the organisation seem to think that the organisation really *ought* to know:
  - Who they are
  - What their personal details are
  - Where they live and how they can be contacted
  - When and where they prefer to be contacted
  - What they have bought from the organisation in the past
  - When (and why) they have contacted the organisation in the past, regardless of who they happened to speak to at that time
  - The information they communicated and the results of the last contact to be carried forward into the current one.

From the customer's perspective, not an unreasonable request – but most customers are still waiting.

The FAQs are:

2 The Customer		
2.1 Who are they?		
2.1.1	How do you describe your existing customer base?	Do you try to describe your customers in terms of their age, their family circumstances, nature of the business that they run, the size of organisation of which they are part or by their geographical location? This is an interesting question because often how organisations describe their customers gives some fairly strong clues as to how they see their customers – and how they treat them. Next, do you have different types of customers or are your customers all the same (see Chapter 8)? How do you describe the different groups of customers that you currently serve? Do you recognise these differences? Expect to hear terms such as larger/smaller/older/younger/northern/southern customers, the list goes on. How people see and describe their customer base often becomes the de facto method of market segmentation. Also, such real or imagined differences can often end up driving (erroneously) new product development, service delivery and promotional activities.

2.1.2	Is there one way of describing the customers, or many?	If you were to ask different people in your organisation to describe your customer base, what do you think might be the reply? Asking different functions, such as finance and accounting, sales, manufacturing and/or service delivery might produce very different answers. Different perceptions of customers (and their needs) can only produce variable response behaviours from an organisation – the result is confused customers who may be unclear as to what the organisation stands for.
2.1.3	What do we know about our customers?	Separately, the various departments/functions in our organisation probably know a lot about our customers. If we could bring together these different pieces of knowledge we would probably be a force in any market. The level of customer knowledge will vary from one organisation to another. Often it depends on how important the customer is thought to be in the overall business and how much time, effort and money has been invested in getting to know and understand the customer. Unfortunately, most of us tend to think we know more about our customers than we really do. Most of our so called 'knowledge' is based on our perception of how some or many of our customers have responded, in the past, to sales activities such as price changes, new product development, product introduction and communication: ● Knowing *what* happened in the past is interesting. ● Knowing *why* it happened is more useful. ● Knowing *what will* happen is worth its weight in gold.
2.1.4	Who collects customer data?	Although vast amounts of customer data are collected (often unconsciously) by every organisation (including yours) it is rarely brought together in any meaningful form. You can probably imagine one set of customer data being collected by the invoicing/accounting procedures, other set collected by customer service, a different set collected by delivery processes and still another by the sales function – there may also be traditional market research. Add to that data you collect in an ad hoc fashion through trade press, national media, conferences, exhibitions as well as passing discussions during social events. The magnitude and diversity of the data as well as the variety of capture mechanisms start to show why aggregating and structuring the data is a mammoth task, especially in larger more diverse organisations. On the other hand, it is doesn't really take very much imagination to see the value that might be tapped.
2.1.5	Where is the customer data held?	Everywhere. Customer data will be found throughout your organisation in written, electronic as well as 'virtual' (in people's heads) format. The first task (certainly before you even start to consider whether you might conduct any expensive market research) is to track down what customer data exists, where it is held and in what format. You must also understand why the data was collected/captured in the first place – you won't understand what it says (and what it doesn't say) otherwise.

2.1.6	Do you conduct product research or market research?	A section on market research in a book about marketing strategy might appear to be out of place. In fact, anyone who thinks beyond the current quarter will need to know what research can do – and cannot do. Usable results are essential – anything else is pointless. But, too much of today's research is *not* market research, but product research. Or, a study into your customers, views on your actual or intended product or service. At the best, product research will only allow you to play with product or service features – it will not allow you to differentiate by making something really different – the making part has already happened. Your marketing strategy needs to recognise the difference between the two.
2.1.7	Who is responsible for the Marketing Information System (MkIS)?	One of the signs of how seriously an organisation values its customers is how much time, effort and money it is prepared to *invest* in getting closer to them. Managing a modern MkIS is no trivial task, it is a strategic issue and ideally one assigned to a manager who can interact both internally and externally at senior levels. Re-labelling a junior market research assistant as 'Market Insight Manager' is fooling nobody! If you really want competitive advantage, you have to invest in it, see chapter 9.

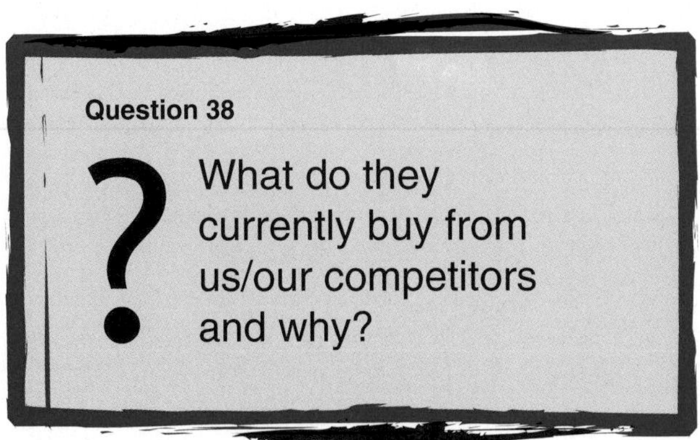

Question 38
?
What do they currently buy from us/our competitors and why?

Rule One – from Day 1 of your basic sales training programme or your first marketing training programme:

- Customers do *not* buy product *features*; they buy *benefits*, or *solutions* to problems.

Levitt said:

- 'A product *is* what a product *does*'.
- 'Customers just need to get things *done*. When people find themselves needing to get a job done, they essentially *hire* products to do that job for them'.
- 'People don't want a quarter inch drill – they want a quarter inch *hole*'.

The biggest single problem with 'theory' is not that it doesn't work because it is untrue – it doesn't work because (almost) nobody tries it. If you really are aiming to develop a marketing strategy that works and that is profitable for your organisation this is where you must start.

MARGIN NOTES

Given (at least for the moment) that customers part with hard earned cash for benefits rather than features, have you any idea at all what your existing customers have been buying from you over the years? Now, before you recoil in disgust at the idea that you may not know your sales results, territory by territory, year by year, quarter by quarter, week by week, line by line, I am confident that you have these figures – and analysed in detailed. No, what you should also have is an analysed breakdown of the different needs or problems that have been *driving* or *motivating* purchase over recent years – what 'jobs' have your products/services been 'hired' to do?

Why is such data rarely held? Quite simply, because it is not the easiest data to collect. Checking off sales by model number or by part number is easy because that is what most organisations deal with. Reassessing current sales and spotting changes in trends in terms of the benefits sought and purchased is much more difficult – we might have to ask the customer, and that would never do.

Rolls-Royce

Our customers across the Marine business within Rolls-Royce are primarily ship owners and operators, ship builders and prime contractor organisations.

We seek to gain a comprehensive understanding of their differing requirements through a market focused, regionally deployed sales and service network supported by product management and other functional personnel based at an increasing number of 'centres of excellence' around the world.

Effective monitoring of customer satisfaction is also valuable to understanding our relative performance against key decision making and partner/supplier evaluation criteria. We undertake this activity on a structured basis and use the output to drive our performance improvement action plans.

In addition, we are actively working to further develop our Customer Relationship and Key Account Management capability as the business in which we are involved becomes increasing more complex, with geographically diverse decision makers and influencers across our customer base.

The FAQs are:

2 The Customer		
2.2 What do they currently buy from us/our competitors and why?		
2.2.1	What solutions/ benefits are they purchasing from us?	We have to break free of the accounting 'yoke' here and stop relying on simple sales or financial data and treating it as marketing information. Customers just *don't* buy product or service features. This data is no different to the old adage of driving a car while only looking through the rear mirror … **1** Step one, is accepting that we don't know the answer. **2** Step two, is starting the process of finding out. In my experience, as soon as we have got this far it is just a matter of time before you work out what is going on.
2.2.2	Do we know their current/recent buying history?	Once we have started to uncover the reasons behind the purchase, (don't forget this should be informed by your business definition) it should start to become easier to understand why certain customers buy certain products or services and not others and why certain brands are less price sensitive than others. It is a truism that any good marketing strategy needs to be based more firmly on the customer needs than on the product or service. Given this, individual customer's or groups of customers' recent buying history starts to become important. Why have sales of particular lines or service areas increased or decreased? If we accept for a moment that price is not the reason (yes I know that is what the sales force says but that's what every sales force always says and it still isn't true) then what has caused these changes in demand? It might be the old 'macro environment' but do you want to stake the future of your business on it?

2.2.3	Have attempts been made to model this data?	Don't let the word *model* frighten you – at least not yet. We needn't be talking about complicated statistical analysis; a model is any kind of number manipulation. For example, as soon as you calculate the number of calls your sales force makes, divide this by the number of orders received (order to call rate) and you have – a model. Sales figures go up and go down; this is the story of life even if most organisations seem to have financial forecasts that only go in one direction. Shareholders simply will not accept downturns so there had better not be any ... Even if we reduced our job to shortening the troughs and increasing the peaks, it would help if we had a better understanding of the reasons for the peaks and troughs. Thinking logically, most people would not imagine that directly following the expensive Christmas period would be a particularly good time to sell equally expensive family summer holidays. Yes I know it is obvious, it is about benefits not features! So where are the *obvious* relationships that affect customer behaviour in your business?
2.2.4	Do we know what percentage of spend we have from our customers?	'*Percentage of what spend?*' I hear you ask. Again this analysis could force you to talk to customers rather than revel in internally produced data – but the results are often worth the effort. You will have to return to your business definition to calculate this properly; the idea is to understand the total customer expenditure in the business you have defined (see Chapter 5) and then calculate the proportion of the total spend that comes to our organisation. Sometimes described as 'share of wallet' this measurement can often be more effective than old-fashioned 'market share' calculations – which are often based on inappropriate definitions of what makes up 'the market'. See?
2.2.5	Who else (competition) gets what percentage?	Once we know what we are getting, we need to find out who else is playing in our market (remember this will be more than just direct (industry) competition – check Porter's Five-Forces model again) and how much of the total potential business each of the major players is managing to capture. Even a rudimentary analysis of this data should start to provide answers to questions such as: ● Who gets what proportion? Why? ● Which organisations are growing? Why? ● Which organisations are declining? Why? ● Where are our significant opportunities and threats for the future? What do you mean you haven't got this data and nobody else in your industry that you know collects and analyses the market in this way? It couldn't be that old product/industry orientation driving the business again could it?

2.2.6	What is our customers' perception of our organisation and brand(s)?	You can't ignore this one. It is just a part of the puzzle but while you are talking to them you may as well start to unravel the qualitative (emotional) issues as well. Finding out what the customers think you are particularly good at (and bad at) might just start to offer some explanations for previously mysterious product or service successes or failures.
2.2.7	Why do they come to us rather than the competition?	By now we should start to understand why you have been successful in the past, why (at least some) people have decided to become customers of your organisation rather than the competitions and what benefits and/or solutions they have been paying you for. It would also be good/helpful to know: • Which customers we have turned off, and why? • Which customers have actually sought to do business with our organisation? • Why? • Which customers have only used our organisation because they have rejected the competition? • Why? The results of these questions should also be used to feed into the 'SWOT' analysis as we are now starting to identify our real strength in the marketplace – the ones our customers and prospects believe that we hold.

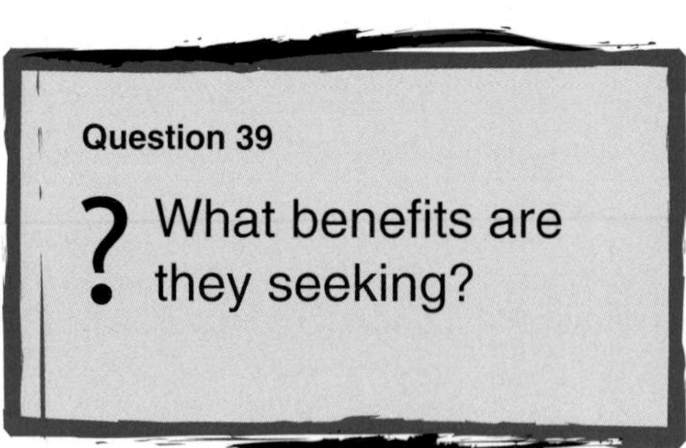
Question 39
?
What benefits are they seeking?

'They want what we give them, we know best' – this is the *wrong* answer.

Practical and profitable marketing strategy will inevitably spring, not necessarily from doing what you are good at, but from doing what your customers want you to do. Inevitably then this means that an understanding of the customer (their needs, wants, problems, motivations and generally how they lead their lives) is the most important ingredient of any marketing strategy. Without the market information, you are left with a product strategy at best.

In simple terms, what you and your organisation needs to find out is:

- What do your customers need or want?
  - What jobs do they have to do?
  - Where does it 'hurt'?

- What do your customers actually need or want – from you?
  - What jobs do they believe you can do for them?
  - What do they believe you are capable/incapable of delivering

- What will your customers need or want from you in 1, 2, 5 years time?

In this section we will deal with the first question, questions 2 and 3 will be covered in the next two sections.

These are deceptively simple questions. Unfortunately, and here comes the really bad news, no one really understands what makes customers behave the way they do. Yes I know that the (other) books are packed with theories and diagrams and complex flowcharts, and as long as these are used to describe past customer behaviour and draw inferences (and sometimes even 'conclusions') based on correlations, then they can do an excellent (if limited) job. Be this as it may, if we are concerned with developing marketing strategy, we need to think about the future, not the past. Only some form of prediction can lead to a proper allocation of investment – in other words:

MARGIN NOTES

- Where do we put our money for maximum return?

- Which customers should we invest our very expensive time and money in?

- Which products and services should we be developing?

- Which products and services should we be putting on 'indefinite hold'?

As we work to achieve an understanding of our customers, we must recognise that we will never achieve a 100% predictability – but as long as it helps reduce some of the more expensive margin of error in our investments this is the best we can hope for.

Looking at customers from the inevitable position of internal (organisation) and product based bias, it often comes as a shock to some practitioners that most customers tend to ask apparently irrational questions such as:

- What job have I got to do/get done?

- What product or service can I 'hire' to do the job for me?

- Where can I get it?
- Can I get it now?
- What's available?
- Who am I buying it for?
- What else is affected by this purchase?
- Can I afford it?
- Should I buy brand A or brand B?
- What do I know about brand A?
- Do I know someone else who has bought brand A?
- Who can I ask about it?
- Do I like the brand A people?
- Will I feel comfortable using brand A?

MARGIN NOTES

Surprisingly few of the questions (in either B2C or B2B markets) have very much at all to do with the detailed technical aspects of any given product or service. Japanese-inspired quality control and production methodologies now adopted by the West have led most buyers to assume that the product or service which they purchase will actually do the job for which it is being 'hired'. This level of expectation has meant that people have started to concentrate much more on the 'softer' aspects of products and services, sometimes described as the intangible elements of a given product or service offering.

The really important questions, at least as far as companies and their customers are (should be) concerned, are issues like:

- What will the purchase and use of this product or service do for me and my status amongst my peers?
- What will other people think of me?
- Will I enjoy consuming this product or service?
- Will I enjoy the relationship which it brings with the producing organisation?

A word on motivation

Your customer has a life, how well do you understand it? Do you understand how your product or service fits into your customer's life?

This essential and the 'headlines' are:

- Our customers will be attracted to products and services which fit into *their* lives, and shun those that don't.
  - The sooner we grasp this idea, the sooner we can stop wasting millions of pounds, dollars and euros developing magnificent products and services that nobody wants.

- Questions such as 'what will this product or service *do* for me?' and 'will I *enjoy* consuming it?' are never easy to answer.
  - The key to understanding the importance of these questions and how this is likely to evolve over time comes from an understanding of what *motivates* the customer to buy certain products and services and to avoid or simply not notice others.
  - This understanding of customer motivation is certainly critical to the development of any practical, profitable and robust marketing strategy.

- One of the true 'missions impossible' of business must be trying to completely understand our customers.
  - Just looking through the following list is enough to demonstrate the complexity involved.
  - These variables are just some (not all) of the elements that come into play when a customer is about to choose between your product or service and that offered by your competitor:
    - Cultural context
    - Social stratification
    - Reference groups and sub-cultural influences
    - Family influences
    - Learning processes
    - Evaluative criteria
    - Attitudes and attitude change
    - Belief systems
    - Personal values
    - Personality
    - Persuasive communications
    - Problem recognition processes
    - Search and evaluation methodology
    - Information processing
    - Brand loyalty
    - Innovation and change
    - Rational economic theory

MARGIN NOTES

    - Environmental pressures (consumerism, environmentalism, green, anti-capitalism, Corporate social responsibility (CSR), etc.)
    - Others …
  - Each one of the variables on this list is currently a specific area of detailed academic research and many of them have been the subject of in-depth research for a number of years – even decades.
  - In each one of these areas, theories and hypotheses have been proposed, and we may be getting closer to understanding why and how people act and react but we are still well short of our ultimate goal of being able to *predict* customer behaviour or reaction in any given market situation.

I know for a fact that marketing practitioners are also consumers, but it constantly amazes me the way that sitting behind a desk can so easily and suddenly turn them from customers into economists. In the structured situation of the typical business environment, there appears to be a change of mindset which says 'I know the world is like that but it shouldn't be'. Consequently we all concentrate on the hard rational issues (such as price!), and we deal with our customers as if they are all rational decision-making machines. Organisations then focus on the economic aspects of their offering such as price, sales, service and delivery terms because these are the things that people ought to be valuing. However, as we all know, they don't, – we don't!

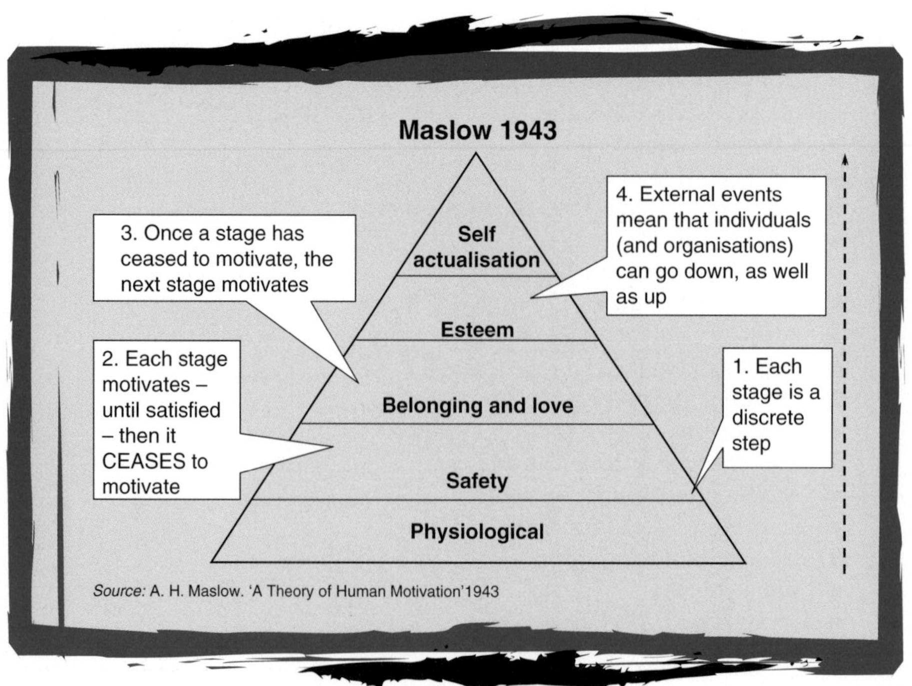

Source: A. H. Maslow. 'A Theory of Human Motivation'1943

To get to the basics of motivation we really ought to go back to the beginnings of the theory and strip away some of the more modern embellishments which, in my view, confuse rather than clarify. One of the early models was produced by Maslow (*'A Theory of Human Motivation'*, A. H. Maslow, *Psychological Review*, 50, 370–396, 1943). Most people have at least heard of his name and it still forms the foundation thinking for many of 'new', 'original', 'radical' and 'proprietary' models which are still being developed.

- Maslow looked at what he called the 'hierarchy of needs'; he put this together into a simple pyramid and his argument is roughly as follows:
  - That man has a number of needs and he will seek to satisfy these needs in a *sequential*, understandable and therefore predictable manner.
  - Only, argues Maslow, once the needs of the lowest levels in the hierarchy have been satisfied do we start to be *motivated* by the next category of needs up the pyramid.
    - This process works as we move upwards, so *satisfied*' physiological' needs then cease motivating and 'safety' needs begin motivating us.
  - Working from the bottom of the pyramid up, we have a series of needs (in a hierarchy) that Maslow described as:
    - Physiological needs
      - These are basically for food, warmth and sex (not necessarily in that order).
    - Safety needs
      - Include the need for protection and for security – the traditional roof over our heads.
      - Naturally enough, different people perceive protection and security in different ways and different people will have different needs in these areas before they can feel 'safe'.
    - Recognition
      - These are the social needs and include a sense of love and belonging.
      - The sense of 'belonging' is a particularly strong motivator especially amongst particular groups in the population such as adolescent children for whom fashion brands are essential badges of membership to select groups.
      - This is definitely a time when you need to have the right trainers not the cheapest trainers!
    - Ego or esteem needs
      - These include the need for self-esteem, status and recognition by others.
    - Self-fulfilment and self-actualisation needs
      - This area includes self-developments and realisation of full internal potential.
      - Thought by many to be more philosophical than realistic, this level is now showing up to be a very strong motivational

MARGIN NOTES

driver for many people although it may not drive many people for more than a short period of time. (The Shirley Valentine effect?)

- However the next decade may show the power of this level as more and more of the 'baby boomers' move from child rearing to retirement and will start to have time and money (we hope) to invest in the search for inner enlightenment that for many started in the 1960s and 1970s!

- The task now is to start to find out exactly what these terms mean within your own business.
  - Given the market, within which you and your organisation operate, you should be asking questions, or rather you should be directing your market research, to finding out the answers to the key questions such as:
    - What are *physiological* needs in my market?
    - What does *safety and security* mean to my customers?
    - Where are the (different) groups to which my customers and prospects are likely to want (or need) to *belong*?
    - What would constitute *recognition* within my target market?
    - How does *self-actualisation* demonstrate itself in my business – is anyone already there, and can I use them as role models in my publicity?

MARGIN NOTES

A word on behaviour

Maslow may give us some clues to motivation, but it is obvious that customers don't always do exactly what they are motivated to do, there is something else going on. Not that motivation is not important (it is) but it is not the whole story.

But with some effort, we can start to get at least a little bit closer to the answer. There are one or two (again basic) models that might help us understand exactly what's going on within our customer base.

The first of these is again quite old (vintage?) and comes from Peter Chisnall (*'Marketing: A behavioural Analysis'*, McGraw Hill, 1985), who attempted to put a number of the more important variables into some sort of overall scheme:

- Chisnall identifies four principle areas of interest to the organisation:
  - Cultural
  - Sociological
  - Economic and
  - Individual aspects to the problem.

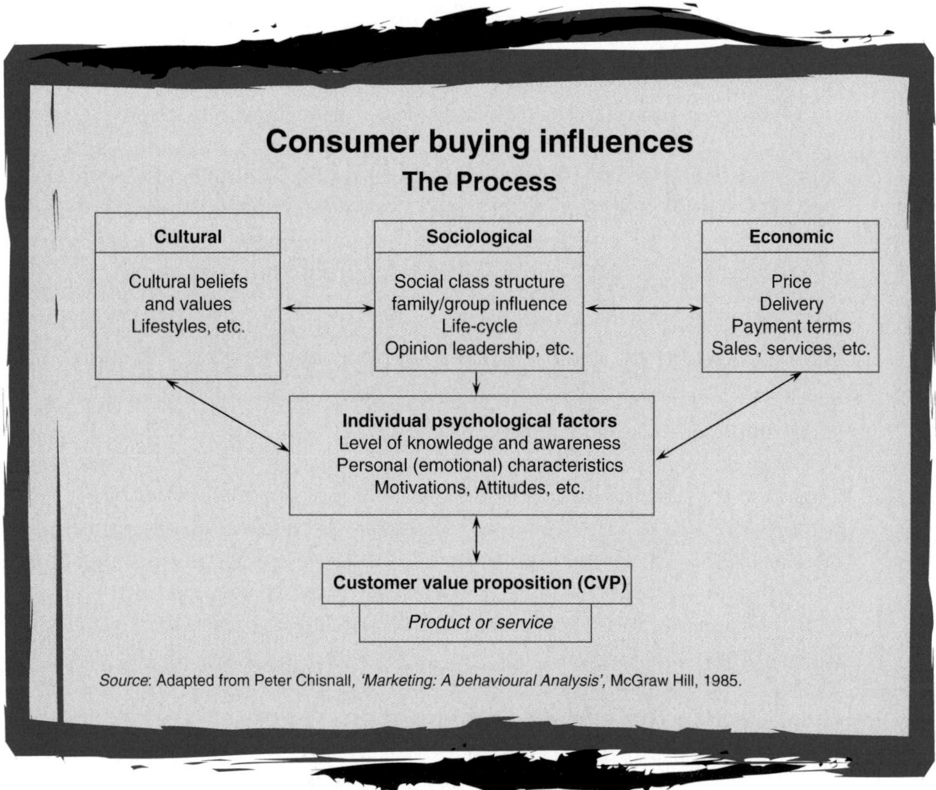

Source: Adapted from Peter Chisnall, *'Marketing: A behavioural Analysis'*, McGraw Hill, 1985.

- Under each of these headings on the diagram you will see some of the key issues at play – of course, the individual issues will vary in importance, not only between individual customers but also for the same customer in differing circumstances.
  - Chisnall does not attempt to put any numbers next to the various factors as do too many authors.
    - This is a wise move on his part since attempting to reduce any of these psychological factors to numbers is necessarily doomed to failure.
  - The diagram is that it shows the wildly differing variables which come into play in customer choice behaviour.
    - These range from the purely economic factors such as:
      - Price
      - Delivery terms
      - Payment terms and
      - Level of after sales service.
    - To cultural beliefs and values and life styles that tend to determine, often at the sub-conscious level, the sorts of problems or needs as well as the products and services which people find intrinsically attractive or instinctively abhorrent.

When I talk to practitioners about these ideas; and identifying needs, wants and problems in their customers' lives, it is always interesting to go through the process imagining yourself to be a customer rather than a producer (it is called 'empathy'). Try it.

It is not difficult to recognise the various factors which you personally bring into play (under each heading) when you are considering the purchase of let us say a motor car, a personal computer or a holiday. Imagine the insight you would have if you had this information from your customers ...

A word on customer satisfaction

What makes a satisfied customer?

MARGIN NOTES

The fact that more and more organisations are now measuring customer satisfaction ('customersat') can only be applauded. Some of these organisations are even starting to use customer satisfaction as an input to employee measurement and reward systems so increasing the chance that people start looking outside the organisation rather than just focusing on internal measures.

Great – But! (Is this man never happy?)

There is a lot more to measuring customer satisfaction than meets the eye. Whether a customer is *satisfied* after the purchase of a particular product or service depends on a number of different things. The crude approach to measuring customer satisfaction will simply pick all (or a sample of) customers, and will ask them whether they are (1) very, (2) somewhat, (3) not really, (4) not at all satisfied with the product/service they have purchased. This is a start but, frankly, a lot more still needs to be done.

Measuring a customer's satisfaction is far more complicated than a simple 'yes/no' answer. Satisfaction has more to do with the customer's emotions than their rational thoughts. It should be about measuring a person's *feelings* of pleasure, disappointment or indifference that has been stimulated by the purchase of a product or service. The feelings will inevitably be linked to what the person *expected* (right or wrong) the performance to be before purchase (*perceptions*).

Obvious, but it needs saying, *expectations* and *perceptions* will vary from customer to customer, and from time to time.

And – lots of studies are showing that a 'satisfied' customer is *no* less likely to defect to the competition than a 'dissatisfied' customer. So why bother measuring customer satisfaction? Well, don't abandon the measuring straight away, it is taken so long to get any measurement at all, it will be easier to change the questions.

'Were you (completely, somewhat, not really, not at all) satisfied with the product/service?' can stay.

For those that answer 'Yes', you can add another question.

'Will you buy the same or another product/service from this company the next time?' This starts to question the customer's *commitment*, not just their satisfaction.

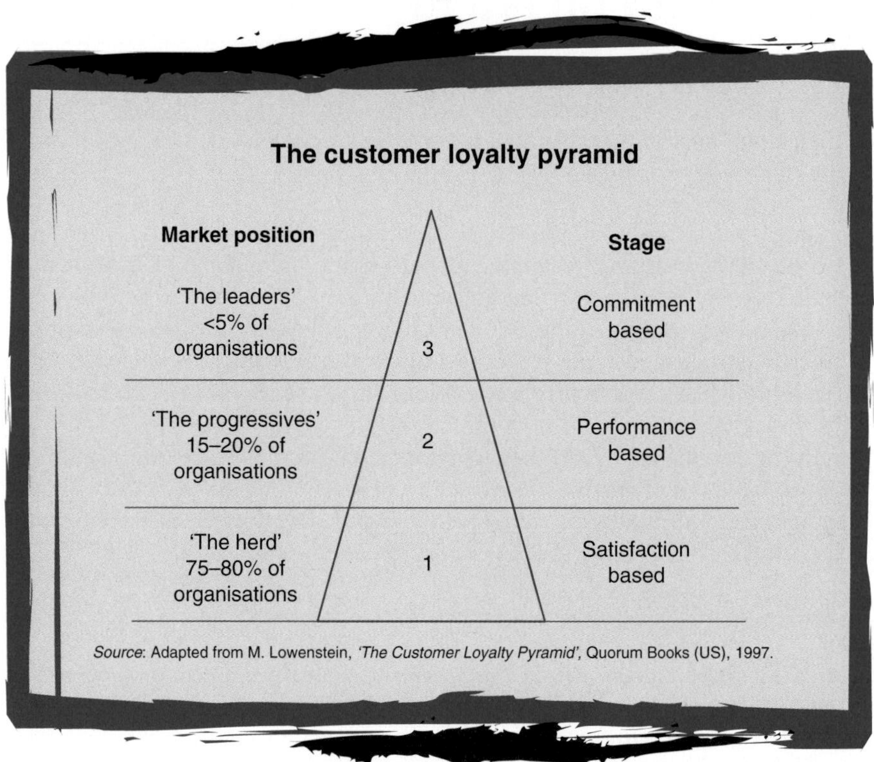

Source: Adapted from M. Lowenstein, *'The Customer Loyalty Pyramid'*, Quorum Books (US), 1997.

A worrying study from Lowenstein (*'The Customer Loyalty Pyramid'*, Quorum Books (US), 1997) has showed that not many organisations can be bothered to go this far! From the Lowenstein study, it seems that:

- Less than 5% of organisations ask about commitment (to buy again)
- 15–20% of organisations ask 'how well did we do?'
- 75–80% of organisations only ask 'were you happy?'

Today, that is no longer enough. The following is a typical dialogue:

Q: Were you happy with our product X?
A: Yes.

Q: Will you buy product X again?
A: Probably Not.

Q: But you said you were happy with the product.
A: It did what it promised, if it hadn't you would have heard from me....

Q: But why not buy again?
A: Because I'll be bored, I will want something different next time....

Sound familiar?

■ A word on latent needs

Just a brief note here on the work conducted by Hamel and Prahaled (see Chapter 5, p. 120) where they made the important distinction between problems/needs/wants which are *evident* to customers and those which are not evident or rather *latent*.

MARGIN NOTES

Hamel and Prahaled made the point that most organisations, when they do conduct customer research, tend to focus on what they have called today's business. On the vertical and horizontal scales you will see that today's business is identified by talking to existing customers about their existing needs. They then go on to suggest that the greatest strategic threats and opportunities for your organisation are not to be found in this small quadrant but in the larger area of customer needs and will only be identified by talking to people who are *not* yet our customers about needs or wants that they *don't* yet know they have. Seems impossible? Not really. All you have to do is take a little longer, talk about their lives rather than your product or service – and listen!

The latent needs to watch for tend to come in two types:

- First there are the needs that customers and prospects may have but for which no solutions are yet available. Examples could be:
  - Cars that run without petrol
  - Completely voice activated computers (Starship Enterprise)
  - Hangover-free alcohol or
  - Safe tobacco products.

- The second category of latent needs includes those issues or solutions that people haven't yet thought about but would be popular (and in demand) if the products or services were made available. Some recent examples of this category include:
  - Email
  - Laptop computers
  - Mobile phones
  - Texting and
  - MP3 players.

Dealing with 'latent' rather than 'evident' needs and wants can, at first glance, appear daunting but this need not be so. Market research methodologies designed to uncover latent needs are well tried and tested. I use them all the time.

■ A word on hygiene factors and motivators?

One final piece of 'theory' (that I use all the time) shows that not all needs and wants motivate the same way – or as strongly.

For a moment, we need to leave Marketing and look at the work carried out by Hertzberg and his 'Two factor theory of motivation' (F. Herzberg, B. Mausner, and B. Snyderman, *'The Motivation to Work'*, Wiley, 1959).

Originally, Hertzberg was conducting research into the motivation of people at work. What Hertzberg found was that there are a number of factors inherent in the workplace which people found essentially

MARGIN NOTES

Hertzberg (1959)
The two-factor theory of motivation

	Hygiene factors	Motivators
Hertzberg	Supervision Salary Work environment Company policies Relationships with colleagues	Responsibility Recognition Promotion Achievement Intrinsic aspects of the job
Marketing	What everybody offers Expected by the customer Not 'news' Ordinary	Special to you Not expected but prized Worth talking about Makes you special
Strategy	**Keeping up with the rest**	**Being different from the rest**

Source: Adapted from F. Herzberg, B. Mausner and B. Snyderman, '*The Motivation to Work*', Wiley, 1959.

dissatisfying about their job – for example, salary. He also found that there are a number of aspects to the work and the place of work that respondents found *motivating* about their work. The most important revelation here, to Hertzberg, was that the two lists were not the same.

When Hertzberg started to dig deeper into these two apparently quite different lists he found that the lists did not contain the same items, which is what he had expected, but contained different items (see the first level of items in the diagram). Looking deeper he discovered that there were two separate lists of items which motivated the people in quite different ways. He titled these two sets of items as 'hygiene factors' and 'motivators'.

- Hygiene factors:
    - These include items such as salary and company policies.
    - Hygiene factors are items and issues which de-motivate quite strongly as long as expectations are not met but, once improved to a position where the expectation is met, then merely become 'neutral' issues and no longer motivate the person.
    - Hygiene factors will de-motivate customers if they are not present but at the very best they will only become *non-issues*.
    - In marketing terms, hygiene factors relate to:
        - Trains running on time
        - Cars starting in the morning and
        - The mobile telephone receiving a signal.
    - We expect these to happen, so no marks awarded.

- Motivators:
    - These consist of items that continue to motivate regardless of the level applied.
    - As Hertzberg noted in his original experiments, the more that responsibility, recognition and promotion were improved, the more productivity and motivation continued to increase.
    - In marketing terms, motivators relate to:
        - The special design of a Bang & Olafson TV,
        - The driving experience of the BMW and
        - The corporate statement made by the organisation's fleet of Mercedes cars.

MARGIN NOTES

So what exactly does this mean for your marketing strategy?

- First there is the question of marketing investment.
    - Once you have identified which of the groups (hygiene factors or motivators) that the identified needs, wants or problems may fall into, it is important that any marketing investment in these areas matches an understanding of the nature of the need.
        - For example, every time I research this phenomenon, service levels are a hygiene factor for customers – not a motivator.

  - The implication is, of course, that the organisation should invest only enough so that any perceived deficiency in customer service is removed from the equation, so that customer service becomes a 'non-issue'.
    - Any additional investment in this area would be wasted since it would not be valued by the target customers.
  - Now, before flinging down the book in disgust, remember that people will scream louder about hygiene factors than motivators – they expect you to deliver on the hygiene factors, and when you don't, you can (rightly) expect uproar
  - When you deliver, it goes quiet just as fast.

- Second, there is the issue of differentiation.
  - If hygiene factors can, at best, become non-issues then they hold *no* potential for differentiation from the competition.
  - In fact *all* potential for differentiation is to be found in the area of motivators not hygiene factors.
  - Given that differentiation is critical for profitability, it must be developed wherever it can be found.
  - It will always be found amongst the *motivators* rather than the hygiene factors because it is here that you can add real customer value.

The FAQs are:

2 The Customer		
2.3 What benefits are they seeking?		
2.3.1	What do you currently know about their lives?	This is where marketing adds value – or should do. The first step to greatness is to focus on customers (their needs, wants and their lives) rather than your organisation's products or services – there are more than enough people in the business already doing that.
2.3.2	What problems/needs/wants do your customers and prospects have?	People don't buy features, they buy benefits – you knew that. Everybody knows that, they just don't believe it. Your job is to convince others – through action. You need to invest in your customers to know what their problems are. If you can show that people buy what the product *does*, not just what it *is* you will attract the converts you need.
2.3.3	What problems/needs/wants are currently 'satisfied', and how well?	Before you even start to think about how you might affect target customers' and prospects' you, how you could measure the current situation. Customer segmentation (see Chapter 3) may be a key aspect here but measuring customer satisfaction in such a way that you can do something with the eventual results is going to need more than a blanket questionnaire.

		First the expectations; these will vary with different customers, different situations and the particular problems or benefits sought from the purchase. So you need to clarify these. This will give us a better understanding of which particular product attributes were seen as the most important in the purchase – this will help explain any satisfaction rating. For example, buying a mobile phone 'that also takes pictures' will disappoint someone expecting high quality images, but not someone who really just wanted to make phone calls – I think you are probably getting the idea!
2.3.4	What problems/needs/ wants are currently 'unsatisfied'?	While the tactical marketer may have their hands full dealing with customer satisfaction results from a (properly constructed) research project, the you need to look beyond this to the size and shape of the offerings that your organisation will be making some years down the line. Let's take an example; detailed research and analysis continues among avid gardeners and in the growing number of garden centres to investigate lawn care. Chemicals are developed and marketed. Tools are designed and manufactured to solve the weed problem and the chase continues. But, as the free time available for gardening and do-it-yourself (DIY) activities decreases, no amount of new chemicals and clever tools are going to solve the real problem. Enter firms such as 'Green Thumb' who simply arrive four times per year and treat your lawn for you.
2.3.5	Which 'satisfaction gaps' are evident and which are latent?	This is key, and it is much easier than it seems. It is your opportunity to develop real customer-driven solutions. Remember, it is not the customers' job to tell you exactly what they want, sometimes (often) they just don't know – until they see it of course. Research in this area is not as complicated as it might appear. It all depends on having good *qualitative* research that: ● Takes time. It is not about rushing through as many 1-hour focus groups as it can manage. I have found that 2-hour sessions (they not only stay that long, they don't want to leave if it is well done) produce much richer, detailed results. ● Focuses on the customer, *not* the product or service. ● Investigates the market-defined business that your organisation is in (see Chapter 5) and not a simplistic industry definition. ● Sets out to understand the customer's life, needs, wants and decision processes. ● Does not expect to come out with an answer – a list of statements or more questions is fine. Invest in developing your qualitative capability – it will give you real advantage.

2.3.6	How 'motivational' are the benefits sought?	Working through the Hertzberg concept with one client organisation, we were having difficulty seeing how to apply the ideas until we linked into the footballing interests of one of the board members – Hygiene Factors became 'Ticket-to-the-game' issues and Motivators became 'Winning factors'. These are in fact excellent labels for Hertzberg's theoretical concepts. As this company found out though, the biggest problem is trying to work out which factor falls into which category.
2.3.7	What role do you want your product or service to play in the customer's life?	Now that we have started to work out exactly what is happening in 'benefit' terms rather than 'product' terms at least we have a truer picture of the market dynamics. The next stage is to decide exactly what role you want to own in the target customers' lives. This really deals with the whole area of positioning which will be covered in much more detail in Chapter 7, however it is noted here for the sake of completeness.

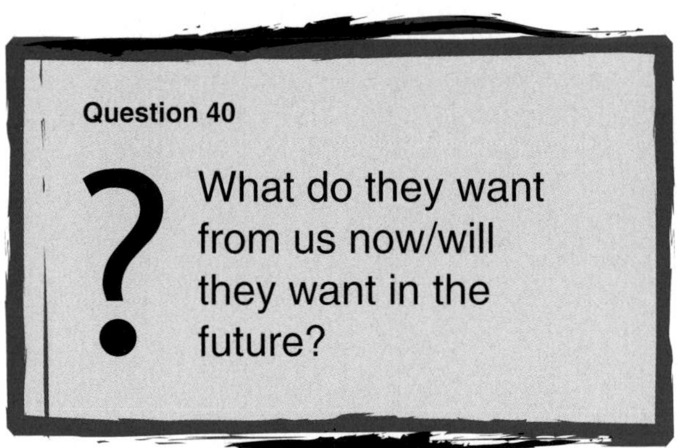

Question 40
?
What do they want from us now/will they want in the future?

MARGIN NOTES

This question encompasses both tactical and strategic activities. Broadening the issue, the questions you need to ask yourself (and then answer) are:

- Are there products/services that you are not offering that your customers would buy from you?
- Are there products/services that you are offering that your customers don't want?
- What will your customers expect to be able to buy from you next month/year/decade?
- What products and services should you be developing for your customers to buy next month/year/decade?

It should go without saying that understanding customer needs ought to be the starting place of any customer-driven organisation and marketing strategy. Unfortunately, it also goes without saying that in most organisations the starting point is the product and 'what can we make'.

'Wrong' it might be, but we understand all the reasons for this state of affairs and I have no intention of wasting more valuable reading time here to bemoan this state of affairs. However, just because everybody else in the organisation is product focused it does not mean that those responsible for developing the marketing strategy have to be product focused too!

Following research and analysis you should now have (at least the start) of an idea where market potential exists in terms of untapped need. First you need to identify the current or existing market need – problems or issues that the target customer base knows and recognises as being unmet. We can leave latent need to one side for the moment.

MARGIN NOTES

Without any value judgments at this stage, we can list the current potential in the marketplace as follows:

- Benefits sought or problems recognised:
  - What does the marketplace say that it wants?
  - Where are the problems that are (currently) either partially satisfied or unsatisfied and (for the moment) your target customers just seem to live with?

- Benefits/solutions:
  - What are the benefits or solutions that would satisfy the identified needs in the market?

- The products or services:
  - What are the product or service packages that would carry the benefits or solutions to the target customers?

- Product or service attributes:
  - What are the specific product or service attributes that would need to be 'bundled' into the product or service offering to make it attractive to customers?
  - Which of these attributes would need to be differentiated in order to make the offering stand apart from the competition?

Again, this list should fall straight out of the (proper) research analysis that you have conducted and, at this stage, should:

- Not be restricted
  - by any pre-conceived ideas of what your product or service or brand/organisation stands for.

- Not be concerned
  - if these offerings might fall outside your current technical expertise.
- Not be worried
  - about whether the markets are too big or too small at present.
- Not be focused
  - on whether you have the ability to make and/or distribute the offer.
- Not even speak about
  - having tried it 10 years ago and it didn't work then!

There will be no shortage of opportunities and you can trim the list down at a later point.

MARGIN NOTES

Bi-focal marketing

We always hear that the important thing about strategy of any sort (business, market, corporate, other) is that it focuses the organisation on the *future*. This is obviously true but it does not mean that we cannot look at today as well. There is a difference between a strategy which is 'future focused' and one which is 'future exclusive'.

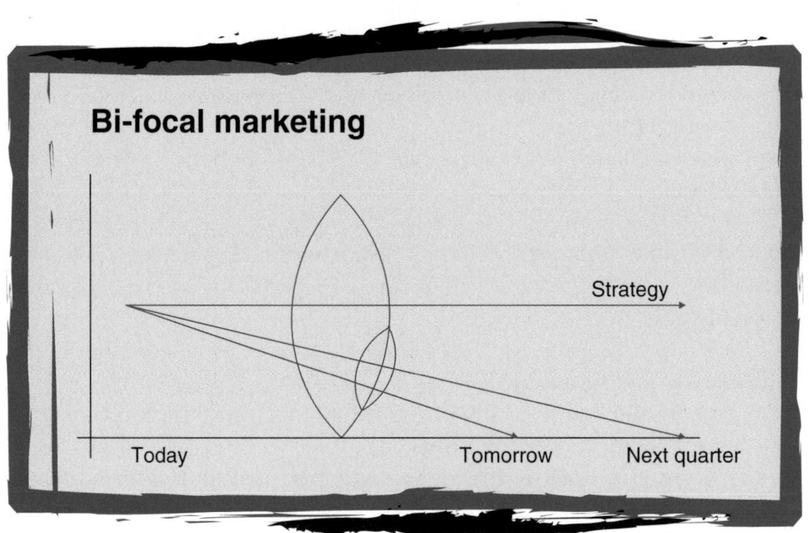

In today's markets, a successful practitioner can't afford to be focussed purely on today. Today is important, but so is tomorrow. But you can't afford to be focused exclusively on tomorrow either. What do you means it is impossible? You can walk and chew gum at the same time can't you?

Doing both means:

- You must be focused on the future but also strongly linked to today's reality.
- As soon as strategic analysis identifies potential opportunities for today's (tactical) marketing these should be considered and acted upon as soon as practically possible.
- There is not a dividing line between strategy and tactics; they are not separate disciplines to be kept apart – in different boxes, departments or functions.
- Present (today) and future (tomorrow, next quarter, next year or decade) exist on a continuum.
- Strategy needs to be rooted in today, but tactics needs to keep an eye on the longer term.

MARGIN NOTES

Forecasting tomorrow

What will our customer want tomorrow? We can't afford to be either surprised – or late.

Certainly there is a lot that can be done in terms of market research but forecasting is a body of expertise that has its own specialists, theories, books and experts. I don't intend to give a full and detailed review of the area of forecasting here but a brief overview is certainly needed.

Broadly speaking, forecasting is what happens when you try to predict future events such as customer needs and behaviours. So that we can separate forecasting from crystal ball gazing, we include some form of quantitative analysis – and that is always historical because it is the only data we have.

Dibb and Simkin ('*Marketing Briefs*', Butterworth Heinemann, 2001) suggest that there are three 'core categories' of forecasting that we should be concerned with:

- Judgemental forecasting:
  - This would involve consulting others and drawing on their opinions of what the future holds.
  - You might decide to consult people inside the organisation, or outside 'experts' (called the Delphi process) to gather the information.
  - If you formalise the process you arrive at Scenario Planning, where we build different scenarios of the future and then assign probabilities to each scenario happening and make plans accordingly.
  - The analysis is quite subjective but not necessarily the worse for that.

- Time series forecasting:
  - This is based on a set of data (usually sales data or similar) that has been collected, on a regular basis, over a period of time.
  - The data is then extrapolated (regression analysis etc) or extended forward in time to identify the results – if the same past trends in the data were to continue into the future.

- Causal forecasting:
  - Covers all the techniques used to study changes in business due to different market and customer variables such as buyer intention surveys and various modelling techniques – an area of significant growth, powered by the increasing capacity of computers to deal with large amounts of data.
  - Beware that computers don't, of themselves, create accurate results.
  - Nor does the amount (or diversity) of data fed into the system necessarily improve the validity of the results.

The FAQs are:

2 The Customer		
2.4 What do they want from us now/will they want in the future?		
2.4.1	What problems/ needs/wants are currently unmet?	The best way of identifying these is to abandon the technical and industry-driven business definitions of the past and re-focus on the customer/market or benefits-driven definitions. It is a matter of changing the *lens* that you use to look at your customers. Just imagine how Harley Davidson managed to identify its unmet customer needs (that it now satisfies) for clothing, accessories, financial services, motorcycle training, rentals and organised tours – it wasn't by looking at motorbikes, but looking at customers.
2.4.2	How and how fast can we meet current unmet needs?	If your customers have unmet needs that is the same as leaving money on the table after a sale. Often, when I find such opportunities it is not due to lack of sales diligence, but usually due to an unreasonably narrow definition of the business we are in, our strengths so what we should be doing. It probably took Harley Davidson a while to realise that if they made (or at least marketed) leather jackets (not really motorbike technology), people would buy them – and it would strengthen the brand (by better filling the space the customer assigned), not weaken it (by stretching the brand beyond the core). How long did it take JCB to work out that there was a market for its brand beyond its back-hoe-diggers?

2.4.3	What needs/wants will be driving in the future?	The customer is the key to the revenues, profits and the future of the business. As we all know, customers' needs, wants and expectations continue to change. That they will change is not the contention here, but ● When they will change ● How fast they will change and ● What they will change to … The question then is, of all the needs, wants and 'whims' that we have identified, which ones are going to be uppermost in our target customers minds, in which order and when? Nobody is expecting the answer from the oracle here but, as the basis for the work which follows, you *must* have a reasoned hypothesis for the rest of your organisation – it is your job to know such things!
2.4.4	When will which needs and/or wants be driving behaviour?	Recalling our discussion on Hertzberg's theory, hygiene factors can never be more than a 'non-issue' while motivational needs and wants are the stuff from which differentiation is made. If you are trying to chart the future development of the market (and so where your organisation should follow), then future needs and wants that you believe are going to be motivational must be worth relatively more investment of your time than the needs and wants we believe are going to be hygiene factors. The decision must be taken, and it is yours …
2.4.5	Which needs and wants will they expect to buy from us?	It all depends on your differentiation and your market position (see Chapter 8) – not on your technology and skill set. What the customer believes you are best at will determine what they will come to you to buy and consume. The better your positioning is executed, the clearer the results and the easier the forecast. Depending on your target and achieved market position, your target customer base should have a very clear idea of what your organisation and brands stand for as well as the scope and nature of benefits which they can receive from you. It then follows that we should only be aiming to invest in future opportunities that the target marketplace believes is a part of the market position you own.
2.4.6	How can we predict critical future problems, needs and wants?	Or in other words where does it go from here? The 'blue-sky' planning, which was much in evidence in the 1970s and 1980s, has fallen away recently. There is nothing wrong with blue-sky thinking as long as everybody recognises what the outputs of such thinking are; 'might be's' rather than 'will be's'. Its popularity decline probably has more to do with the increasingly short-term views and quarter-by-quarter-results mentality than any particular defect in the process. There are a number of very large and successful organisations who wouldn't dream of even trying.

		to develop any form of strategy or plan without a fairly heavy dose of 'blue-sky thinking' at the beginning. Do it, but don't tell too many people. Nevertheless, the question remains – how can we predict future customer needs? The answer, whether you like it or not, is that if you do try and predict future customer needs you are practically certain to produce an inaccurate prediction. How far away you are from the eventual truth would depend on your predictive ability and a fair dose of luck. On the other hand you could say that any form of prediction is futile and not worth the management time or effort in carrying it out. In this case you won't be misled by potentially erroneous forecasts; just jolted from one surprise to the next!
2.4.7	How can we plan future needs into marketing and production?	This question relies strongly on another item in the Scorpio model, 'O' = organisation (see Chapter 10). Research, information and data are useless unless they are communicated to the staff who need to know, and in time for those people to do something with the results. Involving areas of the organisation outside the marketing function in the collection and implications of market data and likely future customer needs is not optional, it is essential. I have said before that marketing is primarily an integrative function; its job is to integrate the customer with the business and to help focus all of the assets and people within the business on its prime objective – satisfying customer needs. There is no doubt that other parts of the organisation also need to take a future view of the business. But the quality of the data on its own is unlikely to achieve this. Even if the highest quality data was collected it needs to be: ● Translated into terms that your target audience can understand. ● Focused on issues that are important to your target audience. ● Communicated in such a way and through such media that the audience find acceptable and relevant. ● Be addressed to an audience that is motivated to listen!

Question 41

? What barriers are getting in the way?

It will probably come as a great shock to some readers to hear that a large proportion of 'missed' business is deflected, not by external competitive or economic activity, but by barriers that the organisation *itself* places in front of it would be customers.

As the driving student was told on his first lesson, if you want to make this car go forward you don't just stamp on the accelerator (gas pedal) – first you release the brake!

Before we get to that though, let's do it by the numbers, and check out the marketplace first, are there any good reasons why we shouldn't be selling more or that sales are going down? For example:

MARGIN NOTES

- Macro issues:
  - There will always be issues that are beyond your control such as recessions, political instability, etc.
  - These don't always affect all companies but can be troubling.
- Competition:
  - Is there strong competition?
  - There will always be 'cheap' or lower-priced competition around but as long as you deliver superior customer value (based on better knowledge of your customer needs) you shouldn't have a problem.
  - But, make sure you are scanning the market for competition from outside your industry, substitute competition can be deadly.
- Are there awareness issues?
  - Has everybody (that you want to attract) heard of you, your organisation and your products or services?
  - There is little point being 'the world's best kept secret' all the time that you have excess capacity.
- If people are aware of you and your offer:
  - Do they have the right awareness?
  - Do they know the right things about you?
  - Do they have a positive image?
- Distribution:
  - Are you managing to get the product or service to the most appropriate point/time for purchase or consumption?
  - Are you and your product or service actually appearing where your prospect expects to find you?
- Value:
  - Is your offer seen as good value for money?
  - STOP!

- Before you rush off following all the lemmings trying to be competitive, value, economical, inexpensive, cost-effective or low price (choose your own euphemism) in the marketplace, offering the appropriate value for money doesn't mean being the cheapest!
- Unless you really do want to present yourself as 'cheap and nasty' to your customers and prospects!

So much for the 'classic' marketing input, nothing there to worry you I am sure. But still we seem to have declining market shares and ever more strident finance directors or CFOs asking 'Why?' But that's the trouble with marketing books; they only ever look at the accelerator. What is the point of putting your foot to the floor if the wheels aren't touching the ground? Lots of noise, steam, sparks but no movement – now that sounds like marketing!

MARGIN NOTES

Shooting ourselves in the foot?

Its time to find some movement. Or 'traction' – as they say in the go-getter seminars. What is happening? We're doing all the right things. We mean well. We really believe in what we do but …

The answer is not necessarily to be found in what you do (or don't do) but what is happening elsewhere in your organisation. Let's leave the external market for a while and start looking at the actions, practices and behaviours of the organisation and how these might create barriers to your prospective buyers.

The first place to look is at 'Customer Relationship Management' (CRM) programmes:

- The growth in the popularity of customer call centres and CRM systems have sometimes produced as many problems as they have brought solutions.
  - While there is no doubt that dedicated call centres have reduced customer contact charges, especially for large service industries and monopolistic public utilities (especially if outsourced to the Indian subcontinent), there may be hidden costs.

- Someone needs to ask whether this increased 'efficiency' may have come at the cost of the 'effectiveness' of customer service.
  - Cost savings from CRM and other 'efficiency' measures are almost instant (at least they can be made to fall into this year's budget) while the effects of reducing customer service may take longer to filter through the system.

- If the negative effects of customers simply not getting through to their provider are not instant, then who is to say that they are not caused by something else?
  - Today's slick, efficient, lean organisation tends to work on a year-by-year financial budgeting system.
  - Today's lean, efficient finance departments focus on trying to match expenditure to returns – within the same accounting period (year).

- A (fictitious) example I am sure you will recognise:
  - Year 1: CRM (financial) investment + headcount (financial) reduction = finance success
  - Year 2: Call centre outsourcing + home headcount (financial) reduction = finance success
  - Year 3: Sales (financial) decline + no direct (financial) activity *this* year = marketing and sales failure.

MARGIN NOTES

But it is not just CRM that could be getting in the way.

- Wider customer service regimes in general are, despite their titles, often little more than internal processes which are put in place that stop rather than aid customers getting what they want from the organisation.
  - Rather then being seen as an 'investment' in the organisation's most precious asset, they are simply 'costs' to be managed and reduced.

- While identifying the customer facing processes that might be getting in the way of customer satisfaction is quite easy, there may be other processes at work that can be more difficult to identify.
  - You need to be looking for the 'hidden' systems and processes that can often deny your company some of its most profitable business.
  - For example, employee measurement, reward and appraisal systems might too easily mean that otherwise profitable customers are excluded from any service because it does not register on this year's appraisal (see Chapter 10).

- Short-term investment payback periods might also mean that certain classes, categories or segments of customers will not be served because an insufficient financial return can be gained from this group of people – within the payback period defined by the organisation.
  - If you really want some customers, you just have to spend money on them, and wait a little longer for them to become profitable.
  - This is the world of 'relationships', but if you're not allowed to make the investment because you can't bring the return into this year's figures …

Identifying the problems and the blockages, from the customer's perspective is actually the easiest part of the process. Doing something about it is quite another matter. You will never find solutions to customer problems unless there is a culture that is supportive of such change. Often the single remedy of changing people's reward or bonus system away from production to consumption (from units sold to customer satisfaction), can have miraculous results. For more ways of solving the problem see Chapter 10.

Some barriers are worth keeping

The needs of sales and finance directors notwithstanding, not every sale is a good one. Not every customer is a good customer. We don't want every customer – we want some customers, not all customers.

How do we do this?

- You need to make sure that you place no barriers in front of the customers that you want to attract, but barriers that reject the customers we don't want are a good thing.
  - Barriers that we don't know we erect might be termed 'unintentional barriers'.
    - They will create 'unintentional rejects'.
    - These 'unintentional rejects' will fall into two separate groups:
      - Customers that we want (we know them and have designed and produced products and services that they want to buy) but they are being rejected by the systems and processes we have put in place.
      - Customers that we don't want (we haven't targeted and haven't really designed the offer for) and are being rejected by our systems and processes.

- The first group of prospects or unintentional rejects we really *don't want to lose.*
  - You need to understand the systems, processes and behavioural problems they have with your organisation – and solve the problems as fast as possible.

- The second group of prospects *you want to lose* – they are a distraction.
  - They should have been turned off by the quality and precision of the organisation's targeted marketing.
  - If you are in the situation of having a clearly defined market position with unique or differentiated and clearly communicated brand values then it is *inevitable* that you will turn parts of the market off.
  - This is a *good* thing, you want this to happen; this is the name of the game.

MARGIN NOTES

MARGIN NOTES

- Remember, some people will *never* buy a BMW just because it *is* a BMW – they don't relate to the projected brand values at all.
- That is absolutely fine, as long as those that are attracted to the brand values are sufficient in number and willing to pay sufficient premium prices to meet required profit levels.

If you want to grow your market in these conditions you have some options:

- Establish whether your organisation's measurement is still profits or has changed (reverted) to sales turnover.
  - Measure profits (that can rise) despite revenues falling.

- Dilute the existing brand position.
  - This will likely 'broaden' appeal for your offering, but will also likely reduce the price premium you are able to command – may not be altogether bad, you need to do the analysis.

- Stretch the brand with variants into new or different areas of the market.
  - Can be very successful although you need to check for dilution effects

Whatever route your organisation takes, the secret is in knowing the difference between the barriers you want to keep (intentional) and those that are there by mistake (unintentional) and are costing you dearly in lost profits.

A measure of the organisation's ability to deal with the market is the degree to which its systems and processes are flexible enough to move with the customer rather than attempt (almost always in vain) to change the customer's expectations or requirements to ones that will fit the systems and processes in place. Jan Carlzon (SAS Airlines) said 'As I learned more about SAS I was amazed at how many of its policies or procedures catered to the equipment or the employees, even if they inconvenienced the passengers'.

The FAQs are:

2 The Customer		
2.5 What barriers are getting in the way?		
2.5.1	What are the external barriers that prevent customers from buying?	This is the easy bit, the stuff that everybody expects you to do. It needs to be done, so that you can tick the box, but don't spend too much time here – the answer is really inside the organisation, not in the market – at least not *only* in the market.

2.5.2	What internal barriers have we constructed against purchase?	It is really a question of organisational culture. If your organisation just doesn't have a customer-driven culture then genuine customer service is going to be a really hard thing to deliver! If you are operating as a monopoly (or as a utility company with a local monopoly) or as an organisation that owns and controls a highly sought after product brand or business solution – where customers frankly will put up with anything, then you can forget about the cultural issues for the moment. In most cases however, competition will give you very little choice – ultimately competitive pressures (especially from lower cost producers) will force you to change the culture in order to deliver the (differentiated) customer service that your target market expects. Can you leverage these forces to get staff to change before it is too late?
2.5.3	How can we make buying easier, better, more fun and satisfying?	Buying doesn't have to be a bind. Really no matter what your product or service, the market is looking for fun, excitement, escapism and generally some enjoyment out of life. Ordinarily, life is hard enough without you adding more pain to the process. Your customers are looking for a little enjoyment and there really is no reason why they can't enjoy buying from you! Remember, if you think buying your products or services is a boring process you cannot help but to communicate this feeling to your marketplace. The first step in the remedial process is to talk to your customers and your prospects and look at the process from *their* point of view. Where do they have issues? Where are the boring, the inconvenient, the unnecessary parts of the process? What systems or procedures do you impose on them that they find particularly onerous or annoying? How can you make it easier, more convenient, faster, slicker ... well I think you probably get the idea.
2.5.4	Are problems highlighted and solved or are they buried?	We will deal with this later but for the moment you should tread carefully. Organisational culture takes no hostages. If the culture is secretive or hostile to change then problems *will* be buried – it is the only safe way. It doesn't solve the problems but it minimises casualties. But, burying problems is a short-term solution. Even the (once) great Marks & Spencer could only bury its corporate head in the sand for about 6 years. Plan your moves carefully and highlight problems only when there is an appetite for change.
2.5.5	Do we understand why non-customers choose to buy elsewhere?	So what about the customers who don't come to you? Every organisation seems to believe that it deserves to grow sales and every organisation includes these 'unknown' customers in next year's sales and turnover forecast. If they were that easy to tie down you would have them already.

		If they don't come to you at the moment you will need to convert them. This obviously means either they are non-users – in other words they don't use the product or service at all – or they are customers of the competition. In any event, converting them to your cause is not going to be an easy or cheap process. Before you have any hope of turning non-customers (call them prospects or suspects if you wish) into customers you will need to invest some time, effort and money in understanding what they want, why they want it and why they don't come to you (or anyone else) already. If you find out the reason why these customers don't come to you is because they've never heard of you, that is probably good news. Awareness campaigns are often the easiest and cheapest to develop. If, on the other hand, they actively choose to buy elsewhere you will have to develop a programme of activity, events and communication designed at 'stealing' these customers from competitors who may not be keen to let them go. Before you go down that route you really ought to how much they are going to be worth and how much it is going to cost to acquire their business.
2.5.6	Are we sure we are turning away the right business?	Now there's an interesting turn of phrase, 'turning away business'. You may be looking at your sales figures and pondering your woefully inadequate market share and wondering how to grow it. Before you just consign that proportion of the market that you don't control as 'the target' you will need to calculate the share of the market that: ● You really don't want (for whatever reason) that you have purposefully avoided ● That you have actively (even if unintentionally) deterred from buying your product or service.
2.5.7	What happens when customer and internal needs collide?	This internal/external collision process is not necessarily a bad thing; it can be a time of great learning for everybody involved. Given that ultimately the outcome can never be in doubt, competitive advantage will lie with those organisations able to deal with the changes fastest. Organisations that come out of the collision process best have a good (market and customer focused) leader.

Question 42

? What will make them come to us?

On the face of it, this seems like just another way of saying 'What is marketing about?'

What will make the (right) customers come to us? Well, just having the right product or service is not going to do it – there are too many of these 'emotional' things wandering about to make a simple economic proposition work.

Remember from the previous discussions, I have suggested that:

- You need to *know* your customers
- You need to *know* what they are looking for
- You need to *know* what they are expecting from your organisation
- You need to beware of erecting 'unintentional' barriers against customers you want, and you should dismantle those barriers when you find them
- There are some customers you don't want to attract

Making the customer (that you want) come to you, instead of to one of the increasing number of competitors is not getting easier with time.

The first question you must ask is, do you understand how and why customers choose to buy from you?

Of course, the question is deceptively simple, and needs some development. Classic product theory suggests that a product or service is a combination of elements, each of which has different importance for different customers and in different combinations, drives different segments (but more of that later, see Chapter 7).

In the meantime, we need to know what the customers (that we want to attract) find particularly valuable in our offer.

It can be to tempting to analyse the technical product or service that you live with (day-in-day-out) and expect to find the answer there. You can always ask customers but I understand how much that worries everybody, so let's look at the product/service in a slightly different way. The concept *of product components* or the 'augmented product concept' has long been understood and comprises a number of broad areas, each offering different value.

- The core component:
  - This is the basic (and obviously critical) component (of a product) or technical know-how (of a service) that ensures the product or services meets the promises that are made for it.

MARGIN NOTES

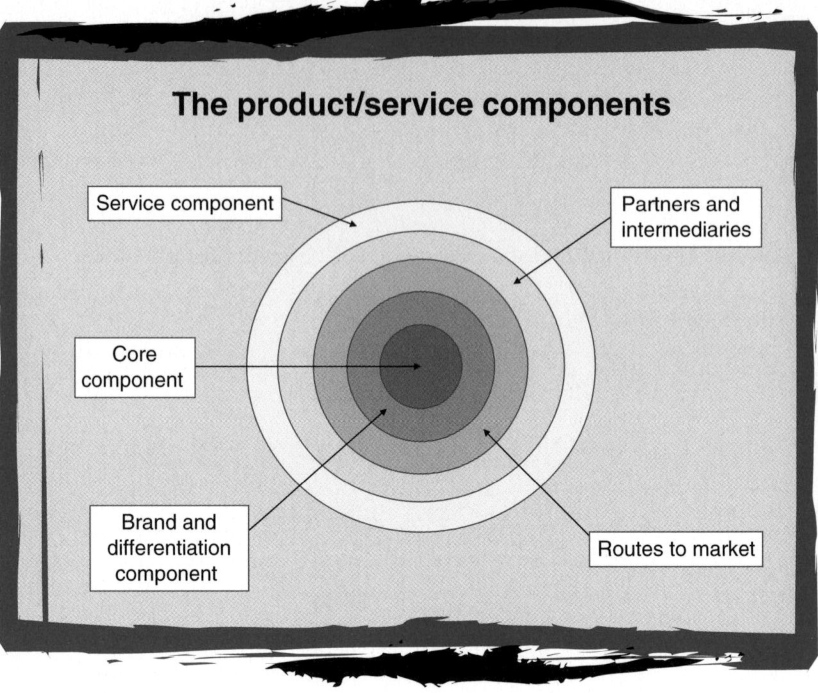

MARGIN NOTES

- That it does what it says it will do.
  - Does it do what it promises?

- The brand and differentiation component:
  - With elements such as design, styling, packaging, brand name and price, these are the elements which begin to differentiate the product or service from the competition.
    - Does it appeal to the targeted customers?

- Routes to market:
  - Where can I get it?
  - Distribution outlets/location and support play an important role of convenience.
    - Is it where your target customers expect to find it?

- Partners and intermediaries:
  - The other people in the process who are able to (and should) add significant value to the offer.
  - Important nowadays with internet services that can 'disintermediate' (cut out the middleman) that intermediaries are there to add customer value, not just add to the price.
    - Are they adding real customer value?

- The services component:
  - Includes issues such as customer care, after sales service, maintenance, warranties, access service points, service delivery mechanisms and so on.
    - Does it (at least) remove anxiety and (better) add real customer value?

Each of these factors, or more than one in combination, can deliver extra value to some customers, you need to make a full review of *all* the components that comprise the offer. As technology plateaus in more industries (cars, mobile phones, laptops) you can expect to find that customers are increasingly unable to distinguish any significant differences in competing core or packaging components – but can find them in service-driven components and choose massively on these components. I know, who is going to tell the engineers?

MARGIN NOTES

A word about service

Engineers and production types notwithstanding, service can make a difference. There are two apparently contradictory aspects to the service question that you need to understand.

First is the importance of service in the overall product/service component mix.

- The past 20 years have witnessed an enormous move in both technology and customer sophistication, both of which have contributed to a significant raising of standards in both manufacturing and service production.
  - Not only have the major players *all* managed to raise their game and been able to meet more customers' needs more regularly than ever before, but technology has allowed smaller and more distant organisations to compete on a more equal basis with the larger organisations than was possible in the past.
  - As more and more organisations are able to achieve better and better technical results there remain fewer ways in which an organisation can differentiate itself on a technical basis.

- This leaves two broad strategies for organisations to follow:
  - Product focused organisations:
    - Still generally, unfortunately the majority!
    - These organisations find it difficult to look beyond the technical aspects of the product/service and focus on getting better and better, often in areas that have only marginal interest or value to the customer.
    - They then end up fighting price wars in commodity markets.
    - Finally they die.

- Customer oriented organisations:
  - Still generally, unfortunately the minority!
  - These organisations tend to look at non-technical bases for differentiation and very soon end up in the whole area of 'service'.
  - So service can become a major differentiator within a technical market otherwise verging towards commodity and standardisation.

On the other hand, service is generally (remembering our previous discussion of Hertzberg's theories) a *hygiene* factor.

- If research within your market confirms this situation too, then you must be aware that you should only be looking at investing *enough* time and effort to get your service levels to where the market expects them because:
  - Service levels can be copied by the competition so only offer you a temporary advantage and
  - Continual investment in service can hurt your sales

MARGIN NOTES

Your job then is to work out where you can differentiate. If there is no opportunity in the core product or service or within basic customer service you are left with branding, routes-to-market and partners/ intermediaries. Invest you resources carefully.

A word about choice

The area of customer choice has fascinated me for years. The more I dig into the concepts and theories behind this idea, the more I realise how little people really understand of the decision-making or selection process made by B2C and B2B customers – oh, that same old story again ...

On the one hand it is clear that choice generally has exploded over the past 10 years. This is certainly true for consumer markets, business markets, industrial, international, global markets – and even commodities. While everybody seems to applaud the explosion of choice as 'a good thing', I remain unconvinced.

Choice is far better than no choice at all but bewildering choice is just *bad marketing.*

Someone (obviously with time on their hands) calculated that Starbucks the coffee (the third place) business had such a range of coffees, toppings, milk and other variants that the customer could in fact choose amongst over 6,000 different combinations of drink from a single outlet. They also calculated (I can feel a PhD coming up here) that if you had a different drink every day of the year, you would need to visit Starbucks for over 17 years to cover the full range. Imagine ... But, thinking of buying a new mobile phone? How many different handsets and tariffs do you need to be able to consider? The same tends to hold for financial services products, paint and industrial fixings – the list goes on.

If you talk to psychologists, they will tell you that human beings make their most effective decisions when confronted with between five and seven options!

So how do customers deal with this often confusing level of (unasked for) choice? What happens is that the customer has to find a way of reducing the 'choice' down to a manageable number of options (between 5 and 7!) – here are a number of solutions that consumer (and professional!) buyers use:

- Use price to differentiate:
  - Amongst a confusing array is a common process but it is not as straight forward as you might believe.
  - Looking for the cheapest is far too simple.
  - There are a number of tactics being used.
  - For example
    - Cheapest first
    - Cheapest last
    - Capping (prices above a certain point which are not to be considered)
    - Averaging (looking for the average price of the providers in the middle of the range)
    - Topping and tailing (reject the most expensive and the cheapest of five detailed technical proposals and just focus on the three in the middle) and so on.
  - There it is, scientific it is not.
- Seek 'independent' advice:
  - And by independent the buyer normally means someone not associated with the people trying to sell the product or service!
  - What is considered independent advice can vary from:
    - Paid experts
    - Independent company specialists
    - Specialist magazines
    - General press
    - Peer group
    - The internet
    - Friends and relatives and
    - Rumour.
  - Remember it is not how independent these advice forces are, it is how much the prospective buyer is prepared to trust them.
- Flex the choice criteria:
  - In exactly the same way that you narrow your choice when looking for something through one of the major internet search engines,

MARGIN NOTES

customers either increase or decrease their criteria for choice so that the outcome produces a manageable number of options.

- Value and ethical concerns:
  - This is currently a popular way of reducing rather than adding choice for most customers.
  - Apart from a small number of dedicated and knowledgeable buyers who will actively select particular producers for their ethical and often environmental behaviour, the majority of customers will find it sufficient to use these measures to remove organisations and/or products and services from the list of choices to produce a more manageable number.

- Brands:
  - This is probably the most important, and effective choice tactic for most buyers.
  - Brands are a short-form methodology by which differences can easily be assessed and choices made (see Chapter 8).
  - In some instances (I must put my hand up here too) customers will actively seek out a dedicated supplier of a particular brand so that they won't have the inconvenience of even seeing competitive products or services – this allows them to make a choice from a very restricted but trusted range of branded products or services.

MARGIN NOTES

What do you mean you didn't know? Now that you do know, we will have to think what you are going to do about it.

What we see is more customers being forced to make choices they would rather not have to make. Branding is one very obvious solution that will allow your customers to cut through the choice process, and save valuable time.

■ A word about relationships

Relationship, relationship marketing, relationship management (RM), managed customer relationships (MCR), customer managed relationships (CMR) and customer relationship management (CRM) are just some of the terms that have been abroad in the past few years. I will deal with these in more depth in Chapter 9, but for the moment it will be more than worthwhile to understand the concept of *relationship* from your customer's point of view.

The classic theory (we will come back to this) involves moving the 'prospect' through customer status up to 'Advocate' and 'Partner' levels. Easy to put in a diagram but difficult, lengthy and expensive to do, especially if the organisation is working on same-year investment and return financing!

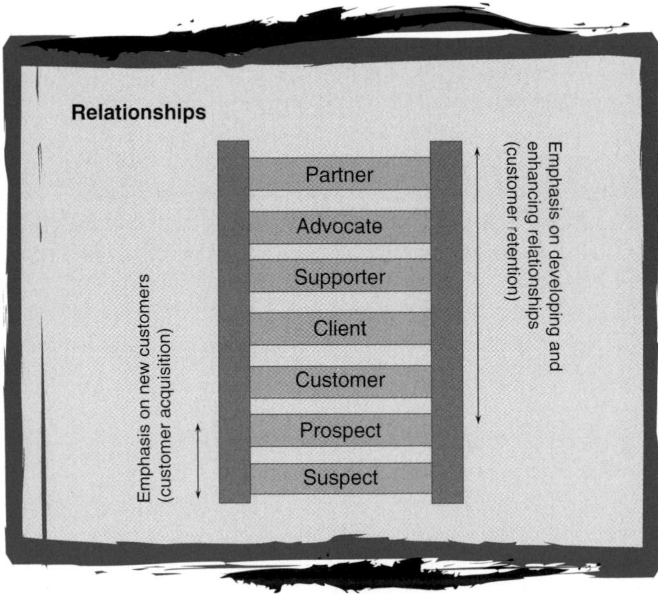

MARGIN NOTES

After years of looking at this question of relationship marketing you would (or maybe not) be amazed at how many times the word 'relationship' is used by organisations – and how rarely it is used by customers! Relationships are necessarily two-way affairs. The one-way relationship has yet to prove itself a viable concept or a rewarding experience, and while we are waiting we need to recognise that although *we* might want a relationship with our customers it all depends on whether our customers want a relationship with us.

The FAQs are:

2 The Customer		
2.6 What will make them come to us?		
2.6.1	Do we understand how and why customers choose to buy from us?	Looking at the customers that you have, do you have a clear idea of *why* those customers come to you in preference to the competition? Do you have a clear idea of the particular and differentiated benefits that they believe (perception) that they will get from buying from your organisation? In particular: ● Why did they choose to come to you rather than the competition? ● How do they rank and compare you with the competition?

		• Who else do they compare you with? • Why do they seem to have a preference for you rather than somebody else? Ideally this analysis should be carried out on a regular basis; it forms the core of the SWOT analysis – your key market analysis tool.
2.6.2	What does the customer particularly value?	More work I'm afraid, no guessing, you know what trouble that gets you into. Don't worry about segmentation yet, that comes soon enough, in the meantime you need to get to grips with what your customers like and don't like – but not with the same old product or concept testing. You need to return to basics and remember that Levitt said '*... people hire products to do jobs for them*'. You need to talk to your customers and find out: • What 'jobs' your customers want done? • Which jobs they 'hire' your company's products or services to do? • Which aspects of the 'job' do you do particularly well?
2.6.3	What is the role of 'service' in the purchase/ repurchase decision?	The more technology becomes all-pervasive, the more similar (undifferentiated) products are becoming. Today almost everything works (well, eventually) and the only areas of differentiation remain softer issues such as design and support. That creates an opportunity but be careful, service area has its own pitfalls.
2.6.4	How do we create 'customer preference' for our offer?	This is ultimately the *name of the game*. If I were asked to explain marketing strategy in a single word, it would be 'preference'. Success is about making sure that the customer prefers *your* offering over the competition's. I particularly like the word 'prefer' because it seems to imply just the right level of rationality and emotion behind most consumer and business buying outcomes. 'Decision' implies a variety of rational and analytical processes which are simply absent. The company that can consistently create and maintain customer preference for its offering at the appropriate price will ultimately win the game.
2.6.5	Can we become the 'obvious choice' (the no-brainer solution)?	Branding is the only safe (if expensive) answer, see Chapter 8.
2.6.6	What will make them stay?	The big job as far as most marketing texts are concerned is customer acquisition. • How do you get customers? • How do you convert customers?

		● How do you bring customers in? ● How do you sell them on new concepts and ideas? This cost, conventional wisdom was upset a few years ago with Frederick Reichheld's book (*'The Loyalty Effect*', 2001) on customer retention and the value (in bottom line terms) of a retained customer (see Chapter 9). It is fair to say that customer acquisition is still probably one of the most expensive aspects of any organisation's job. What surprises me is how few organisations invest anywhere near as much in retaining their customers after (expensive) acquisition. You will get useful insights from talking to customers who have left the organisation and the reasons for the purchase change – did they leave for a better offer? If better, in what way? Where does your offer fail?
2.6.7	How can we move to 'relationships' with customers?	Even if your customers are prepared to use the word 'relationship' to describe their dealings with a company that they buy 'stuff' from, you definitely need to understand the bases that your customers would consider acceptable for such a relationship. If nothing else these will be useful to feed into any later discussion on relationship management or CRM when the mania eventually takes root in your organisation!

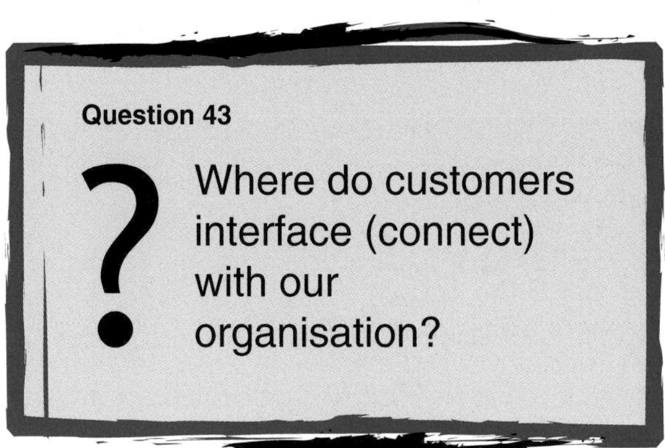

Question 43
?
Where do customers interface (connect) with our organisation?

A small section (not always a popular one) but important. These magical points, sometimes known as *touch-points* other times as *moments of truth*, have been described over the years by many different authors. Compared with the amount of time that organisations spend thinking, planning, designing, developing, producing and delivering new products or service, the actual points of *contact* with real customers (where benefits and money are exchanged) are tantalisingly brief.

■ 'Moments of truth'?

Jan Carlzon first used the term 'moments of truth' (so I tend to quote him at length) in his book (*'Moments of Truth'*, HarperCollins, 1989) on the turnaround of SAS the Scandinavian airline. His view was 'Anytime a customer comes into contact with any aspect of a business, however remote, is an opportunity to form an impression.'

The objective behind his (primarily cultural) turnaround of SAS, he described as 'We have reoriented ourselves to become a customer-driven company – a company that recognises that its only true assets are satisfied customers, all of whom expect to be treated as individuals, and who won't select us as their airline unless we do just that'.

MARGIN NOTES

In his analysis, he looked through the buying and selling process in SAS and tried to identify all the key points of customer–organisation contacts that were in existence and then attempted to isolate those points of contact that were 'make or break' for the business. These points of contact were the ones that would lead the customers to decide whether to buy or not to buy, whether they were going to be satisfied or dissatisfied with the transaction and whether they would come back or find an alternative supplier for the next purchase. He described his dilemma as:

'Last year each of our 10 million customers came in contact with approximately five SAS employees, and this contact lasted an average of 15 seconds each time. The SAS is 'created' 50 million times a year, 15 seconds at a time. These 50 million *'moments of truth'* are the moments that ultimately determine whether SAS will succeed or fail as a company. They are the moments when we must prove to our customers that SAS is their best alternative'.

Some of the moments of truth that Carlzon identified were:

- When you call to make a reservation to take a flight
- When you arrive at the airport and check your bags alongside the curb
- When you go inside and pick up your ticket at the ticket counter
- When you are greeted at the gate
- When you are taken care of by the flight attendants onboard the aircraft and
- When you are greeted at your destination.

You will notice, as he points out in his book, that they are all controlled by people (not machines) and Carlzon suggests there are not many moments of truth that are not controlled by people.

What Carlzon, and other investigators such as Tom Peters found with different organisations, such as Federal Express, is that the organisation's view on what is important and which transaction is key to a purchase (and repeat purchase) situation is not always the same as the customer's! With the result that significant 'moments of truth' for major customers can end up relying upon services or contacts made with staff that are low level, poorly trained, poorly motivated and poorly managed! Carlzon said there are good moments of truth and bad moments of truth. His aim was to create as many good moments of truth as possible.

Little seems to have changed since the late 1980s when the book was written despite the great acclaim it received. Recently I was talking to a manager in a large European retail financial services organisation that professed to be customer focused. I asked why, when every employee who enters the organisation started at the retail counter dealing with customers on a day-by-day basis and, as soon as the best ones were identified they were promoted – always *away* from the customer to internal roles. There then followed a long discussion about culture, systems, processes and structures that will be familiar to you.

MARGIN NOTES

■ Co-ordinating the moments of truth

Once the key, make-or-break, success-or-failure, profit-earning moments of truth have been identified, the next step is to understand exactly what is happening at each point of customer contact – and especially during the moments of truth. Not only what is happening and how the customer is being served from a 'hygiene' (Hertzberg) perspective but also from a qualitative perspective that says – does the way in which the contact is conducted support or detract from the brand position?

Brands are expensive, effective but fragile concepts. Brands are built on foundations of relevance (to the customers' lives) and consistency (at each and every point of contact with the organisation.

But consistency is not enough. The real challenge of points of contact is making every single 'touch' a true experience of the unique characteristics of the brand – when you have a customer contact, the customer is granting you a personal audience, and you should make the most of what is a disappearing opportunity. Don't copy retail banks who pushed their customers away from branches in pursuit or cost reduction, if you are granted the opportunity to bring your brand alive with customers, you would obviously be foolish to ignore it wouldn't you?

And controlling them

Finally the question you hoped I wouldn't ask.

Don't feel too guilty, I have still to find an organisation that has one person in overall direct control and taking direct responsibility for the co-ordination and management of *all the points of customer contact* – that produces *all* the company's revenue and profit. Yes it makes obvious sense but then that's not necessarily the way that organisations tend to work is it?

This is not the place to labour the point, especially given the above average intelligence of my readership; the need for central, co-ordinated overall control of this important activity is obvious. Equally obvious are the historical, structural and cultural reasons why your organisation finds it very difficult to do this.

But don't worry; as long as none of your competitors is actively managing what is arguably the most important area of the business's activity, then you have nothing to worry about. If they ever work it out though ….

The FAQs are:

2 The Customer		
2.7 Where do customers interface (connect) with our organisation?		
2.7.1	Where is the contact (and the money) made?	Are you able to pinpoint the particular times and locations that your company connects with your customers? We are not talking about the points of marketing communication contact but more important, the specific point in space and time where the exchange (product and service benefits for money) takes place. Naturally, everything else the organisation does, thinks about and spends time and effort producing, is important – of course. But you should never forget that the *only* place where all these efforts can be turned to commercial advantage is in *contact* with the customer. In fact, compared with real customer contact, everything else that the organisation does is 'rehearsal'. Do you think everyone else in your organisation understands this?
2.7.2	How many points of contact exist, what is their relative importance?	Can you answer this question and if not, why not? What could possibly be more important? SAS calculated that they had 50 million moments of truth every year, would you have more or less do you think? Although you shouldn't think that this is in any way an easy question to answer.

		It was only 5 or 6 years ago in discussions with a major UK brewing organisation that I asked a simple question, how many public houses do you have in your estate? The answer was, '...well we're not quite sure because we have three separate numbers, one from estates division, one from sales and distribution and one from maintenance and we are currently 6 months into a project to find out the exact numbers of pubs that we own'. Knowing where the contacts exist is the first step. Next is the question of trying to identify the relative importance of the points of contact, both from your customers' point of view and from the organisation's. This has to be the basis of any future market matrix used to control, develop and grow the organisation.
2.7.3	Which of the contacts are 'moments of truth'?	Moments of truth are becoming rare. Customers are learning (being trained/forced?) to deal remotely. Less contact means less cost but it also means less opportunity to demonstrate the (branded) difference between you and others, and the reasons for paying your premium price – short-term economies I feel. Not every contact will be a moment of truth, but more will be than you think – ask the customer and see.
2.7.4	Are the various points integrated to support the brand and/or market position?	The big one. It is one thing just not failing – but that (valuable as it is) only gets you so far. The customer *expects* you not to fail; otherwise they wouldn't even be there. More important, the customer is looking for a reason to enjoy the purchase, and to come back again. Make it easy; let them *feel* the brand, give them something positive to buy into.
2.7.5	Is flexibility built into allow for changes in customer preferences?	No, consistency and flexibility are not incompatible! What satisfies customers today is not necessarily going to satisfy (even the same) customers tomorrow. Consistency is essential throughout all points of contact; however, the contact structure and process needs to be flexible enough to remain in tune with changing customer requirements. For those organisations that don't want to (or can't) keep up with changes in customer preferences there is never a shortage of competitors waiting to steal their customers.
2.7.6	How does it 'feel' from the customer perspective?	Not another one of those 'touchy, feely' questions put in just to fill out the spaces in a book – this is for real. The larger the organisation the more the approaches and procedures need to be systemised, structured, written down and processed. That's fine but for your customer, every contact is a single interaction between two people. So how does the interaction *feel* from your customer's point of view? Like it or not, its feelings that count in this business and emotions not logic drive purchase behaviour.

		This is a difficult area to deal with because people don't like to talk about their feelings, they may not realise they have any, they may wish that their feelings were not driving their purchase behaviour but this is the data and the insight that you need. If you need a structured output try some mystery shopper research but make sure they have the brief to identify more than just the 'logic' of the situation.
2.7.7	Who is in control of the contact with the customer?	Someone needs to be in control – even if the points of contact spread across different areas of your organisational 'turf' or 'baronies'. The customer has no time for all the niceties of turf or due process; they just want to hire a product or service to do a job – now! If they like the way it feels they will expect to come back and do it all again – in the same way. Unless of course the organisation has promised a new benefit to its brand, then they will expect that too – as soon as they turn up. No excuses mind there are lots of other people begging for their money ... I hope whoever controls the contact points has the power and authority to make it happen for the customer, everybody's job depends on it.

■ The strategic questions (37–43)

In this second part of the marketing strategy discussion, we have started to scratch at the surface of the crucial question of 'Who is our customer and what do they want from us?'

The customer is always going to be at the centre of *any* market or marketing debate – although some modern texts seem to think that we should start with the models, theories and processes and then try and *do* something *to* the customer. No, the customer is in control – today more than ever – and they know it. And the organisation that focuses on encouraging its customers to *buy* more instead of trying to *sell* them more stuff will emerge as a clear winner.

It has always come as a surprise to me that the much-vaunted 4Ps, and the 7Ps that followed never had a 'P' that referred to the customer. The SCORPIO model corrects that wrong. This chapter is the longest in the strategy section – not really surprising. What is surprising (at least to me) is that any marketing or business writer could possible think anything else is more important – oh well ...

Here are the next questions for you. Yet more decisions, but there you go. Don't forget the iterative nature of the SCORPIO process, some of the answers you give here will be final; others may not – only time will tell.

As we work through the SCORPIO process, you may not have to cover all of the seven elements in exactly the same depth. Depending on your organisation and your competitive position, you might be able to simply skate over some sections. Unless you are working in a nationalised industry (SNCF), a monopoly (Microsoft) a utility (British Gas) or a dying company (no examples, it would be too embarrassing) then this section is unlikely to be one that you will be able to skip.

No.	Strategic question	Our strategic answer	Importance	✓
	The Customer			
37	Who are they?		Must have	
			Nice to have	
			Not important	
38	What do they currently buy from us/our competitors and why?		Must have	
			Nice to have	
			Not important	
39	What benefits are they seeking?		Must have	
			Nice to have	
			Not important	
40	What do they want from us now/will they want in the future?		Must have	
			Nice to have	
			Not important	
41	What barriers are getting in the way?		Must have	
			Nice to have	
			Not important	
42	What will make them come to us?		Must have	
			Nice to have	
			Not important	
43	Where do customers interface (connect) with our organisation?		Must have	
			Nice to have	
			Not important	

CHAPTER 7

Segmentation and Targeting

> 'We all boil at different degrees'
>
> *Ralph waldo Emerson*
> *US essayist & poet (1803–1882)*

Market segmentation (or, if you insist, customer profiling) is one of the basics of good marketing strategy. The 'mass market' is long dead and today one size no longer fits all.

Levitt said that if the organisation isn't talking segments, it isn't talking markets. That means that without an understanding of the different groupings of needs and wants in the marketplace no organisation can hope to have the necessary customer focus required to stay relevant. That's fine, at least for some organisations. In Chapter 2 we looked at the Product Life Cycle; the importance of segmentation for you depends on the position of your organisation on the life cycle:

MARGIN NOTES

- Introduction and Growth:
  - If you're here, you don't need to segment.
  - As long as you are still on the upwards path, and customers are happy to get whatever is on offer then you can focus on making and selling.
  - Enjoy it while it lasts.

- Maturity:
  - Most organisations are in the mature stage.
  - The market is mainly saturated and sales are replacement rather than first-time sales.
  - Here, professional segmentation is not a 'like-to-have' for practitioners it is a 'must-have' tool.
  - Later we will see why.

- In transition from Rapid Growth to Maturity:
  - The choice is yours.
  - Currently a number of industries are in transition, for example:
    - IT
    - Financial Services
    - Grocery Retailing
    - Satellite TV
  - ... and we see the normal responses to a slow down in growth;
    - A minority:
      - Realise that the good times are not coming back and look to change their ways, they move (often painfully) from emphasis on product-push to customer-pull.

- They start to invest in understanding customers and discovering what they want to buy from them – very soon they discover that not all customers now want the same, standard solution and the chase is on to identify the segment(s) of the market that they want to own, dominate and control.
- Over time, the organisations that evolve to a customer focus will control the majority of the market.

■ The majority of organisations:

- Try to bang away with the same old stuff that worked in the past, big sales forces, aggressive pricing and technological innovation driving undifferentiated (from the customer's perspective) offerings.
- These sales-driven dinosaurs eventually disappear.

MARGIN NOTES

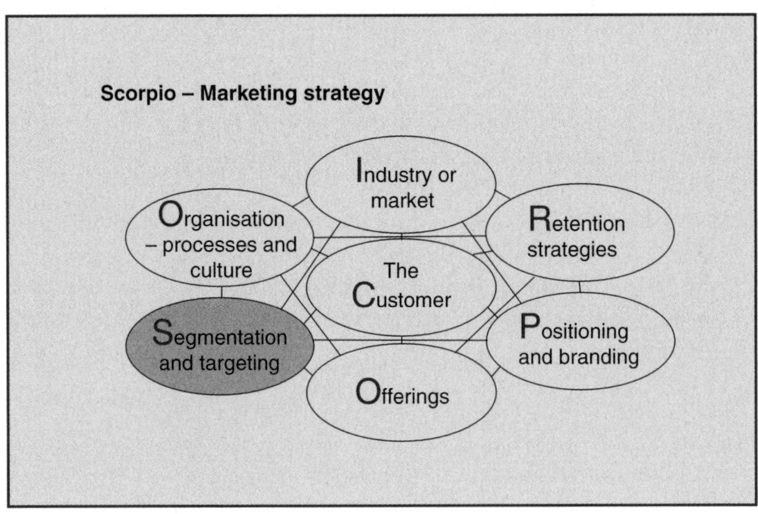

There is no 'one way' of segmenting your markets; it always depends on:

- The sophistication:
  - Of your target market
- The degree of competition:
  - In your market
- The stage of development:
  - Of your organisation (Product/service life cycle)
  - And of your product or service and your industry
- The strategic sophistication of your organisation:
  - And its ability to understand the (customer needs) differences shown by the segmentation analysis

- The ability of your organisation to deal with and implement change:
  - And the 'new' ways of marketing that are normally implied within different segments

- The tactical implementation capabilities of your organisation:
  - And its ability to market to more than one segment at the same time.

The 'headlines' are:

- Market segmentation was first developed as a concept in the late 1950s but started to enter regular marketing parlance in the 1980s:
  - Although it slowly rose in importance during the 1980s and the 1990s it is really only recently that market segmentation is (finally) starting to be recognised as a foundation for the development of any form of customer-driven marketing strategy.
  - The reason for this growth of interest in market segmentation is directly related to the evolution of most market places, especially consumer markets although increasingly it is used in industrial/ B2B markets as well.

- Market segmentation has developed over time:
  - While the 1960s were typified by mass production and volume sales the 1990s started to break this obsession and the new millennium is being typified by people's search for a greater sense of individualism and identity.
  - People nowadays, whether buying for themselves or for their organisation, are less ready to settle for a mass-produced standard item, be it product or service.
  - The search today is for something special, something different, something that reinforces their own sense of identity as a person, as an individual, as a professional buyer – certainly as someone separate from the 'herd'.

- What do we mean by market segmentation?
  - There are very few occasions that I reel out pat definitions but market segmentation is one of the rare instances where a definition can be quite useful.
  - One of the (oldest but) best comes from Kotler:
    - 'Market segmentation is the sub-dividing of a market into homogeneous sub-sets of customers, where any sub-set may conceivably be selected as a market target to be reached with a distinct marketing mix'.
  - From this definition we can see that market segmentation is all about:
    - The identification of *homogeneous sub-sets of customers*, that is, customers who are alike in some way or other.
    - Where any of these groups may *conceivably be selected as a market target*, in other words we can go for one or all of these groups

MARGIN NOTES

but importantly we can treat them as a stand-alone market target.

- The final implication, *a distinct marketing mix*, is that the segments, once identified, may demand something different from us as a producer. In other words, the marketing mix (product/service, pricing, place/distribution, promotion/communication) can conceivably be different from segment to segment.

MARGIN NOTES

- The 'Segment of One'?
  - It has been regularly argued that, given the evolution of society and its need for individualism, the ultimate market segment is a segment of one.
  - Although this idea can be seductive, especially for organisations who are continually trying to keep up with customer demands for greater service, it is only an illusion.
  - Before you go down this route, think – do you really think that Tesco, Eurostar, Marriott Hotels or Group 4 Securicor are going to create an offer just for you alone?
    - I don't think so either.
    - But it might feel like its just for you …
  - A compromise position must be found.

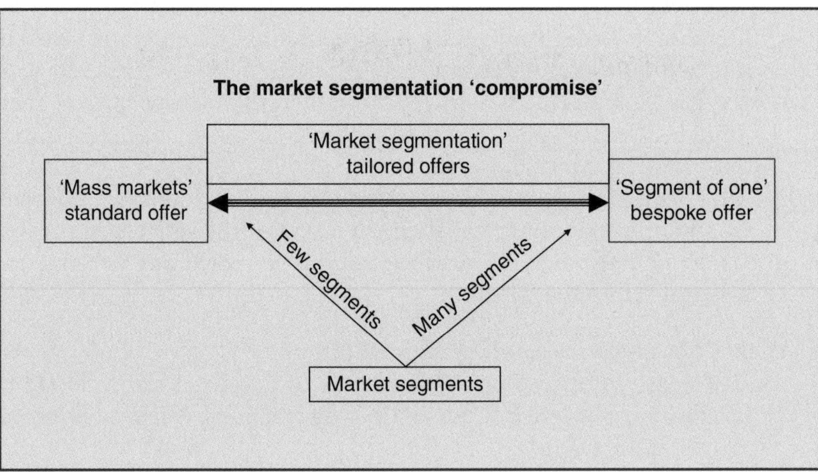

- Market segmentation is the compromise between 'mass markets' one-offer-to-everyone standard offer at one extreme and the 'segment of one' everyone-is-different bespoke offer at the other extreme.

- How bespoke and how *standard* your market segmentation solution should be (whether your chosen and defined market requires just two or three different segmented offerings – or twenty five to cover the range of different needs and wants, will depend on a number of other variables.

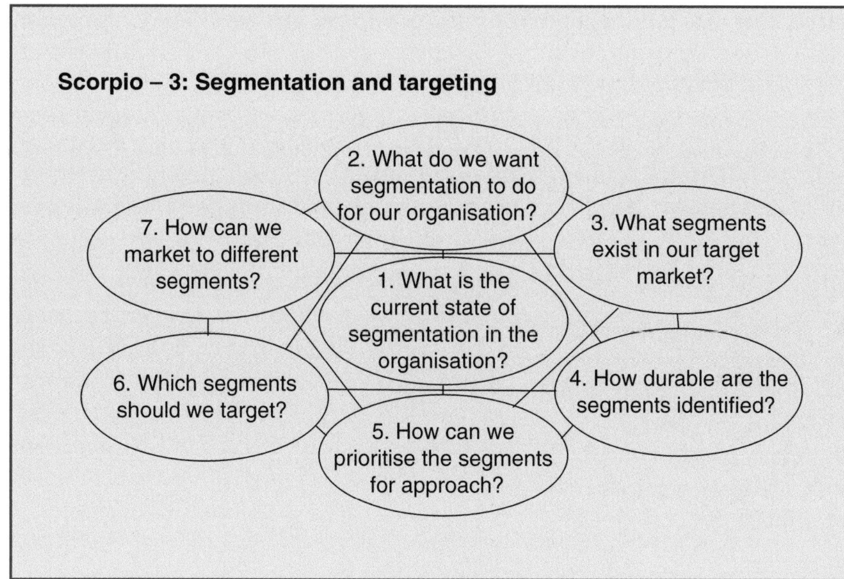

MARGIN NOTES

The rest of this chapter will investigate these questions

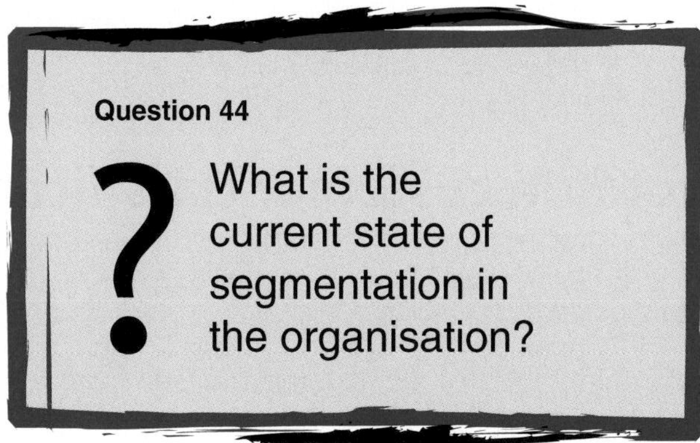

Question 44
?
What is the current state of segmentation in the organisation?

Before we look at market segmentation in any depth you will need to establish exactly how far segmentation (or what may be masquerading as segmentation) has already permeated your organisation, who is using it and what 'segments' people are using.

We do this in the hope that someone will be using something close to a genuine market segmentation approach – this is simply for pragmatic reasons – if the 'not-invented-here-syndrome' can be avoided it should be.

It wouldn't be uncommon to discover that while some people in your organisation are talking about addressing the 'mass market' others, at the same time, are talking about specific groups of customers who appear to want a slightly different service or product delivered in a slightly different way from everybody else!

The next thing to do on your search for a suitable market segmentation approach is to try and track down exactly how many different methods of 'segmentation' are being used in the organisation. A salutary lesson here comes from a large UK based utility organisation – on investigation we discovered that different forms of 'segmentation' were being used by:

- The accounts department
- The maintenance department
- New installations department
- Financial control
- New sales
- Customer service and
- Marketing.

MARGIN NOTES

To be fair, not all of the departments called their approach 'segmentation' but they were all busy dividing up the same market into groups of customers that, at least in their eyes, and for their purposes, had things in common. The scary mathematics of the situation meant when we calculated the total combinations of this organisation-wide 'multi-segmentation approach', we had than 3 million possible individual cells that customers could occupy. The organisation at the time only boasted 2.5 million customers.

■ A word on customer classification

The majority of so-called 'segmentation approaches' are really just methods of customer or *client classification*.

- Classification is an internal methodology that an organisation uses to describe customers for the (internal) convenience of the organisation and its systems and processes.
  - Classification methods (generally) don't identify differences in customer needs or motivations; they describe customer characteristics such as:
    - For B2C:
      - age
      - sex
      - ethnicity
      - culture/sub-culture
      - socio-economic groupings
      - neighbourhood
      - ownership
      - geography, etc.

        - And such as (for B2B):
            - industry/vertical
            - company size
            - location
            - technology
            - company ownership
            - installed base
            - standard industry code (SIC).
    - The advantage of this 'classification' approach is;
        - It's simple
        - It's easily identifiable
        - It's very 'black-and-white' even though the world is predominantly 'grey'.
    - Unfortunately, as we shall see later, such descriptive classifications tend to present quite weak segments.

Segmentation, on the other hand:

MARGIN NOTES

- A segment is about a group of buyers (people or companies) in a *homogeneous sub-set* of the total market that can be selected as a market target to be reached with a distinct marketing mix.
    - If we are to select a target market (segment) in this way, and are expecting to invest in doing something separate, different or unique for this group of people or companies, it is important that they *react in the same manner* to the offer that is made to them, we would hope positively.
    - This will only happen if the group that you identify has a common need or *motivation* for the purchase
    - Rarely do *descriptive* groups demonstrate the same needs and motivations.

- Most B2B marketing today is still wrapped around the beloved *industry vertical* 'segment';
    - There is no denying that this is neat, practical and a simple way to keep the sales force organised against clear industry boundaries.
    - Nevertheless, what this method of classification suggests is that:
        - A start-up organisation of 25 people in the financial services 'industry vertical' will the same issues and concerns as a large, long-established financial services organisation employing 85,000 employees – at least similar enough for the same sales force (with the same offer) to call on both organisations.
    - And ...
        - The start-up organisation of 25 people in the financial services 'industry vertical' will have little in common with another start-up organisation (also of 25 people), in the hospitality/leisure industry vertical – so different that separate sales forces and separate offers are required
    - Really?

Some segmentation bases

CONTEXT©						COMMODITY
	Business to Consumer (B2C) bases					
	Motivations Personality Needs Wants Emotions	Purchase situation Store usage Behavioural Benefits	Family roles Psychographics Reference groups Sagacity	SEG Class Neighbourhood Cultural	Geography Sex/Age Race/Ethnicity Regions Urban/Rural	
	Business to Business (B2B) bases					
	Buyer-seller relationship Risk perception Brand	Urgency Application Order size Importance of purchase	Organisation DMU Purchasing policies Purchasing criteria	Technology User status Customer capabilities (financial)	Industry or 'Vertical' Company size Location SIC	
MOTIVATIONS ←					→ DESCRIPTORS	

MARGIN NOTES

There is no end to the options for segmentation bases – everybody has their favourite!

- To explain the boxes in figure above briefly:
  - The *top row* are bases common in B2C applications
  - *Below* these are bases more common in B2B applications.
  - Generally, bases in boxes towards the *right* are driven by demographic and observable facts.
  - As we move towards the *left*, we start to consider bases that are more needs, wants and motivations driven.

- For the segmentation connoisseurs:
  - The *far right* box (Commodity) is the segment-free marketplace where standardisation and price have been allowed to reign supreme.
  - The *far left* box (CONTEXT©) is a more advanced segmentation approach where we don't consider individual buyers (people or companies) but the situation or occasion (physical or psychological) that the person is in – because its the situation that drives purchase behaviour.
    - Identifying segments that 'everybody is in – some of the time' is tricky and should not be tried at home!
    - We will look more closely at the CONTEXT© approach later.

- Bases that are mostly driven by descriptions or demographics (to the *right* on the model):
  - Are about classification rather than real segmentation
  - Are easier to implement
  - Are more about making the organisation efficient,
  - Promises quick wins especially in marketing communications
  - Are tactical rather than strategic in their implementation, but
  - Threaten little organisational change.
- Bases that are mostly driven by motivations (to the *left* on the model):
  - Are real segmentation bases rather than simple classification
  - Are more difficult to implement
  - Are more effective when they are carried out
  - Work (and pay back) over the longer term
  - Are more Strategic in nature, but
  - Threaten wider organisational change so you should tread very carefully.

From a competitive standpoint, it is useful to identify which box your organisation is currently using as a base for segmentation (if any) and also to assess which box your competitors are using. Competitively, it doesn't really matter which box you are in – as long as you are to the left of your competitors. If they are to the *left* of you, you are probably feeling the effects of being at a competitive disadvantage already.

The FAQs are:

3. Segmentation and Targeting		
3.1 What is the current state of segmentation in the organisation?		
3.1.1	How do we currently categorise/ segment our customer base?	Start by trying to spot what is already being used by the (different) implementers. See if you can identify the differences and then plot them on a motivations-descriptors continuum. Encourage those closer to motivations and discourage those at the other end. Merging them into a single method can come later.
3.1.2	Do we have one method or many inside the organisation?	It goes without saying that the variety of 'segmentation' (or more aptly named customer classification) methods are used, the more confusion will reign. Segmentation will mean different things. Also, your organisation has less chance of developing a cohesive and focused strategy that will make any sense to your target market (customers).
3.1.3	Are categories/ segments based on descriptions or customer needs?	It is normally easier, more convenient and possibly less threatening to develop a company-wide segmentation approach out of an existing method or classification already in use in the organisation. However, before you rush into this you need to ask yourself a few very basic questions. ● What is the basis of the segmentation approach you are studying – where did it come from?

		● Is the base competitive? (Does it compare with what others inside and outside are doing?) ● Will it encourage customer (rather than product/service) orientation inside the organisation?
3.1.4	What are the origins of the current segmentation approach?	It is worth trying to identify the origins of the segmentation or customer classification developments in the organisation not least because they can point to potential sources of resistance to any 'improvement' that might come along. Segmentation, although logical in concept, does tend to imply often quite radical organisational change if it is to be fully and effectively implemented. Many senior managers will resist such change unless there are extremely good reasons for it. Understanding where the current segmentation was born may give some clues as to likely future supporters and challengers.
3.1.5	Are the categories/ segments used as the basis for marketing plans?	How deeply ingrained is the current classification/segmentation process in the business? If you are faced with a plethora of methods then it is likely that these will be used mainly for internal departmental purposes and their effects may not cross departmental boundaries. If, however, the existing procedure is used as a basis for market, business and even sales plans and reward systems, then the eventual effects (and costs) of change are likely to be higher.
3.1.6	Do the categories/ segments drive marketing investments?	Market segmentation, when used by the market driven organisation, tends also to be the primary method of deciding how to invest marketing and financial resources. The enlightened organisation will understand that the product or service does not, of itself, produce profits – profits are produced by customers. It then follows that marketing investment is not made in products (which are simply vehicles to carry the benefits from the organisation to the customer) but in markets and more precisely in segments. ● Which segments will we be investing in for business and financial returns? ● Which segments must we dominate and make our own? ● Which segments are we planning to enter? ● Which segments are we planning to leave alone? ● Which segments are we planning to withdraw from over the planning period? If the organisation already uses market segmentation or classifications as the basis for making these investment decisions then you will be well on the way to developing an effective segmentation approach. If not (as will often be the case) you will have a challenge convincing people why they should bother.
3.1.7	Is segmentation seen as a source of competitive advantage?	In most organisations, market segmentation is a concept that people have heard of but know little about. They know even less about how to implement it. Where it has been recognised, or even applied, it is normally just a method of classifying a relatively large number of existing customers or future prospects into a smaller, more manageable number of groups or categories for internal administrative convenience. If this is the 'state of play' in your organisation then it helps you to understand where people see segmentation and what they expect from its implementation.

Applied properly, on the other hand, market segmentation has the ability (or the potential) of helping your organisation to get closer to its target and its served markets by a better understanding of the different driving needs and motivations that drive your customers.

All other things being equal, the organisation that is closest to its market (and understands the current and likely future needs of its market and customers) will operate at a clear and distinct advantage over the competition.

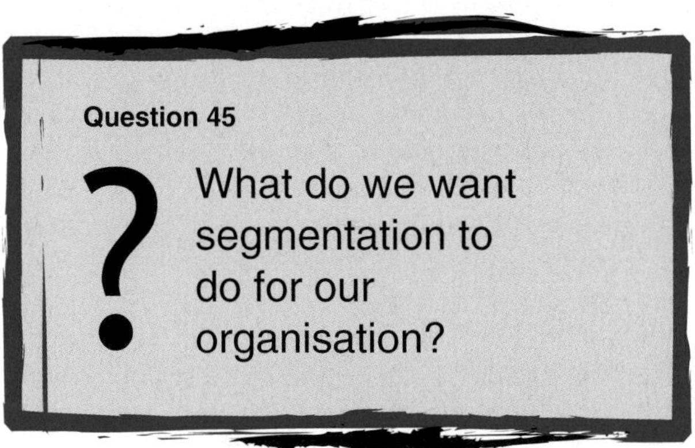

Question 45
?
What do we want segmentation to do for our organisation?

MARGIN NOTES

Market segmentation is just a tool, it is not an end in itself, and it is – and can only ever be a means to an end. It is important to identify the ends before you can work out the most appropriate means (segmentation methodology) to deliver what you need.

- Market segmentation can deliver a wide range of benefits to an organisation – for an equally wide range of budgets!
  - At its simplest level the methodology can be used to identify different groups of interest in a communications audience so that the organisation can either fine tune its message or deliver messages to different parts of the communications audience.
    - This activity is extremely tactical and often carried out as part of the normal marketing communications or advertising agency brief and it can be achieved for a fairly modest amount of money, most of which should easily be recovered in more targeted advertising or marketing communications spend.
  - Your organisation could also decide to embark upon a more detailed market segmentation study to look beyond simple descriptors and identify groups of people with the same need or motivation, attempting to uncover needs or benefits based segments that you can use for the basis of your market plans.
    - The same data would equally be useful in creating an understanding of the market place and helping your organisation to assess its branding requirements and possibly its strategic repositioning needs and even develop new market strategies.

- We will look at the technical differences between these different approaches a little later but for the moment it is worth focusing on the potentially more troublesome 'people aspect' of a market segmentation exercise.
  - If you are considering a simple research programme to help focus advertising and communications activity this probably promises little change to your organisation and behaviours go on as ever.
  - As soon as you develop beyond this level you could be facing more change in your organisation – and we have already see how keen people and organisations are about change!
  - I have helped dozens of organisations move along this route and it matters not one bit the marvels and the golden opportunities that the data or the analysis may turn up, it will be resisted by people in the organisation who see it as 'one change too far'.
  - Overall the lesson here is to proceed carefully and one step at a time. If your organisation has been languishing for a long time in a technology or product-push mode then maybe segmentation has to 'earn its spurs' by demonstrating its value first in improving marketing communications.
  - Later it can be extended to more general marketing tactics, later still as a more narrative and investigative tool that explains some of the market dynamics of the organisation's business.

MARGIN NOTES

The purposes for which you *can* use market segmentation are fairly straightforward. The purpose for which you *should* use market segmentation depends largely upon your current state of activity and, let's be frank, how desperate your competitive situation is.

What can segmentation do for you?

THE PAIN	THE GAIN	
Investment	**Tactics**	**Strategy**
• More Research • Higher Costs of multiple markets • Complicated administration • Possible re-organisation costs • 'Inefficient'production system • Lower economies of scale • Changing 'habits'of the organisation	• Better targeting • More efficient promotion • Less marketing 'wastage' • Improved retention • Improved 'service' levels • More effective production • Higher prices • Focused NPD	• Unique customer propositions • Clear market positioning • Differentiation • Brand values & Personality • Retention,'Loyalty'& 'Relationships' • Sustainable competitive advantage • Market influence • Market leadership • Premium prices & Margin • Profitability

In slightly more detail then, let's look at the Pain-Gain issues involved.

- First, the Investment:
  - Let no one tell you otherwise, segmentation is not a cheap activity – and the more we are talking about 'real' segmentation (rather than classification), the more expensive it will be, because:
    - Research will be required.
      - You probably have lots already (or not) but this is unlikely to be right for segmentation which usually needs different data.
    - Different offerings.
      - Once you have the segmentation solution, you will (I hope) want to deliver different offerings to different segments – expensive.
    - Administration costs.
      - Will rise as you complicate the marketing – you don't want the wrong offering going to the wrong segment after all.
    - There may be some re-organisation costs.
      - As people may be required to do different things.
    - Production costs.
      - And as the production people will scream at you, the 'best' (cheapest) production comes from long runs of standard products, and you want to mess with all that hard work?
    - Economies of scale will suffer.
      - But don't worry, the economies of scale argument is nonsense anyway.
    - Changing the organisational 'habits'.
      - Can be the most expensive of all. 'But we've always done it that way' is all you will hear for a while.

- Second, the Tactical Gains:
  - Depending on how 'motivational' your chosen segmentation approach is, in the short to *medium term* you can expect gains such as:
    - Better targeting:
      - Of your marketing activities to segments that want what you can offer.
    - More efficient promotion:
      - Means that you direct the right messages to the right people (even at the right time, place and occasion).
      - Not always an easy task.
    - Less marketing 'wastage':
      - In communications, sales activity as well as developing offerings that nobody wants.
      - Some marketing will always be wasted but that is normal – minimising the wastage can mean millions of pounds/euros/dollars saved every year.
    - Improved retention:
      - Of customers – that you want to retain.

MARGIN NOTES

- Improved 'service' levels:
  - Doesn't necessarily mean doing more and spending more money but doing the right things; things that targeted segments value.
- More effective production:
  - By making products and services that will be sought out and purchased.
  - Rover cars seems to have spent the past 25 years making cars that sit in fields – never was a sound strategy!
- Higher prices:
  - As targeted customers perceive more value and expect to pay higher prices.
- Focused new product development (NPD):
  - Will reduce risk in another expensive area.

MARGIN NOTES

- Third, the Strategic Gains:
  - Depending on how well you apply marketing to the identified segments, in the *longer term* you can expect gains such as:
    - Unique customer propositions:
      - That are just that; 'unique'.
      - Your insight gives you a lead in seeing customer needs – and acting on it.
    - Clear market positioning:
      - From the customer's perspective so that they understand how you are different and what you stand for.
    - Differentiation:
      - That is clear and has customer value (not based just on what the organisation believes the 'mass' market will buy).
    - Brand values and Personality:
      - And your offering starts to come alive.
      - We will talk more about branding later, but the best brands are not planted at random in the 'mass market' – they are rooted carefully in a specially prepared segment (see Chapter 8).
    - Retention, 'Loyalty' and 'Relationships':
      - Is where we start to see bigger increases in margins because real emotional attachment is worth paying for (see Chapter 9).
    - Sustainable competitive advantage:
      - Rooted carefully in properly researched and prepared segments, competitive advantage can be grown, protected with brands and (unlike simple technological advantage) it cannot be copied.
    - Market influence:
      - Is much better than being at the mercy of customer 'whim'.
      - Have you noticed that only 'follower' companies describe their customers as 'promiscuous'?
    - Market leadership:
      - Is the step beyond influence.

- Not only do customers watch what you do, now they watch to see what lead you are going to take in the market and (almost) learn what is 'right' and what is 'wrong'.
- Premium prices and Margin:
  - And what premiums can be commanded at the leadership end!
- Profitability:
  - Is what it is all about.

Rolls-Royce

The vision of the Marine business within Rolls-Royce is to be 'the Customer's first choice for marine power systems, products and services' with a core focus on power, propulsion and motion control systems.

Whilst these systems are critical to effective and efficient operation of a ship and typically represent a significant proportion

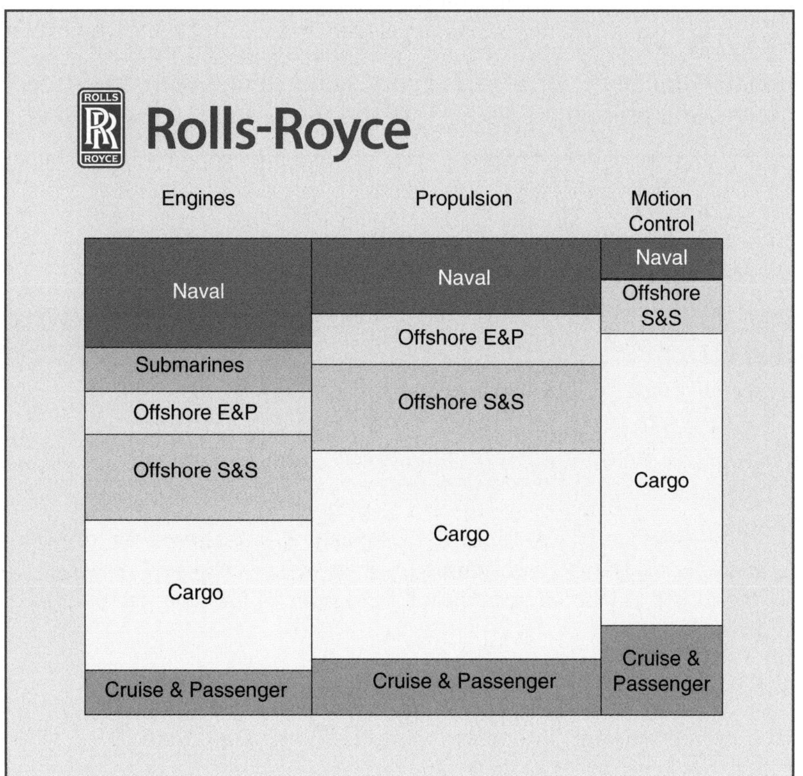

MARGIN NOTES

MARGIN NOTES

of both initial construction and annual operating costs, requirements can vary substantially by ship type.

Consequently our approach to segmentation, and the subsequent development of appropriately targeted offerings, is based on market and customer type.

We segment the marine market into four primary segments – Offshore Oil and Gas, Merchant (commercial shipping), Naval and Submarines – each with further sub-segments, for example, Offshore Exploration and Production, Offshore Supply and Service, comprising groups of similar customers that are sufficiently alike, sizeable and accessible to be treated as standalone markets.

This enables us to gain a clear view of segment and subsegment size, customer requirements, regional variance, relative competitive position etc. through which we develop and apply differing elements of the marketing mix.

In addition, whilst adopting a specific approach to each segment we are also able to identify where common or converging requirements exist. This has helped us apply our capability in one segment across to another, for example the application of a successful Offshore Supply and Service vessel design with integrated power and propulsion system into the Naval patrol vessel market.

The FAQs are:

3. Segmentation and Targeting		
3.2 What do we want segmentation to do for our organisation?		
3.2.1	Segmentation to improve promotion/ communications (spend)?	Segmentation aimed at improving the effectiveness of marketing communications is normally straightforward and often carried out by the advertising agency as part of their normal daily routine. The research involved tends to be straightforward and aims to understand the different demographics of consumer and of B2B targets. It focuses on demographics as primary variable for two reasons. ● It is the simplest and least contentious route to use and ● It is usually the primary variable that determines which media the communication should use to reach the agreed targets.

		The one serious advantage of this type of research is that the cost tends to be self-funding. The relatively small amount of money spent on understanding the different audiences tends to be covered off by the amount of money saved in better focusing and directing of the different messages.
3.2.2	Segmentation to improve current marketing tactics (4P's)?	We have already seen how organisations can start improving the quality of the marketing spend (the P for Promotions) in the mix but what about the other areas? • *Product/service* portfolio and range is more driven by customer and segment insight than product or service technology. • *Market pricing* is a better basis than cost-plus pricing and segment/ customer insight can help here. • *Distribution* (place) policy is also better driven by a better understanding of the market and most appropriate channels can be chosen
3.2.3	Segmentation to explain the market place – the 'battle map'?	In much the same way as a contour map is used by military strategists to plan battles, a properly constructed market segmentation analysis can be used to identify the different groupings of need and motivation in your market place as well as mapping the territory 'owned' by your organisation and competing brands. With this information at its disposal your organisation can then decide which parts of the market would be most profitable for it to 'attack'. Remember, profitability is a function of – the potential size of a market + the seriousness of the need or motivation + customer willingness to pay a price premium for a differentiated offer minus the cost of displacing any entrenched competition!
3.2.4	Segmentation to position the organisation or brand?	Positioning, branding and differentiation are all critical areas of marketing strategy and wealth generation for your organisation. Robust and defensible market positions rarely happen by accident and market segmentation is an indispensable tool in helping your organisation identify those particular parts (segments) of the market that you want to own – and exactly where the barriers to entry should be built.
3.2.5	Segmentation as part of integrated market strategy (SCORPIO)?	It is difficult to conceive of a marketing strategy that does not include elements of market segmentation, since the 'mass market' has now been pronounced dead in every industry, even the British National Health Service (NHS). If you aren't talking segments, then you definitely aren't talking markets (apologies to Levitt) and your *marketing* strategy is really a *sales* strategy. Oh, that hurts ...
3.2.6	Segmentation to develop a competitive advantage?	The key to achieving advantage in practical terms is relatively simple – all you need to do is to gain customer preference for your offering over the competition – easy!

		Segmentation is critical because: • As a marketing technique, it is a well understood tool if not widely implemented. Where it is implemented it will be implemented differently by different organisations. The more professionally it is implemented the more insightful and practical it will be – if you know more about your customers than the competition, you have a better chance of delivering the preferred offerings. • If you get to understand the market and its segments earlier than the competition then you are better placed to get offerings into the market before the competition. The 'first mover advantage' may not be the only thing you have to do to succeed but research at least agrees that it does help. • Any segmentation analysis only really offers a 'snapshot' of the market conditions and likely makeup at a point in time. Markets are dynamic systems and change is constant. Maintaining a regular input from the marketplace and your customers help to renew your segmentation analysis and allows you to change your offerings to keep up with or (even better) to anticipate, customer needs.
3.2.7	Segmentation to do all of the above?	Yes it can, but you need to be careful. The 'advanced level' marketing department here can very easily conduct regular market segmentation analysis to keep abreast of movements in the market place but the key to success comes in knowing which parts of the analysis to reveal and communicate to which parts of the organisation; and in which way. Internal communication is everything because unless you are able to deliver the information people need (and can deal with) at the right time in the right situation the entire process will grind to a halt and will not be used.

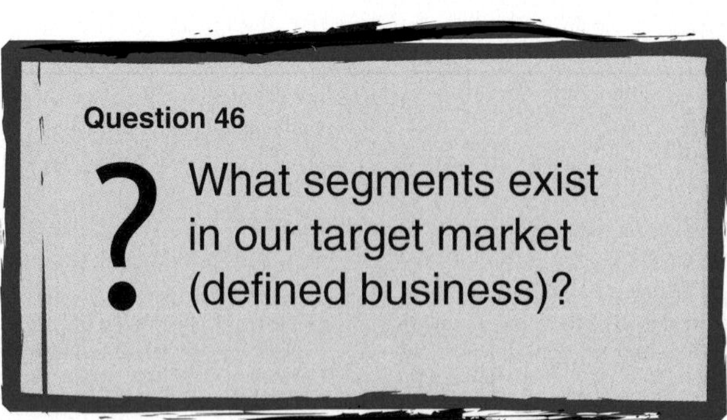

Question 46
?
What segments exist in our target market (defined business)?

Before we launch off into a slightly more detailed analysis of market segmentation and how to do it, there is one lesson that needs to be learned.

- That is, we do not segment markets; *markets segment themselves*.
  - In practice, what this means is that there is little point in us preparing ourselves with 'ideal segmentation bases' or developing

grand theories about how the market will segment – and then trying to find particular segments in certain areas.

- The fact is
  - the market just is
  - customers just are.
- Your organisation needs to face up to the fact that the market you are trying to serve exists as an entity – it has a life of its own and is not somehow our 'creation'.
- Your market will include a number of groups of buyers, people and companies with similar demographic backgrounds or similar needs and wants – all working or living in similar contexts or situations.
  - The idea that the market will reform itself and fit itself into boxes of your organisation's choosing is both widespread and wrong.
  - No, your job is to identify what is going on in the market rather than trying to make the market do what we want it to do.
  - Unless of course you are a Monopoly.
- Be very careful to present segmentation data only to the extent that your organisation (and the senior decision makers) can deal with the change involved and will be willing to implement the segmentation solution.
- If this means progressing stage by stage over a number of years, so be it.

So how might we spot the segments in the market? We're not going to look in depth at the mechanics of the market research involved but, by way of illustration, the following diagram describes a process that I have found useful in uncovering existing or natural segments in any market.

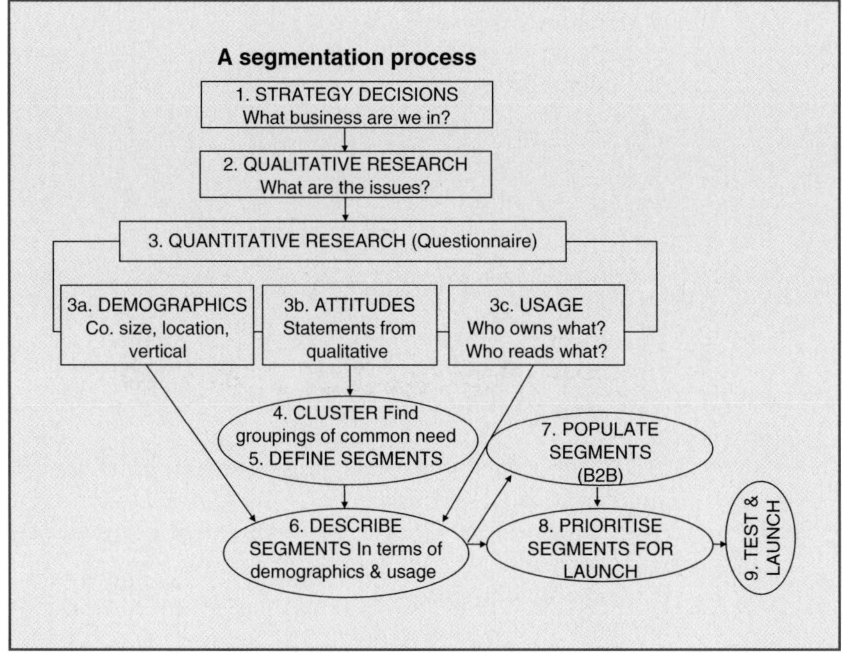

MARGIN NOTES

You will see from the diagram that there are a number of steps to the process and these can be described quite simply (it is, really …) as:

- Agree market definition:
    - This refers back to the previous SCORPIO section (see Chapter 6) and requires that we define our market in customer rather than industry terms.
    - *Why would Rolex attempt to identify segments in the watch business?* – its not in the watch business.
    - This is a point in the process where many organisations go wrong because they attempt to define a market that is described in product terms – never a very successful segmentation exercise!
- Qualitative research:
    - We need to conduct qualitative research, either focus groups or in-depth interviews or a mixture of both, to determine what are the issues driving behaviour in the target market.
    - Good qualitative research will not only focus on today's issues but will also endeavour to flush out 'latent' needs, issues and problems that the respondents aren't yet aware that they have got (don't worry it's much easier than it sounds).
- Quantitative research:
    - Is about putting real numbers into the analysis.
    - The quantitative research questionnaire, I have always found, can most usefully be described as consisting of three parts.
        - Demographics:
            - These are all the relevant demographic and descriptive variables that we need to know about the respondent customer or company.
            - For example (B2C):
                - age,
                - ethnicity,
                - geography,
                - sex,
                - income,
                - postcode.
            - And B2B:
                - company size,
                - location,
                - turnover,
                - geographical reach,
                - SIC (Standard Industry Classification).
        - Usage:
            - This concerns itself with what the respondent purchases on a regular or irregular basis.
            - Which products or services the respondent owns or has regular access to
            - Which channels are used
            - Frequency of purchase

MARGIN NOTES

    - The CONTEXTS© or occasions where consumption takes place.
    - Here we also collect data on different media readership, viewing and listening as well as channel or outlet usage to help with later communications.
  - Attitudes:
    - More accurately defined as 'beliefs, feelings, wants and needs'.
    - These are all the key issues that have been taken out of the qualitative research.
    - In my experience a good qualitative research can identify anything up to 50 or 60 different issues that appear to be influencing demand.
    - These can normally be combined into somewhere around 24–30 key statements, which will cover the full breadth of the issues identified, and will form the battery of questions to set into the quantitative questionnaire.

- Analysis:
  - Normally this is 'cluster analysis' although this method has its critics and new methodologies are now being used.
  - Cluster analysis is a statistical methodology that identifies (through a computer programme) the groups or clusters or segments within the data.
  - It creates these 'clusters' by putting respondents into groups that are, *at the same time*:
    - As alike as possible (homogeneous) *within* the cluster and.
    - As different as possible (heterogeneous) as possible *between* the clusters.
  - Which variables are used for the cluster analysis will, of course, define the clusters of respondents. Here you have a BIG choice. You can search for clusters/segments in any of the three areas that you have used to collect data:
    - Demographics:
      - This is a favourite area for B2C and B2B 'classification' – even though it fails many of the key segmentation tests described below.
      - In B2C there is a historical allegiance to the approach; 20 or 30 years ago society was such that socio-economic groupings (A, B, C1, C2, D, E) were reinforced by society and a person in a particular SEG group would feel *uncomfortable* acting out of character.
      - Today this is no longer the case.
      - The main *advantage* of demographic 'classification' is that it's easy for the sales force to spot the members of the group.
      - Using the popular 'verticals' definition of, say, 'financial services' or 'manufacturing' makes it easy for sales to decide which firms/prospects are in the 'segment' and which are not.

MARGIN NOTES

    - The main *disadvantage* however, is that when the sales team approaches the identified prospects, they are unlikely to all respond the same way to the same offer because their needs are different.
    - Postcode 'segmentation' works for some businesses I suppose, like lawnmower sales, because two houses in the same street might have similar sized lawns; beyond that you just have to look at the people who live next door to you and ask if they want or buy the same things as you do.
  - Usage:
    - Another favourite method of certain industries such as IT where the world is split into 2 broad segments:
      - Existing customers (the installed base) and
      - Others (prospects) – well it's simple.
      - Other approaches include users of different channels or intermediaries and light/heavy users or situation or occasion in which the purchase and/or consumption takes place.
  - Attitudes:
    - The main *advantage* of this approach is that you are likely to get segments that respond the same way to a (differentiated) offer because you will (we hope) have developed an offering based on identified and understood segment customer needs.
    - The main *B2B disadvantage* of this approach is the segments are almost certain to be spread over a number of different industry verticals, industry groupings or other key demographics and are very hard for the sales force to identify.
    - The main *B2C disadvantage* of this approach is that the segments may not split as the internal technical or product/service-focused departments *expect* them to split.
  - Mix and Match:
    - You can try to mix bits of all three types of data but that's like putting starter, savoury and dessert in a blender (and the results look like it too) to save time – why would you?

MARGIN NOTES

- Define Segments from the Clusters:
  - The computer doesn't understand the meaning of the data it is given and is quite capable of producing nonsense groupings as sensible ones. Way back in the 1970s, Yoram Wind ('Market Segmentation', *Journal of Marketing Research*, August 1978) devised a series of tests for good segments. I have added to these but not significantly changed the list that Wind provided. These are:
    - Is the segment identifiable?
      - Can you describe the segment?
      - Can you define the segment, and does it make sense?
      - Remember that sometimes the segment that looks quite good in the computer's 'multidimensional space' but makes no sense in the real world whatsoever.

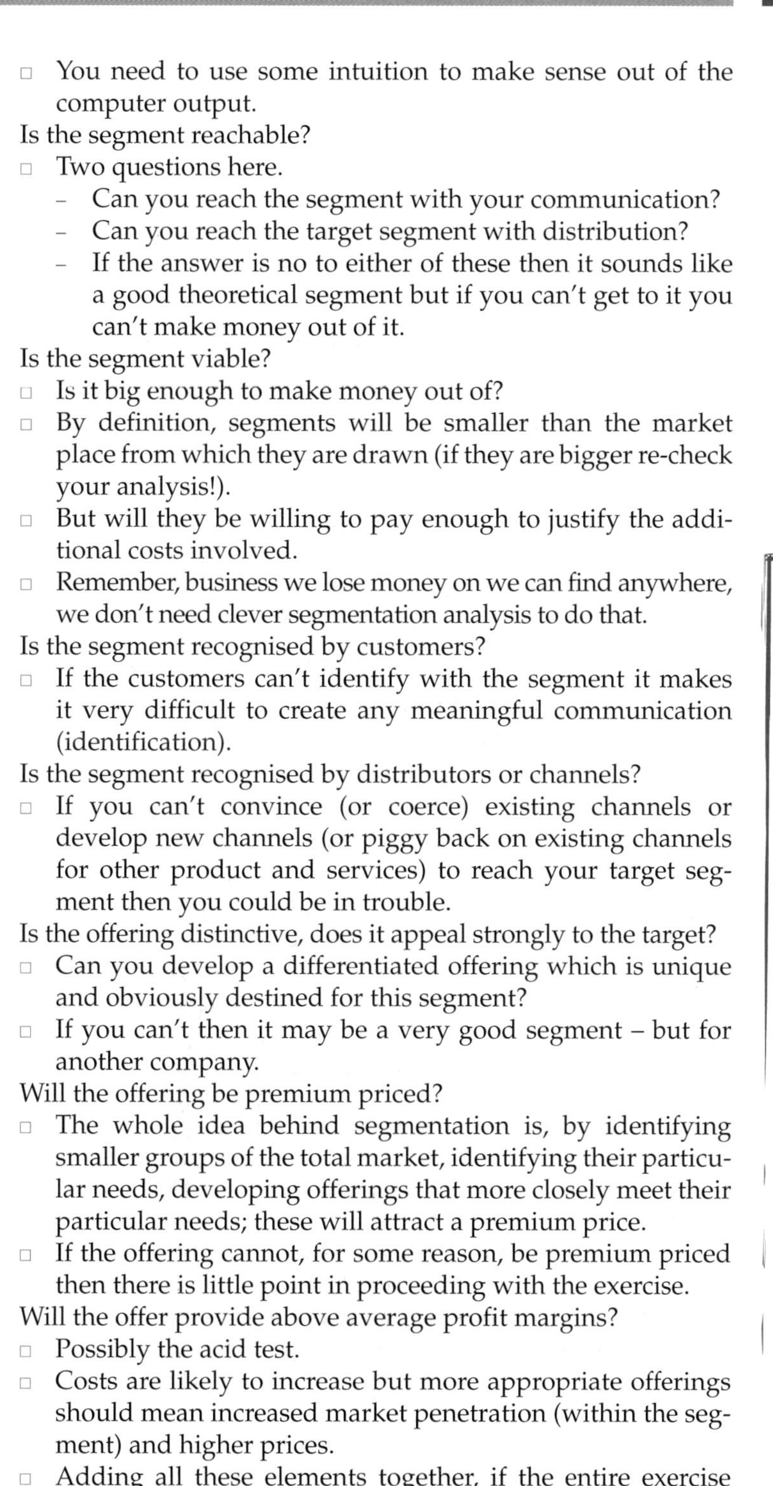

- You need to use some intuition to make sense out of the computer output.
- Is the segment reachable?
  - Two questions here.
    - Can you reach the segment with your communication?
    - Can you reach the target segment with distribution?
    - If the answer is no to either of these then it sounds like a good theoretical segment but if you can't get to it you can't make money out of it.
- Is the segment viable?
  - Is it big enough to make money out of?
  - By definition, segments will be smaller than the market place from which they are drawn (if they are bigger re-check your analysis!).
  - But will they be willing to pay enough to justify the additional costs involved.
  - Remember, business we lose money on we can find anywhere, we don't need clever segmentation analysis to do that.
- Is the segment recognised by customers?
  - If the customers can't identify with the segment it makes it very difficult to create any meaningful communication (identification).
- Is the segment recognised by distributors or channels?
  - If you can't convince (or coerce) existing channels or develop new channels (or piggy back on existing channels for other product and services) to reach your target segment then you could be in trouble.
- Is the offering distinctive, does it appeal strongly to the target?
  - Can you develop a differentiated offering which is unique and obviously destined for this segment?
  - If you can't then it may be a very good segment – but for another company.
- Will the offering be premium priced?
  - The whole idea behind segmentation is, by identifying smaller groups of the total market, identifying their particular needs, developing offerings that more closely meet their particular needs; these will attract a premium price.
  - If the offering cannot, for some reason, be premium priced then there is little point in proceeding with the exercise.
- Will the offer provide above average profit margins?
  - Possibly the acid test.
  - Costs are likely to increase but more appropriate offerings should mean increased market penetration (within the segment) and higher prices.
  - Adding all these elements together, if the entire exercise doesn't give you higher profit margins than you would normally have expected from producing an undifferentiated offer across the wider market then you are advised either not to go ahead or re-analyse the market to find more appropriate segments.

MARGIN NOTES

- Describe the clusters:
  - At this point what we do depends on which method you have used to segment the market;
    - demographics,
    - attitude or
    - usage.
  - You use the *other two* measures to describe the clusters that you have produced through the analysis.
  - For example,
    - If you have used attitudes (motivations, needs) and found groups of people with a common need, problem or motivation, then you 'cross correlate' these motivational segments against the Demographic and Usage data collected to identify any *significant correlations*.
    - This is a fairly standard market research process and produces the large tables which the research agency call the cross tabulations.
    - You just need to remember that *correlation does not imply causality*.

MARGIN NOTES

- Populate segments (B2B):
  - This is a particular requirement of B2B markets rather than B2C.
  - B2B organisations, which have decided to use segmentation on either an attitude or usage basis, may find it difficult to *identify* which prospective buyer may belong to each different segment before they have been approached by the sales force.
  - Spotting members of particular demographics (such as industry or geography) is much easier.
  - There are methodologies available for this and these will be covered in more detail later.
  - B2C markets don't have this issue because there are (normally) larger numbers of customers and, through communications and promotion activities, customers *self-select* themselves into (and out of) particular segments.

- Prioritise and target:
  - Whatever the segmentation solution that comes out of the analysis it is unrealistic (especially in today's competitive market environment) that an organisation could feasibly (or credibly) think it could attack all segments in the market at the same time.
  - In most situations, customers no longer believe this stance and generally prefer a specialist rather than a 'jack-of-all-trades' organisation.
    - If this is the case, then the question arises; which segments should we focus our attention on and which segments should we either leave fallow or leave open to the competition?
  - This is best done using a portfolio management model such as the GE model, the Shell Directional Policy Matrix or the Arthur D

Little model – they are all fairly similar in that they focus on identifying and quantifying two key dimensions for any segment.

- These are:
  - Attractiveness:
    - How 'attractive' is a segment?
    - Is it capable of delivering *what the organisation needs* from its market?
      - What the organisation needs will depend on the organisation and could cover a range of financial and non-financial issues.
      - You will need to uncover the needs (and their relative importance) very slowly and carefully because surprisingly few organisations have thought about what they want or need, and answers like 'All of the above, and lots of it' are not quite precise enough to analyse.
  - Company business strengths:
    - How skilled is the organisation at being able to deliver on the needs of this segment, as we understand it?
    - Do we have (or could we acquire) the skills needed to deliver credibly on the identified needs?
- Combining these two measures together giving a prioritised value to each of the segments will put them in priority order according to your ability to meet the needs of the segment and then the segment's ability to meet the needs of your organisation.

- Test and Launch:

Simple!

MARGIN NOTES

A word on CONTEXT© segments

CONTEXT© segmentation is a proprietary method that I developed with Dr John Marti many years ago. It came originally from work that we had both been developing individually. I have introduced and used CONTEXT© work on a number of occasions but it is for advanced use only!

The problem with this approach is not the intellectual understanding; most people can grasp the concepts instinctively. Neither is the problem in identifying the CONTEXTS through research – we have discovered how to do that successfully.

The main problem is in implementation – most tactical marketing people have simply not been trained to deal with the CONTEXT© approach, and have problems re-aligning the marketing tools to approach the CONTEXTS in the right way.

The 'headlines' are:

- We know from psychology that a person is *not* 'the same person' at all hours of the day and night.

- Different situations and the different roles that people are in, all drive different behaviours.
  - For example, at work the 'businessperson' using day-to-day communications will act in a certain way and will have certain information requirements from the networks that they use.
  - As they leave where (or when) they work they travel home and when they get home they change from business person to a member of a family; mother, father, brother, sister, and their communications (and other) needs are now driven by the new context/situation they are in.
- This CONTEXT© or situation is very different from the one that they were facing at work probably just an hour previously.

MARGIN NOTES

- Imagine a few genuine examples from past research:
  - The first person is at work:
    - The person makes a call on the office landline to a work colleague.
    - There is no reply.
    - After 3 rings, the caller cuts the connection angrily wondering where the person has got to this time.
    - Two (!) minutes later the person picks up the same handset and calls home.
    - There is no reply.
    - After 7 rings, the caller cuts the connection (gently) and worries that everything is all right at home.
  - What have we seen here?
    - Physically the same person using physically the same telephone handset from the same physical location, but with very different needs.
    - In fact we have not seen 'the same person'; we have seen the same person in different CONTEXT©s or two different facets of the same person – the worker/employee and the family/parent.
    - In practical terms (as we would normally categorise customers) we have seen two *different people* – and we will need to market to them as such.
  - The second person is travelling home from work on Tuesday evening and has been asked to bring home some wine on the way back.
    - Looking forward to a restful evening in, the person calls into the local convenience store and considers the wine selection.
    - A bottle of Chilean Dao wine is selected at £3.99 (€$6.00) and a DVD as well.
    - We now move three days forward to Friday evening.
    - The same person is travelling home from work after a hard week and has again been asked to bring home some wine on the way back.

- Looking forward to an interesting evening with friends invited for dinner, this time the person calls into the local wine merchants and considers the wine selection.
- A bottle of Chilean Dao wine is selected at £8.99 (€$11.00) and some dark chocolate as well.

○ What have we seen here?

- Again, the same physical person buying the same technical product (albeit at different quality and price levels through different retail outlets).
- In fact we have *not* seen the same person; we have seen two different facets of the same person in two quite different CONTEXT©s – quiet family at home and the entertainers.
- Once again, in practical terms we have seen *two different* people – and we will need to market to them as such.

It is at this point that most people say, 'You know exactly the same thing happened to me the other night when …' CONTEXT© affects all of us, all of the time.

MARGIN NOTES

The change in CONTEXT© (or occasion or situation or role) affects a wide variety of markets such as food and drink, snacking, entertainments, travel, fashion, information, electronics and many more.

Although I can't categorically say that it drives all behaviour, I can say that I haven't yet found a business or purchase situation that is not driven by CONTEXT©. In B2B as well as B2C markets.

In graphic form we might think of an individual (consumer or business buyer) or company represented by a hexagon, where each segment of the hexagon represents a particular 'facet' of the person or a particular 'role' that the person or company plays in their life:

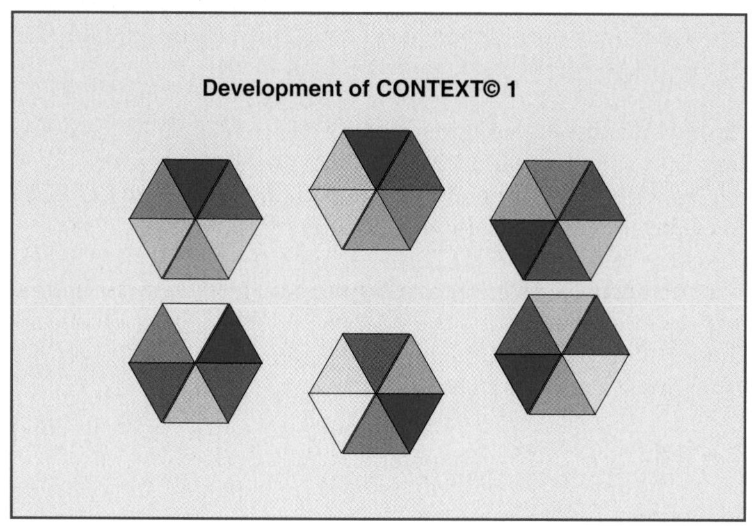

MARGIN NOTES

So that the different 'roles' these people are playing might be:

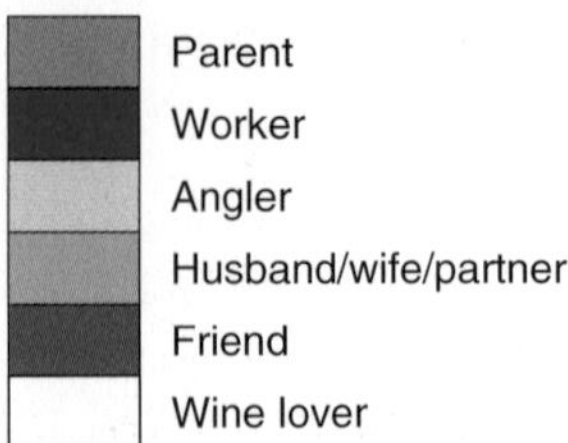

In a B2B situation, the 'roles' these business buyers or DMUs are playing might be:

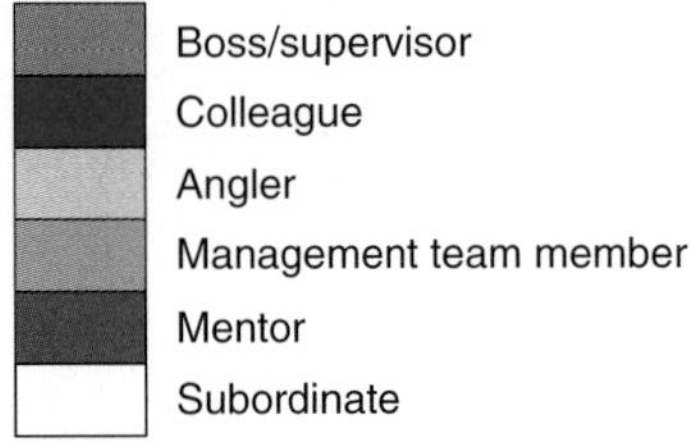

Organisations too can be playing 'roles', such as:

Assuming that in normal circumstances these people or organisations have different demographics and will have nothing in common, they are unlikely to be part of the same traditional segment.

However, if all these (demographically) different people were brought together in a single situation (CONTEXT©) *where they shared a common interest;* we have a very different situation. Situations where CONTEXT©s would create a target for marketing activity might include:

- Demographically different parents meeting at the local school which their children attend
- Fishing on a stretch of river
- On a website
- Waiting for a flight at the airport

- Reacting to a TV or radio message
- At a professional (business) conference or exhibition
- Responding to a business downturn or upturn.

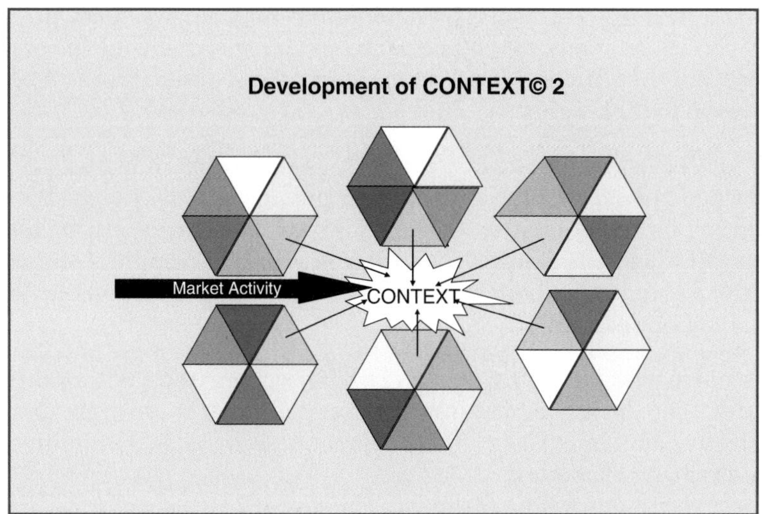

MARGIN NOTES

In these situations, people and organisations would have *predictable interests in common*. While in this CONTEXT© situation, they would be united in a common need or interest – they would certainly act (together) as a market segment. But this CONTEXT© segment could not be identified through any of the traditional approaches to market segmentation.

Since the early 1990s, I have been helping organisations to identify the CONTEXT© situations and/or occasions that drive their purchases – and purchaser roles in their markets. Over the years, I have learned that the greatest challenges arise, not in how to identify the primary roles or CONTEXT© in the market (this, believe it or not, is relatively simple), the problem arises in how to get the organisation to change its market activity to target the opportunities (CONTEXT©) – *and not the people in them*!

For example, if you were to cite any particular CONTEXT© and then ask who was in that market the answer will be quite straight-forward 'Most of the people some of the time'. This raises a very big question; which people at which time? Although even that can be quantified through analysis.

Where the problem arises is in the tactical marketing area – marketers are trained to focus their attention and activities on customers. But with CONTEXT© segmentation, activity now needs to shift *away* from targeting particular customers and *towards* targeting particular CONTEXT© – which are specific geographical (a physical place where people come together) or psychological (a common state of mind that people experience regardless of geographical location) situations that bring people together at a certain time.

We know that whoever is in the right mindstate or place where the CONTEXT© is alive will be part of that segment – and will be driven by the needs and motivations of the CONTEXT©, regardless of their personal needs, want and motivations that might drive them in other CONTEXT©. In many cases this can be too large a challenge for organisations and they find it difficult to market without a clear idea of a physical person in their sights.

CONTEXT© segmentation doesn't try to predict what individual people might do. Instead, it analyses what people are actually doing. By concentrating on these areas or CONTEXT©, a real segment can be identified and targeted. It doesn't deny the value of demographics and other descriptors, but sees them as useful components, not the whole of the segmentation solution.

MARGIN NOTES

If it's not a new idea, why is CONTEXT© segmentation not used more broadly? The answer is, because it is very difficult to do well. Organisations that do target CONTEXT© segments seem to do so intuitively – there are many examples:

- The UK retail chain that focuses its activity on the CONTEXT© of 'motherhood' and attracts mothers, fathers, children, grandparents, friends of the children and parents and anybody with an interest in the babies or children.
- The daily London newspapers that are marketed at the 'commuter' CONTEXT© while all the others focus on reflecting the reader's political views.
- City cafés, bars and public houses that suddenly boast tablecloths and flowers in the afternoon as they move from providing rapid business lunches at noon to a more relaxing drink on the way home in the evening.
- French sparkling wine that (almost) everybody drinks but only on 'special occasions' (CONTEXT©).
- Mobile phone companies that market a package of a 'pair of handsets', one for business use and one for pleasure use, with different features (to use in different CONTEXT©s).
- Bottled water that is provided at formal and business lunches and dinners as an acceptable way of drinking non-alcoholic drinks in formal business company (CONTEXT©).

Finally, a word of caution. You or your organisation might find all this talk about CONTEXT© segmentation just too complicated and even 'academic'. Many organisations that maybe ought to focus on CONTEXT©

segments but are unable to do so, open themselves up to competition. The scheduled airlines knew that their regular business customers also used them for holiday travel but were not receiving the (different) service they needed when in a different (family) CONTEXT© – the 'low cost' airlines entered. The large business and conference hotel that is unable to change its offer will stand empty in the holiday season while smaller, more flexible hotels that can provide both business and holiday offerings are full.

The lesson is – you might find it too difficult to market to context segments, but that doesn't mean you are safe from attack by others who can …

The FAQs are:

3. Segmentation and Targeting		
3.3 What segments exist in our target market (defined business)?		
3.3.1	Have we identified what business you want or need to be in?	Reverting back to Chapter 5, we need to be clear that we have a market-driven definition of the business we want to be in rather than an industry or product driven one. Market segmentation is a process by which we look to identify groups or clusters of customers (not products) that we might approach differently. We can't make this happen with a traditional (wrong) product-defined industry definition. Trying to 'segment' a product-defined business cannot produce market segments – it can only produce product categories. Which probably explains why we see so many product variants desperately seeking markets.
3.3.2	Have you identified the 'natural segments' that exist in your market?	Unfortunately, it is all too easy to begin research with a 'hypothesis' – that the market is split among a particular type of need or a particular type of occasion or according to particular demographics (or even correlates with our sales office locations) and so bias the results in such a way that data is actively sought to support these key dimensions. To find data that completely supports your belief before you started might be good for the ego but might not identify the most profitable areas of market need. Segmentation is an area that is relatively 'new' to many organisations, so the potential for 'slips' in the research process are high.
3.3.3	Have you based segmentation on descriptions, usage, needs/wants or CONTEXT©?	These three approaches to segmentation are intrinsically different. While a case could be made for all three, the worst thing you can possibly do is confuse the different approaches and try and create some sort of complex 'compound' base that stretches into all three areas. Descriptions or demographics are very simple, straightforward and attractive for the researcher, the respondent, the media buyer and all forms of market communication and distribution. Unfortunately,

		experience in most industries has shown that members of similar demographics rarely behave or purchase things in a common way. Sorry … Needs/motivations is traditionally one of the strongest methods of segmentation and has been used successfully by B2C for many years. B2B organisations have more challenges but it still produces good segments. Usage or CONTEXT© (occasion) based segmentation is relatively new – it offers some challenges as well as some serious advantages to the organisation willing (and able) to adapt its marketing away from the person and towards the CONTEXT© that brings the segment members together.
3.3.4	Do you understand the buying motives active in the market?	Regardless of which segmentation approach is preferred and selected you will need to have some idea of the motivations that are driving the different segments. Remember that development of a product or service is about identifying a solution to a problem or a benefit that meets a need. Without at least some insight into the needs and motivations behind the segment that you have identified it will be difficult to develop the other part of the critical product market match.
3.3.5	Do your customers and prospects identify with the segments?	This is not always necessary but it is helpful. As a communication proceeds to a target market (or the target context) it is normally helpful that the prospects can happily identify with the segment characteristics that you are portraying. If they find it difficult to identify with the segment maybe you need to refine the segments further so that they are able to identify with them more easily.
3.3.6	Can distribution and other partners relate to the segments?	If you use partners and channels to distribute your product or service to your end customer it will be important that you engage them in the segmentation process to some degree. Inevitable battles for control of the channel notwithstanding, it is extremely difficult to target particular segments unless you have the willing cooperation of the channels that deliver to that segment. If, of course, you are in the retail business then you need the cooperation of your suppliers to furnish you with suitable products to take to the market segments you have identified.
3.3.7	Have you applied the tests for 'good' segments?	To recap, the tests are: **1** Is the segment identifiable? **2** Is the segment reachable? **3** Is the segment viable? **4** Is the segment recognised by customers? **5** Is the segment recognised by distributors or channels? **6** Is the offering distinctive? **7** Will the offering be premium priced? **8** Will the offer provide above average profit margins? The test must be applied to be sure we are not wasting our time on a whim – or the computer's vivid imagination

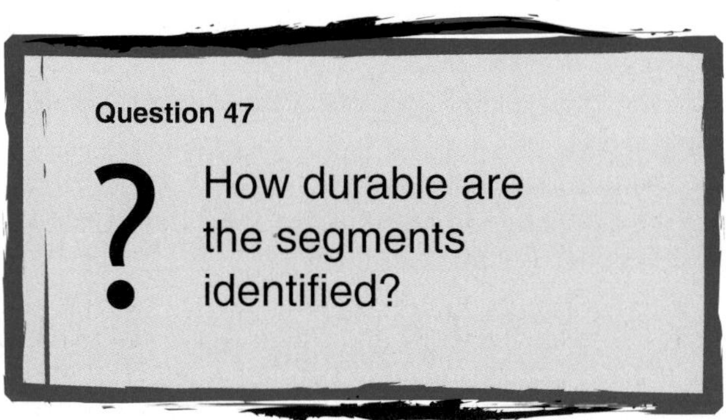

Question 47
?
How durable are the segments identified?

The question about segment durability is important mainly because of the amount of investment involved. As we identify a segment, the logical consequence of this is the development of a special or unique marketing mix that meets the special or unique characteristics and needs of the segment population.

MARGIN NOTES

- Not that you need to be reminded of what constitutes the Marketing Mix, but imagine the potential scope of any investment in the identified segment:
  - Product:
    - NPD (or even simply packaging alterations will affect costs significantly).
    - Not just the NPD costs but also stocking, space insurance, etc.
    - Also, the additional administration costs to ensure that the right product ends up with the right segment!
    - Services may appear simpler but they are not, and they carry the same cost implications
      - Just think, NatWest, Ulster Bank, Royal Bank of Scotland and Coutts & Co. are all the same Bank – well, yes, and no.
      - Just think, Bentley, Audi, Bugatti, Lamborghini, Skoda, Seat, Volkswagen are all the same car – well, yes, and no.
  - Price:
    - Different segments are willing (and expect) to pay different prices for different perceived benefits.
    - But they are not willing to pay extra for nothing at all.
    - The dangers are obvious and the additional costs are significant too.
  - Place:
    - Different routes to market and distribution or supply chain partners.
    - Often spread over smaller volumes with different and additional service requirements make this a potentially costly investment.
  - Promotion:
    - All communications activity is driven by the needs and wants of the target segment.

- As these will be different (by definition) the so will the message –and the media.
- Getting this wrong will certainly kill any chance of success very early.
- As the number of messages and media grow, often while sales volume remains constant, so economies of scale in communication collapses and costs rise.

Of course, increasing costs is not a great problem in itself. As long as the margins increase even faster, then the entire exercise is successful.

- To understand whether it is worth investing in the segment, it will depend on:
  - How much the investment will cost (estimate)
  - How much additional price the segment will pay for the perceived additional value
  - How long it will take to repay the additional investment and move into extra profits
  - How long the segment will exist (and whether this is long enough for the increased revenues to cover the increased outflows).

MARGIN NOTES

These are obviously difficult questions to answer, but even so, it needs to be assessed right from the outset. Obviously, with continuing research that plots the evolution of segments over time, it gets easier.

Much market investment is (all right then, *should be*) driven by our assessment of how the customers, in segments, behave – and will behave in the future. Why would we be interested in knowing how durable the market segments are? – Easy, few sane organisations would continue to invest growing amounts of time and money in a declining or dying market; of course they would insist on knowing how long the market opportunity is expected to last, when the decline is expected to fall below economic levels, when they should abandon the market segment, what new market (segment) opportunities appear to be growing to replace the declining opportunity and where the plans are to access and exploit the new (segment) opportunities.

So much for theory! In practice, rather than a logical seeking of marketing opportunity, the 'insane' behaviour of investing in dying markets goes on all the time. Many organisations, especially those whose markets are moving from rapid growth to maturity (see Chapter 2), appear to spend more and more of their time and money supporting products and services that less people seem to want. But for product oriented organisations, who really have no idea that the market is moving on (and away) from them, this behaviour is quite logical. If you have never had to look beyond the confines of the technical product or service (to the market that consumes the offering), you will have no idea about what else to do. In these circumstances, doing more (but faster and meaner) what worked in the past (even though it fails to bring success today) has to be the right thing to do – lets call it 'inappropriate' rather than 'insane'.

Every market is a dynamic, ever-changing system. Segments ebb and flow, some die and others are created. The practitioner knows this and builds flexibility into the system to deal with constant change. To be able to track (and predict) movements, the five key aspects of segment movement need, wherever possible, to be assessed and (if you can) predicted to determine the most appropriate market spend for the organisation. The key areas you need to be looking at are as follows:

- Growth:
  - Are the segments you have identified growing?
  - Value rather than just volume if possible, and at a rate that make investment worthwhile.
- Fragmentation:
  - One downside of segment growth is that as more and more people enter a segment it is likely to fragment into two or more segments at some later date.
  - Fragmentation can be difficult to predict but if you don't keep an eye on what is happening you could be outflanked by a competitor who makes a more attractive offer to a particularly vulnerable sub-segment.
- Decline:
  - If the segment you have identified is declining in size or number or purchasing value then you have to decide how long it is going to decline and what your response to this decline will be.
- Merge:
  - If two or more segments are declining it is possible that they may merge at some point in time and so expand the overall opportunity.
- Segment member Migration:
  - On top of all the above, we also need to take a view as to the likely migration of customers through different segments over their purchasing lives.
  - Plot the migration if you can, and if you serve more than one segment, welcome them into the new segment as they arrive.

MARGIN NOTES

Nevertheless, the ability of organisations to ignore these migrations is legendary! For years now banks have been offering attractive and special arrangements to university students to encourage people they believe will be tomorrow's 'higher income' earners to sample (and maybe stay with) the brand from an early age. As part of the recruitment process, not only do the banks still try to outdo each other with offers of free CDs, music tickets, tee-shirts and other highly targeted incentives, they also collect important data such as the date of the commencement of studies, the duration of studies and the most likely graduation dates.

It has taken some banks years to work out that the date of graduation, it is not a good time to move the account from 'student' to 'normal banking service' where they receive only the minimum acceptable service levels which befits their beginners' lowly salary rates. The typical response to this 'downgrading' of service is to move to another bank so negating the first bank's years of investment in what might otherwise have been a very profitable long-term relationship.

Prior to their 1990s collapse Marks & Spencer knew that they lost almost all their male (clothing) customers from the age of about 14. They had no idea exactly where they went but knew that they came back about 30 when they had children of their own. Not a good approach, as they later discovered.

The FAQs are:

3. Segmentation and Targeting		
3.4 How durable are the segments identified?		
3.4.1	Are the segments reasonably stable for the period required?	Naturally 'stability' and 'planning period' will be dependent upon the dynamics of the particular industry and your organisation. There will be a big difference between the fashion industries at one end and capital equipment at the other.
3.4.2	Which segments are growing and which declining? Why?	You must try to understand which segments are moving and in which direction – and also *why*? This probably requires more information. When you find the reason, you have to decide whether it is a trend, or a bubble! Investment without understanding the 'why?', is dangerous.
3.4.3	Which segments are fragmenting and which merging? Why?	As important as being able to successfully predict the movements themselves. You might find out the 'why?' if you talk to them … Any activity here needs to be driven by marketing objectives, not just some insane 'growth' ideology.
3.4.4	How do customers 'migrate' between segments?	This is not as complicated a question as it might appear. Many migrations are fairly obvious and can be timed quite precisely. If your organisation targets one particular group of customers and exclude others, this will be less of a problem as long as the entrants to your target segment make up for the people who move out. If your organisation deals with more than one segment you must understand how your customers move from one offering opportunity into another. As they enter the second or third segment on their journey you ought to be able to tap into the marketing investment made on the customer in a previous lifetime, CONTEXT© or segment. Welcome them to their new segment/lifestage/CONTEXT© and they will be much more profitable much earlier. Migration is often correlated to age and follows customers as they move through the various life stages. But, other demographics and environmental influences may also be at play so beware not to assume that it is always customers that are growing up!

3.4.5	Are we working to establish our position in today's or tomorrow's segments?	Investment in customers and markets is traditionally a long-term exercise (yes it is!). Although the national lottery built a top 10 brand position in the UK within a six month period, it did have a large amount of help from the government and the prime national daily press as well as a marketing budget that few of us could even dream about. For most organisations, reputations and brands are built on steady progress over a number of years rather than months! Given that investment is a cumulative activity and takes some time it is important that we build the organisation's reputation, brand and position with a view to the shape and dimension of tomorrow's market – not just today's.
3.4.6	Do we use forecast changes to inform new market strategy?	It makes some sense to say that the better you understand the market, and its constituent segments, the more robust and viable your marketing strategy should be. But of course there is many *a slip twixt cup and lip* and some organisations find it difficult to feed their understanding of the market place (and how it's likely to develop) into profitable actions. The data obtained from a segmentation study generates some of the most powerful information that your marketing strategy will ever receive. Segmentation data needs to feed directly to your marketing strategy decisions – and vice versa.
3.4.7	How do we use these forecasts to form marketing tactics?	A telling analysis (if sometimes rather demoralising) is to match this year's tactical plans (the 4Ps) to our understanding of the current and likely future structure of the market. I know its unkind but what can I say? Ideally: ● Products, services and portfolios should be aimed at the particular needs and wants of your targeted segments, ● Price should be aimed at extracting value differently from different market segments, ● Place/distribution should be about delivering product and/or service benefit differently to different market segments – and so on. You can see why sometimes the analysis is a little embarrassing.

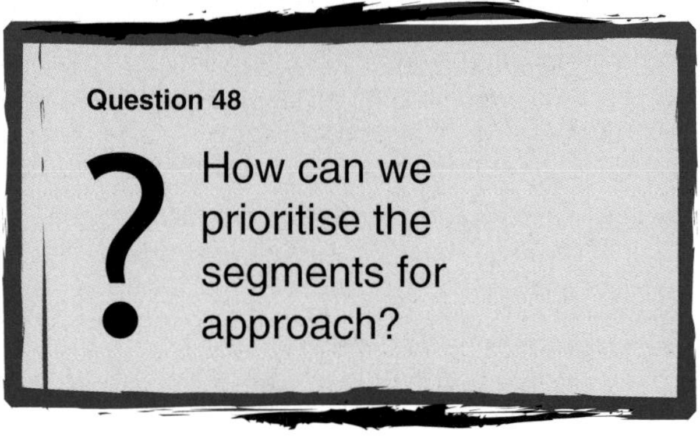

Question 48
?
How can we prioritise the segments for approach?

In today's markets it's difficult to see how a single organisation can *credibly* deliver offerings to all segments at the same time. There was a time that (my more mature readers will remember) the large motor manufacturers such as Ford and General Motors could deliver their branded products to almost all of the market segments in the business. In the past 10 years we have witnessed the acquisition by both these big players, of a number of different brands that they now need to get to parts of the market where the Ford/GM used to be good enough – no longer. Where once the name 'Ford' was sufficient for buyers, now the Ford website used to list Ford as well as Volvo, Mazda, Lincoln, Mercury, Jaguar, Aston Martin and Land Rover (before they started selling off to subsidise record losses). Volkswagen has a very clear market (segment) image while VAG plays across the range of segments – but only with a huge investment in different brands such as Bentley, Audi, Bugatti, Lamborghini, Skoda, Seat as well as Volkswagen. Not a single provider but a stable of specialists! Check Unilever (Van den Bergh foods) and Heineken websites to see how B2C companies use brands to open different segments too.

MARGIN NOTES

This is not the last time that we will see that Branding and *Segmentation need to be considered as joint marketing strategy activities*, not stand-alone issues.

Generally, most customers today seem to feel that an organisation cannot (at least satisfactorily) deal in all segments in a market (at least under the same brand). The 'full range provider' is often seen as a 'jack-of-all-trades', which may not be what they intended. The issue is which segments to approach and which to avoid? To try to approach all segments is unlikely to be successful, customers seem unwilling to accept the 'generalist' approach and just see it as being 'greedy'. How then to prioritise the segments?

There are many ways of prioritising; everyone who does it has their favourite. To give you an idea of what is involved though, I will briefly take you through the approach that I use.

The model I prefer to use for the initial prioritisation is the portfolio model from GE. The other portfolio models would be equally useful and can be used if you prefer. What all the portfolio models have in common is that they take two dimensions to try and assess relative value of the segment. The two dimensions are:

- Industry (or market or segment attractiveness):
  - How attractive is the segment to us?
- Organisation or business strengths:
  - How good would we be at delivering on the needs in the target segment?

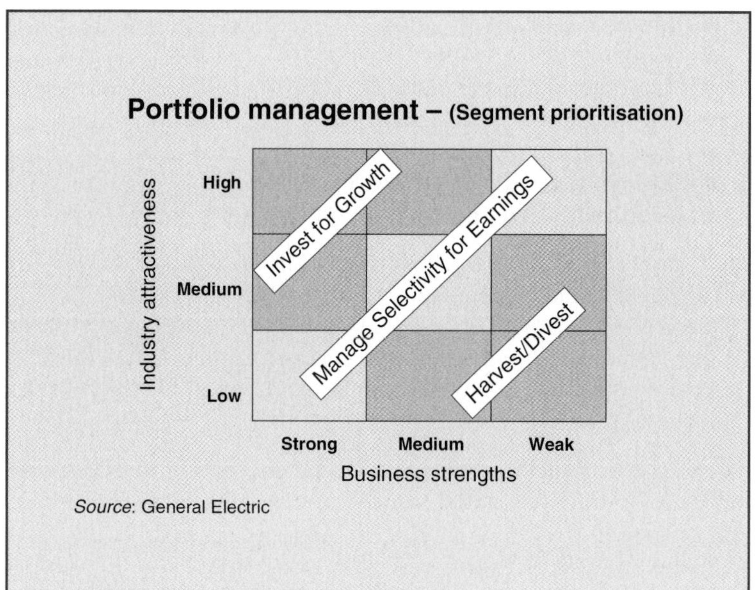

Source: General Electric

MARGIN NOTES

To apply the model in earnest, the steps in the process are:

■ Identify segment attractiveness

- We need to know how attractive each segment is or could be to us, in other words, how good will the segment be at delivering what your organisation needs?
- This means that we have to start by understanding exactly what our organisation needs or requires from the market.
    - This is not just a difficult question to answer; it is a hellish difficult one to ask.
    - If you were to list the possible alternatives, your organisation could decide that it needs some (or all) of the following returns (the list is not exhaustive, you may wish to add your own requirements):
        - Short-term profits
        - Long-term profits
        - Share price growth
        - Turnover growth
        - High margins
        - Margin growth
        - Market/segment share growth
        - Image development growth
        - Brand image (differentiation)
        - Brand value
        - Brand share
        - Barriers to entry
        - Protected market/segment situation

- Differentiation
- Unique selling properties (usp)
- International expansion/growth
- Innovation
- Early Penetration
- Ease of market/segment entry
- (add your own organisation requirements here).

- Then comes the difficult question, what are the *five or six most important* things that the organisation wants from its market?
  - Typically the howls of 'We want them all – and now!' simply disguises the fact that most managers, key implementers (and organisations) haven't really thought through what it is they want most from their market.

- In reality, many of the above tend to be conflicting objectives and to pursue more than one at the same time can only lead to failure in one, both or more.
  - If the analysis is to proceed your organisation needs to agree (at least for this first stage of initial analysis) what are the five or six most important requirements it has – and, the relative importance of these top five requirements.
  - So the steps are:
    - List all the requirements of the organisation (what you need any segment to deliver)
    - Reduce this list to the top 5 (6 absolute maximum)
    - Assess each segment in turn on its ability to deliver on these requirements once the segment has been penetrated.
    - Give marks for each segment ranging from:
      - 1 = the segment won't deliver at all on the selected requirement (0 messes up any analysis)
      - 5 = the segment will deliver 100% of what the organisation needs of the selected requirement.

MARGIN NOTES

■ Identify competitive business strengths

- I work on the belief that comparative strengths are best assessed against some type of measure.
  - To this end I normally work with the group to attempt to work out the ideal set of skills and abilities that *any organisation* would need if it were to completely 'win' in the target market (all the segments) – customers and their needs tell you this – again reducing the key skills down to about five or six.
  - We then try to assess the organisation's skills and competencies against this 'dream ticket' of the ideal competitor. So the steps are:
    - Agree the strengths that *any player* would need to have if they were to win in the segments

- Reduce the strengths down to 5 (6 absolute maximum)
- Consider each segment in turn and assess the organisation's business skills (existing or those that we could easily acquire within a short period of time) against those we believe are needed to win in the market.
- Give marks for each segment ranging from:
  - 1 = we don't have any of the skills required to win the segment (0 messes up any analysis)
  - 5 = we have 100% of the skills required to win in the segment.

Conduct analysis

- All that then remains is to crunch some numbers (find someone who knows how to work a spreadsheet).
  - If you then assess each of the available segments according to its ability (in your estimation) to deliver on the five key requirements of the organisation (I use marks out of five but you can use marks however you want) you get a measure on the scale for market attractiveness for each of the segments.
  - Similarly if you assess each of the segments according to your organisation's ability/competencies to really deliver what the market needs and win the segment from the competition on the same scale as you used for the attractiveness you will get a score for business strengths against each segment.
  - If you then combine the scores you will get a position on the GE matrix.

MARGIN NOTES

Segment prioritisation

Competitive strengths

Market attractiveness

	Strength Criterion 1	Strength Criterion 2	Strength Criterion 3	Strength Criterion 4	Strength Criterion 5
Attractiveness Criterion 1					
Attractiveness Criterion 2					
Attractiveness Criterion 3					
Attractiveness Criterion 4					
Attractiveness Criterion 5					

- Then, if you apply the numbers from the calculation to the standard GE matrix, you can start to see which segments appear to be the most attractive (top left corner) and which are the least attractive (bottom right corner).

Below, is a selection of results which have been produced from a number of different organisations. In the three diagrams the segments (represented by the different sized [relating to the different sizes of the segments] circles of different colours) that tends towards the top left-hand corner are most desirable in that they rank highly on their ability to deliver what the organisation needs and also we have comparatively high strengths in being able to deliver on the market and secure it for our organisation. Then, segments that fall away from the top left corner decline in attractiveness.

MARGIN NOTES

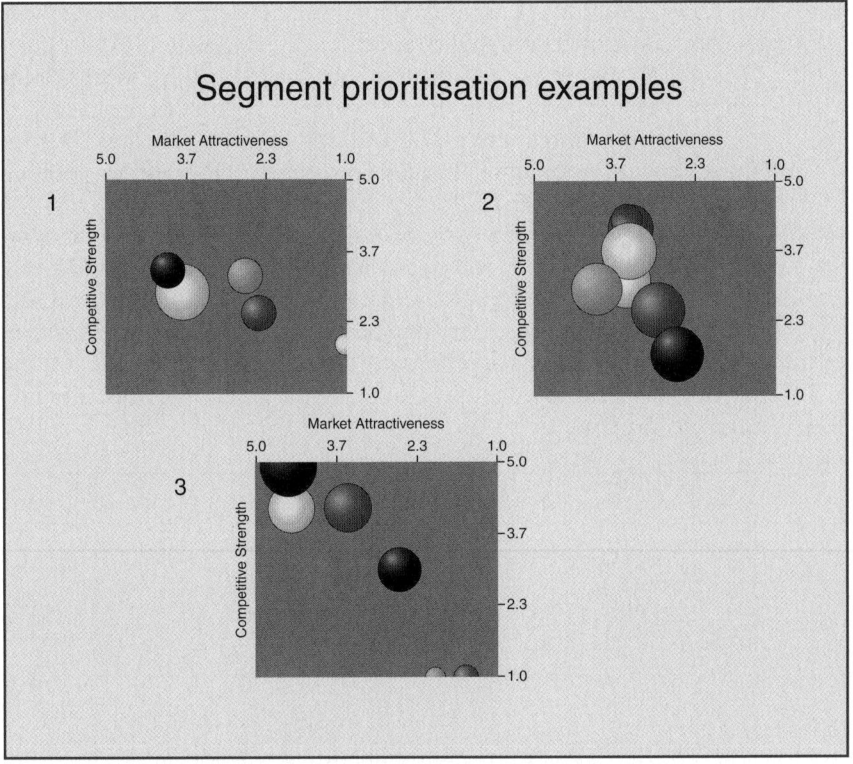

It should be noted though, that any form of analysis is still an exercise in Garbage-In-Garbage-Out (GIGO). The outputs are only as good as the inputs and the inputs are emotionally charged – so beware.

Beware also of the various assumptions that are made about what segments can deliver and what skills are required.

- Diagram 1 was based on a series of assumptions that were particularly negative and showed a very flat spread with no segments being particularly attractive – additional data was collected (based on customer perceptions of attractiveness and skills) and the analysis repeated to get a better view of the vertical dimension.

- There is also a question of timing; for example,
  - diagrams 2 and 3 above are based on the same data for the same organisation.
- The difference between the two analyses is that
  - diagram 2 is based on attractiveness and strengths assumptions over a three-year period;
  - diagram 3 is based on assumptions for a 10-year period.

But, as is the case with any analysis, this is just the first step in the decision making process. If you find that the output is politically unacceptable inside the organisation then obviously some changes will need to be made, different measures and/or weightings can be used for the attractiveness measures and for the business strengths to create a 'sensitivity analysis'. In any event, a lot of the input will be subjective and it is worthwhile seeing how far different numbers and scores change the prioritisation.

Although it is good to be wary of misleading calculations such as this could be, diluting all the results to produce a cluster of segments all around the middle of the diagram serves no useful purpose either. You need to find some way of differentiating those segments that are most attractive to the organisation and those segments that are least attractive.

Remember that ultimately market strategy is all about allocating scarce resource for the highest return – all in a competitive market.

The FAQs are:

3. Segmentation and Targeting		
3.5 How can we prioritise the segments for approach?		
3.5.1	What are the financial and non-financial imperatives (things management MUST deliver) in the organisation?	The list cited above is by no means exclusive and different organisations tend to be driven by different imperatives – at different times. However, in my experience, hardly any organisations ever take the time to sit down to work out exactly what it is they are trying to achieve. Your organisation is obviously an exception. More worrying is the effect on the organisation of different departments and directors pursuing what are tantamount to different corporate objectives. You could find a situation where the finance director is trying to maximise profits, the chief executive officer is trying to maximise share price, the sales director is trying to maximise turnover while the marketing director is trying to maximise his organisation's market share.

		You must have all decision makers (not just marketing) in the room when you identify the segments that will deliver on everyone's agenda items.
3.5.2	What is the relative importance of these attractiveness imperatives (weighting)?	Although it sometimes seems like I am fanning the flames of dissention, if you are to get anywhere close to prioritising particular segments we need, not only to reduce the number of overall 'imperatives' down to a small number that everybody agrees with, but to understand the relative importance within the reduced hierarchy. I tend to aim for a list of five imperatives, award 20 points to each of the imperatives (giving a total of 100) and so starting off with an equal weighted importance to all of the final five imperatives identified. As additional points are 'awarded' to certain imperatives because they are important, they have to be deducted elsewhere to maintain the total of 100. This is an interesting (and rewarding) experience for most managers. It is always heated and it almost always demonstrates the futility of some key assumptions that may have been driving individuals and departments for years – without ever having been questioned.
3.5.3	How might each identified segment deliver on each imperative?	Inevitably we enter the realms of subjectivity because we need to assess how, if all our resources are aimed at any particular segment, would it do against the financial and non-financial imperatives that have been agreed. When the first set of data emerges, just looking at the top and bottom ranked segments against expected attractiveness can be revealing. It can reveal as much about the organisation as the segment.
3.5.4	What are our strengths and weaknesses by segment?	Strengths and weaknesses should be driven by your customers' perceptions rather than internal views and it is important to try and understand the perceived strengths and weaknesses of your organisation through the eyes of the members of the different segments. This will help drive your perceived competencies when it comes to operationalising the different segments.
3.5.5	What competencies do customers perceive we have – by segment?	Your 'real' ability to enter and compete in any particular segment is interesting but not as important as the market's perception of your ability to do so. In the case of a particularly 'flat' set of data you may need to collect some additional data from customers to help you out here
3.5.6	What is the competitive position in a segment?	It is also useful (before you decide finally what to do) to assess your current competitive position in each segment. Are you strongly positioned, weakly positioned or a non-player in the segment. Depending on the time scale for the review and investments, this can dictate what you can achieve in any segment – and help you to prioritise.

3.5.7	How do we assess overall market attractiveness?	You do this (it is important because it figures in the marketing plans as the total potential market that you are targeting) by deciding how many segments the organisation can approach simultaneously (realistically!) and adding up the opportunities in this total number of segments.

Question 49

? Which segments should we target?

MARGIN NOTES

The question of which market segments we should actively target is a function of a number of different and often quite difficult to measure dimensions of the market that can probably be summed up in the following *pseudo*-equation:

$$t = f(v - c \times e \times i)$$

At last, a ridiculous equation that would look more at home in an economics textbook than a practical marketing strategy book. But it means that the intuitive practitioner trying to make a rational decision about where to spend limited budget, is made according to a number of clearly defined issues. Mind you, the issues might be clearly defined but gathering any type of defendable metric from them certainly is not. You will soon see what I mean.

- t = Target segment:
  - So you've identified the segments in your target markets, you've looked at what different people need and you've also tried to assess your ability as an organisation in delivering on the needs of the market and extracting some financial value from that market place.
    - Next comes the difficult decision of which target segments you are going to go for; and which ones you are going to leave, put on the back burner or shelve – or any other euphemism that makes the decision more acceptable!
  - You have limited resources so – no, the problem comes when you try to sell the idea internally, especially if you have a vociferous sales director.
    - The idea of possibly turning your back on any potential sale in any part of the market goes completely against the grain with some people who believe firmly that 'Every sale is a good sale'.

    - In my experience this is not a battle you are going to win with logic and fine words alone.
    - You will need to *prove* your point, I suggest you find a particular part of the market place where you can focus resources and *measure* the return on investment from doing it your way.
  - Age old favourites are of course any segment that includes the managing director or the chairman's wife but once you have tucked these two 'certainties' away you may feel the need to exercise a little more analytical thinking.
  - The following are some of the issues that you need to bear in mind.

- v = our ability to create segment customer Value:
  - Although we will look at this in more detail later (see Chapter 11) it needs to be said that the idea of 'customer value' is not an easy one to grasp, not least because the experts all have different ideas about what the term means.
  - Customers who buy motorcars, desktop computers, designer clothes and mobile ring tones don't want the products that they buy; they buy the benefits or solutions that the product or service will bring them.
    - Levitt said that 'A product is what a product does'.
    - For example a £700/€$1000 suit or business dress from Paul Smith is rarely purchased for warmth or protection from the elements – but if it gives the wearer the confidence to succeed at that important job interview it is an investment to gain promotion and an additional £7,000/€/$10,000 a year it is money well spent.
    - Given that you can buy a perfectly serviceable business suit from a mass retail outlet for under £100/€/$150) 'value' has very little to do with the cost of the product or service on offer but everything to do with the perceived value of what it will do for the customer.
    - In fact Customer Value = Benefit – Effort – Risk – Price (see Chapter 11 for more detailed explanation).
  - No it's too late now to say you should have been an economist, we now need to carry this through to its logical conclusion.
    - It (trust me) follows that the total value of any market or segment is not really made up of product or service sales over a set time period, but is made up of the total amount of money that the customers would be willing to pay for the benefits or solutions they desire.
    - If we follow Levitt's ideas, the total value of a market is the total amount of money that all customers would be willing to pay to get the *job done* for them.
    - Naturally different segments (by their nature) will not only want different things, they will also perceive different values on the same product or service depending upon their perception of what job it can do for them.

MARGIN NOTES

- Assessing the value of a particular segment comes down to a number of key dimensions:
  - The number of people in the segment
  - Their needs and wants in terms of benefits or solutions to problems (or jobs they want done)
  - The perceived value of these benefits or solutions (how much money are they willing to pay for the product or service?)
  - The amount of 'latent value' or potential value which is still not realised by you or the other players in this market
  - The credibility of your offering/brand/company in delivering on the benefits/solutions required by the segment members.

- c = Competitive activity in the target market segment:
  - One thing which is sure about competition is that (whether or not it is good for customers) it certainly succeeds in chasing profits out of a market.
  - The more competition in a market segment the less likely there is to be sizable profits for any of the players in that segment.
  - So, the next dimension you need to assess is how much competition is there in the segment?
  - This might be a function of the number of players or the aggressiveness of the players, or both.

- e = our efficiency in Extracting the value in the market place:
  - Once you have discovered how much potential customer value exists in the market segment and the competitive resistance to that value, the next question is; how good are you and your organisation at extracting that value?
  - This question relates to the efficiency of your total marketing mix and your ability to develop the 'right' products or services at the 'right' price (*not* the cheapest because cheap products have small profit components so are very *bad* at extracting value) through the 'right' channels supported by the 'right' communications.
  - A high total value segment will only be interesting if you can extract that value in a timely and efficient manner.

- i = Indirect (financial) considerations:
  - The numbers, as always, are only ever part of the story.
  - As well as the 'Where is the money?' and 'How much can we grab?' there are other considerations that might prove even more important for your marketing strategy.
  - There may be good reasons why you might decide to enter a particular segment even though it doesn't appear to be offering best value for your organisation.
  - If the reasons are sound, you should resist the short-termist bluster and hold to your beliefs.
  - There are many reasons why you may decide to go against the raw figures, some of these might be:
    - Operating in one segment of relatively low value may enable you to extract much larger value in another segment.

MARGIN NOTES

MARGIN NOTES

  - At the moment most UK, European and US supermarkets are treating food in this way, food retailing has reached a mature stage and sales and profits are fairly stagnant.
  - But it forms the reason for customers to enter the stores where, if they can buy more and more non-food items, profits continue to grow for the retailers.
- History from markets such as the motorcycle business in the US and photocopying machines in Europe have shown that it is often worthwhile controlling a segment, even at little or no value, to stop the competitors entering and gaining a foothold from which they can grow and cause damage in later years.
  - This is sometimes called 'strategic lock-out'.
- The credibility of an organisation may require that it is still seen to be active in a particular 'core' market segment although over time it makes its money in newer different markets.
  - Nowadays people are not surprised that Shell does not import shells; that Radio Rentals Ltd does not rent radios or that Lamborghini no longer makes tractors.

Finally, you must remember that if you are trying to get the organisation to 'change' in some important way they are unlikely to do this without some justification for the 'risk' (see Chapter 11) that they see in the manoeuvre. No doubt your eloquence will carry you a long way down the road but its not likely to be enough on its own. After the eloquence must come the analysis.

The analysis will be looked at by financial and other number experts and you will have a difficult job presenting future unknowns in the same way as they are used to dealing with historical 'facts'. This doesn't mean your analysis is wrong, just different, but you will need to make the case strongly.

The FAQs are:

3. Segmentation and Targeting		
3.6 Which segments should we target?		
3.6.1	Which segments are currently the most 'valuable?'	We have looked at some of the analysis that we can do, and there are other ways of assessing customer value as well. What ever method, you must look beyond the simple list price of the particular products and services. Properly done, any segmentation analysis will identify the different needs and wants of different segments and the importance that different customers give to these needs and wants and the benefits or solutions that they buy or would like to buy from you and other providers. You need to use this data to demonstrate value beyond the over simplistic 'add-up-current-sales' approach.

3.6.2	Which segments are expected to be most valuable in the future?	This is where we get even more future-focused (someone in your organisation has to) and of course, subjective. Strategy is about investing today's money for tomorrow's returns. Investing purely in extracting today's value is interesting but too short term. Value, as we all know, migrates over time and it is unlikely to be in the same place tomorrow as it is today. Unless you are happy to be without any value at all, you need to be investing in tomorrow's most valuable segments – today.
3.6.3	Which segments are the most and least competitive?	Competition chases profits out of a segment; you need a view on which are the most competitive markets today and which are likely to be the most competitive markets tomorrow. Remember of course that you are looking beyond simple industry direct competition to competition in a wider sense as described by the Porter's Five Forces Model. Which competitive forces will be strongest tomorrow? Get some experts around a table and work it out.
3.6.4	Which segments are essential to support our target market position and brand? And which would damage us?	Any brand is an insubstantial concept of promises and beliefs and is as much affected by what the brand holder does as what the brand can do for the customer. It is important that your brand is seen to be active in the market segments where the customer expects to see it. Also, it is as important that you are *not* active in certain market segments (at least with the same brand) if participation in that segment were to be perceived as inappropriate by people who were active in the brand. Presumably the research at Volkswagen said that the VW brand could move up as far as the Phaeton but not down as far as the area now occupied by Skoda. On the other hand only time will tell us whether Porsche's move into 4-wheel drive SUV has been a positive move for their brand.
3.6.5	Do we require profitability by segment or across the market portfolio?	*Ideally*, accounting systems should be a measure on the performance of the whole business rather than a method of inhibiting overall corporate success by measuring component parts of the business as stand-alone activities. There may be good reasons why your organisation may want to incur low profits (or even losses) in a particular segment in order to create even greater returns in other segments. Make sure you know what they are though.
3.6.6	Are there segments we must control to lock out competition?	The downside within organisations that do allow losses to be incurred in some segments is that, unless carefully policed, this can be seen as an excuse not to make profits at all! If we are going to incur low profits or losses in certain areas we need to know exactly *why* we are incurring them and where the compensating returns are being made. Such is the argument behind entering or controlling segments where there is relatively low market value but we are using it to 'lock out' competitors. Apart from hindsight, it is always a difficult case to make. If competitors have been successfully locked out then they are not playing in the market and who can prove that they were going to enter the market anyway? If they're in, its too late …

3.6.7	Which segments should we encourage our competitors to enter?	A final question for the Machiavellian practitioners out there. If you have invested time and money in understanding market segments and the different needs and wants that drive them, then it is only reasonable that you use the data that you have acquired. Knowing where today's value is (and tomorrow's value will be) and which segments you can extract most value from, and why, you might feel encouraged to help your competitors make the *wrong* decisions. This is not intended to be a book on marketing tactics but I am sure you can work the rest out for yourself.

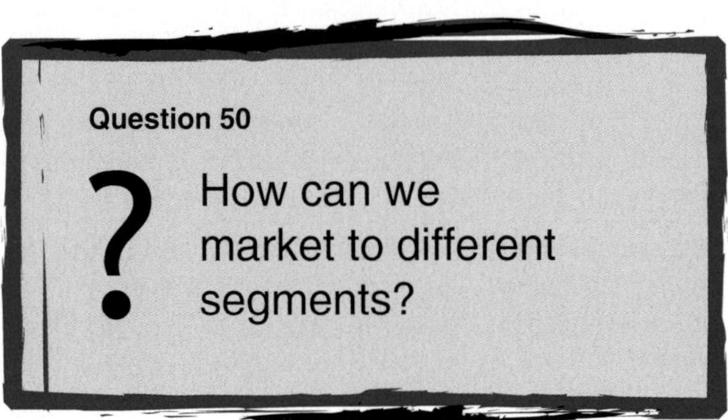

Question 50
?
How can we market to different segments?

MARGIN NOTES

So much for the analysis, what do we do with the results? – how many of the segments should we approach? Marketing to more than one market segment at the same time is 'macho' but difficult. Certainly doing it properly is a major task. There are three different ways of marketing to different segments:

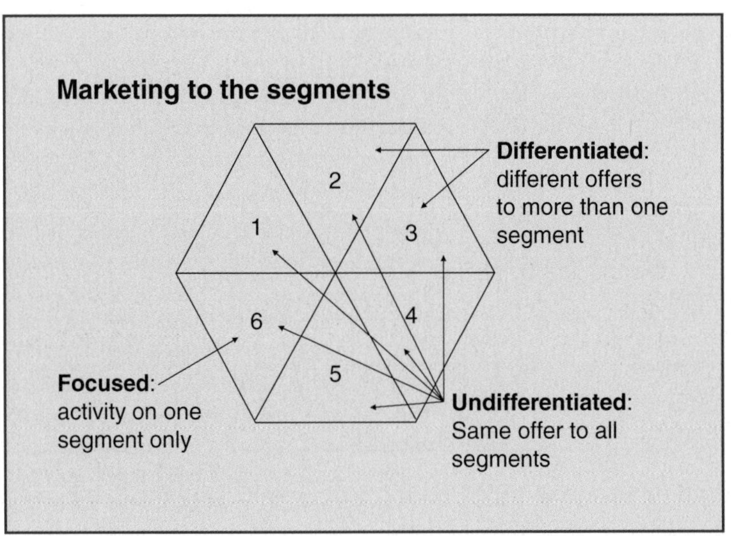

- Undifferentiated marketing:
    - Delivering the same offer to more than one segment.
    - Ignoring all the different segments and doing what you were doing before, is not quite as unrealistic as it might seem – you may have identified the segments and their different needs and wants but also calculated that at the moment there is not enough value to justify the additional cost of developing special marketing mixes for the different segments.
    - You might decide to keep a watching brief on the market and drive down different market segments with different mixes as and when competitors decide to do the same.

- Focused marketing:
    - Delivering a specialised offering to just one segment.
    - Very similar to the case of focused marketing strategy as described by Porter in his generic strategy theory (see Chapter 3) as well as everything you have probably read about 'niche marketing' (no, I don't know why there are three words for the same thing either).
    - This can be quite a successful strategy.
    - However it does tend to put all your eggs into one basket.
    - If the segment you have identified really is a 'niche' (technically quite different from being a single or small segment, a niche is defined as a safe and protected harbour that the larger companies would not find it economic to participate in), then you can do quite well.

- Differentiated marketing:
    - Delivering different offers to different segments.
    - If you are going to approach more than one segment at the same time, then you are taking on quite a serious task.
    - Don't be fooled by those organisations who appear to be working on four or five different segments (effortlessly), they have probably been doing it for many years and have already learned from their mistakes.
    - If you are from the larger number of organisations who move into customer-driven marketing (only) as their market matures, then the idea of designing and maintaining more than one cohesive and integrated marketing mix – at the same time *and* without significant overlap is a challenge indeed.

MARGIN NOTES

You must remember that the entire idea behind segmentation is that we identify different groups of people (with different needs) and we give that group of people, if financially viable, more of what they particularly value, only so that we can gain two important returns:

- We expect and need a greater *penetration* in that segment

- We expect and need to command a *premium price* over an undifferentiated or 'mass' offer.

We will only achieve these returns if we treat the segment customers as intelligent human beings. We need to be able to make an offer that really is different from the competition's and is not seen as just another commodity offer masquerading under a new set of cheap packaging – customers are sophisticated and they have already been caught like that before. Also, the *premium* price must be seen by customers as *reasonable* price considering the special benefits and customer value added in the offer. What this means is that the organisation really is going to have to develop a unique marketing mix to make the offer credible. And for each and every segment that you wish to target. Oh, by the way, if you just happen to target or deliver the wrong offer to the wrong segment you can successfully annoy both segments at the same time! I think that's what they call a 'double whammy'.

MARGIN NOTES

Naturally, the idea that we are going to deliver two or three or four completely different ranges of products, packaging, selections, storage at different price levels, with different advertising and support through different channels – is going to be met with some serious questions inside the organisation. It will be clear to even the weakest manager that this is going to be a serious increase in costs and, even worse, you will appear to be contravening one of the most sacred cows of business – the all-powerful 'economies of scale' argument. The fact that the economies of scale argument rarely holds true beyond the pages of newspapers doesn't seem to worry anybody at all, especially when there is change to resist. You will meet a veritable wall of opposition and complaints that you are destroying their (hard fought for) economies of scale by demanding a number of shorter runs of dissimilar product or service offerings. To help you in your arguments you may want to go back to the original economics text books and polish up on the two concepts that (should be) taught at the same time as the economies of scale argument but seem to be forgotten:

- The 'law of diminishing returns', suggests that the returns from the economies of scale diminish with time rather than grow with time.
- The 'diseconomies of scale', suggests that the additional costs of organisations and production that come with large scale enterprises (such as bureaucracy, slowness to respond to market changes and customer needs) work against and ultimately destroy the gains from the economies of scale.

The fact that you may be helping the organisation out of its death grip on this old fashioned logic obviously won't cut any ice but you need to persevere with the argument.

■ Populating the segments (for B2B)

Finally, a special issue for B2B segmentation – how we can 'populate' the segments for direct sales approach? This supposed 'problem' is at the heart of B2B market segmentation and is the reason why market segmentation tends to be used less in B2B than in B2C organisations.

If there is a process of market segmentation used in B2B, it is likely to be based on demographics (industry classifications such as geography, technology, industry (verticals) or company size) rather than based on more competitive bases such as customer behaviour, needs or motivations.

The standard argument for B2B not being able to use the more motivational approaches runs like this:

- B2C is at the forefront of marketing techniques, really because of the highly competitive nature of many B2C markets
- B2C is a different type of business from B2B because:
  - B2B companies tend to have fewer (larger) customers
  - B2B companies don't deal with a single customer but with a range of buyers, financiers, gatekeepers and influencers (the Decision Making Unit, DMU)
  - Some B2C organisations are so large that different parts or subsidiaries fall into different segments (such as BBC, BT, Deutsche Bundespost, Government Health Services, etc.)
  - B2B product and service offerings are more complex than B2C offerings and need to be explained by specialist sales staff
  - B2B companies still use sizeable direct sales forces to be able to sort all this complexity out on the ground.
- The conventional wisdom is that these two facts mean traditional (B2C) segmentation won't work in B2B because:
  - There are not enough customers for them to 'self-select' themselves into or out of segments based on marketing communications and the offer like B2C markets do
  - Sales forces can only manage to split their markets by observable demographics such as industry (vertical), company location and size, etc.
  - Sales forces can't split their markets by emotional measures such as motivations, customer needs etc. because all the customers look the same.
- Which means that:
  - If motivations based segmentation is ever to be introduced into B2B companies (all the data tells us that it gives better quality B2B segments and competitive advantage), we will have to add one extra step to our analyses
  - We will have to *populate* the prioritised segments with the names and addresses of all the companies and customers/prospects who fall into each (motivational) market segment.

MARGIN NOTES

Populating segments in B2C markets is normally quite straightforward. With the number of potential customers in the market place usually measured in millions, it is normally sufficient for B2C organisation to put together a sufficiently differentiated and attractive offer through broadly the right channels supported by the right message through the right media for:

- Members of the target segment to be attracted to the offer *and*
- Members of other segments to be 'repelled' by the offer *and*
- Members of the target segment to seek out the offer in the market.

For all the reasons explained above, in B2B markets this is believed not to be the case. Whether this is true of a self-fulfilling prophesy, you can decide for yourself – the fact that most B2B organisations *believe* this to be true is enough. If the basis for segmentation is anything other than simple demographic descriptors, then it will be considered incapable of operation, and worse *academic*.

MARGIN NOTES

But it can be done. Having worked with a large number of B2B organisations and helping them to develop market segmentation solutions I have found that there are two useful statistical methods that can deliver the answers that B2B managers need – CHAID analysis and DISCRIMINANT analysis.

You will find more information on these methodologies in the relevant statistics books or the Internet, (or test your research agency knowledge with the questions!) but very briefly:

- CHAID Analysis:
  - (Chi Squared Automatic Interaction Detection – that's got to come up in the pub quiz) is used to build a predictive model, based on a classification system.
  - The output is a 'tree' diagram of which the 'branches' are those questionnaire questions that best predict the membership of one or other of the identified segments.
  - Through this route we can identify which are the most important questions (and order) so that we can replicate just a very small number (usually less than six) of questions with a very good chance of predicting the segments that the buyer or the prospect belongs to.
  - In one organisation we managed to include the CHAID results on to every salesperson's laptop computer and through a maximum of five questions the prospect's segment was identified and immediately the laptop launched into one of four pre-determined sales presentations which highlighted the benefits that had most perceived value to the buyer in the pre-identified segment.
- Discriminant analysis:
  - Is a statistical technique that looks at all the questions that we used to generate the clusters and identifies, for each individual question, the amount of the variance explained by that question in the total cluster (segment) solution.

Populating the segments (B2B)

CHAID analysis

Discriminant analysis

Segmentation questions

Using the scale 1–7, where 1 is strongly disagree and 7 is strongly agree, what scores what you give the following statements.

1. We use our call centre to gain competitive advantage.

- **1–2 Strongly Disagree** → We only use the minimum technology that we need to operate
  - **1–4 Disagree** → **Pragmatists**
  - **5–7 Agree** → **Club 18–80**
- **3 Disagree** → I would prefer that we only use systems that have been tried and tested
  - **1–4 Disagree** → **Club 18–80**
  - **5–7 Agree** → **Henry Fords**
- **4–5 Neutral/ Agree** → Our call centre is our best sales tool for increasing or growing our business in the next few years
  - **1–4 Disagree** → I would prefer that we only use systems that have been tried and tested by others in the industry
    - **Yes** → **Pragmatists**
    - **No** → **Henry Fords**
  - **5 Agree** → Cost is not an issue as long as the call centre achieves its objectives
    - **1–3 Disagree** → **Henry Fords**
    - **4–5 Agree** → **Fire Fighters**
  - **6–7 Strongly Agree** → Key priorities of your customers – always speak to a person and not a system
    - **No** → **Fire Fighters**
    - **Yes** → We only use the min level of technology that we need to operate in
      - **1–3 Disagree** → **Fire Fighters**
      - **4–5 Neutral/ Agree** → **"Club 18–80"**
- **6–7 Strongly Agree** → We only use the minimum technology that we need to operate
  - **1–4 Disagree** → Handling peaks in call traffic (call fluctuations) is an issue
    - **No** → Staff retention is a main issue of importance
      - **1–4 Disagree** → **Henry Fords**
      - **5–7 Agree** → **Fire Fighters**
    - **Yes** → **Fire Fighters**
  - **5–7 Agree** → Reducing cost is the most important objectives for our call centres
    - **1–3 Disagree** → **Club 18–80**
    - **4–7 Agree** → **Henry Fords**

1. XxxxxXxxxXxxxXxxx = 24%
2. XxxxxXxxxXxxxXxxx = 35%
3. XxxxxXxxxXxxxXxxx = 41%
4. XxxxxXxxxXxxxXxxx = 49%
5. XxxxxXxxxXxxxXxxx = 59%
6. XxxxxXxxxXxxxXxxx = 66%
7. XxxxxXxxxXxxxXxxx = 71%
8. XxxxxXxxxXxxxXxxx =
9. XxxxxXxxxXxxxXxxx =
10. XxxxxXxxxXxxxXxxx =
11. XxxxxXxxxXxxxXxxx =
12. XxxxxXxxxXxxxXxxx =
13. XxxxxXxxxXxxxXxxx =
14. XxxxxXxxxXxxxXxxx =
15. XxxxxXxxxXxxxXxxx =
16. XxxxxXxxxXxxxXxxx =
17. XxxxxXxxxXxxxXxxx =
18. XxxxxXxxxXxxxXxxx =
19. XxxxxXxxxXxxxXxxx =
20. XxxxxXxxxXxxxXxxx =
21. XxxxxXxxxXxxxXxxx =
22. XxxxxXxxxXxxxXxxx = 98%

= 100%

- When discriminate analysis works well I have been able to reduce a background questionnaire set of 35 questions down to about seven or eight questions which then give me something in the order of 70% probability of correctly assigning every respondent to the right segment.

In both cases these analyses are ways of trying to reduce the number of questions we need to ask of the respondents so that we needn't burden them with 24–36 individual questions just to make sure we know where they fit into the analysis. It is also possible (one organisation did this for a reasonable cost) to then contact every single client and prospect on the database by telephone and, by asking them a small set of questions, to flag all entries in the company database and reorganise the prospect list by segment.

Remember, it is difficult to attempt any changes in sales force organisation (who are normally organised according to either geography or by industry type) without some very compelling data (even better, real-life experience) first.

The FAQs are:

3. Segmentation and Targeting		
3.7 How can we market to different segments?		
3.7.1	How different are the target segments?	There are different statistical techniques that can be used for segmentation purposes but (different forms of) 'clustering' is the most popular. The statistical process aims to create clusters/segments by organising multidimensional space (don't even ask!) so that the clusters: **1** *Minimise* the differences in the responses *within* the clusters – and **2** *Maximise* the differences in the responses *between* the clusters. So everything is geared to creating clusters/segments that are as different as possible. In other words, the groups of need, want, motivation will be markedly different between the segments so making the job of convincing the organisation that much easier. Where the differences are less clear to the lay observer you may need to build up your proof gradually through experimentation.
3.7.2	Can the same brand be used to cross segments? How many?	We will cover this question in more detail in the positioning and branding sections of the SCORPIO model (see Chapter 8) but, as you would expect, it largely depends upon a number of factors. *A successful brand cannot be grown in the 'mass market'; it needs a correctly defined segment before it can differentiate properly.*

		However, some degree (a shallow form) of differentiation can be achieved by working in less than the whole market. How successfully will depend on the degree of competition and the development of the market.
3.7.3	What level of standardisation is possible in the product or service?	Again, it largely depends upon the degree of difference that exists between the target segments. Very different segments will obviously require very different offers but this doesn't always mean you have to dive into expensive R&D to develop completely different product or service offerings. I remember working for a Japanese producer of telephone exchange equipment. You would expect the telecommunications needs of a major hotel would be different from that of an engineering company which would be different from that of a stock market trading house, and so the organisation marketed quite separate (and quite differentially priced) solutions to various segments of the market it had identified. On closer inspection it turned out that the organisation had not actually identified and created completely different products but rather they had *one* standard product which was capable of doing almost anything that any organisation might demand of it. The secret (and indeed the personalisation) came from the packaging, which included taking a very carefully selected range of options *out* of the core productleaving a dedicated and specialised telecommunications exchange system precisely meeting the need of different segments of the market! Once sensitised to the approach I have found this solution used more than once – in different industries – From cars to mainframe computers to websites The moral of this story is that even quite different segments with very different needs and wants can often be satisfied by different *packaging* rather than different core products – but it needs to be very carefully done.
3.7.4	What are the costs of necessary adaptations	The answer here is zero. (Maybe I ought to explain ...) If the adaptations really are necessary, then they will have to be done. On the other hand, to give way to the idea that these are *costs* may be the first step in the defeat of the entire segmentation process inside the organisation. You need to demonstrate from the outset that we are *investing* in particular customers and segments by making the adaptations they require – so that they can buy more and pay more. The earlier the argument is started, the faster others in your organisation can respond.
3.7.5	What are the price premiums available?	This should come out of your analysis. An assessment of market value should identify what price premiums are available. This should become a base target for your operations and you should measure your success in gathering increasing premiums year on year.

3.7.6	How do we 'populate' the segments?	We have spoken about populating segments for B2B sales forces. However, this is a lengthy process and, of course, it is not 100% accurate. Sales people are also keen to avoid change wherever possible, even if that change might promise some improvement, so they will focus on anything less than 100% accuracy – as a 'fault'. Alternatives to this approach might be considered: ● Get the sales force to recognise the customers and prospects on their own – this can be done through training or by questions. Not an easy task but it builds flexibility into the system, which will be useful for later changes. ● If you have the volume, use B2C communications techniques to allow self-selection procedures and get customers to classify themselves – you can see this approach on major B2B web sites such as Dell and HP already – who said it couldn't be done?
3.7.7	Can the organisation successfully manage multiple marketing mixes?	The final and possibly the 'crunch' question. Two shorter sub-questions here, if the organisation can't manage submixes very well you may need to scale back your ambitions and the speed at which you change from undifferentiated to differentiated marketing. If your analysis leads you to believe that you don't have the time to spend learning to deal with multiple mixes successfully, you may need to acquire the skill from the outside so that you don't lose your position against competitive pressure. If you can't do this, your options are either: ● Focus your operations on a single segment and command premium prices from a specialisation ● Ignore the segmentation analysis, trust in the 'mass market' and produce a standard, undifferentiated offer. The prices will be low and volume will decline as your sales are attacked by specialist providers. Commodity markets always beckon; I hope you can beat the Chinese prices.

■ The strategic questions (44–50)

In this third part of the marketing strategy discussion, we have broached the unnecessarily tangled question of market segmentation.

Segmentation has been around for a long time now and most managers have heard the word. But it is not easy to do. The analysis is quite costly (collecting the customer data) and takes time to complete. Not only that, but it can sometimes suggest what appear to be quite radical change for the business. Sometimes, it's just too difficult.

The trouble is, the organisation who is saying it can't be done is the one interrupted by another organisation that is doing it. Market segmentation is not a luxury any longer – it is a key tool in the battle for customers.

Here are the next questions for you. Normally segmentation is the area of SCORPIO where I get most 'nice-to-have' or even 'not-important' responses. Before you tick these boxes, remind yourself that I haven't included a 'too-hard' option and that may be what you are really looking for

No.	Strategic question	Our strategic answer	Importance	✓
	Segmentation and Targeting			
44	What is the current state of segmentation in the organisation?		Must have	
			Nice to have	
			Not important	
45	What do we want segmentation to do for our organisation?		Must have	
			Nice to have	
			Not important	
46	What segments exist in our target market (defined business)?		Must have	
			Nice to have	
			Not important	
47	How durable are the segments identified?		Must have	
			Nice to have	
			Not important	
48	How can we prioritise the segments for approach?		Must have	
			Nice to have	
			Not important	
49	Which segments should we target?		Must have	
			Nice to have	
			Not important	
50	How can we market to different segments?		Must have	
			Nice to have	
			Not important	

CHAPTER 8

Positioning and Branding

> 'In order to be irreplaceable one must always be different'
>
> *Coco Chanel (1883–1971)*
> *French fashion designer & perfumer*

For a subject which makes organisations so much money (and could make them even more), it has always amazed me that branding doesn't sit anywhere in the traditional marketing mix. It is squeezed into all parts of the mix, sometimes it is inserted into product and packaging, everything is inserted into promotion, in fact its spread all over the place – so thinly nobody gets to concentrate exclusively on the important issues of branding.

Brand is absolutely *not* a tactical issue, something that even the writers of tactical textbooks have recognised, because investment in brand rarely has an immediate (in the same financial year) return. But neither does it, at least up to now, have anywhere to sit in the overall structure of marketing strategy. Of course there are books written just on branding, I know that, but where does it fit in the organisation's planning structure? How does anybody know what to do about planning brand growth? Now that the SCORPIO concept has arrived (I hope) all this is behind us!

MARGIN NOTES

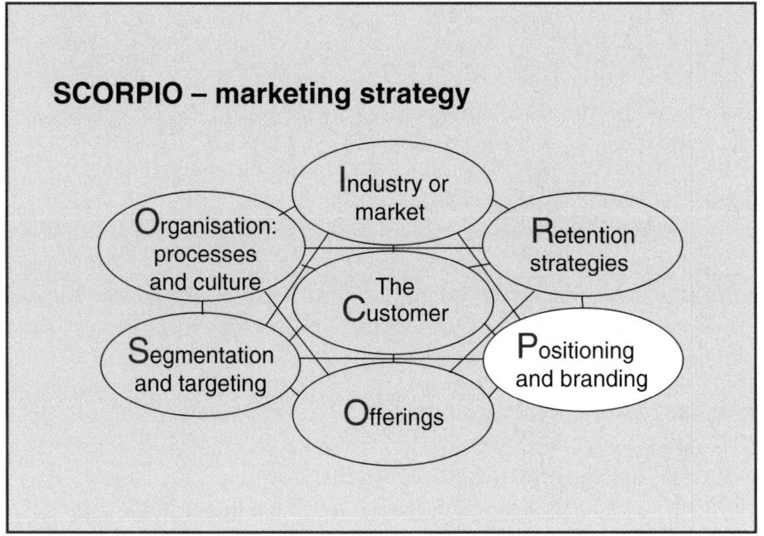

Branding

I won't insult you with a long diatribe about the importance of branding, you know all that, so let's focus on a list of the most important 'headlines' so that we remember the sheer scale of what we are discussing:

- Every year Interbrand and Business Week calculate the value of the top 100 global brands and publish the results online.
  - Most years Coca-Cola comes out as number one with an estimated brand value of around $70 billion (that's $70,000,000,000).
  - Interbrand's value for the top 100, comes to just shy of $1 trillion (that's $1,000,000,000,000) and of course there are more than just 100 brands alive in the world.

- Simon Anholt (*'Brand New Justice'*, Butterworth Heinemann, 2003) has compared this global brand value as:
  - Equal to the combined gross national incomes of the 63 countries defined by the World Bank as 'low income'.
  - Almost one-third of the entire value of global wealth.

MARGIN NOTES

- Almost all of this value exists off-balance sheet, since most 'intangibles' are not yet included under the list of the company's assets.

- A brand isn't a name, a product or a service, it is more precisely:
  - A set of consistent meanings which belong to and exist separately from the product or service offering.
  - A set of feelings and beliefs that exist in the customer's mind.

- Not everybody likes brands (some writers hate them and would like to prove that brands are a form of confidence trick aimed at overcharging the customer). The 'death of brands' was announced (prematurely) in 1993. On 'Marlboro Friday', Friday, 2 April, 1993, Philip Morris, the maker of Marlboro cigarettes, announced that it would be cutting the price of Marlboros to compete with generic cigarette makers. Everybody is still buying brands.

- Customers really like brands because:
  - We use the brands we buy to make statements about ourselves to other people.
  - They make decisions easier so that we can get round the supermarket in under an hour, buying brands we trust, and get on with our lives.

- Brands come from different places:
  - Real or perceived experience of the product or service offering
  - Advertising and promotion history
  - Word-of-mouth communication in its various forms
  - The customer's perception of how the brand owners appear to behave
  - The importance and role of the brand in our everyday lives.

We will discuss brands and branding in much more detail soon but before we do that, we need to concentrate on one other important but often overlooked aspect, that of market position.

Positioning

Much of the work on positioning comes from advertising and marketing communications research and especially the books written by Reis and Trout (*'Positioning: the Battle for Your Mind'*, McGraw-Hill, 2001). The basic idea behind positioning is not what you do to your product or service but *it is all about what you do to the mind of the prospect*.

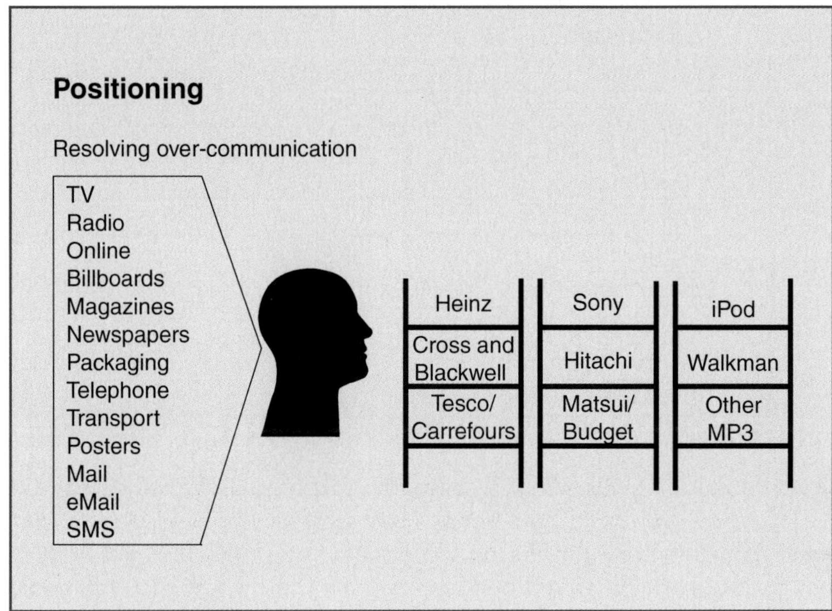

MARGIN NOTES

The 'headlines' are:

- Positioning is about owning a word or a concept in the customer's mind.
- Positioning is about resolving the chronic 'over-communication' in today's consumer and industrial markets.
  - Research (various) suggests that we are bombarded by something between 600 and 1,000 separate messages every day of our life.
  - Customers are forming short 'ladders' in their mind for each product or service category which has any relevance to them.
- Different customers have different ladders, but generally
  - The top position is the one that customer believes 'owns' the word or the category
  - The second position is that owned by the runner-up and
  - The third position is often either a local or a budget supplier
  - People tend to lose interest in most categories after three positions on the ladder.
  - 'Specialist' customers might have ladders that reach a maximum of seven rungs.
- The category leader is the one that 'owns' the top position on the ladder

To illustrate the point, a simple word association test.

Positioning and the 'Word Association' test

Category	Your answer
Economy airline	
Baked beans	
Chocolate	
Coffee	
Personal computer	
Cornflakes	
Business hotel	
Fast motor cars	
Safe motor cars	
Mobile phone	
White rum	
Trainers	

MARGIN NOTES

Look at this form and, *thinking* as little as possible; simply write any brand names in the right-hand column that spring to your mind. I realise that the categories may not be to everyone's choice, and that you could have selected better ones, and who does this author think he is trying to tell me which products and services I should like? – I know all this – but

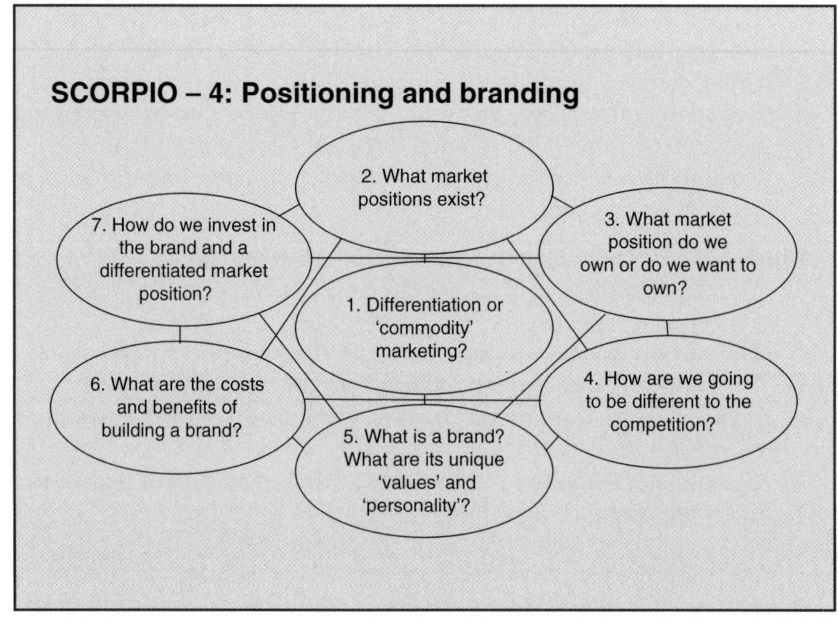
SCORPIO – 4: Positioning and branding
1. Differentiation or 'commodity' marketing?
2. What market positions exist?
3. What market position do we own or do we want to own?
4. How are we going to be different to the competition?
5. What is a brand? What are its unique 'values' and 'personality'?
6. What are the costs and benefits of building a brand?
7. How do we invest in the brand and a differentiated market position?

just look at the half a dozen or so answers that you managed to complete and ask yourself, how much this top ladder position is worth to these companies' results?

If you have worked out that positioning and branding is definitely not about trying to work on a 'level playing field' but about finding ways of tilting the playing field so that it works in our favour – you could be right.

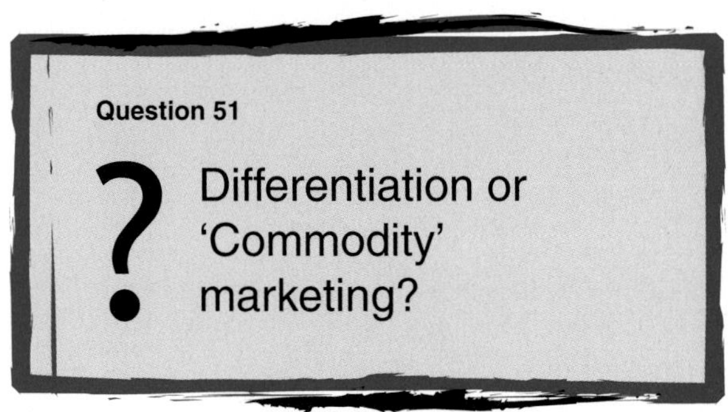
Question 51
?
Differentiation or 'Commodity' marketing?

MARGIN NOTES

Levitt said that there is no such thing as 'commodity markets' only 'commodity marketing'. In other words, markets don't insist on consuming commodities – bad marketing ensures that they are offered nothing else.

First, the 'headlines':

- Commoditisation of markets is *not* a foregone conclusion
- Commoditisation is *not* something that is out of your control
- Because everyone else is reducing prices does *not* mean that you have to follow
- Continual price reduction is *not* an immutable law that must be followed
- Customers don'*t* always buy on price alone
- You are *not* serving your organisation if you let profits slide – even to maintain market share!
- Lemmings are *not* the brightest animals in the world
- If the market price collapses 'on your watch' and you collapse your prices to match the market, you *are* at fault

The very first thing we must do here is to ask you whether you realise that every time you look at 'reducing prices', 'becoming more competitive', 'employing aggressive pricing', or any other euphemism that you may care to use; you could actually be taking your organisation one step further towards its death?

The commodity slide is the most dangerous ride in the amusement park and it is waiting for you.

MARGIN NOTES

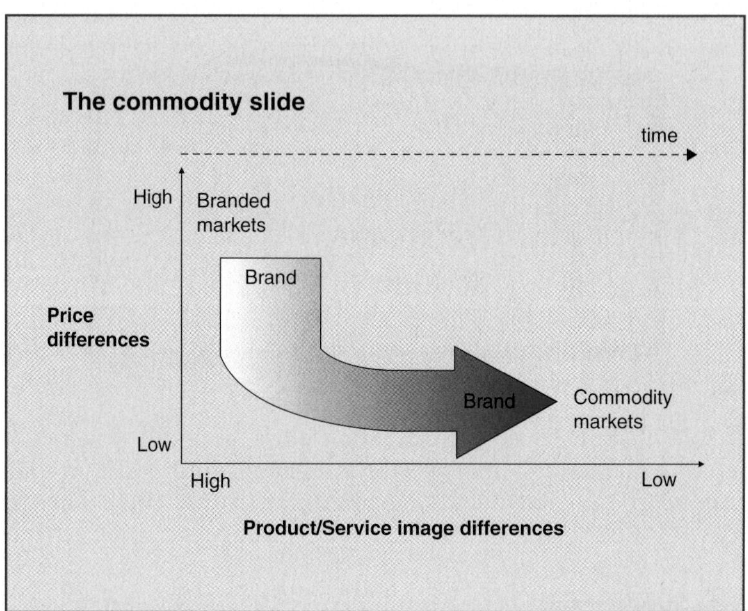

The commodity slide is an idea that has been around for a very long time although it does not seem to have penetrated the day-to-day lives of many (certainly not enough) practising managers. From the diagram, you can see that all products and services exist somewhere on a continuum between 'brand' and 'bland' – between highly priced and highly differentiated offerings at the top left-hand corner known as branded offerings and low priced with little or no differentiation in the bottom right-hand corner called the commodity markets.

For most managers (who prefer not to think unless they really have to) the commodity position seems to exert a powerful attraction. These are markets (and there are *far too many*) where most customers find it almost impossible to see any real differences between the competing products or services on offer, and are forced to make a choice just on price! That is the only difference that customers can see.

Remember, they may not have been looking to choose on price, but they can't see any other differences. Nevertheless this is all it needs for the price-driven specialists to say that the market is obviously driven solely by price – so we have to be the cheapest if we want to sell the most. It is not true, but it is what a lot of managers want to see.

A word on commodity markets

This is where so many decision makers are headed.

In a commodity market:

- Everyone is competing on the same variable – price
- The organisation that can offer at the lowest price, wins
- Success is about being able to produce at the *lowest cost*
- There can only be *one* winner in the commodity battle.

Before to start cutting prices, you should ask yourself a few questions:

- Are you (or can you become) the lowest cost producer in your business?
  - If the answer is '*Yes*':
    - Can you remain the lowest cost producer?
    - What do you plan to do when you have removed all the competition?
    - Do you want to invest your profits this way?
  - If the answer is '*No*':
    - Why are you cutting prices when you know you cannot win the end game?
    - What, haven't you got another plan?

MARGIN NOTES

A word on branded markets

If we look at the other end of the continuum we see the B2C and B2B branded markets.

These are characterised by a rich assortment of product and service offerings that are recognisably different in the customer's perception. All offer clear and distinct benefits and together make for a sensible range of choices, in that the customer isn't forced to choose on price; there are other variables that can be used as well.

The advantages of heading towards a branded option are:

- First, sales volume is likely to be smaller at the branded end of the market than it is at the commodity end. However, as we all really know from experience:
  - Revenue is 'vanity'
  - Only Profit is 'sanity'.
  - We would expect to see profit margins far in excess of those which allow organisations to eke out a survival living at the commodity end.
- Second, there is room for more than one 'winner'.

- ○ There will be as many winners as there are credible market positions (in customer's perception) to be owned.
- ○ Depending on the market, there can be three, 10 even 20 or more viable and profitable organisations all making a good living out in a properly branded environment.
- ○ Customers are happier too because they have more options to choose from and they are not just forced to use price as the discriminator.

So why do organisations appear to be driving, lemming-like, to create a significant market position in a commodity business?

- An unreformed sales culture will only allow anyone to see sales revenue as the ultimate measure of the organisation's success. But as market share explodes and margins disappear …
- Rewards and assessments are often a hangover from the rapid growth stage of an organisation's development and, unless changed, will continue to drive sales turnover growth rather than on customer satisfaction, commitment and retention.
- Some organisations (for example, IT) have a business model where they can survive for four or five quarters without making a profit but they cannot survive one quarter without meeting their revenue targets, which they need to pay their staff. If it is revenue at all costs then short-term thinking drives.
- Rather than benchmark their activities against customer measures, too many organisations benchmark performance against others in the industry where lemmings are cutting cost, price and value. Everybody else is doing it so it must be the right solution.
- For too many organisations, it is just easier to do what we have always done than to think about new ways of doing things. For the lazy, cutting price beats thinking any day. And of course, cutting price doesn't kill the business instantly, we run away to fight another day. As long as we can keep on our feet until after I have collected my pension then I will have done my job.
- For some managers it is simply fear of the unknown. We know all the reasons why we shouldn't do it, but, we don't know what to do – because there is nobody else to follow.

MARGIN NOTES

■ An important word on price

Before we go on, a brief word about the nonsense that is talked about price.

Message 1 – *Customers don't want to buy on price.*

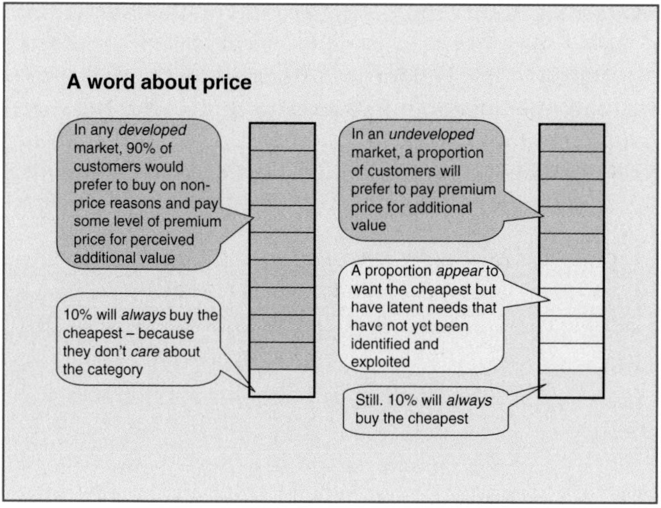

MARGIN NOTES

All the research I have ever conducted for clients (a lot) and other research that I have seen (more) show the same message every time (read this list carefully):

- In a developed market (one where 'real marketing' has been exercised and research conducted to understand customers driving and latent needs):
  - 90% of customers would *prefer* to buy on non-price issues
  - 10% of customers will always buy on price because they *don't care* about the category and are not engaged in the issues (everybody has some categorise that they buy but just don't care about)

- In an undeveloped market (one where 'so-called marketing' is all about sales support and key decisions are made by sales and production departments in ignorance of customer needs):
  - A given (variable) proportion of customers would *prefer* to buy on non-price value issues
  - 10% of customers will (always) buy on price because they don't care about the category and are not engaged in the issues
  - A given proportion of customers will *appear to buy on price* because nobody has worked out what additional benefits they would be willing to pay a premium for. This is *latent* need.

Professional, practicing managers have a complete marketing mix at their disposal; price is *not* the only element they can use.

■ Why not decommoditise?

Before you even start thinking that its all too late and some previous short-sighted manager has messed up the whole business by dragging you down the commodity route – dig around on the Internet for an inspirational (its not often I say that) article 'Shedding the commodity mindset', by Forsyth, Gupta, Haldar and Marn (*McKinsey Quarterly*, No. 4, 2000). They talk mostly about B2B organisations who have decided not to 'just go along with' the commodity mindset and have looked for areas to differentiate their offers and improve their marketing – and their prices.

They make much of 'conjoint analysis' for market segmentation (a method that I use when I can and is not anywhere as complicated as the name implies) and show, in one example after another, how to identify latent needs within their markets. But beware, we are talking exciting markets such as industrial resins, bulk chemicals, refractory bricks and printing here.

MARGIN NOTES

The authors also found that the typical company's sales force was *not* representative of the customers they serve and customers, when interviewed, highlighted all sorts of other areas where they would welcome more help.

For the manager who really doesn't want to go down with the ship there are some interesting lessons from this research:

- Commoditisation is not a one-way street.
- Sales forces are not a good guide to what customers really want (and are willing to pay extra for).
- As the authors say, *'For all practical reasons, the B2B market has no commodities'*.

Differentiation

Differentiation is a term that we all know, we all use – and some of us understand.

Differentiation is the foundation of professional marketing:

- Customers like it – they find it much easier to choose on non-price variables than on price alone.
- It makes choice easier.
- Various researches have suggested that differentiation is about three times more effective than cost advantage at producing long-term returns to shareholders.

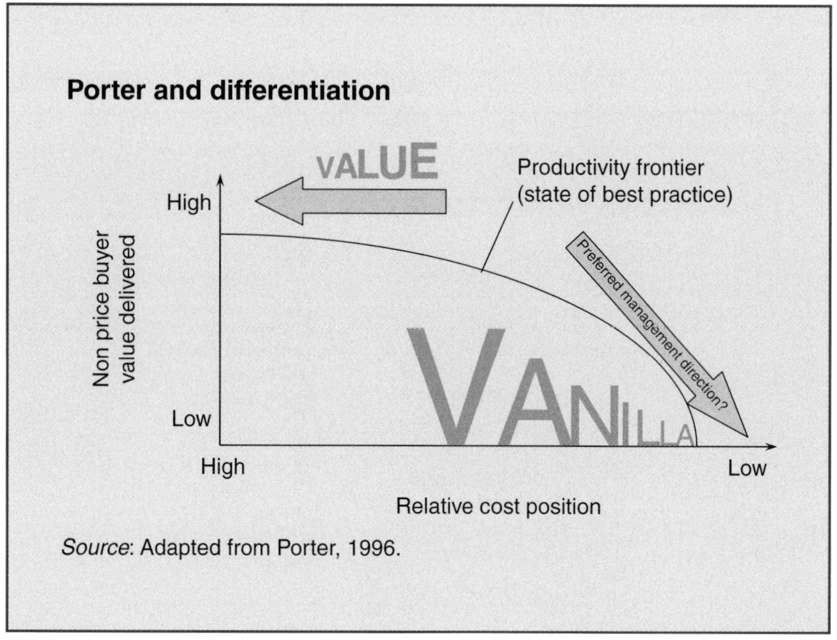

Source: Adapted from Porter, 1996.

MARGIN NOTES

Michael Porter in his HBR article ('What is Strategy' *Harvard Business Review*, November 1996) suggested that the reasons for lack of differentiation in most organisations, and the dire consequences that the activity produces, is all down to the rather unhealthy level of internal focus of most organisations. He suggested that there is an obsession with what organisations call *operational effectiveness*. He maintains that operational effectiveness is necessary, but it is not sufficient to win – and it is not strategy. Porter finishes his (quite long) article by suggesting that:

- Winning is about having a competitive strategy
- Competitive strategy is about being different.

He then goes on to suggest that there are two ways the organisation can be different

- They can perform *different* activities from rivals
- They can perform similar activities in *different* ways.

Building on the work done by Porter, Nora A. Aufreiter, David Elzinga and Jonathan W. Gordon ('Better Branding', *The McKinsey Quarterly*, November 2003) looked at what makes good brands compared to just names and commodity offerings. I have adapted the Aufreiter,

Elzinga and Gordon approach and have used it very successfully with clients:

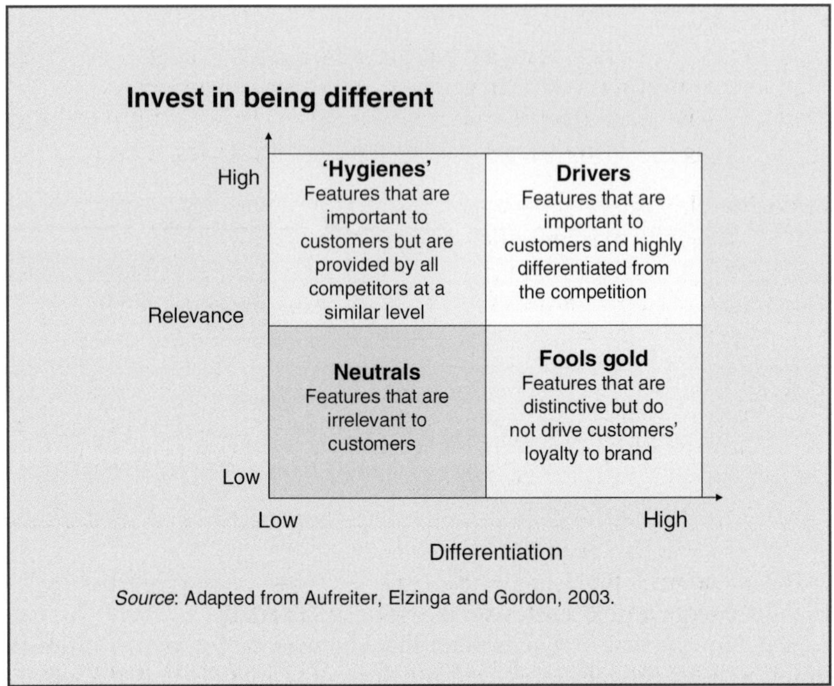
Invest in being different
High
Relevance
Low
Low
High
Differentiation
'Hygienes'
Features that are important to customers but are provided by all competitors at a similar level
Drivers
Features that are important to customers and highly differentiated from the competition
Neutrals
Features that are irrelevant to customers
Fools gold
Features that are distinctive but do not drive customers' loyalty to brand

Source: Adapted from Aufreiter, Elzinga and Gordon, 2003.

MARGIN NOTES

The work harks back to Hertzberg's work (see Chapter 6) and suggests that being different isn't the whole story. We need to find ways of making our offer(s) different in two main ways:

- Differentiated:
  - From the competition in the customers' perception.
  - That means different in terms the customer can understand.
  - Also, customers may compare your offering with offerings from another technology (substitute competition) – you need to be different from these.

- Relevant:
  - Your offering needs to have some relevance to your customers' lives.
  - This means possessing some information of your customers' needs, wants, aspirations, lifestyles and culture.
  - Technological or scientific knowledge is not enough.

Within these two categories, offerings fall, broadly, into four categories:

- Neutrals:
  - These offerings are typical commodity offerings.

- They are not different to any other offerings and have no features that are particularly relevant to your customers.
- They do the job but are, well, boring.

- Hygiene:
  - These offerings have all the right features – and they are what customers want, but they are the same as everyone else.
  - This is better than the neutral offers but there is still no way of telling these offers from the other (also good) competition.

- Fools Gold:
  - These offerings are different; there is no doubt about that.
  - But, perhaps because you have given the R&D boffins their head, you are now launching offerings that are packed with clever 'gismos' that no customers understand, want or ever asked for.

- Drivers:
  - These offerings are not only clearly different from the competition, they are different with features and benefits that customers really want – and value!
  - The 'drivers', if they have been properly identified, will be the 'motivators' identified by Hertzberg.
  - Remember that customers really can't get enough of these additional features, each time more value is added.

Just in case anybody missed the point of all this – *the opportunity is in the top right box*. The value is here because segmentation works in our favour. We have talked about market segmentation previously (see Chapter 7),

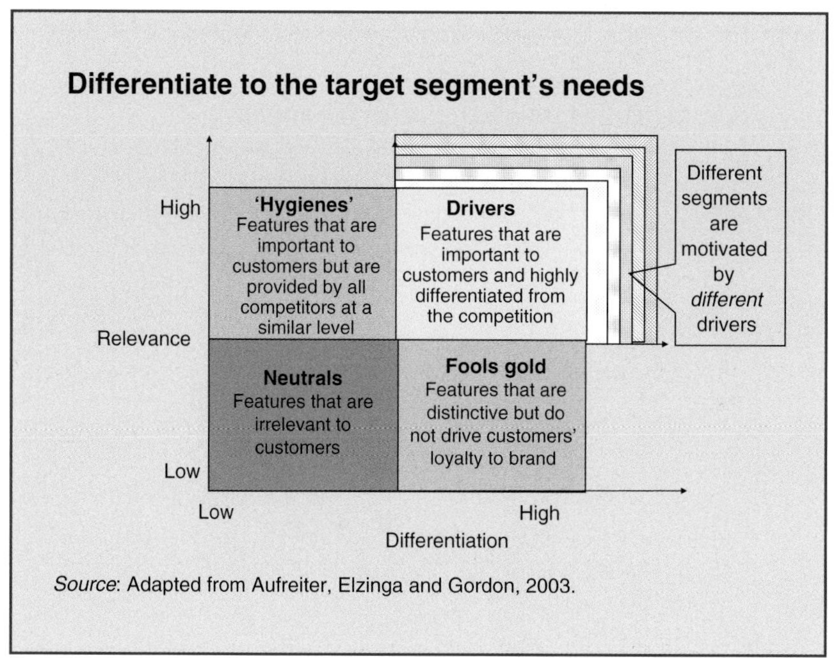
Differentiate to the target segment's needs
High
Relevance
Low
'Hygienes'
Features that are important to customers but are provided by all competitors at a similar level
Drivers
Features that are important to customers and highly differentiated from the competition
Different segments are motivated by *different* drivers
Neutrals
Features that are irrelevant to customers
Fools gold
Features that are distinctive but do not drive customers' loyalty to brand
Low
High
Differentiation

Source: Adapted from Aufreiter, Elzinga and Gordon, 2003.

MARGIN NOTES

here you can see that the area to investigate for segments is where the different motivational drivers exist.

The different drivers in the top right box are the building blocks of successful (and profitable) marketing. Attempting segmentation from any other box is simply nonsense.

Now the *bad news.*

Up to now, differentiation has been a good thing to do, but largely an 'option' for companies who were happy to take risks and were hungry for success. Those that wanted it bad enough could get it if they differentiated – and they did!

Those that preferred a quiet and uneventful life could still take undifferentiated route as long as they were willing to live off the lower returns. Up until now, mediocre companies had a future. Not a great one, but a future nevertheless. The risk averse and the amateurs so beloved of British Industry could still make a living, and play golf at weekends, amateur dramatics in the evenings …

MARGIN NOTES

Now, I fear the game rules may have changed forever. China, and soon India (then you should be very afraid indeed), have decided to enter the game. Now, the neutrals and fools gold boxes are beginning to shrink – and unless you can produce at a unit cost cheaper than the Chinese (I thought not) then it really is a case of differentiate or die.

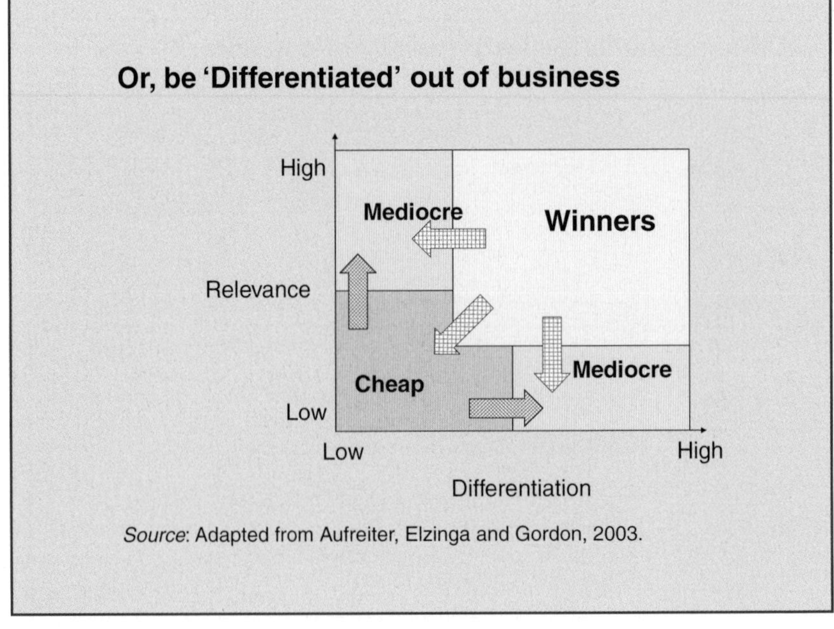

Source: Adapted from Aufreiter, Elzinga and Gordon, 2003.

The future looks bleak for the mediocre company. I know I should feel more compassionate – but I don't. The mediocre organisations have been coasting for so long – and all at the expense of the customer, who has been short-changed continually. They have been content to make and sell what *they* wanted, considering the customer difficult or stupid or both for wanting something different. Now that they absolutely can't drop the price to a level that they will still sell something, they will have no alternative but to pay more attention to their customers.

It looks as if Marketing might finally come of age – even if it took the Chinese to do it!

The FAQs are:

4 Positioning and Branding		
4.1 Differentiation or 'commodity' marketing?		
4.1.1	Is the concept of 'commodity' accepted in your business or industry?	If people in your industry or organisation accept the concept of a commodity market (at all) then you probably have an uphill battle to fight. This type of conventional wisdom tends to make managers fatalistic and suggest that the only way they can win any battle is by a brutal price war and face-to-face competition with their main antagonists. Unfortunately, the most attractive thing about a commodity market is that it doesn't seem to demand much in the way of brains – just lots of muscle. You can take it from me (so it must be true ...) that *real* examples of commodity markets (not ones created against customer desires by *bad marketing*) are amazingly difficult to find. If your market was really a commodity market then the lowest price offering would be by far and away the biggest seller. My 'in-depth' researches over the year have only uncovered a real commodity market in the area of saline drips (as used in hospitals) but nowhere else. I am sure now that I will receive suggestions from all over the world, but check figures before you write. If you think about all those markets that are rumoured to be commodity markets (like insurance) the genuinely cheapest offers rarely have much of a market.
4.1.2	Do we and/or our organisation's key decision makers believe that differentiation is possible in our defined market?	The power of belief! If an organisation doesn't believe it can differentiate its offering it will never try. And no matter how many good examples we bring in from other industries the cry of 'Oh yes but here it is different' will bounce off the walls from morning to night. The problem is that the organisations involved and the managers who make the key decisions probably have no direct experience of differentiation nor can they point at anyone in *their industry* that has successfully differentiated. And they will probably continue protesting that it is impossible to differentiate – until somebody does it.

		Even pointing at everyday B2C products and services that are technically commodity but very successfully differentiated (Heinz Baked Beans, McDonald's potato fries, Perrier bottled water) will don'thing to weaken their resolve. Talking about successful B2B differentiation (Caterpillar, Komatsu, Volvo, IBM, GE, JCB, Heidleberg, Microsoft, Airbus, Boeing, Rolls-Royce, Otis, Pfizer, Pratt & Whitney, Accenture, PwC, American Express, SAP, Sage, Reuters) meets equal 'death-wish' scepticism. There are ways to overcome this scepticism but they are long and they are slow. However, if you don't overcome this perception that change is not possible your organisation has a future once described to me as 'death by a thousand price cuts'.
4.1.3	What is (believed) to be the role of price in the purchase decision?	The traditional, rational, economics view on the world is that price and delivery are the two most important factors in every purchase decision. Many organisations, especially if they are led by accountants, engineers or other managers with a scientific background will tend to follow this reasoning. In many cases the feeling is that getting the right price is about 90% of the battle. In fact these people are just about 90% wrong! But of course it is about *belief*, and this is the problem. If people believe that the price is all that matters then they tend to act accordingly. Your job then is to try and change this belief – in any way you can.
4.1.4	What (or who) does our organisation 'benchmark'?	When benchmarking takes place in an organisation it is typically carried out on a fairly rigorous and mathematical basis – and that tends to lead organisations to benchmark themselves against other businesses in the same *industry*. Acting on these results will drive you towards the 'vanilla' position highlighted in Porter's research. Benchmarking itself is not an unrealistic process and the results can be quite useful but you need to be benchmarking the sort of organisations that your customer will compare you with. To remind yourself what sort of organisations these might be you need to look back to Chapter 5 of the SCORPIO process where we were working out what business we were in.
4.1.5	What differences/ added value are customers willing to pay for?	Well, this is the crunch. There is no alternative but to talk to some customers or conduct some research. It doesn't have to be complicated or expensive but if you are trying to find a *unique* differentiation, you will only find it in *unique* research. Go on, invest some money on your customers, they will love you for it. Of course, you have a problem if your organisation doesn't believe that differentiation is possible in this business it certainly won't be willing to spend the money on research to find out what the differences are or could be. You will have to be creative.
4.1.6	Is it worth being different?	Another step in the process of changing your (internal) people's perceptions is working out what differentiation could mean to your business – in hard financial terms.

		You will have noticed that I quoted 'three times' improvement for differentiated companies over cost-driven companies. It takes a while to achieve this but even so, it must be worth some more on the bottom line to add customer value and maintain real increased prices. It could be time for marketer to turn financial expert here and start doing some numbers. If you don't, nobody will believe you.
4.1.7	Does our organisation really want to be different?	Yes it is another one of those questions. Some organisations do want to be different but don't know how to start, other organisations don't want to be different at all and don't want to change and frankly there is little you can do apart from stay if they are going to survive beyond your pension date or get out and find a better job somewhere with decent survival prospects. Never forget that some organisations would rather die than change. Who are we to get in their way?

Question 52

? What market positions exist?

MARGIN NOTES

Now that we have all (I hope) bought into the idea of being different rather than being the same, the next question starts to loom on the horizon.

Exactly *how* are we going to be different from the competition?

Here you must remember your customers' needs, wants and wishes as well as your own ambitions. Before you start looking at which different market positions you might like to occupy and which market positions you would be qualified and able to occupy, maybe you need to start with your customer and find out which market positions exist out there – from their point of view. Remember, if the customers don't see a particular market position, then for them it does not exist and any money spent supposedly differentiating the offer to make it unique within this position would be a completely wasted investment.

If you rake through the books and articles then a number of possible market positions are suggested by various authors. An example of the range can be seen by looking at the car/automobile category:

The positions outlined in this table are obvious and will probably exist in many markets or categories. I have added some examples just to make

Some 'common positions'

Positions	Examples ...
Best quality	*Rolls Royce*
Best service	
Lowest price	*Skoda*
Best value	
Safest	*Volvo*
Fastest	*Porsche*
Most customised	
Most convenient	*Ford*
Most advanced technology	

MARGIN NOTES

sure you get the general drift but have refrained from filling in the table completely for three reasons:

- I am not as fast as my publishers would like in creating new and updated versions so the more examples I put in the more likely they are to be out of date before I come round to organising the next edition of this book.
- Each reader has a different background and understanding of market positions depending on their overall experience. Also, there is a difference between 'reality' and 'perception'. If Volvo is perceived as the safest car, the fact that it really isn't the safest doesn't matter because enough customers will act (purchase) as if it is. The more examples I cite the more likely it is that some of them will be contested by different readers – and we don't need that.
- Audience participation is 'must' nowadays so feel free to engage in this and complete the table with your own examples!

This list is by no means exhaustive and there are many finely tuned positions which may exist in between and around the ones described on this table. The most important criteria are:

- The customer absolutely must believe that the position exists
- The position has additional (beyond commodity) value for the customer.

But digging further through the literature there are even more options cited for potential market positions like the ones you will find on the next table. This time I have completed the examples, I suppose it is a need to live dangerously.

Some further options for positioning/differentiation

	Options – You could position by ...	Examples ...
a	**Attribute** (for example, *size*, speed, colour, age, complexity)	Microsoft?
b	**Benefit** (for example, *easiest, fastest*, strongest)	Porsche?
c	**Use/application** (for example, for holidays, for *celebrations*)	Bollinger?
d	**User** (for example, for *young/old*, for experts, commuters)	iPod? Saga?
e	**Competitor** (for example, *better* than 'x', cheaper than y)	Nokia?
f	**Product category** (for example, *yoga* holiday, *computer game*)	PS2?
g	**Quality/price** (for example, best, most expensive, *cheapest*)	Easyjet?

You should start to see from these two (far from exhaustive) lists that the customer has a very wide understanding of different market positions and, depending on the category or segment involved, you will probably have a fairly wide choice of positions that you may decide you want to own.

MARGIN NOTES

OLYMPIC DIFFERENTIATION

A friend finally explained just how far differentiation can go, the Winter Olympics were on at the time so:

- Ski Freestyle
- Ski Cross Country
- Ski Combined
- Ski Nordic Combined
- Ski Alpine
- Ski Jumping
- Biathlon
- Ice Hockey
- Figure Skating
- Speed Skating
- Short Track
- Snowboard Freestyle
- Snowboard Alpine
- Luge
- Curling
- Bobsleigh
- Skeleton

are, as he carefully explained, all just 'sliding' games!

■ Checking for incumbents

Assume that you have identified one or two positions that you feel could be valuable, could hold some attraction for your target customers and for which you may be able to develop offerings; think first and check for incumbents. Someone may already be sitting pretty in the position you are coveting. As you know, I am always wary about trying to teach grandma to suck eggs but there are one or two points you might like to bear in mind:

- Is there an incumbent?
  - You may, or may not see an incumbent, but we are not as interested in your opinion as that of your target customers.
  - You need to find out whether your customers believe that there is anybody holding this position – and how well they are holding it.
- Is the position empty?
  - If so, why?
  - Is there a good reason why the position is empty?
  - For example, is there any potential business there?
- Does the target position hold any value for your customers?
  - You are going to have to ask them.
  - Would your customers perceive any additional value in a product or service offering specially directed at the user in your particular category?
  - If they would, would they be willing to pay extra money for it?
- Would an offer from your organisation be credible?
  - If all the answers so far are positive don't forget to ask this one, would the target customers believe an offering in this position if it came from your organisation?
  - If the answer is yes you could be seriously cooking, if the answer is no you could still own and develop a solution for this position but you may need to do it under a separate brand.
- Does the position integrate or contradict our segmentation solution?
  - You will remember back to the amount of work and effort we put in to looking at market segments and coming to an understanding of:
    - which segments we need to target and
    - which segments we should leave to the competition
  - Does the ideal position also fit the needs of your target segment customers exclusively, is there some degree of potential overlap, or (least positive of all) does the position only appeal strongly to customers in non-targeted segments?

MARGIN NOTES

Questions like these can make a section look problematic, but remember these are only simple questions and while we use the words 'market research' it doesn't mean you have to put everything on hold for two years while you do an in-depth analysis of every single thing the customer wants, needs or has ever dreamed about. We are talking about simple, straightforward exploratory research to identify opportunities in markets. While a few weeks may be needed to do this type of work it is far better than continuing to guess.

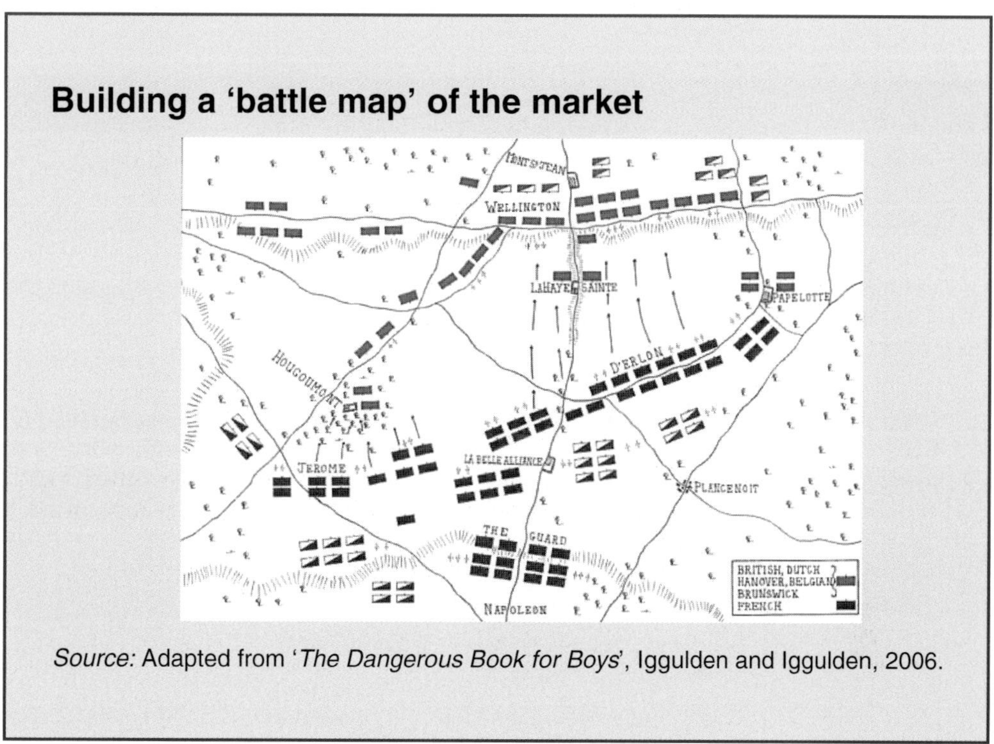

Source: Adapted from '*The Dangerous Book for Boys*', Iggulden and Iggulden, 2006.

■ Building a 'Battle Map' of your market place

Working to identify the different market positions that you and other organisations hold is like building a 3D relief map of the marketplace. Each market position is like a 'high point', 'hill' or defensive position from which the owner gains a strategic advantage.

Finding out who owns which strategic offensive or defensive position, how well they hold the position, what parts of the map (market) they control from their vantage point and how easy or difficult it might be to unseat them is key information that the General (you!) needs *before* committing troops and resources to win market share.

Remember, all but the most developed markets are still forming their strategic positions. It is like looking at the marketplace and seeing a battle map shrouded in fog. What you and the competition can't yet see is hiding away in the customer's subconscious. Unlock the knowledge and you might find that it is more profitable to start building defences around overlooked positions that will be big and profitable tomorrow rather than fighting for positions that are visibly profitable today.

The FAQs are:

4 Positioning and Branding		
4.2 What market positions exist?		
4.2.1	What market positions does the target market deem credible?	Marketing as we (ought to) know is about perceptions rather than fact or reality. In terms of market positions it is always important to start the search with your target customers (and maybe prospects) and to look at uncovering positions that *they* believe to be credible. And for which they are willing to pay some form of premium price.
4.2.2	What positions have 'value' to target customers?	Leading from the previous question, this is slightly more detailed but even more important. Trying to understand the potential value within a position is difficult, especially if nobody has yet established their brand as the owner of this position then the customers will find it quite difficult to understand what a Ryan Air or a Stella Artois offer actually looks like. Nevertheless, we need to grasp some idea of value and the level of premium price the customer would be willing to pay for this particular value added position. This is similar to the question of assessing the value of a market segment (see Chapter 7).
4.2.3	Are the positions held within, or across segments?	In the past, I have always found a strong correlation between credible market positions and membership of particular segments – in any market or category. This is not really surprising given that most proper market segmentation ideas are based on grouping customers with common or similar needs, wants and aspirations rather than just common descriptors. Having said that, the correlation is rarely perfect and there is usually some degree of overlap. For example, people who aspire to a certain added value may not *all* fall within the target market segment that we have developed and identified. Positions that fall primarily (or exclusively) within a target segment are obviously better since you can focus your activities and your communications on a known and understood group of people and you need not be unduly worried about competition from outside the

		segment. When a position is credible across two or three segments then the competitive situation is slightly more complicated.
4.2.4	What positions do the competitors hold?	If you have correctly identified your competition (as in Chapter 5) you will be dealing with a mixture of direct industry competitors as well as substitute competition from other industries. These competitors may or may not see the same market positions, depending on the level of customer insight that they have been able to gather, but you need to understand who currently 'owns' which position – in the customer's mind. Remember, owning a position of the biggest, the best, the cleanest, the fastest, etc. is *only* about the customer's perception of things. I have come across situations in the past where competitive organisations didn't even know they owned a particular market position because they never asked the customer.
4.2.5	How strongly do the competitors hold their positions?	This is important because it will give you some idea of the level of competition which you could be facing as you encroach on these or adjacent positions. We have said this before and we will say it again – competition is sometimes good and sometimes bad but if it does nothing else, it *always* reduces profits. The more competition you face in a particular market position will definitely affect the amount of profit which you (and the competitor) can extract from the position. This being said, it doesn't mean that you shouldn't go head to head, it doesn't mean that just because an organisation or a collection of brands have owned the market position for decades that their time is now not over and the market is ready for the pretender to take the throne – but it does mean that you need to think and assess how much the competition is going to cost you before you get into a fight.
4.2.6	Are there 'empty' or latent positions, not currently held by anyone?	Because a particular market position is empty or vacant could mean that the competitive response will be less (and therefore the drain on your profits will be less as well). It could also mean that there is no real value to be had in achieving the position or positions that are vacant because companies and/or brands owning adjacent positions wish them to remain so. In any event you are well advised to look before you leap into action.
4.2.7	How should we evaluate/ prioritise these existing positions?	At the very least you need to have some idea of how credible and valuable these market positions appear to be. How much additional value (premium prices or margins) could you extract from these new market positions minus the cost of competitive response? Assessing all the potentials against this will give you the best idea of the best and worst opportunities for your organisation.

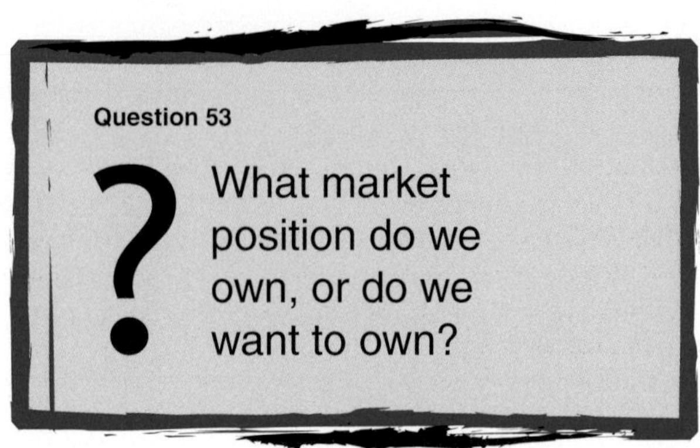

Question 53
?
What market position do we own, or do we want to own?

First, find out where you are

MARGIN NOTES

Unless your organisation is a new entrant to this market, you have already been operating for a number of years (perhaps as a product-push rather than a customer-pull organisation) and you will probably have achieved some level of reputation and position already in (your customer's mind) the market. Find out what position you already have.

Your customers will tell you this – if you ask them properly. While you are talking to them you should also find out how strongly the position(s) are held in the customers' mind and roughly how much value they ascribe to the position or positions which you appear to own.

If you like what you hear (some organisations do) then your marketing activity for the next few years is decided – driving to establish your ownership of the position and the enhancement of the value of the position in the minds of your targeted customers and prospects.

If you don't like the answer you get, then you will have to change something. Ask yourself:

- What position would you like to hold in the customer's mind?
- What is the value of holding this ideal market position compared to holding the existing (or improved existing) position?
- Is it worth changing position?
- If so, how are you going to do it? You must have a reasonable idea about which position you are going to drive to own over the next three, five or ten years, it is a lengthy and expensive process, one you really don't want to get wrong.

A word on the rules

Reis and Trout have a number of pointers for you. The rules of the game are simple, but too often ignored (with devastating consequences):

- There are a number of positioning 'traps'.
  - Two companies cannot own the same word in the customer's mind.
  - You have to give up something in order to get something – you cannot be 'unique' and 'all-things-to-all-men' at the same time.
  - Marketing is not a battle of products it is a battle of perceptions – focus on what the product/service *does*, not what it *is*.
  - Positioning from the company's viewpoint, not the customer's, will not work.
  - If it doesn't relate to the customers' life it will be rejected.
- If you can't be first in a category, set up a new category to be first in.
  - 'First' sticks in customers' mind (although this isn't necessarily the well known 'first mover advantage'), this is the first offer the customer hears.
  - Once the 'first' has gone, 'second' really is the first-among-the-losers and has much less value.
  - But 'first' depends on the category. For instance, IBM might have been first in the 'computer' category, but its power got chipped away by the arrival, not of 'seconds', but by new 'firsts' such as first in mini-computers, first in PCs, first in laptops, first in hand-helds, first in educational computers, first in …
  - More aware readers will have spotted *market segmentation* there in the discussion, and not for the last time.
- The technology trap.
  - Too important to be listed as just another 'trap', the great technological leap forward will fail if it doesn't relate to the customer's life and needs.
- If you can't re-position yourself, you can re-position the competition.
  - If there seems to be nowhere to go, you can start working on the competition.
  - Coca-Cola successfully re-positioned Virgin from 'giant-killer' to 'cheap substitute' when it tried to take Coke on in the beverages business.
  - Bottled water had to re-position wine, beer and tap water to achieve its position in the UK market.

MARGIN NOTES

Future positions

All markets develop, grow and evolve and market positions do the same. It may be that your assessment of the market is that new and potentially more exciting positions will start to make an appearance in the not too distant future.

- Some examples of where this has happened in the recent past might include:
  - Low cost airlines
  - Video mobile phones
  - Superglue
  - Organic food
  - Organic clothing
  - Fair-trade
  - Internet retailing
  - Four-wheel drive/sports utility vehicles (4WD/AWD/SUV)
  - Digital photography
  - High definition TV and DVD
  - Farmers markets
  - Electric/green vehicles
  - MP3 players
  - Mobile Internet (PDAs, WiFi, WiMax, etc.)
  - Internet computing/web services
  - Social networking
  - Green/renewable energy
  - Sustainable.

MARGIN NOTES

You can probably see the obvious ones that I have deliberately missed off the list – I thought so. But beware, there are more examples (no, I don't know them all) of product and services that did not make a mark because the customers rejected them. Any marketing book will tell you that far more products and services are launched than are successful. The same goes for market positions.

In each of the cases above there is a positioning issue at stake as well as potentially major changes in technology or product life cycle. In some instances incumbents have re-positioned quite successfully to own new positions as well as old positions (for example, Nokia in mobile handsets) and in other markets the incumbents appear to have been completely shocked by the appearance of a new position (for example, airlines) and in other markets the result is more 50-50 with positions being dominated partially by incumbents and partially by new players (digital cameras).

The ability to forecast the appearance of a new position arising in the marketplace is only half the battle. More often than not, the winner is the one who is able to time the run to own a position correctly. Too early and nobody understands the position they are trying to create, too late and somebody is there already.

The FAQs are:

<table>
<tr><th colspan="3">4 Positioning and Branding</th></tr>
<tr><th colspan="3">4.3 What market position do we own, or do we want to own?</th></tr>
<tr><td>4.3.1</td><td>What position(s) do we already hold?</td><td>Focus market research (qual as well as quant is preferable here) to talk to existing prospects, customers and competitors' customers about their perception of your company and your offering and (possibly) your brands. Also their understanding of the differentiation or uniqueness of your offering as well as the market position it is most closely related to.</td></tr>
<tr><td>4.3.2</td><td>How strongly are those positions held in the customers' minds?</td><td>Do you own these positions because you are clearly and demonstrably unique in this regard and promise and deliver benefits that no other player is deemed capable of offering? Or do you 'own' this position in a more passive sense in that you don't do anything particularly special but neither does anybody else?
Naturally the stronger that your positions are held in the customer's mind at the moment:
• The more value that position will currently have
• The easier it may be to develop, entrench and make that position defensible and
• The more difficult it might be to move from that to another position.</td></tr>
<tr><td>4.3.3</td><td>Are our positions held within, or across segments?</td><td>This issue has risen before – if there is a disparity between the market positions and market segments it may lead to confusing marketing and overlapping communications and distribution. The stronger the correlation between your target market positions and the target market segments the better for all of your plans.</td></tr>
<tr><td>4.3.4</td><td>What position(s) do we want to hold in the future?</td><td>It may be that the view from your analysis is that your current position is not the one you want to hold. This can happen for a number of reasons:
• Organisations who are looking at market position for the first time (maybe your organisation is maturing and starting to move from product-push to customer-pull practices) might think that there is more long-term mileage in a position other than the one that they have owned up to now – albeit unwittingly.
• Organisations who assess their market positions on a more regular basis find that market positions ebb and flow and change with changes in customer perceived needs and sometimes even fashion. It might be that, as part of a regular audit, the organisation decides that some of its current market positions don't hold enough long-term growth potential and they need to re-position their offering for more profitable growth in the future.
In either event the activity is neither cheap nor fast and needs to be planned quite carefully so as not to confuse customers any more than is necessary.</td></tr>
</table>

4.3.5	What positions will come 'available' in the future?	Life, and markets, move on. Nothing stands still and you need to evolve, at least in line with the market, if you are not to be left behind. Market positions too, need to evolve and sometimes a position loses its appeal completely. In this case, we need to look to the future. But, the future must be assessed in customer, not in industry terms. Future positions are not always easy to spot, but can be 'suggested' to customers – market research is a powerful tool. In any event, future positions will be found more easily in a market defined business.
4.3.6	What do we have to do to own the position in the customers' mind?	Again your customer will tell you; it differs from market to market, category to category and position to position. It is all about credibility and the customer will tell you more or less what you have to do in order to be the credible owner of your target position.
4.3.7	How can we calculate the financial value of holding the position?	The answer here is 'with difficulty' until you have actually created the offering and real customers have parted with real money. Up to that point we are left with the always inferior market research insight that might help us to understand: ● How many people would be attracted by this position and would want to buy from a company with this offer. ● What value they would give this position in terms of additional premium price they would be willing to pay. ● How often/frequently they will be expected to purchase. ● The likely competitive response to our attempt to own this position and the costs of such competitive responsive activity.

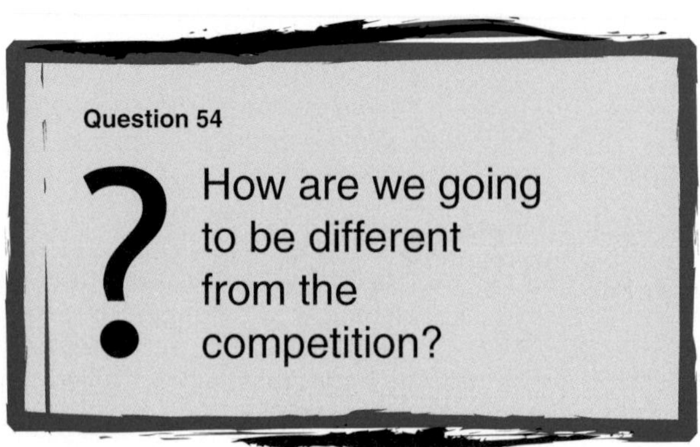

Question 54
?
How are we going to be different from the competition?

This is the point at which you start to align market position with differentiation.

What we are going to do now is to try and turn the target market position (the word or concept that we want to own in the customer's mind), into a clear and distinct set of differences that will mark us out from the competition.

■ Different is not an option: it is a 'must be'

We have already seen the additional value (this is extra money you can add to the bottom line) that comes from being different rather than just being the same (or as close to the same as the customer can't see the difference) as the competition. In case you skipped that part (or were planning to go back) we established that differentiation was about *three times* more effective than cost advantage in delivering long-term value to shareholders.

So let us hope that we can settle the question about whether we should be different or not once and for all. There is no money at all to be had in being the same as everyone else and all the profit you need is to be found in differentiation. Levitt ('Differentiation – of Anything', *The Marketing Imagination, Free Press*, 1986) had it right years ago when he said: 'There is no such thing as a commodity. All goods and services can be differentiated and usually are. Though the usual presumption is that this is true more of consumer goods than of industrial goods and services, the opposite is the actual case. The only exception to this proposition is in the minds of people who profess that exception.'

Maybe it is a strange trait of the human race that we have to prove everything for ourselves before we accept an obvious, if minority, idea. Maybe we need the pain before we can learn the right route to take. In any event, we need to know which direction to take …

■ How are *you* going to be different?

If I really have got you thinking about *how* to be different rather than *whether* to be different, the question is – How are you going to be different from the competition?

Yet again (no, I never did promise originality) the answer is not going to be found inside your organisation, or its history but is going to be found

MARGIN NOTES

in the market, in the minds and hearts of your today's customers and tomorrow's prospects.

Which differences are best?

1.	Which market segment(s) are you targeting?	Different people want/value different things.
2.	Where does your customer or prospect perceive the most value?	Always work with the customers. Aim to target the greatest store of market value.
3.	Where is most of your competition concentrated?	Look for gaps in the marketplace and exploit them. Only attack competitors'positions if there is no alternative.
4.	Where is your offer most/least credible?	Relate to perceived strengths and weaknesses. Aim for credible areas first.
5.	Where is the differentiation easiest for your company to maintain?	Profit is key and differentiation can be expensive to maintain over time.
6.	Where is the differentiation easiest for your company to protect?	Do not create a position for others to steal. Balance cost and costs against defensibility.
7.	Where are the opportunities that fall outside your technical/scientific expertise but within your 'market' definition?	You will only find the opportunities that you look for – if you look in the 'industry'rather than the 'market'area you may not find the best differentiation opportunities.

You should be asking yourself a few key questions:

- Which market segment(s) are you targeting?
  - The 'mass market' is dead – it is now a thing of mystery and folklore – you should not be attempting to market to it.
  - Different customers want different things for themselves and their lives; they can see very different value in the same offering.
  - Attempting to differentiate an offering so that everybody is attracted to it can only place you at the centre, by definition, the position that everyone else differentiates away from – cruel isn't it?

 - To be successful you need to move from away from 'same' towards 'different' and aspire to 'unique'. The further you get away from 'same' the more value you add to the offer, but the more potential prospects you alienate because they don't value the differentiation. You know this is going to happen so choose your target segment(s) with care and make sure you know what they value – and what they don't.

- Where does your customer and prospect perceive the most value?
  - It is important, that from all the possible ways that you could differentiate your offer, you choose the ways that actively support the needs of the market segment and the market position that you wish to own. For example, a food company wishing to own the 'pure or purist' position in its category would be unlikely to differentiate itself by adding more chemicals or preservatives than anybody else.
  - Before you start to reinvest in differentiation according to particular features and benefits that you 'just know' are the right ones for your market, check! Many managers are disadvantaged by knowing (technically) more than their customers about what the product or service is and how it works, sometimes leading to the addition of features that the customer just doesn't believe supports the market position or adds any value.
  - Always work with the customers. Aim to target the greatest store of market value with the fewest features.

- Where is most of your competition concentrated?
  - Simple strategy is called for here – and some intuitive thinking.
  - First, establish the criteria by which companies have been designated 'competitors'. If they are just the 'industry competitors' (of the Porter Five-Forces diagram) then you are missing *big* opportunities and *bigger* threats. Assess the marketplace again and identify the real competition (see Chapter 2).
  - Second, identify where (around which market positions or points of differentiation) your competitors are concentrated.
  - Third, take a view (supported by insight of course) on whether the perceived customer value is really where the competition is concentrated – or whether the competition is playing that favourite game of follow-the-lemming.
  - Look for gaps in the marketplace and exploit them. Only attack competitors' positions directly if there is no alternative.

- Where is your offer most/least credible?
  - Unless you are coming to the market for the very first time, you will have a track record, a history and many customers may already have experience of your offer. It is important, when you

MARGIN NOTES

  differentiate, to make sure that you don't add aspects that the market simply doesn't believe.
  - Customers and prospects may find it difficult to believe some claims, not necessarily because they are technically too difficult for you to achieve, but simply because (for whatever reason) they just don't believe that you have the ability to carry through on the promise that you are making. Test and retest before you launch rather than making a fool of yourselves.
  - Relate the differentiation to your *perceived* strengths and weaknesses. Always aim for credible areas first.

- Where is the differentiation easiest for your company to maintain?
  - Markets (made up of customers needs and perceived value) tend to change over time. Some markets move fast and others more slowly. No markets stand still.
  - The choice of differentiation is not just a question of 'what is available?' or 'what should we do?' The question should be about owning the selected position over a number of years. Rapidly changing differentiations/positions are more difficult to win and cost more resource to retain – don't move unless you are sure that you will be able to 'keep up the payments'.

MARGIN NOTES

- Where is the differentiation easiest for your company to protect?
  - There is simply no point in spending money to differentiate your offer if the competition can copy what you have done in a matter of weeks. Or if you are in the fashion industry and you show your product on the Paris fashion catwalks then it can be copied before you even launch your product.
  - When it comes down to the ability to copy don't assume that just because a differentiation is complicated or scientific or technical it can't be copied. Today this is not the barrier that it used to be. Of course, if you differentiate in ways that can be protected legally (patents, copyright or more importantly branding) then you stand a better chance of making some market impact – and profiting from it.

- Where are the opportunities that fall outside your technical/scientific expertise but within your 'market' definition?
  - If you limit yourself to the technical or scientific product aspects of your offer and consider only potential differentiations that you are (technically) able to create and deliver, you will expose yourself to technological leapfrog (copying) as well as missing more profitable opportunities.

Looking inside (just this once I promise) at the organisation, Grant ('*Contemporary Strategy Analysis*', Blackwell, 2005) suggests that successful positioning (differentiation) is about matching customers' demand for difference with the organisation's capacity to supply differentiation:

Matching customers with the organisation

Demand side	Supply side
• Reason for purchase • Motivation for purchase • Choice criteria used • Perception of available offerings • Preferences • Perceptions of different product or service attributes • Price/value perceptions	• Product features • Product performance • Complementary services (credit, delivery, etc.) • Intensity of marketing activities (advertisement spend, etc.) • Technology embedded in design and manufacture • Quality of purchased inputs • Processes influencing conduct of each activity (quality control, service procedures, etc.) • Skill and experience of employees • Location (with retail and service outlets, etc.) • Degree of vertical integration (and process control)

Source: Grant, '*Contemporary Strategy Analysis*', Blackwell, 2005.

The best approach here is to work through the lists, first on the 'demand side' and then on the 'supply side' and look for opportunities that:

- Are different from the competition
- Are valued by the target customers
- Are aligned with the position you want to own.

MANOEUVRING FOR POSITION

Take a lesson from the consumer area. At the end of 2006, Men's Skincare was starting to establish itself as a profitable category in UK supermarkets. As 'new' category, positions were still being fought over and the combatants included:

- *Adidas*: from footwear and sports
- *Ben Sherman*: from the rejuvenated men's clothing brand from the 1960s

- *Lambretta*: from the men's clothing range drawing from the brand of Italian scooters of the 1960s
- *Nivea for Men*: men's range from the female skincare company
- *L'Oreal men expert*: men's range from the female cosmetics products
- *Gillette*: from men's shaving products company
- *Sure*: from Unilever's unisex deodorant range
- *Sanex*: from the bath and shower products range.

Who will win is (still) anybody's guess, but none of them is letting the past, technical aspects of the brand, stop positioning in a new category where there are profits to be made.

The FAQs are:

4 Positioning and Branding		
4.4 How are we going to be different from the competition?		
4.4.1	What differentiation is required by the target market position?	Always try to understand the deepest needs of your target segment and what the market position (the word or concept you want to own in their minds) requires that you do. Did you follow that, it is not easy. The market (your customers) will tell you, if you ask them, what you will have to do, and how you will need to be different if you are to own the position. Remember, the position only exists in the customers' heads, you have to look there to understand it. It is important that you choose differentiators that support this position – and that don't detract from it.
4.4.2	Where is your brand or offering most and least credible?	Never forget that perception *is* marketing reality. Whatever people in the organisation or the people who make the product or service may believe to be the unvarnished 'truth', what the customer believes is always going to be more important because what they believe will drive how they behave. The 'truth' is that if your organisation is technically competent to deliver a particular differentiation but the market doesn't believe it – they will not buy – it will not be successful. If on the other hand, you have no particular expertise in creating a given differentiation and you have to buy expertise in from the outside – but the marketplace believes that you would understand this differentiation – they will buy and it will be successful. Don't cave into the logic pedlars; this is an emotional situation – for everyone.

4.4.3	Where is the differentiation easier to protect and maintain?	There is little point in investing in differentiation, the objective of which is to be able to draw you away from the pack, if everyone in the pack then instantly adopts your differentiation and brings you back into line again. You need to look for differentiators that either can't or won't be copied by the competition. It can't be copied if you have a reasonable brand to protect you or if you have patents or other legal protection. They won't copy the differentiation if they don't understand why you are using it. This can often be the case if you have identified differentiation from a customer perspective rather than a technical one; competitors may not be that far behind in their capability but may be looking for technical differentiators rather than customer ones.
4.4.4	Where is the most competition concentrated?	As always, your problem is a difficult one. Everyone in your organisation will be able to see market potential, especially when every type of company is trying to stake a claim. But like sharks circling a shoal of fish, this may not be the healthiest part of the sea to dive into. Competition is fun but it does tend to depress profits. You might find more profits are to be extracted in areas where there are less fish, but also less sharks. For example, as soon as EasyJet and Ryanair started to demonstrate the viability of low cost airlines (in fact their service was based on services already existing in the US) then all of a sudden every man and his dog wants to be part of the action. British Airways starts Go and later sells it when it realises it just can't run a low cost offer. The slightly more creative marketer might decide that there is a range of possibilities which exist between the low cost airlines at one end and the over-priced flag carriers at the other and search for different market positions and use different differentiators to make their case. In late 2006, a number of niche players are just starting to make an appearance.
4.4.5	What if the potential differentiation comes from outside our existing 'technical' or product expertise?	Well there is no reason not to use it. Yes, you will be assailed by (internal) complaints and forecasts of doom and destruction by all those people who espouse the 'push mentality' – but this is no reason to hold back. Remember (I am now starting to lose track of how many times I have said this) customer perceptions are more important to your organisation than technical or scientific reality. If the customers require you 'flex' your offer into adjacent technologies, and they receive more customer value from this, then go ahead. Remember, its not the technology they are buying but what they believe it can do for them – if the same technology has greater value if it comes from you, you can't lose.
4.4.6	How can we differentiate (and add value) through partnerships?	Don't forget (although more will become apparent when you read Chapter 11 (Offerings) ultimate customer satisfaction is produced by much more than the simple product or service on its own. Routes to market including distributors, retailers or other forms of intermediaries can not only add significant value they can also help you differentiate your offer from competitors.

		A good historical example (for the more mature reader) involves the re-positioning of potato crisps from 'drinks ancillary' to 'snack'. This was achieved primarily by moving the distribution from public houses and off-licences to petrol service stations. A slightly more modern example would include Dell which used the Internet and its direct distribution channels to reinforce the idea that it is a lower cost producer than competitors such as IBM and HP. It remains to be seen whether either Sony or Ericsson gain from their association in the mobile telephony area. You can use intermediaries to support and enhance the differentiation. In partnership with your customers, choose them carefully.
4.4.7	Can the organisation *deliver* a truly differentiated offering?	We will cover this in more detail in Chapter 10, the marketing organisation. Here the most important thing to recognise is the ability of your organisation to deliver the differentiated offer – in a way that your customers find credible. If people in your business believe that the differentiator is in fact no more than a 'fluffy sugar coating' over a standard offer, their attitude will convey this message only too clearly. Even worse, promising a real differentiation promises real customer value – if you can't deliver on the promise your customers will disappear for ever. The organisation really is the 'weakest link' in the chain and if you are convinced the organisation won't or can't deliver the differentiation you are strongly advised to look for a differentiation that the organisation can deliver.

Branding is one of the most important missing links between corporate strategy and maketing tactics. Branding is probably the greatest store of value open to the organisation today.

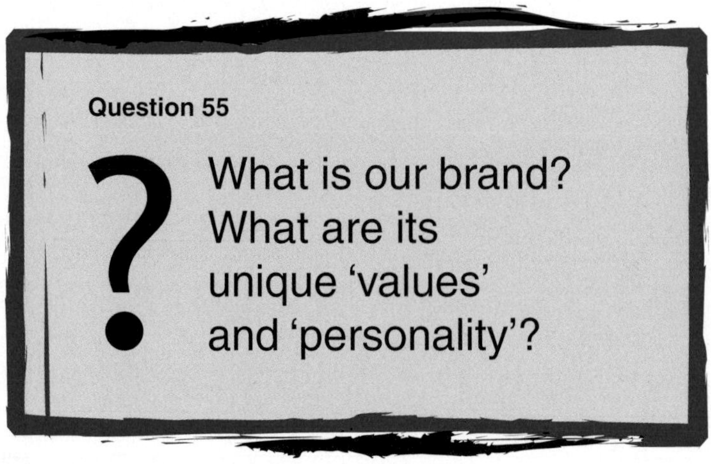

Question 55
?
What is our brand?
What are its
unique 'values'
and 'personality'?

Books and articles (thick and thin) are written every year on the 'alchemy' of branding – many using words and concepts that make no sense to anyone but the author. Feel free to buy the books and hone your skills – this is an area where you can make serious money if you do it right. For most of us though, we only need to know enough to be competent in the area and not make costly mistakes. Here is what you need to know.

■ What is a brand?

A brand is described properly as *a set of consistent meanings which exist in addition to the product or service* offering. This means that a brand is not the same as a product or service. Branding is something that exists over and above the physical product or service. This also means (get ready for this) that doing more and more work on the product or service, won't necessarily enhance the brand – working on what your customers' believe the brand *promises* them will.

MARGIN NOTES

So we can see that a brand is:

- A set of *beliefs and feelings existing* in the customers' minds (rather than in the fabric or workings of the product or service).
  - These convince customers that they will receive certain *specific benefits* from using the brand rather than a competing offer.

Where do these beliefs and feelings come from? We believe (no, we don't 'know', we're dealing with people here, not products) that they are derived from a complex of:

- Actual experience of the product/service.
  - Using, testing and living with the product or service will certainly communicate what it does and how it is different or unique from other offerings.
  - Of course, you might want to communicate to customers as well and give them an idea of what differences to look out for.
- Word-of-mouth communication
  - Talking to others and hearing what their experiences were.
  - We take word of mouth to include telephone and Internet communications too.
- Advertising and communications history
  - And what promises you have been making.
  - The general rule is, under-promising and over-delivering is better than over-promising and under-delivering.
- What the brand owners do more than what they say
  - Remember the sad stories of Barclays and South Africa, Nike and child labour, Nestle and baby formula in Africa, Mercedes and the 'elk test', the list goes on.

  - How the brand owner behaves is becoming more and more important to the success of a brand in more cynical times.
- The role of the brand in our lives and purchasing behaviour
  - The big one.
  - Forget what the brand *is*; understand what the brand does for the customer.
  - Every successful brand has a role in the customer's life (things without a role are peripheral and are just products, services, stuff, who cares …). Find the role, understand its importance, and design your brand to fit the role – easy!

Importantly, *a brand is not the same as a name*. Just putting a name on a product (even as good as my snappily named printer the '*7301*') does not automatically confer a set of consistent meanings, beliefs and feelings to a standard (undifferentiated) product or service. No really. Just because you know all about your product or service, and could pick it out of a crowd at a hundred paces does not mean the customer can or wants to.

MARGIN NOTES

Don't continue deluding yourself; ask the customers what they see in the offer. The sooner you find out whether you have a brand or just a name the sooner you can start the marketing job proper.

B2B has brands too		
3M	Hewlett Packard	Pfizer
Accenture	IBM	Pratt & Whitney engines
BAE systems	Intel	PriceWaterhouseCoopers
Boeing	International Harvester	Reuters
Caterpillar	JCB	Rolls-Royce engines
Chubb security	Komatsu	SAP
Cisco	Lloyds of London	Salamander Grills
Dell	Merrill Lynch	Sikorsky helicopters
DHL express	McKinsey	Smith Kline
GE	Oracle	Sun Microsystems
Group 4 Securicor	Otis Elevators	Tetra packaging
Heidelberg printers	Perkins engines	TNT delivery

■ Different types of brand

Unless you have a range or portfolio of brands you probably won't need to worry about this. But, if you have more than one brand in your care – or more than one segment to market to – and you really don't want confused customers, then you need to follow this section carefully.

There are a number ways to arrange the 'portfolio' (a big word if you only have two brands, but bear with me). It is important because we need to make sure that the story is as simple as possible *for the customer*. You remember I am sure that we need to make it simple, not because the customer is stupid, but because they have a busy life to lead and no time to invest in understanding subtle differences. Your options are:

- Monolithic brands
  - Here we arrange all (both) the brands under a common monolithic name. Examples would be Siemens, BT and British Airways.
  - A monolithic approach then conveys a guarantee of overall corporate excellence (or failure) and differentiation.
    - Just think what guarantees are promised by monolithic brands such as IBM, Dell, Google, Microsoft, Lidl, Marks & Spencer, DHL, Parcelforce, Amazon and Tesco. This is a 'swings and roundabouts' game;
  - Advantages:
    - Any investment in communications or research benefits all the products/services under the common banner.
  - Disadvantages:
    - A failure in one area can have effects in all other areas with the same name. Makes segmented marketing quite difficult because works on a standardised approach.

- Umbrella brands
  - Are different from Monolithic brands in that there is more focus on the individual brand's meaning and specific promise but the customer knows that it exists within a broader range and the parent brand exists as an overall quality endorser.
  - Examples would include Dulux paints, Heinz, Airbus, Virgin and Ford.
  - Advantages:
    - This approach is popular because it allows a degree of variability in the promises but also permits some economies of scale as investment in communications and distribution can be spread.
    - Can be a useful way of addressing more than one segment if not too different.
  - Disadvantages:
    - It can limit the degree of individuality you can create in the brands, for example, it doesn't help working in segments that are very different, only those that are more common.

MARGIN NOTES

- Single line brands
  - Are where each brand is a stand-alone offering and no connection or lineage is provided.
  - The usual example here is Van den Berghs (who they??) who produce a wide range of edible oils/yellow fats (margarine to you and me) that you probably have heard of – they own all these brands – Flora, Stork, Echo, Krona, Outline, Olivio, ICBINB, Becel, Blue Band, Rama, Country Crock, Doriana, Family, Delma and many more.
  - Advantages:
    - This allows the brand to provide maximum focus in its meaning.
    - It is not a cheap approach but you create a lot of separate brand value and a failure in one brand does not affect any other.
    - The best way of addressing many segments – each segment gets its own, unique offer.
  - Disadvantages:
    - It is expensive, especially with more than one brand to worry about.

MARGIN NOTES

- Brands and sub-brands
  - This approach rather falls in between the two previous approaches, Umbrella and Single line.
  - The 'parent' brand can have different relationships with its sub-brands, some parents are 'public' parents (Heinz and WeightWatchers) while others are less obvious (Toyota and Lexus).
  - Sub-branding works best when the parent brand has a broad meaning and can encompass a wide range of 'offspring' without negative effects on its own brand.
  - Advantages:
    - Allows the sub brand to develop its own life while creating some 'back office' economies of scale. It can be sold at a later date if required.
    - Can be a useful way of addressing different segments.
  - Disadvantages:
    - Only limited economies of scale in market investment.

- Brand 'halos'
  - Brand 'halos' describe a special 'attribute' or 'promise' that has a meaning that can be used across the entire brand range to enhance offerings. Classic examples who really started the trend are Saab *Turbo* and Audi *Quattro*.
  - Advantages:
    - Enhancing every offering attached to the halo can improve differentiation, penetration and profits.
  - Disadvantages:
    - If you haven't got it, you haven't got it. Lots of companies have tried to emulate the Saab/Audi success but haven't done quite so well.

- Brand portfolios
  - Where the organisation owns and markets an interlocking range of separate brands, which together give reach to all or most parts of the marketplace.
  - Classical examples include:
    - VAG with VW, Audi, Skoda, Seat, Bentley, Lamborghini, Bugatti
    - Royal Bank of Scotland with RBS, Coutts & Co, Child & Co, NatWest Bank, Isle of Man Bank, Ulster Bank and Direct Line Insurance.
  - Often the result of consolidation as a sector moves from rapid growth to maturity stages of the life cycle, the acquiring organisation can decide whether to bring all the acquired companies into the main brand – or it can keep the acquired brands and use them to position in different segments.
  - However, treading the line between 'real' differences between the brands and just 'packaging' differences can be difficult – especially with knowledgeable customers.
  - Advantages:
    - If organised properly, can create enormous economies of scale in production and distribution (but not necessarily in marketing).
    - Can deliver routes to most segments with different offerings and deeper penetration than with more shallow offerings.
  - Disadvantages:
    - Can be expensive, depending on how different the needs of the segments and how much adaptation is required.
    - Can be tricky stopping the organisation not driving for the low-cost routes automatically and destroying any difference between the brands – the customer will notice and margins will suffer.

- Ingredient brands
  - Many brands are successful, unique and never purchased on their own.
  - An ingredient brand exists only as a part of another brand or offering. Examples would include: Intel, Goretex, Nutrasweet, Lycra, Teflon, Triplex and Rolls-Royce (aero engines).
  - Consider the role and power of these important brands and how they affect the perception, sales and margins of the brands that they are in.
  - Advantages:
    - Good way for B2B brands to get exposure in other and even B2C markets.
    - Helps fight constant price pressure from powerful customers who probably buy in large volumes.
    - Low costs of distribution.
  - Disadvantages:
    - Still requires large investment.

MARGIN NOTES

- May not make your customers very happy as you stretch beyond them to create a brand franchise with their customers.
- If you can live with the extra business and unhappy immediate customers who will look for ways of avoiding having to buy your ingredient if they can get away with it, you will be fine.
- Difficult concept for many B2B cultures to understand.

Franchising has brands too		
Amtrak Express Parcels Limited	Interlink Express Parcels Ltd	Pronuptia Bridal and Men's Formal Wear
ANC	Kall-Kwik Printing (UK) Ltd	Rosemary Conley Diet and Fitness Clubs
Bang & Olufsen	Kumon Educational UK	Saks Hair and Beauty
Budgens Stores Ltd	McDonald's	Scottish and Newcastle Pub Enterprises
Cash Converters	Nevada Bob UK Ltd	Snack in the Box
Clarks Shoes	Perfect Pizza	Snap-on-Tools
Dairy Crest	Pirtek Europe plc	Subway
Domino's Pizza	Pitman Training Group	TaxAssist Accountants
Drain Doctor Ltd	Post Office Ltd	Thrifty Car Rental
Express Dairies	Prontaprint Ltd	Vision Express

Source: The British Franchise Association, http://www.thefa.org/.

MARGIN NOTES

Why do brands work?

Brands work simply because customers really like them.

- Brands make our decision making easier
  - It was fine all the time that we didn't know just how many products and services were out there to choose from. With the arrival of hypermarkets, supermarkets and the Internet we now know for a fact that there is too much choice.
  - Without brands to guide me, I wouldn't get out of the supermarket inside three hours – and frankly there are better things to do with my life.
  - Brands act as 'shorthand'

  - They help me choose within a category and for specific purposes.
  - If I am looking for a hotel in an unknown European city, I can choose one I have never heard of before (for the excitement) or I can choose among Hilton, Ibis, Sheraton, Formule 1, Holiday Inn, Meridien, Novotel, Intercontinental and Travelodge as well as others – each brand gives me a faster way of understanding what I will get if I buy.
- Brands help me reduce the risk in the purchase;
  - If a box of paperclips are not fit for purpose there is not too much problem, if a new car fails to live up to expectations then I am badly out of pocket. The bigger the purchase, the bigger the risk, and the more we worry. Brands can help us reduce some of the risk (see Chapter 11).
  - In a straightforward re-purchase there is little or no risk. Buying something for the first time is very different and brands that we know can be a guide. For example, buying the first MP3 player, iPod, the leader or Sony where my walkman comes from? Does my regular brand make a good decaffeinated coffee too? Does my preferred car brand do a people carrier for the growing family?
- Brands allow me to buy on 'automatic pilot', especially for everyday purchases
  - With an entire supermarket gondola dedicated to tea and coffee, and another to washing powder, if it wasn't for brands we would have to make a new set of decisions every week!

MARGIN NOTES

- Brands make statements about ourselves to others
  - And to ourselves
  - On a more personal level, brands are public property and when we buy into a brand, everyone else is likely to see. If I drive a Volkswagen, a BMW or a Mercedes it says something about me and the type of person I am.
  - Within certain circles (or CONTEXT©) the same could be said about the food I eat the shops I use, the holidays I take and the clothes I wear.
  - I am what I buy
    - Many people use brands to project their identity and to signal the type of person they are to others, both friends and strangers.
    - In case you think we are getting too carried away with the over-emotional consumer, what do you think the road maintenance companies are doing when they use (branded) Volvo, Caterpillar and JCB diggers and earthmovers beside the busy roads? Or the local printing company that places its least used machine (the Heidelberg) closest to visitor reception?
  - I would like to be what I buy
    - Aspiration is a wonderful thing.
    - It explains why the 1.6 basic model is always one of BMW's highest selling lines.

Brand leadership

There are lots of reasons why everybody wants to be the brand leader, most of them obvious and to do with ego, money and power. So we won't waste time explaining all that. What I do want to do is to show you how there can be *more than one winner* in the leadership game. There are three types of brand leadership:

- The Brand Leader
  - The one that everybody thinks about
  - The biggest in the market or the category
  - The one that makes all the profit
  - The one that spends its days fighting off the young pretenders.
- The Niche Brand Leader
  - Another option is to differentiate away from the brand leader and become leader of a sub-category or niche.
  - Companies such as Porsche, Bang & Olufsen, and Club Med are good examples.
- The Thought Leader
  - The one everybody is talking about.
  - The one that people are watching.
  - The one that people are interested in, even if they haven't tried it yet. BMW has been doing this for years and hold a reputation far above the relatively small numbers of cars produced.

MARGIN NOTES

Who owns who?

FORD	*FIAT*
Ford, Mazda, Volvo, Lincoln (Land Rover & Jaguar sold to Tata in 2008)	Alfa Romeo, Ferrari, Fiat, Iveco, Lancia, Maserati
BMW	*TOYOTA*
Mini, Rolls-Royce	Daihatsu(51%), Lexus
VOLKSWAGEN	*GM*
Audi, Bentley, Bugatti, Lamborghini, Skoda, Seat, Volkswagen	Buick, Cadillac, Chevrolet, GMC, GMDaewoo, Holden, Hummer Oldsmobile, Opel, Pontiac, Saab, Saturn Vauxhall

Note: all subject to change over time.
There was a time when the single brand 'Ford' or Volkswagen' was sufficient to enter, and succeed, in a number of different market segments. No longer.

Brands and segments

Finally, there is a question that the branding books don't often cover; the role of market segmentation in the branding decision. Brand and segmentation cannot be separated, any calculations on brand need to include a deep understanding of the target audience for the brand or all will be for nothing. Let's follow the logic:

- A successful brand:
  - Will be one that is different and has specific promises attached
  - The more specific the offer the more some people will be attracted, and others repelled – the rules of segmentation.

- An unsuccessful brand:
  - Will have a fairly undifferentiated offer
  - An offer that 'sort of' attracts a wide number of people but only slightly – the un-segmented approach.

- The most successful organisations:
  - Will first identify the segments (see Chapter 7) in their market
  - Will prioritise the segments they want to enter or dominate
  - Will design the branded offer required to penetrate the segment(s).

- Failure comes from a number of routes:
  - Planting a brand in any number of segments – and watching it die.
  - Planting a brand in all segments (the 'mass market') – and watching it die.
  - Developing a brand and not knowing where to plant it – and watching it die.
  - Developing a brand from one segment and trying to plant it in another segment – and watching it die.

MARGIN NOTES

A word on brand values and personality

We have spoken (at length I fear) about successful brands and how they must be different. Customers (we will see later) feel they are building a relationship with an important (to them) brand, in much the same way they would build a relationship with another person. This is why so much of the research and theory around branding talks about:

- *Values*: what the brand stands for and

- *Personality*: how it feels to be in a relationship with this almost – person.

MARGIN NOTES

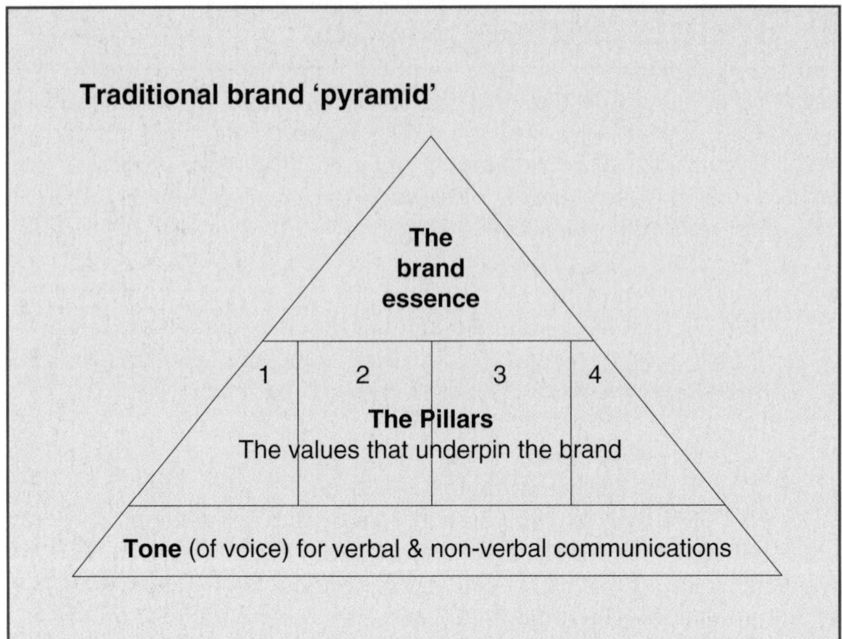

The concept of the traditional 'Brand Pyramid' is well known but too superficial to be a working tool. I have tried to develop this basic idea into a structure that looks more complicated but actually contains all the *decisions* you need to make about your brand – if you want to own more than just a name.

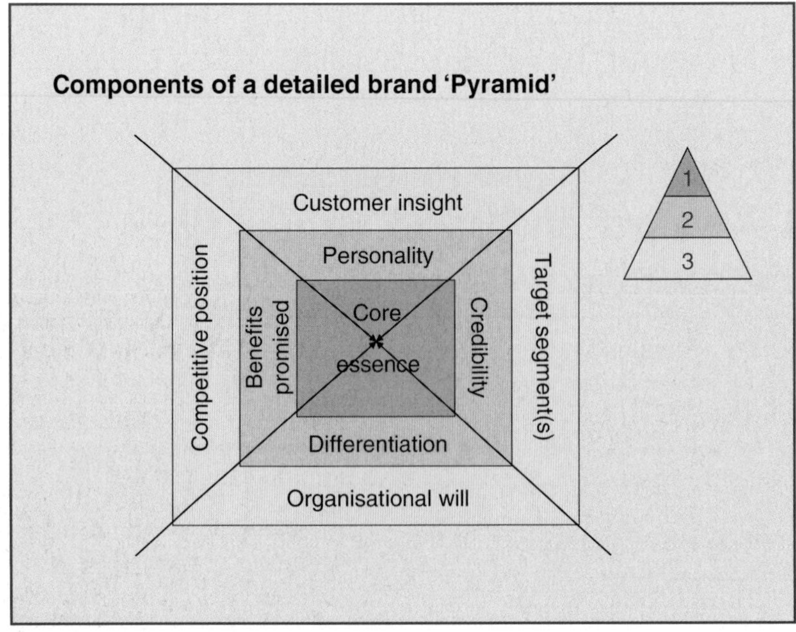

The following is a decisions checklist that you will need to revisit reasonably regularly to keep your brand(s) fresh. If you reach a section you cannot answer, I would hope that, by now, you might at least think about how to acquire the information before you dump the section in frustration:

- Customer insights
  - Exactly how does the brand fit the research?
  - You have carried out some customer research because you know that customers don't buy products or services, they buy what the products and services do for them.
  - While you were there you also found out a little more about how customers would like those jobs done.
  - How will the proposed brand match the needs, wants and motivations you have uncovered?
- Target segment(s)
  - Exactly who is the brand aimed at?
  - From the customer research you analysed the data for groups of customers who wanted the same things.
  - You identified the segments in the target market.
  - Which segment (or two segments, but not too many!) is the brand directed at?
  - Remember, too bland an offer, the less chance the brand has of being unique.
- Competitive position
  - Exactly how will it be better than the competition?
  - Life is competitive and the ultimate game is that the customer needs to prefer your brand over a competing brand.
  - This is not a game of chance though. You need to work out exactly how your brand is better than the others – and tell them.
- Organisational will
  - Does the organisation really want to do this?
  - A bit of a tricky question as we haven't yet been honest about what it is the organisation has to accept, that comes later (see Chapter 10).
  - At this stage we are talking about 100% support from the whole organisation driving the brand in the market and everybody inside the business living the unique brand values at every customer contact. Not an easy task.
  - If the organisation doesn't sign up for this the branding exercise will not succeed. If there is not internal hostility, just lack of awareness, then an internal marketing exercise will be needed.
- Personality
  - What precise traits will drive the relationship?
  - If the brand were a person what would it be like?

MARGIN NOTES

  - What personality traits (good and bad) will this brand have?
  - If the customer were to enter a relationship with this brand what sort of person (friend, confidant, elder sibling, parent, wise counsellor, expert, cruel-to-be-kind, shoulder to cry on, taskmaster, change agent, teacher, mentor, safe haven, guide/Sherpa) be?
  - No, you absolutely can't leave this to those nice but crazy people at the agency; this is your brand – your decision.

- Credibility
  - Will the target (segment) customer really believe this?
  - If not, why not?
  - What proof or evidence do they require?
  - How can you convince them?

- Benefits promised
  - Exactly what is the brand offering?
  - What are the specific benefits that you are promising the customer can get nowhere else but with your brand?
  - Not getting worried now are you?
  - If you can't be this specific then:
    - You don't really have a brand yet or,
    - You don't yet really know what the customer wants.
  - Whatever the reason, this is the level of specificity the customer requires before they will think about getting involved with the brand.

- Differentiation
  - Exactly how is the brand unique?
  - Not shades of meaning or legalese here, we are looking for the big, straightforward, up front, shame-the-devil promise that you and your organisation are willing to live (or die) by. Nothing less will do.
  - Getting worried again?
  - Wanting to be BMW all the time is easy but promising to be the 'ultimate driving machine' for 30 years – and delivering on the promise takes some doing.

- Core Essence
  - What is the big idea?
  - If you were to boil it all down to what the pundits call the 'essence' what would your brand be about?
  - Essence is not easy to define but is sometimes found by adding '-ness' to the end of the brand.
  - For example, how is 'Sony-ness' different from 'Bang & Olufsen-ness' or 'Coke-ness'? Harley Davidson owners have been known to describe their bikes as 'companions' rather than just a bike. Hallmark cards cite their brand essence as 'enriching lives'.
  - But seriously, if you can't do this your brand probably doesn't stand much of a chance out there.

MARGIN NOTES

- If you can't distil the brand down to the essence, your organisation has nothing to get behind, the communications has nothing to hang on and the customer has nothing to covet.

You just don't get your share of the estimated one-third total world wealth that is represented by brand value without doing some work!

Rolls-Royce

When Rolls-Royce plc acquired Vickers in 1999 and became a world-leading supplier of marine equipment, the Group also became owner of an extensive portfolio of brands, including Kamewa, Aquamaster and Brown Brothers, that were more established within the marine equipment industry than Rolls-Royce.

These recognised names were subsequently managed as product names under the Rolls-Royce brand to build association with the new owner, for example, 'Rolls-Royce Kamewa waterjets'. However, this was complex given the extensive product portfolio and required multiple product names to be maintained and promoted.

After a sustained period of focused promotional activity, customer research supported the view that a strong association with Rolls-Royce had been built and that 'Rolls-Royce' was now clearly recognised as the driver brand.

In addition, whilst national attachment remains internally to a number of product names, for example, Sweden and Kamewa, the strength and driver role of the Rolls-Royce brand that has been widely established within our target markets is recognised across the Marine business.

This has enabled us to adopt a more structured and consistent approach to branding, for example, 'Rolls-Royce waterjets', which emphasises the Rolls-Royce brand and has substantially reduced the number of product names that need to be maintained and actively promoted.

In addition, we have established a formal process to ensure that new product names are only introduced where there is a compelling need to provide a specific identity or competitive differentiation under the Rolls-Royce brand.

MARGIN NOTES

The FAQs are:

4 Positioning and Branding		
4.5 What is our brand? What are its unique 'values' and 'personality'?		
4.5.1	What is the difference between 'a brand' and 'a name'?	A world of difference exists between the two. A name is just that – a product or a service with a name attached. It can do well enough in the market but it is unlikely to earn the extra margin that goes to a brand because its not differentiated in any meaningful way. To turn a name into a brand it needs at least a set of consistent meanings attached to the name that starts to set it apart from the rest of the names. Then it needs to arouse some unique beliefs and feelings within the minds of the customers. Easy – No. There are many more names out there and far fewer brands – for obvious reasons.
4.5.2	How will our brand be different from the competition?	You obviously have a choice as to how you differentiate the brand but: ● The brand must be at least different, at best unique ● Differentiation needs to be sufficiently attractive to a sufficient number of prospects and customers to be commercially viable ● The differentiation must be: ○ Credible to your customers ○ The one your organisation can support.
4.5.3	What brand values should be created, and how?	The secret here is to find brand values that are, at the same time: ● Attractive to the market segment you have targeted ● Significantly different from the competition to stand out to the target customers ○ Attractive to your organisation, staff and partners so that everybody can: ○ Believe in them ○ Be part of the brand effort ○ Live the value inside the organisation – and in every contact with the customer. So take your time and get it right.
4.5.4	What is our target brand personality?	Customer relationships are difficult to achieve but profitable if you can. Customers will find it difficult to have a relationship with anything than another person – that is the way we are programmed. Customer relationship management (CRM, more of that later) must not start with a mechanical IT system, it starts with the brand. If you have no brand personality to begin with, relationship can be nothing but a hollow word and no amount of systems and IT programming can make a wallflower the queen of the ball.

4.5.5	How are the personality and values to be kept relevant over time?	Time changes whether we like it or not. Brands must remain relevant and as times change so must brands. Any serious student of changing times should visit the Robert Opie Museum of Brands, Packaging and Advertising in London (http://www.robertopiecollection.com) and plot the, often gradual, changes that major brands have used to stay in business for so long. Suddenly coming across other brands that have quietly disappeared because they failed to keep up is also instructive.
4.5.6	What is the relationship between brands and segments?	Similar to the flower and the pot (I am sure I will think up a better example eventually). The brand makes all the money but it can't just be cast adrift in the 'mass market' – it needs to be looked after. It needs to be planted in the area of the market (segment or segments) where it is unique character, personality and promise will be most attractive.
4.5.7	How 'deep' must the brand go to be successful?	I ask the questions … and then can't answer them. It all depends on a number of interconnected issues, such as: ● The degree of competition ● The level of customer sophistication and expectation ● The level of customer cynicism in the market or segment to be overcome ● The level of brand management experience in the organisation ● The overall organisational 'will' to succeed ● The amount of 'patient money' and how long investment (to take it deep) can continue before returns are required.

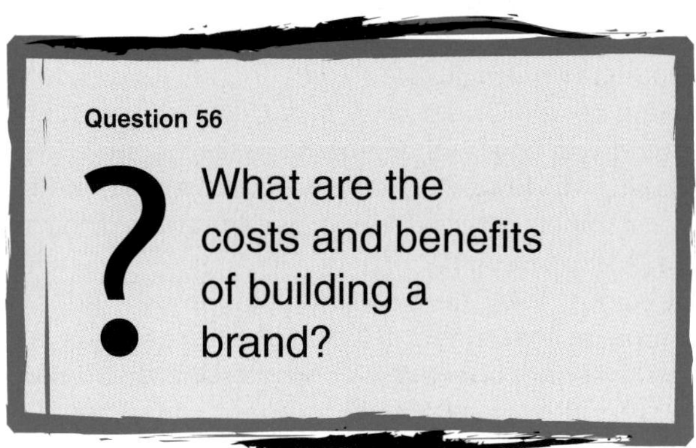

Question 56
?
What are the costs and benefits of building a brand?

The answer is, as always, it depends.

Branding (a little like marriage) is not an estate to be entered into lightly. It must be said that branding is not a 'no-cost' exercise, but neither does it have to be on the scale that Proctor & Gamble, Unilever or McDonalds lavish upon their advertising agencies – although they do reap the rewards.

But, it all really hangs on what you (and your organisation) mean by a brand.

Two approaches to branding

Supply side thinking	Demand side thinking
• Products • Do what can be measured • Cross selling & cost savings • CRM, the 'numbers game' and ROI	• Customers • Build trust • Long-term value • Relationships stimulate demand

MARGIN NOTES

There has been some debate over the past few years about exactly what a brand is, and what it can do. There are two broad schools of thought (I say 'thought', although in fact one is wrong and the other right – I leave it to you to work out which is which from my impartial explanation).

- Supply-side branding:
  - The constant ascendancy of IT and Finance specialists have finally learned that branding means real money, not just costs.
  - Consequently we have seen the rise of the 'Supply-side brand thinker'. To this person, a brand is all about:
    - Products and services.
    - Doing to the brand only what can be measured, how else would you know what worked and what didn't?
    - Making additional gains by 'cross-selling' and 'up-selling' to customers who will buy just about anything with a fancy name slapped on it.
    - Doing anything necessary to show a year-on-year growth of return on investment (ROI). All returns in the same year as the investment of course or we don't invest. CRM is excellent because the returns (headcount reduction) come in within 12 months, let's have some more.
- Demand-side branding
  - On the other hand, fighting something of a rearguard action, are the 'Demand-side brand thinkers'. To these people:
    - Customers are key to the brand success, not the products.
    - They believe the organisation needs to invest in the customer rather than the products or services to remain flexible and relevant.

    - Building trust in the minds of the customers is the key activity for longer-term success. Not easily measured but the organisation's most valuable activity.
    - Long-term value is the name of the game – in terms of margin, retention and brand equity. It is a strategic game that cannot be measured in tactical space of a financial year without damaging the future of the brand. We cannot mortgage tomorrow's success for short-term gain.
    - They believe that relationships stimulate demand and attempt to build real, human relationships into the brand by increasing the level of human-to-human contact rather than rationalising it out of the process.

- The 'Demand-side' brand thinkers – and I (Oh, I may have given away my allegiance there) believe that:
  - The value to the company (in the brand) is based on the relationship between the customer and the brand
  - Relationships (an imprecise term) will span a spectrum ranging from complete ignorance to satisfaction (think about that one)
  - Relationships can be translated directly into sales, volume and margins
  - The role of marketing is to influence those relationships in such a way that will produce a return. It must:
    - Identify the different relationships within the target market or segment
    - Identify the return that can be obtained from transforming the relationships from 'distant' to 'closer'
    - Allocate resources to changing those relationships that will maximise return – over the longer term.

Benefits of brands

These are many and varied and will depend largely on the organisation, the market/segment and the level and nature of competition.

- Many benefits have been noted by organisations and they suggest that a brand can:
  - Differentiate your product or service from the competition
  - Allow you to introduce new products or services more quickly (the name is already known and trusted)
  - Make it more difficult for competitors to steal your customers
  - Attract a higher price (your brand has particular meanings and promises attached and these are valued by your target market)
  - Communicate with your customers with consistent messages (not easy but consistent messages mean they are received more easily and are more effective)

MARGIN NOTES

- Provide some level of legal protection
- Build a positive image of your business
- Make your company look bigger
- Create an identity that is bigger than you (especially for the smaller business)
- Convey stability in your business (organisations that have been around longer are trusted more)
- Ensure consistency in your materials (if you do it right and you police it, the communications materials are produced to a constant, and recognised theme)
- Lower marketing expenses over time (as less marketing spend is wasted by 'off-message' communications)
- Attract more customers than an invisible commodity (over time)
- Create internal commitment and personal pride of the staff in the business
- Create more memorable offerings
- Create customer loyalty (maybe, see Chapter 9)
- Premium price (the real name of the game)
- Greater business equity. For the smaller business as well as the subsidiary, brand can mean that your business (brand owner) commands more money should it be sold.

MARGIN NOTES

David Aaker ('*Building Strong Brands*', Free Press, 1996) has looked at the benefits of brand and has highlighted a number of *financial benefits* that can be traced back to good branding. His argument goes as follows:

- Price premium:
  - A strong brand identity commands a price-premium.
  - The value proposition (see Chapter 11), if it is wrapped around the brand, should ensure that your brands are worth more in the minds of consumers regardless of whether the product actually functions better.

- Perception of quality:
  - A price premium creates the perception of quality.
  - People will still pay more for what they perceive to be a better- or higher-quality brand.

- Customer usage:
  - Perceived quality increases customer usage.
  - Customers select brands they believe to be quality brands and they tend to keep them as long as they reward them with a good experience.

- Return on investment:
  - According to Aaker's research, perceived quality is the single most-important contributor to a company's ROI.

- He suggests that it has more impact than market share, R&D, or marketing expenditures.

- Perceived value:
  - Customers relate value with quality.
  - If one brand is perceived to be of higher quality than another brand, customers tend to perceive that the higher-quality brand is a better value.

- Differentiation:
  - Perceived quality can be a point of differentiation.
  - Perceived quality can be used to differentiate, and in doing so, enable the company to loop back to Benefit 1 (Price) and charge a premium for their brand.

HOW TO *MAKE* BRANDS

- Make promises
  - That are valued by the market or segment, you will know this from the research you have conducted

- Keep those promises
  - Every time and at every point of customer contact

- Consistency of delivery
  - This ultimately generates trust because it meets expectations
  - This is more difficult with a service, but *must* be done regardless

- Create a trusted brand
  - The less the perceived risk in the equation and the higher the perceived customer value

- Develop and grow over time
  - Reflect the environmental conditions and change with them.
  - This needs significant investment and commitment over the longer term.

MARGIN NOTES

Costs of branding

'Almost everyone' says that branding is an expensive business.

'Almost everyone' finds it difficult to tell the difference between a *cost* and an *investment*.

There are some obvious costs involved in building a brand – but not as fearsome as some people would pretend.

There are all the 'normal' costs associated with developing, producing, distributing and supporting any new product or service in the market-place, and nobody has a problem with these, so why the horror? Or is it just an excuse not to bother?

There is some conventional wisdom that a brand must, in some way, be more expensive than a 'normal' or undifferentiated product or service. I have never worked out where that idea came from. Unless you believe that, for some reason, a brand has to go deeper, wider and faster than a 'normal' offering, and then there are few particular differences.

MARGIN NOTES

Of course, there are fewer options to cut the marketing corners and still hope a brand will be more successful than an unbranded offer – but maybe that is the issue, the internal expectations are different. Maybe, because it is going to be a 'brand' we really ought to do *proper* research, assessment, screening, testing, packaging and name research as well as dry run the distribution and communications to weed out problems *before* we launch. Maybe we ought to be doing that for every product or service we launch, it is called professional marketing.

So, apart from the 'additional' costs of doing a *proper* marketing launch job, what else needs to be done – well, here the additional investments (don't forget that you will get *additional returns* from a brand) are specific. A brand will not survive and grow unless it is consistent. This means that the organisation behind the brand has organised itself behind the unique values and personality of the brand. Every time the prospect or customer touches the brand (and its parent organisation) it must sense the values running through the system, like the lettering inside a seaside rock. This means that:

- You must develop a 'brand manual'
  - This contains all the key dimensions of the brand, such as value proposition, personality, feeling, tone of voice, font styles, colours, logos and position, etc.
  - A complete 'idiot's guide' to the brand that guides the teams of people who will be working on it.

- An internal 'brand police' role is also essential.
  - The role of these caring individuals is to police the execution of the brand and to identify any transgression of the brand manual.
  - Everyone knows better, everyone is a soon-to-be-discovered-genius, but make your own brand to play with.
  - Customers demand consistency and that doesn't include constant 'improvements' and changes in font size and shifts of the colour references – if it isn't updated in the brand manual, it doesn't happen.

- All points of customer contact need to be identified and co-ordinated
  - So that they communicate the same message every time.
  - This is a tricky role as it will probably cover different internal 'silos' and 'baronies' – now you start to see why branding isn't easy?

- All external points of contact (distribution, agents and other partners) need to be co-ordinated
  - With the internal contact points so that only one message is communicated.
  - This is trickier, at least for those starting off down the branding route.
  - Early branders don't have much leverage yet – threatening to withdraw the product/service of a new/starting brand will not leave as big a hole as if BMW, McDonalds or Heinz removed its entire brand.

So, how much do you want the additional margins and higher share prices?

MARGIN NOTES

HOW TO *BREAK* BRANDS

- Confuse a 'brand' with a 'name' or 'label'
  - A name is not the same as a brand.
  - A successful brand makes a clear promise about valuable and unique qualities.

- Fail to deliver on the promises made
  - The most dangerous of all, make a promise and fail to deliver.
  - Customers today are not fools and have been around long enough to know when they are being misled.

- Fail to keep the brand up to date
  - Customer needs and tastes change with time.
  - Brands must be kept relevant if they are not to be swept aside by more modern and fashionable offers.

- Communicate the wrong messages
  - Not explaining how the brand offers unique value.

- Communicate different messages through different media
  - When customers receive different messages about the same brand from different sources within the same organisation ...

MARGIN NOTES

Costs of not branding

The simplest and shortest section of the chapter – if you don't have brands, then you have commodities.

If you are in the commodity business you will eventually end up in a price war because price is the only differentiator you have.

If you are the lowest cost producer, you will win the war. Otherwise you won't.

Times change – and brands must keep up		
1960s	*A snapshot of Britain*	*2004*
52,807,000	Population	59,432,000
17,481	Miles of rail route	9,983
0.46	Litres of wine consumed per person per year	2.98
24	Number of hours of TV available per day	3,000
30,000	Prison population	75,065
25,000	Number of first degrees awarded annually	250,000
56.5%	Percentage of population smoking	27%
3m	Number of Britons taking overseas annual holidays	39.9m
5,776,000	Number of cars registered	24,543,000

The FAQs are:

4 Positioning and Branding		
4.6 What are the costs and benefits of building a brand?		
4.6.1	How much will it cost to create a brand?	Are we talking 'costs' or 'investment'? The answer will say a lot about your organisation and its attitude to its customers and brand building. The 'costs' camp are unlikely to be successful over the long term. Investments are always a function of the organisation's ambitions in the market. Brands are not cheap to build, but the returns can be impressive. Investment needs to be calculated in terms of time as well as money and will depend on how deep, how wide (market area) and how fast you want to go. The Proctor & Gamble and Unilever's of the world want to own a category, globally, very fast – that costs a lot of money.

		If your ambitions are more limited so will be the size of the investment required.
4.6.2	How long will it take to create a brand?	It all depends on the customers. Customers tend not to learn very fast, not because they aren't interested but because they have a life – and other things to do. As a rough rule of thumb, customers are just starting to hear and understand your brand promise as you are getting bored with it and are briefing your agency to update everything.
4.6.3	What constitutes a viable brand in our target segment(s)?	Talk to your target customers and test the idea. 'Viable' suggests a return on investment calculation – and that will depend on assessing the number of customers willing to buy into the brand, the level of repeat purchase and the level of premium price they are willing to pay.
4.6.4	What skills are required to develop and maintain a brand?	• Customer empathy • Identified market segments as target(s) • A fully supportive organisation • The ability to control all points of customer contact whether with the organisation and/or it is partners in the supply chain.
4.6.5	What are the financial and non-financial benefits of a brand?	See the full list above, in the meantime remember that brands can give you: • Superior return on investment • Above average prices, margins and profits • Above average customer retention • A leadership position in the marketplace.
4.6.6	What are the costs of not developing a brand?	If you haven't got a brand, you only, at best, have a name – a commodity all the same. If you only have commodities in your stable, you had better make sure that you are the lowest cost producer, or find another job.
4.6.7	Can we win in a price war?	Absolutely, we just make sure that we aren't involved – a brand sells on difference and quality, price wars are only for the commodity offerings.

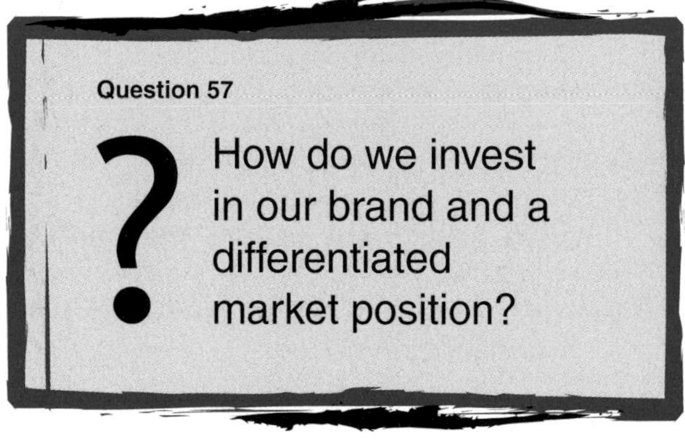

Question 57
?
How do we invest in our brand and a differentiated market position?

The word 'investment' here has been chosen carefully – branding is all about investing in what will probably be the organisation's *most valuable asset*. As an asset, your brand needs to be maintained and regular investments are needed to keep it in top, returns delivering, shape.

As soon as you, or others in the organisation start talking about the 'costs' of keeping the brand going you can probably kiss goodbye to the big gains – the organisation doesn't 'get' branding and is probably sharpening its claws for the price war already.

A word on brand valuation

MARGIN NOTES

We know that brands are 'worth a lot of money' but what exactly does that mean? Coca-Cola is valued by Interbrand as the most valuable brand in the world and is valued at $70 billion – which means? Broadly this means that if Coca-Cola were sold tomorrow, the purchase price would be the total price of all its net assets – plus $70 billion.

How is this worked out? – well it all depends. If the company is up for sale it is easy – it is worth what the buyer will pay for it. The Economist magazine called 1988, '*The year of the brand*':

- In the US, Phillip Morris took over Kraft and paid four times the value of Kraft's tangible assets.
- In Europe, Nestle bought Rowntree and paid over five times the value of Rowntree's tangible assets.

These payments for 'names' were a reflection of the value placed on the brands in terms of their long-term profit expectancy (customer sales over a number of years), and what they could do for the acquiring company. Kraft helped Phillip Morris extend its portfolio outside tobacco, Rowntree offered Nestle one metre of shelf space throughout UK distribution.

- The phenomenon was not just a feature of 1988 and 'those crazy old days', it continues today with recent acquisitions well above net asset value including:
  - Seagram buys Polygram
  - Times Warner buys AOL
  - eBay buys Skype
  - Oracle buys PeopleSoft and Siebel
  - Ford buys Volvo
  - Lenovo buys IBM pc
  - Proctor & Gamble buys Gillette
  - Cadbury buys Green & Blacks
  - Nestle buys Perrier and San Pellegrino
  - Adidas buys Reebok
  - And we are still wondering what Microsoft is going to do with its $56 billion cash pile.

If you aren't selling the brand how can you value it? Well, first, you can have a go yourself. There are two crude methods that might give you an indication of how much your brand is worth:

- Market capitalisation minus net assets:
  - This shows the stock market's idea of what you are worth
  - Total value of all shares less net assets and the difference = brand.

- Price per share/earnings per share:
  - This is an attempt to calculate brand value from the extra length of time that profits will continue to flow if you have a brand.
  - The idea is that brand = loyalty = customers retained for longer, so investors will pay more per share if income flows are 'guaranteed' for longer.
  - This method is better at assessing relative brand value within a category such as 'supermarkets'.

Second method, get the brand valued by the specialist consultants (who will do all of the above but give you a 'branded' report that will have more power internally). Fun, but its not an exact science.

Brand valuation models

Interbrand	Young and Rubicam 'Brand Assett Valuator'	Millward Brown 'Brand Dynamics'	Brand Finance
• Leadership • Stability • Market • International scope • Profit trend • Support • Protection	• Differentiation • Relevance • Esteem • Knowledge	• Customers' predisposition towards the brand • Size of the brand • Type of consumer • Relative price	• Financial forecasts • Brand's contribution to demand • The risk attached to future earnings • Value and sensitivity analysis

The specialists keep their exact methodologies confidential (obviously) but do publish the broad parameters that they use. Each camp has its supporters and its detractors.

Interbrand is probably the market leader and says that its methodology is based on the net present value or today's value of the earnings the brand is expected to generate in the future. It says there are three 'elements' to this assessment:

- Financial Forecasting
  - Identifying the revenues from products or services that are generated with the brand.
- Role of Branding
  - Identifying the earnings that are specifically attributable to the brand.
- Brand Strength
  - Identifying a discount rate that represents the risk profile of these earnings.

MARGIN NOTES

These are really all ways of deciding what the future cash flow is likely to be, and the number of years it can be valued at so that there is a number to add to the net assets.

A word on brands and balance sheets

It is estimated (Interbrand/Business Week) that almost £1 trillion of brand value exists in the world – almost all of it not included in the balance sheets of the organisations that own the brands.

The balance sheet is one of the financial statements that companies must produce every year for their shareholders. It is described as a financial 'snapshot' of the organisation's financial situation giving the company's assets and liabilities at that moment in time. The balance sheet is typically presented in two halves – the top half shows where the money is currently being used in the organisation (the net assets), and the bottom half shows where that money came from (the capital employed). The value of the two halves must be the same – Capital employed = net assets, hence the term '*balance* sheet'.

The money invested in the organisation may have been used to buy long-term assets or short-term assets. The long-term assets are known as fixed assets, and help the firm to produce its offerings. Typical examples always include plant, machinery, equipment, computers and buildings. A brand also helps an organisation produce its offerings but is rarely listed. Until recently, when a company was purchased for more than its asset value (the difference = the value of the brand purchased) this excess would be termed 'goodwill' and would be written off in the books over time!

To some extent we can see the accountants' problem (no, really)

- They tend to like things that are not too exciting; and brand values have been known to go up and down like a yo-yo.

- They have been using their traditional 'performance ratios' for years and if we were to add Coca-Cola's brand value, estimated at about $70,000,000,000 to its assets, then its Return on Asset ratio would fall through the floor.

On the other hand, if brand value were added to the balance sheet, marketing and market managers could point more convincingly to the value that they add to the organisation. Others might be more prepared to invest in marketing strategy too.

There is pressure to find a way of including brands on the balance sheet with the organisation's other assets but progress is patchy; while the Gucci brand is included on the balance sheet of its parent as intangible asset, the Louis Vuitton brand does not show up on the balance sheet of its parent (LVMH) even though it accounts for about 44% of the group's market capitalisation.

MARGIN NOTES

Changes are afoot, we are told, and the rules on listing 'intangible assets' are moving too – watch this space.

■ Managing your brands for maximum value

Brands and brand value can be seen as the storehouse of future profits that result from past marketing activities. It is also a way of 'evening out' annual performance, sometimes described as the organisation's 'suspension system' in an uncertain environment.

Assuming that eventually you will value your brands or, you will sell the business or, all brands will end up on the balance sheet or, your organisation will understand the importance and value of brands all on their own, then you need to know what to do:

- Invest in your brand asset to make sure that it is in good shape.
  - The building needs maintenance, the cars need servicing, the brand needs a regular makeover before it gets 'tired'.

- Base the regular 'makeover' on a continual investment in customer insight (market research).
  - Markets don't stand still and customers (and their perceptions) change.

    - Make sure that you know what is going on.
    - Make sure you have a good idea what is going to happen/be demanded next.

- Engage the whole organisation.
    - Your staff will make or break the brand, keep them 'onside' with what you are trying to do.
    - Make sure they don't get bored with the brand and its values.

- Integrate the brand into the fabric of the organisation.
    - Make sure that processes and systems are driven by the needs of the brand, not the other way round.
    - People should be recruited to support the brand and trained for the job.
    - If you recruit for the (technical) job first and the brand second, you can expect the differentiation (and those wonderful margins) to slip.

Remember, nothing lasts forever and, unless you are ready to work for your brand, it will stop working for you – like a reforming alcoholic, you are just a single mistake away from a commodity.

The FAQs are:

4 Positioning and Branding		
4.7 How do we invest in our brand and a differentiated market position?		
4.7.1	How do we measure brand value/brand equity?	There are a number of methods, and the differences in the approach really don't matter. What matters is that the decision makers in the organisation start to understand that a brand is an *asset*. Once you have that understanding, you start to place the market and branding activities on a completely new plane – you move from a cost centre activity to a revenue or profit centre activity. Choose whichever valuation method will allow you to get through to the organisation in this way.
4.7.2	Is brand or differentiation used as a key metric for controlling marketing activity?	If its not – it just won't happen. Customers take much longer to get to grips with an idea or a claim to 'uniqueness', much longer than the staff inside the organisation. It doesn't mean they don't care; they are too busy with their lives to take it all in. So the metric must take up the slack and stop people thinking there is a better way to success. There are no short cuts where customers are concerned; day-in-day-out work to convince the market of a differentiation pays off eventually – as long as nothing gets in the way.

4.7.3	Are *all* our marketing activities coordinated to create, support and maintain the brand?	The best brands come from organisations that understand their job – to protect and cherish the brand with all the resources at their disposal – that is why they are there. When people start to think they are paid by the organisation for some other reason than to satisfy customers and support the brand, it all starts to fall apart.
4.7.4	Are our people part of the brand (and our competitive position)?	If you don't have your people (internal and in partners' organisations) lined up behind the unique values and personality of the brand, then you probably won't succeed. In the most competitive markets, it is not a battle of products; it is a battle of ideas. To win the battle of ideas requires every single person you have.
4.7.5	Are we monitoring all levels of our brand's 'promise'?	Please, *please*, please measure exactly what you are promising; over-deliver on what you promise, by all means. But, your brand cannot afford to under-deliver on its promise, ever.
4.7.6	Can we create a 'philosophy' of brands?	Yes. First buy the book – ('*The Philosophy of Branding*', Thom Braun, Kogan Page, 2004) and immerse yourself in the branding 'top tips' the author draws from Heraclitus, Socrates, Plato, Aristotle, Descartes, Spinoza, Leibniz, Locke, Hume, Rousseau, Kant, Hegel, Nietzsche, Wittgenstein, Existentialism and Popper … Enjoy.
4.7.7	What is the planning horizon for brand development?	Branding is a long game. Thousands of brands (including most of the big ones) are over 50 years old, many hundreds are over 100 years old and some brands can trace their lineage back over a thousand years. But branding is a short-term business too – customers are concerned with the 'now and immediate future' that is their life. Brands need to be managed on a two-to-three year basis, where all the two-to-three years are joined up. Difficult, of course it is difficult; you don't earn your share of $1 trillion for doing the easy jobs!

■ The strategic questions (51–57)

In this fourth part of the market strategy discussion, we have looked at:

- Positioning
  - Which has not really escaped the realm of advertising, although it deserves a wider audience.

- Branding
  - Which, on the other hand, has attracted so many words; books and articles continue to flow from the pens of authors who know what they are talking about – and those who don't.

But for the hard-working practitioner the story never seems to get any clearer. But, given the advantages of establishing a clear and distinct position and brand I hope I have convinced you that it is worth trying. Also, I hope that this section has encouraged you to have a little more patience with your branding activities; most things really do come to those who can bear to wait.

And then we have the questions. Take all the time you need here, this is where the organisations who know what is going on make all their money.

No.	Strategic question	Our strategic answer	Importance	✓
	Positioning and Branding			
51	Differentiation or 'Commodity' marketing?		Must have	
			Nice to have	
			Not important	
52	What market positions exist?		Must have	
			Nice to have	
			Not important	
53	What market position do we own, or do we want to own?		Must have	
			Nice to have	
			Not important	
54	How are we going to be different from the competition?		Must have	
			Nice to have	
			Not important	
55	What is our brand? What are its unique 'values' and 'personality'?		Must have	
			Nice to have	
			Not important	
56	What are the costs and benefits of building a brand?		Must have	
			Nice to have	
			Not important	
57	How do we invest in our brand and a differentiated market position?		Must have	
			Nice to have	
			Not important	

CHAPTER 9

Customer Retention

> 'I am a deeply superficial person'.
>
> *Andy Warhol (1928–1987), American artist*

Now we move SCORPIO on to the (sometimes) less exciting areas that don't involve all that macho 'hunter' style customer acquisition stuff – but might make you even more money.

The 'challenge' of customer retention has always been with us but not really brought to centre stage, at least for larger organisations, until the arrival of Frederick Reichheld's book (*'The Loyalty Effect'*, Harvard Business School Press 1996).

MARGIN NOTES

Most importantly, why is retention in the SCORPIO model at all? Because, if you *really* want to retain more (lose fewer) customers, the solution is strategic, not a tactical one. Customer retention has to be planned and built into the organisation – the businesses that have seen it as a quick fix or just something to be sorted out by 'tweaking the bonus system' have achieved little or nothing from their efforts.

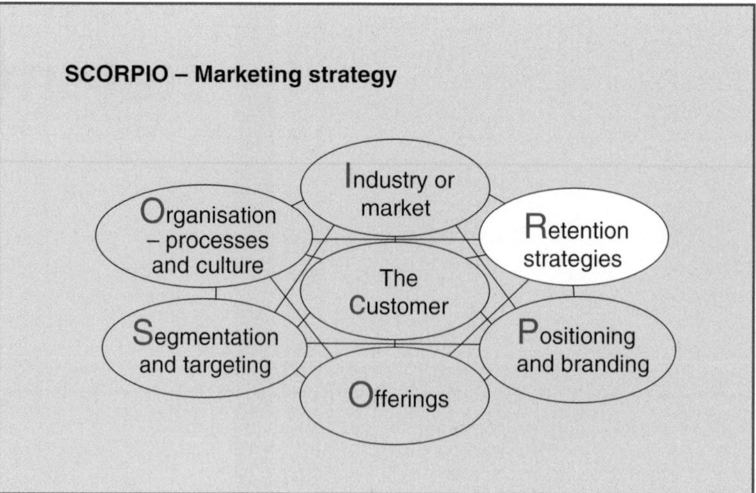

Reichheld, a member of the consultancy Bain & Company, conducted some simple research among typical large organisations and discovered what happened if these companies managed to *lose fewer customers* every year. Serious lateral thinking …

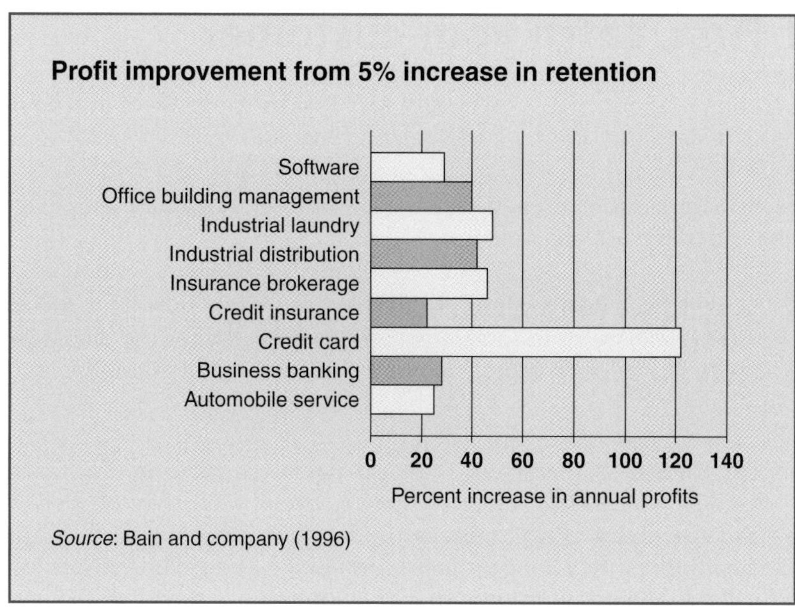

MARGIN NOTES

The results varied from industry to industry depending on costs but the numbers managed to attract everybody's attention – at least until they worked out just how difficult customer retention can be.

The examples cited by Bain/Reichheld were all based on US organisations but were still impressive, based on the firms increasing retention (losing fewer customers) by just 5%. What this means is of all the customers that they expected to lose in a year, they retained 5% (they still lost 95%), then credit insurance was the lowest benefiting industry with just below 20% *increase in profits* (not bad). Credit cards increased their annual profits by 120% (doubling profits by only losing 5% less customers should impress us all).

How would you like to increase your annual profits (not sales turnover though, profit) by just the lowest figure of 20%? I always hope to have people's attention by this point but some people just seem to take a lot of impressing.

In this chapter we will look at a few key questions that might help you jump your annual profit levels significantly:

- What is retention all about?
- Why is it important?
- How do you do it?
- What gets in the way?

First, catch your customer

Marketing is about customers. Levitt said that the purpose of every business is: 'To *create* and *keep* a customer'.

'Create' is obvious; everybody reads that far – but not many people read to the end of the 6-word sentence.

This focus is probably because we all think we know how to create customers (it's called sales in some businesses) and everybody in the organisation sees the value in more customers, so the plaudits lie thick on the ground.

MARGIN NOTES

Generally, business managers think so narrowly that, as long as the organisation is acquiring more customers every year, they believe that they and the organisation must be doing well – when it all falls apart underneath them they are genuinely surprised – and instantly start looking for the saboteurs in their midst. They don't for a moment imagine it could be their fault, they have done their bit and brought in more new customers every year – all those experts in accounting and production had to do was to keep service up … It's not that simple, or is it?

Well, no. There is a larger problem (challenge) of organisations, silos, organisational design, empires and baronies involved here as well as appraisal, reward and bonus systems that make it very personal – and deadly. But we tread these dangerous waters in Chapter 10.

I still remember the discussion with the Sales Director of a UK Life Assurance company; I asked why he continued to raise the sales incentives for the direct sales force so that they received an increased bonus for every personal pension product sold, even though:

- The prices had been reduced in an attempt to retain market share in a price war.
- The new economics meant that it then took *eight years* to recoup (break even) the costs of sale
- Intermediary (Independent Financial Advisors) commissions and sales bonuses needed to be paid before any profits were calculated
- But the intermediary sales contract had not been changed meaning that the intermediary still had to wait just *five years* before he could 'churn' the customer (cash in the old pension and buy a new one (obviously on better customer terms) and make another full intermediary commission on the new sale from the new provider.

The response was 'Paul, you just don't get it'. Eight months later they were out of business.

The morale of the story is simple; catching more and more customers is *not* the name of the game. Unprofitable customers you don't need – the problem is, they are often the easiest to find. Too many customers aren't necessarily unprofitable – they just need to stay long enough to 'go into the black'. The more investment (discounts, incentives, intermediary and channel costs, lower prices, sales and promotions activities) you lavish on acquiring customers, the longer they have to stay before the investment is paid back.

■ Second, keep your customer

MARGIN NOTES

How do you keep your customers? Customers are supremely selfish, will stay with you as long as they believe they are getting something out of the deal.

Just to be sure we understand each other here; customers will stay with you as long as *they* believe *they* are getting something out of the deal. I know you need something as well but that's not doing anything for the customer. Tune into the famous radio station – W11*fm* – (What's *In It* For *Me*?)

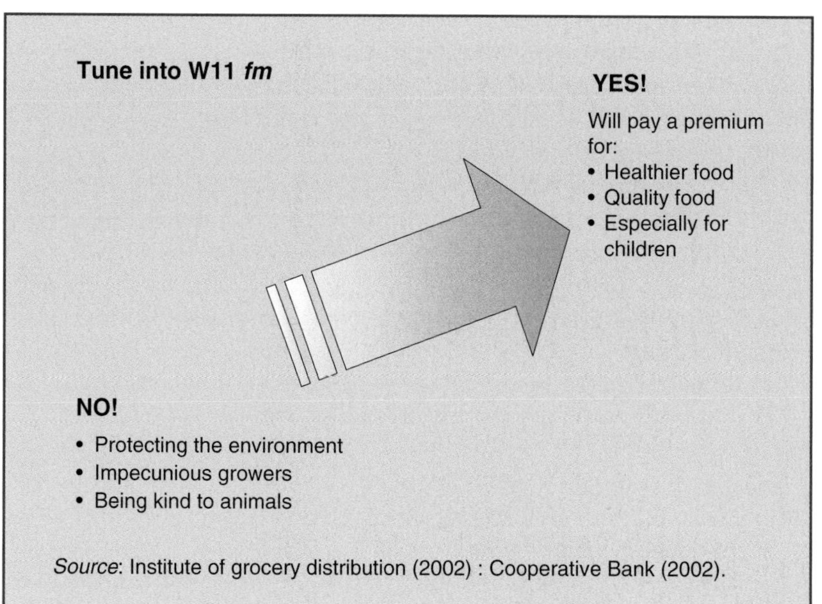

Tune into W11 *fm*
YES!
Will pay a premium for:
• Healthier food
• Quality food
• Especially for children
NO!
• Protecting the environment
• Impecunious growers
• Being kind to animals

Source: Institute of grocery distribution (2002) : Cooperative Bank (2002).

Imagine that you are trying to get Fair Trade products to differentiate your offer (they have been around for a long time). You have invested in market research and you know from the customer insight people that:

- You won't succeed just by making morally correct claims like:
  - Protecting the environment
  - Caring for the rights of poor, third world growers
  - Being kind to animals
  - Add as many to the list as you want …
- Everyone *will* agree but *won't* buy. What's in it for them? Making claims that offer something for them (or better, the people they love) will be much more successful.
  - Healthier food
  - Quality food
  - Fewer allergies
  - Especially for children.

MARGIN NOTES

So, at the risk of seriously annoying you if you have come directly from Chapter 6, the steps in retaining customers are really obvious:

- Constantly add customer value
  - That means delivering offers that make sense to them and clearly contain something for them (W11fm).
  - Bear in mind that 'what they want' changes over time (see 'value migration' later). To do this:
- Find out what they want
  - Its not complicated, I'm sure you'll agree.
  - Don't guess or assume, ask them what they want. Then:
- Satisfy their needs and wants
  - Or, give them what they want.
  - Don't give them what you 'think they want', what 'they should want' or 'what you would want if you were them'.
- Make sure that they can get more of what they want with you than anywhere else
  - If you are really intent on adding customer value, make sure that they really can't get more of what they want anywhere else.
- Make sure that they know it
  - Then, and only then, bring the marketing communications to bear on the target customers.
  - Make sure that they all know what you have and that nobody else does it better.

If you can do this more than once in the face of constant changing customer needs, wants and perception; not only are you very good, you have a Strategy!

Looking more broadly at the retention issue we can see that there are some interesting questions for us to answer:

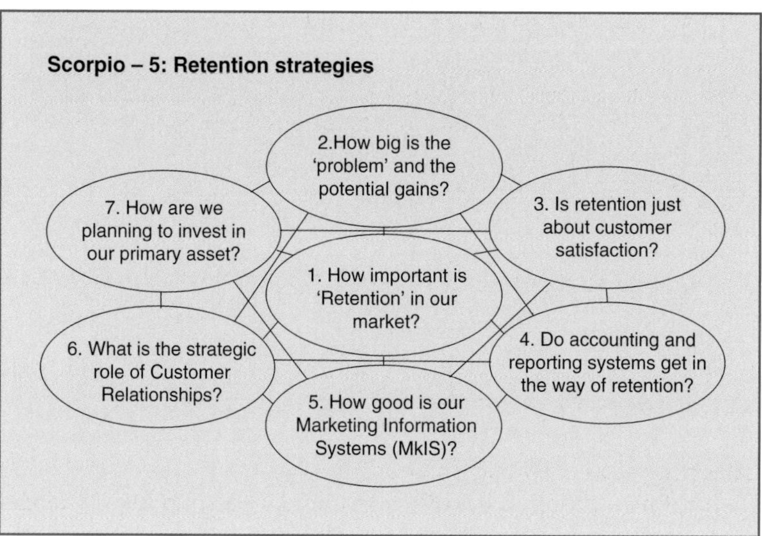

Scorpio – 5: Retention strategies
1. How important is 'Retention' in our market?
2.How big is the 'problem' and the potential gains?
3. Is retention just about customer satisfaction?
4. Do accounting and reporting systems get in the way of retention?
5. How good is our Marketing Information Systems (MkIS)?
6. What is the strategic role of Customer Relationships?
7. How are we planning to invest in our primary asset?

Taking these, short but difficult questions one by one:

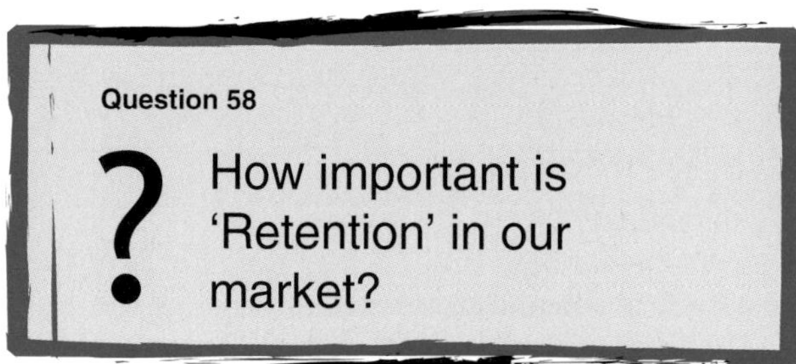

Question 58
?
How important is 'Retention' in our market?

MARGIN NOTES

We have already seen from Reichheld that customer retention, while valuable for all organisations, is startlingly more valuable for some.

Unfortunately, few organisations have any idea where they stand in the retention stakes or how bad the 'lapse' situation is currently. It's because it looks a bit like accountants' work I suppose, but bear with me …

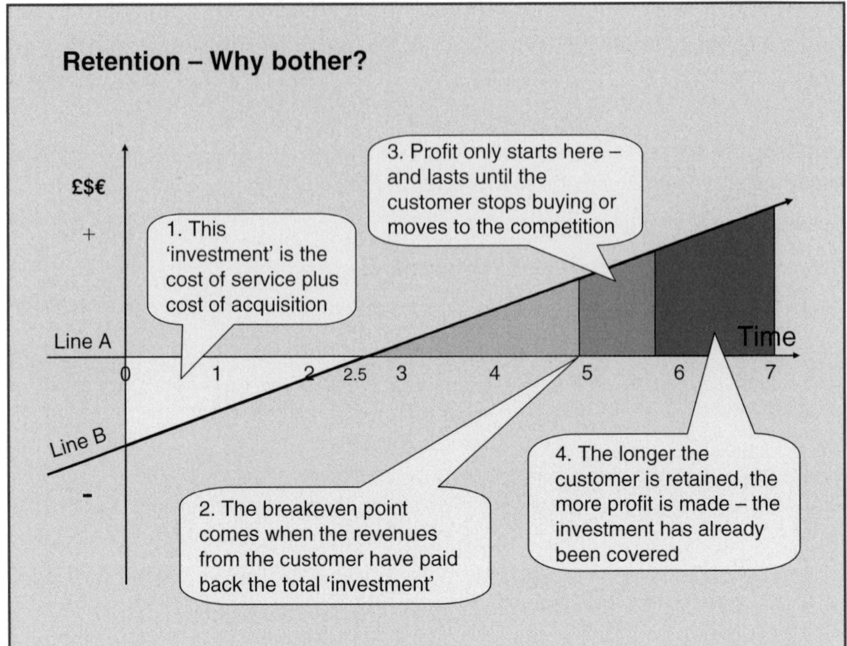

MARGIN NOTES

Picking the diagram apart to make some sense, we can see:

- Line A:
  - Is the time line and shows the progress of an organisation measured in years (might be useful for a common B2B organisation), or in months (might be better for a fast moving B2C organisation)
  - No, these are just random numbers, fill in your own timescale that makes sense – weeks, months or years all work.

- Line B:
  - Shows the money.
  - At the very beginning, Time '0', say the launch of the product or service, there is a negative balance (it is below the horizontal year line A). This is because of all the special costs associated with acquiring customers in the first place.
  - This example doesn't include costs of the product or service itself that is part of other, unnecessarily complex diagrams that we don't need to worry about here.
  - It should though, include expenses such as sales forces (with their overheads, cars and expense accounts), intermediary commissions and discounts, special offers, marketing communications (advertising, direct marketing and PR) and sales collateral as well as special prices or offers.

- At time '2.5':
  - With the passage of time, the organisation gradually acquires new customers so that by the time '2.5' (years or months) the figures stabilise and the organisation stops losing money.
  - After this time, there are enough customers (and they aren't leaving yet) that the money 'inflows' match the money 'outflows' on a daily or quarterly basis.
  - But the capital investment in acquiring customers (the first shaded area to the left of this point) remains.

- At time '5':
  - By the time the organisation gets to time 5, the second shaded area (between time points 2.5 and 5) equals the first shaded area (between time points 0 and 2.5) and, finally, the investment has been paid back
  - The activity has *broken even*
  - No profit has yet been made.

- Beyond time '5':
  - As soon as customers stay (keep buying) beyond time 5, we move into profit.
  - The profit per customer goes through the roof because there is no longer any cost of acquisition cost to offset.

- Beyond time '6':

- Move beyond time six or seven the profitability per customer per year accelerates further.

- Longer:
  - The longer customers stay with us, the more profitable they become.

We will dig into these figures as we work through this chapter. But at this point, let's look at the departing customers.

There is normally no shortage of information on the newly acquired customers – you are told even if you don't want to know, but leaving customers – who are they?

Some customers should leave, it is best for them and for the organisation. Their needs and wants will naturally change and sometimes this will be beyond what we want or are able to offer from our unique market position. You will (?) remember our discussion on Positioning (Chapter 8) and the need to keep to our market position rather than succumb to the all-things-to-all-men approach, sometimes customers must leave because they naturally move segments and into positions controlled by other organisations.

For those that should not be leaving – where are they going? Importantly, can you tell the difference between the two types of leavers?

MARGIN NOTES

The FAQs are:

5 Customer Retention		
5.1 How important is 'Retention' in our market?		
5.1.1	Apart from the customers that we have intentionally relinquished, how many have defected?	I know these aren't the numbers that every organisation keeps, but they are essential. The old story about the leaky bucket (as fast as you pour water in the top it leaks out of the bottom) is referenced everywhere – and by everyone but nobody keeps the numbers! All the effort that goes into new customer acquisition is put at risk – if 50% of customers are 'lapsing' every month or year how much harder does everybody have to work to fill the leaky bucket? Hard numbers please: ● How many customers have we lost? ● By product or service? ● By segment? ● By month/quarter? ● Over the past x years? What percentage of those were we happy to see go?
5.1.2	What is the current customer defection rate?	What are the current numbers like this month or quarter? How do these numbers relate to similar periods? No, don't start feeling inadequate – it's not a failing, its normal – and we need to know the state of play to see if it's worthwhile doing something about it. Maybe we are 'on the case' but are simply not reacting fast enough to stem the tide
5.1.3	Has the rate increased or decreased over the past few years? Why?	What is the trend? Up or down, both could be OK; it all depends on the reasons behind the trend. ● Are you changing your market stance or position? ● Are you working to change/modify or re-position the brand(s)? ● Has there been any change in competitor activity? ● Do you measure competitive activity beyond the direct industry definition? (See Chapter 2)
5.1.4	What are the reasons for customer defection?	You probably conduct 'exit interviews' on staff when they leave, do you do it for leaving customers? Why the amusement? – We do it on the costs (staff) but not on the revenue (customers) as they leave the organisation – why is that? Exit research is easy, simple and effective. Beware B2B, you must conduct independent research here (or you must talk to exiting customers personally), sales forces always believe it about price – and we know that it is not – you must dig for the real reasons.
5.1.5	Have the reasons changed over the past few years? Why?	Is there any evidence of 'value outflow' with your customers moving away from the 'old' (you) to buy the 'new' somewhere else?

		Remember, the outflows are often between (rather than within) industries so you need to be looking across a wide area. Check that you are asking the right questions. Do you recall a few years ago there were reports of teenaged girls cutting back on their chocolate expenditure to top up their mobile phones? 'Which brand of chocolate are you moving to?' would have been the wrong question to ask ...
5.1.6	How does our defection rate compare with our competition?	It depends who you consider to be the competition of course. Where are you placed in your customer's comparative review? Are you losing customers faster or slower than your unique market position would explain?
5.1.7	Who is losing and gaining which customers? Why?	Is the entire sector up or down or are there identifiable winners and losers? If it is sector wide, is the category under threat from cross-industry substitution? If so, where? What is to be done about it?

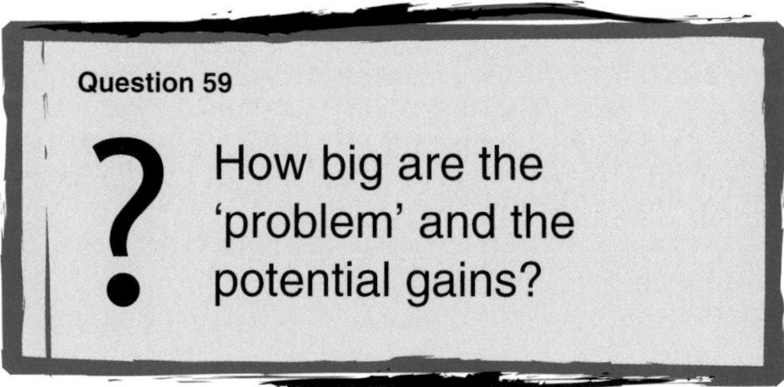

Question 59
?
How big are the 'problem' and the potential gains?

So is it worth looking further?

Calculating the opportunity

Total expenditure on new customer acquisition		#1
Total number of new customers acquired		#2
What is the cost per new customer acquired		#3 (=#1÷#2)
How long does an average customer stay with us (time periods)		#4
Average net income* received per customer per time period		#5
Number of (time periods) before acquisition cost repaid (break-even)		#6 (=#3÷#5)
How many customers do we lose per (time period)		#7
What is the financial cost per (time period) of all lost customers		#8 (=#7×#5)
How much additional revenue would be achieved by 5% reduction in lost customers		#9 (=#8÷20)
** Net of direct costs*		

MARGIN NOTES

Well, first there are some numbers to collect. You may have to be subtle here; some people might think you were collecting negative data with another agenda in mind.

Let's look at how we might calculate the size of the problem and opportunity. We need to identify:

	(No/£€$)
• Total expenditure on new customer acquisition in time period ○ We need to know exactly how much we spend on attracting new business (be careful how you ask/collect this data it will be sensitive). ○ Imagine that you decided to outsource the entire new business acquisition activity (some organisations do), what are *all* the activities (and people) that would disappear? You should include things like: ■ Sales force salaries ■ Expenses ■ Transport, etc. ■ Incentives (including sporting events) ■ All sales support staff costs ■ All external agency costs (visuals, collateral, recruitment, training, etc.) ■ All sales overheads including central services, rent heating, communications, etc. ■ Total costs of new customer communications including above and below the line communications, promotions to intermediaries and end users ■ Other, I'm sure to have forgotten something.	#1
• Total number of new customers acquired in time period ○ How many new customers have you added to the books in the time period? ○ These need to be real customers rather than anything else, beware of double counting.	#2
• What is the cost per new customer acquired ○ Calculate: Total expenditure on new customer acquisition in time period *divided by* Total number of new customers acquired in time period ○ This will give you a total cost of acquisition, per new customer.	#3(=#1/#2)
• How long does an average customer stay with us (time periods) ○ Go back an agreed number of time periods, it depends on you, and your business how far this can or should be, but 5 to 10 time periods back should give a reasonable view	#4

○ Find out how many customers joined during that period ○ Find out how long each one stayed. ■ It can be difficult to agree when a customer has 'left', at the date of the last order or the date of the order that they did not place – as long as you keep to the same definition, any will do ■ If you find significant differences by product, service and segment (I would expect it) than you may need to calculate these figures separately for different groups.	
● Average net income (*net of direct costs)* received per customer per time period ○ How much money have you taken from the average customer? ○ This is best calculated by taking gross income per customer, and ○ Deducting the direct costs, which might include: ■ Intermediary costs ■ Production costs of product or service, etc.	#5
● Number of (time periods) before acquisition cost is repaid (break-even) ○ Calculate: The cost per new customer acquired *divided by* Average net income (*net of direct costs*) received per customer per time period. ○ This will give you the number of time periods required for the average customer (or by segment/product/service) to repay the cost of acquiring the customer in the first instance.	#6(=#3/#5)
● How many customers do we lose per (time period) ○ What is the rate of defection? ○ How many customers do you lose every time period?	#7
● What is the financial cost per (time period) of all lost customers ○ Its getting tense now ○ Calculate: The number of customers you lose per (time period) *divided by* Average net income (*net of direct costs*) received per customer per time period ○ This will give you the cost, per time period of the lost business – expressed in terms of the income you aren't receiving from these defected customers.	#8(=#7×#5)
● How much additional revenue would be achieved by 5% reduction in lost customers: ○ This measures the effect of Reichheld's 5% reduction ○ Calculate: The financial cost per (time period) of all lost customers *divided by* 20 (gives the 5%).	#9(=#8/20)

MARGIN NOTES

You may wish to flex this calculation process to meet the special needs of your organisation. Fine, it is a guide rather than a blueprint, so feel free.

The numbers almost certainly exist, but they may be hidden. Equally, they are probably not together because they have not been analysed yet.

Tread carefully; carry out the analysis before you give in to the need to talk to anyone about it. And, don't turn up at a meeting with the figures as a problem, unless you also have a solution – you need to know what to do about it.

As soon as you have a (strategic) solution and it has been costed, the you can present the data:

- The size of the problem
- The value of a 5% reduction in defection (#9 in the calculation)
- The cost (investment) of achieving that reduction
- The return on the investment.

Make your case carefully – even increasing profits is a 'change' so will be treated with suspicion. Not only that, you will see later that some of the changes required might be just 'too difficult to deal with' anyway. Oh well …

The FAQs are:

5 Customer Retention		
5.2 How big are the 'problem' and the potential gains?		
5.2.1	How much do we spend on acquiring new customers?	Here you should ignore all the costs (direct and indirect) associated with the product or service; they aren't relevant for this discussion. What you should include, for an agreed time period, for example a year, is for you to decide, every organisation is different. But the number is likely to be large. Obviously life is not that simple. Almost though! You can allow for acquisition work carried out and customers not acquired yet if you want to – 'accruals' – (you can see that I have been through all this more than once) but then don't forget to deduct from the analysis all the customers acquired from the previous period's effort and cost … You can assess by segment too – an excellent idea as long as it doesn't water down the central idea. Stay focused.
5.2.2	How long do our customers stay with us? (Average & by segment)	Simply work out when customers first buy and when they last buy. More adventurous analysis might contain some modelling allowing for different groups or segments of buyers re-purchase cycles but the idea is straightforward.

5.2.3	How long must a new customer stay before they become profitable after acquisition costs?	A simple but worrying analysis. First you need to calculate the *net* revenue from a customer. This is called different things in different organisations (no, I don't know why either) and may be called 'contribution' but it is really the total revenue less the cost of sales (the cost of making and delivering the product/service). Don't worry about getting the 'right' calculation – far too many critical decisions get bogged down in such useless niceties – you know what I mean, any measure your organisation agrees within the area will do. Second, you need to work out how many months/quarters/years (you choose) the customer has to stay with you to pay back the total cost. Check with the diagram in the previous section, this is not just when the customer's account goes 'cash positive' (at time 2.5) but when the full payback is made (at time 5). You could add a discount factor for the time value of money if the payback is a particularly long time.
5.2.4	Are our acquisition cost and payback periods comparable with competitors?	Are the results 'normal'? It all depends on the type of business you think you are in and whether your payback periods are longer, shorter or the same as your competitors. Of course, that depends on who the competitors are, and we don't just mean direct competition. It also depends on your own, particular, unique market position – if your position means you take longer to acquire but keep customers longer, then don't expect to be 'normal' at all.
5.2.5	How much do you spend on retaining existing customers?	If you spend any time or effort, how much do you invest in this important area? The amount needs to be isolated from the new customer acquisition areas, so calculate carefully.
5.2.6	What is the annual financial cost (lost income) to your organisation for customer defection?	This can be calculated by adding up the total of all the defecting customers' business that you have lost – if they had continued to remain a customer for a further full time period, for example a full year. The real financial cost must relate to the loss of net profit because they have left. Fall back on the figure you agreed in 5.2.3 above.
5.2.7	How much additional profit would be generated by an annual 5% increase in retention?	Finally, divide the above figure by 20 and what do you get? Beware – if the result is a paltry figure then you have probably miscalculated. The normal problem is around how organisations calculate profits: • On an annual, financial accounting period basis • Linked to products and services, rarely customers • Including the cost as acquisition as a 'general overhead' (for example as a cost against retained as well as new business). It is too complicated to explain in detail here but a friendly accountant will help.

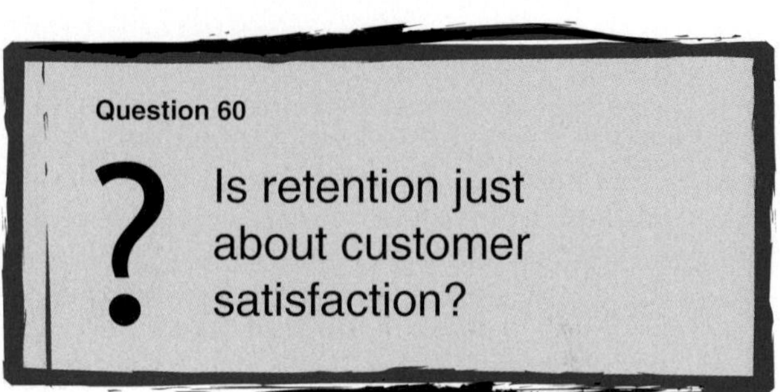

The short answer here (in case you were in any doubt) is No.

There has been lots of research over recent years to show that the so-called 'satisfied customers' are likely to 'defect' about as readily as dis-satisfied ones. So just focusing on *keeping the customer satisfied* (did the strains of Simon and Garfunkel sound in your mind there?) is no longer enough. But, as we have already seen, not very many organisations seem to be doing much about it.

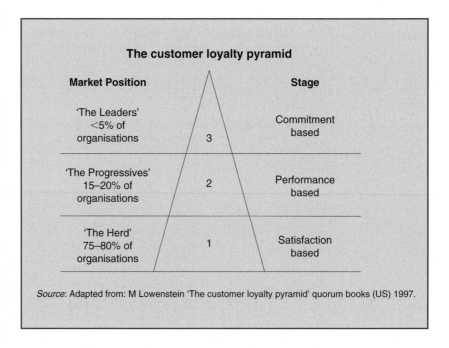

MARGIN NOTES

The customer loyalty pyramid

Market Position		Stage
'The Leaders' <5% of organisations	3	Commitment based
'The Progressives' 15–20% of organisations	2	Performance based
'The Herd' 75–80% of organisations	1	Satisfaction based

Source: Adapted from: M Lowenstein 'The customer loyalty pyramid' quorum books (US) 1997.

Lowenstein showed that less than 5% of organisations were even bothering to measure commitment (to come back and buy again) among its customers. Granted it was 1997 but things really don't change that fast in the real world where many of the organisations I meet are still grappling with whether to or how to add 'flaky' measures like customer satisfaction to the measurements they take.

Other (very large) organisations measure customer satisfaction on a regular basis but still do nothing worthwhile with the results. By worthwhile I mean incorporate the results into everybody's staff appraisal and reward systems – so that satisfying customers gets rewarded. When selling stuff (to whoever is in the firing line) adds so much bonus to the annual salary, which turkeys are going to vote for Christmas? So much for progress.

Despite all this, we are told by every organisation that they are investing 'fortunes' in creating loyal customers. Show some people a bandwagon and they can't help but clamber aboard. What too many organisations don't seem to realise is that loyalty is about more than 'bribery'.

If you want mindless 'loyalty', then buy a dog.

If you want committed customers who keep coming back, then you have to give them a very good reason to be 'loyal' – and that means much more than just being who you are or selling what you happen to sell. Even knowing what the 'good reason to stay' might be all depends on how well you understand them and their needs. Here we go again …

MARGIN NOTES

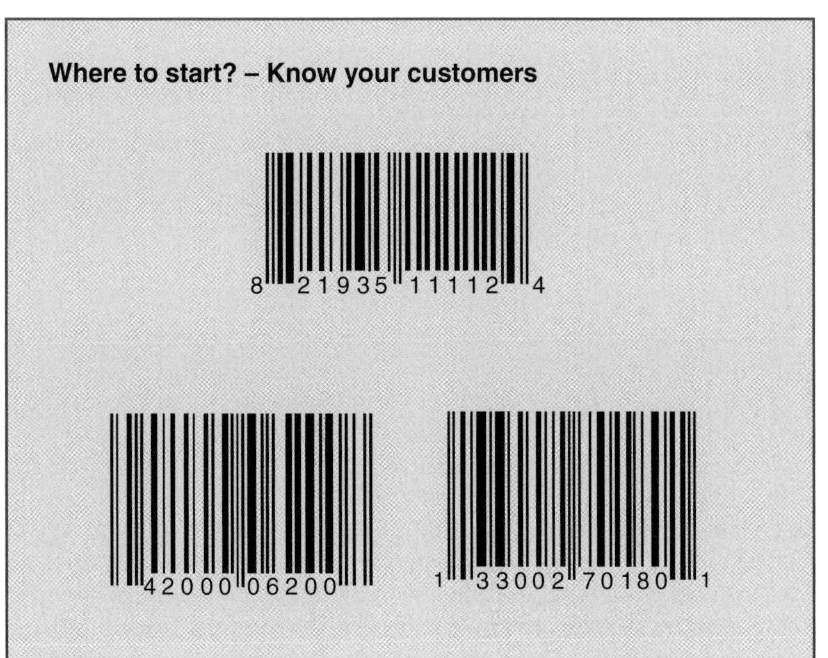

Barcodes *don't* make customers.

Understanding your products to an insane level of granularity is *not* the same thing as understanding your customers and empathising with their needs, wants, fear and aspirations.

Loyalty is what you want, but how do you get it? Issuing everyone with a discount card has nothing to do with either 'loyalty' or 'relationships'. Loyalty is about customers coming back because they want to. How do we get there?

Maybe a better way of asking the question is to ask, what gets in the way of customers coming back? The answer, unsurprisingly, is a lot of things – which ones are driving your business will depend on you, your organisation, its unique market position and its customers. The (not exhaustive) list of items to think about might include:

MARGIN NOTES

- Competition:
  - Have there been any moves by the competition that may have put you and your offer at a disadvantage?
  - Has there been any evidence of competitive entry, perhaps from outside the industry or in the form of substitute competition?

- Value migration:
  - Is there any evidence of value migration in the marketplace?
  - Are customers being attracted away to a new, more satisfying solution?

- Changing customer needs and wants:
  - Are customers' needs changing?
  - Have needs and wants changed so that your offering no longer has the same interest or following that it used to enjoy?
  - Are you the 'Sony Walkman' of your business who thought your dominant reign would go on for ever?

- Changing customer circumstances:
  - Customers are on a journey. They change, grow older, pass through life transitions (school, work, marriage, children, empty nest, divorce, retirement, illness, wealth/poverty) and as they do, their needs, wants and perceptions of value change too.
  - Not only will they possibly leave, they may also significantly change their purchasing behaviour, buying more, more often or less, less frequently as a result.
  - These are 'intermediate stages' between being a customer and defecting, sometimes called upward migration (buying more, more often) or downwards migration (buying less, less frequently).
  - The attentive organisation will be tracking and understanding these changes closely. Firstborn children are notorious at changing their parents' perceptions and buying behaviours.

- Internal changes:
  - Finally, check inside for something that your organisation has done that has caused (or contributed to) the decline in loyalty.

- We all know that we ought to check these things out with customers before we do anything, but we all know that we just don't.
- Sometimes simple administrative changes or minor cost efficiency changes can be enough to tip the scales for a customer who was 'just thinking' about changing.
- Range rationalisation is a well-known irritant for many, often long-standing, customers who feel they are no longer valued as their regular purchase is suddenly withdrawn – with no explanation.

Customers change like everything else. Loyalty requires different actions at different times, if you believe you have found the sure-fire-silver-bullet and you are bound to be disappointed.

A word on 'value migration'

MARGIN NOTES

There is a book you need to read (after you have finished this one of course), '*Value Migration, How to Think Several Moves Ahead of the Competition*' by Adrian Slywotzky (Harvard Business School Press, 1996).

In case you have trouble getting on to Amazon, briefly, Slywotzky is talking about the way that customers, (consumer and business/industrial) tend to change their minds. He looks at this and decides that there is a process at work that we should be able to identify and use. He considers that (at least some) of the changes in demand can be put down to *value migrating* in a marketplace.

Much of the thinking will remind you of Hertzberg theory (see Chapter 6) and the way that 'hygiene factors' will drive behaviour until they are satisfied, then they cease to drive or motivate. To give an example of Slywotzky's quite able arguments, we can think back to the long development of the car/automobile business:

- In the early days, (up to the 1960s):
  - There were lots of producers and the products were fun but not always reliable.
  - But they did not really have to be, shops and work was reasonably close by and public transport still worked so …
- Then the Japanese arrived:
  - With a car that started first time, every time.
  - Everybody wanted it.
  - Customers saw value in the offering.
  - Producers who could not deliver this reliability suffered.
- Then everybody had reliability:
  - And the customer wanted more 'styling'.
  - No value was attached to simple reliability, everyone had that.
  - Value had migrated in the market from reliability to style.

- Then everybody had 'style':
  - And the customer wanted 'performance'.
  - No value was attached any more to either reliability or style, all (at least most) had these.
  - Value had migrated again, this time to performance.

So the progress moves on, with the customers seeing different value in the marketplace over time, and then wanting and buying different solutions.

The Slywotzky 'headlines' are:

- Marketing strategy:
  - Is the art of creating value for the customer (I particularly like that one).

MARGIN NOTES

- Customer Value:
  - This can only be delivered by offering a product or service that corresponds to customer needs.

- Change:
  - In a fast changing business environment, the factors that determine value (customer perceptions of what they think they need or want) are constantly changing.

- Value migrates:
  - From outmoded business models to business designs that are better able to satisfy customers' new needs/wants.
  - For example, yesterday's customers were fighting to own Walkmans, colour televisions, video recorders and a second home in Wales.
  - Today its mp3 players, HDTV, DVD recorders and a holiday home in Switzerland or Croatia.

According to Slywotzky, there are three phases of what he calls *value migration*:

- In 'Inflow':
  - The initial phase, a company starts to grow by taking value from other parts of its industry because its business design proves superior in satisfying customers' priorities.
  - It has more of what the customers want now than the other players (iPod takes value from Sony?).

- In 'Stability':
  - The second phase, business designs are well matched to customer priorities and by overall competitive equilibrium.
  - The organisation grows on its successful base and spreads its offer through the innovation diffusion categories from the early adopters to the rest of the population (now everybody has a mobile phone).

- In 'Outflow':
  - The third phase, value starts to move away from an organisation's traditional activities toward business designs that more effectively meet evolving customer priorities.
  - Today's early adopters are on the move again, looking for the next big idea (Interactive gaming? Voice over IP? Hybrid cars?).

We all knew that nothing lasts forever – now we know what it's called – 'Value Migration'.

Value migration is an unstoppable force but it need not be a lethal one. For the product-focused organisation, value migration will likely prove fatal but there needs be no fear for the organisation that keeps its focus firmly on its customers. By focusing on perceptions of needs and wants (customer value) it should be able to move with its customer base, not away from it.

MARGIN NOTES

Rolls-Royce

One of the success stories within the Marine business of Rolls-Royce has been the market leading position gained by our series of 'UT' ship design and integrated systems within the Offshore Supply and Service vessel market, with over 500 such ships now at sea.

This success, which has been driven by significant customer loyalty, has been built on close co-operation with customers to continuously develop new, value-adding solutions that meet specific operating requirements, with the ship design and installed equipment working effectively together as one integrated unit.

We take the need to understand value from our customers' perspective extremely seriously and are continuously working to improve our organisational capability in this area and apply this knowledge across the range of products, systems and services that we offer.

Effective monitoring of customer satisfaction is a key input to understanding what is important to our customers and Rolls-Royce performance against these factors, as we seek to further increase customer loyalty and retention.

We use a balanced scorecard across the Marine business, of which 'Improve Customer Satisfaction' is a key element. This provides an effective mechanism to focus on priorities for improvement and an ability to communicate these effectively throughout the organisation, with annually agreed improvement targets embedded within individual objectives and reward systems.

The FAQs are:

5 Customer Retention		
5.3 Is retention just about customer satisfaction?		
5.3.1	Is 'customer satisfaction' a key marketing metric?	What this means is, is it: ● Collected ● Analysed and ● Used. To improve the organisation's market performance? Just collecting it is pointless – and costly. 'CustomerSat' is not a business 'ritual' that, like the traditional SWOT analysis, we carry out but treat as window dressing. Using it, even if its use annoys some internal people (often a good thing), is the point of collecting it in the first place.
5.3.2	What constitutes a 'satisfied' customer?	Frankly who cares any more? Really, I wonder if this question, so often heard, is worth the effort that it could soak up. The reasons for this outrageous statement are: ● It is difficult ● What does 'satisfied' mean? ● Customers may not know what makes them 'satisfied' ● They will be tempted to tell you what you want to know ● If you find out, it could all change tomorrow as value migrates constantly Much better that we invest the time and effort in maintaining an organisation that has the flexibility to deal with constantly changing markets.
5.3.3	What is the relationship between 'satisfaction' and 'commitment'?	A committed customer is one who wants to come back and, barring any obvious disasters on your part, (or surprising developments on the part of your competitors) will come back. Commitment is really the only thing worth measuring nowadays, so jump the lets-measure-satisfaction brigade and get straight to the metric that means something.
5.3.4	Is 'customer loyalty' a key marketing metric?	Yes – and no. The idea is right but the word conjures up all the stereotypical ideas that are wrong about customers. Loyalty should really be kept for 'man's best friend' and customers should be treated with the respect due to the people who are solely responsible for the survival and success of the organisation. Just because customers appear to be coming back because they want to ... For many years IBM was the 'safest' option and many organisations were almost frightened into buying IBM. As soon as the organisation began to acquire some knowledge in the IT area, the tables turned.

5.3.5	What else gets in the way of creating loyalty?	If you don't check for the things that *will* get in the way then you won't get a committed customer – or even a loyal one! ● Competition – is somebody doing it better? ● Value migration – are you about to be consigned to history? ● Changing customer needs and wants – are they bored or do they want something else? ● Changing customer circumstances – have they grown up/older and moved on? ● Internal changes – have you messed up? Nobody leaves without a reason – but 'I'm bored' and 'I could not be bothered any more' are both excellent reasons to move on. No organisation has the excuse to be boring!
5.3.6	Is marketing activity aimed at creating 'sales' or 'relationships'?	If it's 'sales' you will still be all right – as long as you remain in the rapid growth stage of the product life cycle (see Chapter 2). If you want to move into the 'maturity' stage you will have to leave the sales obsession behind you.
5.3.7	What will make the customer want to come back again and again?	Ah. If I knew the exact answer to that one I would be running your business instead of you. But you can find out – ask your customer.

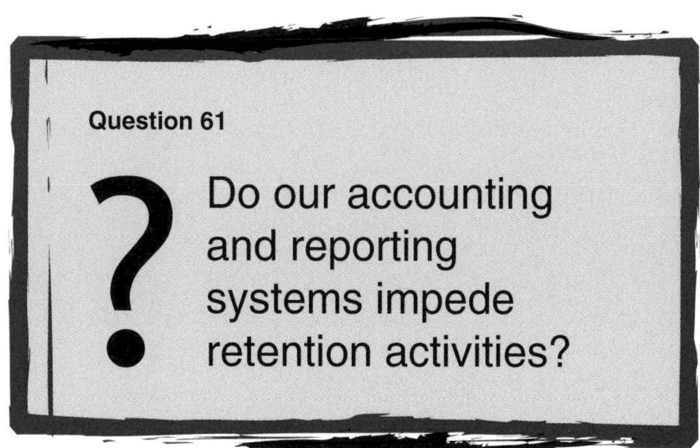

Question 61
?
Do our accounting and reporting systems impede retention activities?

Possibly the shortest section in the book, this part is less like reading and more like an internal project assignment.

If you read Reichheld (and subsequent writings by Reichheld and other commentators) carefully one problem comes through all the work, there is not very much chance of customer retention happening in an organisation – at least a large, shareholder-owned organisation.

The success stories of customer retention all tend to showcase organisations that are private, owner-managed or co-operative – examples of successful retention projects in exchange listed companies are as rare as hens' teeth. Why is this? The answer seems to lie in the accounting and finance systems – the processes which once served these organisations now controls them. Once again we are faced with an external (customer) versus internal (company) argument.

- The External View:
  - The customer is the name of the game and organisational profits only come from happy customers – who come back.
  - We maximise the profits by maximising customer commitment.
    - To do this we have to take a customer view of the world to be able to empathise with their needs and wants and to be able to develop new products and services that always meet their changing needs.
    - If we can keep the customer committed, the bottom line will look after itself.
  - Profits and margins are all about brands, market position and relationships.
  - Customers who *prefer* to do business with us are committed and profitable customers and (reasonably) safe from competitive poaching.
    - Our investments are always investments in customers, not just products, because customers give us our best returns.
    - We maximise the return on customers by taking a view of the investment over the lifetime of our relationship – some investments in our customers might not payback for five years, in this way we are sure to maximise the *lifetime value* of every customer.
- The Internal View:
  - The shareholder owns the business and needs to receive ever increasing returns on their investment.
    - Business is about being lean and mean and constantly looking for ways of reducing costs and being price competitive in the market – there is no 'loyalty that 10% off can't overcome'.
  - The secret to our success is simple.
    - Keeping a very close eye on the bottom line and making sure the costs are under control.
    - Everybody knows that they have a part to play in keeping the share price high and the returns on investment attractive – we do that by fearless control of spending and rigorous monitoring of every investment.
    - Either it comes good by the end of the year or we cut our losses fast.

It's your organisation, so it's your choice

Where does your organisation fit on this continuum?

MARGIN NOTES

The returns from customer retention activities will accrue more to the externally focused organisation because it, rather than the internally focused organisation, will be able to do what needs to be done to secure those returns.

The FAQs are:

5 Customer Retention		
5.4 Do our accounting and reporting systems impede retention activities?		
5.4.1	Is financial return an objective or a 'hurdle' in the business?	This takes us back to the first stages of strategy and understanding the organisation (see Chapter 1). Too many organisations confuse 'objectives' with 'measures of success' and think that they *exist* to maximise profits. Too often this is a part of the organisation culture and very difficult to change. If you can change the perspective (maybe in a small part of the business or a subsidiary where things are left to run themselves as long as the returns are made) then retention might just be on the cards.
5.4.2	Is success based on analysis of *product* or *customer* profitability?	Older style organisations still believe that products and services make profits rather than customers. As long as they believe this they will be looking in the wrong place to achieve any profit increase and will be pulling at the only levers they can see – the wrong ones.
5.4.3	Is success driven by quarterly, annual or longer returns?	The more business apes American practices, the more it all becomes shorter-term and the tyranny of the quarter dominates all thinking. Customers don't think in quarters ... Relationships aren't a series of quarterly liaisons ...
5.4.4	Can our systems account for lifetime value analysis?	Many systems 'can' account for any period that you want – the problem (challenge) is for you to explain to the masters of the systems why anyone would want to use a different or longer period.
5.4.5	How 'loyal' are our stakeholders?	Reichheld's original work showed that (in the US) shareholders were even less 'loyal' than customers and many organisations turned over their entire shareholder base faster than they turned over their customer base. Investors can also be described as 'fickle', 'disloyal' or 'promiscuous', names not just reserved for customers. In this case, the organisation has probably fallen down on its communications to this important stakeholder group. Investors, like customers, exist in different segments. If you need/want to attract long-term investors you need to explain why the organisation is focused on lifetime value and what it means for their long-term investment.

5.4.6	Have we calculated the (discounted) cost of the existing systems?	No discussion with the guardians of the 'accepted wisdom' of financial prudence will ever get off the ground unless you have some evidence of untapped financial returns from improved retention.
5.4.7	Do the financial decision-makers understand the issues?	You're the communications expert, its down to you.

MARGIN NOTES

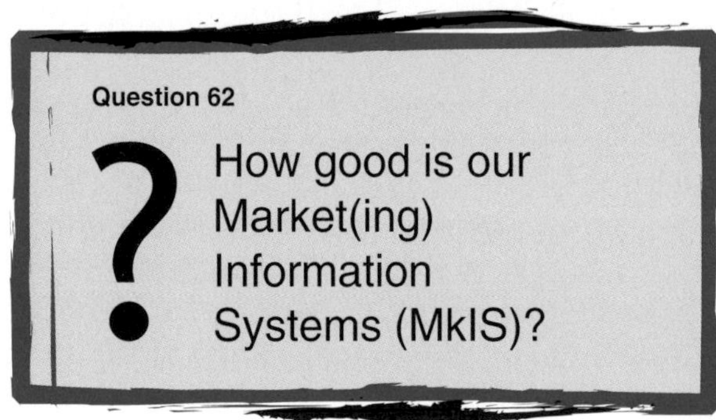

Question 62
?
How good is our Market(ing) Information Systems (MkIS)?

We won't dwell too long on what is a painful issue in almost every organisation I have ever met. If you have rubbish information, you will make rubbish decisions.

But – information is not a cost – information is a source of competitive advantage. How good is yours? The Marketing Information System (MkIS) is a good place to start, but it may not be called a 'system' or even be overtly concerned with marketing information – but it always exists (in some form) in every organisation.

Kotler (*'Principles of Marketing'* Kotler, Wong, Saunders & Armstrong, Pearson 2005) defines a marketing information system as a system which 'consists of people, equipment and procedures to gather, sort, analyse, evaluate and distribute needed, timely and accurate information to marketing decision-makers'. But, it should be clear from the preceding sections that assembling, analysing and disseminating information is far too important a process to be left to chance.

The market(ing) information system has gained a whole new lease of life recently with the creation of a new area of academic research, 'knowledge management'. Knowledge Management (KM) is the process through which an organisation generates value from its intellectual and knowledge-based assets. Most often, generating value from such assets involves 'codifying' what employees, partners and customers know, and sharing that information among employees, departments and even with other companies in an effort to devise best practices. You will have noticed, I'm sure that technology is not mentioned! KM is often facilitated by IT, but technology itself is not KM.

Call it what you will, information is the lifeblood of any organisation in a competitive marketplace. It is often the source of true competitive advantage. If an organisation is better informed on the needs of its target customers then it has a better chance of developing and offering products and solutions than the competition. Faster too.

Unfortunately, there is more to developing an effective market(ing) information system than simply piling miscellaneous data into a computer database – and hoping. One of the most common problems is that the systems simply become too complex and too data-heavy. To be effective, the system needs to:

- Produce information in a form that is really needed, and
- Deliver it to the people who need it most.

MARGIN NOTES

From the diagram it can be seen that a MkIS has four principle components.

- The external record system:
  - This which may include data on orders and invoicing, pricing stock levels, sales and payments.
- The marketing intelligence system:
  - Which may consist of regular data flows on market and product developments in the market and customer environment (often gleaned from trade press, media, conferences, exhibitions) to monitor trends and flag any unexpected changes.
- The market research system:
  - As described above (see Chapter 6).
- The marketing decision support system:
  - Which may include any tools or statistical decision models (including simple ratios) that the organisation uses to make sense of the data and turn it into useful information for decision-making managers.

The best test of any information system must be the extent to which it *contributes to the decision-making process* – that helps managers to make better, faster and more informed decisions. Obviously, to do this it must be updated regularly, be easily accessible – and produce information in a form that managers find usable. Of course none of this is possible unless we have a reasonably good idea of the marketing strategy's information needs. Without this it is likely that any system will prove both unfocused and unusable.

Moving from today's *data*-rich world to an *information*-rich environment in which marketing strategy can be developed and implemented is not as easy as it might sound. The faster that data grows (compounded by the IT department's ability to store more and more of the stuff) the greater becomes the problem of winnowing the wheat from the chaff.

Frankly, there is little point in congratulating yourself upon your ability to store six quarters worth of transactional data in your brand new data warehouse if you lack the skills to:

- Analyse the data for trends and changes and the ability to
- Understand the reason behind any movement in customer behaviour and
- The strategic marketing skills to do something about the changes you have identified.

MARGIN NOTES

The market(ing) information system

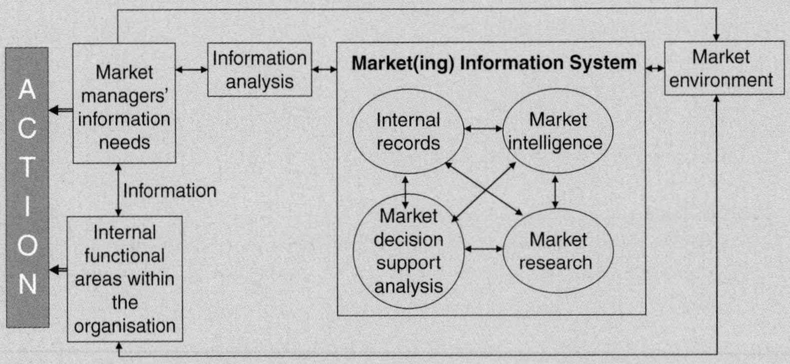

Source: Adapted from: Fifield & Gilligan (2000).

A sensible MkIS is more than just a database – although we all have to start somewhere. The basics have been covered in many specialist texts, but to make sure that we have no gaps, here is what you need to know:

- Market environment – what is going on out there?
  - Remembering the debate about what business we are in (see Chapter 5) the environment drives everything we do.
  - The better organisations work to tune broad antennae to the trends and ideas that flow around the environment so that they are never surprised – a big task.
  - Environmental scanning techniques are described in the main texts as well as other approaches.

- If we don't understand our environment (and our place within it) it can quickly turn from a nurturing one to a dangerous one.

- Market managers' information needs:
  - Information is only useful if it answers a question, otherwise it is just 'data' and there is far too much of that floating around already.
  - Start by understanding what questions the decision-maker has and that will help you understand what information is needed.

- Internal functional areas within the organisation:
  - The same applies to other areas in the organisation – their questions may be concerned with their day-to-day operations as well as a broader remit to understand the relevance of the customer information to their area of operations.

- Market(ing) information system – is made up of a number of ingredients:
  - Internal records
    - From sales or finance or customer returns – all types of data comes back to the organisation from these administrative systems.
    - They can be used but include the reasons why the data has been collected and allow for any bias this may introduce
  - Market intelligence
    - Refers to the various input of ideas and pieces of data that filter back through our connection with the marketplace.
    - These pieces need to be collected, collated and trends assessed.
  - Market research
    - Any specific research studies undertaken.
  - Market decision support analysis
    - Models used to analyse and make sense of the data.
    - No, don't turn off, a 'model' can mean anything from the UK Treasury Office model of the economy to the small sales company that measures the 'order-to-call-rate' on a spreadsheet to assess the effectiveness of its sales force – both are models, which ones do you use?
  - Information analysis
    - The bit that makes all the difference, how we translate the data and the analysis into terms that implementers can understand and use.

- Action
  - It all must point to something *happening* with the results, or there is just no point in the exercise.
  - Traditionally there are three activities that the MkIS needs to feed into:
    - *Planning*: Organising tomorrow's activities
    - *Execution*: Doing what the plans say
    - *Control*: Making sure what the plans say, gets done.

MARGIN NOTES

The FAQs are:

5 Customer Retention		
5.5 How good is our Market(ing) Information Systems (MkIS)?		
5.5.1	Are your database and/or management systems based on market needs?	Collecting data for its own sake is pointless, the idea is to understand market needs and allow relationships to be established and nurtured.
5.5.2	How accurate and flexible is your customer data?	Rigid systems are favoured by some systems people because they allow very fast processing – in set directions. Try and change the directions though! But, customers change their minds and their perceptions all the time – you need to keep up.
5.5.3	How accurate and flexible is your prospect data?	Typically we know less about our prospects than our customers – so the systems need to be even more flexible.
5.5.4	Do you make use of the MkIS for planning, execution and controlling?	MkIS needs to be *used*. • *Planning*: How we will execute better and differently tomorrow to meet new customer needs • *Executing*: Getting activity going in the market to satisfy more customers • *Controlling*: How well we are meeting our customers' needs compared to the competition.
5.5.5	How responsive is your MkIS for market feedback?	We don't (should not) operate a purely 'push' system – we need some feedback on how well we are doing. The better and faster the feedback the stronger your competitive advantage.
5.5.6	Do you use your MkIS as a source of competitive advantage?	If you don't you probably won't last very long. Customers search for value – for the perfect solution to their problem. If you aren't nearest to a perfect solution in the marketplace, they will buy somewhere else.
5.5.7	Is 'KM' used within our organisation?	We will deal with the issue of KM later. However, here we should state that we will soon start to see organisations differentiating themselves by how they retain and manage knowledge. KM is a simple concept but one that is desperately difficult to implement, it will grow, if slowly, as organisations discover that the market advantage it can bring will offset the investment in developing internal KM processes.

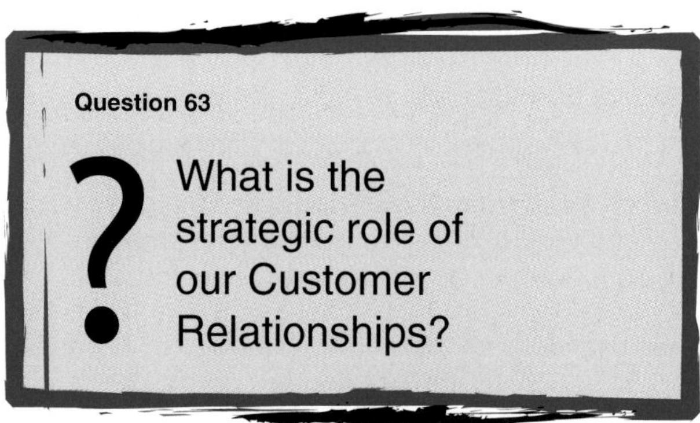

Question 63
?
What is the strategic role of our Customer Relationships?

So much nonsense has been written about 'relationships' and 'relationship management' over the past few years that it is barely credible.

Mediocre managers love bandwagons, especially very expensive ones.

In this section we aren't going to criticise all those very expensive CRM systems that organisations have purchased and now complain about – I have done that elsewhere. Here we will look at the basics of *relationships* and relationship building and leave you to make your own mistakes.

MARGIN NOTES

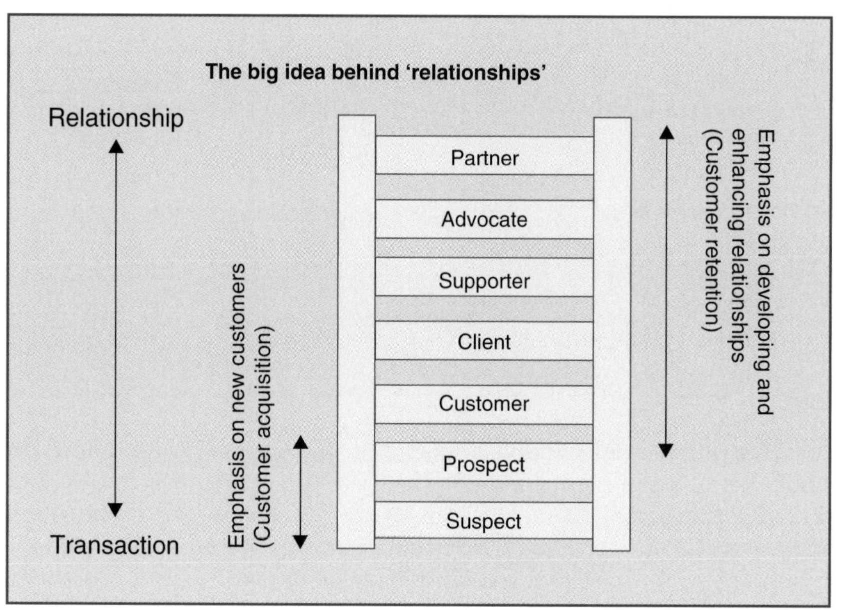

The big idea behind 'relationships' (not a very good word really) is that if we work at moving beyond the simple *transaction* to a 'deeper', more *relationship* basis we will make more money from customers who buy more, better and more often.

Different commentators have chosen interesting labels for this phenomenon but always it is presented as our view on what should happen; little account is taken of the customer.

Also, where most attempts at forging relationships go astray is in the implementation. One day organisations are going to get used to the idea that customers aren't happy just to have things imposed on them without asking by organisations that think they know best.

If we really want a *relationship* with our customers, we are going to have to stop 'doing things to' customers without asking them. A relationship needs two parties to be successful, not just one. Relationship is a *two-way* bridge that allows customers the freedom to take what they want and need from our organisation, not just to soak up what we want to give them.

I can see the high-need-for-control managers running for cover already.

MARGIN NOTES

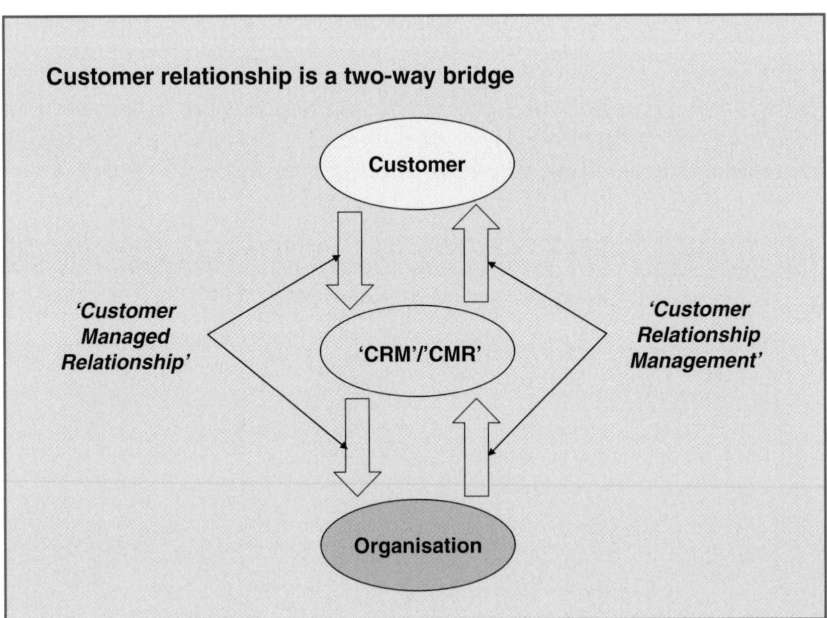

One of the few books I have found that makes some sense about the whole relationship area is called *'The Customer Differential'* by Melinda Nykamp, (Amacom, 2001). Nycamp keeps reasonably clear of the whole CRM debacle and focuses on what relationships are all about and how to build them, but without the normal obsession with heavy IT systems that allow the whole relationship process to be de-personalised.

- Has nobody else seen a flaw in that argument yet?
- Has nobody else worked out that 'relationship' is a human process not a systems one?

- Has nobody else worked out that people are better at differentiating your offer than systems?
- Has nobody else worked out that customer service is not excellent if delivered by automated call systems and cheap outsourced call centres on the Indian sub continent with a language problem?
- But the bottom line has improved this year so why bother?

Nycamp explains that the relationship process starts with the customer.

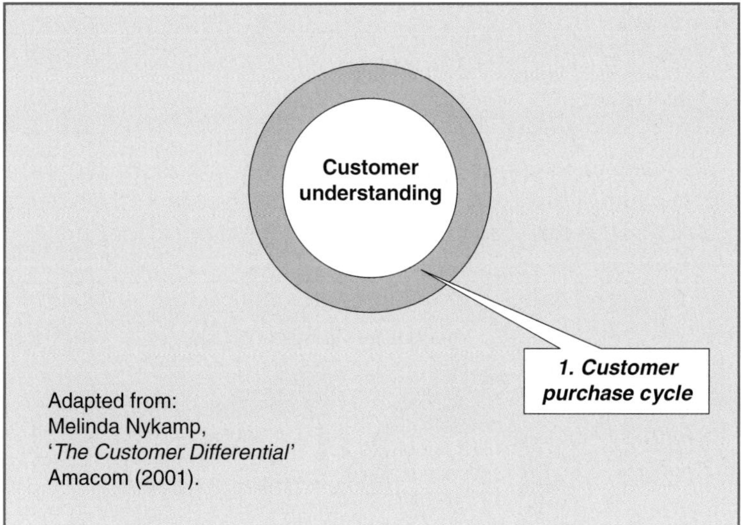

MARGIN NOTES

We need to know all about the customer as we have explained above – there really is no escape from this. We also need to know about the customer's normal purchase cycle. Nycamp suggest we understand:

- Stages of the Purchase Cycle
- Length of each Stage
- Related Complexity of Each Stage
- Indicators of When a Customer Enters a Stage
- Frequency at Which a Customer Repeats the Cycle
- Level of Resources Directed at Each Stage.

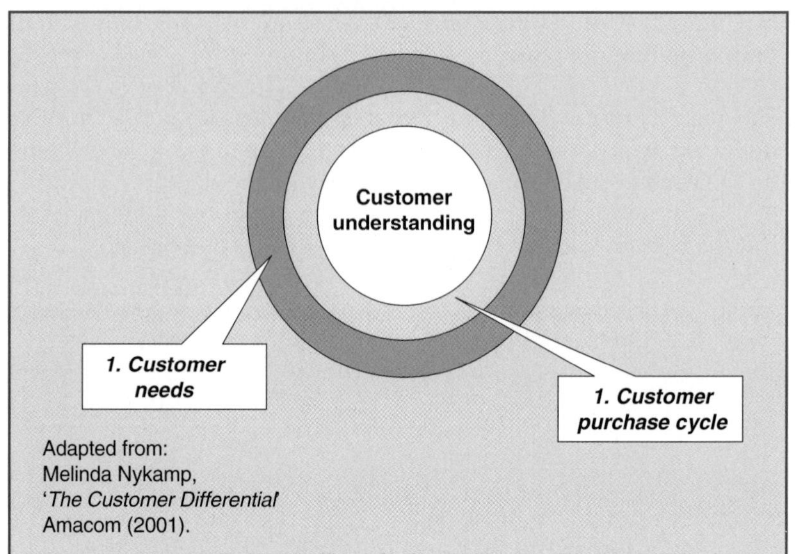

MARGIN NOTES

Next, we need to know how the customers needs affect the purchase cycle. For example, how different levels of information, convenience, efficiency, price and reputation might affect purchase behaviour.

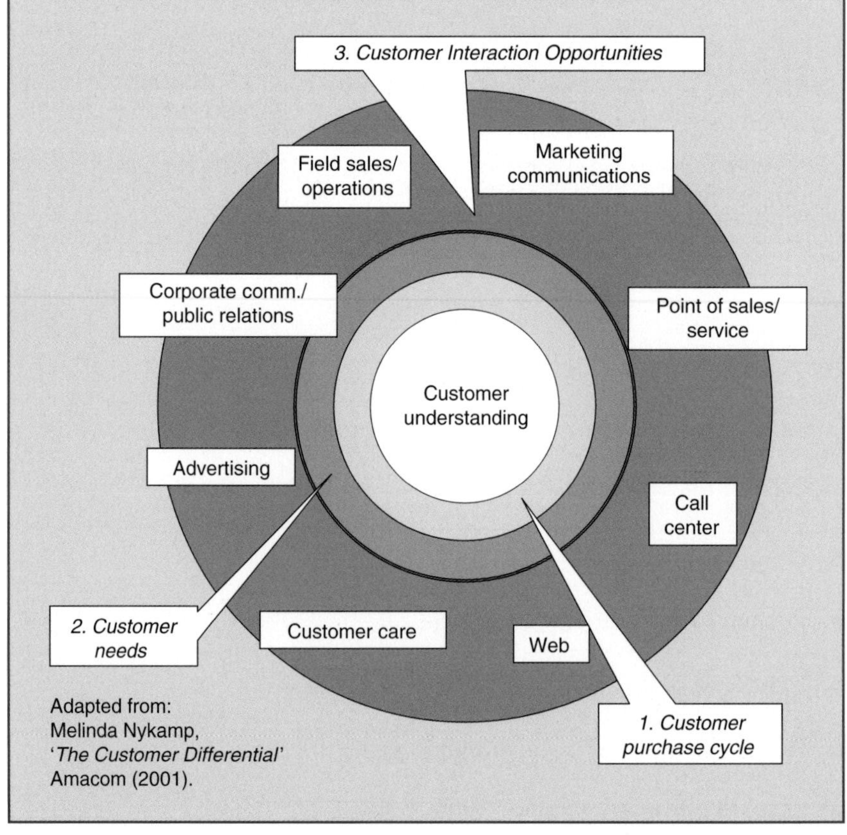

Next, we need to understand the opportunities we might have to interact with the customer. Nycamp suggest that we look for opportunities that are:

- Tied to specific stages of the purchase cycle.
- Cross-channel and cross-media, not just the normal ones.
- Situation-driven or driven by a deeper understanding of customer needs and behaviours, not simple driven by demographic differences (see Chapter 7 and the discussion on 'CONTEXT© marketing').

Some of these interaction opportunities can be seen in the diagram:

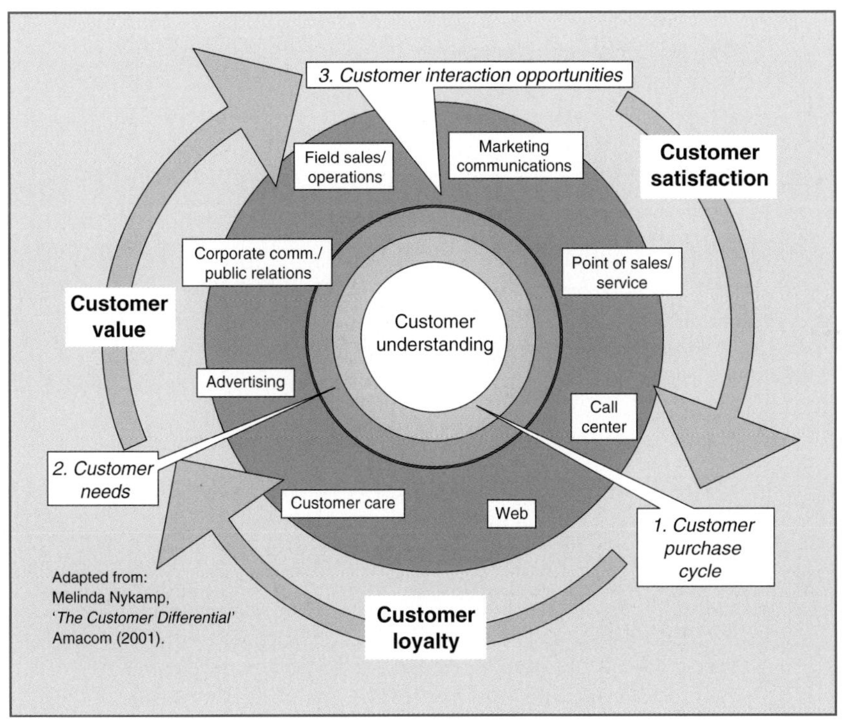

Adapted from: Melinda Nykamp, *'The Customer Differential'* Amacom (2001).

MARGIN NOTES

Finally, Nycamp draws out the idea 'virtuous circle' and places the important 'strategic' arrows in and we can see a flow of investment in:

1. Driving for customer satisfaction, that leads to
2. Driving for customer loyalty, that leads to
3. Driving for customer value, that leads to …

One more time

Just in case you lost sight of things in that run-through of key steps, this *doesn't* have to be done by a large and very expensive IT system. Nor is this just for the bigger companies; although the smaller companies will be wondering what all the fuss is about, they know that they have relationships with their customers or they have no business.

The FAQs are:

5 Customer Retention		
5.6 What is the strategic role of our Customer Relationships?		
5.6.1	Have we/are we considering implementing CRM?	Most companies have at least considered it although more and more now are starting to wonder if they need a system to do it. If it is on your agenda, you need to ask: ● Why is it on the agenda? ○ For cost saving? ○ For growth? ○ For customer satisfaction/commitment? ● Who is responsible for the assessment? Head of IT, Finance, Operations, Marketing ...
5.6.2	Does CRM have to be IT based?	No
5.6.3	Is the CRM based on clear marketing objectives and strategy?	If you don't have these you will have enormous problems. To be fair to the large proprietary IT systems, they all have (small) print that says that you need to have agreed the objectives and strategy before you install the CRM. The reason is, a well designed system will move you along quite fast – but unless you have a very clear idea of exactly where you want to be (unique market position and differentiation ...) then you will get a 'standard system' that takes you to, well, the same place as everybody else.
5.6.4	Is the CRM built on the 'customer-centric' organisation?	CRM built over a product centric organisation will move products and customers along very nicely and will provide an *efficient* if soulless support service. CRM built over a customer-centric organisation will move customers and relationships along very nicely and will provide an *effective* if sometimes erratic support service. Which one would your customers prefer?

5.6.5	Is the CRM designed to target customers or 'woo' them?	The former is a lot cheaper than the latter. If all you have (and all you want) is a prospecting database, then don't call it a CRM system and expect great things from it.
5.6.6	Are we talking CRM or CMR?	Ah. Which way would your customers like the relationship to go? Where would they like the power and control to lie?
5.6.7	Is our CRM future-proofed?	Everything (especially if in contact with customers) changes all the time. Systems and processes (whether IT or people systems) tend to be inflexible. The good thing about 'inflexible' is that you get conformity and consistency, important if there is a brand to be built. The bad thing about 'inflexibility' is that it may not cater for customers changing their minds and wanting different offerings and service over time.

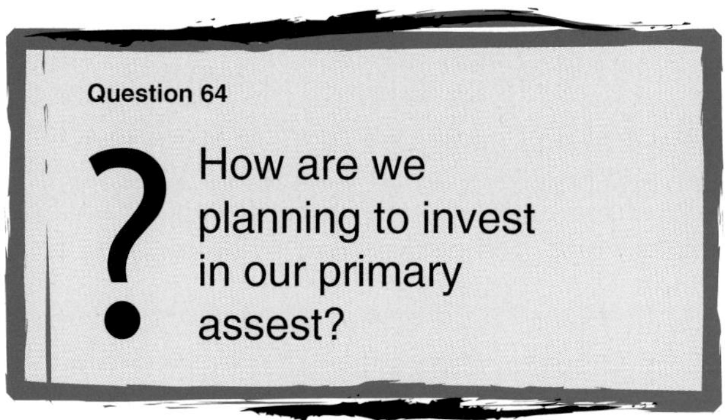
Question 64
?
How are we planning to invest in our primary assest?

This section is placed here, more as a precursor to the following, important chapter on the Marketing Organisation than as a self-standing unit.

Up to this point we have looked at the technical and the 'hard' aspects of customer retention – the things we need to do to retain more customers and to improve the bottom line.

If only it was that easy.

Knowing what to do (assuming what I have said makes sense and you have managed to retain enough of it) is just not enough – *wanting to do it* is what counts, and that's a human thing.

LOYALTY'S SIX PRINCIPLES

- Preach what you practice
  - Clarify your values and hammer them home to customers, employees, suppliers and shareholders – by words *and deeds*
- Play to win-win
  - Loyalty means your competitors lose and your partners win
- Be picky over your customers
  - At high-loyalty companies, membership is a privilege
- Keep it simple
  - Small teams for responsibility and simple rules for decision-making
- Reward the right results
  - Save your best deals for your most loyal customers
- Listen hard, talk straight
  - Make it safe for employees to offer candid criticism.

Source: Frederick Reichheld, '*Lead for Loyalty*', HBR July 2001.

The questions in this section are more for guidance than for eliciting answers – you and I both know the answers to some of them and know that no amount of logical argument is going to change anyone's mind. For these managers, often in the rapid growth stage of business or the more protected backwaters of industries, they have not yet had to face the concerted price competition that will force them to re-think the accepted wisdom of their calling.

If you have been through that particular fire and come out the other side, you know who really pays the bills, and who is really in control of the business – the customer.

The FAQs are:

5 Customer Retention		
5.7 How are we planning to invest in our primary asset?		
5.7.1	Is the customer currently regarded as the most important asset in the organisation?	Not in many organisations. But, when I have approached the problem from an 'asset basis' with finance directors, they really start to understand some of the issues involved. Try it, have patience, you have nothing to lose.

5.7.2	Have we calculated the 'return-on-assets' we get from customers?	Now here's a calculation worth doing. Everybody gets very excited about all those other assets but nobody calculates the return on the big one
5.7.3	Do we know the value we extract from each customer or segment?	We have looked at this already in the segmentation area. We need to know where the money comes from to know where (which customers/segments) are worth investing in.
5.7.4	Have we calculated the value we could extract from the market?	If we know what we get, we ought to have an idea (calculated on a spreadsheet of course) of what we don't get – because of ineffective marketing – but could get. Retention will be the big one of course.
5.7.5	What investment is needed to extract this value?	Just a simple financial case here, how much will it cost? How long will it take? How much will we make? Be impersonal.
5.7.6	Over what time period, with what returns?	If you are feeling up to it, (or you have an MBA, or you trained as an Accountant but daren't let anybody know or if you know a tame accountant) calculate a DCF (discounted cash flow – look it up) of all the future returns from improved retention that fall outside the current year. You never know ...
5.7.7	Do the financial decision-makers agree with our view?	They have been trained to seek out the sources of revenue open to the organisation. Just help them see that revenue can come from previously unexpected quarters. How can you get them to agree?

■ The strategic questions (58–64)

The fifth part of the Market strategy discussion, Customer retention

Retention, in the guise of CRM has become one of the big bandwagons of the past decade, which is unfortunate. Retention and relationships (and to some extent even CRM) are definitely not a waste of time like some of the bandwagons we have seen in the past. Dealt with properly, the returns to be gained from good retention practice are astounding. But every task needs the right tool.

I wonder whether IT has been the 'right' tool for implementing relationships – I suspect not. Some organisations are no re-trenching in the face of customer revolt and bringing call centres back from India. Will it be enough? Typically with relationships, it will take as long to fix as it took to be messed up in the first place. Short-term obsessed managers who believe their future hangs by a quarter-by-quarter thread will just make life increasingly difficult for themselves if they don't deal with strategic issues like retention, on a strategic timescale.

Approach retention as a tactical problem and it certainly it won't pay off within the year and you scrap it. The problem only gets worse as customers defect because they absolutely believe you don't care about them any longer. And they are right.

So we arrive at the questions again. Do the calculations and then be honest with your answers.

No.	Strategic question	Our strategic answer	Importance	✓
	Retention			
58	How important is 'Retention' in our market?		Must have	
			Nice to have	
			Not important	
59	How big are the 'problem' and the potential gains?		Must have	
			Nice to have	
			Not important	
60	Is retention just about customer satisfaction?		Must have	
			Nice to have	
			Not important	
61	Do our accounting and reporting systems impede retention activities?		Must have	
			Nice to have	
			Not important	
62	How good is our MkIS?		Must have	
			Nice to have	
			Not important	
63	What is the strategic role of our Customer Relationships?		Must have	
			Nice to have	
			Not important	
64	How are we planning to invest in our primary asset?		Must have	
			Nice to have	
			Not important	

CHAPTER 10

Organisation: Processes and Culture (with Hamish Mackay)

> 'He who has not first laid his foundations may be able with great ability to lay them afterwards, but they will be laid with trouble to the architect and danger to the building. (The Prince)'
>
> *Niccolo Machiavelli (1469–1527), Italian diplomat, political philosopher, musician, poet, and playwright*

MARGIN NOTES

Ever since the SCORPIO approach first appeared with 'the organisation' as one of its integral components, people have been asking why a subject area that is obviously outside the traditional confines of 'Marketing – the MBA subject', is included in an approach that is obviously all about the customer.

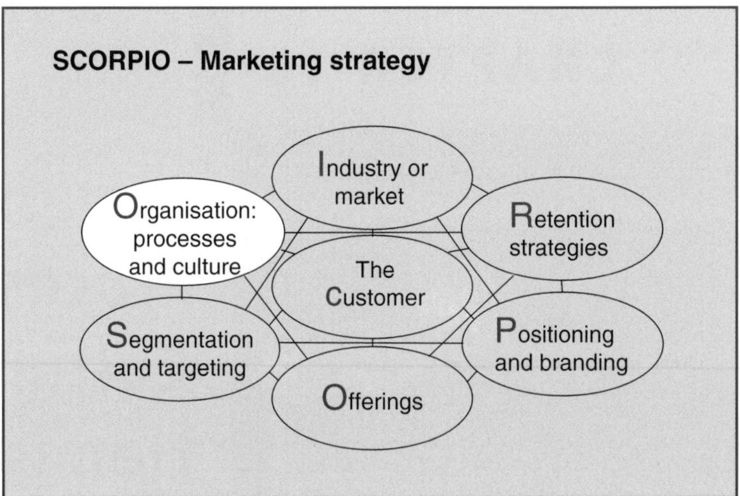

The answer is frighteningly simple: marketing strategy that is not *implemented* is a pointless waste of everybody's time.

We will look and ponder on the internal working of the organisation because there is no point in dissecting the marketing strategy of an organisation if you don't also consider what is required to give that strategy life.

Individuals can achieve very little on their own, only organisations (a formal group of people with one or more shared goals) can get *big* things done. But, as we all know, each organisation has its own way of doing things. What we are trying to do in this chapter is give you an understanding of the 'organisational levers' so that you can relate these levers back to the rest of the SCORPIO content – and maybe get (the right) things done!

We won't spend time looking at 'the organisation' in general; there are too many excellent books that do that job already. We are only interested in 'the marketing organisation'.

First, some basics on the organisation, management, staff/employees and process:

■ A word on 'the organisation'

MARGIN NOTES

Maybe a definition or two:

- 'An organised body of people with a particular purpose, for example, a business' (Oxford)
- 'An official group of people who work together for the same purpose' (Cambridge)

And the 'headlines':

- Organisations are about people.
- An organisation is a group of people who come together with shared objectives.
- Most of what an organisation does is to 'organise' (see?) the energy of those inside the organisation – the staff or employees – to deliver benefit to those outside the organisation – the customers.
- What we know about how all these people (inside and outside) think and behave has everything to do with how successful the organisation will be in the short, medium and long term.
- The organisation needs first to recognise what it is in business to achieve (see Chapter 2) and that doesn't mean 'handsome returns for shareholders' (see Chapter 3).
  - Financial returns are clearly necessary, but they cannot guide the organisation.
  - An organisation needs to be striving to be something.
- This 'something' gives a purpose and a rationale to an organisation.
  - If the organisation is customer focused (we have not yet come across an organisation that did not *believe* it was customer

focused) then this must guide you to the goal of delivering benefits that the customer wants, values and is willing to pay for.

A word on 'management'

But first, a definition or three:

- 'Directing and controlling a group of one or more people or entities for the purpose of co-ordinating and harmonizing that group towards accomplishing a goal' (Wikipedia)
- 'The process of managing' (Oxford)
- 'The control and organization of something' (Cambridge)
- 'Getting things done through people' (Fifield)

MARGIN NOTES

And the 'headlines':

- There is, we believe, an irrefutable logic about management.
  - The logic is that once the objective is set and the full *customer value proposition* (CVP) (see Chapter 11) is worked out, the rest is as natural as light follows day.
  - The key is to work out the Value Proposition *in sufficient detail* knowing that the detail informs everybody in the organisation about how to deliver what the customer wants (the benefit).
- As long as you really understand the customer and everybody else agrees with both the direction and the importance of the customer focus, then you hold the moral high ground.
  - If one part of the organisation would seem to be out of line then you use the logic to bring them back into line.
  - We will see how this logic works as we go through this chapter.
- Management clearly have a role but it is not in delivering benefit to customers.
  - For those of you who are concerned with why management – here is what I believe management were put on this earth to do:
    - Determine strategy – or as Edith Penrose from the LSE elegantly phrased it a long time ago – 'the search for profitable business plans'
    - Put the machine in place to deliver strategy
    - Make the organisation optimally efficient
    - Resolve conflict
    - Manage change
- So now you know what the manager's job is all about.

A word on staff or employees

Looking at definitions again:

- 'An employee contributes labour and expertise to an endeavour. Employees perform the discrete activity of economic production. Of the three factors of production, employees usually provide the labour' (Wikipedia)

- 'A person employed for wages or salary' (Oxford)

- 'Someone who is paid to work for someone else' (Cambridge)

And the 'headlines':

- Staff (or employees) are the people who do the work, who deliver the benefits that satisfy (we hope) the customers.
    - This is not about management style, whether an organisation is consensus managed or autocratic or any other style – they all work if applied consistently.
    - The most important element of 'staff' for us, in the marketing strategy context, is how we can ensure that the staff delivers on the promises that we make to customers.
    - And that they do so in a way that re-enforces the unique characteristics and values of our brand. How do we do that?

- What matters is that the 'natural laws' of organisational life are respected. These are:
    - Staff need to understand *why* they need to do certain things, in certain ways.
    - There needs to be a common understanding of the *why*
    - Staff need to understand in what way they are contributing to the *why*
    - Staff means all staff

- So what matters in an organisation is what the staff are doing, in every way, to deliver benefit to the customers. For example:
    - Are they doing the right tasks?
    - Are tasks being carried out in the right way?
    - Are staff aware of what is happening elsewhere in the organisation which affects how they operate?

- It is a natural human trait; we all try to improve what we are doing, so changing in some small (or maybe very large) way the overall outcome. How do we know if this change was optimal for the organisation as well as our own small unit and how do we harness the ideas that are all around us for the benefit of *all parts of the* organisation?

MARGIN NOTES

A word on the importance of process

A definition:

- 'A series of actions or steps towards achieving a particular end' (Oxford)

And the 'headlines':

- There is a very simple way of linking what the organisation wants to achieve as expressed in its objectives (see Chapter 3) to what and how the customer benefit is delivered. This is called *process*.

MARGIN NOTES

- Every organisation has several key processes but surprisingly few organisations actively recognise processes and use the management of process as an organisational lever.
  - Process is the 'glue' that holds the organisation together and the easiest way (by far) of affecting and changing what is done in the organisation.
  - Process (properly identified and managed) allows the customer and the staff to be united.

- If process 'achieves the particular end', the monitoring of process should help the organisation to know what is happening – how progress towards the particular end is progressing.
  - Then, with the aid of management information (MI), benchmarks and objectives we can find out how far away from the 'particular end' we are likely to arrive.
  - This, ultimately, is defined as the performance of the organisation.

There we have the basics of the marketing organisation, not an unbiased list but tailored to the needs of the marketing strategy:

- The organisation
- Management
- Staff/employees
- Process

Each of the sections of this chapter deals with part of the logic described above. In addition, as we develop the ideas on the organisation, we will build them into lessons for the customer value proposition (see Chapter 11), the key tool for organisational behaviour and outputs.

This is *not* an either/or question, the successful organisation will be focused externally and internally – certainly not just internally.

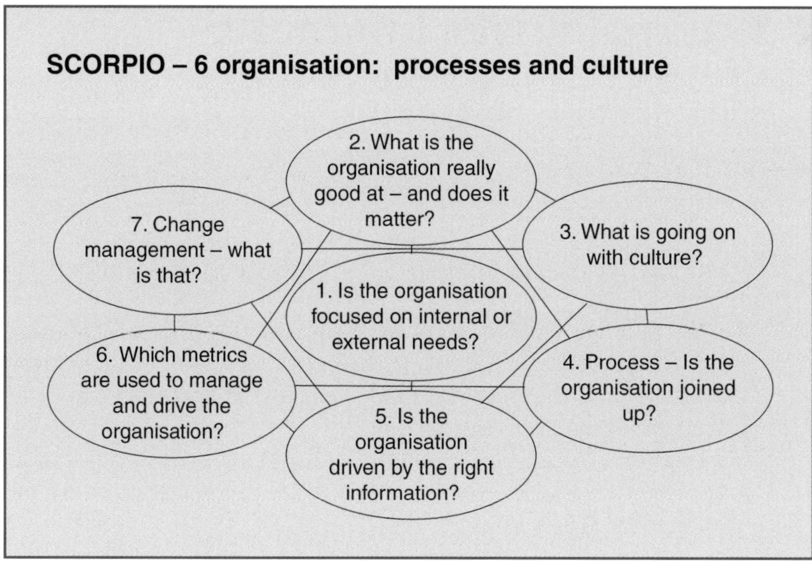

SCORPIO – 6 organisation: processes and culture
2. What is the organisation really good at – and does it matter?
7. Change management – what is that?
3. What is going on with culture?
1. Is the organisation focused on internal or external needs?
6. Which metrics are used to manage and drive the organisation?
4. Process – Is the organisation joined up?
5. Is the organisation driven by the right information?

MARGIN NOTES

Question 65

? Is our organisation focused on internal or external issues?

As with 'customer or market orientation', all organisations *claim* that they are externally focused, even if their strategy and their product development are driven exclusively by internal measures and their key performance indicators (KPIs, see Chapter 5) are all internally focused. 'After all, we sell to customers who are external don't we?'

It is time to be honest. Organisations are naturally internally focused. This is not how it should be but in most cases that is the way it is – people go to work, they meet the same people every day, many staff never see, much less talk to, a customer as long as they work in an organisation. This can make involving staff in the implementation of the marketing strategy very difficult.

External drives internal

The marketing strategy requires that the internal focus be driven by external (customer and competitive) issues – they are the most important issues are they not?

- We have to be concerned with how an organisation 'organises' itself to *deliver* the marketing strategy – by delivering on identified customer needs.
  - To do that we need to pay attention to the natural default of people (and so organisations) to be concerned with what is immediately around them, rather than what is perhaps more important but further away and less visible.
  - The right focus can be created and supported by internal marketing programmes (see below) and will be delivered more by process than by structure.
  - An organisational structure can help to make an organisation more efficient in the delivery of customer benefit but it won't ensure that the focus is maintained (effectiveness).

- The focus of the staff/organisation's activities will be set, first of all by the marketing objectives and these, as we saw in Chapter 5, should be translated directly into the KPIs.
  - The organisation's performance is then measured and compared to the KPIs so informing the organisation whether it is on track or not.
  - In the same way that the objective should not be financial (see Chapter 3) neither should the KPIs; they should be about what matters to the organisation if it is to succeed in achieving its strategic goals.
  - Financial objectives are about whether the performance is being translated into profit and cash and enough of each to satisfy all the stakeholders in the organisation.
  - If this seems intuitively 'wrong' to you, read Chapter 1 again – carefully.

- KPIs can focus the activities of the organisation on market penetration, name awareness or margin, depending on the marketing objectives you have selected.
  - KPIs will normally stand as 'proxies' for the marketing and business goals – proxies that allow staff (and sometimes management) to identify more closely with what the organisation is trying to achieve.
  - Assuming the decision makers (you?) have followed the SCORPIO process, your objectives will be customer based and the marketing strategy will have been based on customer insight.

MARGIN NOTES

The organisation will have a clear view of what it wants to be and how it wishes to compete.
   - This organisational 'self-view' should demonstrate to all staff how the KPIs reflect the marketing objectives – imagine the power in that.
   - Bringing the unique identity and business purpose alive for the staff is critical, unless you are intent on running an undifferentiated, price competitive business.

- Unfortunately, the reality is that too many organisations will short circuit the objective setting process and some will even simply decide empirically what the objectives are to be – 'that is management's job after all is not it?'
   - The problem with this (traditional) route is that it will be almost impossible to convince anybody that the objectives are sensible – or that the objectives have anything to do with them, or their job.
   - That sounds more like the organisations we know …

MARGIN NOTES

The power of the 'strategic process'

The biggest and most serious mistake managers (and commentators) can make is to forget that organisations are collections of people – it always comes back to people.

- To succeed in business we need the staff (people) or workforce (people) to carry out certain tasks and behave in a certain way.
   - Just because they are paid to do the job as the organisation determines it, doesn't mean it will happen that way.
   - If we are looking for excellence, we need the staff to believe in what the organisation is doing.
   - To do that, they need to *understand* – and someone needs to explain why!

- Strategic decisions that are arrived at without 'due process' – a series of visible steps that everybody can see and understand, will normally lack the rationale needed to take the staff with you.
   - It is often the strategic process itself that allows you to communicate *the why* to the people who will have to implement.
   - The strategic process that is visibly and demonstrably based on an understanding of customer need and customer value has further benefit; it ensures that the organisational focus is external rather than internal.

- An organisation won't survive very long if its focus is purely internal, at least not beyond the move from rapid growth into maturity.

Contributing to the value proposition

As explained above, the most important tool for co-ordinating and directing organisational behaviour and outputs to meet identified customer needs is the CVP.

A customer value proposition (CVP) can be defined as:

MARGIN NOTES

- A written statement that focuses all the organisation's market activities onto customer-critical elements that create a significant differential within the customer's decision process to prefer/purchase the organisation's offering over a competitor's.
- 'An implicit promise a company makes to customers to deliver a particular combination of values' (Treacy and Wiersema).
- Internally, the CVP is a statement summarising the customer targets, competitor targets and the core strategy for how you intend to differentiate your product or service from the offerings of competitors.

At the end of each of the seven sections in this chapter, we will look at how the ideas we have discussed might inform the CVP.

The value proposition lessons here are:

Your organisation's value proposition need to show how the objectives translate into staff issues:

- Who are your customers?
- What do they want (in terms of benefits)?
- Why are one set of customers different from another (segmentation)?
- What does that mean for your staff?
- How have these customer needs been identified and the resulting strategy agreed (the strategy process)?

The FAQs are:

6 Organisation: processes and culture		
6.1 Is our organisation focused on internal or external issues?		
6.1.1	What dictates the organisational design?	The prime driver for organisational design tends to be the *efficient* running of the business. Thus the divisional splits will accommodate the natural grouping of skills and work tasks (for instance accountants and book keeping will collect in the Finance Department). This makes everything easier and simpler to manage. Concerns about structure will be more about the eternal debate over centralisation versus decentralisation than about which structure will best facilitate the marketing strategy. There is now more of a move to identify *process* within structure, so that rather than have artificial links between functions all the process is managed within one area (not one function). This will take greater hold as process is better understood and organisations will change shape as a result.
6.1.2	Where is the customer in the 'structure'?	If you are internally focused then the customer won't feature in the structure! It is far too easy for an organisation to slip into the habit of believing its own thinking. To combat this, *customer champions* need to be located strategically in the organisation. There are two key areas where this can take place: ● First, in the marketing department. o Charged with understanding the customer, the role of customer champion is generally filled in this area. ● The second is within the *process* – more of how that works later.
6.1.3	How are objectives reviewed?	We have already seen that there are different ways in which objectives can be set. Of equal importance is how they are reviewed and how often. Objectives need to evolve with the changing fortunes of the organisation – not so that they are made easier but that they stay relevant. The target customers and segments is constantly evolving as well, so without review the organisation could easily find itself falling behind the competition or worse, following false shadows. Organisations generally have an (short-term) annual budget review cycle and often follow three-year planning periods. It never fails to amaze us that organisations should follow this course and effectively end up with a one-year plan before the next three-year planning review is completed. Of course this is driven by stock market analyst requirements, but a rolling plan with continuous review at whatever frequency would be a more appropriate approach. The main point is that there should be constant review of all objectives to ensure that they remain relevant to the organisation and its long-term goals.

6.1.4	What happens when the objectives are in conflict?	Unless an organisation is unusually fortunate, the objectives they set themselves will be in conflict. This is quite normal and brought about by circumstances in the environment which have not been foreseen, as well as management's preference for multiple objectives rather than single objectives (see Chapter 3). However, one of management's key roles is to resolve conflict. To avoid unnecessary 'fall out' from these conflict-resolving discussions, the organisation should have in place a set of *design principles*. Design principles set out the rules and preferred behaviours of the organisation (for instance that service quality is more important than the cost of service) that: • Are applicable to all situations, events and processes • Are rooted in the unique market position of the organisation (see Chapter 8) • Are the way that the organisation believes it will create the unique behaviours that support its differentiation and brand. Design principles are never absolutes, but being brand based, they help to bring alive what is the desired attitude and behaviour needed to deliver your unique strategy.
6.1.5	How effective is organisation-wide communications?	If your organisation is not good at communicating internally, don't worry, you aren't alone. This area of a business almost always gets a big 'thumbs down' from staff. (*In all the companies I have worked in, we have never seemed to get this right, either it is too much or it is too little or it is too late. But that doesn't mean that you should not try. You always get points for trying – Hamish Mackay*). Staff want to know how well they are performing and how the organisation is getting on. Try always to tell the staff what is going on before you tell the outside world get into the habit of regular briefings. If (as we hope) customer value and satisfaction is top of your agenda – and part of staff appraisal, then make sure that you tell staff how your customers think they are performing. Market research is not just an information tool – it should be part of internal communications too.
6.1.6	How responsive is the organisation to customer demands?	Without a good flow of accurate information, you won't know what customer needs are – or how to respond to them – that could be comforting of course ... Not just whether you respond, but *how well* you respond will ultimately determine your competitive position. Are you going to position yourself as the one that gives its customers what they want, or the one that doesn't really care? Remember, customers can be unforgiving. This is where management (should) earn their salaries, your organisation must respond. Not to respond will deliver exactly the same result as if there were no strategy, and success becomes a game of chance.

6.1.7	How resistant is the organisation design to change?	This question looks the same as the last but is very different. Management can make it easier to change by giving itself a flexible structure; one that is built to last – by being built to change. All organisations will *claim* that they can change-in reality most cannot. We look at the levers of 'change' later, but a great opportunity still lies out there for the nimble organisation – customers and markets are changing so fast nowadays that you can probably keep *ahead* of your competitors just by keeping *up* with your customers.

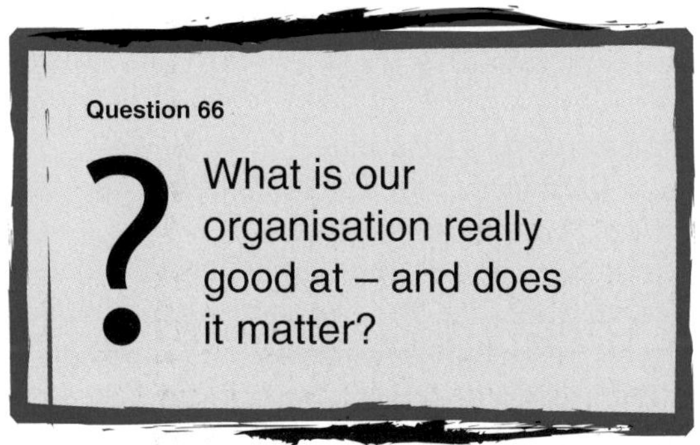

Question 66
?
What is our organisation really good at – and does it matter?

MARGIN NOTES

Customers aren't all the same and don't all want the same things. It follows then that customers will prefer to buy from organisations that are better or different in some important way.

Most organisations have aspects of their business which they consider themselves to be particularly good at, an understanding, an expertise or a methodology that is unique to them in terms of the extent and depth of that *competence*.

If organisations are to be (really) different from each other, then it follows that they will be better (and worse) and doing certain things. Then, different organisations will have what Hamel and Prahalad ('*Competing for the Future*', Harvard Business School Press, 1996) have called different core competences.

■ A word on 'core competences'

The ideas of core competences have been around for a while now. It is well defined as:

- 'A core competence is a combination of complementary skills and knowledge bases embedded in a group or team that results in the ability to execute one or more critical processes to a world-class standard.' (Coyne, Hall and Clifford, *McKinsey Quarterly review*, 1997/1)

Hamel and Prahalad said that a core competence is something that an organisation can do well – and set the following three conditions:

- It provides customer benefits:
  - The most important, the competence must add customer value.
  - This means that if the organisation is particularly good at doing something that the customer doesn't want or is not interested in, then it is not a core competence.
  - Core competences are the special skills that should enable a business to deliver a differentiated customer benefit.
  - Core competences are what should cause customers to prefer one offering over another.

MARGIN NOTES

- It is hard for competitors to imitate:
  - So it has a life that is longer than a simple process or technology lead that gets copied quickly.
  - A genuine core competence should be 'competitively unique' – if the organisation just has the same special skills as every other player in the same industry, these aren't unique.
  - A core competence must be something that other competitors wish they had.

- It can be leveraged widely to many products and markets:
  - The idea that the competence is not just specific to one product – but belongs to the organisation rather than just a single product, service or brand.
  - The key here is that the core competences allow/enable the creation and development of unique new products and services.

Since Hamel and Prahalad's work, many authors have tried to specify and organise the different types, nature and sources of core competences. In fact this is quite difficult since unique market positions aren't created out of standard analyses! Of the different attempts, an interesting one comes from Coyne, Hall and Clifford, who suggest that core competences can come from five different areas:

- Technical or scientific knowledge
  - For example, knowledge that produces a series of unique and difficult to copy inventions.

- Proprietary data
  - For example, the data that is (probably) held by the UK's National Health Service and allows them to negotiate with drugs companies.
  - The very biggest supermarkets may also have such data from loyalty card programmes.

- Information derived from having the largest share of leading-edge transactions in the deal flow
  - For example, the information controlled by eBay and Amazon.

- Pure creative flair in inventing successful products
  - For example, Disney's continued success in family entertainment and Nokia's series of high design telephone handsets.

- Superior analysis and inference
  - For example, the development of the iPod by Apple, based on the same technical knowledge possessed by other manufacturers – but applied in a unique way.

A competence may be central to the organisation's operations but if it is not unique in some way, it is *not* a core competence – it *won't* differentiate the organisation within its marketplace. Therefore:

MARGIN NOTES

- It follows that internal skills and resources that are standardised or easily available to all organisations won't enable a business to achieve a sustainable competitive advantage over rivals.
  - You cannot be good at everything.
  - Much of the research in the area suggests that if you have more than two or three core competences then the focus of the organisation will be diluted and the 'core' part of the term will change to just 'useful', which is just not good enough.
  - Many organisations will find that they have some competences that have been built up over the years and which mark out the organisation as what it stands for – but which don't really matter (to the customer) anymore.
  - Some organisations even delude themselves that because they are good at something; what they are good at is also important to the customer. Now where did that come from?
  - We have spoken about the need for a clear differentiation in Chapter 8 and Core competences are the means by which the organisation becomes different, the customer receives superior customer value and the organisation derives superior returns.
  - None of this is possible without investing in and developing the right core competences.

There is a strong link between the brand and the core competences of the organisation – 'we are the people who …'

- If you need a good reason to command most of the resources available for investment, there it is – the brand needs it.

- On the other hand, if you find that you have some competences that no longer make a difference, then you need to be equally ruthless and cut off the investment flow and maybe jettison the expertise completely.

- Generally the most challenging role for senior management is moving on from former core competences which probably what made them the senior management in the first place – you are asking senior managers to discard their own history.
- Good managers can do this but inferior managers may need to be replaced by new management (often from outside the organisation) to do the job and save the organisation.
- Venture capital organisations are excellent at this.

Core competences aren't fixed in time:

- Core competences need to change in response to changes in the company's business and market environment.
  - They are flexible and must evolve over time.
  - As an organisation evolves and adapts to new circumstances and opportunities, so its core competences will have to adapt and change.

MARGIN NOTES

- Not everything that an organisation needs to be good at is a 'core' competence.
  - Good quality service and innovative product development are too generic and not specific enough and probably aren't differentiated enough in the minds of the customers.
  - Nor are today's core competences necessarily what will be needed tomorrow.
  - Its management's job is to *manage the competence portfolio.*

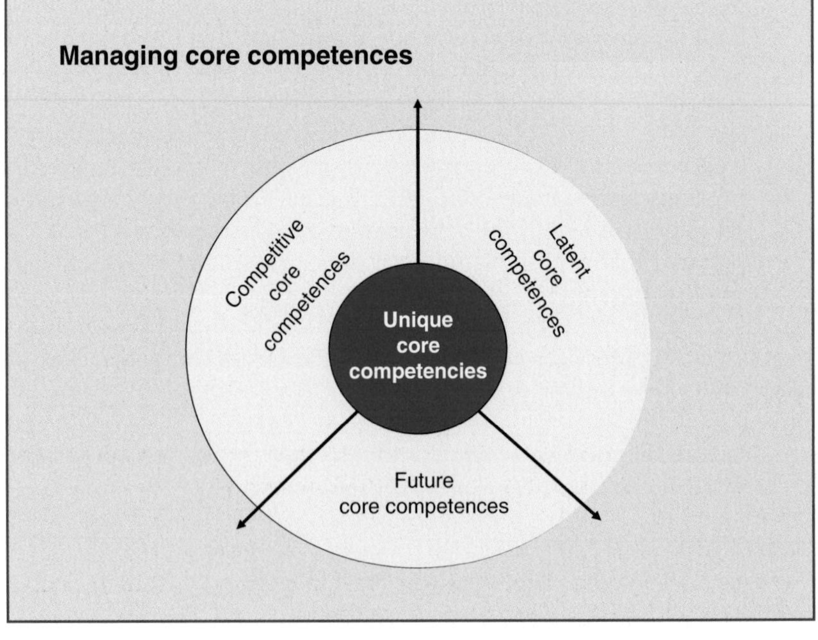

There are in fact four different types of what is commonly called core competence:

- Unique core competences:
  - If these are what you think they are, they are the unique, uncopyable 'skills and knowledge bases' that set you apart in the eyes of your customers.
  - They allow you to deliver superior customer value for superior returns.
- Latent core competences:
  - Every organisation will have competences that are 'latent' but allow it to operate in its chosen market.
    - For example, hotels will cite competitive competences (such as location, supply chain management and reservations systems) and unique core competences in abundance.
    - However, the people management skills within the hotel business are both complex (different people with a wide range of skills and abilities for a very wide range of time critical tasks) and simply assumed – the organisation's latent core competence.
- Competitive core competences:
  - Every organisation needs core competences that simply allow it to compete in its chosen market.
  - If you wish, these competences are the 'hygiene factors' that permit the organisation to 'be in the game'.
    - For example, today's major retail organisations need strong core skills in supply chain management simply to survive in the business – but supply chain skills, on their own, don't qualify as unique core competences so won't be sufficient to 'win' the game against the competitors.
- Future core competences:
  - Customers' needs change over time and value migrates constantly.
  - This is not unusual and this must not come as a surprise.
  - The organisation that is intent on retaining its unique position will have understood the inherent transience of its market and will be busy developing the core competences that it will need to dominate tomorrow's markets in the same way.

MARGIN NOTES

If you have some competences that are fundamental to the delivery of the proposition and the organisation's differentiation from the competition, then you need to put them at the very heart of the business.

- If possible you should structure around them to give them the importance that they deserve.

- You need to invest in them – heavily, not just in terms of investment projects but also in terms of the acquisition of skills and the development of those skills.
- They need their own development strategy.
- The whole organisation should understand what the competences are and why they are important.
- They need to be built into the very fabric of the organisation.

- If the organisation really wants success badly, then it won't only know what it is good at today, it will also have a good understanding of what it will need to be good at tomorrow.
  - Very few market disrupting phenomena that are invisible to the alert organisation.
  - Unless a new entrant has some new and totally proprietary technology, what the competition can see coming should be just as visible to you.

MARGIN NOTES

- As always, flexibility is the key.
  - The organisation needs to be constantly reviewing the environment, the market, and its objectives to be sure that its core competences remain relevant and aligned to customer value, and, where necessary, make changes.
  - Earlier changes are always less dramatic than changes that have been ignored, postponed or discarded as 'too scary' – evolution is always better than revolution.

■ Consequently, a word on outsourcing

This is a big debate, one that has grown recently with the widely publicised outsourcing of some service elements of business (such as telephone call centres) to Asia and India, mainly on a cost basis. If a core competence yields a long-term advantage to the company, it is said to be a sustainable competitive advantage. The extension of core competence in modern business theory suggests that most activities that *aren't* part of a company's core competency should be outsourced:

- Although we agree (in principle) that the organisation should not be investing heavily in areas that could be outsourced to far better qualified organisations, this 'obvious and unavoidable truth' needs to be tempered slightly before handed over to managers incapable of thinking for themselves.
  - In the same way that every large amount is *not* automatically a 'cost', then everything that is *not* a clear core competence should *not* be outsourced.

- The organisation needs to make allowances for (and think twice before outsourcing) non-core competence activity that:
  - May be unavoidably connected to the core competence
  - May be the foundation of the core competence
  - May be a 'latent' core competence
  - May be a 'competitive' core competence
  - May be tomorrow's core competence
  - May be none of these but the morale, enthusiasm of the staff and customers would be seriously affected by its outsourcing.

MARGIN NOTES

Your organisation's value proposition needs to show:

- What your competences are that make the difference in customer perceptions
- Why these core competences are unique and important to customers
- What areas of the competences to focus on
- What parts of the competences to strengthen or develop
- What tomorrow's core competences are going to be
- How you are working on tomorrow's core competences now

The FAQs are:

6 Organisation: Processes and Culture		
6.2 What is our organisation really good at – and does it matter?		
6.2.1	How does the organisation know what it is really good at?	The point of this question is to focus on the *relativity* of 'good'. How good you are is only important – relative to what competitors are doing and what the customer is expecting. You cannot assess this for yourselves by just taking an internal view of the organisation. Does it matter? Yes, if the customer cares. No-one else's opinion really matters, if the customers aren't impressed, you can blow your own trumpet all day long and it won't do you any good! Ask the customers and keep asking them at regular intervals, they will give you an honest view of life.
6.2.2	Do these competences make enough of a difference?	Core competences are central to a differentiated strategy. They are supposed to be *the* difference. So, 'enough' is only *enough* when the customer says it is. If the customer is prepared to pay more for your proposition because of what your core competences deliver, then you are making a difference.

6.2.3	How do you ensure that the core competences get the lion's share of the investment?	Nothing happens naturally in an organisation. If you want to ensure that something happens then you have to: ● Plan it ● Build it into a process and ● Make someone accountable for it. For the core competences, there needs to be a documented development strategy within a development plan. In addition, the process by which investment is assessed needs to be given a bias towards the core competences. This may still not be enough – every competence needs a *champion*, someone who will ensure that all this happens as intended.
6.2.4	Does the organisation know what needs to get done to compete?	The way the core competences are managed matters. The CVPs will require that the competences are used and developed in a certain way. What the competitors are doing will also have an impact on how they are managed. This should all be reflected in the competence development plan and should be reviewed in line with the regular information about the customers and the competitors. The core competences help the organisation maintain a distance from its competitors as well as help build the brand for the customers.
6.2.5	Does the organisation normally do everything itself?	It is not necessary these days for an organisation to do everything itself. Outsourcing is a well developed industry delivering great benefit by making something core for the outsourcing company, what is not core to another organisation. The rule should be that you manage in-house those aspects of the business that add customer value and outsource where possible those aspects that don't, but need to be done efficiently. The more that aspects of the business which aren't core are outsourced the easier it is to invest money and management attention on the core aspects of the business that really add value. Ask the customer how much they care about you doing yourself – don't do more if it can be done better by someone else.
6.2.6	'Marketing' as a core competence?	This book is more about marketing strategy than tactics. It is about the whole organisation being involved in that strategy. However, we should not ignore the role of the Marketing function it needs to guide the process and translate the needs of the customer into language that the organisation can understand – and can work with. The Marketing function was never intended to be an operational function, but always an integrating and organising one. If the organisation doesn't deliver on its promise, that is an operational matter. If it doesn't understand how the customer wants that delivery or why, that is a marketing issue. If the information about the changes in the customer's needs is not understood, the Marketing function is not doing its job. If market changes aren't reacted to quickly and effectively, Operations has a problem, but the responsibility lies with Marketing.

		Marketing as a core competence? We probably cannot say until we can agree what 'marketing' means. If we mean the co-ordinating function that enables the entire organisation to be (and remain) closer to the customer than any of the competitors then *yes*, it can be a valuable core competence. If we mean just 'marketing communications', then *no* – this is just another tactic and unlikely to make any difference to the long-term prosperity of the organisation.
6.2.7	What will the organisation need to be good at tomorrow?	Here comes that tricky question again. In the short to medium term, it should be answered in the context of the current customer propositions. In the longer term we may need to be looking at totally different propositions. It need not take that long to build new core competences. If it needs to be done quickly you just have to buy them in. When IBM decided that it needed to be excellent at business solutions and not just IT, it found and bought the PriceWaterhouseCoopers consulting arm.

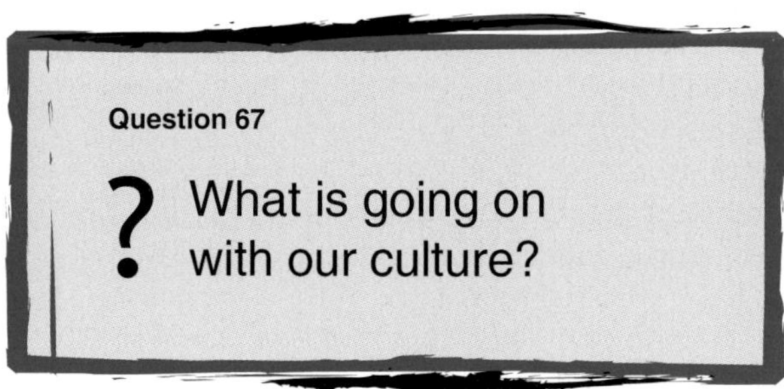

Question 67
?
What is going on with our culture?

MARGIN NOTES

What is culture?

- 'The customs, institutions, and achievements of a particular nation, people, or group' (Oxford)
- 'The way of life, especially the general customs and beliefs, of a particular group of people at a particular time' (Cambridge)
- 'The way things are done around here' (Anon)
- 'An organisation's culture is an evolution of history and not necessarily forward looking. Take this, together with the fact that most of management issues are internal, it is understandable that organisations structure themselves to deal with and manage internal issues.' (Larry Greiner in '*Evolution and Revolution as Organisations Grow*'. Harvard Business Review, May–June 1998).

The last quote from Greiner suggest that there are some important lessons here for the (would be) customer-focused manager and marketing strategy implementation:

- Lesson one; the culture of an organisation is like an iceberg.
  - Most of it is invisible below the 'water line' just waiting to cause an accident (or sink the 'unsinkable' strategy).
  - Culture is all-pervasive and most people who are part of 'it', have difficulty seeing 'it' or explaining what 'it' is.

- Lesson two; culture is self-protecting and will resist attempts (threats) to change it.
  - New staff (and managers!) are generally not listened to until they have been in the organisation for about three months.
  - The process of 'enculturation' (becoming part of and displaying the behaviours required by the culture – or leaving) takes about three months ...

MARGIN NOTES

- Lesson three; the culture of an organisation is not what managers say that it is.
  - Whenever we have carried out an audit of a business and analysed what managers think is the culture of that organisation, and then looked at what the staff say it is, there is always a sizeable gap between the two.
  - Just because managers are in charge doesn't mean that they control culture, they don't. They can influence it, but they cannot ordain that a certain culture should exist and simply have it happen.

- Lesson four; culture is best described as 'the way things are done around here'.
  - It is an expression of the attitudes and behaviours of the staff – not the management.

- Lesson five; culture is desperately important because:
  - It affects every aspect of how customers are engaged (by staff who are part of the culture) and
  - Service is delivered (by staff who are part of the culture) and
  - Customers retained (by staff who are part of the culture).
  - Your organisation cannot engender trust with the customer if the staff, who are dealing with the customers, don't feel that they are trusted by the organisation.
  - It just doesn't work, somehow or other the feelings and internal relationships always get through to the customer.

- Lesson six; you need to behave internally as you want your staff to behave externally.
  - If you are intent on delivering a low cost solution (see Chapter 6.4 if you still think this is a great idea), then management cannot

behave as though it lives in a high margin business and money grows on trees.
- Staff will see through the veneer and soon customers will see through the offer too.

You ignore culture at your peril, and never underestimate its strength and importance; if the culture of the organisation is not understood then management is flying blind in all its endeavours.

Before we look a little closer at what you could be doing about your organisational culture, one final assessment, are you primarily a 'theory X' or a 'theory Y' type company. Be truthful now ...

Douglas McGregor

'The human side of enterprise', 1960	
Theory X	**Theory Y**
'reflects an underlying belief that management must counteract an inherent human tendency to avoid work'	*'assumes that people will exercise self-direction and self-control in the achievement of organisational objectives to the degree that they are committed to those objectives'*
Devise the right STICKS with which to prod work-shy labour	Look for the CARROTS that will induce them to stay/perform

MARGIN NOTES

Theory is all very well, but what should you be *doing* about your culture? There are a number of factors that need to be considered in arriving at the 'right' culture for an organisation.

- What do the customers want?
  - Well it had to be number one.
  - Customers will want to deal with a certain type of organisation when they are looking to 'hire a product (or service) to get a job done'.
  - Understanding what this is and reflecting that into the organisation builds differentiation and credibility.
    - For example, if you are offering a solution for 'small businesses', there is no point employing staff who have only ever

worked for large corporations; they won't be able to relate to and empathise with the small business customer.
  - At the very beginning of any relationship, is when potential customers are at their most alert – if the customer doesn't 'feel' that he or she is talking to someone who understands them then that process won't progress. This doesn't apply to public utilities and other monopolies which offer no customer choice.
  - If your organisation offers fashion clothing to upwardly mobile 'thirty-something's', there is no point staffing your shops (or your switchboards) with either teenagers/students or people approaching retirement, they cannot represent the style of the organisation in the same way as people of the same age wearing the apparel.

- What do the staff want and what do they believe?
  - Staff are the culture and what they believe *is* 'the way things are done round here'.
  - Staff are the recipients of all the information that management gives them and where they are in contact with the customer then they will represent the organisation.
  - Inside the organisation, they can also represent the customer.
    - A salutary example comes from the UK retail store Marks & Spencer; for so many years the UK byword in customer excellence. During the six years that it took for the fortunes of the organisation to collapse, the staff became very disenchanted as management ignored them – even when they gave valuable information about how customers were reacting. The Marks & Spencer culture became one of 'management think they know best and aren't interested in staff views', this was bad for management/staff relations and customer/Marks & Spencer relations – it was obvious to the outside world what was going on and the demise accelerated.
  - If senior management wants a culture of staff involvement, believing it to be important for the brand, but engenders a culture of 'keep to your place, we know what we are doing', staff will simply 'do what they are paid for', leaving the 'extra mile' for the new recruits.

MARGIN NOTES

- What does management want and how do they behave?
  - Management need to understand what the culture should be (as determined by the target customers) and then need to act the part themselves.
  - Often a culture audit will reveal that an organisation is not adopting the culture required by its customers, but also that management aren't themselves adopting that culture.
  - Staff will take their lead from management.
    - For example, if staff are expected to exercise discretion with customers in sorting out a customer's problem then management need to give staff the space and support to do that; it won't work (for customers) if staff are required to justify every

decision taken and are taken to task when the manager would have acted differently.
    - On the other hand, if management want to engender a culture that supports innovative thinking, it should follow up on ideas put forward by staff – and not rubbish those that don't work!
- You might be thinking now that this is all 'common sense' – most of management is.
- You might also be wondering how often management seem *not* to act sensibly. Hmmm
- Culture can be much worse than a 'negative influence', when it is no influence at all. If management chooses to ignore culture altogether, what it gets is little cells of culture throughout the organisation (based on functional background, geography of 'baronies') which are totally inconsistent with each other and a disaster for the customer.
- This is worse because it is much more difficult to change.
- It should follow then, that if it is obvious that management can create (albeit unwittingly) a negative culture then they can also create (through positive influence) a positive culture.

At best, the wrong culture will stop the organisation being excellent; at worst it will stop the organisation.

MARGIN NOTES

Your organisation's value proposition needs to identify the important aspects of culture from the customer's point of view:

- Differentiating elements of your culture that support the unique offering
- Standards of service sought by your customers
- Style and nature of 'relationships'
- Tone of voice.

The FAQs are:

6 Organisation: Processes and Culture		
6.3 What is going on with our culture?		
6.3.1	How do you know how 'things are done around here'?	It is unlikely that management will know what the culture actually is; and if they were to ask the staff, they would probably not get the right answer. Culture tends to be invisible to those within it, so you will have to use an independent agent to assess (confidentially in discussion with the staff) what actually happens. Staff aren't going to open up if they think that they will be held to account for having 'non-conformist' views.

		It is best to use specialists who are experienced at carrying out 'culture audits' and will know best what questions to ask – and how to ask those questions.
6.3.2	What are the 'levers' that create culture?	There are two principal levers that affect culture: ● Management action and behaviour which we looked at earlier in this section and ● The personal/individual appraisal system together with any bonus and reward. The appraisal system is the only tool available to managers that can directly influence staff behaviour. Qualitative objectives can be used to direct the way staff act in certain circumstances. Unfortunately, it is more difficult to measure qualitative objectives so too many managers shy away from using them – but an assessment does need to be made. Management action can also play a part in the way that appropriate attitudes are applauded in a visible manner.
6.3.3	Do we understand the effects of the culture on the business results?	Culture might be driven by management desire rather than the CVP – in which case there will probably be little impact on results and rather more on the frustration levels of management if it doesn't hit the mark. Some managers will never learn. The value or impact of the right culture, where this is driven by the value proposition can be considerable depending upon the importance that the particular cultural traits have on customers. Research will identify which components of the value proposition are sensitive to organisational culture and follow-up research should elicit how customers see cultural performance (in terms of behaviours produced).
6.3.4	Does management inspired culture matter in the organisation?	Right at the beginning of this chapter we made the comment that different management styles, as long as they are applied consistently, don't matter much in performance terms – all styles can work. However, the style needs to be *consistent* and to the extent that management is not normally very good at reading culture, consistency may be an issue. Management will take decisions in the belief that certain results will follow. If the real culture creates 'unexpected' outcomes, performance and results can be affected.
6.3.5	What does the culture need to do or deliver today and tomorrow?	The optimum word here is *harmony*. The culture of the organisation needs to deliver harmony with the customer (through the value propositions) and with management. This is not a goal that, once achieved, can be considered as 'done and dusted'. Unfortunately, culture is liable to change all the time and will need constant reinforcement. New staff and new management will affect the culture, as will the changing working environment.

		Add to that the changes in culture made necessary by changes in customer needs and we have a potentially explosive situation. Culture needs to deliver a consistent *harmony over time* in support of the business.
6.3.6	How can culture be changed if necessary?	Culture, by its very nature is ingrained in the behaviours of people. To change that culture takes time and effort – and sometimes a change of the people themselves. The levers have been discussed above (management action and personal appraisals), change is made by using these levers, but it depends greatly upon: ● How important the change is to the organisation ● How much time is available to make that change It is always preferable to help people make the necessary changes. Properly explained, rational people will understand why changes are necessary and, with the appropriate help and support – perhaps with training, culture will change. Irrational people won't change and cannot be managed because they cannot be reasoned with. If the culture is important enough the people would have to change. The best advice I ever received from a HR director when discussing culture change was, 'We have two options, either we change the people, or we will have to change the people'.
6.3.7	How do you know if the culture has changed?	The same way you know that the culture is not right. You carry out an audit and take the temperature of the organisation. This needs to be done on a frequent basis because management will be trying a number of initiatives to help mould the culture in (what they see as) the right way. You need to know which initiatives are working and which aren't. If the culture is important to the success of the organisation then this spend is essential and will never stop as we replace 'frequent' by 'regular' assessments of the cultures and customer needs.

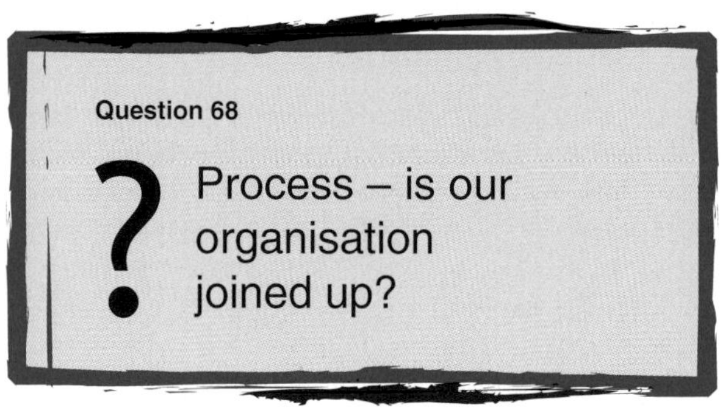

Question 68
?
Process – is our organisation joined up?

Now we get to the 'organise' part of organisation.

Organisations are primarily self-serving edifices – such is human nature. They are structured mainly for efficiency (doing things right) rather than for effectiveness (doing the right things) and so we tend to build functional units around similar tasks performed with similar skills and experience, such as operations, accounting, human resources and even, marketing.

To get anything useful done, the different functions need to work together – or, be joined up.

Unfortunately, functions can take on a separate existence within an organisation and will naturally default to being inward looking. This can give them a 'silo' mentality (like missiles, things go up and down very fast but nothing goes side-to-side), lacking in communication with the world outside of their function as well as outside of their organisation.

MARGIN NOTES

Organisations will attempt to manage the different functions by way of the 'group strategy', which will have a functional strategy showing how each function should fit in and develop with the whole.

All this serves the system that is the organisation, but may not provide the outputs that the customer requires. Luckily, there is another facet of organisational life that we can focus on when we consider whether we are joined up and how we deliver a customer benefit – *process*.

A word on process

- 'A series of actions or steps towards achieving a particular end' (Oxford)
- 'A series of actions that you take in order to achieve a result' (Cambridge)
- 'A particular course of action intended to achieve a result' (Webster's)

And the 'headlines':

- Process is the term given to a continuous stream of tasks which are designed to deliver a given benefit (generally to the customer).
  - Because of the functional structures used in most organisations, a *customer process* will tend to flow through several function.
  - A process in its simplest form (say, a sale), may start with a customer order (in the sales department or call centre) be passed for fulfilment (in deliveries) and end with a payment for the benefit (in customer accounts) following the successful delivery of the product or service.

- Each function may have several *tasks* in which it is involved, and the process may move back and forth between the functions – thus accounts may be involved at the outset to ensure that the customer has an account with the organisation or to set one up and then at the end to send out an invoice and collect payment.

- Process is the 'glue' between the functions.
  - For an organisation to be joined up, each function has to understand the role of the other functions, and each member of staff in each of the functions needs to understand what he or she is required to do in order to fulfil the customer benefit to the required (differentiated) standard.
  - Process is, therefore, the way in which an organisation joins up its functions; it is the glue holding the organisation together.

- Process is also the way in which the strategy and the CVP are reflected into what people do in the organisation.
  - A process defines the tasks, how those tasks are performed, why they are performed, what the particular task delivers and how they contribute to the end delivery of the customer benefit.

- Understanding processes can give the market-focused manager a wonderful tool for helping the rest of the organisation to focus on, and work towards, creating customer value.
  - Although the organisation is full of functions that seem to be self-propagating and self-fulfilling, these august groups of technically minded people don't generate very much of value, at least to the customer. They can do, but they are, by their very nature, product or input focused.
  - Customers are, by their very nature, output focused.
  - Processes are the only way we can hope to channel input-focused functions into meeting the needs of output-focused customers.

MARGIN NOTES

Working across any organisation, depending on the organisation's particular market and competitive position, are a small number of 'macro' processes which, if managed carefully, can focus the whole organisation on delivering what really matters – customer value. These *macro* processes are:

- The customer proximity process:
  - More than just 'data', 'information' or 'knowledge' (although all these play a part), the process by which we position ourselves *closer to our customer than the competition* and so are able meet their needs and wants well enough that the customer comes back again – and again.
  - Enough of this book is spent on this subject so I won't explain it all again here.

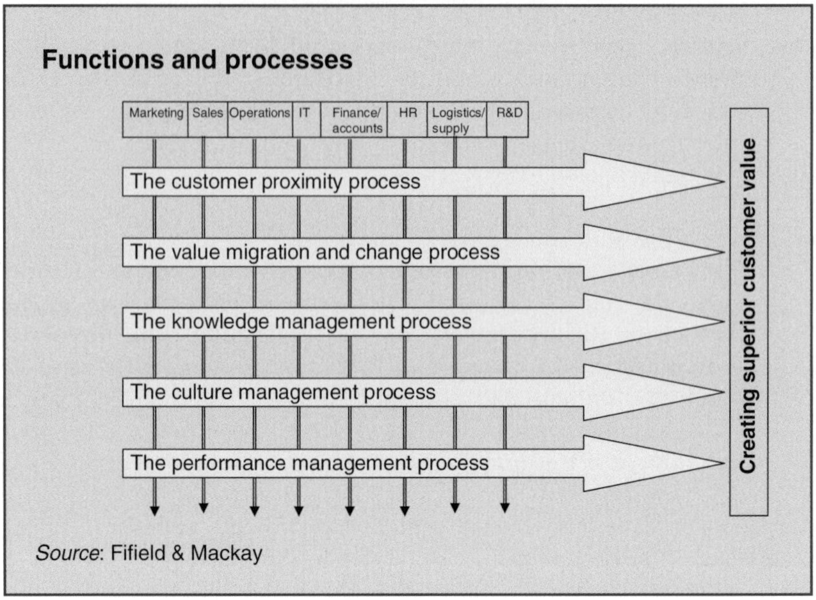

Functions and processes

Source: Fifield & Mackay

MARGIN NOTES

- What is critical is the process of transferring and translating that sense of customer proximity to everybody else in the organisation, sufficiently well, that they know what they have to do to create differentiated and superior customer value.

- The value migration and change process:
  - The process by which everybody in all the functions understands the current customer value as well as the likely future shape and directions of value (migration).
  - Consequently, the organisation (and its functions) not only understands the need to change on a regular basis but contributes positively to the constant organisational change process.

- The knowledge management (KM) process:
  - The process by which the organisation collects data and information from the market environment and converts it into knowledge (data made meaningful).
  - And then pushes specific parts of the knowledge to those people (in all parts of the organisation) who need it – to improve the quality of the differentiated customer value they create.

- The culture management process:
  - The process by which the most appropriate culture for delivering benefit to the customer is understood and sustained throughout the organisation.
  - Bearing in mind that customers (bless them) will change their minds on a regular (or irregular) basis.

- The performance management process:
  - The process by which the organisation tracks performance towards the market objectives and manages the situation as and when the organisation deviates from the chosen path.

All organisations have processes, but not all recognise that they exist in this way; and many don't *micro*-manage them as the discreet and integral units that they are:

- Processes should not be confused with the functions of the organisation, but they do determine how the functions should operate in respect of customer delivery.
  - It is not good enough for a function just to be efficient; it has to recognise that optimal efficiency for that function may not mean optimal efficiency for the process as a whole and therefore for the customer.

- All processes will work at the outset
  - The problem/challenge is, as always, people.
  - People are always trying to 'improve' matters and change them to be better or easier.
  - Because of the link that all tasks in a process have to all other tasks and also to the ultimate customer value created, you cannot allow anyone to change anything in a process without reference to the process owner – who can decide (in consultation with others in the process) whether that change will improve the overall result. In other words, make sure any proposed change is optimal to the whole process.

- The Process needs an Owner
  - There has to be a higher authority that has overall responsibility for the process – a process owner or manager.
  - This person is the key to everything concerning that process, and ultimately, customer satisfaction.
  - Here is a *key issue*: The functional managers must defer to the process owner, otherwise you will have silo-based management and the organisation won't be joined up. We hope you got that one … .
  - The process owner also has a role in determining how the process can deliver the customer value more efficiently or where the process is falling down – and what remedial action is required to repair the process.

MARGIN NOTES

We have now identified a *customer champion* in the heart of Operations. The process owner is the ideal person.

- The process owner is also:
  - Responsible for the organisation delivering the benefit to the customer effectively and to the right standard.

- Responsible for ensuring that the value proposition is reflected into the process and the performance of the individual tasks.
- Perfectly placed to act on behalf of the customer within operations.
- The link to marketing and through marketing to the customer.
- The means by which marketing communicates to the whole of operations.

Joining up the dots (functions) happens when you use the macro processes (with their process owners) to join up the different functions behind the need to deliver differentiated customer value.

- Sometimes the different functions will need their own 'strategies', and in this event it is essential that they are aligned with the overall market strategy – we are, after all, on the same mission, to create and keep customers.

MARGIN NOTES

- The processes are needed to join up, at least
  - Financial strategy
  - Human resources strategy
  - Operations strategy.

We need to cover just the 'headlines' of these three functions to understand how to join them up.

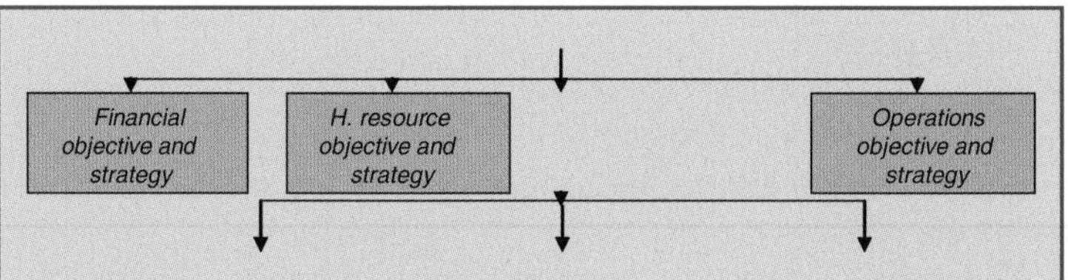

2 Financial strategy

According to most of the major texts on finance, the financial management of any organization can be seen as having four separate tasks:

- The acquisition of funds
- The investing of funds in economically productive assets
- The managing of these assets and
- The eventual re-conversion of some (or all) of the productive assets into future returns to the original investors, creditors, suppliers, employees and other interested groups.

To these tasks we could probably add:

- Keeping a record of revenues and expenses, and
- Achievement of the long-term financial objective (hurdle).

Although all these aspects of financial strategy and management impinge on marketing strategy, the biggest area of interest centres on the discussion of the word 'assets':

- A customer is an asset that is usually more precious than the tangible assets on the balance sheet.
- You can usually buy balance sheet assets, there are lots of willing sellers.
- You cannot so easily buy customers; they are far less willing than are sellers and have lots of eager sellers offering them many choices.
- A customer is a double asset:
    - First, he/she is the direct source of cash from sale and
    - Second, his/her existence can be used to raise cash from bankers and investors, cash that can be converted into tangible assets.

- The 'customer-as-asset' view has a number of advantages for the organisation as market and customer expenditure is not seen as a cost but an investment and is treated as such.
    - Cutting marketing expenditure in the bad times is not managing costs; it is withholding investment on which the future of the organisation may depend.
    - The nature of customer investment is often seen as risky and cavalier – this is often a justified criticism.
    - Customer investment is often more uncertain due to the unpredictable nature of the asset, the customer.
    - While too many so called marketers still revel in the mystique of this unpredictability, many more are working hard to create a closer understanding of the target market's needs and so reduce the uncertainty to more manageable and acceptable levels.

- Ultimately, it all comes down to cash.
    - Cash is 'king'.
    - Nobody has understood this better than the venture capitalists and is a major aspect of their continuing success.
    - If you cannot convert an asset or profit into cash in some way then what is it really worth? (Answers on a postcard …)

- In the same way, we can look at the value of the brand (see Chapter 8).
    - This is represented (essentially) by the cash that customers will create for the organisation in the future.
    - The ability of any company to support a valuation on the basis of future earnings comes down to this – how long, in the opinion of the buyer, will the customers keep buying and at what rate?

MARGIN NOTES

2 Human resource strategy

Distilled to its very essence (and greatly simplified) the strategic human resource (HR) function is responsible for three broad areas within the organisation:

- Recruitment and selection
- Motivation and reward systems
- Training

- The market – HR strategy will centre on similar areas to those already seen above.
  - In the market-focused organisation, is it the job of HR strategy to recruit, select, motivate and reward in order to improve internal efficiency?
  - Or is it to maximise the organisation's external effectiveness (creation of differentiated customer value) within its market?

MARGIN NOTES

- Potentially, the most serious area of strategic conflict is in how different roles in the organization are seen.
  - The best way of explaining this is through a practical example.
    - If we consider two roles which the HR function is currently trying to fill. The two vacant positions are for a call centre receptionist and for a manager in the payroll department. HR has limited resources and is concerned with how best to use this limited resource to achieve its objectives.
    - From a purely internal perspective, the position of payroll manager is the more senior position and will require relatively more resource recruit than the call centre receptionist.
    - From the external or customer perspective, the relative importance of the two positions is reversed. When customers attempt to make contact with the organisation directly, the call centre receptionist is the first point of contact with the organisation and capable of representing (and misrepresenting) your organisation and everything it stands for in your customer's eyes.
    - It is this inferior role that has the greater power to either reinforce your expensive marketing messages or destroy the marketing investment instantly.

- The aligned HR function will understand the different levels of importance and its role in differentiating the organisation.

3 Operations strategy

According to most of the major texts on operations management, the function can be seen as having seven principal tasks:

- Process planning and control
- Operations planning

- Operations control
- Scheduling
- Inventory planning and control
- Facilities design, location, layout, materials handling, equipment maintenance
- Quality control.

We are using the word operations to cover both the manufacturing and the processing that will be required in any organisation, manufacturing or services, to deliver customer value.

- While no organization can prosper in its business activity without careful regard to efficient and effective operations management, it is not, and cannot be regarded as, 'the sole aim and objective of industry'.
  - Adam Smith noted this in the 18th century and, despite the apparent unwillingness of too many organizations to accept consumption as the ultimate end and object of all industry and commerce, Adam Smith's words are as true today as they were 200 years ago.

- There is no doubt that what the organisation produces must be driven solely by customer needs and not simply by what the organisation is able to produce.
  - While with other areas of the organisation, a certain degree of collaboration is required (albeit led by the marketing strategy), operations strategy is best driven exclusively by the organisation's KPIs (based on the marketing objectives, see Chapter 4).
  - Once the marketing objectives have laid down what the organisation has to produce, it is then the role of the operations function to mobilise its resource in order to produce what the market wants in the most efficient and effective manner possible.
  - Most conflict arises from different perceptions on what is important. What is important when considering facilities design, scheduling, inventory, quality and forecasting could differ markedly from what the customer deems most important – and ...
  - The customers *must* win ...

- And, there is no law that says Research and Development (R&D) must be part of operations
  - There is generally, much confusion over the relative roles of marketing and operations strategy in the control of the research and development function.
  - R&D is often placed within operations because of the (often) technical nature of the work.
  - Wherever the activity is placed, unless it is led by customer insight it will produce little of real (customer) value.
  - R&D, to be a profitable investment, needs to find practical, technical solutions to problems which the customer already has – or is expected to have in the future.

MARGIN NOTES

- Effectively this is really part of new product development (NPD) (albeit of products and services in the future) and seen in this light it would be natural (and pretty obvious) that this must at least be *guided* by the Marketing function, even if it is managed by operations.
- Only if R&D is linked to the perceived future requirements of the customer will the customer win.
- If not we will simply create more 'heroic failures' such as the Sinclair C5, the Ford Edsell, Boo.com (or insert your favourite dot. com disaster story), Ratners, the new Multiplex Wembley football ground or Northern Rock.

One method of joining-the-dots, internal marketing.

MARGIN NOTES

Every organisation needs specialists if they are to achieve the level of efficiency necessary to guarantee profits in ever more competitive marketplaces. Unfortunately, with every specialist comes a separate (and different) set of priorities and 'right' ways to do things.

But, unless a common sense of external, customer-based purpose can be instilled within the organisation, then we will risk the possibility of internal squabbles over procedure, 'turf' or priorities becoming lengthy discussions about how best to arrange the deck chairs on the Titanic as the ship slowly sinks into the sea. Our competitors will love us forever.

Aligning the organisation (and its different specialisms, experts, functions and 'best practices' – whatever *they* are) to meet the needs of ever

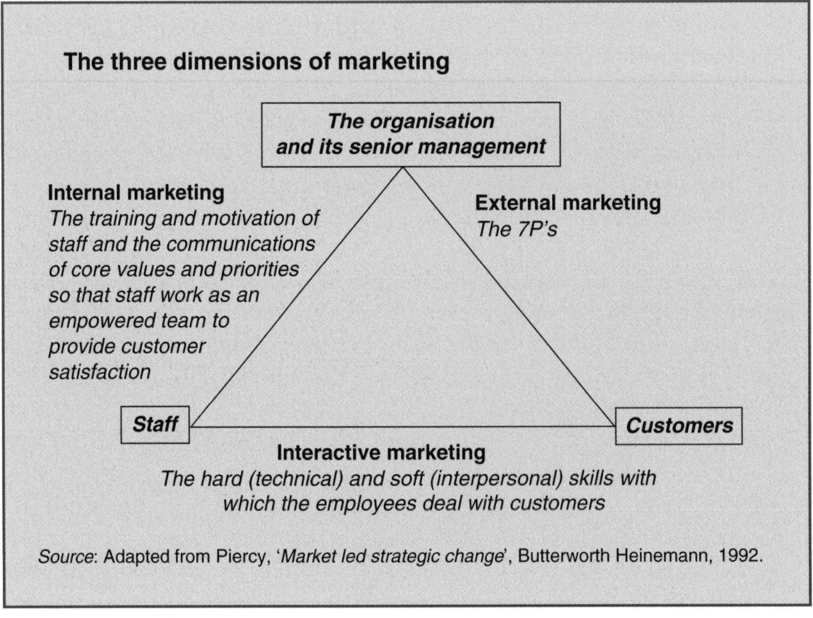
The three dimensions of marketing
The organisation and its senior management
Internal marketing
The training and motivation of staff and the communications of core values and priorities so that staff work as an empowered team to provide customer satisfaction
External marketing
The 7P's
Staff
Customers
Interactive marketing
The hard (technical) and soft (interpersonal) skills with which the employees deal with customers

Source: Adapted from Piercy, '*Market led strategic change*', Butterworth Heinemann, 1992.

more sophisticated and demanding customers is not an option, it is a necessity. Internal marketing is the approach:

Internal marketing involves linking the three important 'publics' of an organisation, the organisation's senior management, its staff and its customers. Looking at this issue we can see that there are in fact, three different types of marketing the organisation's marketing specialists should be focusing on:

- External marketing:
  - The traditional body of knowledge and techniques traditionally employed by marketing professionals.
  - This focuses on the *interaction between the organisation and its external customers* – identifying, anticipating and meeting the needs of target customers.

- Interactive marketing:
  - The marketing techniques employed to manage the *interaction between the staff and customers*.
  - In all types of business, staff and prospects and customers meet and interact.
  - In all (but some internet offerings), there exists an element of person-to-person (sometimes called P2P) business.
  - Some organisations try to remove any form of personal contact because it is 'uncontrollable' while others try to 'manage cost downwards' on what they see as an unavoidably expensive area – hence the rise of Indian and Asian call centres.
  - Other organisations see staff–customer interaction as another opportunity to demonstrate the unique brand values and to differentiate their offer.
  - Which type of organisation are you?

- Internal marketing:
  - The marketing techniques employed to *train and motivate the staff* so that the culture is part of the 'solution' (it supports and differentiates the offer) rather than part of the 'problem' (it does as it damn well pleases, regardless of what the brand or the customer wants from it).
  - The benefits of a well funded, well researched and well implemented internal marketing programme are so obvious; they won't be elaborated here.
  - The most successful examples (B2B as well as B2C) are where the organisation invests in internal marketing on a constant basis – it is not a one-off event.
  - Customer needs change and value migrates, continually.
  - To do this, there are some requirements, as pointed out by Wilson and Gilligan.

MARGIN NOTES

Wilson and Gilligan (*'Strategic Marketing Planning'*, Butterworth Heinemann, 2000) suggest that a successful internal marketing programme requires:

- Senior management to accept the strategic importance of internal marketing
- A willingness to change structure so that the importance of front-line staff is recognised
- The development and communication of clear organisational values
- The empowerment of front-line staff so that they are given greater freedom to make decisions that will solve customers' problems
- A commitment to staff training and development
- A system that recognises staff excellence and rewards it accordingly
- The development of strong teams
- The identification of 'moments of truth' and the conscious thinking through of the ways in which these can be capitalised on by staff training and behaviour
- The setting of particular standards, a fundamental commitment to their achievement and a total lack of willingness to compromise
- The development of effective feedback systems so that the effectiveness of the internal marketing programmes can be monitored.

MARGIN NOTES

The 'joined up' organisation is efficient – and effective. The organisation that is not 'joined up' risks not meeting customer needs, and wasting a lot of valuable resource along the way.

Muddling through in this fashion is no longer an option in most industries and all organisations, apart from the lazy public authority monopolies, need to join up or die – customers have so much choice that they don't have to put up with organisational incompetence any longer.

Your organisation's value proposition needs to identify how the organisation joins up the dots:

- The outputs which are important to your customers
- How these outputs drive internal processes
- The customer objectives for internal marketing investments.

The FAQs are:

6 Organisation: Processes and Culture		
6.4 Is our organisation joined up?		
6.4.1	How does the organisation resolve conflict between function and process?	Where only process issues are in question, the process owner should be the final arbiter, but life is not always that simple. Conflict may arise because other issues than delivery on customer needs may be at risk – organisational security for instance. There needs to be a process for resolving such conflicts – an escalation procedure. How senior management deal with these situations is important, because process must be respected unless some over-riding business issue carries more weight.
6.4.2	How are customer segments reflected in process?	If the segments require the same tasks carried out in a different manner, then the task descriptions will detail how this should be done and the process will be the same. If the tasks themselves are different, then a different process is required. Either way, it should always be clear to the staff involved in the process, how to deal with any customer in any segment and to understand why that difference is important.
6.4.3	Is IT part of the process?	We have come across many organisations where IT was considered a part of the process, that is, they carried out a process task. In other organisations IT believes that they control the process. Neither should be the case. Systems and therefore IT can only 'support' a task, by automating an operation which would otherwise be carried out manually – They aren't intrinsically part of the process. IT should never control the process as 'process owner' – it would be in conflict as both the supplier and the customer of their own services.
6.4.4	Should functions be built around process?	Ideally yes. In practice, however, this is very difficult. Once again people are the issue and there is a human 'herd' instinct to group together with like-minded people. Staff roles are typically made up of multiple tasks (which will generally not be part of the same process) and unless all the staff in a process are dedicated to that process, management would become very difficult and the process very expensive.
6.4.5	How effective are cross-organisation initiatives and tasks?	You guessed. This is often a big problem for organisations. Functional issues are easy to deal with because the levers of change and the benefit of the initiative tend to be under the same control. Cross-organisational or cross-functional initiatives require much more co-ordination. First there needs to be an organisational recognition of the (customer) need, then assuming it is important enough, a team of people with the requisite skills can be formed (from the functions involved) to carry out the initiative.

		Where a major initiative is concerned, people may need to be taken out of the function, temporarily, and dedicated to the new team. Management needs to be careful that people have a role to go back to at the end of the initiative, otherwise the number of people willing to accept a temporary role in the future will dwindle to nothing!
6.4.6	How does the organisation ensure that customer value is created?	The emphasis of this question must be on the word 'value'. Most organisations will ensure that the customer receives something, although generally of a value that is attributed by the organisation itself! Customer value can only mean that the customer perceives value in the product or service and this is communicated to the organisation through the regular research. The value should be ensured through a regular dialogue between the customer (via research), the marketing function (as the medium or interpreter of the messages from the customer) and the rest of the organisation, to ensure that value continues to be delivered. Process is part of this, in fact there needs to be a process to review the customer offering and the process owner should be an integral part of the 'product review' process.
6.4.7	Who should take the role of the customer champion in the organisation?	If it were possible to have a dedicated but independent senior executive who could carry out this role, that would be ideal. However, in many organisations a 'non-line' role is seen as lacking credibility and a 'powerbase' and the role would be unlikely to survive. This is a cultural issue and the culture needs to be strong enough to support such a role. Those organisations that have a customer champion (most don't!) will ask the executive closest to the customer to perform this role, this is likely to be in the Marketing function. Whoever takes on the role, what is important is that the organisation listens intently to what the 'champion' has to say. The customer's view is often an awkward one and will usually cost the organisation money in the short term.

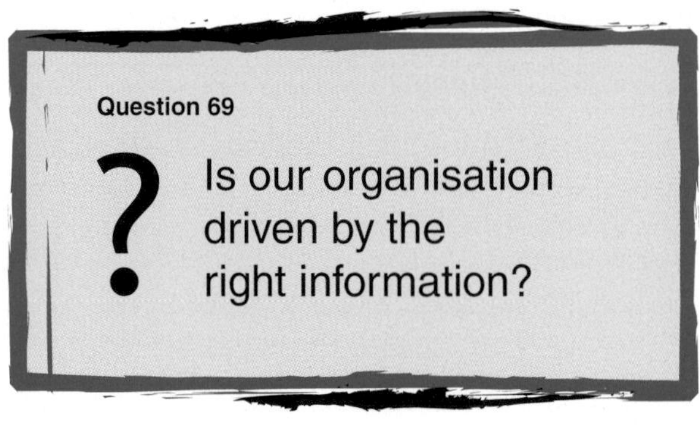

Question 69
?
Is our organisation driven by the right information?

We are all awash on a rising sea of data. Researchers from University of California, Berkeley said, that in 2002:

- 800 megabytes of data (roughly equivalent to 800 books) was created for every man, woman and child.
- The new information, stored on everything from hard disk drives to paper, added up to 5 m terabytes (5 million, million MB) in 2002 alone.

Whether this is all driven by a newfound desire to document all that happens around us, an explosion of *data* doesn't mean we have more *information* about what is going on. To explain:

- *Data* – Facts and statistics used for reference or analysis
- *Information* – Facts or knowledge provided or learned
- *Knowledge* – Information and skills acquired through experience or education (Oxford).

MARGIN NOTES

Which has to make us wonder, whether the organisation is using or being driven by the right (or the wrong) information.

Data, information and knowledge collection, management, and dissemination can be a time consuming process. There are three principal pitfalls for the unwary:

- Collecting data and then doing nothing with it:
  - A classic mistake.
  - This may be because too much data is collected and, generally, there is not enough resource to sort it, understand it and manage it.
  - Sometimes nothing is done because the organisation takes too long to review the data and the data becomes too old to use.
  - Data must be reviewed and assessed immediately. In the same way that an army marches on its stomach, an organisation progresses on its information feed; stale data won't satisfy the organisation's hunger or need for information.
  - Finally, data might not be used because the managers (and the organisation) are confused about their purpose – the point of the exercise is to *use* the data, not just collect it (see also Chapter 6).

- Accessing what is relevant to the organisation:
  - This is not easy, but very necessary.
  - Much data will be gathered which is 'interesting' but not relevant to the organisation.
  - This must be assessed carefully by people who understand the market strategy intimately and are in a position to make the necessary judgements.
  - If you try to work on all the data that comes into the organisation you will drown and nothing of any use will emerge.

  - Mistakes will occur and you will, on occasion, miss something that might be important, but normally you will have an opportunity to rectify that mistake when the same data comes in again and prompts further review.

- Turning the relevant data into information:
  - The data that is relevant to the organisation needs to be turned into useful information which can be used by the organisation (to create customer value).
  - This transformation takes place by answering some of the following points:
    - Why is the data relevant?
    - How does it relate to the organisation?
    - How important might be the impact of the information?
    - How urgent is the review of the information?
  - If the data is not transformed into information, then either it won't have any impact at all or everyone will put their own skew on the data and use their own analysis of the data to pursue their own agendas.

MARGIN NOTES

Remembering the marketing information system (MkIS) diagram (see Chapter 9), we know that we only collect information so that we can use it – turning it into answers to managers needs and ultimately into marketplace action.

There are many sources of data and information, from the obvious trade journals and financial news to your own customer research. There are also many ways of accessing those sources, you need not be restricted to the efforts of a team with designated responsibility, the whole workforce can be employed, particularly in watching what the competition is up to. (*I have always regarded as a standard and valuable information source the interviews with potential recruits. Most of them come from the competition and will have some useful insight into part of another organisation's business. On its own, this data is not very useful, but you would be amazed how you can gradually build up a picture of what is going on around you – turning the data into useful information – Hamish Mackay*).

Resource is needed to *manage* the information process.

- Of course it costs hard won resource, but; if it reveals the organisation position – relative to its objectives, customers and competitors – it is an invaluable investment.

- The process of information retrieval doesn't stop with the review of the information, the information feed needs to translate into action where required.
  - An organisation creates its objectives and measures its success in relation to others (both competitors and customers).

- This process is the 'compass' that keeps the organisation on track in relation to the constantly changing market.
- Without this process the organisation runs the risk of wandering off into the market desert and finding more and more price battles to fight.

The information we have considered so far is what is needed to inform the organisation about itself and the outside world. There is another form of information which is increasingly important; we can call this information – *knowledge*.

Rolls-Royce

The Rolls-Royce business strategy has been consistent over many years and is built around five core strategic drivers:

- Address four global markets
- Invest in technology, capability and infrastructure
- Develop a competitive portfolio of products and services
- Grow market share and installed product base
- Add value for our customers through the provision of product-related services.

This provides the basis for the Group strategic and financial planning process which has a 10-year horizon, sub-divided into 'first three' and 'next seven' year plans to provide a shorter- and longer-term perspective.

The Marine strategic plan is described in summary through a 'Roadmap' document that provides an overview of the key elements we believe will be important in the realisation of our growth objectives.

The Roadmap provides the basis on which the Marine strategy is communicated throughout the organisation using a variety of media to provide clarity and understanding of the major areas that we will be focusing on to drive growth.

In addition, we use a 'Marine Card' that is updated each year to provide a reminder of our vision, values, key behaviours and critical success factors, together with a summary of objectives for that year.

MARGIN NOTES

Monitoring and management of performance against these objectives is achieved through the use of balanced scorecards across the business and integration with individual objectives and reward schemes.

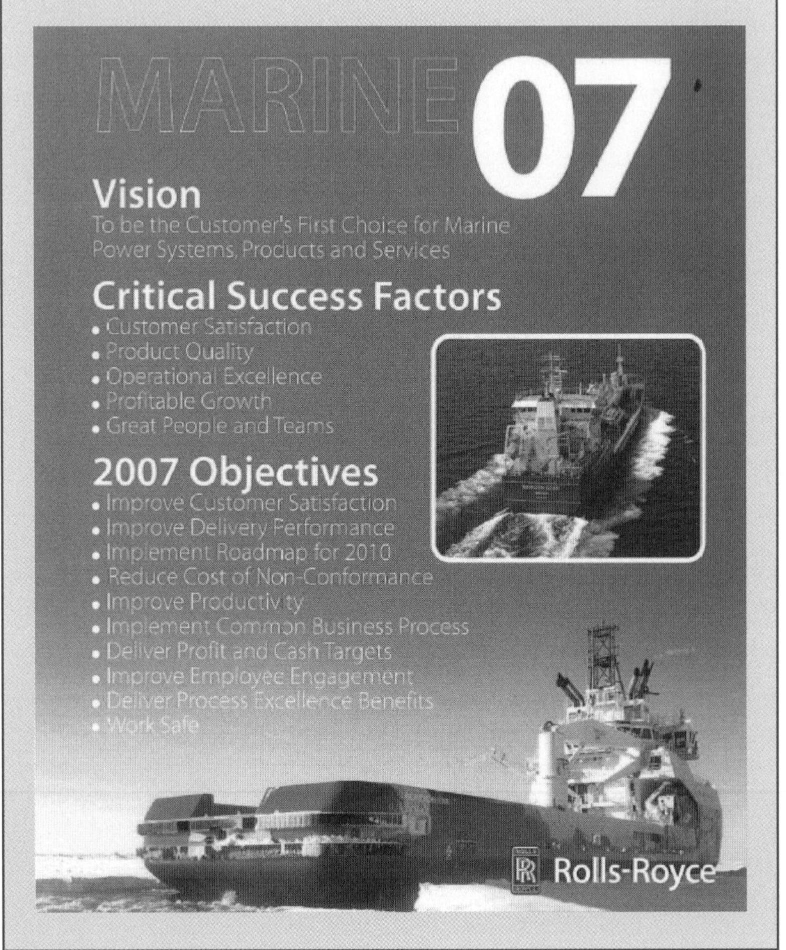

MARGIN NOTES

The KM is a relatively new area of research and it is distinguished from 'information' by the way it is used as an essential ingredient in the customer offering and business purpose.

First a definition:

- 'The explicit and systematic management of vital knowledge and its associated processes of creating, gathering, organising, diffusion, use and exploitation. It requires turning personal knowledge into corporate knowledge that can be widely shared throughout an organisation and appropriately applied.' (Skyrme, '*Knowledge management: making sense of an oxymoron*', Management Insight, 2nd series, No. 2, 1997).

And, the 'headlines':

- Gradually and inexorably, organisations will differentiate themselves by how they retain and manage knowledge.
  - A relatively new management area, KM made an appearance at the end of the 1990s.
  - A simple concept but one that is desperately difficult to implement, it is growing – but slowly – as organisations discover that the market advantage it can bring offsets the investment in developing internal KM processes.
  - The essence of KM is about creating a competitive advantage by:
    - Collecting relevant data from the environment
    - Analysis, turning that information into knowledge
    - Pushing that knowledge to staff that need it to be used in the market
    - Using the knowledge to enhance the customer offering and experience

- KM is slowly trying to bring together a collection of recent 'good ideas' proposed in different business and management articles and provide a good home for 'orphaned ideas' – So if you see these buzz words in your wanderings ...
  - Intellectual capital
  - The knowledge worker
  - The learning organization
  - Communities of practice
  - Knowledge bases
  - Expert systems
  - Help desks
  - Corporate intranets and extranets
  - Content management and
  - Document management.

- The other reason why KM has been slow in taking off is because many different academic and business function areas have been looking at KM from their own perspective.
  - KM is currently being 'explained' from a variety of different angles, among which you will find focuses on:
    - Technologies (especially those that are information based)
    - Theories underlying the concepts of knowledge and truth
    - People, and bringing people together and helping them exchange knowledge
    - Processes that may drive knowledge creation, transmission and transformation

MARGIN NOTES

- Organisation needs to be designed to facilitate knowledge processes
- Ecology and its focus on the interaction of people, identity, knowledge and environmental factors as a complex adaptive system.

- How 'knowledge' is managed and made available will grow in importance, particularly in this age where the manufacturing and delivery of basic services is increasingly being sent offshore to countries like India and China.
  - European organisations will never compete with the cost base available in these countries and in the future we will sometimes struggle to meet the quality as well.
  - What we will have to concentrate on is the knowledge that we have (and can develop and *use*) to enhance customer value.
  - We have a long way to go, to really exploit the potential available from KM.
  - Toyota is a good example of how we might develop KM.
    - Toyota have deemed that all the knowledge that has been collected and developed in any of their manufacturing or distribution processes is available free to all of its customers.
    - The price of this largesse is that all of its customers have to do the same-share all their knowledge with other Toyota customers and Toyota itself – even if they are competitors.
    - Toyota believes that everyone benefits from this knowledge sharing and the net revenue that results is better for all.
    - Their success seems to bear this out.
    - The process is managed very carefully and anyone not 'playing ball' loses the Toyota 'franchise' and is ejected from the family.

- The KM is one the keys to the future and all organisations would be wise to give this some airtime in their businesses.

- Modern technology has changed the way people support each other, there is a great opportunity for organisations to capture the attention of the customer by providing some of that vital support.

MARGIN NOTES

Your organisation's value proposition needs to build in the unique advantages of KM by identifying:

- What knowledge is important about your customers
- What knowledge is important about your competition
- Who needs the knowledge to make customer decisions
- What support your customers are looking for
- How the knowledge adds customer value.

The FAQs are:

6 Organisation: Processes and Culture		
6.5 Is our organisation driven by the right information?		
6.5.1	First – how do we get focused on today's customers?	The attention of the whole staff (and almost the whole organisation) should be on today's customers. So all processes, all communications and training should be helping the staff to understand what is important and how they can help make a difference. The whole process of objective and KPI setting, design principles and task definitions is designed to focus the organisation on what is important – its customers. If management understands this importance then that is what the process will be used for, if they don't understand, then a miscellany of other objectives such as cost minimisation or productivity improvement will dominate the agenda. Ultimately this is a cultural issue, the organisation will focus on what management *believes* and demonstrates through its actions is the primary focus – staff take their lead from management.
6.5.2	Is market information retained systematically?	If your organisation has designed an information retrieval process then it would be foolhardy for that process not to be carried out on a systematic basis. It should not be something that gets done 'as and when' there is some spare resource available. Unfortunately this is what often happens. If you are serious about it, the only way to make retention systematic, is to give this to someone as their prime responsibility – with full accountability for a set of objectives. Otherwise there will *always* be other issues or tasks which are more visible or more immediate.
6.5.3	How much does the organisation know about the competition?	We have already looked at the inclusion of competitor data in the information retrieval process. However, the question that is really interesting is – 'Is your organisation looking at the right competition?' This is not so easy, for new competition can come from many angles, particularly if new technology is playing a part (see Chapter 2). ● Did Kodak see mobile telephony as a potential source of competition? ● Did IBM see the threat from the PC? ● Did Sony expect the iPod? The answer is 'no' – and these organisation were never considered slouches at customer orientation. This puts the spotlight firmly onto the PEST analysis (see Chapter 2) and a clear understanding of *what business* your organisation is really in (see Chapter 5). Having worked out who the competitors are, your organisation should always know 'as much as possible' about your (real) competition – once you put your mind to finding out, managers are always surprised about how much good quality information is available.

6.5.4	How do we know what information we need?	It is important to focus the available resources where they can do the most good – obviously. It must follow then that, as far as possible, your information requirements should not be left to the discretion of those managers in charge of the retrieval process; that can lead to: ● Collection of what is easy to get rather than what is most urgently required ● Information (data?) overload ● An inability to understand what to *do* with it when it arrives. The 'first' information you should be seeking is for the implementers – who need to know what to implement. The 'second' information you should be seeking is to understand how the organisation is progressing against your agreed objectives – of satisfying customers' needs.
6.5.5	Who sees the information produced?	There is a tendency with modern technology (and particularly with the 'reply to all' email button) not to be too selective in communicating information. The lazy managers and organisations *won't know* who needs the information – and who doesn't, and will fire all the information to all the management and maybe a good number of staff as well. This: ● Turns information into data ● Creates email overload ● Produces very poor productivity as everyone has to read everything to work out what is relevant to them. As we have seen though, with a clear link from the market all the way through to the task definitions, you should be able to work out whose roles and responsibilities need which information feeds. Where it is not clear, there are individuals who can help you work that out – for instance, process owners and functional managers.
6.5.6	How do we focus on tomorrow's (new and retained) customers?	Tomorrow's retained customers are (of course) today's existing and new customers (see Chapter 9). We will maintain the right focus on today's business and tomorrow's business by tracking customer needs as they change. The *trick* here is to focus your organisation on your customers' needs and wants, and not on internal issues. But you also have to be careful to monitor the changing shape of the market. Will today's segments also be there tomorrow?
6.5.7	What is driving new product and service development?	Every organisation focuses on new product and service development. You cannot stand still, because the competition – and customers, keep moving on. NPD is just one of the beneficiaries of the information retrieval process. Some information will suggest changes to your existing products and services, other information will move your organisation to new products or service areas.

What is important is that there is a constant marriage between the ideas generated internally and the information coming in from the market:

- How do the customers react to the new ideas?
- Are the new products and services or enhancements generating real customer value?
- Or are they merely interesting features, which carry no real value?

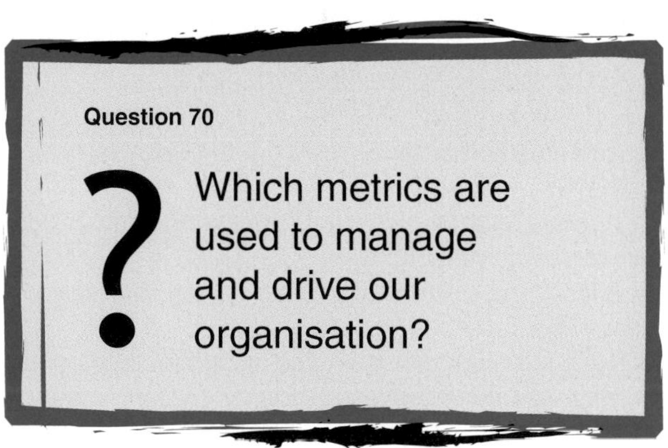

Question 70
?
Which metrics are used to manage and drive our organisation?

MARGIN NOTES

So how important do you think metrics are? The saying goes:

- What gets measured, gets done
- You get what you *inspect*, not what you *expect*
- There is measure in all things.

The 'headlines':

- The specific metrics used to manage the organisation will go to the heart of how and what is being managed in the organisation. Because *measurements drive behaviour*.
  - The metrics are the measures that tell the organisation how it is *performing* in relation to any and every aspect that the organisation considers important.
  - The results are the basis of the MI pack reviewed on a regular basis by senior management.
    - Metrics go further; they also deliver any information at any level to enable management to manage.
    - What gets measured is therefore very important, this is about the right metrics being measured and informing the right people.

  - The tendency, therefore, is to measure everything in sight, producing reams of statistics, most of which don't matter and aren't reviewed.

- All metrics should be driven by an objective.
  - If there is no objective set then it is difficult to know whether the performance is satisfactory or not.
  - There may be any number of metrics for one objective so, in looking at the process of delivering customer benefit, every task will have a metric attached to it:
    - Was the task carried out within allowed time span?
    - Was quality satisfactory – perhaps measured by error rates? And the like.

- Metrics are also used to monitor functional performance.
  - For example
    - In human relations we might measure numbers of candidates per recruitment campaign
    - In marketing communications we might measure effectiveness of the advertising
    - In sales we might measure the orders received per calls made.
    - To measure the relative experience of staff in the organisation, we might measure staff turnover in relation to length of service.
  - Each function will follow its own metrics, against its own view of best practice, to monitor the functional efficiency.
  - These measures may not necessarily be required by senior management, which is concerned with monitoring the overall organisational effectiveness.

MARGIN NOTES

- We don't intend, in this Chapter, to look at what metrics are needed in any particular organisation. This is individual to your organisation and your objectives, and generalisations would be pointless. However, we would expect your measures to cover four broad areas:
  - Process efficiency
  - Organisational effectiveness
  - Functional efficiency
  - Cultural behaviour

- Some organisations use a 'balanced business scorecard' approach which has the benefit of showing that there are other organisation performance measures apart from just the traditional financial ones.

Kaplan and Norton (*'Balanced Scorecard: Translating Strategy into Action'*, Harvard Business School Press, 1996) suggest that we view the organisation from four perspectives:

- The financial perspective:
  - Obvious, but not the only one.

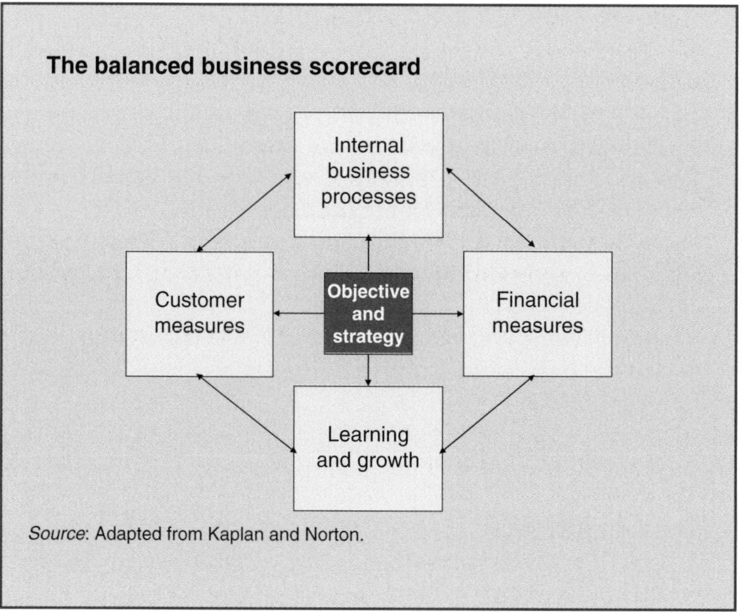

Source: Adapted from Kaplan and Norton.

MARGIN NOTES

  - Timely and accurate funding data will always be a priority, and managers will do whatever is necessary to provide it.
  - There is perhaps a need to include additional financial-related data, such as risk assessment and cost-benefit data, in this category.

- The learning and growth perspective:
  - Includes staff training and corporate cultural attitudes related to both individual and corporate self-improvement.

- The customer perspective:
  - Customer focus and customer satisfaction is essential in any business.
  - These are leading indicators: if customers aren't satisfied, they will eventually find other suppliers that will meet their needs.

- The business process perspective:
  - Refers to internal business processes.
  - Metrics based on this perspective allow the managers to know how well their business is running, and whether its products and services conform to customer requirements.

Not a bad approach. If it were *applied* as well in the organisations that 'flirt' with the approach we are sure it would do a better job at prizing managers away from their 'all-that-matters-is-the-money' obsession.

But what are the 'best' or 'right'; metrics to use?

- It is obvious but – the best metrics aren't always the easiest metrics.
  - Sometimes, the easiest metrics to use will be the wrong ones – they will create the wrong behaviours and will displease customers.
  - If it is difficult, it is probably even more important to measure because it will matter more to the organisation.
  - In their article on 'Creative destruction', (*The McKinsey Quarterly*, 2001/3) Foster and Kaplan had it exactly right when they determined that an organisation should 'Control what you must, not what you can and control – when you must not when you can'.

- Is that measure you have been using since, well forever really, creating the behaviours that customers say they want and you have promised them?
  - No, we are serious.
  - Are you absolutely sure that that traditional quarterly sales budget (and associated bonuses and rewards) doesn't ever result in customers being sold something on March 33rd that they did not really want or need?
  - Does it really support your brand promise of only providing 'solutions', never selling stuff they don't want?
  - While you are there, you might want to calculate the financial advantage of being on sales target in Q1 against the brand investment that you have just destroyed (see Chapter 8 for the costs of building a brand).

MARGIN NOTES

- Information technology is now the mainstay of all organisations, particularly in the realm of MI, and, unfortunately, IT tends to determine what can be measured. (*I have often found in looking at operational effectiveness of an organisation that management information stops where IT stops. This is not only a complete nonsense but an aberration of management duty – Hamish Mackay*)
  - Dependence on IT is the course of least resistance
    - What has IT got to *do* with anything?
    - Before the advent of the electronic organisation, if something was important it was measured manually – it simply took more resource to do it.
    - If cost is an issue then the metric is probably not important enough and should be ignored.

- We need to be able to react to the results.
  - If we are deviating from the path of meeting our objectives, then we need to react and do something about it – as fast as possible.
  - The whole point of metrics and the resulting MI is the call to action when we are off-course.
  - We call this the *control process*.

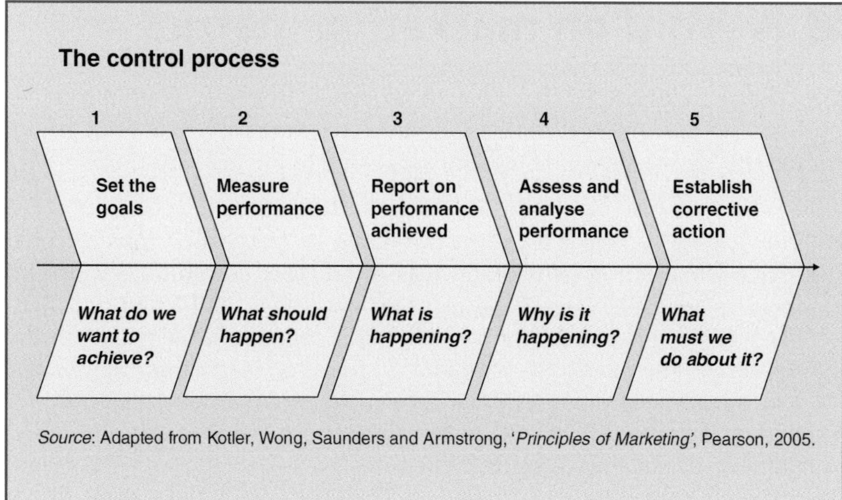
The control process
1
2
3
4
5
Set the goals
Measure performance
Report on performance achieved
Assess and analyse performance
Establish corrective action
What do we want to achieve?
What should happen?
What is happening?
Why is it happening?
What must we do about it?

Source: Adapted from Kotler, Wong, Saunders and Armstrong, '*Principles of Marketing*', Pearson, 2005.

MARGIN NOTES

We will cover the control process in more detail (see Chapter 11), but for now all we need to see is that there are five key stages in any project of activity – and each has a very simple but serious question attached:

- Setting goals
  - What do we want to achieve?
- Measuring performance
  - What should happen if everything goes to plan (we can dream)?
- Reporting on performance
  - What is (really) happening?
- Assessing performance
  - Why has it happened?
  - No, don't get excited, these things happen, but we cannot do anything about it unless we know why it happened differently from what was expected
- Establishing corrective action
  - What should we do about putting it 'right'?
  - If anything?

Without the processes in place to answer these questions, only an amateur manager (or one that has already landed the next job) would consider wasting resources by starting the activity in the first place.

A word on marketing metrics

Ever since a consulting firm wrote an article entitled 'Has Marketing outlived its usefulness?' the entire marketing fraternity has been trying to find the 'right' measures to justify its value to the organisation.

- The original article was, in fact, right in its suggestion, given that it defined marketing as it really was (marketing communications and services) and bemoaned the fact that marketing (still) had not managed to do the real job of co-ordinating organisational focus on the customer. The resulting 'scramble' to identify Marketing metrics has had a beneficial effect – it has shown that if 'real' marketing (rather than just communications) were employed by an organisation, then there would be very significant benefits.

MARGIN NOTES

- There is nothing different about how marketing will measure itself from any other function. Recently, the UK's Chartered Institute of Marketing (www.cim.uk) has sifted through all the data and suggested the following list of marketing metrics:
  - Financial, for example:
    - profit
    - turnover
    - cost base
    - return on sales
    - share price
    - earnings per share, etc.
  - Operational, for example:
    - percentage capacity in use
    - bed/seat occupancy
    - time to complete production
    - waiting lists, etc
  - Market position, for example:
    - percentage market share
    - position relative to market leader
    - size of operation
    - geographic distribution
  - Reputation, for example:
    - awareness
    - positioning, etc.
  - Loyalty assessment, for example
    - customer 'churn'
    - percentage repeat business
    - percentage of wallet of target customers (particularly key customers).

Your organisation's value proposition will dictate those metrics that are needed to track:

- customer satisfaction (the things that count)
- staff behaviour (culture) and relations to brand promise
- the processes that deliver customer satisfaction and staff behaviours.

The FAQs are:

6 Organisation: processes and culture		
6.6 Which metrics are used to manage and drive our organisation?		
6.6.1	Does it all make sense?	Sometimes you just have to stand back and ask this question: • Are the right metrics being used? • Are they being reviewed frequently enough and fast enough? • Does it still make sense? An independent and objective mind is needed to carry out such a review; this could be a role for Internal Audit or an external consultant. Is all the MI being put to good purpose or has the reason that the metric was put in place now disappeared? This 'sanity check' will save a deal of time spent in creating unnecessary management data and should find out if there are any gaps in the information as well. This check ought to be carried out with every planning review.
6.6.2	Who sees the management information (MI)?	A balance needs to be struck in the communication of MI. More will be *interested* than are directly affected by certain aspects of the MI. If every manager is not to 'wade through' irrelevant data, each measure needs to be considered in turn: • Who is affected by the metric? • Who is affected by the result? There are cultural issues at play here as well. Is the organisation an 'open' or 'closed' society? If 'open', then only information that is confidential should be withheld and there is not usually much of that. If 'closed', then only information that directly relates to any member of staff will be revealed. (*I am in the 'open' camp. Good staff will manage their time effectively and will ultimately only review information which is important to them. An 'open' organisation will create a much more inclusive and involved team – Hamish Mackay*).

6.6.3	How do the financials fit into the organisational drivers?	This point has been referred to several times without really being addressed directly: • The MI is about metrics and measures of performance. So results are related in units, time, percentages, etc. • Financial information is all in £€$¥s and shows how the organisation has *translated* the performance into profit and cash. • Financial information is controlled by the stock exchange and is price sensitive, if you are a public company. • This can and should be reviewed as often as is required to ensure continued good performance. • Therefore, the *financials aren't measures* but are 'results', which can be compared to targets or hurdles that are required by the organisation to satisfy the different stakeholders (see chapter 3). Financials cannot be metric measures (unless they relate to units) because you cannot identify an action that will result in a change in performance. Hmmmm
6.6.4	What are the informal measurement systems?	It won't surprise you to hear that every organisation has *informal* as well as *formal* measurement systems. Informal measures will be created by a local need to monitor some performance not captured by the formal MI processes. The informal metrics are important because: • They can reveal much about the function or the manager involved. • They can utilise considerable resource. Ask yourself also: • Why does the formal process not capture this information? • Are the informal metrics consistent with the culture and objectives of the organisation? • Is the resource used being used wisely? • If it is important, should the metric be supported by IT and brought into the MI pack reviewed at a more senior level? • If not, why was it started in the first place? The 'sanity check' referred to above should also review the informal information created.
6.6.5	How are metrics used to track behaviours?	There is no limit to the metrics available to measure performance but they won't help a great deal with behavioural change. The more qualitative the objective, the more difficult it is to measure – and behavioural aspects are the most difficult. If performance needs to be monitored then it can be reviewed by: • Video or by tape recording and played back after the event. • Mystery shopper research on service levels • Customer research can be asked if performance was satisfactory. Generally – and unfortunately – behaviour won't easily allow a metric to track conveniently what the organisation is looking for, but that doesn't obviate the need for the metric.

6.6.6	Are we using the most appropriate marketing metrics?	There are two ways of answering this question: First we need to measure the performance of the marketing function or activity: ● There are a number of standard performance measures – see above. ● These are straightforward but are essentially 'efficiency' measures – as long as nothing is 'wrong' doesn't automatically mean that things are 'right'. Second, and more importantly, we need to measure the effectiveness of the organisation in creating customer value (marketing strategy): ● Technically, this is both very difficult – and very easy. ● Very difficult because the key (see Chapter 8, and the whole book really) is differentiation. ● If you are investing in being unique, then how can you find any benchmark to measure how well you are doing? ● You cannot, so don't look. ● Now the simple stuff, if what you are doing is working, it will be showing up in the financials! Beware though, real marketing strategy is not aimed at the short term, so won't produce cash or profit returns in this period – choose the appropriate timescale.
6.6.7	Should you use proprietary measurement tools?	This depends upon what you are using the tools to do. Proprietary tools can be used to carry out the measurement efficiently and then present a MI type *dashboard* with graphs and diagrams to bring the results alive. Never let the salesman talk you into buying a tool set without having already worked exactly what you need from the tool set. Tools can make data capture too easy in some ways and allow capture of unnecessary information. Then again in the wrong hands, they can become (heaven forbid) a form of creative self-expression? However, if it makes life easier why not? This is a case of making an investment like any other. The hard costs (purchase and time involved in set up and maintenance) and benefits (time saved in capturing and presenting the MI) should be assessed and the soft benefits (improved presentation of results) only be taken into account if the decision is not clear cut. Your next question (but not for this book) is which one of the many types would/should you use?

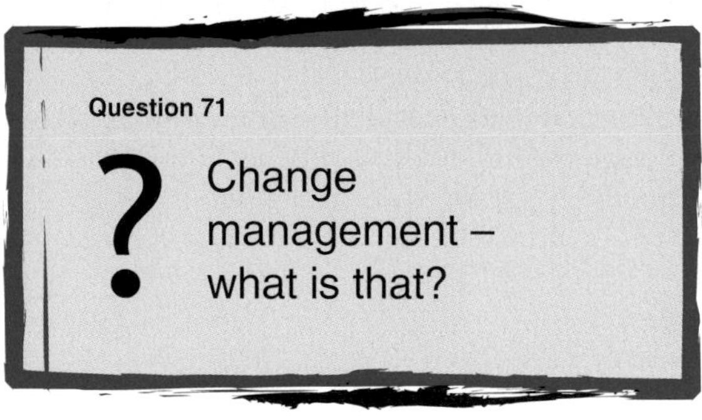
Question 71
?
Change management – what is that?

There's nothing like finishing a section on organisation on a real high.

You (and your organisation) have no choice, *you will have to change*:

- Customers change and value migrates
  - When value moves, either your organisation moves to follow the value – or you starve.
  - Allow visions of the Lapp herders following the wandering herds of reindeer and you are probably not far off the mark! Further survival guidance can be found in '*Who Moved My Cheese?*' (Johnson, Vermillion, 1999).

- Change management is the most important of the management disciplines and unfortunately it is also the least understood.
  - Organisations will want or need to change for many reasons.
  - Some of these have been discussed in previous sections of this chapter.
  - Whether new systems are being introduced, the organisation is evolving to keep abreast of the market or it simply needs to be that much more efficient, change needs to be planned carefully.

- Change is never simple.
  - If you think it is, then it is likely you have missed a trick or two, somewhere.
  - If you are changing an organisation in however small a manner then at the very least you will have to look at:
    - Working practices
    - Measurement metrics
    - Staff communication and
    - Project monitoring.
  - Changes in process or tasks within a process need just as careful management as large and complex change projects.
  - It is the role of management to effect that change and manage the required transition in that part of the organisation.
  - The problem is that management will almost always underestimate the effort required and the difficulty involved in making change.

- Change always involves *people*.
  - You won't be able to change the organisation successfully in the manner required unless you can not only take the people with you but actively get them on your side.
  - It is generally accepted that two-third of change projects fail and mostly because the impact on staff is either not recognised or underplayed.
  - It is undeniable that if you don't change behaviour in some way then you have not changed the organisation.

MARGIN NOTES

  - You will be able to make changes in working practices or systems but if care is not taken with the people side of things then the organisation will regress and you will be worse off than before.
  - This part of a project is sometimes called 'internal marketing' (see above), although this is sometimes just a fancy term for communicating what is happening, when and why, what is expected of staff involved and how they are impacted when the change is made.

- Like any good story, *A Change Project* needs a beginning, a middle (muddle?) and an end.
  - The beginning is *the plan*.
    - This should be formally documented and is sometimes known as the 'project initiation document' (PID).
    - This ensures that what is intended, how it is to be carried out, what the intended impact is and what the resultant costs and benefits are, are agreed by all the relevant parties.
    - It also allows any variations during the project to be compared to the original plan and cost/benefit analysis so that if the project ceases to be viable then a timely halt can be brought to the project before more money is wasted or appropriate remedial action can be taken to bring the project back on course.
    - The plan needs to indicate who is involved and what resource is required to achieve the change. If staff are to be dedicated to the project for a time – and the bigger the change project, the more important this will be – then re-entry plans for the staff involved need to be agreed in advance.
  - The middle is the *management* of the change itself.
    - A complex project will need a programme office to track all the sub-projects which go to make up the entire event – and a project plan.
    - Smaller projects will need the same methodology but not necessarily with a dedicated team or specialist project management.
    - A complex project will require regular and frequent management reporting on progress.
    - Red/Amber/Green (RAG) reports are often used, reporting each facet of the project as Red, Amber or Green at each report.
    - This is simple and effective, as long as it is honestly carried out.
    - This point is important as most project reporting is subjectively carried out by the project team.
    - As the changes are put into place then metrics will need to change, management reports will alter and new processes may need to be understood.

MARGIN NOTES

        - The organisation should have changed and therefore management and controls need to reflect the changed state of the organisation.
    - The end is the *realisation* of the benefits.
        - This takes place after the changes have been put into effect. It is surprising how often major projects leave this aspect of change management out altogether.
        - The benefits need to be positively managed or they won't happen.
        - The actions required to deliver the benefits should have been detailed in the original plan, so there should be no need to work out what needs to be done to deliver the financial result which justified the original investment of resource.
        - This is the point where regression is a serious threat.
        - Even if the benefits are realised, it is still possible for the organisation to regress to its former state.
        - Management and management controls should be monitoring the changes to ensure that this doesn't happen.

MARGIN NOTES

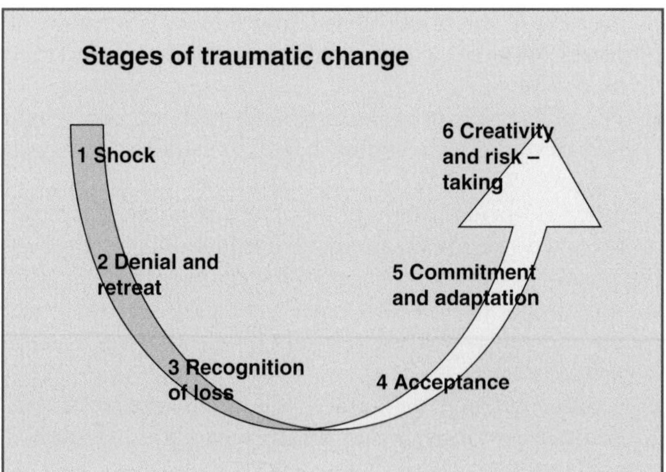

There should be no surprises to anyone about the impact that change (of any sort) will have on your staff.

- Staff are intelligent (if not why are you employing them?) and can work out for themselves if there is a likelihood of redundancies or aspects of change that they won't like.
    - If this is the case, you must face this head on and work out a satisfactory solution for all, those who stay are just as vulnerable as those who may have to go.

- The change process is well documented and, depending on the *perceived* severity of the change, is similar in all cases. The steps are clear:
  - *Shock*: this cannot be happening
  - *Denial and Retreat*: – there must be some mistake
  - *Recognition of loss*: coming to terms with the facts and that the future will be different
  - *Acceptance*: I can see the future, it is really happening
  - *Commitment and adaptation*: I want to be part of the future
  - Creativity *and risk taking*: I will do things differently
- What is less well understood is that progress through these steps is difficult to forecast.
  - First, progress is not linear; people tend to take two steps forward and one step back.
  - Secondly, different people progress through the change at different rates, so beware achieving critical mass and having the right people come through.
- Survivors of trauma often feel very guilty that they are the ones to survive. Change can sometimes resemble a trauma situation if it is not handled properly.
- Unless this is managed then the staff won't be with you and if they aren't with you, they are likely to be against you – and you *will* fail.

MARGIN NOTES

- As we have seen elsewhere in this chapter, organisations must change – and constantly– to stay healthy; there is little real choice in the matter.
  - It is imperative, therefore, that organisations learn how to do this effectively.
  - Business and people are naturally static, seeking firm ground on which to get organised; markets, customers and the business environment aren't.
  - The more easily that an organisation can change itself the better it will be for the organisation and its people.

- What is really important is that change is taken on willingly and wherever possible, managed without pressure.
  - It should be timely and appropriate.
  - If the organisation has waited until the last moment to make a change then it will always be under pressure and won't have the luxury of doing it properly. Corners will be cut. (*In my experience, whenever I have delayed a change decision, because I thought that later would be easier or less traumatic or that the organisation would be more ready to accept a given change…I have regretted it. If change is needed then get on with it – Hamish Mackay*).

So the principles of change management are:

- Plan the changes well

- Communicate and explain the changes

- Monitor the change project
- Redesign the organisation for the impending change then
- Monitor carefully, the areas of the organisation that have been subjected to the change and finally
- Manage the benefits positively, don't expect them to happen of their own accord

Above all, if everyone in the organisation understands that 'change is normal – steady state is dangerous' you won't only have less resistance, you will also have help.

> *Your organisation's value proposition*:
>
> - Won't throw any light on change management – there are limits to what it can be used for!

The FAQs are:

6 Organisation: processes and culture		
6.7 Change management – what is that?		
6.7.1	How resistant is the organisation to change?	Organisations can be very resistant to change. Ultimately, this spells doom for the change manager. Where this is the case, the methodology stays the same but nothing should start until the right environment has been created to make the change acceptable. It could well be that staff have never been taken into the confidence of management and so a complete understanding of the current strategy (and how it was arrived at) may be required to understand *the need for the change*. You just cannot get away from the need to communicate with staff eventually. Resistance will always come down to two issues: • The organisation doesn't normally carry out change, so the status quo is where staff are most comfortable. • Staff don't understand why it is necessary to change. If this is the case in your organisation, then don't wait until these effects are felt, employ a 'safety first' principle, assume that they exist and manage accordingly.

6.7.2	How do we remain relevant as value migrates in the market?	Essential for every organisation that faces competition. For an organisation to remain relevant it must create a 'change is normal' culture. To survive and prosper, you have to be able to do this as and when customer value migrates, without major fuss or heartache. Good research should give us warning that things outside are changing and that the organisation needs to change or realign. Following the SCORPIO logic, we ought to be able to see that the best profits are created by customers who come back (retention). Retention means customer relationships. Relationships are built, not with the first offering but with a series of offerings – that change to meet ever-changing customer needs.
6.7.3	Can change be organised methodically?	There is now an accepted methodology called Prince 2 (PRINCE – 'Projects in Controlled Environments' – was first developed by the UK government in 1989 as the standard approach to IT project management for central government). This details a process of change management from the PID through to the realisation of the benefits. Specialist project managers can be hired who are experienced in this methodology and have undergone large and complex projects in other companies. Most organisations don't employ this expertise on a permanent basis, it is simply not justified and most very experienced project managers are only available as contractors anyway. There is no reason why management should not be trained in the basic elements of Prince 2 methodology. This would help managers understand the pitfalls better and also give valuable skills which can be applied to normal management situations.
6.7.4	How do you monitor the change project itself?	We mentioned that most project reporting is subjectively carried out by the project management itself. This is inevitable as only those involved in a project will understand it well enough to know whether it is on or off-target. In large projects, lasting many months or even a few years, this approach should be mitigated by an independent audit half way through the project or every six months. *(I am generally met with howls of anguish at this suggestion because of the expense. To carry out such an audit needs experienced people who need to take the time to understand the project. But this should all be built into the original cost and not be seen as an add-on. When a project fails, it is bad for everyone and very, very expensive. This sort of audit can be regarded as a form of insurance for senior management who can never hope to really understand a project deeply enough to know that all is well. Where projects are going off the rails, there may still be time to take action if it is realised early enough. If the basis upon which the project investment was agreed has changed then positive management would recognise that fact and stop any further cash drain out of the organisation – Hamish Mackay).*
6.7.5	How do you make change to be non-threatening?	In absolute terms, the only change which is not threatening is one that doesn't upset the employees' own sense of worth or livelihood. In other words, after the change they will still have a job that they consider to be valuable.

		Sometimes, where redundancy is in synch with an employee's (or manager's) personal agenda, voluntary redundancy schemes can come in. Barring this, the most important is to communicate properly so that surprise and all the associated emotions are minimised. Change needs to be commonplace. In a culture where change is happening on a constant basis, not only will the organisation be very experienced at making the changes effectively but the staff will also regard this as a normal part of their role.
6.7.6	What to do about the impact of change on the customer?	Customers will only be concerned with changes they can see. That is, changes in the offering or in the marketing mix. If these changes flow from customer research then you are starting from a point where you expect them to be positive, but any change that doesn't flow directly from an understanding about the customers needs to be monitored very carefully. You have to earn the right to serve customers by demonstrating that you understand the customer and can meet his or her needs – constantly. You will put that 'right' in jeopardy if you start making changes that move you in the wrong direction. This is why changes are often tested before being rolled out. Even if the change flows directly from customer research, test how well you have interpreted the data. 'Carefully does it'!
6.7.7	What to do if resistance is so strong that change is not possible	If you work in one of the following, you have no problem: ● A public utility or nationalised industry (for example, UK water, electric or gas 'services', France Telecom) ● A local monopoly where the customer has no real choice (for example, rail services) ● A global monopoly where the customer has no real choice (for example, Microsoft) ● A service that is controlled by government to limit competition (for example, UK Actuaries, Belgian pharmacists) ● An organisation or industry that is effectively controlled by a profession or union as a closed shop. If you are in *any* other type of organisation, one that faces national and international competition, you must either change – or die. If you really cannot change ...

■ The strategic questions (65–71)

The sixth part of the marketing strategy discussion, organisation – processes and culture.

The organisation is too often seen as a problem (challenge) that exists outside the normal boundaries of what we call 'marketing'. This is a great shame because, along with the unhealthy obsession with marketing communications, it is the single reason why marketing has never lived up to its promise as a business process.

Marketing is, and was always meant to be, a co-ordinating function that aligns everybody *inside* the organisation with what the customer wants (and is willing to pay for) *outside* the organisation. With access to the workings of the organisation denied, real marketing has little of value to contribute.

In this chapter we have tried to give you an overview of the issues you need to know if you are planning to implement your Marketing strategy. We have touched on the main elements of the management skill-set and showed how the actions of managers can and should link together and to the market. It can all be looked at in greater detail but, from the marketing strategy viewpoint, you just need to understand why and how.

So we arrive at the questions again. Fewer calculations to do here, but some quite deep analysis – many marketing people are skilled at dealing with people (customers), just re-apply your skills inside the organisation and understand the needs and wants of managers and staff (internal customers) in the same way.

No.	Strategic question	Our strategic answer	Importance	✓
	Organisation: Processes and Culture			
65	Is our organisation focused on internal or external issues?		Must have	
			Nice to have	
			Not important	
66	What is our organisation really good at – and does it matter?		Must have	
			Nice to have	
			Not important	
67	What is going on with our culture?		Must have	
			Nice to have	
			Not important	
68	Is our organisation joined up?		Must have	
			Nice to have	
			Not important	
69	Is our organisation driven by the right information?		Must have	
			Nice to have	
			Not important	

70	Which metrics are used to manage and drive our organisation?		Must have	
			Nice to have	
			Not important	
71	Change management – what is that?		Must have	
			Nice to have	
			Not important	

MARGIN NOTES

HAMISH MACKAY

Following a successful career in financial services, Hamish has been involved over the last 10 years in creating and implementing marketing strategy for different companies, many with Paul Fifield. He now acts as a consultant ensuring operational effectiveness and alignment with market strategy. Email: hamish.mackay@wanadoo.fr or call on 0044 7768 848598.

CHAPTER 11

Offerings

> 'What is a cynic? A man who knows the price of everything and the value of nothing'. (Lady Windermere's Fan, 1982, Act III)
>
> *Oscar Wilde (1854–1900), Irish writer*

Before you start complaining, no this is not just a re-work of the 'product' section of the marketing mix, that comes later (very briefly in Chapter 13).

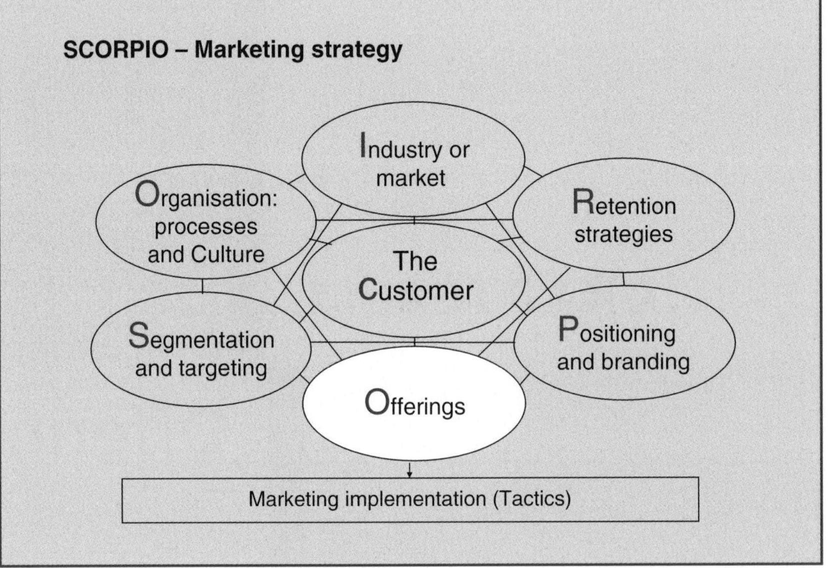

MARGIN NOTES

Given that 'Offer' and 'Product' aren't the same word, maybe there is more going on here than it might seem – indeed there is, we are going to look at the whole 'system' of thinking, planning and implementation that attempts to meet the customer's need to *get a job done*. That includes a lot more than just producing products and services – and hoping.

The (strategic) Offerings section of SCORPIO will include:

- (Another) review of customers and their needs/wants
- A review of the product or service provided currently
- How the product or service needs to adapt over time
- The development of new offerings
- The organisation's customer Value Proposition

- The organisation's business model (how it plans to make money from the transactions)
- Assessing risk
- Managing the life cycle
- Working with the most appropriate routes to market.

Before we start, let's take a 'refresher' look at the marketing process. The overall idea is to make money (cash, profits and revenues) from satisfying customers' needs and wants. (No, not just from selling stuff – did you start the book at this chapter?).

Ideally the process includes information flow from the customer to the organisation (so that we get a better idea of what the needs and wants are) and a flow of communication from the organisation to the customer giving the market good reasons why they should prefer our offer over the competition's. But that is just the surface noise.

MARGIN NOTES

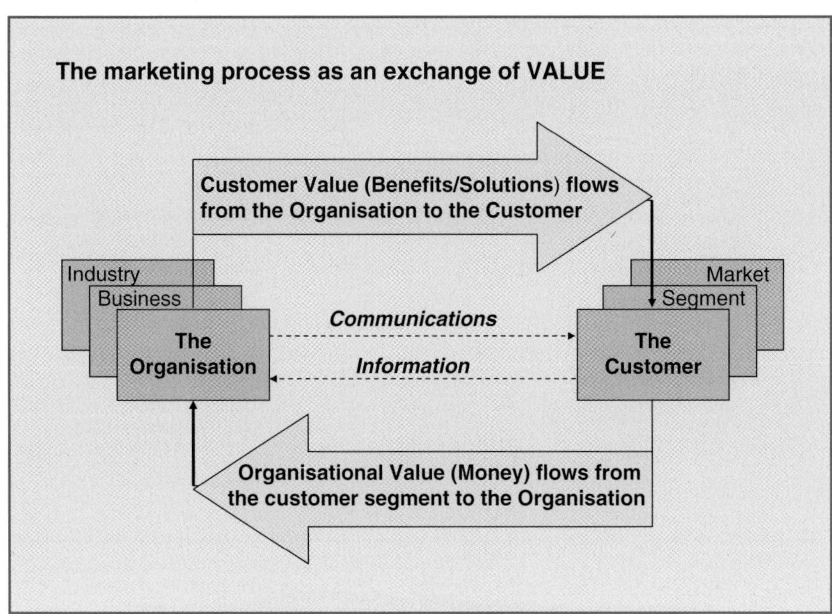

Underneath the surface we have the real game:

- The organisation receives 'value' from the transaction:
  - More is received if it's a 'relationship' (see Chapter 6.5 Retention).
  - The very successful organisation will receive much more money back than it has spent (profit) because the customer believes that it solves their problems best.

  - The mediocre organisation will receive more money back than it spent, but less than the best organisations.
  - The failing organisation will receive less money back than it has spent and will be wondering why …

- The customer receives 'value' from the transaction or relationship:
  - Because they perceive some special benefits or solutions in the offer that allows them to 'get a job done' in precisely the way that they want it done.
  - The more 'value' that the customer perceives in an offer, the more they are willing to pay for it.

- Its all about 'value' – understand 'value' and you control the game.

To understand offerings, we will look at the role and position of 'value' in the process.

MARGIN NOTES

Look at each one and discount the parts that (you think) don't matter – at least not yet – and focus on the ones that do.

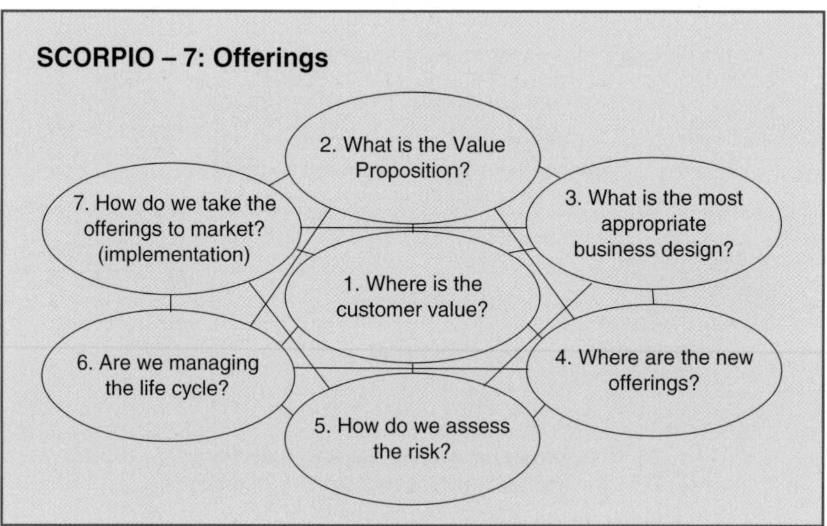
SCORPIO – 7: Offerings
1. Where is the customer value?
2. What is the Value Proposition?
3. What is the most appropriate business design?
4. Where are the new offerings?
5. How do we assess the risk?
6. Are we managing the life cycle?
7. How do we take the offerings to market? (implementation)

Question 72

? Where is the Customer value?

What does our target customer (really) want – now that's a serious question. You might have got the idea so far that market research is the solution to everything – it is not.

Sometimes you have to ask the difficult (if simple) questions to get to grips with the reasons for the continued survival and growth of your organisation.

To survive and grow, you need customers. Customers will only turn up if they see something of 'value' in your offering.

To make sure that your offering is full with the value your target customers crave, you need to understand what value they are seeking, and why ...

It's all about *'value'*

Some Definitions:

- 'The importance or worth of something for someone' (Cambridge)
- 'Perceived benefits minus perceived sacrifice' (McGraw Hill)
- 'A firm is profitable if the value it commands exceeds the costs involved in creating the product' (Michael Porter).

And the 'headlines'

- Customers understand 'value' intuitively – which makes it difficult for us to measure dispassionately.
  - Customers buy value and they spend much of their active consumer lives searching for it.
  - Smart customers actively search it out and weigh up the relevant 'pros-and-cons' of each 'proposition' to be able to judge 'best value' – to them.
  - We already know (unless you have jumped to this chapter of course) that *best 'value' doesn't mean cheapest price,* despite some commentators continuing to confuse the 'Value' end of the market with the 'cheap and nasty' end.
  - Customer value can involve small or large amounts of money.
  - All that matters is what the economists call the customers' perception of the overall *'utility'* of the product/service-or what *they* believe the offer will do for *them.*
  - Customers (just like you and me) will spend lots of time 'trading off' different 'perceived values' of different offers against the price demanded.

MARGIN NOTES

- For all these reasons, the term 'Value' is probably one of the most over-used and misunderstood terms in business today. Why?
  - The first reason is because 'value' is too often simply linked with the issue of pricing, which itself is a subject that is hugely under-researched.
    - We don't understand enough about pricing yet either.
  - Also, 'value' means different things to different people, and it is not easy to define and quantify.

- Customer value is the ultimate in insight and bankable profits.
  - If you know what your customers 'value' – and can deliver it, you have success within your grasp.
  - But we have already said that customer value is more intuitive than scientific, not a reason not to understand it, but that makes it more difficult to measure.
  - More important but more difficult too.
  - Maybe it is easier if we measure the component parts of customer value, then we might have a chance of understanding the 'whole'.

MARGIN NOTES

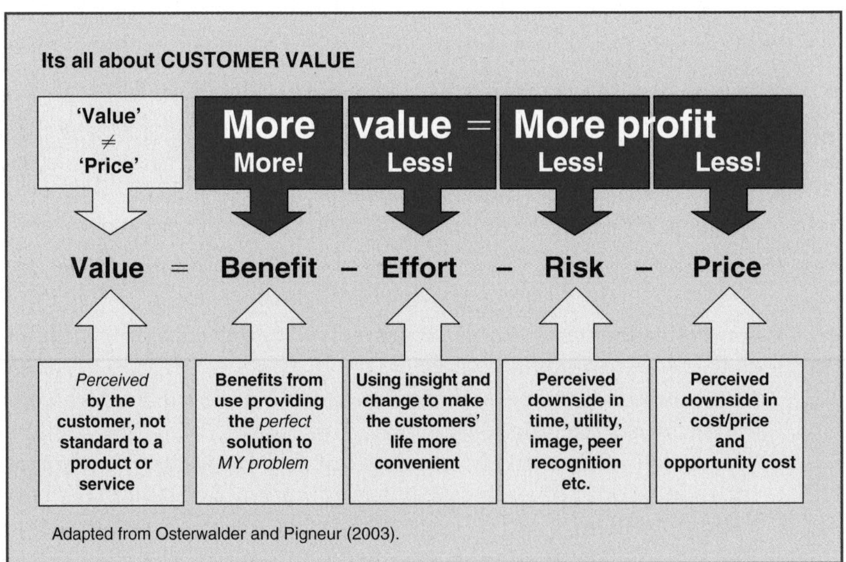

Adapted from Osterwalder and Pigneur (2003).

Developing some work carried out by Osterwalder and Pigneur (University of Lausanne 2002) I have created a practical equation that enables organisations to do something practical about measuring and plotting changes in customer value. This is not meant to be the quickest or simplest model, but the one that constantly reminds you of the components you have to play with.

- The basic equation is: *Customer value = Benefit – Effort – Risk – Price*

This means that any customer's perceived value (what they see in the offer that they are willing to pay for) is made up of separate elements. The key elements of the equation (CV = B − E − R − P) need to be explained:

- Customer value:
  - This is NOT about price and especially not about being cheap.
  - Customer value is about the value that the customer *perceives* in the offer (and its promise) and the value that the customer sees in getting the job done in the particular way that the offer promises.
  - The perceived customer value is made up of three separate components:
    - Benefit
    - Effort
    - Risk
    - Price.
- Benefit:
  - By using the product or service the benefit or solution becomes obvious.
  - The customer is always looking for one thing – the perfect solution to his/her problem.
  - The closer the offer is to the perfect solution, then the greater the perceived customer value and the greater the price the customer is willing to pay. Easy!
  - All you need to find out is the nature of the customer's problem, what the customer believes would be the perfect solution to that problem, where exactly you fit on that scale and where you fall short.
  - It goes without saying that every customer's perception will be unique, every problem will be unique and every solution will be unique – although you may find ways of grouping customers with similar perceptions in segments.
  - Aren't you glad you're in marketing?
- Effort:
  - How much effort will the customer have to put into solving their problem?
  - Life generally is about ease and convenience.
  - The customer will take a view on all the offerings (and different ways of solving the problem) and will see greater value in offerings that are more convenient than ones that are (perceived as) inconvenient.
  - Generally, there will be greater customer value attached to those offerings where the organisation has spent time, research, effort and insight into finding new ways of making the old jobs easier.
  - This perceived value will extend to acquiring the product or service (channels and route to market decisions) as well as the usage of the product or service itself.

MARGIN NOTES

- Risk:
  - The interesting question.
  - Customers perceive 'risk' in all sorts of choice and purchasing situations.
  - Much perceived risk is caused by lack of experience or knowledge.
  - The greater the level of risk that the customer sees, the lower the perceived customer value – got that?
  - Some of the risks that you should investigate here might include perceived downsides (things that could go wrong) in:
    - Time taken in choosing
    - Waiting for delivery or for the benefits to flow (set-up times and problems with 'learning' to use new products)
    - Image risk (what others will think of me)
    - Utility (the product or service doesn't do what it promises) then how will I feel?

MARGIN NOTES

- Price:
  - The obvious one, but last in the order of things, just where the customer places it.
  - This component does NOT just cover the price being too high – a producer perspective – but from the customer's perspective covers more complex and interesting issues such as:
    - Paying too much (obviously)
    - Seeing the same thing cheaper elsewhere
    - Paying too little (inferior quality or maybe not fit for purpose)
    - Opportunity cost (if I buy this, what offerings cannot I buy)
    - Not buying early enough and missing out (waiting too long for the price to fall)
    - Spending too long searching for the lowest price (opportunity cost of time).

How then can you manipulate the levers of customer value to make sure that your offering is perceived as the one with most value? There are a number of ways of doing this, not just price cutting, the one way favoured by the dinosaurs.

Remembering your school maths lessons (I know how you feel), we are dealing with an 'equation' ($CV = B - E - R - P$), so we can increase the left side (CV) by:

- Reduce price:
  - The obvious one and one we have already spoken about – it is a way of increasing customer value – getting more for less – but less successful than most people seem to think (see Chapter 6.3).
  - There are customer costs in reducing the price too far, too unevenly or too fast, so think it through before you act.

  - Price reduction is not only a very crude way of competing; it is also very expensive compared to other ways of increasing customer value.
  - Before you take a lemming-like lunge at price reduction, look to see if there is not a better way; for example:

- Increase benefits from usage:
  - Adding more benefits (make sure that they are real benefits, things that customers really want) will increase perceived customer value.
  - Remember that if you are seeking differentiation, you are unlikely to have a competitor to follow and imitate – you will need to be close to customers to add real benefit.
  - Check back to Chapter 6 and the ideas of latent need.

- Reduce effort:
  - Make it easier to use and acquire the benefits.
  - But not *too easy*, check your target customers or segments, sometimes if a solution is too easy it can lose its appeal.

- Reduce risk:
  - So much time is spent worrying about price that the non-price risks seems to fade away – but here are the even bigger issues.
  - You can reduce these risks by offering guarantees and warranties, free-trial periods and
  - Above all, you can offer a *brand* to believe in.
  - Branding is the most effective way of reducing perceived risk (by making valued promises that will be kept (see Chapter 8)) and so of increasing perceived customer value.

Now that we have learned the term, we can rephrase the question, from 'What does our target customer (really) want?' to 'Where is the customer value?'

Customer value is a more precise definition of customer 'needs and wants' and is a combination of *customer perceptions of*:

- The problem (the job that needs to be done)
- The 'perfect solution' to the problem
- The effort required to get the job done
- The value of reducing that effort
- The risk in the offering not 'getting the job done'
- The image risk
- The opportunity cost risk

MARGIN NOTES

- The risk in spending too much time in choosing and/or waiting, etc.
- The risk in paying too much or too little.

It's no use saying it's too difficult, these are your customers we are talking about and *they* decide where to spend their money. If, one day, they decide to spend their money with one of your competitors because they can see greater customer value there than with you, they will leave. If you have invested enough in getting as close to understanding where your target customer sees the customer value, you might be able to modify your offer enough to save (and even grow) the business. If not …

We will look more carefully at the question of Value Propositions later. For the moment, Osterwalder and Pigneur also suggest that there is a life cycle for customer value – this provides us with some fascinating insight.

MARGIN NOTES

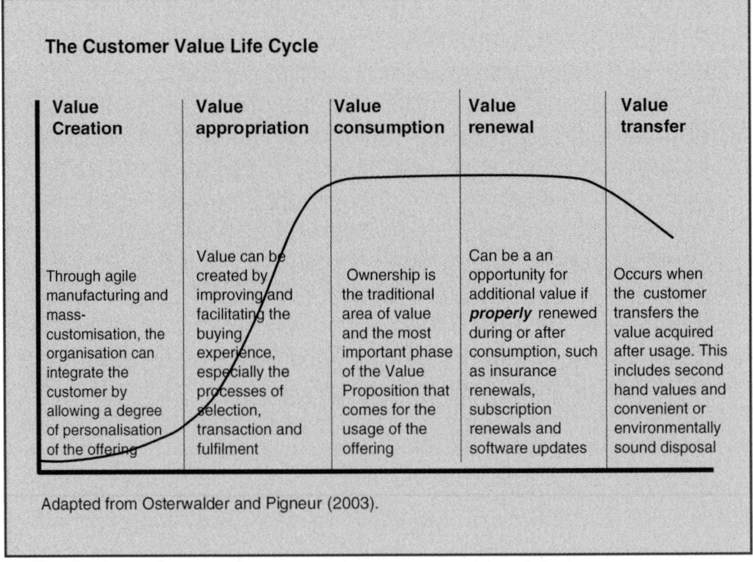
The Customer Value Life Cycle
Value Creation
Value appropriation
Value consumption
Value renewal
Value transfer
Through agile manufacturing and mass-customisation, the organisation can integrate the customer by allowing a degree of personalisation of the offering
Value can be created by improving and facilitating the buying experience, especially the processes of selection, transaction and fulfilment
Ownership is the traditional area of value and the most important phase of the Value Proposition that comes for the usage of the offering
Can be a an opportunity for additional value if *properly* renewed during or after consumption, such as insurance renewals, subscription renewals and software updates
Occurs when the customer transfers the value acquired after usage. This includes second hand values and convenient or environmentally sound disposal
Adapted from Osterwalder and Pigneur (2003).

Remembering the section on Customer retention (see Chapter 9) we saw that best returns come from retained customers and best retention comes from working with customers' timescales (lifetime value) rather than the artificial construct of the financial year. This work develops those ideas and gives us some strong indications on how to integrate the customers' lifecycle into our offerings.

Your customers perceive value in the lifetime of the relationship with your organisation; it is up to you whether you maximise on these opportunities:

- Value Creation:
  - Boeing involves its key airline clients in the planning and development of its next generation of planes to make sure that the

client feels involved and that the product does what the client needs it to do.
  - Many sandwich bars make sandwiches to customer order rather than simply offer pre-packed sandwiches.
  - But, for most business laptops its still 'any colour you want as long as its black'

- Value Appropriation:
  - UK supermarkets invest millions every year to improve the 'shopping experience'.
  - Mercedes invites buyers of its top models to its German factories to visit and collect their car in person.
  - But, still telecommunications tariffs proliferate so nobody knows if they are getting the best deal

- Value Consumption:
  - Restaurant waiters ask you if you are enjoying the meal.
  - IBM has dedicated after-sales teams to ensure continuing client satisfaction.
  - But, if you miss a Flybe flight you get no refunds – 'its not company policy'

- Value Renewal:
  - Microsoft and McAfee/Symantec offer regular updates to their software products during the life of the subscription.
  - Harley Davidson enrols all customers in one of its Harley Owners Groups (HOGs) where they can share experiences and engage in the lifestyle.
  - But, insurance companies don't talk to you at all until they ask you for more money to renew your insurance at the end of the year.

- Value Transfer:
  - Most car companies actively manage the second-hand market for their cars and continuing warranty on their 'pre-owned' cars and trucks maintained and re-furbished by them.
  - Growing numbers of European food processors are providing product in bio-degradable packaging to deal with customers' growing environmental concerns.
  - But, electronics manufacturers still prefer to mare 'throwaway' TVs and radios rather than invest in repair facilities

MARGIN NOTES

ROLLS ROYCE **Rolls-Royce**

Across the Marine business, we aim to deliver value through the provision of products, systems and services developed as a result of effective segmentation and targeting and a clear

MARGIN NOTES

understanding of our sources of competitive advantage applied within the markets in which we operate.

We seek to differentiate through effective application of our capabilities in:

- Innovation and technical leadership
- Systems integration
- Modern and cost-efficient manufacturing
- Provision of world-class service and support
- Development of strong customer relationships.

We are actively using our knowledge and capability to support the development of complex ice-class vessels required to explore and produce oil and gas within the harsh Arctic environment, thereby expanding our ship design and integrated systems business in the Offshore and Merchant shipping markets.

In a very different area, we are working jointly with the UK Ministry of Defence to ensure cost-effective availability of Royal Navy submarines through an innovative contract that provides support for the powerplant installed across the fleet.

This contract, which is an example of our ability to add value to customers' operations through the development of long-term support agreements, provides for payment against agreed service level targets and sharing of cost savings made through improvements in business efficiency and effectiveness.

The FAQs are:

7 Offerings		
7.1 Where is the customer value?		
7.1.1	What are the needs and wants of the target customers?	I know – I keep going on, and on, and on, but it really does matter. There is just no point being an expert on your product or service if you don't know what it can *do* for the customer – that is the only reason they buy it, for what it can do for them. But we have had this discussion before .... You don't have to spend lots of money, you just have to listen – talk to your customers and they will tell you.

7.1.2	Where is the customer value in the marketplace?	It seems to spend a lot of time hiding in the strangest places – who would have guessed that the iPod would be such a runaway success (certainly Apple did not) and who would have guessed the amount of customer value in having white plastic wires to the earpieces rather than black ones? First you have to put your pre-conceived ideas of 'logical value' behind you before you try and see the 'emotional value' that hides in previously ignored recesses of the market. How did Apple find the customer value in: ● New application of existing, hard disc technology ● 'Cool' design ● White wires ● Countering the staid image of incumbent brand (Walkman). Can they do it again? Ah.
7.1.3	Who else is competing for the customer value?	Until you discover where the customer value is hiding in your market, you cannot spot the likely competitors. ● Look again at the organisations, businesses and brands that your organisation believes it is competing with ● Look again at Porter's Five Forces diagram and the different types of competition out there ● Look now at what you believe the customer sees as value in your offering: ○ Think of the 'Benefit–Effort–Risk–Price' equation ○ Think of the Value Lifecycle. ● Are you sure that you have a good idea of who is trying to steal your business at the moment – and what you should be doing about it? You could always ask the customer – but only if all else fails you understand ...
7.1.4	Which customer value should we target (segmentation)?	My but this SCORPIO business gets complicated the way it links all over the place ... Remember all that discussion about market segmentation (see Chapter 7). And the discussion about positioning and branding (see Chapter 8). Well, nothing has changed – you can try and go for all the customer value you can find and you can become 'Jack of all trades, master of none' and be happy with the margins that come from the generalist position. Or, you can decide to specialise – on delivering those customer values that you can deliver best. Your choice (– sorry).
7.1.5	Where will the customer value be tomorrow (migration)?	And of course what constitutes customer value today will probably be different tomorrow. How fast things change will depend on your target customers as well as the ferocity or desperation of your competitors, but change it will.

		Value migrates in every market, only the speed of migration changes. You job is not to be surprised by the migration but to be there at the same speed as the customers you want to retain (see Chapter 10). Dell was the darling of the computer business all the time that price (driven by make-to-order) was all that mattered, when the value migrated to customer service Dell did not do so well. Dell did not really change but customer value migrated and perception shifted.
7.1.6	How much of the value can we expect to be able to extract?	This will depend largely on your market position, brand and general credibility more than physical ability to deliver. Remember, practical and efficient operations are only half the battle, the first part certainly but not enough on their own. Much of your ability to extract value will depend upon your organisation's alignment to the needs of your customer rather than its alignment to the product, service or industry. You can't extract the value you don't see or don't understand.
7.1.7	Do we have the skills and credibility to be able to extract this value?	Once your internal, technological, logical processes and systems have been aligned so that you are technically capable of delivering on the value, the serious (and often more expensive job) of convincing the market can begin. Credibility is key and if you don't have credibility in what you see as a critical area, you will have to develop it. Credibility also has a time-lag. Customers (because they have their own lives) tend not to think about you all day so take some time to learn (or re-learn) your capabilities. When Ford acquired Jaguar it suffered from a bad reputation in both technical build quality and service compared with Mercedes. Ford put much of the quality issues right reasonably fast but it took almost a decade before the customers started to change their opinions of the two offerings – and Jaguar (Ford) could start to deliver on some of the critical customer values demanded of such a prestige marque.

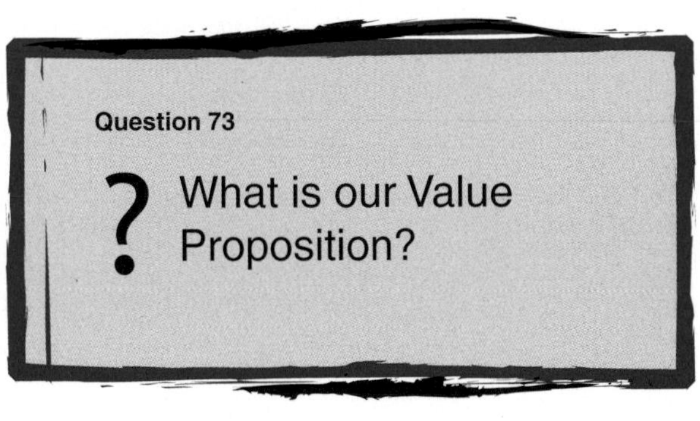
Question 73
?
What is our Value Proposition?

Trust me; you are going to love this part.

The key to successful marketing (and successful business) is 'preference'. If we can somehow make customers prefer our offering over the competition's then we have done our job. But how exactly do we do that? The more people that are involved in the process, the greater the chance that things can go wrong. We have seen (see Chapter 10) that this is not malicious, it is how things happen. But the customers aren't concerned with our problems, they just insist on capturing as much customer value as possible, and will go wherever the value seems greatest.

How do we ensure the customer comes to us? By being clearly different (see Chapter 8) from everyone else. And how do we do that, with people on the inside all trying to do (what they think is) their best and customers on the outside not knowing where to go – and changing their minds over what constitutes customer value over time?

We (all) need a customer Value Proposition.

MARGIN NOTES

- By 'we all' I mean that:
  - Your target customer needs a Value Proposition
  - Your target prospect needs a Value Proposition
  - Your marketing department and brand/product/segment groups need a Value Proposition
  - Your internal staff need a Value Proposition
  - Your sales force needs a Value Proposition
  - Your intermediaries/channel partners need a Value Proposition
  - Your agencies all need a Value Proposition
  - Your shareholders need a Value Proposition.

What do you mean you have not got one?

First, let's begin with a definition or two, a Value Proposition is:

- 'A written statement that focuses all the organisation's market activities onto customer-critical elements that create a significant differential within the customer's decision process to prefer and/or purchase the organisation's offering over a competitor's'

- 'The combination of product, service, pricing and delivery system offered to the customer'. (Bain & Co)

- 'An implicit promise a company makes to customers to deliver a particular combination of values'. (Treacy and Wiersema).
  - Treacy and Wiersema have also identified organisations as offering three (generic) kinds of Value Propositions (see Chapter 3):
    - Management efficiency/Operational excellence
    - Product leadership
    - Customer intimacy.

And the 'headlines'

- A Value Proposition is a clear, concise series of factual statements on what the customer can expect to be the tangible results from purchasing and consuming your products or services.
  - Externally, a Value Proposition is an offer to the target customers or segment(s) in which the purchaser gets more value than they give up, as perceived by them, and in relationship to competitive alternatives, including doing nothing.
  - Internally, a Value Proposition is an internal statement summarising the customer targets, competitor targets and the core strategy for how you intend to differentiate your product/service from the offerings of competitors.

MARGIN NOTES

- The Treacy and Wiersema definition of a Value Proposition is about the very least you should expect your Value Proposition to achieve.
  - Their approach is rather too external communications-led than I would like.
  - For the Value Proposition to drive the organisation as we need, it must also:
    - Relate to all the different 'publics' that are listed at the very beginning of this chapter and earlier in the 'stakeholder' map (see Chapter 1)
    - Integrate all these essential 'publics' so that they are aligned to meet the customers needs
    - Inform all the essential 'stakeholder publics' where they fit into the customer value process and how they relate to each other
    - Specify (exactly) *how* the organisation (and each of the stakeholder publics) will create customer value. The differentiated organisation will do this in a unique way, this must be carefully specified within the Value Proposition.

- A successfully tested and proven Value Proposition is essential to a successfully differentiated business. It can:
  - Open more doors and close more sales
  - Create strong customer propositions that deliver results
  - Increase revenue from clearer positions
  - Speed time to market as internal staff align their efforts
  - Decrease costs as agreed 'wastage' (in customer value terms) is removed
  - Improve operational efficiency from agreed and understood customer-centric targets
  - Increase market share
  - Decrease employee turnover as staff identify with the differentiation – and the customer value
  - Improve customer retention levels.

A word on creating your own Value Proposition(s)

Bain & Co, extended their definition of the Value Proposition somewhat to give a deeper idea of what it should do for you:

- 'The combination of product, service, pricing and delivery system offered to the customer:
  - To maximise customer demand, an individual Value Proposition should be created for each target customer segment by strategically balancing these four factors.
  - A clear understanding of a firm's sources of advantage in providing value and creating fit with target customer segments is important to defining the firm's Value Proposition.
  - In addition, anticipating customer value migration and shifting or expanding the firm's offering appropriately is required to sustain competitive advantage'.

If your Value Proposition process is going to work, you really need:

- A 'cascade' or 'hierarchy' of Value Propositions that follow that of your brand(s) and/or your market segment(s) and position(s).
- The format for each Value Proposition needs to be the same, although you can chose your own format that best suits your internal and external needs.
  - Remember though, that to be successful, your Value Proposition must be differentiated, compelling and clearly communicate best value to *all* your audiences and/or stakeholders.

The (minimum) Value Proposition worksheet

Who is your target market?	
What are their needs or problems?	
What is your target Context© or Occasion	
What will your product or service do for them?	
How is your offering unique? (in customer perception terms)	
Why should they prefer your offer over the competition?	
So your statement is:	
The 'elevator pitch'	

MARGIN NOTES

- To get you on the road, here are a few 'worksheets' that you can use to start the process inside your organisation.

In the basic version, you need to answer the following questions:

- Who is your target market?
  - Describe the customers and/or segments that you are targeting.
  - Preferably you should focus on describing the target customers by their unique or special needs, motivations or required customer value and describe them then by demographics as required.
  - Always remember that internal audiences less well versed in the intricacies of segmentation will still believe that demographics drive everything (see Chapter 7), so use these as little as possible.
  - One of the primary uses of the Value Proposition is to explain to internal audiences how the market works; how customer groupings are different, why we have chosen the target customers we have chosen and how they are unique.
  - Internal audiences (in-company and intermediary or channel partners) must completely understand (if possible believe) this if they are to be part of the solution rather than part of the problem.
  - Remember, marketing should be a co-ordinating, not executive, function – we need others to get things done, we cannot do it all ourselves. Don't try.

MARGIN NOTES

- What are their needs or problems?
  - Exactly now, you have (should have) done enough research to know what your target customers (really) want.
  - You must describe these needs and wants carefully and succinctly so that all your audiences (internal and external) understand.
  - What jobs to your target customers what to get done?
  - What is the problem?
  - Where do they see the real customer value (in Benefit, Effort, Risk and Price)?
  - Internal audiences need to understand the scale of the task – and their role in it.
  - External audiences need to be able to identify with the problems and recognise that they are part of the target market for the offer.

- What is your target Context© or Occasion?
  - Refer back to the debate about Context© segmentation (Chapter 7)
  - Which events, occasions (Context©s) are driving needs, wants and purchasing behaviour?
  - Where (physical location) are your customers likely to be in the Context©?
  - When (time of day, week, season, year) are your customers likely to be in the Context©?
  - Which (mind state, emotions, feelings) are your customers likely to be in when in the Context©?

    - You *might* still think that Context© is too advanced for your market, but what that really means is:
        - Your customers are being driven by Context©s, but
        - It is one step too advanced for you and your organisation at the moment
        - You hope that none of your competitors start working on it already

- What will your product or service do for them?
    - Just as precisely, exactly what will your offer do for the customer?
    - We need 'exactly' if we are to create and maintain a profitable market position, brand and reputation for differentiated products or services.
    - An answer that is just 'almost' or 'about' will absolutely guarantee you a place in the great bloodletting that we call the price war among the commodity players.
    - Much of marketing is 'woolly' and 'vague' because customers make it so.
    - But not here, again because customers make it so – either you are different or you are an 'also-ran', there is no middle ground.
    - Internal audiences will push to move you to the 'killing ground' of the commodity because they just don't understand the absolute need to differentiate.
    - Use your Value Proposition to convince everyone why they should be behind the offer, or look for a new job.

- How is your offering unique?
    - This must be in customer perception terms; in-depth technical or operational reasons won't do at all here.
    - Also, no complaints about how the internal technical departments might feel about their highly prestigious work being 'dumbed down' for the benefit of 'ignorant customers'.
    - The only reason they get to do their highly prestigious work is so that 'ignorant customers' can pay us to 'get their jobs done' easily.
    - It will be your job to explain all this to the technical departments so that they start to understand how all their hard work is actually used – and they can start to imagine even better ways of 'getting jobs done'.
    - Are you starting to see the power of the value statement in bringing the internal and external parts of an organisation together (alignment) – so that *everyone* benefits.

- Why should they prefer your offer over the competition?
    - This is the ultimate test.
    - If customers prefer your offer over the competition's then you get the sales, and they don't.
    - But how do we make that happen?
    - Easy, we tell them *exactly* why they should prefer our offer.
    - This is just too important to leave to chance; we cannot just 'hope' that customers work out for themselves why they should prefer

MARGIN NOTES

your offer – they have busy lives and might just miss the too-subtle signals in the hustle-and-bustle and the competitive noise.
  - Also, all those communications agencies need some very clear guidance if they aren't to run off doing very interesting but different things.
  - If you don't yet know (precisely) why customers should prefer your offer over the competition, then you have some more work to do.

- So your statement is:
  - You put all the answers together into a single statement.
  - It doesn't have to be good English/French/German/Dutch/Other, it is just to make a point.
  - Also, *this statement is not the final 'tag line'* or any other version of any advertising copy – the agencies and other wordsmiths will still have their work to do later.

- The 'elevator pitch:'
  - Its précis time.
  - The term comes from the American for lift (elevator) and the idea is that you have your ideal prospect in the list with you and he/she is getting off in just two floors – how can you reduce the above value statement down to the barest minimum – to make you prospect want to find out more?
  - If you cannot do it, then you don't understand you offering
  - *This statement is also not a final advertising tag line*, stop worrying.

MARGIN NOTES

Take your time, these questions are both difficult – and essential.

Below is a worked example based on a European motor car. It has been created working off the company's promotional material and doesn't set out to be accurate, only illustrative.

The Value Proposition worksheet

Who is your target market?	High mileage drivers
What are their needs or problems?	Want performance without the show
What is your target Context© or Occasion?	Inconspicuous enjoyment
What will your product or service do for them?	Affordable performance
How is your offering unique? (in customer perception terms)	You wouldn't know it was diesel
Why should they prefer your offer over the competition?	It is a diesel that performs better than a petro carl
So your statement is:	[For] high mileage drivers [who] want performance without the show [we offer] affordable performance, [uniquely,] you wouldn't know it was diesel [it offers you] a diesel that performs better than a petrol car
The 'elevator pitch'	**Real GTI performance – driven by diesel**

MARGIN NOTES

In the event that you need to include more data in your Value Proposition, you could look at the second example worksheet. This approach may be better for organisations who are either starting up in a sector and need to explain the (new) concepts in more detail, and for organisations that have wide product or service ranges or operate in a number of different market segments and need to describe what might be more minor differences carefully.

The additional questions are, I think, self-explanatory:

Another version

ISSUE	QUESTION	ANSWER
Market description	Who is our target market?	
Market sizing	How big is our target market (segment)	
Needs and Wants	What are this particular segment's needs and/or wants?	
Context© or Occasion	Which situations, events or occasions drive needs?	
The Benefits	What will our product or service do for them?	
Differentiation	How is our offering unique? (in customer perception terms)	
Competition	Who is the closest competitor?	
Preference	Why should they prefer our offer over the competition?	
Brand	What will be the brand promise to this market (segment)?	
Offering	The (minimum) key elements which are fundamental for any offering to be credible	
Route-to-market	What are the (customer) preferred routes to market/channel partners?	
Alliances	What are the critical partnerships/alliances required to launch	
Price	The strategy of pricing the service packages	
'Elevator pitch'	Strip the proposition down to the essentials	

If neither of these worksheets do it for you, please compile your own. But, the first worksheet really carries the absolute minimum of questions you need to answer (for every separate product or service variant, market segment and brand. You can add more questions to worksheet one, but don't try to remove any. Even if it would be a lot easier!

The FAQs are:

7 Offerings		
7.2 What is our Value Proposition?		
7.2.1	What is a Value Proposition?	In case you missed it, a Value Proposition is: A written ● *statement* that ● *focuses all* the organisation's ● *market activities* onto ● *customer-critical elements* that create a ● *significant differential* within the customer's

		● *decision process* to ● *prefer and/or purchase* the organisation's offering ● *over a competitor's*.
7.2.2	What is the role and purpose of a Value Proposition?	A Value Proposition is a wonderfully versatile tool, it can: ● Help you to answer all the most important questions to a level where you are able to respond to the key questions on the Value Proposition ● Help you identify gaps in your market/customer knowledge ● Help you explain the market, customers to internal staff ● Help you explain to internal staff their role in profit generation via customer satisfaction ● Help link internal staff effort to customer value, perhaps by rewards, incentives and appraisal too ● Help align internal processes to the end output (customer value generation) so reducing wastage and conflict ● Align all internal and external communications ● Align sales force activity behind the differentiated position ● Align and coordinate all external agency communications activities. If you don't have a Value Proposition, there is a strong chance that you will end up undifferentiated and competing on price. Not intentionally perhaps, but because you don't have the *same hymn sheet* for everyone in your organisation to sing from.
7.2.3	How many Value Propositions?	At least one – for your organisation – it codifies what you are, what you stand for and why/how you are unique. If you want to turn it into a woolly 'mission statement' later on that's fine, but at least start with something focused and accurate. Then you will need a separate proposition for each: ● Product or service in the range ● Brand ● Brand variants or extensions ● Segment. Everywhere there is a real danger of confusion; your range of Value Propositions must make even the most subtle differences clear – as well as the absolute need to maintain the subtle differences. If you need a different offer, you need a different Value Proposition.
7.2.4	How do we create our Value Proposition(s)?	Carefully and slowly – don't rush this. Value propositions are always a group activity. They might start individually but they will need to be agreed within the core group that will be responsible for its policing *and implementation*. The group process makes for a slow process but that is the way it always is. A Value Proposition always takes a long time. This can be useful as it chases out areas where there is internal confusion but nobody was aware of the problem. A Value Proposition simply won't work without internal and external buy-in. Your Value Proposition should always be based on customer knowledge and insight rather than informed guesses.

7.2.5	How do we use our Value Proposition(s)?	Once it/they have been developed, agreed and set – it absolutely needs to be used. There is no point hiding the Value Proposition in the drawer (next to the SWOT and PEST analyses) and expecting any benefit to arise. If you have done the job properly and key people feel they 'own' the content, it needs to be the blueprint for all the organisation's key business and market activities. All the internal and external people who will be feeding into the proposition need to have it explained (slowly) to them so that they can contribute fully. The Value Proposition should also be used as a measure of internal and external activity that doesn't add customer value and so should be halted.
7.2.6	How do we gain active support for the Value Proposition(s)?	The Value Proposition must form the basis of *all* the organisation's marketing, including its internal marketing communications campaign. (see Chapter 10)
7.2.7	How do we police the implementation of our Value Proposition(s)?	The other side to the Value Proposition – the stick. Once the Value Proposition (s) have been approved, explained and the subject of internal and external marketing communications campaigns, some people will still want to 'do their own thing', 'be creative', 'demonstrate their individuality', 'play a hunch' or 'try something new'. Depending on the organisational culture these people may be allowed to keep their jobs but such activities cannot be allowed to take root. Assuming that the Value Propositions are accurate (based on accurate data and updated regularly to plot value migration), then any attempt to divert effort can only result in diluting differentiation, with a corresponding dilution of market position, brand value and profitability. This is about very serious stakes indeed.

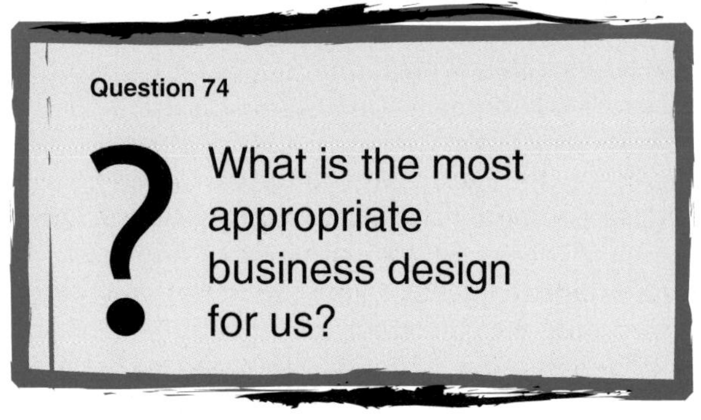

Question 74
?
What is the most appropriate business design for us?

The most appropriate business model is the one that allows the organisation to extract the most value from the marketplace.

So, customers (specifically the ones you have targeted) are the most important factor when deciding on the 'right' business model, not internal consideration such as finance. As customers and their perception of what constitutes customer value changes over time (value migration) then an organisation will need to look at whether it needs to change its business model over time to keep up with customers and continue extracting most value.

For those who wish to investigate all the potential business models, a good selection of 22 of the most common can be found in '*The Art of Profitability*', (Slywotzky, Little, Brown & Company, 2004).

MARGIN NOTES

First, some Definitions:

- 'A company's business model deals with whether the revenue-cost-profit economics of its strategy demonstrate the viability of the enterprise as a whole' (McGraw Hill)
- 'A business model (also called a business design) is the mechanism by which a business intends to generate revenue and profits. It is a summary of how a company plans to serve its customers. It involves both strategy and implementation' (wikipedia)
- 'A business model is the answer to a few questions. What is my unique Value Proposition? Who are my customers? How do I make money? What is my strategic control and how do I protect it?' (Slywotsky).

The 'headlines' are:

- What is the best way of assessing whether we have the most appropriate design for extracting value currently? There are a number of steps in the process:
- Identify the target customers:
  - Which customers are we targeting?
  - How are they different?
  - Why have we decided to target these customers?
  - These answers should drop out of the work you have carried out in the area of Market Segmentation (see Chapter 7).
  - It is important to identify your organisation's particular target market because the customers (perceptions) determine the nature of the customer value to be delivered and so the best way of the organisation extracting that value.

   - As the nature of customers (their needs or the customers themselves) changes over time, it is unreasonable to expect a single business design to always be the best way of extracting value/profit from the market.

- Create the Value Proposition:
   - The Value Proposition will clearly define the nature and quality of the value to be delivered – and extracted.

- Identify how Value is captured currently:
   - How does the organisation capture value/profit from its customers at the moment?
   - Is the profit received through, for example, cost reduction, customer service or standardisation?
   - Are all subsidiaries, business units, brands capturing value/profit in the same way or are there different approaches?
   - Which ones seem to be working best?
   - Why?

- Identify potential strategic market control:
   - How is your target market influenced or controlled to create and protect profit flows over time?
   - Techniques such as differentiation, branding, supply chain partnerships, innovation, design and low price might be successful.
   - How are your organisation and different competitors using different controls?
   - How successful are you?
   - How successful are the competitors?

- Identify the critical activities required by the Value Proposition:
   - What does your (unique) Value Proposition require you to deliver to customers?
   - What are the absolutely essential activities that the proposition promises?
   - Who has to deliver on these (you, channel partners, the customer)?

From these analytical steps, you should be able to assess whether you currently have the most effective business design for what your Value Proposition requires you to do, whether competitors are doing it better, whether you should think about moving to a new business design.

There is more than one way to skin a cat – and many more ways of making a profit.

But you would think that most organisations have only one way of working and making profits – and that the day it stops working, everybody is out of business. It is unusual for an organisation to think about its business design – it started with it, it has worked, so ... But it is not necessarily so.

MARGIN NOTES

What was a good way of working years ago won't necessarily last forever – equally, there is no reason why an organisation should be saddled with the same design for the duration of its business life – change is possible and should be considered. As with any type of change, it will be resisted ferociously – simply because it is 'change' and so, 'bad'. That way lies death and destruction.

Customers are all that matter and they change all the time – they revel in change, because they can. Remember, if you don't change (just to keep up with your customers) they will leave you.

There is nothing sacrosanct about a business design, longer-lived organisations change them all the time – they have to.

It has to be worth thinking about.

MARGIN NOTES

A longer list of 22 business designs is contained in Slywotzky's book (see above). Some of the ones you may have heard of include:

- Product Pyramid:
  - An approach more common in a market with high variation in customer budget and preferences, such as motor cars.
  - It is quite likely that not all the products (or services) in the range will make profits in their own right.
  - On one hand, it might be that profit is extracted only on the offerings with high prices and low volume; in this case bottom end products are marketed as a 'firewall' to protect the more profitable products or services from competitive attack.
    - Some of the flag-carrier airlines tried to develop their own low-cost variants to protect themselves against Easyjet and Ryanair.
  - On the other hand, profits may only come from the lower priced products with the most expensive losing money; in this case top end products or services act as a 'brand halo' to set the tone for the rest of the brand.
    - VAG did this with its Bugatti (Veyron) brand, which loses money on each car sold but raises the image of the entire VAG range.
  - As long as the 'pyramid' makes profits, in total, and these are greater than if all the individual products or services were marketed separately, the approach is successful.

- The switchboard:
  - The switchboard creates value and profits by lowering the transaction costs in a crowded marketplace.
  - This means that when there is a market with a large number of buyers and sellers, and the buyers don't necessarily know the sellers, then the organisation that owns the 'switchboard' that connects them is well placed to extract high value and profits.

  - The greater the number of buyers and sellers, the more benefit each accrues.
    - eBay is a good example of this design.

- Profit multiplier:
  - In this approach, the organisation invests heavily in the development of a core asset (this could be a brand, trademark or technology) that it maintains and protects fiercely.
  - The organisation has high investment in the core asset, and makes good returns.
  - However, 'derivative' offerings cost much less to develop but still carry high margins because of the association with the core asset.
    - Disney is one of the prime examples of this approach.

- Installed base:
  - Using the installed base approach, the organisation builds a sizeable installed base of customers, often around a lower-margin offering.
  - The organisation then sells follow-on products and services to the 'captive' customer base, with much higher margins.
  - The key to this model is to be able to build a large installed base first.
    - The classic examples include Hewlett-Packard (HP) printers (sell the low-margin printers and follow with high-margin ink cartridges) and Mobile phone companies (sell low-margin handsets and sell high-margin airtime).
    - The path was probably pioneered by Gillette.

- De facto standard:
  - Next, the Microsoft approach.
  - An organisation that holds the standard within an industry can experience increasing returns as the scale of operations increases.
  - But, the opposite is also true; companies that lose the battle to establish a market standard can experience diminishing margins over time.
    - The classic example of a winner in this model is Microsoft.
    - Sony lost to VHS in the fight over standards in VCRs, but is trying again, this time to establish its standard (Blu-ray) in hi definition DVD.

- After sales:
  - In some industries, it is not the sale of the offering that generates profit, but the after-sale financing or servicing of the offering, which typically enjoys a long life.
    - A typical example would be Boeing and Airbus where the value/profit opportunities don't lie in the cost of the plane itself, but in other opportunities such as financing the aircraft (leasing companies), fitting out the plane to the buyer's

MARGIN NOTES

specifications, maintenance of the plane during its life, re-sale of the plane to secondary and tertiary owners.

You can see that the choice of business design is not limited. You should also see that these models are quite versatile and can be used in many different markets. Once Gillette decided to almost give the razors away and make the profit (extract value) from the razor blades (history lesson), it was then copied by HP for printers and Vodafone for mobile telephony.

The FAQs are:

7 Offerings		
7.3 What is the most appropriate business design for us?		
7.3.1	What are the different ways we can extract value (business profit models)?	There are 22 listed in Slywotzky's book, although these aren't the only ones. Look around you at the players in your market (and associated markets) and see what is going on. Just because an approach is being used in one market/ industry doesn't mean that it cannot be used in a different one. There is no such thing as 'the only way to extract value/ make money'.
7.3.2	Which model(s) do we use at present?	It is a fairly safe bet to say that your approach to extracting value/profit is a historical one. Can you find out where it came from, whether it was chosen specifically, why it was chosen, what the prevailing customer conditions were at the time that it was chosen and whether those customer conditions have changed.
7.3.3	How effective are they at extracting ALL the value?	Now the difficult bit. Is the existing approach working? Well, if you're earning enough money to stay afloat, then something is working – but that was not the question. Is the current approach extracting *all* the value/profit that it could be extracting? Not an easy question to answer but you could: ● Look at organisations that you (and that the key decisions-makers inside your organisation) admire and assess how they extract value – could you mimic their approach in your market? (Be open minded, don't even listen to the 'but we're different claims') ● If you have them, look at other business units, subsidiaries or international operations with different approaches and assess how well they do ● Look at other members of your industry or local business network with a different approach and assess how well they do ● Ask your customers (really).

7.3.4	Which models do our competitors use?	Bearing in mind that competition is a complicated subject, can you identify the current approach that they are using to extract the value/profit from your collective market? ● Look at direct competitors with a different business model and assess how well they do ● Look at indirect competitors (maybe from a different industry) with a different business model and assess how well they do ● Look at potential entrants with a different business model and assess how well they do – this one might galvanise activity.
7.3.5	Could we increase the value extracted by using a different model?	And could you do it enough to convince the decision makers that it's worth changing? You might have to think about trying out the new approach in a small part of the market as a test before trying to convince people inside the organisation.
7.3.6	Does this influence how we allocate resources?	Spot the rhetorical questions! The question is really, *how* will this affect the way you invest money at the moment – and what will be the new level of returns? If you can prove it you might get some support.
7.3.7	How can we measure how much value we extract (customer conversion)?	Not easily at all – but you will have to 'prove' it before any change is possible. This is not a scientific question *don't* just try and measure what you think is a sufficient level of customer acquisition and/or retention – that is *not* the problem. You must start with the decision makers and the questions they have in their minds. Once you have found where the real barriers to change lie, then you can start to collect measurements that might have the right effects.

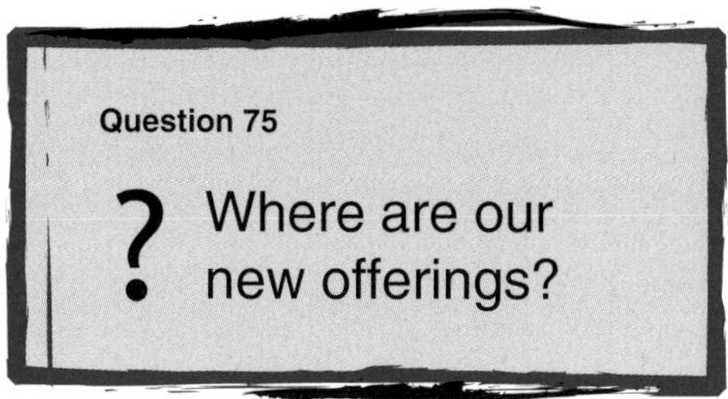
Question 75
?
Where are our new offerings?

That's the trouble with customers, they're never happy – just as you think you have them in the palm of your hand, they are queuing up to buy what you are very happy making, then they just decide that they want something else.

The message here is:

- Innovate or die, but
- Don't make a big thing about it, change *is* business as usual (see Chapter 10)
- Not everything that is new will sell
- No matter what you do or how good you are, you will still mess up from time to time because customers will never be completely predictable.

MARGIN NOTES

Still, we cannot just sit back and accept what comes, that's not the Western way, we have been trained to predict and anticipate rather than just react – but we have not been trained to accept that anticipation is never 100% accurate.

The innovation 'headlines' are:

- Innovation is the topic of so many articles and books that it almost seems as if there are some people out there who *can* really predict customer behaviour – and they don't seem to be multi-billionaires yet – strange.
- Customers, B2B as well as B2C, are human beings rather than computer programmes. They run on emotion and not on logic and, like it or not (it doesn't much matter either way) customers won't always act or react as we might expect them to – they (as the maxim goes) will do as they damn well please. Nevertheless, there are a few rules and we know that:
    - Customers will change their minds at some point (how fast depends on the business you are in).
    - Customers have been known (surprisingly frequently, and in B2B as well as B2C) to buy without knowing why. They will rationalise after the fact but that's not the point.
    - Generally it is a better idea to be ahead of the change curve than behind it and to have the new or modified offer ready when the customer wants it.
    - Customer change can be modelled in a market but it only looks at historic changes and may or may not predict the future.
    - Not all customers want 'new' in the same way or the same order (see Innovation Diffusion model below).
    - The jury is (still) out on the 'customers-drive-innovation' versus 'innovation-drives-customers' argument. I tend towards the

former but I am willing to be swayed in some market circumstances towards the latter.
- ○ Value migrates in every market – all the time.

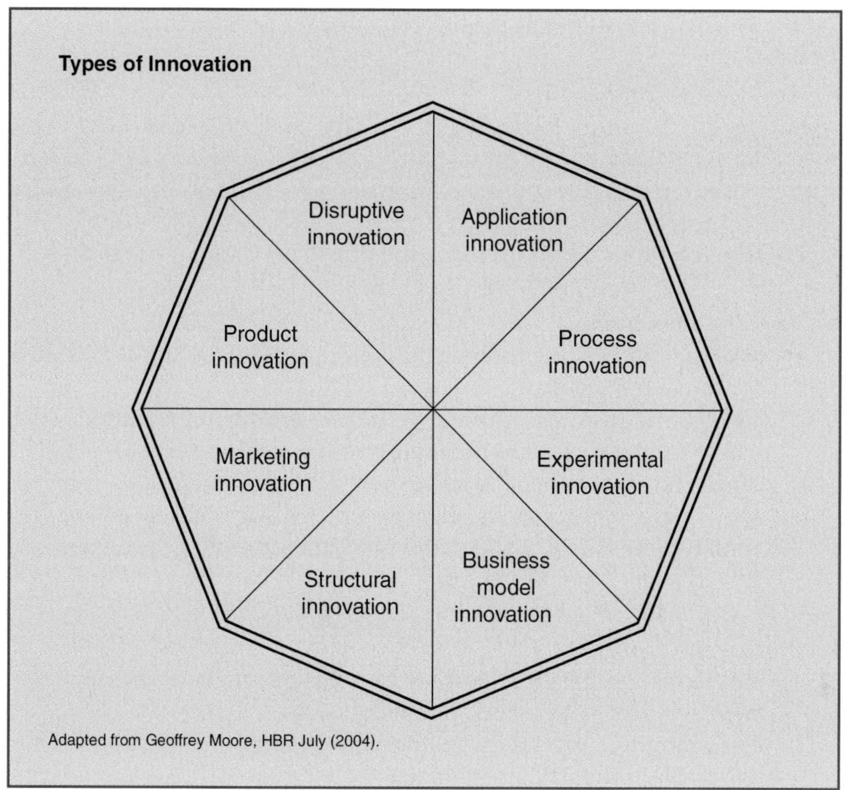

Adapted from Geoffrey Moore, HBR July (2004).

MARGIN NOTES

None of this, of course, makes innovation a 'science' no matter how you try to dress it up. On the other hand, we can look at the different ways that innovation has happened and been generated in other markets to gain some idea of what might be happening.

One of the most succinct descriptions of the different types of innovation comes from a recent article by Geoffrey Moore (HBR July 2004), of '*Crossing the Chasm*' fame. Although Moore's list is neat and precise it still won't guarantee that you will have the 'right' innovation in front of the 'right' customers at the 'right' time so work hard to reduce the risk of uncertainty but don't expect to get it 'right' every time.

- Disruptive Innovation:
  - ○ Has its roots in technological discontinuities (an unexpected innovation that topples the incumbent usually from outside the dominant technology) and causes much noise as it seems to appear from nowhere.
  - ○ An example might be mobile phones which upset the fixed line providers who had invested years and millions in the 'copper

MARGIN NOTES

wire network' that was now to be simply by-passed by wireless technology.
  - The 'disruptor' needs to focus on customer needs first and technology second.
  - The incumbent needs to scan for substitute competition.

- Application Innovation:
  - Takes existing technologies in to new markets and new applications.
  - For example, the military defence network became the global communications Internet.
  - The iPod took hard discs into the music-on-the-move business.

- Product Innovation:
  - Works with existing offers in existing segments to the next logical level in a benefit area.
  - One of the most common innovations producing examples such as the safer car, the smaller laptop or the faster delivery service.
  - Here, innovators need to make sure that customers actually want the 'safer car' or the 'smaller laptop' – always check where customer value exists in the market before 'improving' products and services just because you can.

- Process Innovation:
  - Improves the existing process for existing offers in existing segments, either in efficiency or effectiveness.
  - For example, longer service intervals for cars, airplanes and white goods and industrial machinery.

- Experimental Innovation:
  - The 'surface' modifications (that don't affect the functioning of the product or service) that will improve customers' experience of consumption.
  - For example, the special design features of a Morphy Richards kettle, the white iPod leads or the headquarters design of an engineering consultancy.

- Marketing Innovation:
  - Includes improvements in customer communications and service 'touch-points'.
  - Examples might include high-service support call centres from some IT providers, low-service from Ryanair and the forthcoming web 2.0 Internet.

- Business Model Innovation:
  - Repositions an existing offer within a new business model and so improves customer value.

- For example, IBM's move from computing to business services (including its US stock market listing) to improve value provided to its customers.

- Structural Innovation:
  - Often using disruption or political change to re-structure industry operations and processes.
  - Examples include deregulation of telecoms and banking to change the nature of competition and operations.

These examples, while quite 'neat' still only give you a list of types of innovations that commentators have noted in different markets – apart from impressing your peers on the quality of your reading, I am not sure it really helps you do anything practical about it in your organisation. What you need is to be able to spot sensible ideas for innovation and change in what you do day-to-day.

MARGIN NOTES

Most of the people I talk to aren't so much interested in what 'types' of innovation to look for or whether to worry about 'discontinuities' but what they *can do*, within an already too busy schedule, to try and keep up with what customers might want next. How then do we integrate innovation within the normal marketing day job? There are four main ways of thinking about this:

- First, Redefine the business you are in:
  - This approach takes us all the way back to the very first part of the SCORPIO discussion, 'Industry or Market thinking' (see Chapter 5).
  - Imagine that you are re-defining the nature of the business or market you are in from the industry/product definition to the market/customer definition as Harley Davidson, Swatch, Louis Vuitton or Google have done.
  - If you have not already done this, start by listing all the possible 'businesses' that you might be in.
  - For example, Mercedes might list its 'possible businesses' as:
    - Cars
    - Tracks
    - Prestige cars/trucks
    - Business transport
    - Supply chain
    - Engineering
    - Status
    - Moving.
  - For each of these 'possible businesses' you then need to ask yourself:
    - Who would the customer be?
    - What would the customer want in this business?
    - How might we satisfy the customer (in the new business(es)) in a different way?

- Who would we be competing with?
- How would we compete differently?

- You can decide to keep the 'radical' nature of this approach to yourself if you don't want to frighten too many of your colleagues, but the analysis (if properly re-packaged) can deliver some very insightful innovations – that meet some 'difficult' customer needs by stretching the existing technology base in an 'unusual' way.

- Second, Re-segment the market:
  - This approach also takes us back to the earlier parts of the SCORPIO discussion, Market segmentation and targeting (see Chapter 7). There are many ways that a market can be segmented and here we see just a few of the segmentation 'bases' that are used. To use this approach you need to ask yourself:
    - How do you currently segment your market?
    - What other ways might you also look at segmenting the market?
      - Geography?
      - Life stage (sagacity)?
      - Psychographics?
      - Motivations?
      - Education/knowledge?
      - Technology?
      - Purchasing Criteria?
      - Context©?
  - Based on the analysis that you carry out, you need to ask yourself:
    - What would be motivating/driving the customer?
    - What would the customer want in this segment?
    - How might we satisfy the customer (in the new segment(s)) in a different way?
    - Who would we be competing with?
    - How would we compete differently?
    - What would be the implications (operationally and competitively) from a re-segmenting exercise?

- Third, Track customer value:
  - If in doubt – follow the customer value.
  - Obvious, but sometimes it gets lost in the excitement. Although we need to return to a previous SCORPIO section, the Customer (see Chapter 6), I think the role of research and customer insight is best explained by the 'Kano' Model (*'Kano's Methods for Understanding Customer-defined Quality'* by Berger, Blauth, Boger, Bolster, Burchill, DuMouchel, Pouliot, Richter, Rubinoff, Shen, Timko and Walden. *Centre for Quality Management Journal*, Vol. 4, 1993). Here we see that any offering can be split into its component parts and these components assessed in terms of the amount of customer value that they deliver.
  - Above, we saw that customer value is a matter of perception and a function of 'usage', 'effort' and 'risk'.

MARGIN NOTES

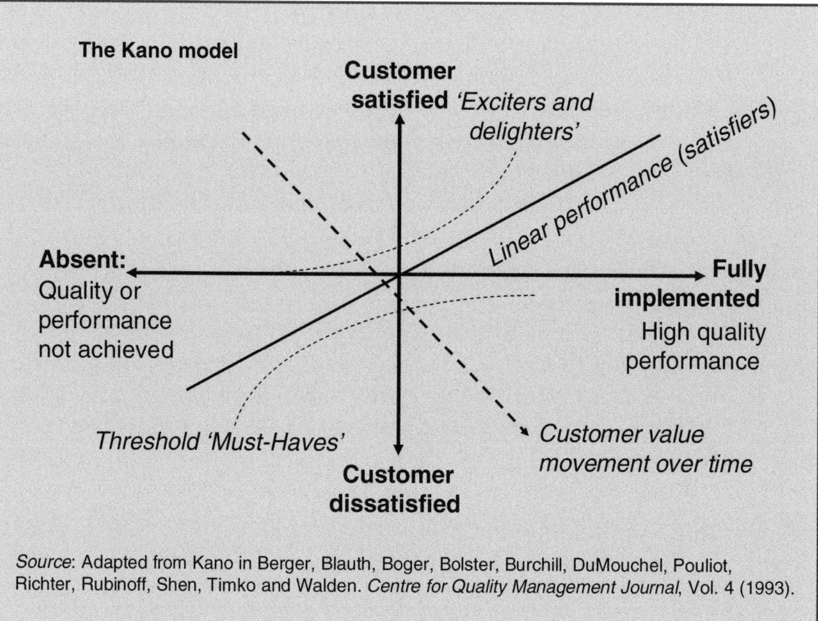

Source: Adapted from Kano in Berger, Blauth, Boger, Bolster, Burchill, DuMouchel, Pouliot, Richter, Rubinoff, Shen, Timko and Walden. *Centre for Quality Management Journal*, Vol. 4 (1993).

MARGIN NOTES

- The 'Kano' model simply shows us that:
  - Certain components or features have more customer value than others
  - Some components or features actively 'delight' and some are 'must-haves', which corresponds with our previous discussion on Hetrzberg's 'motivators' and 'hygiene factors' (see Chapter 6)
  - Over time (how fast depends on your particular market and competition) the components or features will move from 'delighters/motivators' into 'must-haves/hygiene factors'. The perceived customer value will decline.
    - For example, the today's 'must-have/hygiene factors' in a new motor car (power assisted steering, anti-lock breaking, air conditioning) are yesterday's 'delighters/motivators'.
- If you can plot the components or features that have moved from 'delighters' to 'must-haves' in your market you may be able to start plotting:
  - The speed of movement
  - The 'triggers' of the movement
  - The nature of the customer value in your market
  - The likely nature of future customer value
  - (Possibly) tomorrow's delighters
- None of this guarantees success of course, but it can help reduce the likelihood of making simple, avoidable mistakes.

- Fourth, Work with your customers:
  - Finally, we can look at how we might use some of our customers to help us uncover innovations. Many years ago, Everett Rogers

developed the 'Innovation Diffusion' model – this suggested that a new idea, concept, product or service would pass through a population (segment) of people (customers) in an understandable way:

- Innovators:
  - Would be first into the new idea, purely because it was 'new'.
- Early Adopters:
  - Would follow hard on the heels of the Innovators but would not want to be first into any market, preferring the 'teething problems' to be fixed first
- Early Majority:
  - Then brings the first part of the volume customers
- Late Majority:
  - Arrives later on, when the idea is no longer new and a majority of the target market has already purchased
- Laggards:
  - Arrive as the innovation has started to flag.

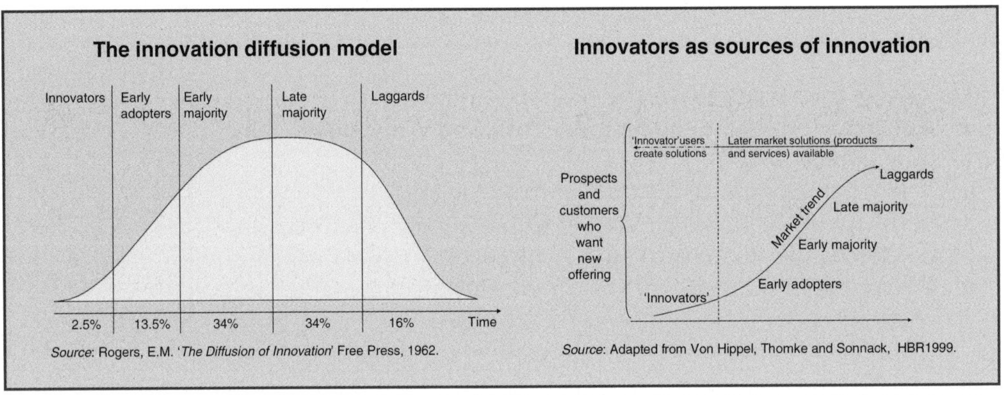

Source: Rogers, E.M. '*The Diffusion of Innovation*' Free Press, 1962.

Source: Adapted from Von Hippel, Thomke and Sonnack, HBR1999.

- Of all these groups, the Innovators are the most interesting and, if properly researched, can help us spot innovations that may be worth investing in.
  - I use this method quite frequently and some research organisations specialise in this type of research (see for example www.futurefeaturing.com).
  - Innovators, by their very nature are more aware of tomorrow's customer value in an offering than the later groups – it is what they are attuned to. If we can identify these customers from our existing base, and talk to them more deeply, we might gain some valuable insight in tomorrow's products and services.
    - Many innovators are simply more interested, more involved in the offering than other groups.

    - Your (and the competitors!) offering plays a more important part in their life and they have a greater awareness of the customer value that they receive now – and the nature of the customer value that they want to receive in the future.
    - Carefully recruited and groomed, your innovators can become your in-company innovations department.
- Beware though, innovators in one business/segment won't necessarily be innovators in another – you cannot use the same 'panel' for different product or service categories.
    - Given that the same person can be an innovator in, say, prestige cars and a laggard in, say, personal computing means that customers have to be recruited very carefully.
- A word of caution, the identification of the innovators will depend hugely on the way that you have defined both 'the business' and 'the segment' (see above).
    - For example, for Mercedes, an innovator in 'moving' will be different from an innovator in 'prestige cars' and will have different interests, different priorities – and will see different customer value in offerings.

The FAQs are:

7 Offerings		
7.4 Where are our new offerings?		
7.4.1	How much customer value is there in innovation and NPD?	Of course you can measure it. It means asking the customers but you should be getting used to that by now. Your target customers will be able to tell you (not in figures of course, there has to be something left for you to do) the value they see in the current offer and the value they see in potential new offerings.
7.4.2	What is 'innovation?' New to who?	Beware the word 'innovation', it's a little like 'solutions', so over-used that nobody is very clear what it means any more. The only 'innovations' that add customer value. That means that the innovation will: • Add benefit – be a better solution to the customer's problem • Reduce effort • Reduce price • Reduce risk. 'New' to the internal technology people is something else, as is 'new ideas that seem to create a whole set of new customer problems'.
7.4.3	What is 'new product or service development?'	Here you need to refer to the marketing tactics books and the diagrams that show the 'funnel' of (usually about) 100 ideas that might eventually turn into (usually

		only ever quoting B2C examples, about) 1 innovation launched into the market. There is a whole process (and associated industry) linked to the origination, screening, development, testing, launching and marketing of innovations – more than we can cover here.
7.4.4	Where can innovation come from?	'New' ideas can come from all over the place, and invariably do. Innovations that have some additional customer value tend to come from customers. BUT – the research required to uncover the areas of latent customer value are more complicated than the common-or-garden variety of research so need to be commissioned carefully.
7.4.5	Can customers be a prime source of innovation?	The most important – but not always the easiest to tap. As a rule of thumb, I always *start* with customers before I go anywhere else.
7.4.6	How can we take innovation to market?	Carefully. Depending on the type of innovation, the new product or service might flow through the existing routes to market – or it may require new routes. Ask the customers again.
7.4.7	What are the tests of good innovation?	Every book and writer has his or her favourite test. There are many to choose from. For me there is only one test – a good innovation increases customer value, which increases profit. What else is there?

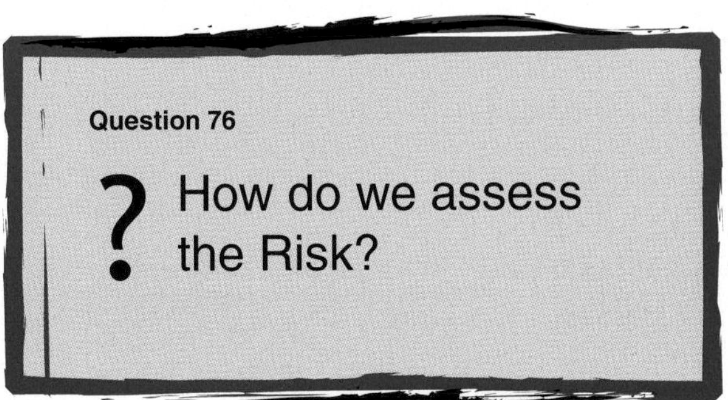

Question 76
?
How do we assess the Risk?

'Life is risk' I hear you cry, and you are right. The nature of business is all about risk.

The definitions of Risk are interesting too:

- 'Is an event or action that may adversely affect an organisation's ability to survive and compete in its chosen market as well as to maintain its financial strength, positive public image and the overall quality of its people and services'

- 'Can arise from failure to exploit opportunities as well as from threats materialising'

- 'Entrepreneur' = 'Owner or manager of a business enterprise who through risk and initiative attempts to make a profit' (Oxford).

I particularly like the use of the word 'attempts'! In the past, the entrepreneur 'used initiative', 'attempted' and 'used risk' and either made a profit – or not, some were always better than others.

Today life is more controlled and managers and directors need to demonstrate that they have assessed the business for risk and carried out all reasonable and necessary measures to reduce business risk. For good or bad, the days of *laissez-faire* are past and have been replaced with 'accountability'.

MARGIN NOTES

So, what is this risk business all about? Essentially it is about you taking some time to think through the things out there that could mess up your plan(s)-and then think about what you might do about it, *before it happens*. Sounds quite professional to me.

The risk 'headlines' are:

- Larger organisations have seen the value in managing business risk closely for a long time, employing professional Risk Managers.

- More recently, the professional bodies in the Risk areas have come together with the European Union to clarify the risk situation and to promote the benefits of risk management to smaller organisations. They have started by clarifying what we mean by risk. The UK Institute of Risk Management (IRM) have done this and suggest that there are four key areas of business risk:
  - Financial Risk
  - Strategic Risk
  - Operational Risk
  - Hazard Risk.

- They also suggest that the risks can be broken down into:
  - Those driven internally within the organisation, and which should be under the organisation's control
  - Those driven by external events and forces that are outside the organisation's direct control

- The individual risks in each of these categories are self-explanatory.

Types of business risk

	Financial	Strategic	Operational	Hazard
Internally driven	• Liquidity and cash flow	• Research and development • Intellectual capital • Mergers and acquisition integration	• Accounting controls • Information systems • Recruitment • Supply chain	• Public access • Employers • Properties • Products and services
Externally driven	• Interest rates • Foreign • Credit	• Competition • Customer changes • Industry changes • Customer demand	• Regulators • Culture • Board composition	• Contracts • Natural events • Suppliers • Environment

Source: Institute of Risk Management (UK) 2002.

- You can see immediately that business risk, defined this way, goes far beyond simple financial risk and covers all aspects of business activity.
- Apart from just complying with government regulations (a stand-alone activity in its own right), managing business risk better can lead to clear and obvious business benefits for the organisation. It has been suggested that some of these might include:
    - Stronger and better quality Growth
    - More Stable business and less prone to environment/market changes
    - Better quality Staff as clearer responsibilities emerge
    - Stronger Suppliers attracted by more stable business
    - Better quality Channels to market as business stabilises
    - Better Customer acquisition and stronger, more stable brand
    - Better Customer retention through consistency of operations
    - Obtains Cheaper finance through lower perceived business risk
    - Drives Lower costs (for example insurance).

MARGIN NOTES

■ A word on marketing risk

There is more to risk in the market/marketing area than you might imagine although there should be no surprises, apart maybe from the format.

There are two key areas of marketing risk:

- Primary demand risk
    - These risks are quite similar to financial risks in that they are based on factors largely beyond the control of marketers and other managers.

- The 'primary demand risk' relates to the general level of effective demand in the marketplace and the ability to pay.
- This will be driven by factors such as:
    - Economic life cycles
    - Currency and exchange fluctuations
    - Government regulations
    - Technology changes.

- Market share risk:
    - These are different from the organisation's primary demand risk in that they aren't 'absolute'; it is always 'relative' – to the competition.
    - The organisation might be world class in the way it identifies, assesses and manages marketing, risk but if its competition is even better it will still be at a disadvantage.
    - These risks should be within the control of the organisation and better organisations will reduce these risks further (and make more profits) than poor (less customer focused) organisations.
    - The factors included in this section are:
        - The possibility of not acquiring customer
        - The possibility of not retaining (losing) a customer.
    - The market share risk will be directly affected by the amount of consideration and company investment (time, attention and money) in:
        - Customer research and understanding
        - Product and service development
        - Price maintenance (not discounting)
        - Brand and differentiation
        - Communications activities.

As you work to first assess and then to reduce the risk in this area, you need to remember that your activities are affected, not only by your actions over time, but also by the quality and quantity of our different competitors' investments in customers, product or service, pricing, brand and differentiation and communications.

- The best way of reducing marketing risk is to focus on three activities (as if you did not know already):
    - Get closer to your target customers
    - Improve the quality of your organisation's marketing efforts
    - Increase the share of marketing investment – relative to your competition.

- Typically, the Risk Management process the organisation follows is:
    - Identify the risks:
        - Working against the types of list that are submitted above, identify all the possible risks that confront the organisation.
        - This is not a bad exercise really; it can help communicate to others in the organisation the nature and complexity of the customer task.

MARGIN NOTES

- The 'build-a-better-mousetrap' brigade could do with understanding how things really work.
- Assess the impact of the risks:
  - Which risks should we be worried about and which can we leave 'till later?'
  - The diagram shows that you need to assess each risk on two dimensions:
    - The likelihood of the risk occurring and
    - The significance of the risk should it occur.
  - The traditional 2 × 2 grid shows the output with 'Primary Risks' (high impact and high likelihood) coming top of the list to worry about with 'Irrelevant Risks' (low impact and low likelihood) coming last.
  - And yes, we have all noticed that scoring the risks could be a highly subjective matter – although time will tell just how good you are at this.

MARGIN NOTES

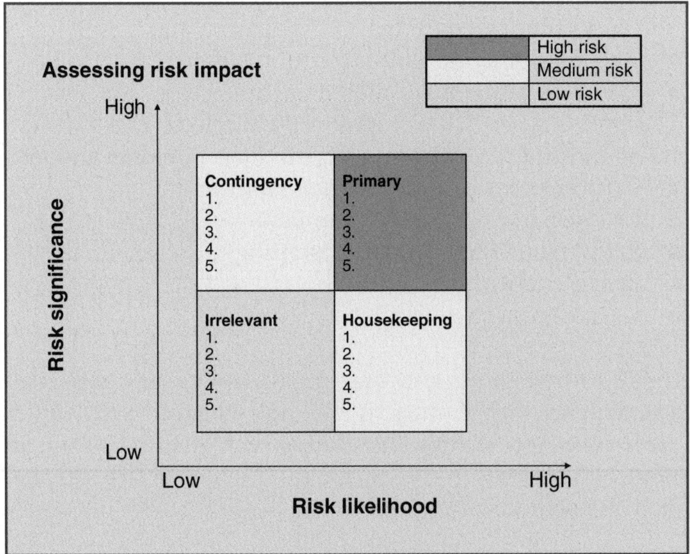

- Create a risk map – Not as complicated as it sounds – it rarely is. A 'risk map' is just a simple way of making sure that you know where to focus your effort – and what can wait for when you have some free time on your hands (what was that sigh for?). All you need to do is:
  - Take the outputs of the previous 'analysis'
  - Place the 'primary', 'contingency and housekeeping' and 'irrelevant' into three groups as shown in the 'risk map' diagram
  - Assess each identified risk according to the effectiveness of the available controls to manage the risk
  - Re-position the risk (see arrows on diagram) into one of the three horizontal squares depending on whether the controls we have will work weakly, moderately or strongly on the risk.

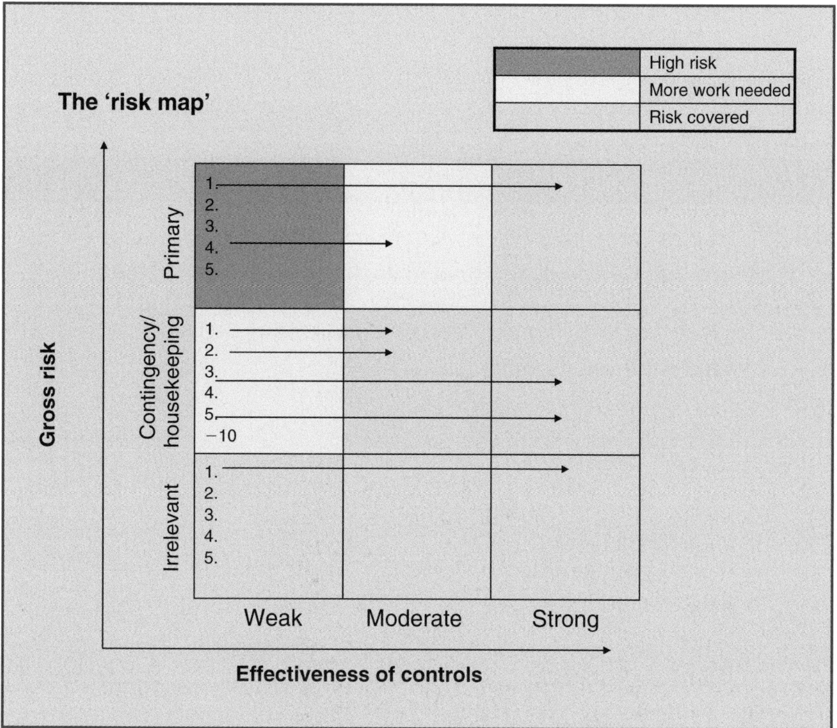

MARGIN NOTES

- Use the risk map to highlight priorities for action:
  - The top left are the risks that actively threaten the organisation, you should focus your immediate attention here.
  - Then focus on the second level risks.
- Develop risk management strategies:
  - Risks are unlikely to go away; they are a natural part of being in business.
  - Given that they, like competition, are always with us and always changing, we need some form of 'strategy' to deal with them – continual tactical meddling is not likely to do much good.
  - The important risks will be the strategic ones – these will need strategic responses.
  - Don't get downhearted; this is a great opportunity to recruit support to the cause.
  - Imagine, constant competitive pressure on prices is identified as a primary risk that current controls don't affect.
  - Suddenly you have an audience that will be receptive to a strategic solution such as differentiation and branding – and will see the need to invest in such a programme.
  - I can see you are getting the idea …
- Monitor and review progress:
  - The well-known 'return arrow' in the diagram that takes you back to the beginning, because everything changes, all the time.

Easy.

The FAQs are:

7 Offerings		
7.5 How do we assess the Risk?		
7.5.1	What is 'Risk?'	Risk is natural and it is normal in business. Without risk there would only be what the economists call 'normal profit' and every organisation would make the same (minimum) profit. Where is the fun in that?
7.5.2	How do we assess business risk?	Being aware of risk is the first hurdle. The second step is to understand the broad nature of business risk, covering: ● Strategic ● Operational and ● Hazard risks as well as the better known ● Financial risks. The third step is to realise that business risk is a normal part of business and removing it is impossible. We only aim to understand it and protect ourselves from its worse effects. The fourth step is to assess the nature of the risk that, unless we take preventative action, could cause the organisation serious harm.
7.5.3	How do we assess environmental marketing risk?	Some elements of marketing risk are inherent in the nature of markets and will affect all organisations equally – such as the broad economic cycle and customers' general wealth and ability to purchase (disposable income). These risks need to be assessed and preventative action taken, if possible.
7.5.4	How do we assess competitive marketing risk?	Other elements of marketing risk are competitive and depend upon your organisation's ability to gain customer preference. These risks need to be assessed and additional investment in marketing and customer insight made where possible.
7.5.5	How do we assess the impact of these risks?	If the risk were to turn into reality would it hurt? If all players in your market dropped sales revenues by 5% because of, say, an increased interest rate, would it really matter? If you lost 40% of your sales because of the arrival of low cost Chinese imports, would it matter? Worry only about what would matter to you.
7.5.6	What is our existing risk management strategy?	Do you have a strategy for dealing with risk? If so, what is it? Would it be sufficient?

7.5.7	What are the implications of the assessment?	How confident do you feel? We aren't trying to de-risk business-that is not possible. We are trying to take elementary precautions that might stop us losing the business if we were better prepared.

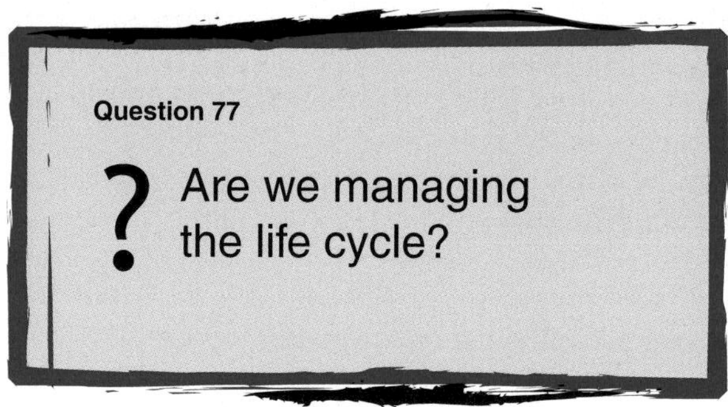

Question 77
?
Are we managing
the life cycle?

MARGIN NOTES

What on earth can the venerable Product Life Cycle (PLC) model tell us about the offerings component of SCORPIO marketing strategy? Probably more than you thought. We dealt with the basics of the PLC in Chapter 2 when we were looking at the business environment.

Now we are looking at how to develop and manage the offerings part of the marketing strategy, we can start to use the PLC in a more creative way.

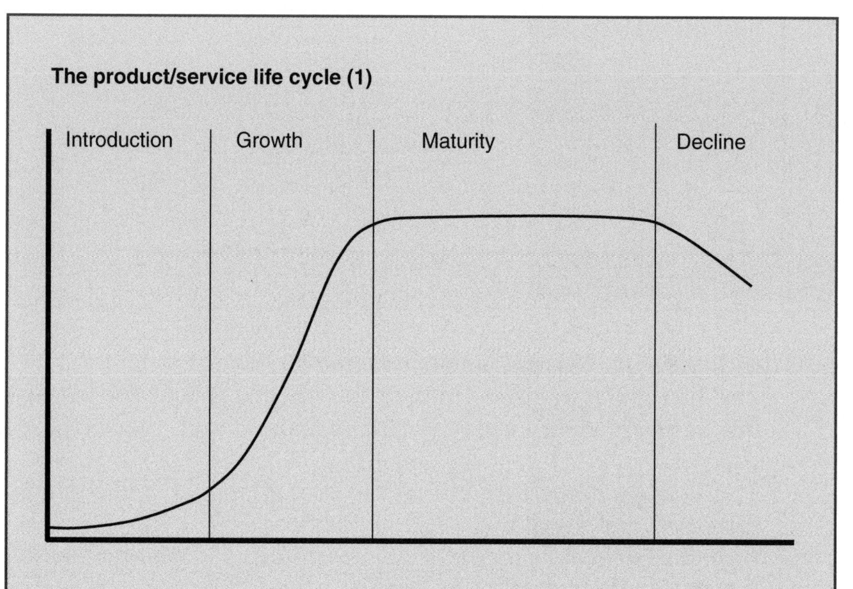

The 'headlines' are:

- The PLC is just a model, it's not set in stone so you can *use* it
  - The way that the PLC is taught and written about (just as I did in Chapter 2) always gives the impression that the PLC is a 'given', that it is almost cast in stone and that our products and services will, if we get beyond the introduction stage, pass through the different stages until it eventually passes into decline and death.
    - The very first thing to realise, is that this is not so. You do have some power to play with the PLC for your benefit.
  - The first question facing you though, is the BIG question, where are you now on the curve?
    - I know it's a big issue and we never know for sure until we are past the stage and can say for certain where we were, but take an educated guess.
    - You can always replay the ideas if you find that you were wrong. Go on, what have you got to lose?

MARGIN NOTES

There are four 'games' you might want to play with the PLC to support your offerings.

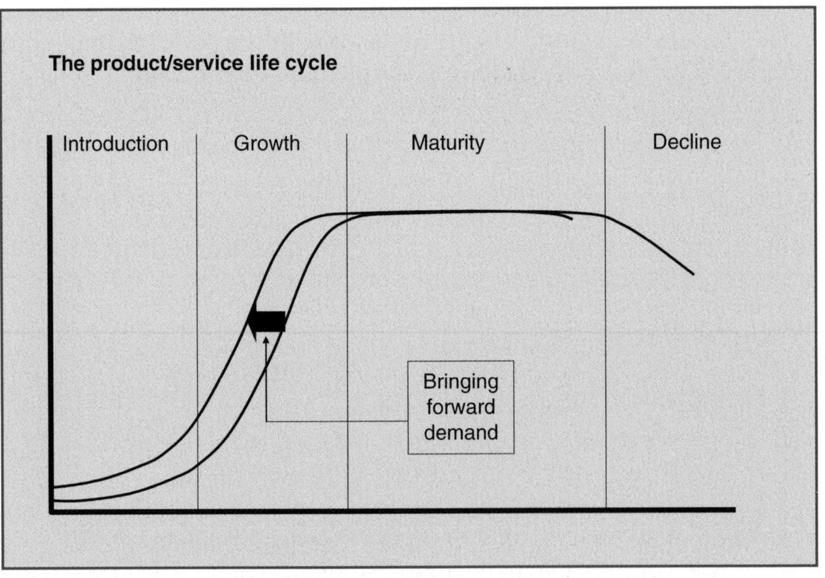

- Game 1, Bringing forward the demand curve
  - The first game involves shifting the whole curve to the left and bringing in more demand earlier than would otherwise be expected.
  - This activity doesn't mean that the overall market is likely to be increased, just the timing of the demand.
  - Bringing demand 'forward' is no different from stimulating demand in the normal ways (4Ps).

- Just that in this case you know what you are going to do and you prepare product stocks or service capacity to deliver on the demand when it arrives early.
- The competition, of course won't be prepared and, as a result you might expect to increase your overall market share.

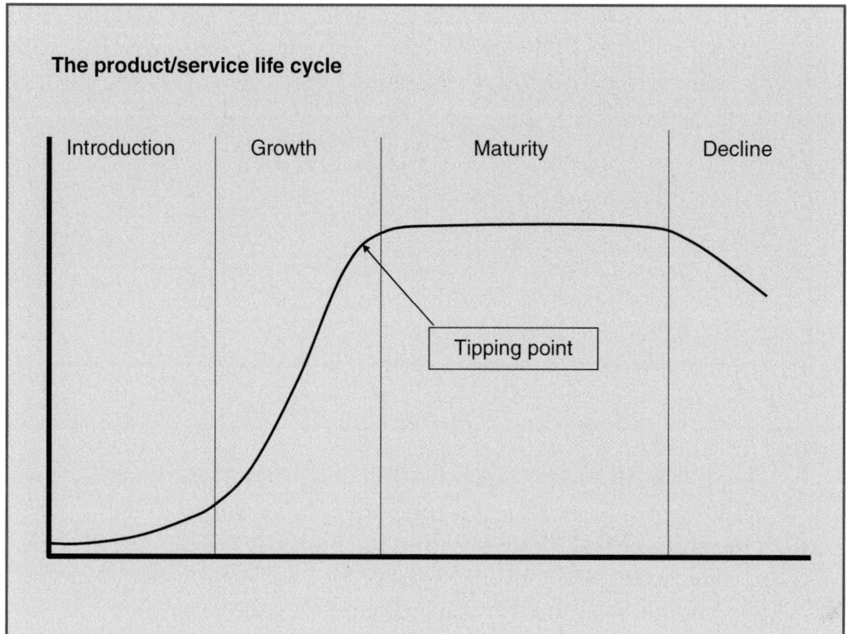

- Game 2, Getting to the 'Tipping Point' first
  - In Chapter 2 we looked at the problems with the move from 'rapid growth' stage to the 'maturity' stage.
  - It is a time for 'consolidation' and many organisations don't survive this difficult transition.
  - Knowing this, and being prepared for the inevitable transition from rapid growth/sales emphasis to maturity and customer emphasis, if you can get to the transition stage or tipping point – (named after the book by the same name *'The Tipping Point'* Malcolm Gladwell, Abacus, 2001) before the competition, you could make early and significant wins in the maturity stage.
  - If you played games 1 and 2 sequentially, you would absorb demand before the competition – and stimulate the arrival of the transition to maturity faster than would normally be the case – and if you were prepared for this change before the others …
- Game 3, Stimulating demand
  - Just because the product or service has moved into the maturity stage doesn't mean that subsequent growth is now impossible.
  - True, we expect that the majority of customers who are going to be attracted to the offering class have now purchased.

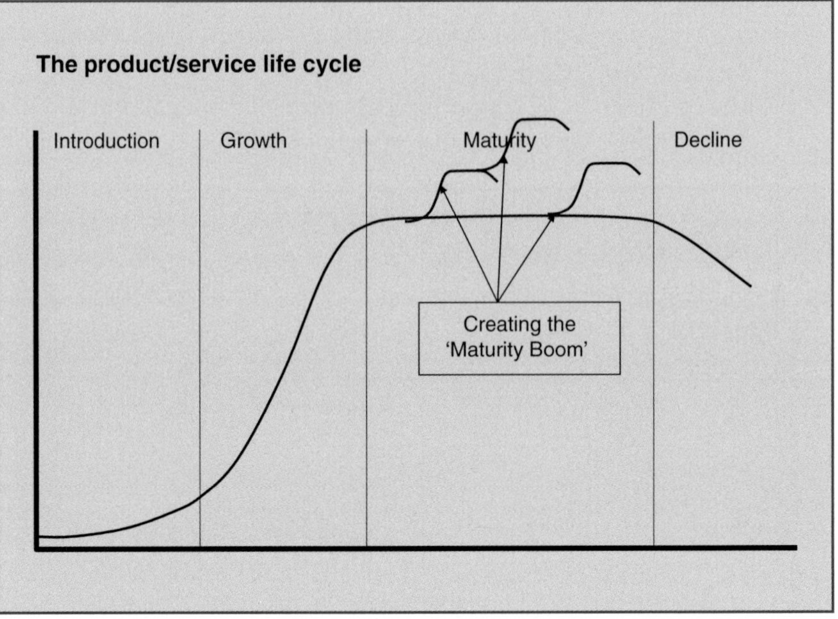

'Replacement' purchasing doesn't mean that we have to wait until the product or service is completely used up.

- We can create sales *booms* within the maturity stage.
- Good examples of maturity booms over the years would include:
  - Manual to automatic transmission for cars
  - Black and white to colour TV
  - Vinyl to CD's for music
  - Videotape to DVDs for films
  - Coal to diesel for shipping
  - Coal to gas for electricity generation.
- Maturity booms aren't the same thing as normal product or service development that continues throughout the maturity stage.
- A maturity boom must be important enough to encourage a significant proportion of the customer base to 'trade up' and exchange or replace their existing model well before normal replacement would be expected.

- Game 4, Extending the maturity stage
  - The maturity stage is recognised as being the longest of the stages.
  - How long depends on the organisation's closeness to the customer and the resulting quality of the marketing involved.
  - Products and services don't 'have to' die, it is not fore-ordained by some superior law, it all comes down to the skills of managers in keeping the offer relevant amid changing customer perceptions and needs.
  - Ask yourself:
    - Why does Guinness continue to hold its position while other traditional beers are falling behind lagers and wine?

MARGIN NOTES

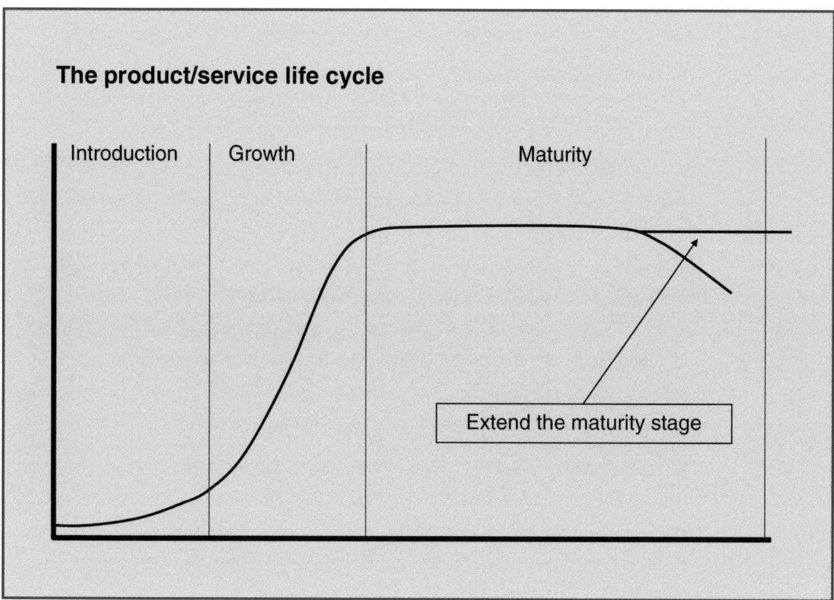

MARGIN NOTES

- How does the Heidelberg printing machine retain its prestige position and hold out against the Far Eastern onslaught of printing machines?
- Why does Coca Cola dominate supermarket shelves while the other 'seltzer brands' of the period now just exist as magnetic advertising plates on refrigerator doors?
- Why does your organisation survive and others go to the wall?

- The answer is *relatively* better marketing.
- The longer the offer is seen as worthwhile, having a role in the customers' life and possessing Value to the customer it will survive and even flourish.
- Remember, nothing is 'written' it depends on you.

The FAQs are:

7 Offerings		
7.6 Are we managing the life cycle?		
7.6.1	Does the organisation believe that the product life cycle is NOT a self-fulfilling prophesy?	If everyone (you included) believes that the PLC is effectively 'in control' and there is nothing we can do, then. Nobody 'does' anything to change the PLC progress-or our progress within the PLC. As a result, the PLC carries on – as expected. This is termed a 'self-fulfilling prophesy'.

7.6.2	Where are we on the curve?	Not easy but it doesn't mean you should not have a go at working it out. Very few products or services are true innovations so normally comparisons can be made with previous offerings. If 'similar' offerings of yours (or to yours) have turned into maturity at 45% of market capacity and you are moving close to 35% already ...
7.6.3	How can we bring demand forward?	Nothing complicated here, increased communications, sales and channel offers and promotions. Wider testing and encouragement to 'try' the offer, perhaps with an integrated price offer can all help stimulate trial and purchase. But don't be surprised by increased demand, have the capacity ready to grow your share of the market.
7.6.4	How can we get to the 'tipping point' first or fast?	I am normally wary of 'buying market share' but if here it is to a purpose and you plan to increase returns and margins later on ... Only race to get the transfer into maturity if you are certain that your organisation is ready to deal with the structural changes required. If you have worked in maturity already, you will know how (and why) to get there.
7.6.5	How can we stimulate growth?	Maturity booms are driven primarily by customers. Customers today are aware and sophisticated and if they feel they are being 'blackmailed' into early change and spending more money unnecessarily, they will rebel. If they see a clear and compelling increase in customer value, however, they will need no encouragement.
7.6.6	How can we grow in maturity?	There need be no practical 'end' to the maturity stage, it all really depends on how good (and flexible) the organisation can be when assessing and meeting customer needs. A recent survey (*The Economist* 18/12/04) on Europe's oldest companies revealed that: ● The world's oldest firms are all family owned ● Hoshi Ryokan, a Japanese Inn founded in 718 is now being run by the 46th generation of the family ● Europe's oldest firm is Chateau de Goulaine, a French vineyard founded in 1000 ● Britain's oldest is John Brooke & Sons, a 1541 founded textile maker that has turned its mills into a business park ● One third of the firms in the Fortune 500 in 1970 no longer existed in 1983, killed by merger, acquisition, bankruptcy or break-up. The report concludes that evolving is key to longevity: ● Kikkoman, founded in 1630, the world's leading provider of soy sauce is also in food flavourings, and now biotech. ● Survivors are good at following a set of unchanged values and separating what they do and how they do it – from who they are.

7.6.7	What are the best metrics to use to plot progress	Metrics are always an issue ● Find the ones that are best at assessing a position ● Find the ones that managers will believe and accept ● Find the ones that will generate the (customer) required behaviours. Choose the metrics that suit you best, but the PLC suggests at first glance, that profits are finite and somehow circumscribed by the line of the curve itself. This is not so and even the 'flat line' of the maturity stage can create ever-growing margins, profits and returns on investment.

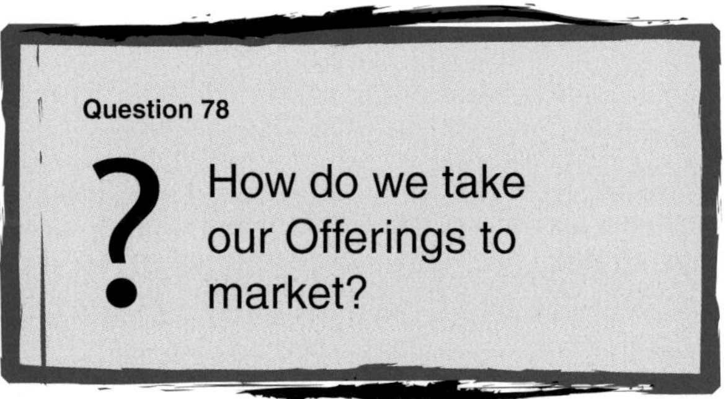

Question 78
?
How do we take our Offerings to market?

MARGIN NOTES

This section is about lots more than just 'distribution', 'logistics', 'supply chain' or 'routes to market' or whatever is the next definition of moving stuff and people around the country or the world.

How we get the offerings to market is about implementation in its broadest and narrowest sense.

- Setting the strategy is important, but without implementation, all your work will be *pointless*
- You *have to* cross the line from strategy to implementation – if only to make sure that what you planned is how it gets done
- But, you cannot focus on strategy and implementation and expect to complete both tasks to *the same level*
- Let's cover those points one more time:
    - Strategy is a pointless exercise without implementation
    - A strategy that cannot be implemented is just a management 'whim'
    - The best plan cannot be expected to implement itself

  - Implementers won't implement as *you* wish without some involvement from *you* in the process
  - A complete strategy includes a plan for its implementation
  - The marketing strategy *won't happen* unless you protect and nurture it during its early stages; why go to all the hard work of creating a differentiated strategy just to 'orphan' it when it needs you most?

The 'headlines' are:

- There is no end of things you can worry about when looking at implementation – just look at how many people are paid to worry about the tactics of life.
  - But, implementation *per se* is not our problem, what is our problem is setting the critical implementation issues that will ensure that the strategy is a success or a failure.

MARGIN NOTES

- Every business, market and organisation will be unique and the very idea of prescriptive cure-all remedies is laughable.

- You will have to decide for yourself which of the issues could be critical to your strategy. The most important areas of implementation you need to consider are probably in 'The marketing mix', especially (and traditionally):
  - *Product*: Or service that carries the benefits that have maximum customer value

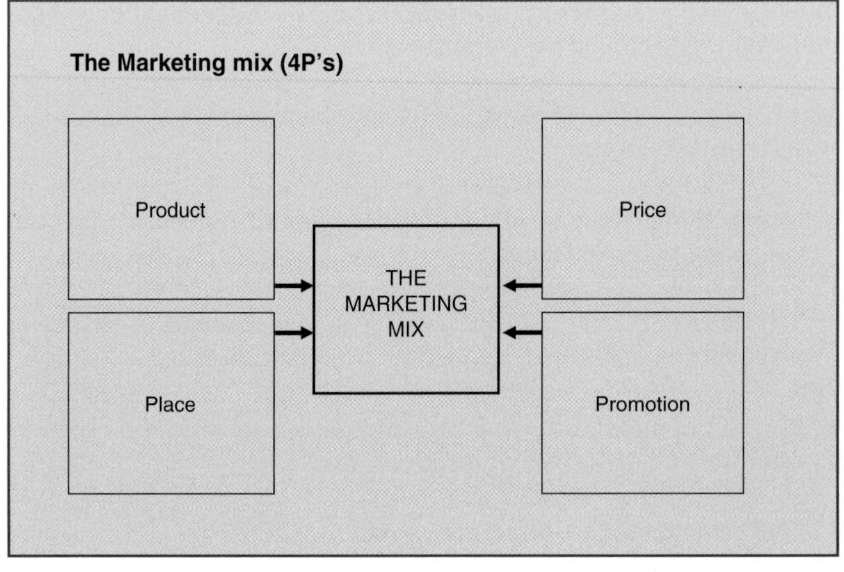

- *Pricing*: To extract maximum value from the market
- *Place*: Routes to market
- *Promotion*: Communications.

- Again, *your job is not to implement*, there are people much better at that than you (or there should be) and you have other things to worry about.
  - Your job is to highlight areas where implementation can make or break the strategy; and to make sure that the strategy is not broken.

- The tacticians know their job, but differentiation is rarely achieved by doing what everybody else does.
  - Remember that some functionally driven idea of *'best practice' alone will never create superior customer value* – that's where you come in and what this section is all about.

- The 'me-too's', the 'also-ran's' and the other organisations heading towards the commodity end of the market will all focus on making-no-mistakes-with-the-components of the marketing mix.
  - Organisations intent on reaping the rewards of differentiation will be focusing their attention on creating-superior-customer-value-from-innovative-blending-of-the-components of the marketing mix.
  - Which type of organisation is yours?

- If you have researched the market and gleaned sufficient insight to create a winning Value Proposition, you must make clear to the organisation what needs to be done to achieve success.
  - Your strategy will undoubtedly depend on certain components being blended in a certain way – you must specify these to the implementers if you are to avoid the possibility of 'things being done the way we have always done them'.

To finish this section, we will look, very briefly, at the major components of the marketing mix and consider the very minimum controls that you need to manage as the strategy moves from formulation to implementation. A slightly (but not much) wider explanation of the mix elements is covered in Chapter 13.

Although I fully accept that each and every organisation and marketing strategy is different. I also suggest that every marketing strategy can be reduced to a common theme that ties your strategy together; and you will need to clarify this before you pass the strategy over to the implementers.

MARGIN NOTES

■ Your Value Proposition is the most important control measure you possess

- The best way to do this is to translate the *Value Proposition* into marketing mix terms that the implementers will be able to use.
  - They were involved in the creation and development of the Value Proposition and agreed with the decisions made.
  - They were also involved in agreeing the control measures – the time you invested will now pay off.
- This is not doing the implementers jobs for them, it is handing over enough detail in a 'specification' that they can implement what (they have already agreed) is the 'right' job for your customers.

MARGIN NOTES

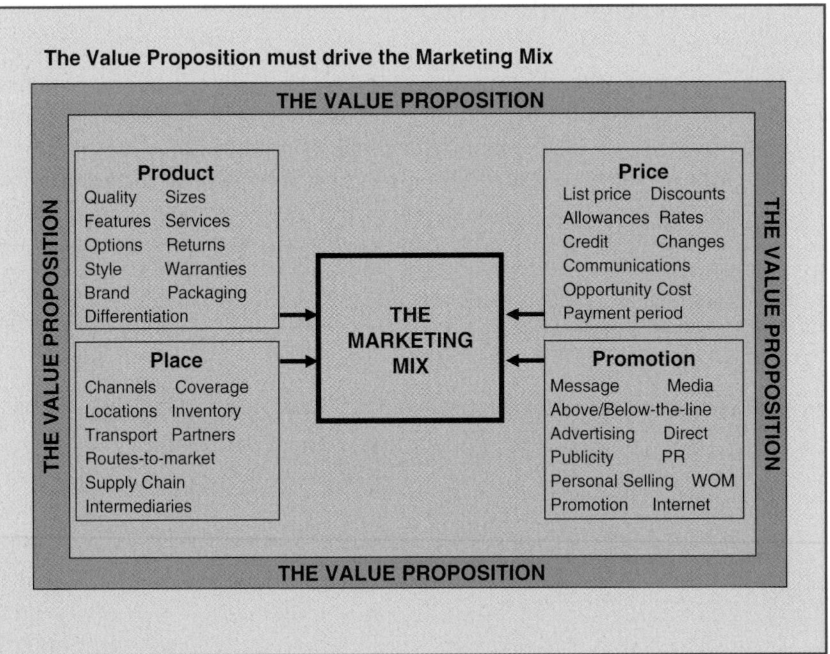

- Your organisation may be unique, but the key issues generally associated with Product, Price, Place and Promotion Policy must be directly aligned with the agreed Value Proposition, these are:
  - Target Market (Customer) needs and wants
    - The Value Proposition will define these, follow this lead only
  - Differentiation
    - How does the Value Proposition say you will be different?
  - Brand
    - What does the Value Proposition say that you brand values and personality will be?
    - What tactical activities are on line with this?
    - What tactical activities are off-line with this?

A word on measuring progress

The marketing mix is obviously more complicated and detailed than the points I have covered – I agree. There are (very thick) books dedicated to understanding and manipulating the elements of the marketing mix – and they do the job very well indeed.

But, they don't worry too much about longer term marketing strategy, and that is my main concern.

The secret remains, *what gets measured – gets done*. If the marketing strategy is important to you, then you will absolutely need to measure progress – against the strategic levers that you have identified, communicated and agreed (through the Value Propositions) with the implementers – regularly.

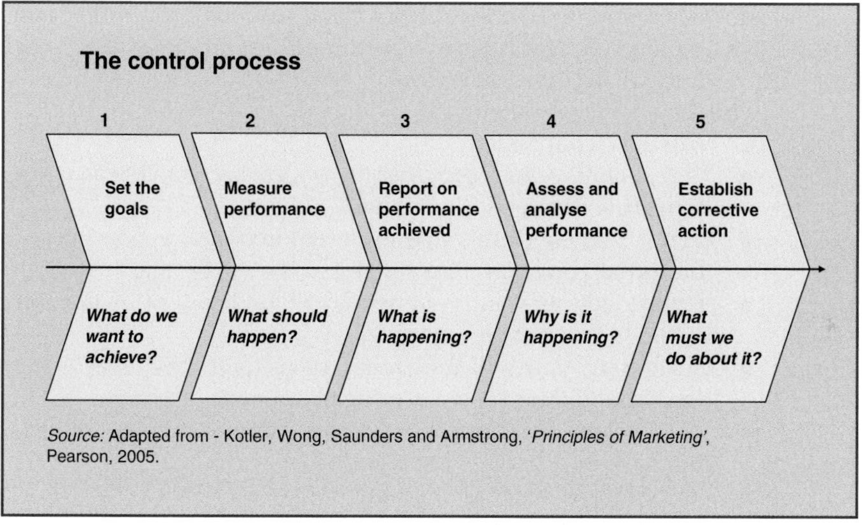
The control process
1
2
3
4
5
Set the goals
Measure performance
Report on performance achieved
Assess and analyse performance
Establish corrective action
What do we want to achieve?
What should happen?
What is happening?
Why is it happening?
What must we do about it?

Source: Adapted from - Kotler, Wong, Saunders and Armstrong, '*Principles of Marketing*', Pearson, 2005.

MARGIN NOTES

- As we have already seen (Chapter 10), the classic control process has a few, very simple stages, here applied to controlling the implementation of your marketing strategy:
  - Goal setting:
    - What do we want to achieve?
    - Use this stage to set the critical outputs from the strategic levers as discussed above.
    - For example, customer perception of value received from the offerings, or degree of differentiation from competing offers.
    - Don't set too many measures (the implementers will have batteries of their own to apply); focus on the important ones for you and for the marketing strategy.
  - Performance Measurement:
    - What should happen if everything goes to plan?
    - Here you must be specific.

        - Based on the research that you have carried out, where do we need to be?
        - These measures won't be 'hopes' based on random feelings or aspirations but will be clear, defined measures that have been based on where your organisation needs to be relative to the market, customer requirements and competition.
        - As soon as you are told that the measures you ask for are, 'not normal', 'not industry standard', 'not easy to measure' and finally 'far too expensive to carry out' then you know you are getting somewhere.
        - Hold to your measures or kiss the market strategy goodbye.
    - Performance Reporting:
        - What is (really) happening?
        - Agree the time scales and get the feedback.
        - When you receive the results make sure they are in the terms you agreed, and have not been modified to make them more 'normal' or 'easier to obtain'.
    - Performance Assessment:
        - Why has it happened?
        - Here, you have to accept that the original objective was wrong in the first place – it can happen.
        - Unless you cover this (too often ignored) stage, you have no idea what you should do about it in the next stage.
        - Beware here that all your work can be heading in the right direction, but not fast enough.
        - Customers, you will remember, have their own lives – they don't spend their time worrying about your offerings.
        - Just because your response times have not been achieved don't assume that it is not working.
        - Customers work at their speed, not yours.
    - Corrective Action:
        - What should we do about putting it 'right?' If anything? If it is not a question of customer speed or faulty forecasting, it comes down to one of just two possibilities:
            - The Market Strategy is faulty – re-assess and correct
            - The Implementation is faulty – review and correct.

MARGIN NOTES

If you hold tight to the handful of levers that I have pointed out, you might just succeed in sending your strategy off to the market, intact, (at least) in the most important parts.

Naturally, every strategy changes between formulation and implementation. This is true; but putting down some strong markers about routes to market, pricing and communications you will ensure that any changes made are 'necessary' and not just 'convenient'.

The FAQs are:

7 Offerings		
7.7 How do we take our Offerings to market?		
7.7.1	How do we ensure the marketing mix is designed to 'enshrine' the customer Value Proposition?	You won't enshrine anything unless you keep some form of control over the key areas of the mix. *The (agreed) Customer Value Proposition(s) are your primary control tool – use it* You cannot simply pass over control to the implementers and expect the strategy to be implemented as you imagine it. As a minimum, you need to: ● Identify the key strategic levers for your market strategy ● Communicate properly (think, internal marketing) the aims and ambitions of the strategy to those who will be implementing. Answer all their questions about the things that aren't going to be done the 'normal' way so that they understand and are 'on side' ● Use this process to agree the Value Proposition ● Agree the continuing controls you will retain over key levers ● Agree measurements and report-backs on implementation progress – against the agreed strategic levers ● Take corrective action when you need to.
7.7.2	How can we ensure continued customer focus into implementation?	You will only have to hold the implementers' hands' if this is the first time that they have implemented a customer-focused strategy. After the first time, you can normally rely on self-interest to carry the day for you – when everyone sees that the results are better, then the arguments stop. Until, that is, you start to make changes to a 'winning formula'... Nothing is better than constant and effective communication
7.7.3	What is the right speed-to-market?	Customer speed is the right speed, nothing else matters If you don't know what speed the customer wants, ask them. Make sure that you ask all the different segments, they are likely to have different requirements. When you are informed on the speed-to-market achieved by the competition you may wish to feign interest but you don't have to take any notice – after all, your offering, brand promise and unique market position is not the same as theirs so ...
7.7.4	How do we build in 'change' to the implementation programme?	Right from the very start, don't even let anybody think that they will be getting comfortable with a 'standard' way of doing things. Actions are always more powerful than words so as soon as you have a success on your hands – and you are seen to be working on its replacement already ...

7.7.5	How do we avoid tactics-led strategy?	By being vigilant. There is no malice here, it's a matter of culture (see Chapter 10) and the day-to-day is everywhere and (obviously) responsible for all the sales and riches in the organisation. Without your key strategic levers (and Value Proposition) you have no control over what tactics are used at all. If you don't specify the routes to market that customers and brand would prefer, and the implementers use the routes to market that everyone else in the industry uses, and your proposed offer doesn't meet the needs of the normal routes then the offer will be changed-back to an undifferentiated offer; that the routes to market understand. Now you have a tactics-led strategy, not a market-led strategy.
7.7.6	Where is the 'lifetime value' assessment?	This is one to rub salt in the wounds – and rightly so. Now that you have control of the key strategic 'levers', it's about time you started your assault on the 'quarter-by-quarter-financials-are-all-that-count' managers. Lifetime value (see Chapter 9) is the important measure, but not favoured by internal accounting systems. However, if you give in to the short-term approach, your marketing strategy will always be short-term in nature as longer-term investments will be disadvantaged by short-term repayment requirements. Pick your time but do the calculations. Choose a moment when your 'stock' is high and see how much support you can gather for the lifetime value approach.
7.7.7	How do we ensure feedback from the market operations?	Knowledge Management will soon be a key element of competitive advantage (see Chapter 10). This is another longer-term investment but one that will pay off handsomely. In my experience, people are far happier to do the work and collect the data (and feed it back to you) if they can see the benefits – being a 'good thing' just is not enough but when *knowledge* is pushed back to them to make their job easier ... Too many managers think that data collection and feedback is a one-way process. Historical mistakes *don't have* to be repeated ...

■ The strategic questions (72–78)

We arrive, finally (I can hear the sighs) at the end of the central SCORPIO modules.

I hope that you have seen now that the order that you take through the seven modules is largely up to you, it's all interconnected, and it all leads to the customer.

In this section on Offerings, I have tried to make a sensible link from strategy (three-year thinking) to tactics (this quarter). If we (strategy and tactics) all work for the same organisation (subject to all the 'issues' highlighted in Chapter 10) then we need to find a way of working together so that the customer benefits – only customer value can create organisational value.

In this final chapter I have tried to look at those areas where a managed handover is needed from the strategy to the implementation. Some of the issues are technical although most are cultural. How well your organisation succeeds with the handover is less a measure of its ability than just how badly it wants to win.

And the questions. This time the stakes are high, for you and for your organisation. These questions are some of the most difficult that we have looked at so far, because they imply a lot of work. Value Propositions aren't easy. But, this is much more a measure of whether you are happy just to calculate and design strategies – or whether you want to see them implemented.

Its not just about how good to are, its about how bad you want it …

No.	Strategic question	Our strategic answer	Importance	✓
	Offerings			
72	Where is the customer value?		Must have	
			Nice to have	
			Not important	
73	What is our Value Proposition?		Must have	
			Nice to have	
			Not important	
74	What is the most appropriate business design for us?		Must have	
			Nice to have	
			Not important	
75	Where are our new offerings?		Must have	
			Nice to have	
			Not important	
76	How do we assess the risk?		Must have	
			Nice to have	
			Not important	
77	Are we managing the life cycle?		Must have	
			Nice to have	
			Not important	
78	How do we take our offerings to market?		Must have	
			Nice to have	
			Not important	

PART III

Co-ordinating your marketing strategy stances

> 'It is not from the benevolence of the butcher, the brewer, or the baker, that we expect our dinner, but from their regard to their own interest. We address ourselves, not to their humanity but to their self-love, and never talk to them of our necessities but of their advantages.'
>
> *Adam Smith (1723–1790), Scottish moral philosopher and political economist*

This section is much smaller than the previous strategy section, but nevertheless important.

The SCORPIO approach to marketing strategy seems, at least by number of pages, to be deep and complicated. In fact it is neither. I should carry no additional information, it is *not a new model* but an 'aide-memoire' that supports the busy practitioner, and does not give him or her lots more to learn.

Nevertheless, I thought it prudent to add a short section on co-ordinating the elements of the SCORPIO approach, so that you can break down the process into bite-sized pieces.

In this part, we will look at creating the building blocks of good marketing strategy.

- This third section will look at:
  - What makes 'good' marketing strategy?
  - How to plan with SCORPIO?
  - What is the minimum SCORPIO?
  - What is the defensive SCORPIO?
  - What is the offensive SCORPIO?

CHAPTER 12

Co-ordinating your marketing strategy

> '[I am] opposed to the laying down of rules or conditions to be observed in the construction of bridges lest the progress of improvement tomorrow might be embarrassed or shackled by recording or registering as law the prejudices or errors of today'
>
> *Isambard Kingdom Brunel (1806–1859), Engineer, Creator of Great Western Railway and other significant works*

MARGIN NOTES

Now that we have covered all the individual components of marketing strategy, in this short section I intend to look at what makes 'good' marketing strategy, and how to manipulate SCORPIO to get great results.

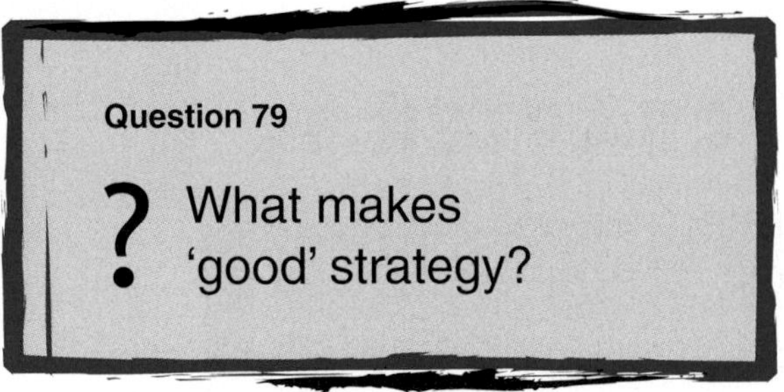
Question 79
?
What makes
'good' strategy?

Looking at the options for 'good' marketing strategy is interesting. Culling some ideas from various sources, we soon have a long list:

- Market dominance:
  - Leader
  - Challenger
  - Follower
  - Nicher
- Porter's generic strategies:
  - Cost leadership
  - Product differentiation
  - Market segmentation
- Treacy and Wiersema's excellence strategies:
  - Product leadership
  - Management efficiency
  - Customer intimacy

- Innovation strategies:
  - Pioneers
  - Close followers
  - Late followers
- Growth strategies:
  - Horizontal integration
  - Vertical integration
  - Diversification (or conglomeration)
  - Intensification
- Aggressiveness strategies: (1)
  - Building
  - Holding
  - Harvesting
- Aggressiveness strategies: (2)
  - Prospector
  - Analyser
  - Defender
  - Reactor
- Warfare-based strategies:
  - Offensive marketing warfare strategies
  - Defensive marketing warfare strategies
  - Flanking marketing warfare strategies
  - Guerrilla marketing warfare strategies.

All make good books but leave some basics unattended.

What makes a 'good' strategy depends entirely on what the strategy is intended to do. The manager is faced with three separate but related questions:

- What objective(s) was the strategy (originally) designed to achieve?
- What choice criteria should be used?
- How can we evaluate alternative options that appear to be open to the organisation?

MARGIN NOTES

A word on the time scale

The word is, long. Strategy is not the same as tactics and should not be treated as such.

If marketing strategy is about the long-term success of the organisation, its success or failure must be measured by procedures that take into account this long-term view. The choice of evaluation methods is critical because quickly they can become the *raison d'être* for the organisation's activities and we have to be careful that the evaluation methods are aimed at assessing how well the intended strategies will achieve set objectives (may be difficult to measure) and not how well they will meet current sales or revenue targets (probably easier to measure).

■ A word on financial versus non-financial measurement

There is far too little debate about the difference between those measures which assess *efficiency* and those which assess *effectiveness*.

MARGIN NOTES

- Efficiency:
  - Defined as 'doing things right'
  - The most common in business
  - Tend to evaluate, often on an ongoing basis, the efficiency or precision with which actions are carried out by the organisation
  - Are mostly internal measures
  - The majority of financial and accountant-driven measures also fall into this category.

- Effectiveness:
  - Is defined as 'doing the right things'
  - Are less common business measures
  - Are concerned with how well the organisation is doing the right things – how well the organisation is meeting its paying customers' needs
  - Are mostly external measures.

Most of the traditional financial measures we all know concentrate on some notion of 'return' – they will include:

- Profit
  - Profit is essential to any business but is not the only reason why we are here (see Chapter 1)
  - Evaluation and appraisal processes which rely exclusively on profitability can overshadow the fact that the only way we make profits is by satisfying customers

- Profitability

- Shareholder return

- Cash flow/liquidity

- Share price

- Earnings per share
- EBITDA
- Return on net assets
- Return on sales.

Of course, liquidity/cash flow evaluation is essential. Cash flow problems can even eliminate companies with a rising order book. Despite everything we have said about strategy, without cash there is no longer term. However, the laws of physics apply to all activities, even financial returns:

- Financial returns can only be created by sales revenue
  - Customers recognising and purchasing value
- Short-term returns above the average often have to be paid for in the long term.
- When profits continue while sales and customers are disappearing a company is simply taking value from its brand
  - The brand value exists off balance sheet
  - This is called 'mortgaging the future'
- Strangely enough, stock markets and investors don't seem to worry about long-term returns as much as the short-term human nature?

The non-financial measures of performance tend to measure effectiveness rather than efficiency although not exclusively so.

- Non-financial measures may include:
  - Market share
  - Growth
  - Competitive advantage
  - Competitive position
  - Sales volume
  - Market penetration levels
  - New product development
  - Customer satisfaction
  - Customer retention
  - Customer franchise
  - Market image and awareness levels.

Bear in mind though, there are caveats:

- First, that any one of these measures taken in isolation is unlikely to be sufficient to guarantee the long-term survival and development of the organisation.

MARGIN NOTES

- Second, growth is always a good thing.
  - The growth aspect to strategy is very much a development of the heydays of the 1970s and remains dangerously unquestioned in most texts.
  - Certainly the organisation must *develop* if it is to continue to adapt and remain in touch with its marketplace. But growth?
  - Growth of what?
  - Growth can be a good and healthy influence but if pursued for its own sake can lead to problems.
  - Sales maximisation and volume growth can often lead to serious declines in profitability especially in highly competitive marketplaces.
  - Directed and controlled growth based on a qualified and detailed analysis of the marketplace and potential business opportunities can lead to a flourishing organisation.
  - As author Ed Abbey has noted: "growth for the sake of growth is the ideology of the cancer cell".

MARGIN NOTES

In almost every situation the dependence upon a *single* criterion for evaluating and appraising strategy is likely to be dangerous.

- Organisations behave ineffectively from some points of view if a single criterion is used.

- Organisations fulfil multiple functions and have multiple goals, some of which may be in conflict. It would be inappropriate to assess market strategy purely on the basis of any one criterion.

How can we make sure that we are choosing *the right criterion* against which to evaluate our longer-term market strategy? Although you should always treat these models with great care, some indications might come from:

- Product life cycle
  - What is our organisation's position on this cycle?
  - Whether we consider this cycle applicable for the organisation, the industry, the product or service category or even the particular brand it might help us to select those criteria which are of most relevance in the situation at hand.

- Boston Consulting Group (BCG) Matrix
  - There is much debate about the continuing validity of the Boston matrix, and much care must be taken in its use.
  - It can still be useful for conceptually placing products or businesses in the overall organisation's portfolio.
  - Different forms of evaluation need to take place depending on the market and business situation of the product or the business considered. For example:

- 'Dog' products or businesses need to be measured according to the net free cash flow that they generate
- 'Question marks' are best evaluated by the sales volume and revenue that they are able to generate in their particular market situation
- 'Stars' are best evaluated by an assessment of net present value
- 'Cash cows' need to be assessed, evaluated and managed to generate the maximum return on investment.

- GEC/McKinsey matrix (and similar portfolio models)
  - This can also be used, with a little common sense, to ensure that we are measuring strategies within a sensible context of the business conditions that the company faces.
  - The common use of a standard set of criteria to assess any strategic option is both naïve and dangerous.
  - Of course, that is what analysts do all the time.

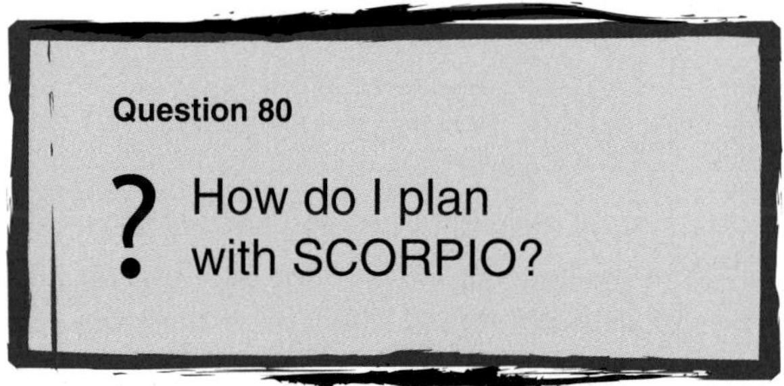
Question 80
?
How do I plan
with SCORPIO?

MARGIN NOTES

Effectively, SCORPIO becomes the template for your organisation's strategic market plans, ultimately you should be able to plot:

- Where you are on each SCORPIO dimension
- Where you need to be
- How to get there by actions on each SCORPIO dimension.

Every organisation and every market and brand position is unique. It follows then that no two organisations will need to approach SCORPIO in exactly the same way.

- Depending on a number of factors, your own blend of SCORPIO will constitute your market strategy for the future.
- Consequently, it will be extremely unlikely that you will need to go into the full depth on all of the seven elements but on those one or two that you really need to dig quite deeply I hope I will have allowed you the data to carry out your search.
- For the other areas where you don't need to dig so deeply you need only skim the information to assess how well you are doing versus the competition.

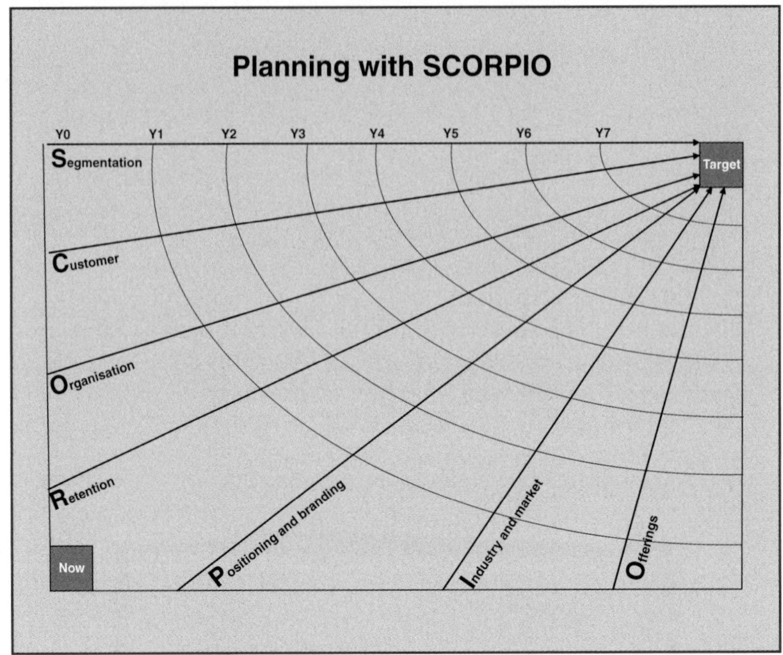

MARGIN NOTES

The process of market planning and marketing plans has been described at some length – and in some detail – in a number of specific and specialised marketing texts, so I shall not repeat their efforts here, beyond offering an example of my own marketing plans template (template means that it is a pro-forma, that always gets modified) for you to try (see Appendix).

This (unsurprising) process is the traditional approach of sequential thinking that proceeds step by step with back steps as we adapt through learning.

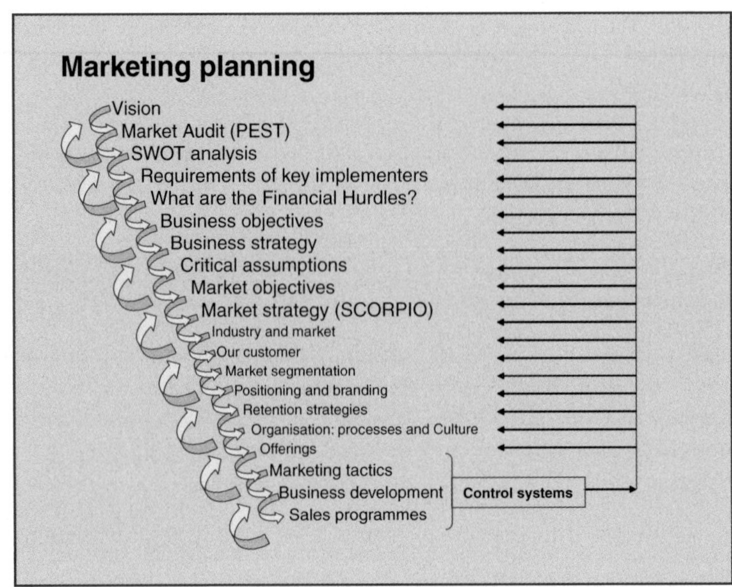

From the strategy perspective, the marketing planning process fills the gap between the strategic process and specific, market or segment-based activities.

The marketing planning headlines are:

- The marketing strategy process is concerned with taking various elements of it into a strategic marketing mix.
  - The strategic marketing mix can also be seen as a set of interrelated sub-objectives which are passed down to the relevant marketing function to be turned into more detailed operational plans, with a small number of strategic control levers maintained by the strategy manager or team to control implementation.
  - It is these later detailed plans, when combined, which form the basis of the organisation's marketing plans.

- There is one final aspect which marketing strategy *must* bring to the marketing plans – an effective and functioning control system.
  - The only true test of the marketing strategy is marketplace response – the final verdict always lies with the customer.
  - A marketing control system is essential if the organisation, and its market strategy, is to be validated by real, unbiased market response.
  - Essentially, the control system will detail the controls that will be applied to monitor the progress of the marketing plans and their success (or otherwise) in achieving the market objectives/key performance indicators.
  - Often, market control systems tend to be spelled out in budgets and budgeting terms.
    - Product, pricing, distribution and other objectives will have been broken down, on a monthly basis, and transformed into a set of targets.
    - These subsidiary targets are merely surrogates for sales turnover and (sometimes for) profit and profitability.
    - Few control systems even mention profitability (I have found none that mention Customer Value) let alone relate profitability to the various marketing activities.
  - The ideal control system will contain some element of contingency planning.
    - A contingency plan is an outline plan for additional or alternate activity which management would initiate if specific correctional activity were required.
    - The idea behind contingency planning is to encourage managers to think forward through some of the difficulties which might arise in the marketplace.
    - It encourages pre-planning in case the marketing strategy and plans don't operate like clockwork.

MARGIN NOTES

- Because of the fundamental inter-connectedness of the SCORPIO elements, contingency planning of this sort should not be restricted purely to implementation activity.
- The effects of such contingency plans on other areas of the organisation, human resource, finance and operations, must not only be communicated to other functions, but their active help in developing contingency plans must be sought.
- If this is not done, then contingency planning is purely an exercise to keep the strategy team quiet – it should be much more than that if it is to be taken seriously.

- The last comment to be made on marketing control systems is the use to which they are put.
  - Control systems should be seen as a method of improving performance, not a way of identifying and punishing under-achievers.
  - Some organisations even prohibit the development of marketing control systems in their market plan in the belief that this is defeatist thinking and that it will – of itself – produce plans that are bound to fail.
    - Frankly, it is very difficult to know how to respond to this type of organisation, apart from saying that it is completely wrong.
    - This thinking is symptomatic of an organisation that believes market strategy and implementation is a science that can be practised and controlled according to well understood rules.
  - Unfortunately (or fortunately?), customers remain unpredictable.
  - Market control systems and contingency planning are essential tools.
  - Never leave home without them.

MARGIN NOTES

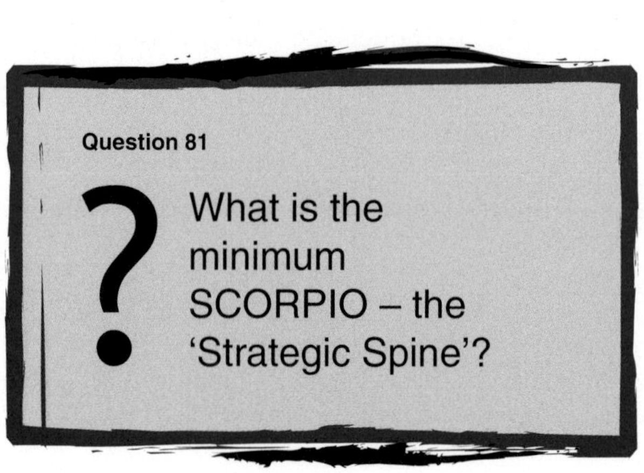

Question 81
?
What is the minimum SCORPIO – the 'Strategic Spine'?

In case it just seems 'all too much', I have spent some time working out how we can deal with the SCORPIO approach, but in bite-sized pieces.

Working with a client we have produced the divisions I was looking for:

- The 'strategic spine'
- The 'defensive strategy'
- The 'offensive strategy'.

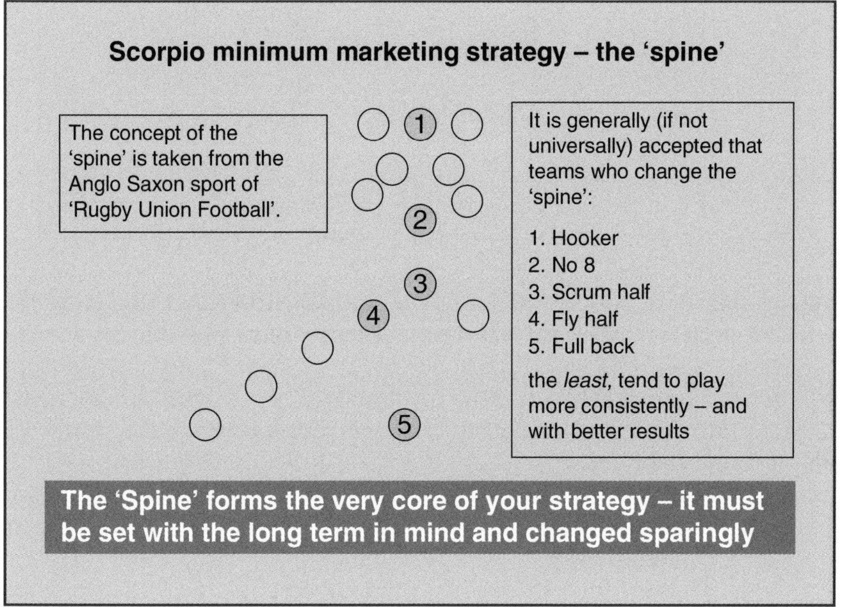

Scorpio minimum marketing strategy – the 'spine'
The concept of the 'spine' is taken from the Anglo Saxon sport of 'Rugby Union Football'.
1
2
3
4
5
It is generally (if not universally) accepted that teams who change the 'spine':
1. Hooker
2. No 8
3. Scrum half
4. Fly half
5. Full back
the *least*, tend to play more consistently – and with better results
The 'Spine' forms the very core of your strategy – it must be set with the long term in mind and changed sparingly

MARGIN NOTES

First, the 'strategic spine' was taken, I must admit, from the only sport that I follow, Rugby Union. An analysis of the six Nations tournament in 2006 (the year before the World Cup) stated that the reason why the French team had performed so well was down to stability and minimum changes – in the key areas of the team described as the 'spine'.

In the case of rugby, the 'spine' positions were:

- Hooker
- No 8
- Scrum Half
- Fly Half
- Full Back

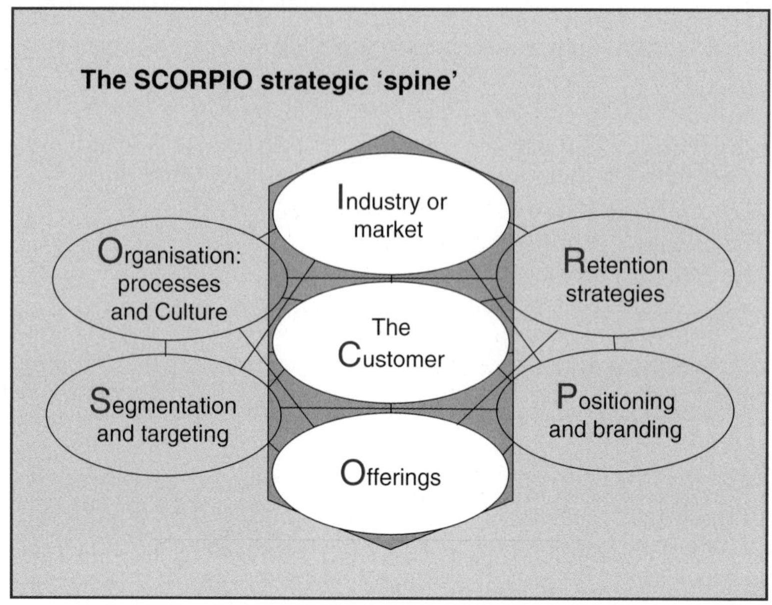

MARGIN NOTES

Taking this lead, the key elements of the SCORPIO that you must set with the long term in mind – and changed as little as possible, are:

- Industry or market
  - What business are you in, and what business should you or do you need to be in?
  - This key question is *fundamental* for any serious strategy, because
    - It determines your (real) competition and keeps you aware to vulnerabilities
    - It determines the market to be segmented and which customers to serve
    - It determines your Customers' needs and identifies how you could differentiate your offer
    - It determines your strategic threats and opportunities
    - It determines directions for growth and for effort
    - It determines your organisation's processes and culture (that will deliver customer value – and those that won't).

- The customer
  - By now (Chapter 12) it should go without saying that understanding your customer is key to any sort of marketing strategy.
  - At the very least, you *must* know
    - Who they are
    - What they currently buy from you (benefits or a job to be done) and why
    - What benefits they are seeking (and maybe not receiving yet)
    - What they want from us – and they might want in the future
    - The barriers that are getting in the way.

- Offerings
  - Once (and only once) you have understood
    - What business you are in and
    - Who your customers are and what they want from you
  - Then you can start to create the offerings that will deliver real customer value
  - To be clear – developing offerings (products and services) that aren't preceded by understanding your business and your customers, *is not marketing, it is called selling*
  - If you are intent on marketing to your customers, you need to
    - Agree and write as many value propositions as required to control implementation
    - Agree the most appropriate business design to extract value from the market
    - Have a programme of new offerings that will arrive as value migrates in your marketplace
    - Manage the life cycle to maximise (at the same time);
      - Customer value
      - Competitor discomfort
    - Have a clear plan for taking your offerings to market in the most customer-convenient fashion.

MARGIN NOTES

To re-cap:

- These are the minimum steps you need to have for a marketing strategy
- The steps must be co-ordinated carefully
- The steps in the spine, should be changed the least.

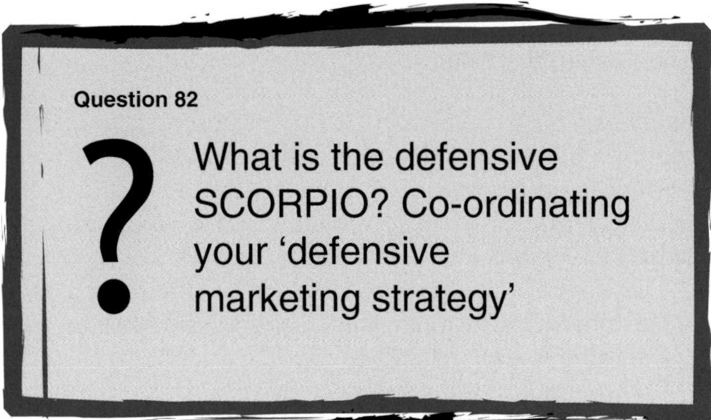

Question 82
?
What is the defensive SCORPIO? Co-ordinating your 'defensive marketing strategy'

Defensive strategy is not a game for the faint hearted; it has its place and must be managed carefully. I remember (years ago) talking to a major high street bank about how they rewarded their managers. The banking system had just emerged from tough regulation and wanted to flex their muscles, unfortunately that led to years of selling rather than marketing but that is another story. To demonstrate their new macho nature they decided to bonus all new business (loans, mortgages, etc.) – but nobody thought to worry about redemptions (paid off loans, mortgages, etc.). All 'offence' with no 'defence' means *no progress.*

MARGIN NOTES

The key elements of the SCORPIO that you must set with defence in mind are:

- Industry or market
  - Central to the defensive strategy because we need to understand how the customer sees us and sees our actions
  - Details covered above.

- The customer
  - Without a deep understanding of the customer we have no hope of defending ourselves.
  - Ultimately, any defence must be about not losing customers, this can be subdivided:
    - Customers move to competitor who's offer is seen as better.
    - Customers move to a cheaper offering because they don't see the value in your offering.
    - Customers leave the category because they no longer see relevance to their lives.
  - Details covered above.

- Organisation: processes and culture
  - The organisation only survives as long as it delivers value to customers

- Customers, by exchanging money for solutions are the only source of revenue
- Customers pay everybody's salaries
- If the organisation does things that customers don't value, they will take their business elsewhere. A critical part of your defence strategy is to *make sure that all your hard work in attracting customers is not squandered by your organisation acting in an inappropriate way.*
- It seems reasonable therefore, to spend some time on making sure that your organisation understands what it has to do, and why. At the least, you need to know
  - Whether your organisation is focused on internal or external issues – understand what is driving behaviour?
  - What your organisation is really good at (core competencies) – and whether it matters to your customers (perceived customer value).
  - What is your organisation's culture?
    - The culture drives behaviours of your staff.
    - As long as these behaviours are valued by your customers you are OK – you can build new business and it will be kept by the organisation.
    - If the behaviours and the requirements of your customers start to diverge, you have a major defensive problem.
    - If the promises you make aren't met by the organisation, you will lose customers.
  - How well your organisation is joined up. If your processes are customer driven and customer managed you have a chance of delivering on your promises. If not ...
  - That your organisation collects the right information (current and future customer perceptions, needs and wants) – and that the information is driven to those who need it for their decisions.
  - That the metrics which are used to manage and drive your organisation are creating the values and behaviours that customers want.
  - Change management happens, as regularly as required by the market.

- Retention
  - The second, important string to the defensive strategy is retention.
  - Acquiring new customers is fine, but can also be very expensive.
  - Investing in customer acquisition is excellent, but unless to make a return on the investment, you will lose money and go out of business.
  - Customers are expensive to acquire.
    - The longer they stay (repeat business) the more profitable they will become.
    - If they leave before you have recover the cost of acquiring them they will make a loss.

MARGIN NOTES

- Retention must be planned – it is not sufficient just to *hope* that they will come back while counting the commission you made on the sale!
- At the least, you need to know
    - How important 'Retention' is in your business
        - How much you invest on acquiring each new customer
        - How long the customer must stay to break even
        - How much profit you will make for every week/month/year you keep the customer beyond that.
    - Retention is not just about customer satisfaction, it is about *commitment* to come back.
        - Make sure you measure the right thing
        - Invest in a Marketing Information Systems that delivers *usable* information.
    - Your accounting and reporting systems may be getting in the way of retaining customers. If it is stopping you making the necessary investments in your customers:
        - You need to establish the strategic role of your customer relationships
        - Establish the concept of *lifetime value* of customers
        - Establish and act in a way that recognises that your customers are your most important business asset – and need to be managed accordingly.

MARGIN NOTES

To re-cap:

- These are the defensive steps you need to have in place if your investment in marketing strategy is not to be put at risk
- Defence is the first stage of growth
- *"The transition from the defensive to the offensive is one of the most delicate operations in war."* Napoleon Bonaparte, Emperor of the French.

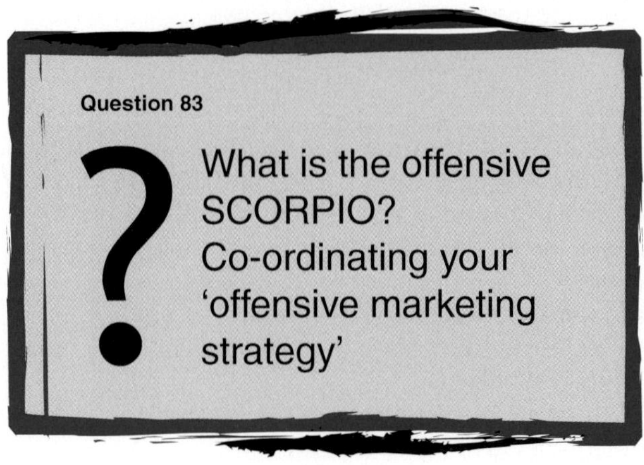

Question 83
?
What is the offensive SCORPIO?
Co-ordinating your 'offensive marketing strategy'

But, you cannot spend your life worrying about looking after what you have, sometimes you just need to go and get some more. As the proverb has it, "Attack is the best form of defence". Sometimes nothing else will do ...

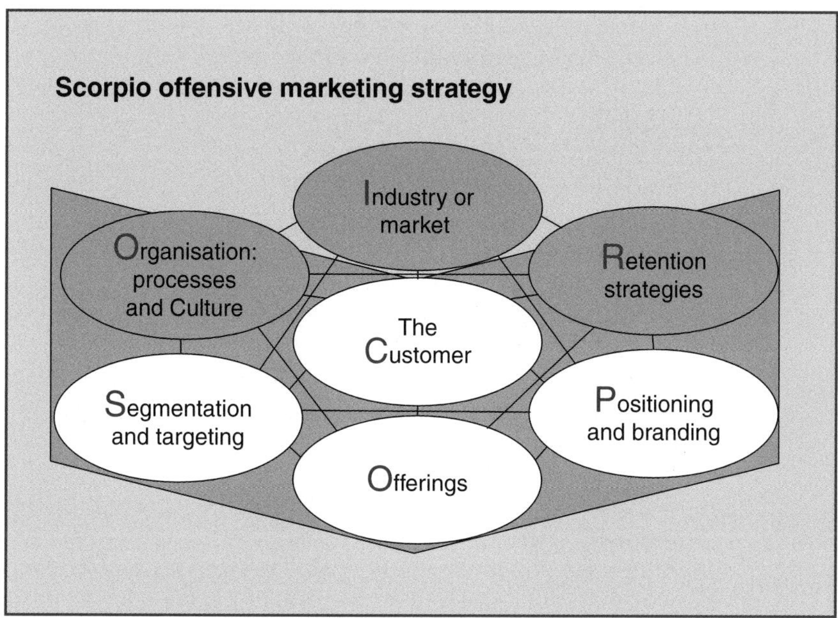

MARGIN NOTES

The key elements of the SCORPIO that you must set with offence in mind are:

- The customer
  - Customers are essential for the offensive strategy:
    - More customers who buy more or pay more are normally the minimum for growth
    - Customers are unlikely to do any of these things unless they can see something in it for them
  - Details covered above.

- Offerings
  - Customers will buy into offerings that (*they believe will*) deliver customer value
  - Discovering what customer value is – and then delivering on it is not easy
  - Details covered above

- Segmentation and targeting
  - Segmentation takes your marketing strategy to a new level of competitiveness
  - Segmentation allows you to exit the so called *level playing field* and 'tilt' the table in your favour

- You can set objectives for segments (dominate, control, lead) that are impossible in the wider, undifferentiated, more competitive marketplace
- To achieve this, you must (through research, not just guessed) know
  - How your organisation currently 'segments' the market. It may not be correct, it may not be pretty but it is an open door
  - What you want segmentation to do for you, it can
    - Make your communications more effective and more efficient
    - Reduce wastage in your marketing spend
    - Avoid price and other competition
    - Allow you to be different
    - Allow you to create loyal customers and defensible business propositions
    - Be the first step in building a brand.
  - What segments exist in your target market; the market 'is'-look for the natural segments, don't try to manufacture them for internal convenience.
  - Which segment (or segments if you are very good) you should focus on and make your own
    - Segments will have to be prioritised and the most attractive targeted
    - Internally, you must win the value versus volume debate.
  - How to market to different segments if you have selected more than one target.

MARGIN NOTES

- Positioning and branding
  - Branding and positioning (only if linked to identified market segments), can create the greatest store of value for your organisation.
  - Brand value is calculated in a number of different ways but always *exists over and above* net asset value.
  - But, brands aren't easily created, nor are they created fast.
  - Where *names* are important, *brands* include a set of consistent meanings which exist in addition to the product or service offering.
  - If you hope to create profitable brands, you will need to know:
    - Whether your organisation is really prepared to differentiate its offerings or whether it would prefer to play the 'commodity' marketing game. If everyone is not prepared to play the full game, don't start.
    - If there is a willingness (better a need) to be different, how are you going to be different?
    - What market positions exist in your target market. There will be as many positions as the customers deem credible.
    - What market position you own at the moment.
      - Customers will tell you.
      - If you don't like it, you will have to change it.
      - Then you must have a clear idea what market position(s) you want to own in the future.

- The unique 'values' and 'personality' of your brand must be agreed and driven into the market – and your organization.
- Finally, everyone in your organisation needs to know (and be committed to) investing in the brand every year, year-in-year-out. Branding is not a quick fix or a tactical solution – it is a strategic activity with strategic returns.

MARGIN NOTES

To re-cap:

- These are the offensive steps you need to consider if you want to achieve more than ordinary or 'normal' returns on your investments.
- If you want higher profits, you will have to be different from everyone else – in ways that customers value.
- That means driving for special segments with unique, branded solutions.

The strategic questions (79–83)

This section is not about SCORPIO, as much as what you should be doing with it.

I have tried to look at SCORPIO from a simpler viewpoint and it seems to me that the 'generic' strategies make understanding easier – and so helps implementation more structured.

And the questions. This time they are more straightforward, although the additional discipline of looking at Spine. Defensive and Offensive may not be easy for some. Nevertheless …

No.	Strategic question	Our strategic answer	Importance	✓
	Part Three: Co-ordinating your marketing strategy stances			
79	What makes 'good' strategy?		Must have	
			Nice to have	
			Not important	
80	How do I plan with SCORPIO?		Must have	
			Nice to have	
			Not important	

81	What is the minimum SCORPIO – the 'strategic spine'?		Must have	
			Nice to have	
			Not important	
82	What is the defensive SCORPIO? Co-ordinating your 'defensive marketing strategy'		Must have	
			Nice to have	
			Not important	
83	What is the offensive SCORPIO? Co-ordinating your 'offensive marketing strategy'		Must have	
			Nice to have	
			Not important	

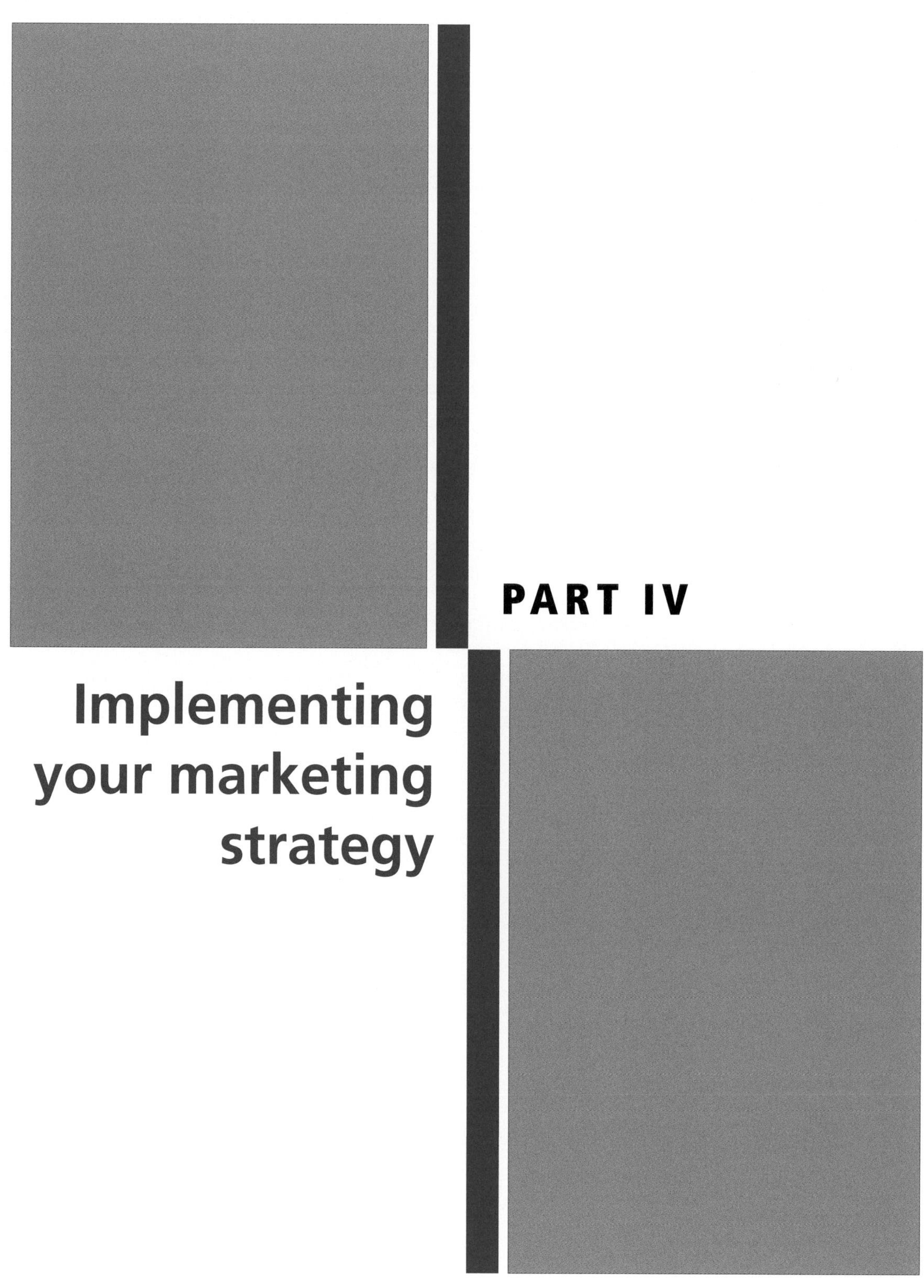

PART IV

Implementing your marketing strategy

> 'However beautiful the strategy, you should occasionally look at the results.'
>
> *Sir Winston Churchill (1874–1965), British Statesman*

This section is much smaller than the previous strategy sections, but strategy was always the main reason for the book.

However, to write a book on strategy, without worrying about implementation would be at best remiss and, at worse, negligent.

- This final section will look at:
  - How do we implement the strategy, and turn our thinking into action?
  - The most important elements of the marketing mix and how to control implementation of
    - Product policy
    - Pricing policy
    - Place/distribution policy
    - Promotion policy
  - The 'Very Important Tactics' that are around at the moment and whether they need to treated strategically or not.

CHAPTER 13

Making it happen

> 'An ounce of performance is worth pounds of promises.'
>
> *Mae West (1893–1980)*
> *American actress, playwright,*
> *screenwriter, and sex symbol*

How, exactly do we make it happen?

Planning and strategy are important but, without implementation, it is a pointless and expensive exercise which will probably take the organisation backwards rather than forward.

But we should be clear; 'implementation' is NOT the same as 'tactics. This section is not a shortened overview of marketing tactics – we aren't concerned with the short-lived intricacies of web analytics or the role of social networks on viral campaigns. Our concern here is solely how to move our longer term plans into action. Possibly against the wishes of some other functions in the organisation – sometimes against the marketing tacticians too…

MARGIN NOTES

You may be involved with implementation directly or you may not. All that matters is that what you planned to happen – happens. This may not be as easy as you think.

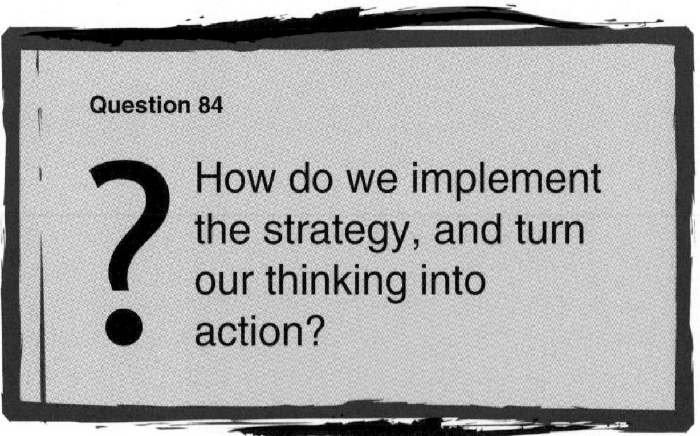

Question 84
?
How do we implement the strategy, and turn our thinking into action?

We are dealing with marketing – and marketing is all about customers. Any system based on customers will necessarily be volatile and difficult to predict accurately.

Before you become too depressed, the constantly changing place we call home can have a positive side too, we can use change as a driver for implementation. As we saw in Chapter 10, (if you have not read it yet, go there now) *implementation will depend entirely on the people in your organisation*. You might need some help in getting them to implement your strategy in the way you envisioned.

First, catch your wave ...

Let's look at what might be going on out there; maybe we can hitch a ride:

- Customer expectations:
  - Customers in all markets are now demanding the 'impossible' on a regular basis.
  - Customers are prepared to leave brands and organisations if these fail to provide what is wanted, when it is wanted, at what the customer sees as a reasonable price.
  - The explosion of choice means that customers don't have to put up with second best – loyalty has to be earned, it is not given as of right.
  - If others in the organisation are feeling these effects too, you may be able to use the 'discomfort' to implement change.
- Revenues:
  - And cash and profits are the life blood of any organisation.
  - Recessions drive deep spending cuts that make the thirst for revenues stronger.
  - Booming markets fuel the addiction so that organisations need more and more revenues.
  - Once the quick wins (cost cutting and financial manoeuvring) have wrung out all the spare revenues, the only source of further revenue and profit growth is now the *customer*.
  - Eventually all senior managers work out that to make more money, they will need more happy customers ...
  - Now, there's an open door worth pushing at
- Competition:
  - Not only is technology driving down entry barriers everywhere,
  - Markets are beginning to fragment in many and devious ways, and
  - Competition is intensifying in practically every business sector:
    - Existing players fighting to gain and retain customers
    - New entrants are often being attracted by more substantial profits than they can gain in their hard-pressed home markets.
  - Product and service offerings are proliferating and customers are now faced with a greater (confusing?) choice than in the past.
  - You could decide to compete on price – but if you would rather grow a profitable business;
    - The only way is to establish a clear and differentiated position in the market, and
    - Give customers good, simple and relevant reasons why they should come to them rather than the competition – the *Value Proposition.*
- Innovation:
  - Innovation for its own sake is unlikely to create additional *customer value.*
  - But innovation directed at supplying more relevant products to customers (more customer value) will.

MARGIN NOTES

- Innovation, like all other potential business 'saviours' is a dangerous path to travel:
  - Simply doing new things is unlikely to be enough
  - 'New' things could even be a way of hastening commercial suicide.
  - Too much innovation does no more than create more choice and complication in customers' lives.
- Clearly identified (existing and latent) customer needs and wants are the starting point for productive innovation.

- Cheap imports from China/India/and …
  - Are a good thing!
  - Organisations that have 'muddled through' for years must now either decide to change (finally become more customer focused) or try to compete on price with those 'unfair' costs of developing economies.
  - This is exactly what we need to put the customer back at the head of the list, and get organisations focused on delivering customer value not just more 'stuff'.

MARGIN NOTES

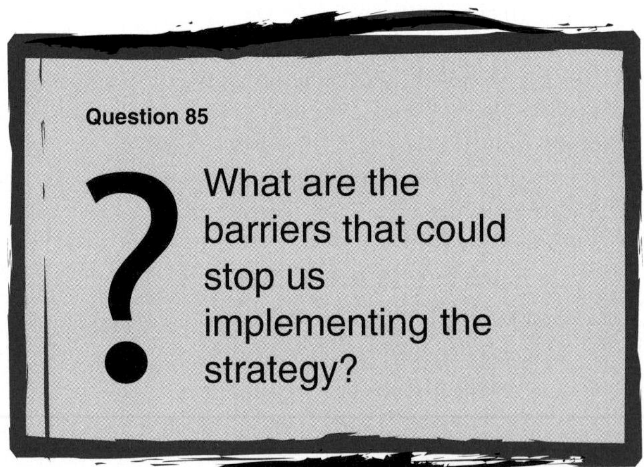

Question 85
?
What are the barriers that could stop us implementing the strategy?

From the positive- to what could be the negative. What are the barriers that are – or might – get in the way of putting your strategy into practice?

Some barriers can be avoided, others cannot. But ignoring them and being surprised is the least helpful (and least professional) alternative open.

There are many barriers that can stand in the way of successful implementation of marketing strategy, some evident, some not so.

- First, there are the external pressures on the organisation:
  - Social factors:
    - Changing demographic and social patterns, such as
      - Ageing population
      - Fewer school leavers
      - The migration to knowledge workers

    - Changes will affect plans that require implementation over the next five to ten years.
    - Structural changes such as environment, individualism and immigration need to be accounted for too.
- Legal factors:
    - More laws affect business, such as
        - Employment
        - Pay and price policies
        - Health and safety
        - Discrimination and diversity
        - Specific acts to control particular industries
    - European Union (EU) based laws.
- Economic factors:
    - Where will future European policy go – towards greater business freedom or greater control?
    - What other events might appear in your market?
        - Mergers
        - Joint ventures
        - Share price movement and investment
        - Trade union activities
        - Suppliers' actions
        - Changes to include vertical integration and disintermediation.
    - Distribution changes need to be assessed:
        - Distribution infrastructure
        - Transportation
        - Supply chain
        - Channel management and control
        - Internationalisation.
    - Competition itself is one of the most important factors to forecast in strategic implementation since no marketing strategy ever operates in a vacuum.
        - Direct (own industry or business) competition
        - Indirect/substitute competition from outside your traditional industry base
        - Competition is expected to increase in all sectors over the next 10 years driven primarily by the internationalisation of business, the fragmentation of many markets and the continued rise of China, India and eventually Africa.
- Political factors:
    - There is a general trend in most western markets for governments to take an increasingly active role in business and influencing competitive activity.
    - Whatever the intention behind political actions, the result is always some form of restriction over the organisation's activities and these restrictions need to be forecasted and attempts made to modify implementation of the strategic plan within this developing framework.

MARGIN NOTES

- Technological factors:
  - Technology has made radical change in manufacturing possible and has been a major catalyst in the recent proliferation of new products and services.
  - The application of modern technology has enabled small- and medium-sized organisations to operate at cost levels previously the exclusive preserve of much larger organisations.
  - Economies of scale are no longer the barriers they used to be.

- Second, the internal barriers that may affect your ability to turn plans into action:
  - Leadership:
    - Does top management buy in to the objectives and process?
    - Does the plan involve any form of significant change?
    - Unless strong leaders are 'bought in' to the vision and strategy completely, little progress is likely to be made.
  - Organisational culture and structure:
    - Implementation is a people process.
    - In an organisation with a non-customer/market culture, the chances of successfully implementing a true marketing strategy will be severely limited.
    - As today's markets become more and more competitive, the options are becoming clearer – change the culture or the organisation may not survive.
    - If the culture won't change, goals and strategies must be changed to something which the organisational culture can implement.
    - In many organisations the structure is designed for the convenience of those that work inside and is simply not able to deliver the proposed marketing strategy.
    - You just cannot design a marketing strategy without factoring in the organisation realities
    - Remember, an organisation is nothing without the people who work inside it.
  - Functional policies:
    - Most functions in an organisation (finance, operations, human resources, sales- and marketing) tend to operate according to their own idea of what constitutes 'best practice'.
    - If the intended marketing strategy contradicts these best practice processes, they could be blocked.
  - Resources:
    - Do you need significant resources to implement? Its not always necessary
    - Are these additional to existing spending?
    - Or, can to re-direct spending away from what was good use of resources in the past but is not now?
  - Evaluation and control procedures:
    - What gets measured; gets done.
    - Are you measuring the right things?

MARGIN NOTES

        - As long as the proper (appropriate) control measures are installed there need be no problems in implementation.

- Third, there are barriers that marketing sometimes puts in the way:
    - Marketing's interface with other functions:
        - Delivering satisfactions to customers may be the responsibility of the marketing function but it is not a job that marketing can carry out on its own.
        - Abrasive relationships may get in the way of implementation.
        - The role of tactical marketing will also affect implementation:
            - Is it mainly 'advertising and promotion?'
            - Or mainly sales support?
            - A catalyst for organisational change toward a more customer oriented position?
            - Used to identify, anticipate and satisfy customer needs profitably?
    - Market Research:
        - How well the strategy is implemented will depend on how much, how relevant and how good the information is and how well it is interpreted and acted upon.
        - Customer information is the marketing powerbase, although too few marketing professionals use it as such.

MARGIN NOTES

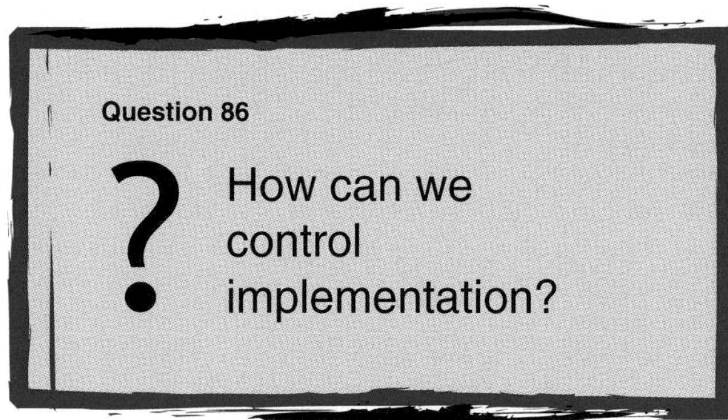
Question 86
?
How can we control implementation?

What gets measured gets done. If you don't measure the marketing strategy implementation, it won't get done

The Control systems 'headlines' are:

- Strategic decisions have long-term implications and organisational momentum has to be built over a planned period.
    - Constant change of strategy produces uncertainty, confusion, misdirection and wastage – not results.
    - Tactics are designed to change on a weekly or even a daily basis in response to changes in the marketplace, tactical change causes no problems of uncertainty as long as the strategy, the broad overall direction of the organisation, remains constant.

- Control systems which drive regular tactical changes to keep the strategy on course are a positive boon to any organisation.
  - But, if the control systems allow managers to make constant changes to strategy and direction, the organisation will end up achieving nothing and going nowhere.
- There are many and various different measures available and selecting the right method will depend upon:
  - The market you are addressing
  - The particular goals and objectives set
  - Your organisation structure, design and culture.
- Effective controls should be driven by the following principles:
  - Formality:
    - Firm rituals that are applied generally and in a standard manner
  - Necessity:
    - Should be seen as useful by the organisation and not just a ritualistic process
  - Priority:
    - To be concerned with those elements which the organisation *needs* to control, not with everything capable of control
  - Veracity:
    - Need to be data based, not based solely on intuition or subjective opinion
  - Regularity:
    - As regular as is affordable and useful depending on the activity measured and the dynamics of the market situation
- Control systems can become the reasons for the organisation's existence quite soon after their introduction:
  - Managers and staff focus on the achievement of agreed targets
  - Targets are often the primary focus of appraisals and rewards
  - Achievement of the tasks-behind-the-targets is rarely noted or measured
  - The reasons for the existence of the targets are rarely questioned.
  - In some organisations, the accepted behaviour (culture) is to exceed targets not just meet them.
  - There is often no thinking involved; it is just 'the way things are done around here'.

MARGIN NOTES

Selecting the 'right' control systems that will support the implementation of your marketing strategy is a matter of balancing four primary issues:

- Standard setting:
  - The goals and objectives which fall out of the business and marketing strategy process are translated into 'standards' that drive the organisation.
  - The standards will have been set within an understanding of what the organisation is currently able to deliver to its customers.
- Performance measurement and

- Reporting results:
  - Most discussion will centre on:
    - Which performances should be measured
    - How results should be reported.
  - The measurement activities of the planning achievements can be broken down into three broad areas:
    - *Quantity*: How much was achieved? How much should have been achieved?
    - *Quality*: How good was that which was achieved? How good was it meant to be?
    - *Cost*: How much did the achievement cost? How much was it planned to cost?
  - These basic parameters of the plan can then be quantified through an analysis of one or more of five distinct areas of operation which are:
    - Financial analysis
    - Market analysis
    - Sales and Distribution analysis
    - Physical Resources analysis
    - Human Resources analysis
  - Then, the three most common measures-also-used-as-reporting-tools are:
    - Audits:
      - The market audit can be used to monitor the successful implementation of marketing strategy.
      - All areas of marketing activity must be regularly monitored and their performance measured against pre-set standards.
    - Budgets:
      - Probably the most common form of control mechanism for marketing implementation as well as financial housekeeping.
      - Budgets tend to be short term, typically based on the annual plan for the achievement of that year's profit and turnover forecasts – these may not be relevant for the measurement and control of longer term strategy.
      - Beware – budgeting is not the same as management
        - Budgets are based on estimates rather than reality
        - Estimates are someone's idea of how the future will happen
        - When deviations from budgeted figures arise, you must ask:

          Are the deviations are significant?
          Do they require corrective action?
          But-how valid were the original estimates?
    - Variance analysis:
      - The detailed analysis of the variance (difference between actual and expected results) that arises from the organisation's activities.
      - Variances of a number of different items can be measured and assessed

MARGIN NOTES

- Typical variance measures will include
  - Sales price variance
  - Sales quantity variance
  - Sales volume variance
  - Profit variance
  - Market size variance
  - Market share variance
  - Whatever-you-want-to-measure-over-time variance.
- Whatever the method of analysis and evaluation is used, analysis on its own is not sufficient to monitor and implement market strategy properly.

- Taking corrective action:
  - Once any divergences or deviations from the estimated results have been highlighted, the task is to decide whether corrective action is required – and if so, how to implement this action in time to bring the plan back on target.
  - What is done, will depend on the reasons behind the variance.
    - Environmental changes:
      - If the environmental factors are thought to be temporary then a modification to the tactics can be considered.
      - If the external changes are judged to be fundamental or 'structural' then the organisation may need to revisit the original strategy and its objectives.
    - Internal problems:
      - If the variances are caused by internal problems, the organisation has to decide whether this is a shortfall in performance or is caused by active blockages in the organisation.
      - Corrective action must be directed at these points.
    - Faulty estimating:
      - If the original estimates were wrong, the organisation needs to re-estimate the rate at which it will achieve its strategic objectives.

MARGIN NOTES

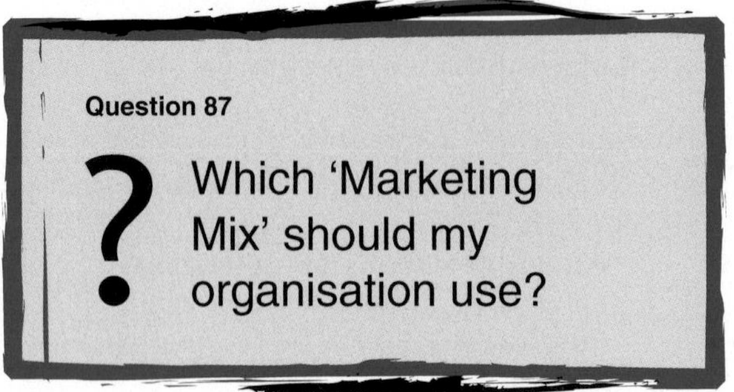

Question 87
?
Which 'Marketing Mix' should my organisation use?

Today, everyone is an expert; whether it is in packaging, supply chain, communications or just knowing who to talk to, everyone knows more and more-about less and less.

Everyone has heard of the marketing mix, most people know it's about lots of P's and some people can name them.

REFERENCING THE MARKETING MIX

1. Bordon, N.H., 'The concept of the marketing mix', in G. Schwartz (ed.) *Science in Marketing* (Wiley, Chichester, 1965), pp. 386–397.
2. McCarthy, E.J., *Basic Marketing* (Irwin, 1975).
3. Booms, B.H. and Bitner, M.J. 'Marketing strategy and organization structures for service firms' in J. Donnelly and W.R. George (eds) *Marketing of Services* (American Marketing Association, 1981).
4. Lauterborn, B. 'New marketing litany: Four Ps passé: C-words take over', *Advertising Age*, 61(41), 1990, 26.

MARGIN NOTES

Not enough people know that the most important word is *Mix* and the whole skill is in *blending* the ingredients to create differentiated customer value.

The history o the marketing mix and offers some insight regarding what we should be doing:

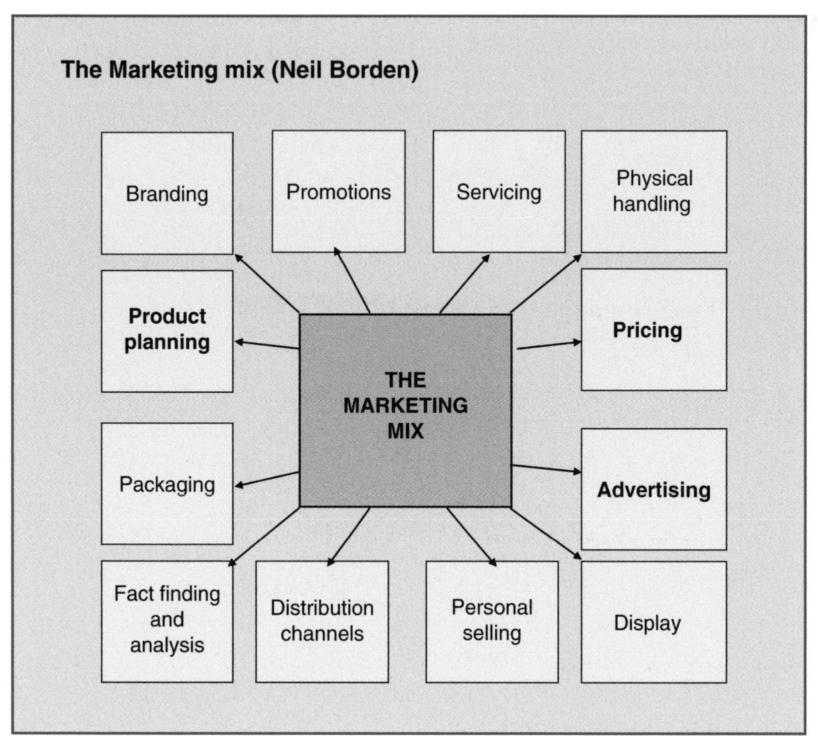

Borden's launched his original marketing mix in 1953 and included 12 elements – including the all important 'branding' which soon disappeared, never to re-surface in the mix.

The model focused on the 'mix' element, and it obviously reflected the concerns of the day – physical products marketing.

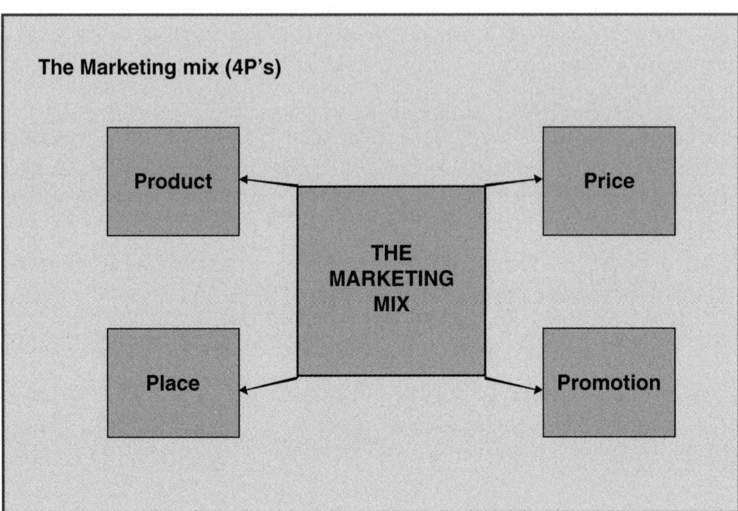

MARGIN NOTES

In 1975, McCarthy produced the famous 4Ps, which was meant to include all of Borden's elements but in a new, easy to remember format. In fact it was strongly simplified

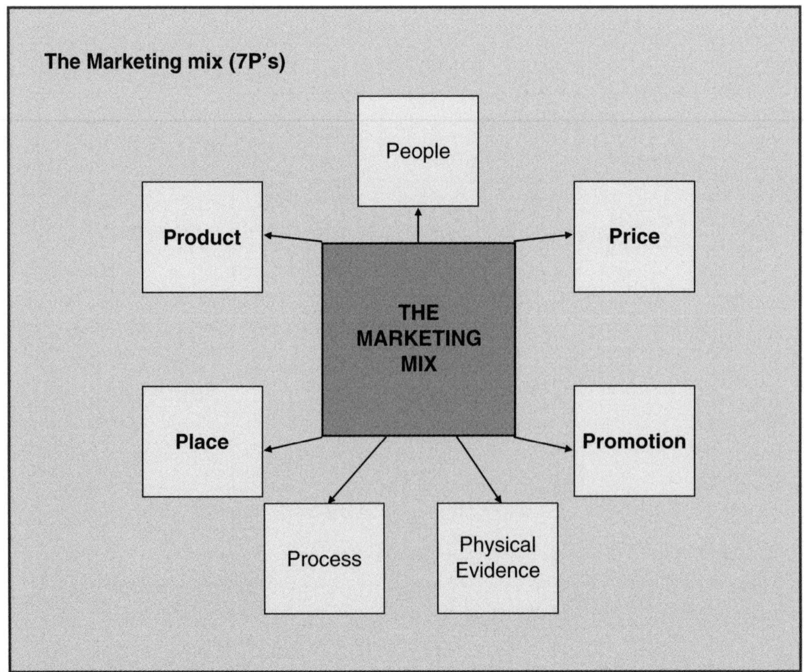

By 1981, everyone had recognised that services were overtaking products in importance and Booms and Bitner created the 7P's to allow for the different nature of services. The original 4P's were retained and 3 more added.

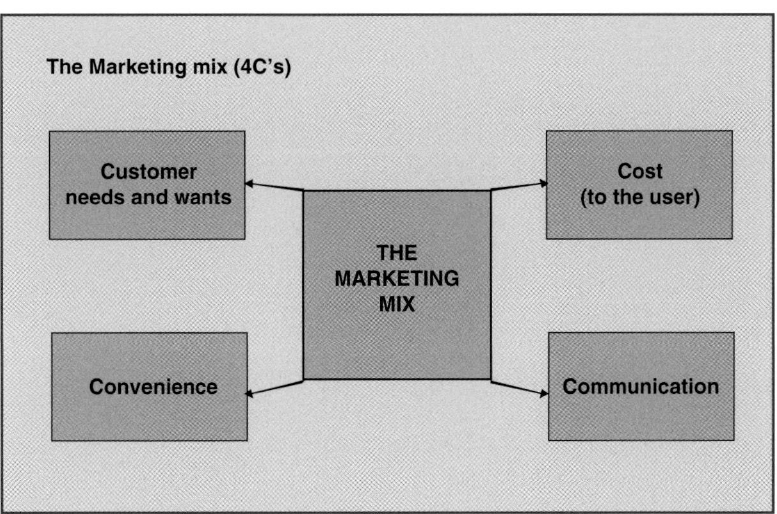

MARGIN NOTES

In 1990, Lauterborn responded to the idea that the marketing mix of the P's seemed to do something to the customer. Marketing was about putting the customer in charge so we should see things from the customer's perspective, not the supplier's. The 4C's was born – but never went anywhere.

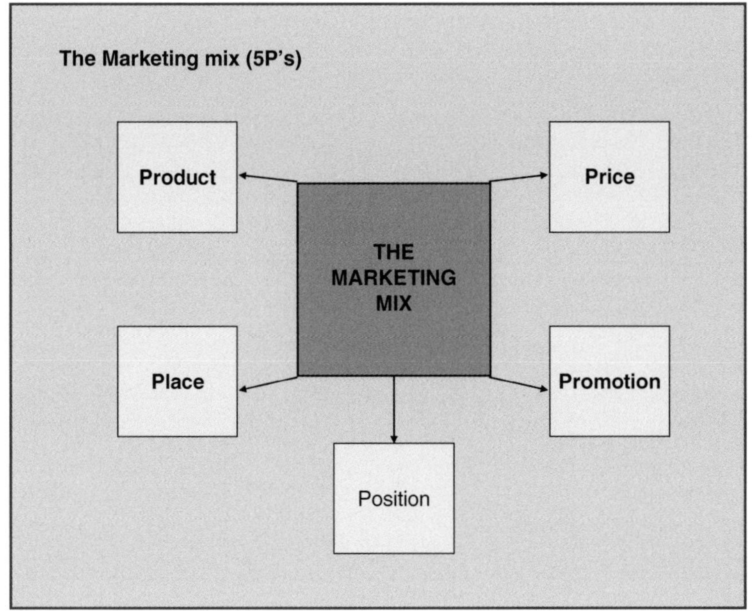

Nowadays, we can often see the 5P's. Take the original 4 and add something about position, branding and differentiation. Not a bad idea really.

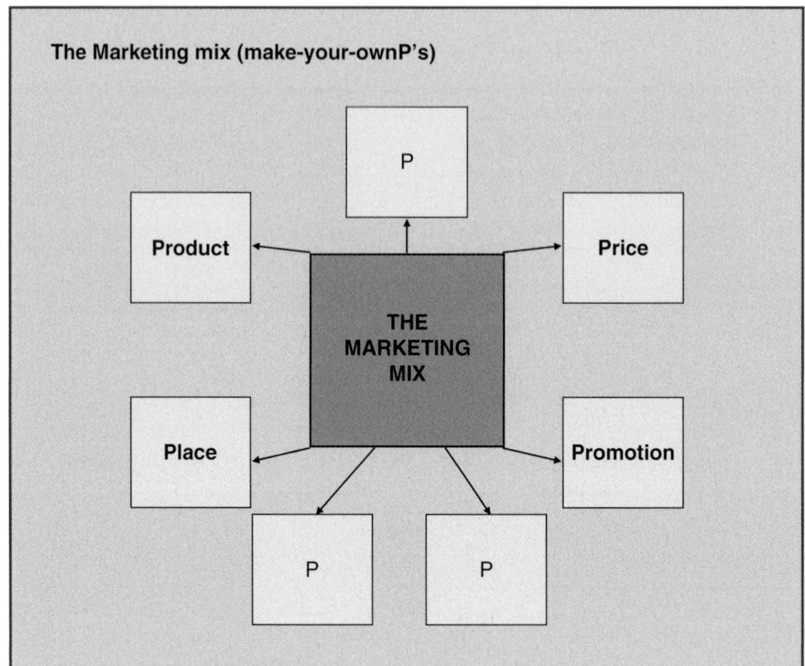

So what not make up your own mix? Decide on the elements that are most important for you and enjoy. Just make sure that everything starts with a P though, it would not do to break with tradition.

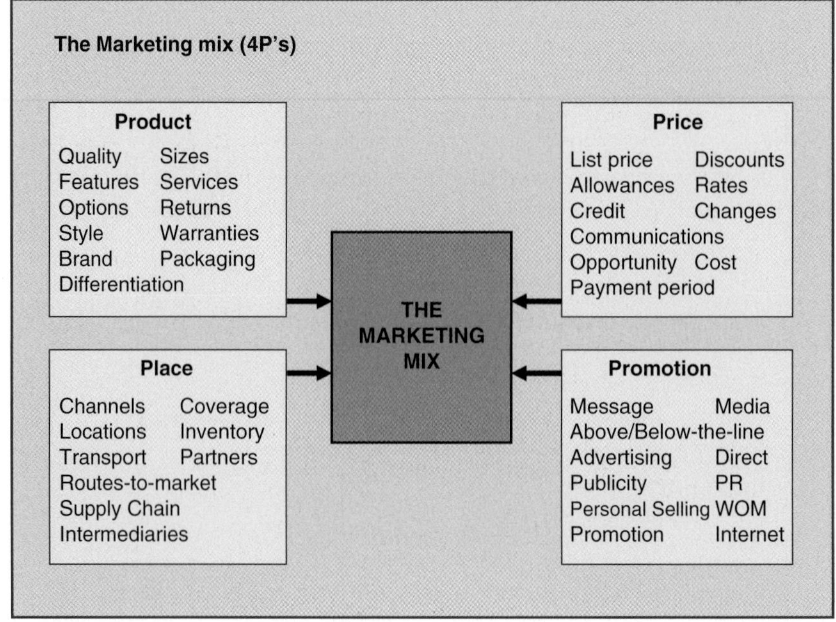

MARGIN NOTES

I still prefer the 4P's, not because it's better but because:

- Everybody has heard of it, even people who aren't 'in marketing' (they think!)
- The SCORPIO model covers the major omissions such as Customer and Branding
- Its easy and in all of the text books.

Using the 4P's approach, we will look, very briefly, at the key issues and questions that should concern you when implementing the marketing strategy.

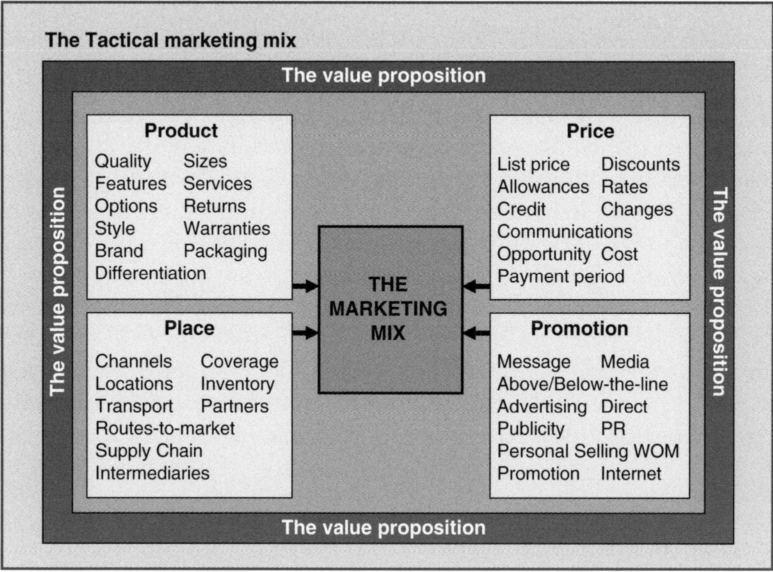

Lesson One – whichever marketing mix model you decide to use, make completely sure that it fits neatly within the Value Proposition(s) that you have generated and agreed within your organisation. Also make sure that everybody sees that the mix is driven by the Value Proposition, and nothing else.

Your Value Proposition is your most important control tool over implementation

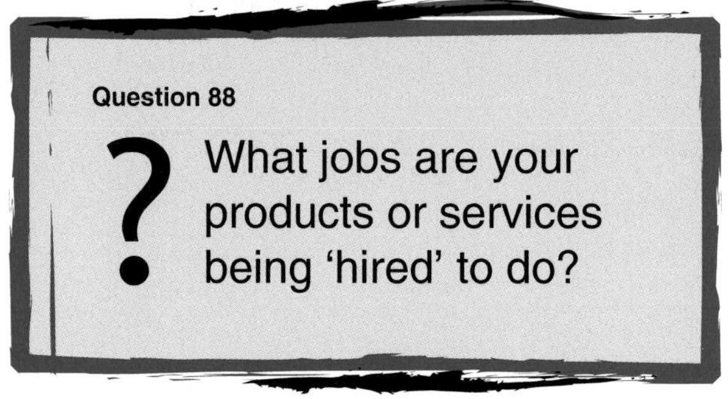

Question 88
?
What jobs are your products or services being 'hired' to do?

MARGIN NOTES

How can I break this to you? … Products and services are key to any organisation's survival and growth – but only as far and as long as they continue to deliver the solutions and benefits that the customers want from them.

At the risk of repeating myself, (Levitt can bear plenty of repetition) Levitt said 'Customers just need to get things done. When people find themselves needing to get a job done, they essentially hire products to do that job for them'. You will notice (I hope) that the emphasis here, at least from the customers' perspective, is on the *job* that needs to get done – not on the products that they may hire to get the job done.

This means that, over time, customers might just move from one product to another to get the same job done – but maybe better, cleaner, easier, faster, more environmentally – or whatever differential the customer or segment feels has additional value.

MARGIN NOTES

This in turn means that, no matter how good your product or service might be, if the customers believe that there is a better (they define 'better') way to '*get the job done*' then your organisation and its superior product or service is history. And don't for a moment think that it cannot happen to you. The pages of history are filled with organisations and industries that believed they were so important to their customers that they were 'indispensable' in day-to-day living. From agriculture to coal to steel to shipping to railroads to clothing manufacturers to flag-carrier airlines to who knows what next have been secure in the knowledge that they are the pinnacle of demand and life would be unthinkable if they no longer existed. But they exist no more.

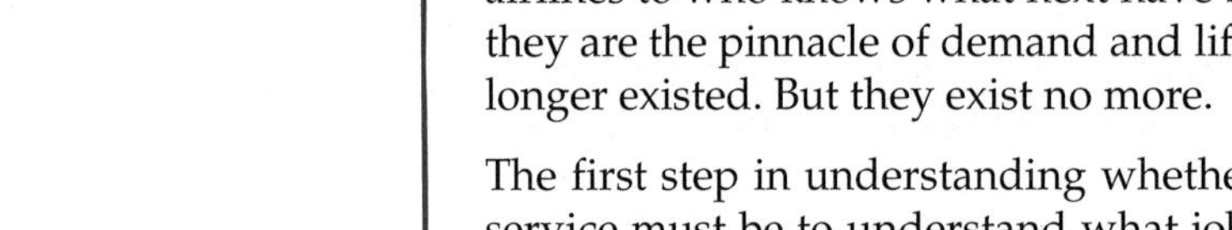

The first step in understanding whether you have the 'right' product or service must be to understand what jobs the customers are 'hiring' your product or service to do for them.

We covered this idea way back in Chapter 6 and it is simply critical for managing the implementation stage. There will necessarily be 'issues' when implementing and, as long as *what the product or service does* always triumphs over *what the product or service is*, then you have a chance of implementing according to plan.

The Product

4. Potential benefits
3. Augmented benefits
2. Expected benefits
1. Core functional benefits

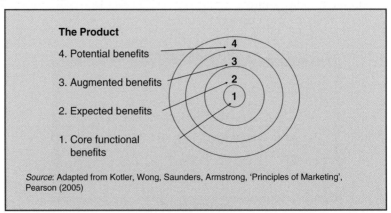

Source: Adapted from Kotler, Wong, Saunders, Armstrong, 'Principles of Marketing', Pearson (2005)

Getting to grips with what your product or service could be doing for your customers, you might consider Kotler's approach:

- Core functional benefits:
  - What is the product or service designed to do?
  - These are the basics (hygiene factors) that the product/service must deliver upon
  - For example, a car is expected to transport people (and luggage) from A to B in a certain way.

- Expected benefits:
  - What, in additional to the functional benefits, is your product or service expected to do
  - These are the additional benefits that the customer expects to receive simply because they are buying from you rather than an unknown product/service from an invisible source
  - For example, the car will also be expected to travel with safety and economy and last a fixed period between service or breakdown.

- Augmented benefits:
  - What benefits will your product or service offering on top of the 'hard' offers?
  - These benefits start to differentiate your offer and lift you product or service away from the 'noise' created by technically similar offerings.
  - For example, the car may also be expected to add to the owner's status or prestige.

- Potential benefits:
  - What else could your product or service offer, that the customer is either not yet aware of or doesn't yet expect from you
  - These benefits are the growth area-commodities yesterday, differentiated today, unique tomorrow – you need to specify the future benefits that your customers will expect in the future
  - For example, the car may be purchased to meet needs of a particular context or situation (see Chapter 7) and be a stylist work car. It may also be ideal for transporting family at weekends and holidays (in another Context).

Your job is *to specify the benefits that the customer requires* – how the product/service delivers these benefits is a tactical issue, what the benefits are (today – and then tomorrow) is a strategic one that you cannot abdicate.

See Chapter 6 (and Chapter 5 for what business you should be in) for more help here.

MARGIN NOTES

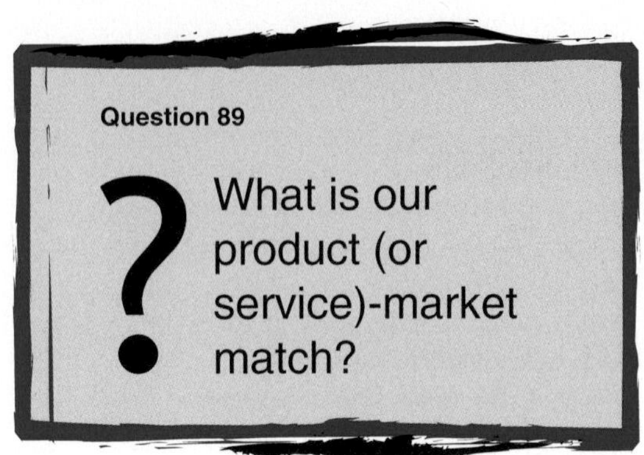

MARGIN NOTES

The absolute core of tactical marketing either you have a positive match between:

- What your target *customer needs and wants*, and
- What your product or service *does for them.*

Or you don't have a business

Amazingly, few businesses actually audit and monitor the effectiveness of this match.

Given that products and services change over time and, perceived customer value changes and migrates too, it is unlikely that the product/service-market match will remain solid for very long. If you don't monitor this regularly, the first you will hear of the

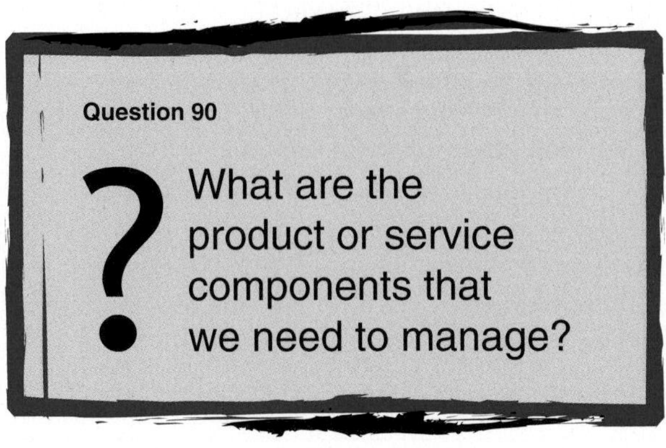

Question 90
?
What are the product or service components that we need to manage?

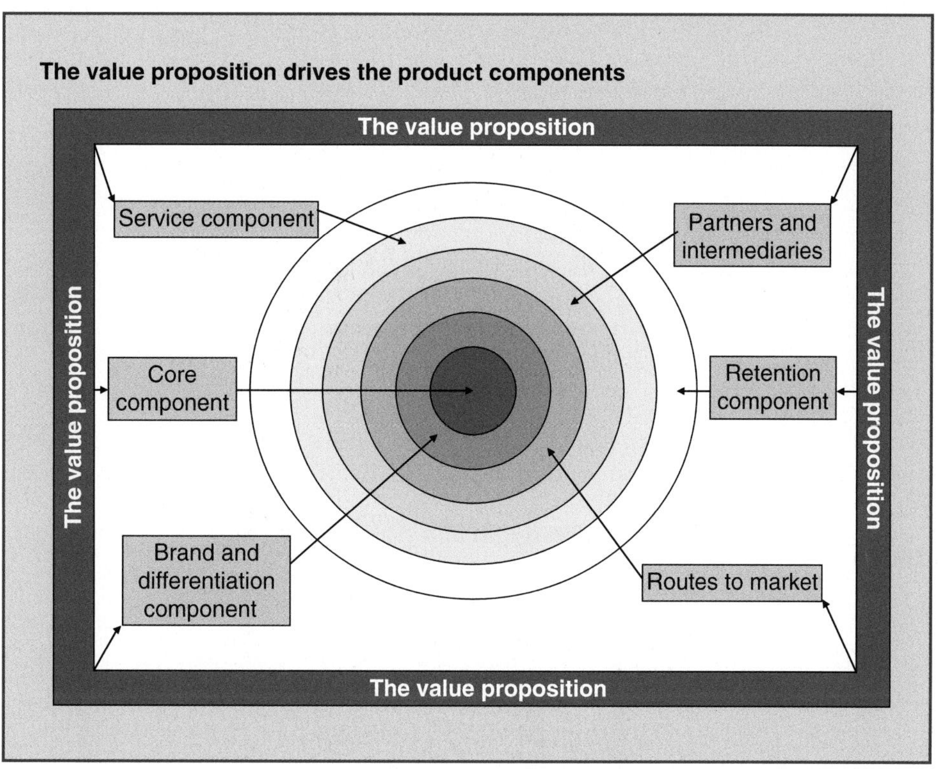

Your Customer Value Proposition (I hope you didn't jump that stage) will allow you to specify:

- The Core Component:
  - Specify the precise benefits that must flow from the product or service to maximise customer value.
  - Make sure that you monitor for changes over time.

- The Brand and Differentiation Component:
  - Specify the precise way that customers will perceive your offer.
  - Specify exactly how it is unique in the market, and what needs to be done to achieve that uniqueness.
  - Specify the brand's value and personality.
  - Specify things the brand *won't* be associated with.

- Routes-to-Market:
  - Specify how and where routes-to-market contributes to customer value.
  - Specify where and how routes-to-market can support and destroy brand.

- Partners and Intermediaries:
    - Specify how, where and when intermediaries and partners will add value to the overall offering.
    - Specify what that value is.
- The Service Component:
    - Specify exactly the nature and importance of customer service, both before and after sales.
    - Specify the exact role of service in differentiation and brand and retention.
    - Specify customer or segment required service levels and methods of forward monitoring.
- The Retention Component:
    - Specify the level and timing of customer re-purchase and the service and communications activities required to meet these objectives.

MARGIN NOTES

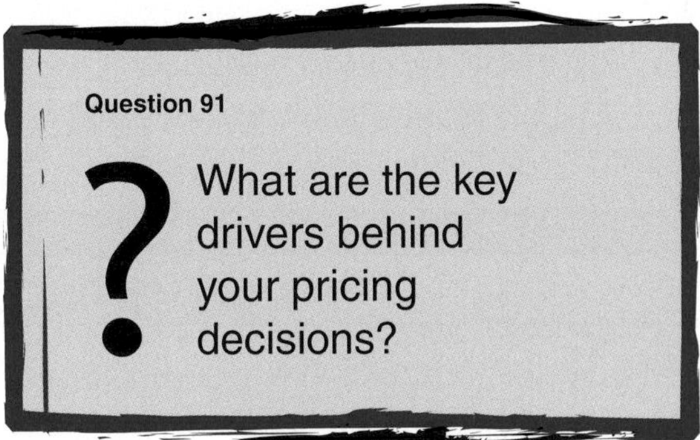

Question 91
?
What are the key drivers behind your pricing decisions?

Of all the P's in the marketing mix, only one – Price – is about revenues (and cash, and profits), the others are all costs.

Give the implementers as much room as possible, by all means, but don't lose control over pricing.

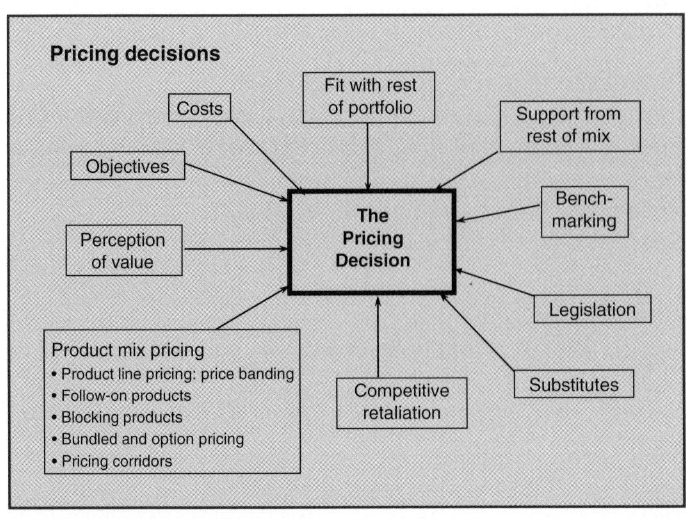

Fit with rest of portfolio
Support from rest of mix

Product mix pricing
• Product line pricing: price banding

• Blocking products
• Bundled and option pricing
• Pricing corridors

If you are wondering at this new idea, you only have to remember:

- Price is not, not, NOT just what you drop any time you need to meet some arbitrary product or service sales target.
- Price is where all your revenues, profits and CASH comes from – not something to be 'tinkered' with.
- There is no evidence that allowing sales people latitude in setting prices does anything positive for the bottom line.
- Pricing decisions are very complicated and need to be managed at a high, if not strategic level.

The price you set needs to be driven by a number of interrelated considerations:

- Costs:
  - Only important to know whether you make a profit.
  - Costs do NOT drive prices, customers do
- The mix:
  - Prices must synchronise with the other elements to blend into a simple and coherent offer
- Benchmarking:
  - Customers will compare your price – but to what?
  - Make sure you know and the comparison is what you want it to be
- Legislation:
  - Can affect certain products and services
- Substitutes:
  - Measure your prices against non-direct competitors
- Competition:
  - What retaliation can you expect against your prices?
- Communication effect:
  - Price suggest quality to customers
- Objectives:
  - Make sure that your price supports your business, marketing objectives and strategy – it should not conflict.

You can see that price is far too difficult to allow it to 'float' free or be decided at tactical levels.

MARGIN NOTES

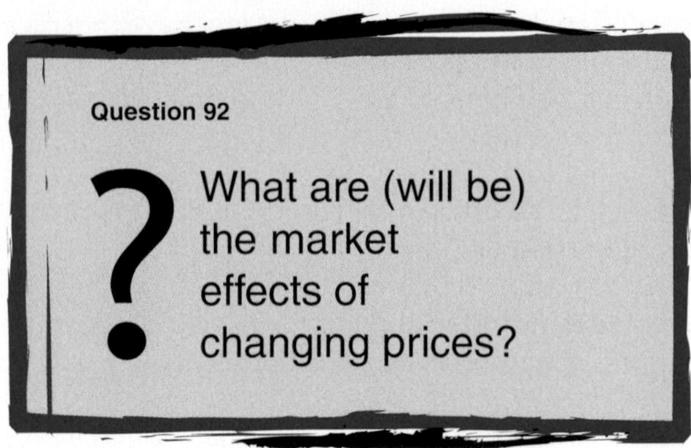

The communication effect of pricing is surprisingly strong. We know from research that:

MARGIN NOTES

- Reducing prices has been known to make customers think:
  - The item is about to be replaced by another model-so will postpone purchase
  - The firm is in financial trouble, needs the cash, may not stay in business long enough to supply future parts
  - Price will come down further and so better to wait
  - The quality or size (or both) has been reduced.
- Raising prices has been known to make customers think:
  - Price is an indicator of quality
  - They are unsure and require quality reassurance
  - They perceive quality differences in competitive offerings and are prepared to pay for quality (expensive but worth it)
  - They are concerned to be seen to buy the most expensive.

Don't mess with prices unless you know what effects it will have over the short, medium and long term.

If you want/need to increase profits, reducing price is a really BAD way to try and do it.

Increasing sales is better, decreasing costs is better still, increasing price is best!

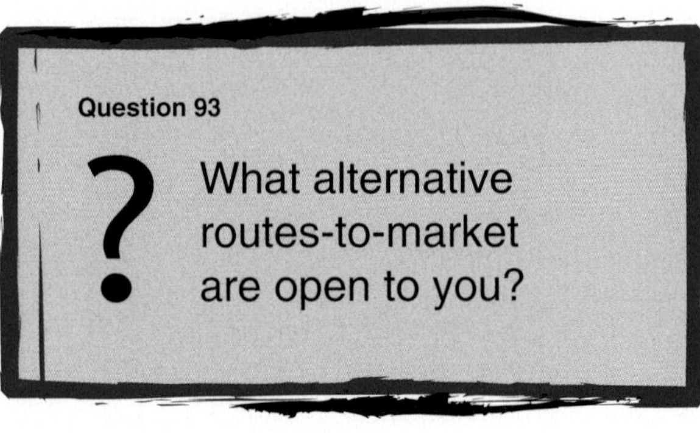

Question 93
?
What alternative routes-to-market are open to you?

The whole issue of routes-to-market – supply chain – distribution is complicated, it involves a lot of people, a lot of time, a lot of expense and so much can go wrong that it needs looking at carefully, all the time.

Products and (some) services need to get from where they are produced to where they are to be consumed. Some services (such as hotels and laboratories) are fixed so we need to find ways of getting customers to the service – to consume. Different organisations decide to do this differently, either doing it all themselves (direct) or doing it all through a range of channels, or somewhere in between.

Every step in the process that is owned by someone outside the organisation needs to be paid – and motivated to do things the 'right' way. The more steps in the process, the more this gets complicated – and expensive.

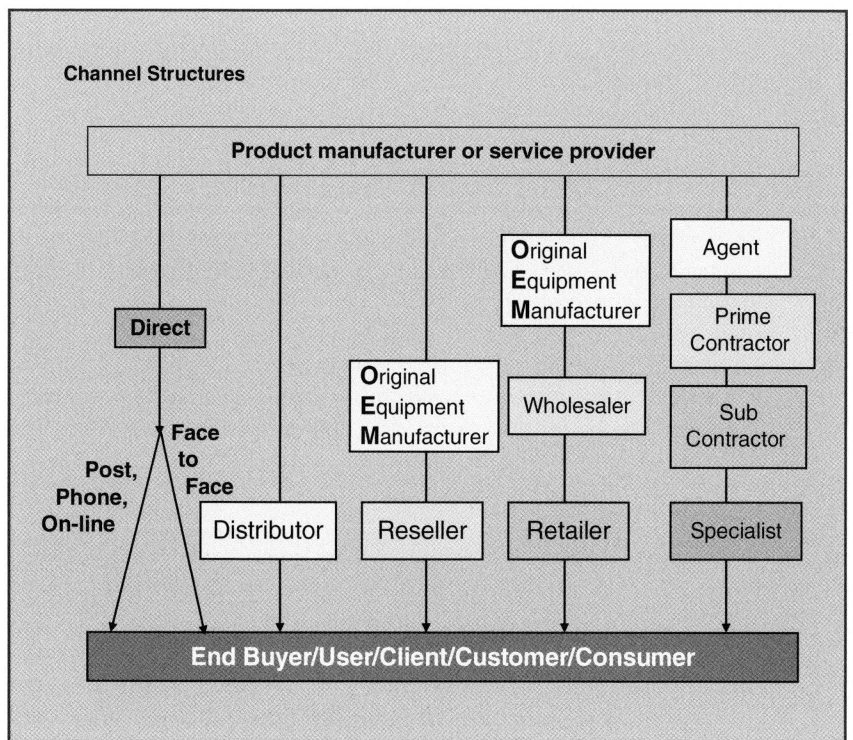

Some areas you might think about are:

- Conventional Wisdom:
  - If there is an 'accepted way' of distributing your product or service, do you really have to follow it?
  - I know nobody questions it but that's the point.
  - Some of the biggest (most profitable) 'innovations' have come from taking another view on distribution.

- From repositioning potato crisps (chips) from drinks accessories to snacks supported by introducing them to petrol service stations (Golden Wonder), to launching cars through farm suppliers (Subaru) rather than create expensive car dealerships, to telephone banking (First Direct) so avoiding the need for an expensive branch network, to Internet bookshops (Amazon).

- Customer Convenience:
  - Should be top of the list really but …
  - Where is the customer in all this?
  - Convenience is the name of the game here, how convenient is your system for customers?
  - If it's not convenient why on earth are you doing it this way?
  - What do you mean you have not asked the customer yet?

- Customer Value:
  - The 'big' one, what value does the customer get from the distribution process?
  - If its 'none' then you need to cut costs wherever you can.
  - What value could the customer get from the process?
  - Who should be delivering the additional value?
  - You or some specialist in the chain? 'Value-added reseller' is not just a term that applies to IT, it should apply everywhere that intermediaries are used – what additional value do they offer to the customer?
  - Which leads into:

- Cost–Benefit:
  - What benefits are we/our customers receiving from the intermediaries in the system, and what is it costing us/our customers?
  - Is what we pay worth it to us?
  - Is it worth it to our customers?

- Differentiation:
  - Differentiation is always complicated, is the distribution system part of the solution – or part of the problem?
  - Do the various intermediaries support your attempts at differentiation your offer and establishing you unique brand values – or do they work against you because they don't believe it's worth the hassle?
  - If they are part of the problem, are they doing it out of ignorance (so educate and train them) or on purpose (see battle for control below)

- Segmentation:
  - Segmentation comes before Branding (you cannot have one without the other, see Chapter 8).
  - Delivering on the special needs of different segments is difficult without active support from the channels. (VAG had to invest in

MARGIN NOTES

a new chain of outlets for its Audi brand, previously sold through the Volkswagen outlets, before it could re-position Audi more accurately against BMW)
  - Do the intermediaries work with you or against you in delivering to different segments?
  - If they are part of the problem, are they doing it out of ignorance (so educate and train them) or on purpose (see battle for control below)

- Where is the battle for control?
  - Every distribution system has a battle going on – are you winning or losing?

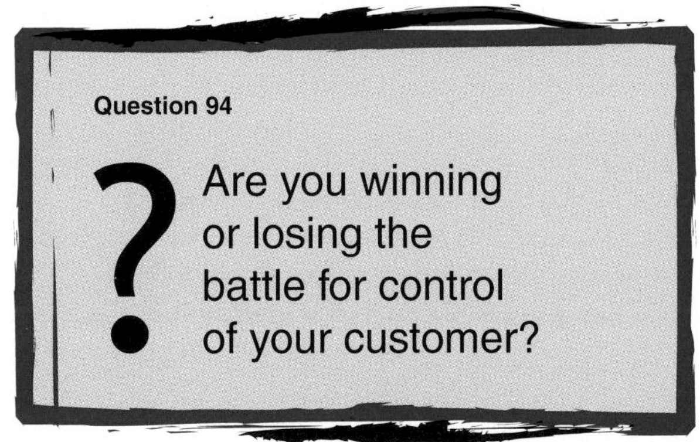

Question 94
?
Are you winning or losing the battle for control of your customer?

MARGIN NOTES

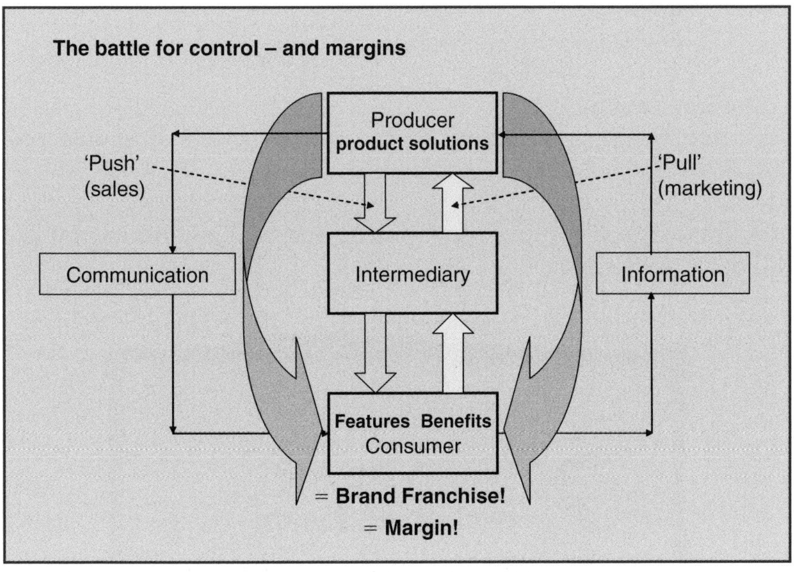

Every distribution system or network has its battle for control – it's where the money is. Who controls the customer, controls the margin.

- Intermediaries in the system:
  - Tend to be closer to the end customer (they try to serve them)
  - So they should be better positioned to understand and satisfy their needs.
  - If they can do this (some can, some cannot) then they can pick and choose which suppliers to support or stock and can effectively control access to customers and revenues.
  - Intermediaries in this position have the power to dictate terms to producers.
  - Often the intermediaries are given this position of power by producers who aren't customer or market oriented – they are only interested in making what they make and are happy to rely on the channel to know the customer and inform them of new trends and needs as they arise.
  - 'Slave' producers such as these survive as long as the channel wishes them to survive and tend to be prey to cheap imports.

MARGIN NOTES

- Where producers are in control of the distribution system:
  - They tend to be customer and market oriented
  - They don't 'push' their products/services through the system
  - They invest in creating a brand franchise with the customer so that they are 'pulled' through the intermediary system.

If you want to take control of your distribution system you will need to invest in

- Information:
  - On what your customers want and value

- Communication:
  - To your target customers on the reasons why they should prefer your offering over the competitive offerings.

Not a low-cost route, but an investment that will pay off (if you get it right) in increased margin.

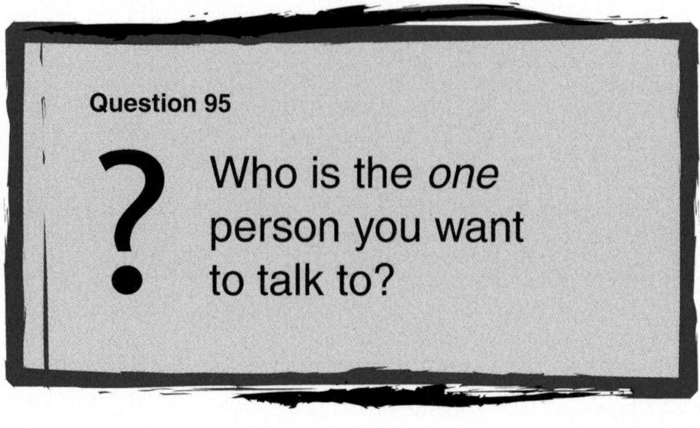
Question 95
?
Who is the *one* person you want to talk to?

We finish this section on the marketing mix – where too many people start – with Promotion.

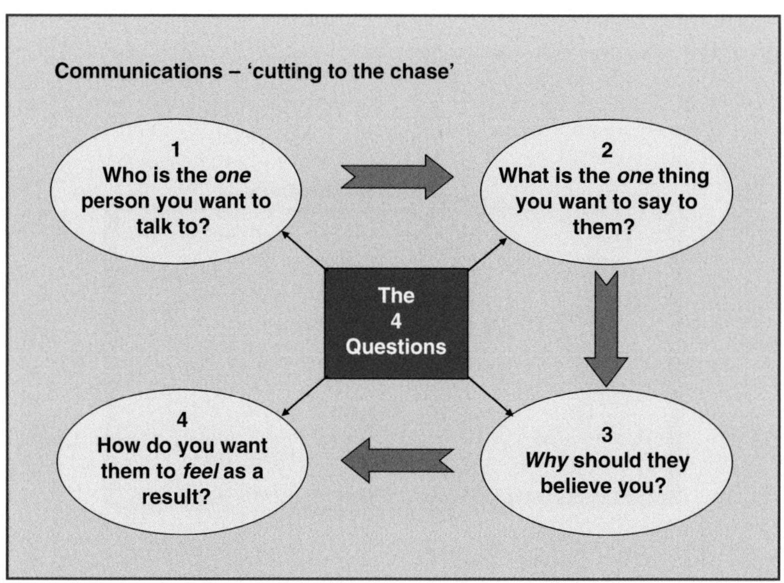
Communications – 'cutting to the chase'
1
Who is the *one* person you want to talk to?
2
What is the *one* thing you want to say to them?
The 4 Questions
3
Why should they believe you?
4
How do you want them to *feel* as a result?

MARGIN NOTES

So much nonsense has been written about marketing communications over the years that I am always wary about coming near the subject. Nevertheless, over the years I have found that there are four key questions that allow me to focus and manage all communications – and link them to marketing strategy.

There is nothing very clever about the 'four questions' apart from the way that they are (still after all these years) able to cut right to the core of any communications problem – no matter how much hubris has been piled on top.

I have also discovered that these questions apply to any type of communications, from the 'above-the-line', 'below-the-line' and 'online'. The first question you should ask of any communications issue is:

Who is the one *person you want to talk to?*

- Effective communications need to be focused
- We all know that you are communicating to lots of people, but it has to feel like its one-to-one
- People aren't all the same and the mass market is really dead
- Segments are the order of the day

- Different segments want different things and need to hear different things from you – and everyone is an individual, so make it personal or don't talk at all.

- Don't know who the 'one person' is?

- Don't waste money on communication until you find out.

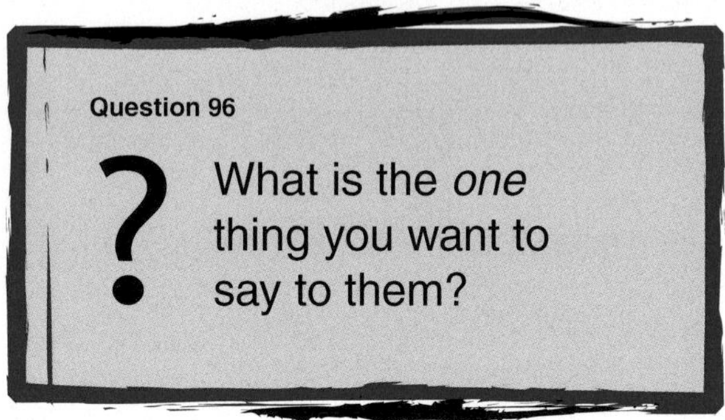
Question 96
What is the *one* thing you want to say to them?

MARGIN NOTES

The second question you should ask of any communications issue is:

What is the one *thing you want to say to them?*

- An effective message says *one* thing only

- More than one message just confuses so better not to say anything than to confuse your audience

- Don't get convinced that because the communications is so expensive you need to get more than one message included, it doesn't work

- Don't know what the 'one thing' is?

- Don't waste money on communication until you find out.

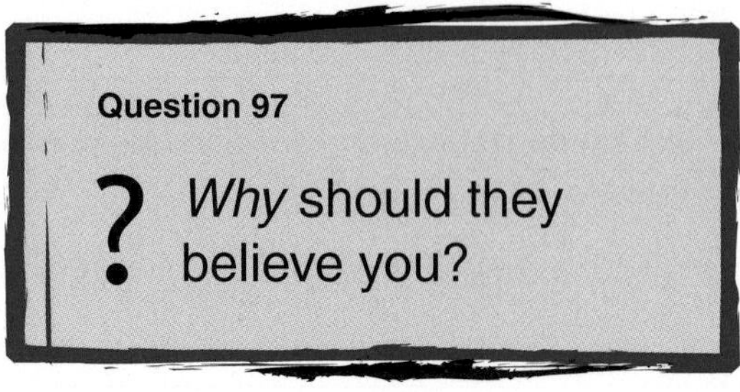
Question 97
Why should they believe you?

The third question you should ask of any communications issue is:

Why should they believe you?

- If they don't or won't believe you, why would you communicate – just to give the audience an opportunity to recall how untrustworthy you are?
- You need to give them the reason why you should be believed, they won't necessarily work it out for themselves
- Don't know why they should believe you?
- Don't waste money on communication until you find out.

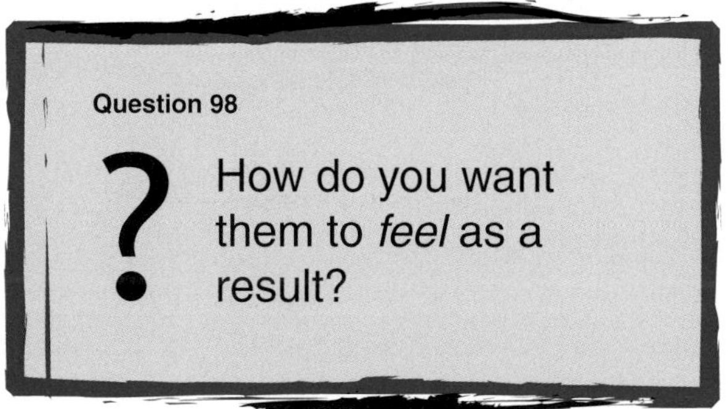
Question 98
?
How do you want them to *feel* as a result?

MARGIN NOTES

The fourth and final question you should ask of any communications issue is:

How do you want them to feel *as a result?*

- Communicating is all about feelings – that ultimately lead to purchase
- Communications need to generate some key feeling in your audience's mind – that can open the way for the unique benefits of your offering
- Whether it is 'peace of mind, 'reassurance', 'relief', 'smugness' or any emotion of your choice, there needs to be an outcome
- Don't know what emotion you want them, to feel as a result of the communication?
- Don't waste money on communication until you find out.

The more adventurous among you might also want to try applying these ideas to your internal audiences as well as you external ones – some internal marketing will be essential if the old lines of demarcation between strategy and tactics aren't going to limit your chances of market success.

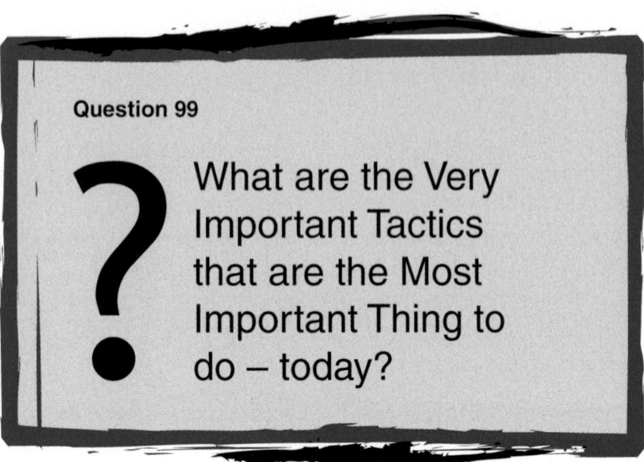

Question 99
?
What are the Very Important Tactics that are the Most Important Thing to do – today?

MARGIN NOTES

Any sensible and independent study of management (including marketing), must come to the conclusion that managers follow a cycle of surfing one management 'fad' after another.

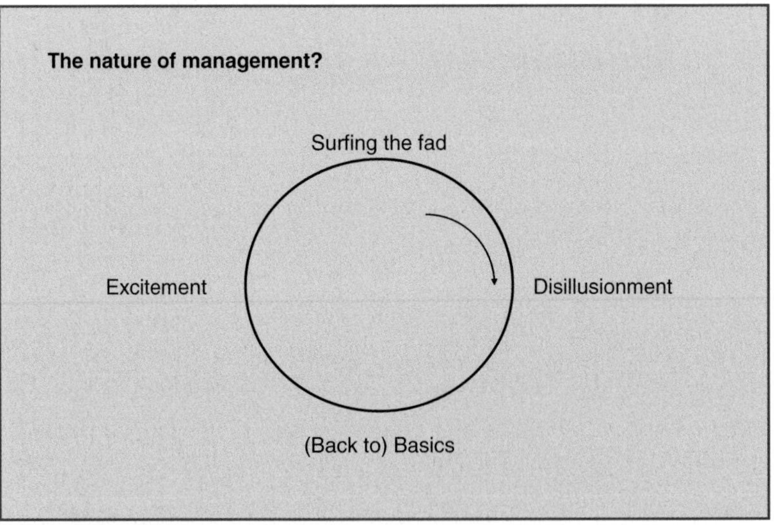

- A list of some of the fads that have been surfed over the years include:
  - Time and Motion
  - Management by objectives
  - Management by walking about
  - Portfolio management (BCG)
  - Strategic business units
  - Time management
  - Customer care

- Globalisation
- 'Excellence'
- Total quality management
- BS5750/EN29000/ISO9000
- Just-in-time (JIT)
- Kaizen
- Re-engineering
- Business process redesign
- Benchmarking
- Micro-marketing
- One-to-one marketing
- Customer service
- Investors in people (IIP)
- Relationship marketing
- Internet marketing
- Millennium bug (Y2K)
- E-Commerce
- Customer relationship management (CRM)
- Dot.com revolution
- Outsourcing
- Post-modernism
- Post-materialism
- Post 9/11
- Cause-related marketing

- Are today Very Important Tactics (VITs) fads or trends?
  - Web services
  - Viral marketing
  - Environmental/Green business
  - Post consumerism
  - Low Carbon marketing
  - Social networking
  - Sustainability
  - … and next???

But at any 'today' all we hear is an almost overwhelming chorus in support of the latest panacea. There are almost no critics so what are we to believe?

At the time of writing – Autumn 2007 (it may have changed by the time this book is published) all I can hear at the moment is:

- Social networking is the *only* thing on the horizon (Wikipedia lists almost 100 popular sites, Bibo, Facebook, Friendster and Myspace seem to be leading the field with a clutch of 'Senior' (55+) sites bursting on to the scene more recently) although nobody seems to know exactly where it is all going, what to do with them and why they are the only thing on the horizon.

MARGIN NOTES

- Climate change and global warming
- Low carbon footprints for everybody and every product or service
- Sustainable business.

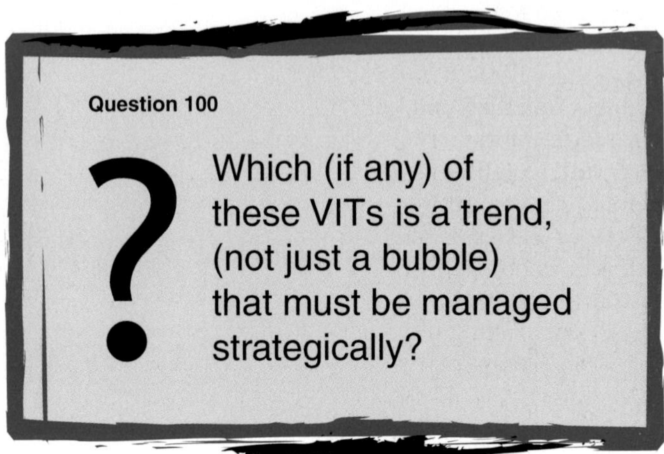

Question 100
?
Which (if any) of these VITs is a trend, (not just a bubble) that must be managed strategically?

MARGIN NOTES

As Kipling said, 'If you can keep your head while all about you are losing theirs and blaming it on you', then you may have a chance of implementing your strategy professionally.

These VITs are:

- Very Important:
  - At least everyone is talking about them and getting involved
- Tactics:
  - NOT strategy

The BIG question is, which of the VITs are doomed to be 'bubbles' and which ones might be destined to be 'trends'.

You must work with the trends because they will affect and be affected by your marketing strategy.

You must do what you can with the bubbles but *you must NOT be drawn in to the 'feeding frenzy'*, because they will soon sink without trace and they must not affect your strategy in passing.

Which fad is which? Ah, now that's the difficult question

My view as a non-clairvoyant is that *sustainability is the one to watch*, here are my reasons:

- Tactical VITs (like social networking) tend to be:
  - Very specific, focused in one area, technology or interest
  - Action-oriented, and one particular sector or group of society becomes mildly obsessed with the activity

    - Expected to move from an obsessed minority to the mainstream
    - Offering little real 'human benefit'

- VITs that might turn into a trend (like Sustainability), are often:
    - Slower burning
        - Sustainability was first raised seriously by Schumacher in his book *Small is Beautiful* (1973)
    - Engage more than one 'proposer' in society
        - Sustainability is currently supported by Government, Scientists (although both these groups aren't seen as particularly trustworthy by large sections of the population), UN, respected NGOs and corporations
        - Much more importantly, there are early signs of more 'ordinary' consumers recognising *customer value* in sustainable offerings. All governments believe they affect things but simple legislation really does very little – now, when legislation is replaced by *customer motivation* you have to take notice.
    - Composed of a number of separate but connected trends
        - Sustainability is driven by movement in areas such as:
            - Energy prices
            - Use of energy as a political weapon
            - Possible demise of consumerism
            - Wider social change.
            - The gathering global recession.

But my views aren't guaranteed, and you are responsible for your own organisation's future …

MARGIN NOTES

■ The strategic questions (84–100)

Strategy without implementation is pointless. But, to spend time and effort developing a good marketing strategy for it to be practically ignored by the implementers and tacticians is equally pointless.

The golden rules are:

- Develop the strategy based on identified customer needs and wants
- Make allowances for organisational capabilities but:
    - Don't limit your strategy and aspirations to only what the organisation can do now
    - Raise the game to what the organisation could achieve with some effort
- Engage the decision makers and implementers in the Value Proposition work
- Use the Value Proposition as your main control measure
- Manage the key aspects of the marketing mix as implementation continues.

And the questions. There are a lot this time, but in more familiar areas. Just because you might know the subject matter, don't be tempted to jump over the answers – make sure you (or someone in the organisation) really knows.

No.	Strategic question	Our strategic answer	Importance	✓
	Part Four – Implementing the Marketing Strategy – Making it Happen			
84	How do we implement the strategy, and turn our thinking into action?		Must have	
			Nice to have	
			Not important	
85	What are the barriers that could stop us implementing the strategy?		Must have	
			Nice to have	
			Not important	
86	How can we control implementation?		Must have	
			Nice to have	
			Not important	
87	Which 'Marketing Mix' should my organisation use?		Must have	
			Nice to have	
			Not important	
	Product or Service Policy			
88	What jobs are your products or services being 'hired' to do?		Must have	
			Nice to have	
			Not important	
89	What is our product (or service)-market match?		Must have	
			Nice to have	
			Not important	
90	What are the product or service components that we need to manage?		Must have	
			Nice to have	
			Not important	
	Pricing Policy			
91	What are the key drivers behind your pricing decisions?		Must have	
			Nice to have	
			Not important	

92	What are (will be) the market effects of changing prices?		Must have	
			Nice to have	
			Not important	
	Place/Distribution Policy			
93	What alternative routes-to-market are open to you?		Must have	
			Nice to have	
			Not important	
94	Are you winning or losing the battle for control of your customer?		Must have	
			Nice to have	
			Not important	
	Promotion/ Communications Policy			
95	Who is the *one* person you want to talk to?		Must have	
			Nice to have	
			Not important	
96	What is the *one* thing you want to say to them?		Must have	
			Nice to have	
			Not important	
97	*Why* should they believe you?		Must have	
			Nice to have	
			Not important	
98	How do you want them to *feel* as a result?		Must have	
			Nice to have	
			Not important	
	Other VIT (Very Important Tactics)			
99	What are the VITs that are the Most Important Thing to do – today?		Must have	
			Nice to have	
			Not important	
100	Which (if any) of these VITs is a trend, (not just a bubble) that must be managed strategically?		Must have	
			Nice to have	
			Not important	

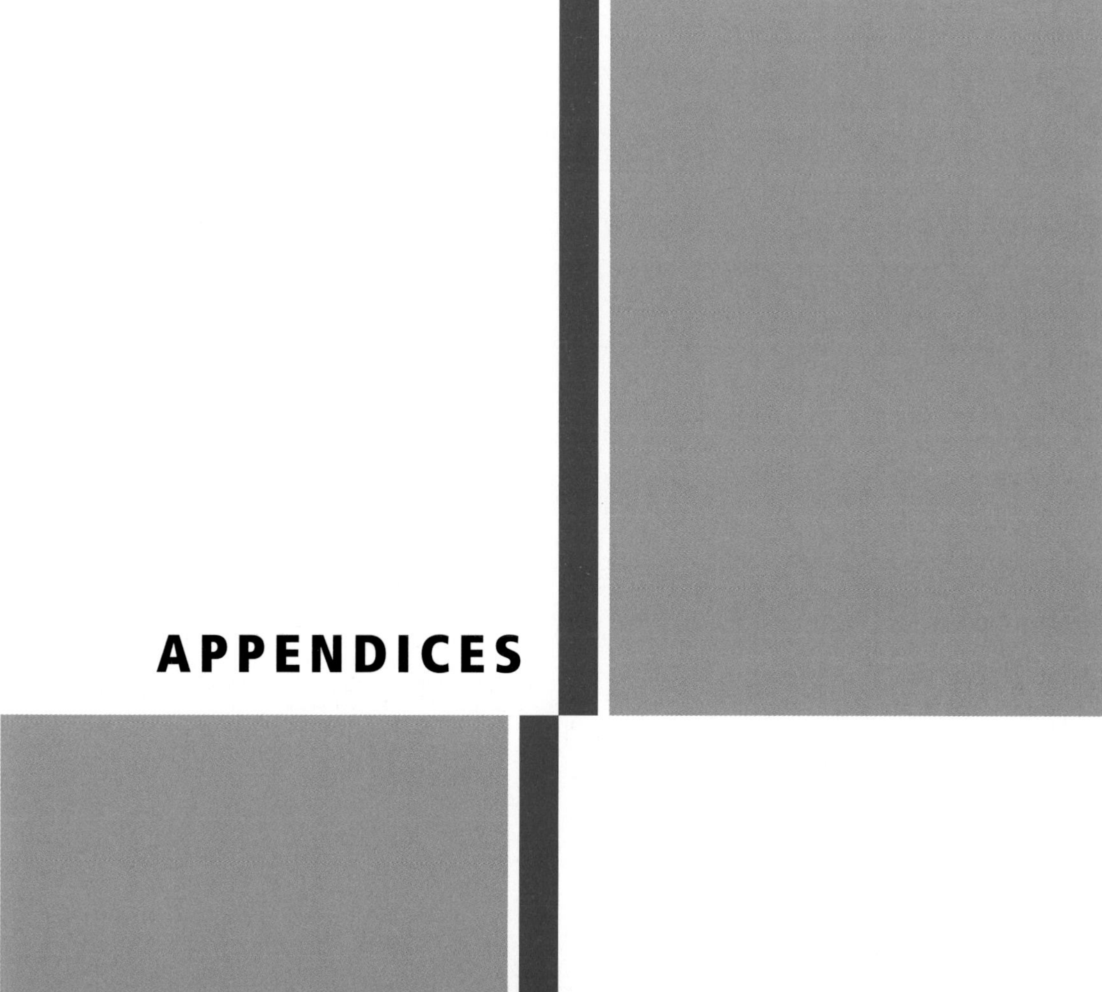

APPENDICES

Come to the edge.
We might fall.
Come to the edge.
It's too high!
COME TO THE EDGE!
And they came,
and he pushed,
and they flew.

Christopher Logue (1926-),
English poet

MARGIN NOTES

1 The 100 questions for your marketing strategy

No.	Ref:	Strategic question	Notes	Our strategic answer	Importance	✓
	Chap	**Part One: Preparing for Marketing Strategy**				
	1	*Internal business drivers*				
1		What do our shareholders require from us?			Must have	
					Nice to have	
					Not important	
2		What do our stakeholders require from us?			Must have	
					Nice to have	
					Not important	
3		Who are the key implementers in the organisation and what are their personal values and requirements?	1	1	Must have	
			2	2	Nice to have	
			3	3	Not important	
4		How should we best describe their/our strategic intent?			Must have	
					Nice to have	
					Not important	
5		Out of these various factors do we have a clear statement or understanding of the corporate/business mission?			Must have	
					Nice to have	
					Not important	
6		What is the long-term financial objective that the organisation is dedicated to achieving?			Must have	
					Nice to have	
					Not important	

No.	Ref:	Strategic question	Notes	Our strategic answer	Importance	✓
	Chap	**Part One: Preparing for Marketing Strategy**				
7		What are the financial hurdles?	1	1	Must have	
			2	2	Nice to have	
			3	3	Not important	
			4	4		
8		What is the vision of the organisation? What should it be?			Must have	
					Nice to have	
					Not important	
	2	*External business drivers*				
9		What resources do we have and how are they being utilised?			Must have	
					Nice to have	
					Not important	
10		What are the strengths and weaknesses of the organisation?			Must have	
					Nice to have	
					Not important	
11		What is the 'Environment Audit' and how do we create one?			Must have	
					Nice to have	
					Not important	
12		What opportunities and threats exist in our broad macro-environment?			Must have	
					Nice to have	
					Not important	

13		Are we (really) customer focused?			Must have	
					Nice to have	
					Not important	
14		How is our industry put together? What business are we in? (see 'Industry or Market')			Must have	
					Nice to have	
					Not important	
15		Are there opportunities arising from the structure of our business/industry?			Must have	
					Nice to have	
					Not important	
16		Who are our real competitors and what are their competencies?			Must have	
					Nice to have	
					Not important	
17		What are the opportunities for our organisation in the competitive environment?			Must have	
					Nice to have	
					Not important	
18		Are we internally or externally driven?			Must have	
					Nice to have	
					Not important	
	3	*The business strategy*				
19		What is our business/corporate objective?			Must have	
					Nice to have	
					Not important	
20		What is our business/corporate strategy?			Must have	
					Nice to have	
					Not important	

No.	Ref:	Strategic question	Notes	Our strategic answer	Importance	✓
	Chap	**Part One: Preparing for Marketing Strategy**				
21		What are the options for sustainable competitive advantage?			Must have	
					Nice to have	
					Not important	
22		What do we believe is the most appropriate sustainable competitive advantage we should be seeking? – Our competitive strategy			Must have	
					Nice to have	
					Not important	
	4	*The marketing objectives*				
23		What are the marketing objective(s)? (*Note*: these will become the KPIs of our organisation)	1	1	Must have	
			2	2	Nice to have	
			3	3	Not important	
			4	4		
			5	5		
24		How do I develop the KPIs from the marketing objectives?			Must have	
					Nice to have	
					Not important	
		Part Two: Developing the Marketing Strategy				
25		What is marketing strategy?			Must have	
					Nice to have	
					Not important	

26		What are the steps involved in developing marketing strategy?			Must have	
					Nice to have	
					Not important	
27		What does marketing strategy mean for my organisation?			Must have	
					Nice to have	
					Not important	
28		Should I prepare my organisation for marketing strategy?			Must have	
					Nice to have	
					Not important	
29		Who do I involve in the marketing strategy process?			Must have	
					Nice to have	
					Not important	
	5	*Industry or Market?*				
30		What business are we in?			Must have	
					Nice to have	
					Not important	
31		What business do we want to be in or should we be in?			Must have	
					Nice to have	
					Not important	
32		How does this define the market/ customer needs we should be satisfying?			Must have	
					Nice to have	
					Not important	
33		Where/how should we be growing the business?			Must have	
					Nice to have	
					Not important	

No.	Ref:	Strategic question	Notes	Our strategic answer	Importance	✓
	Chap	**Part Two: Developing the Marketing Strategy**				
34		What are our strategic opportunities and threats?			Must have	
					Nice to have	
					Not important	
35		What competition are we (really) facing?			Must have	
					Nice to have	
					Not important	
36		What are the boundaries for effort?			Must have	
					Nice to have	
					Not important	
	6	*The Customer*				
37		Who are they?			Must have	
					Nice to have	
					Not important	
38		What do they currently buy from us/our competitors and why?			Must have	
					Nice to have	
					Not important	
39		What benefits are they seeking?			Must have	
					Nice to have	
					Not important	
40		What do they want from us now/will they want in the future?			Must have	
					Nice to have	
					Not important	

41		What barriers are getting in the way?			Must have	
					Nice to have	
					Not important	
42		What will make them come to us?			Must have	
					Nice to have	
					Not important	
43		Where do customers interface (connect) with our organisation?			Must have	
					Nice to have	
					Not important	
	7	*Segmentation and Targeting*				
44		What is the current state of segmentation in the organisation?			Must have	
					Nice to have	
					Not important	
45		What do we want segmentation to do for our organisation?			Must have	
					Nice to have	
					Not important	
46		What segments exist in our target market (defined business)?			Must have	
					Nice to have	
					Not important	
47		How durable are the segments identified?			Must have	
					Nice to have	
					Not important	
48		How can we prioritise the segments for approach?			Must have	
					Nice to have	
					Not important	

No.	Ref:	Strategic question	Notes	Our strategic answer	Importance	✓
	Chap	**Part Two: Developing the Marketing Strategy**				
49		Which segments should we target?			Must have	
					Nice to have	
					Not important	
50		How can we market to different segments?			Must have	
					Nice to have	
					Not important	
	8	*Positioning and Branding*				
51		Differentiation or 'Commodity' marketing?			Must have	
					Nice to have	
					Not important	
52		What market positions exist?			Must have	
					Nice to have	
					Not important	
53		What market position do we own, or do we want to own?			Must have	
					Nice to have	
					Not important	
54		How are we going to be different from the competition?			Must have	
					Nice to have	
					Not important	
55		What is our brand? What are its unique 'values' and 'personality?'			Must have	
					Nice to have	
					Not important	

56		What are the costs and benefits of building a brand?			Must have	
					Nice to have	
					Not important	
57		How do we invest in our brand and a differentiated market position?			Must have	
					Nice to have	
					Not important	
	9	*Retention*				
58		How important is 'Retention' in our market?			Must have	
					Nice to have	
					Not important	
59		How big are the 'problem' and the potential gains?			Must have	
					Nice to have	
					Not important	
60		Is retention just about customer satisfaction?			Must have	
					Nice to have	
					Not important	
61		Do our accounting and reporting systems impede retention activities?			Must have	
					Nice to have	
					Not important	
62		How good is our Market(ing) Information Systems (MkIS)?			Must have	
					Nice to have	
					Not important	
63		What is the strategic role of our customer relationships?			Must have	
					Nice to have	
					Not important	

No.	Ref:	Strategic question	Notes	Our strategic answer	Importance	✓
	Chap	**Part Two: Developing the Marketing Strategy**				
64		How are we planning to invest in our primary asset?			Must have	
					Nice to have	
					Not important	
	10	*Organisation Processes and Culture*				
65		Is our organisation focused on internal or external issues?			Must have	
					Nice to have	
					Not important	
66		What is our organisation really good at – and does it matter?			Must have	
					Nice to have	
					Not important	
67		What is going on with our culture?			Must have	
					Nice to have	
					Not important	
68		Is our organisation joined up?			Must have	
					Nice to have	
					Not important	
69		Is our organisation driven by the right information?			Must have	
					Nice to have	
					Not important	
70		Which metrics are used to manage and drive our organisation?			Must have	
					Nice to have	
					Not important	

71		Change management – what is that?			Must have	
					Nice to have	
					Not important	
	11	*Offerings*				
72		Where is the customer value?			Must have	
					Nice to have	
					Not important	
73		What is our value proposition?			Must have	
					Nice to have	
					Not important	
74		What is the most appropriate business design for us?			Must have	
					Nice to have	
					Not important	
75		Where are our new offerings?			Must have	
					Nice to have	
					Not important	
76		How do we assess the risk?			Must have	
					Nice to have	
					Not important	
77		Are we managing the life cycle?			Must have	
					Nice to have	
					Not important	
78		How do we take our Offerings to market?			Must have	
					Nice to have	
					Not important	

No.	Ref:	Strategic question	Notes	Our strategic answer	Importance	✓
	Chap	**Part Three: Coordinating your Marketing Strategy Stances**				
79		What makes 'good' strategy?			Must have	
					Nice to have	
					Not important	
80		How do I plan with SCORPIO?			Must have	
					Nice to have	
					Not important	
81		What is the minimum SCORPIO – the 'strategic spine'?			Must have	
					Nice to have	
					Not important	
82		What is the defensive SCORPIO? – coordinating your 'defensive marketing Strategy'			Must have	
					Nice to have	
					Not important	
83		What is the offensive SCORPIO? – coordinating your 'offensive marketing strategy'			Must have	
					Nice to have	
					Not important	
		Part Four: Implementing the Marketing Strategy – Making it Happen				
84		How do we implement the strategy, and turn our thinking into action?			Must have	
					Nice to have	
					Not important	
85		What are the barriers that could stop us implementing the strategy?			Must have	
					Nice to have	
					Not important	

86		How can we control implementation?			Must have	
					Nice to have	
					Not important	
87		Which 'Marketing mix' should my organisation use?			Must have	
					Nice to have	
					Not important	
		Product or Service Policy				
88		What jobs are your products or services being 'hired' to do?			Must have	
					Nice to have	
					Not important	
89		What is our product (or service)-market match?			Must have	
					Nice to have	
					Not important	
90		What are the product or service components that we need to manage?			Must have	
					Nice to have	
					Not important	
		Pricing Policy				
91		What are the key drivers behind your pricing decisions?			Must have	
					Nice to have	
					Not important	
92		What are (will be) the market effects of changing prices?			Must have	
					Nice to have	
					Not important	
		Place/Distribution Policy				
93		What alternative routes-to-market are open to you?			Must have	
					Nice to have	
					Not important	

No.	Ref:	Strategic question	Notes	Our strategic answer	Importance	✓
	Chap	**Part Four: Implementing the Marketing Strategy – Making it Happen**				
94		Are you winning or losing the battle for control of your customer?			Must have	
					Nice to have	
					Not important	
		Promotion/Communications Policy				
95		Who is the *one* person you want to talk to?			Must have	
					Nice to have	
					Not important	
96		What is the *one* thing you want to say to them?			Must have	
					Nice to have	
					Not important	
97		*Why* should they believe you?			Must have	
					Nice to have	
					Not important	
98		How do you want them to *feel* as a result?			Must have	
					Nice to have	
					Not important	
		Other VIT (Very Important Tactics)				
99		What are the VITs that are the Most Important Thing to do – today?			Must have	
					Nice to have	
					Not important	
100		Which (if any) of these VITs is a trend, (not just a bubble) that must be managed strategically?			Must have	
					Nice to have	
					Not important	

2 FAQS – Frequently asked questions in market(ing) strategy

1 Industry or Market?		
1.1 What business are we in (now)?		
1.1.1	Is the definition product or technology based?	
1.1.2	Do we understand where the current definition came from?	
1.1.3	Understanding past and future value (migration)	
1.1.4	What are the likely effects of staying with the current definition?	
1.1.5	Does our current marketing make sense to the customer?	
1.1.6	How does it affect our planning and marketing?	
1.1.7	Who in the organisation is most attached to the current definition?	
1.2 What business do we want to be in or should we be in?		
1.2.1	Will the customer understand it?	
1.2.2	What does the 'SWOT' analysis tell us about the business definition?	
1.2.3	Is there a gap in the market – and a market in the gap?	
1.2.4	Where is the 'value' in the market and can we extract it?	
1.2.5	Is there room to differentiate and grow?	
1.2.6	Will the staff and other stakeholders understand the business definition?	
1.2.7	Can we do it? Do we (really) want to do it?	
1.3 How does this define the market/customer needs we should be satisfying?		
1.3.1	Does it help us understand the customer better?	
1.3.2	How does it add to current knowledge?	
1.3.3	Does it clearly aid differentiation?	
1.3.4	Does it clearly identify needs we should NOT be satisfying?	
1.3.5	How far does it take us from our product/technology competencies?	
1.3.6	Can we satisfy the needs identified?	
1.3.7	Do we have the people and culture to make it happen?	

1.4 Where/how should we be growing the business?		
1.4.1	Do the growth prospects excite the organisation, management and staff?	
1.4.2	Does it show potential areas of significant market growth (gap)?	
1.4.3	Are the growth areas 'innovative?'	
1.4.4	Are the growth areas profitable?	
1.4.5	Are the growth areas 'logical' to the customer?	
1.4.6	Are there sufficient growth prospects for at least 3–5 years?	
1.4.7	How different is the route from that planned before?	
1.5 What are our strategic opportunities and threats?		
1.5.1	Does our 'PEST' analysis change in the new market definition?	
1.5.2	SWOT– what are the new opportunities?	
1.5.3	SWOT – what are the new threats?	
1.5.4	SWOT – what are the new weaknesses?	
1.5.5	SWOT – what are the new strengths?	
1.5.6	SWOT – how do the 'new' and 'old' compare?	
1.5.7	What actions result from this analysis?	
1.6 What competition are we (really) facing?		
1.6.1	Who are the competitors in the 'new space'?	
1.6.2	Does Porter's Five Forces analysis show new threats?	
1.6.3	Do we understand the new and potential competition?	
1.6.4	What business do new/potential competitors believe they are in?	
1.6.5	How does 'substitute competition' in the new business affect us?	
1.6.6	What are the competitors' plans and ambitions in our market?	
1.6.7	How do we build competitive response into our plans?	
1.7 What are the boundaries for effort?		
1.7.1	What should we be doing MORE of?	
1.7.2	What should we be doing LESS of?	
1.7.3	Where are the 'quick wins' in the market?	

1.7.4	What are the skills and/or knowledge gaps that must be filled?	
1.7.5	How should we reallocate marketing investments?	
1.7.6	What are the implications for strategy and planning?	
1.7.7	What are the implications for the organisation and its people?	
2 The Customer		
2.1 Who are they?		
2.1.1	How do you describe your existing customer base?	
2.1.2	Is there one way of describing the customers, or many?	
2.1.3	What do we know about our customers?	
2.1.4	Who collects customer data?	
2.1.5	Where is the customer data held?	
2.1.6	Do you conduct product research or market research?	
2.1.7	Who is responsible for the Marketing Information System (MkIS)?	
2.2 What do they currently buy from us/our competitors and why?		
2.2.1	What solutions/benefits are they purchasing from us?	
2.2.2	Do we know their current/recent buying history?	
2.2.3	Have attempts been made to model this data?	
2.2.4	Do we know what percentage of spend we have from our customers?	
2.2.5	Who else (competition) gets what percentage?	
2.2.6	What is our customers' perception of our organisation and brand(s)?	
2.2.7	Why do they come to us rather than the competition?	
2.3 What benefits are they seeking?		
2.3.1	What do you currently know about their lives?	
2.3.2	What problems/needs/wants do your customers and prospects have?	
2.3.3	What problems/needs/wants are currently 'satisfied', and how well?	
2.3.4	What problems/needs/wants are currently 'unsatisfied?'	
2.3.5	Which 'satisfaction gaps' are evident and which are latent?	
2.3.6	How 'motivational' are the benefits sought?	

2.3.7	What role do you want your product or service to play in the customer's life?	
2.4 What do they want from us now/will they want in the future?		
2.4.1	What problems/needs/wants are currently unmet?	
2.4.2	How and how fast can we meet current unmet needs?	
2.4.3	What needs/wants will be driving in the future?	
2.4.4	When will which needs and/or wants be driving behaviour?	
2.4.5	Which needs and wants will they expect to buy from us?	
2.4.6	How can we predict critical future problems, needs and wants?	
2.4.7	How can we plan future needs into marketing and production?	
2.5 What barriers are getting in the way?		
2.5.1	What are the external barriers that prevent customers from buying?	
2.5.2	What internal barriers have we constructed against purchase?	
2.5.3	How can we make buying easier, better, more fun, and satisfying?	
2.5.4	Are problems highlighted and solved or are they buried?	
2.5.5	Do we understand why non-customers choose to buy elsewhere?	
2.5.6	Are we sure we are turning away the right business?	
2.5.7	What happens when customer and internal needs collide?	
2.6 What will make them come to us?		
2.6.1	Do we understand how and Why customers choose to buy from us?	
2.6.2	What does the customer particularly value?	
2.6.3	What is the role of 'service' in the purchase/repurchase decision?	
2.6.4	How do we create 'customer preference' for our offer?	
2.6.5	Can we become the 'obvious choice' (the no-brainer solution)?	
2.6.6	What will make them stay?	

2.6.7	How can we move to 'relationships' with customers?	
2.7 Where do customers interface (connect) with our organisation?		
2.7.1	Where is the contact (and the money) made?	
2.7.2	How many points of contact exist, what is their relative importance?	
2.7.3	Which of the contacts are 'moments of truth?'	
2.7.4	Are the various points integrated to support the brand and/or market position?	
2.7.5	Is flexibility built in to allow for changes in customer preferences?	
2.7.6	How does it 'feel' from the customer perspective?	
2.7.7	Who is in control of the contact with the customer?	
3 Segmentation and Targeting		
3.1 What is the current state of segmentation in the organisation?		
3.1.1	How do we currently categorise/segment our customer base?	
3.1.2	Do we have one method or many inside the organisation?	
3.1.3	Are categories/segments based on descriptions or customer needs?	
3.1.4	What are the origins of the current segmentation approach?	
3.1.5	Are the categories/segments used as the basis for marketing plans?	
3.1.6	Do the categories/segments drive marketing investments?	
3.1.7	Is segmentation seen as a source of competitive advantage?	
3.2 What do we want segmentation to do for our organisation?		
3.2.1	Segmentation to improve promotion/communications (spend)?	
3.2.2	Segmentation to improve current marketing tactics (4P's)?	
3.2.3	Segmentation to explain the market place – the 'battle map?'	
3.2.4	Segmentation to position the organisation or brand?	
3.2.5	Segmentation as part of integrated market strategy (SCORPIO)?	
3.2.6	Segmentation to develop a competitive advantage?	

3.2.7	Segmentation to do all of the above?	
3.3 What segments exist in our target market (defined business)?		
3.3.1	Have we identified what business you want or need to be in?	
3.3.2	Have you identified the 'natural segments' that exist in your market?	
3.3.3	Have you based segmentation on descriptions, usage, needs/wants or CONTEXT©?	
3.3.4	Do you understand the buying motives active in the market?	
3.3.5	Do your customers and prospects identify with the segments?	
3.3.6	Can distribution and other partners relate to the segments?	
3.3.7	Have you applied the tests for 'good' segments?	
3.4 How durable are the segments identified?		
3.4.1	Are the segments reasonably stable for the period required?	
3.4.2	Which segments are growing and which declining? Why?	
3.4.3	Which segments are fragmenting and which merging? Why?	
3.4.4	How do customers 'migrate' between segments?	
3.4.5	Are we working to establish our position in today's or tomorrow's segments?	
3.4.6	Do we use forecast changes to inform new market strategy?	
3.4.7	How do we use these forecasts to form marketing tactics?	
3.5 How can we prioritise the segments for approach?		
3.5.1	What are the financial and non-financial imperatives (things management MUST deliver) in the organisation?	
3.5.2	What is the relative importance of these attractiveness imperatives (weighting)?	
3.5.3	How might each identified segment deliver on each imperative?	
3.5.4	What are our strengths and weaknesses by segment?	
3.5.5	What competencies do customers perceive we have – by segment?	

3.5.6	What is the competitive position in a segment?	
3.5.7	How do we assess overall market attractiveness?	
3.6 Which segments should we target?		
3.6.1	Which segments are currently the most 'valuable?'	
3.6.2	Which segments are expected to be most valuable in the future?	
3.6.3	Which segments are the most and least competitive?	
3.6.4	Which segments are essential to support our target market position and brand? And which would damage us?	
3.6.5	Do we require profitability by segment or across the market portfolio?	
3.6.6	Are there segments we must control to lock out competition?	
3.6.7	Which segments should we encourage our competitors to enter?	
3.7 How can we market to different segments?		
3.7.1	How different are the target segments?	
3.7.2	Can the same brand be used to cross segments? How many?	
3.7.3	What level of standardisation is possible in the product or service?	
3.7.4	What are the costs of necessary adaptations?	
3.7.5	What are the price premiums available?	
3.7.6	How do we 'populate' the segments?	
3.7.7	Can the organisation successfully manage multiple marketing mixes?	
4 Positioning and Branding		
4.1 Differentiation or 'Commodity' marketing?		
4.1.1	Is the concept of 'commodity' accepted in your business or industry?	
4.1.2	Do we and/or our organisation's key decision makers believe that differentiation is possible in our defined market?	
4.1.3	What is (believed) to be the role of price in the purchase decision?	
4.1.4	What (or who) does our organisation 'benchmark?'	
4.1.5	What differences/added value are customers willing to pay for?	

4.1.6	Is it worth being different?	
4.1.7	Does our organisation really want to be different?	
4.2 What market positions exist?		
4.2.1	What market positions does the target market deem credible?	
4.2.2	What positions have 'value' to target customers?	
4.2.3	Are the positions held within, or across segments?	
4.2.4	What positions do the competitors hold?	
4.2.5	How strongly do the competitors hold their positions?	
4.2.6	Are there 'empty' or latent positions, not currently held by anyone?	
4.2.7	How should we evaluate/prioritise these existing positions?	
4.3 What market position do we own, or do we want to own?		
4.3.1	What position(s) do we already hold?	
4.3.2	How strongly are those positions held in the customers' minds?	
4.3.3	Are our positions held within, or across segments?	
4.3.4	What position(s) do we want to hold in the future?	
4.3.5	What positions will come 'available' in the future?	
4.3.6	What do we have to do to own the position in the customers' mind?	
4.3.7	How can we calculate the financial value of holding the position?	
4.4 How are we going to be different from the competition?		
4.4.1	What differentiation is required by the target market position?	
4.4.2	Where is your brand or offering most and least credible?	
4.4.3	Where is the differentiation easier to protect and maintain?	
4.4.4	Where is the most competition concentrated?	
4.4.5	What if the potential differentiation comes from outside our existing 'technical' or product expertise?	
4.4.6	How can we differentiate (and add value) through partnerships?	
4.4.7	Can the organisation *deliver* a truly differentiated offering?	

4.5 What is our brand? What are its unique 'values' and 'personality?'		
4.5.1	What is the difference between 'a brand' and 'a name?'	
4.5.2	How will our brand be different from the competition?	
4.5.3	What brand values should be created, and how?	
4.5.4	What is our target brand personality?	
4.5.5	How are the personality and values to be kept relevant over time?	
4.5.6	What is the relationship between brands and segments?	
4.5.7	How 'deep' must the brand go to be successful?	
4.6 What are the costs and benefits of building a brand?		
4.6.1	How much will it cost to create a brand?	
4.6.2	How long will it take to create a brand?	
4.6.3	What constitutes a viable brand in our target segment(s)?	
4.6.4	What skills are required to develop and maintain a brand?	
4.6.5	What are the financial and non-financial benefits of a brand?	
4.6.6	What are the costs of not developing a brand?	
4.6.7	Can we win in a price war?	
4.7 How do we invest in our brand and a differentiated market position?		
4.7.1	How do we measure brand value/brand equity?	
4.7.2	Is brand or differentiation used as a key metric for controlling marketing activity?	
4.7.3	Are *all* our marketing activities coordinated to create, support and maintain the brand?	
4.7.4	Are our people part of the brand (and our competitive position)?	
4.7.5	Are we monitoring all levels of our brand's 'promise?'	
4.7.6	Can we create a 'philosophy' of brands?	
4.7.7	What is the planning horizon for brand development?	
5 Customer Retention		
5.1 How important is 'Retention' in our market?		
5.1.1	Apart from the customers that we have intentionally relinquished, how many have defected?	

5.1.2	What is the current customer defection rate?	
5.1.3	Has the rate increased or decreased over the past few years? Why?	
5.1.4	What are the reasons for customer defection?	
5.1.5	Have the reasons changed over the past few years? Why?	
5.1.6	How does our defection rate compare with our competition?	
5.1.7	Who is losing and gaining which customers? Why?	
5.2 How big are the 'problem' and the potential gains?		
5.2.1	How much do we spend on acquiring new customers?	
5.2.2	How long do our customers stay with us? (Average and by segment)	
5.2.3	How long must a new customer stay before they become profitable after acquisition costs?	
5.2.4	Are our acquisition cost and payback periods comparable with competitors?	
5.2.5	How much do you spend on retaining existing customers?	
5.2.6	What is the annual financial cost (lost income) to your organisation for customer defection?	
5.2.7	How much additional profit would be generated by an annual 5% increase in retention?	
5.3 Is retention just about customer satisfaction?		
5.3.1	Is 'customer satisfaction' a key marketing metric?	
5.3.2	What constitutes a 'satisfied' customer?	
5.3.3	What is the relationship between 'satisfaction' and 'commitment?'	
5.3.4	Is 'customer loyalty' a key marketing metric?	
5.3.5	What else gets in the way of creating loyalty?	
5.3.6	Is marketing activity aimed at creating 'sales' or 'relationships?'	
5.3.7	What will make the customer *want* to come back again and again?	
5.4 Do our accounting and reporting systems impede retention activities?		
5.4.1	Is financial return an objective or a 'hurdle' in the business?	
5.4.2	Is success based on analysis of *product* or *customer* profitability?	

5.4.3	Is success driven by quarterly, annual or longer returns?	
5.4.4	Can our systems account for lifetime value analysis?	
5.4.5	How 'loyal' are our stakeholders?	
5.4.6	Have we calculated the (discounted) cost of the existing systems?	
5.4.7	Do the financial decision- makers understand the issues?	
5.5 How good is our Market(ing) Information Systems (MkIS)?		
5.5.1	Are your database and/or management systems based on market needs?	
5.5.2	How accurate and flexible is your customer data?	
5.5.3	How accurate and flexible is your prospect data?	
5.5.4	Do you make use of the MkIS for planning, execution and controlling?	
5.5.5	How responsive is your MkIS for market feedback?	
5.5.6	Do you use your MkIS as a source of competitive advantage?	
5.5.7	Is 'knowledge management' used within our organisation?	
5.6 What is the strategic role of our Customer Relationships?		
5.6.1	Have we/are we considering implementing CRM?	
5.6.2	Does CRM have to be IT based?	
5.6.3	Is the CRM based on clear marketing objectives and strategy?	
5.6.4	Is the CRM built on the 'customer-centric' organisation?	
5.6.5	Is the CRM designed to target customers or 'woo' them?	
5.6.6	Are we talking CRM or CMR?	
5.6.7	Is our CRM future-proofed?	
5.7 How are we planning to invest in our primary asset?		
5.7.1	Is the customer currently regarded as the most important asset in the organisation?	
5.7.2	Have we calculated the 'return-on-assets' we get from customers?	
5.7.3	Do we know the value we extract from each customer or segment?	
5.7.4	Have we calculated the value we could extract from the market?	

5.7.5	What investment is needed to extract this value?	
5.7.6	Over what time period, with what returns?	
5.7.7	Do the financial decision-makers agree with our view?	
6 Organisation: Processes and Culture		
6.1 Is our organisation focused on internal or external issues?		
6.1.1	What dictates the organisational design?	
6.1.2	Where is the customer in the 'structure?'	
6.1.3	How are objectives reviewed?	
6.1.4	What happens when the objectives are in conflict?	
6.1.5	How effective is organisation-wide communications?	
6.1.6	How responsive is the organisation to customer demands?	
6.1.7	How resistant is the organisation design to change?	
6.2 What is our organisation really good at – and does it matter?		
6.2.1	How does the organisation know what it is really good at?	
6.2.2	Do these competences make enough of a difference?	
6.2.3	How do you ensure that the core competences get the lion's share of the investment?	
6.2.4	Does the organisation know what needs to get done to compete?	
6.2.5	Does the organisation normally do everything itself?	
6.2.6	'Marketing' as a core competence?	
6.2.7	What will the organisation need to be good at tomorrow?	
6.3 What is going on with our Culture?		
6.3.1	How do you know how 'things are done around here?'	
6.3.2	What are the 'levers' that create culture?	
6.3.3	Do we understand the effects of the culture on the business results?	
6.3.4	Does management inspired culture matter in the organisation?	
6.3.5	What does the culture need to do or deliver today and tomorrow?	
6.3.6	How can culture be changed if necessary?	
6.3.7	How do you know if the culture has changed?	

6.4 Is our organisation joined up?		
6.4.1	How does the organisation resolve conflict between function and process?	
6.4.2	How are customer segments reflected in process?	
6.4.3	Is IT part of the process?	
6.4.4	Should functions be built around process?	
6.4.5	How effective are cross-organisation initiatives and tasks?	
6.4.6	How does the organisation ensure that customer value is created?	
6.4.7	Who should take the role of the customer champion in the organisation?	
6.5 Is our organisation driven by the right information?		
6.5.1	First – how do we get focused on today's customers?	
6.5.2	Is market information retained systematically?	
6.5.3	How much does the organisation know about the competition?	
6.5.4	How do we know what information we need?	
6.5.5	Who sees the information produced?	
6.5.6	How do we focus on tomorrow's (new and retained) customers?	
6.5.7	What is driving new product and service development?	
6.6 Which metrics are used to manage and drive our organisation?		
6.6.1	Does it all make sense?	
6.6.2	Who sees the management information (MI)?	
6.6.3	How do the financials fit into the organisational drivers?	
6.6.4	What are the informal measurement systems?	
6.6.5	How are metrics used to track behaviours?	
6.6.6	Are we using the most appropriate marketing metrics?	
6.6.7	Should you use proprietary measurement tools?	
6.7 Change management – what is that?		
6.7.1	How resistant is the organisation to change?	
6.7.2	How do we remain relevant as value migrates in the market?	
6.7.3	Can change be organised methodically?	

6.7.4	How do you monitor the change project itself?	
6.7.5	How do you make change to be non-threatening?	
6.7.6	What to do about the impact of change on the customer?	
6.7.7	What to do if resistance is so strong that change is not possible?	
7 Offerings		
7.1 Where is the customer value?		
7.1.1	What are the needs and wants of the target customers?	
7.1.2	Where is the customer value in the marketplace?	
7.1.3	Who else is competing for the customer value?	
7.1.4	Which customer value should we target (segmentation)?	
7.1.5	Where will the customer value be tomorrow (migration)?	
7.1.6	How much of the value can we expect to be able to extract?	
7.1.7	Do we have the skills and credibility to be able to extract this value?	
7.2 What is our value proposition?		
7.2.1	What is a value proposition?	
7.2.2	What is the role and purpose of a value proposition?	
7.2.3	How many value propositions?	
7.2.4	How do we create our value proposition(s)?	
7.2.5	How do we use our value proposition(s)?	
7.2.6	How do we gain active support for the value proposition(s)?	
7.2.7	How do we police the implementation of our value proposition(s)?	
7.3 What is the most appropriate business design for us?		
7.3.1	What are the different ways we can extract value (business profit models)?	
7.3.2	Which model(s) do we use at present?	
7.3.3	How effective are they at extracting ALL the value?	
7.3.4	Which models do our competitors use?	
7.3.5	Could we increase the value extracted by using a different model?	

7.3.6	Does this influence how we allocate resources?	
7.3.7	How can we measure how much value we extract (customer conversion)?	
7.4 Where are our new offerings?		
7.4.1	How much customer value is there in innovation and NPD?	
7.4.2	What is 'innovation?' New to who?	
7.4.3	What is 'new product or service development?'	
7.4.4	Where can innovation come from?	
7.4.5	Can customers be a prime source of innovation?	
7.4.6	How can we take innovation to market?	
7.4.7	What are the tests of good innovation?	
7.5 How do we assess the Risk?		
7.5.1	What is 'Risk?'	
7.5.2	How do we assess business risk?	
7.5.3	How do we assess environmental marketing risk?	
7.5.4	How do we assess competitive marketing risk?	
7.5.5	How do we assess the impact of these risks?	
7.5.6	What is our existing risk management strategy?	
7.5.7	What are the implications of the assessment?	
7.6 Are we managing the life cycle?		
7.6.1	Does the organisation believe that the product life cycle is NOT a self-fulfilling prophesy?	
7.6.2	Where are we on the curve?	
7.6.3	How can we bring demand forward?	
7.6.4	How can we get to the 'tipping point' first or fast?	
7.6.5	How can we stimulate growth?	
7.6.6	How can we grow in maturity?	
7.6.7	What are the best metrics to use to plot progress?	
7.7 How do we take our Offerings to market?		
7.7.1	How do we ensure the marketing mix is designed to 'enshrine' the customer value proposition?	
7.7.2	How can we ensure continued customer focus into implementation?	
7.7.3	What is the right speed to market?	

7.7.4	How do we build in 'change' to the implementation programme?	
7.7.5	How do we avoid tactics-led strategy?	
7.7.6	Where is the 'lifetime value' assessment?	
7.7.7	How do we ensure feedback from the market operations?	

MARGIN NOTES

3 Marketing and sales plan template

Strategic Marketing and Sales Plan

Paul Fifield

CONTENTS

<table>
<tr><th></th><th>Strategic questions</th><th>Strategic answers</th></tr>
<tr><td>1</td><td>EXECUTIVE SUMMARY:</td><td></td></tr>
<tr><td></td><td>The executive summary should be limited to ONE page and should describe the inputs and outputs from the plan as well as a brief rationale for the activities</td><td></td></tr>
<tr><td>2</td><td>BACKGROUND</td><td></td></tr>
<tr><td>3</td><td>STRATEGIC MARKETING PLAN:</td><td></td></tr>
<tr><td></td><td></td><td>This marketing plan is a ____ year ____ strategic plan, from [date] ____ to [date] ____. More detail is included on the first 12-month period of the plan, since this covers the ____ period.</td></tr>
<tr><td>4</td><td>MARKET AUDIT (PEST):</td><td></td></tr>
<tr><td></td><td>What are the key Social, cultural, economic and technological circumstances and the environmental factors that will affect or drive the plan?</td><td></td></tr>
<tr><td></td><td colspan="2">(External audit/PEST/Uncontrollables)
<table>
<tr><td>Social/Cultural
1
2
3
4
5</td><td>Economic
1
2
3
4
5</td></tr>
<tr><td>Political
1
2
3
4
5</td><td>Technological
1
2
3
4
5</td></tr>
<tr><td>The market
1
2
3
4
5
For example Size of market: What is the overall size of the market?This could be calculated in terms of:
1 Total addressable market
2 Target market for all players
3 Target market for us</td><td>Competition
1
2
3
4
5</td></tr>
</table>
</td></tr>
</table>

<table>
<tr><td>5</td><td>SWOT ANALYSIS:</td><td></td></tr>
<tr><td></td><td>Identify the key (not 'all') strengths, weaknesses that the organisation has and should use/protect.Maximum of 6 in each box and SWOT items have to be assessed from the customers' point of view. A quick guide to strategy can be gained by asking three questions (convergence):
(a) How are we going to convert weaknesses into strengths?
(b) How can we convert threats into opportunities?
(c) How can we convert strengths into opportunities?</td><td></td></tr>
<tr><td></td><td colspan="2">(Internal/Controllable) (External/Uncontrollable)
Strengths: 1 2 3 4 5 6 | Opportunities: 1 2 3 4 5 6
Weaknesses: 1 2 3 4 5 6 | Threats: 1 2 3 4 5 6</td></tr>
<tr><td>6</td><td>REQUIREMENTS OF KEY IMPLEMENTERS</td><td></td></tr>
<tr><td></td><td></td><td>1
2
3</td></tr>
<tr><td>7</td><td>WHAT ARE THE FINANCIAL HURDLES?</td><td></td></tr>
<tr><td></td><td></td><td>1
2
3
4</td></tr>
<tr><td>8</td><td>BUSINESS OBJECTIVE</td><td></td></tr>
<tr><td></td><td>The aim or goal to which all the resources of the organisation are directed</td><td>'To … '</td></tr>
<tr><td>9</td><td>BUSINESS STRATEGY:</td><td></td></tr>
<tr><td></td><td>The means by which we will achieve the objective. The strategy has to be both 'Necessary' and 'Sufficient' to achieve the objective</td><td>'By … '</td></tr>
</table>

10	**CRITICAL ASSUMPTIONS:**	
	What are the 'unknowns' that we are still unsure of and that have the power to disrupt the plans that we are laying – these uncertainties should be reduced as we progress to implementation.	1 2 3 4 5
11	**MARKETING OBJECTIVES:**	
	These translate the business objective into market (street) terms.	'To … '
	The marketing objectives (not too many now) will become the organisation's Key Performance Indicators (KPIs) – choose with care	1 2 3 4
12	**MARKETING STRATEGY:**	
	The means by which we will achieve the marketing objective – and align the business to the market(s) that it wishes to serve. *Will involve some combination of the Scorpio model as below*	
	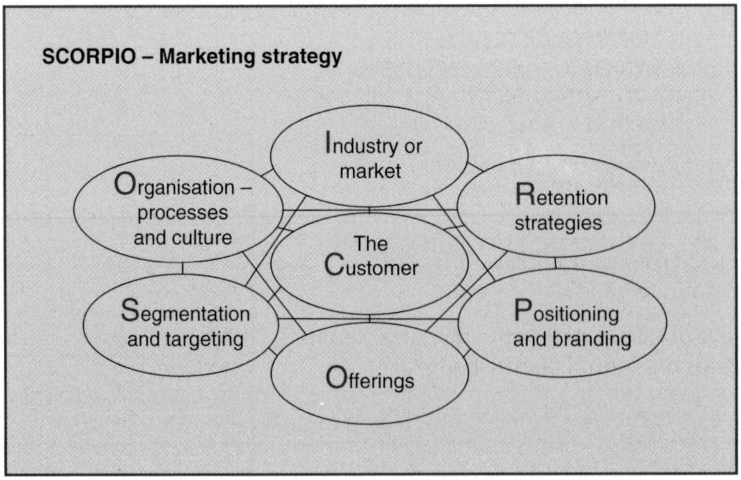 **SCORPIO – Marketing strategy** Industry or market Organisation – processes and culture Retention strategies The Customer Segmentation and targeting Positioning and branding Offerings	
	In the early stages, you may wish the plan to concentrate on, as an absolute minimum, the four following areas: (a) *Industry or Market* (b) *The Customer* (c) *Segmentation and Targeting* (d) *Positioning and Branding*	

	This focus may + be appropriate: (a) *Because these are the key customer-facing issues* (b) *The organisation may be early in the development of marketing/customer focus and other issues are still developing, and will be fully developed during the next few months/quarters.*	
12a	**Industry or Market**	
	One of the oldest, and most vexing questions facing business managers – 'what business are we in?' and, 'what business should we be in'? First raised in Levitt's article 'Marketing Myopia' in 1960, and rarely answered since then, this is the central question behind any practical marketing strategy. If you do not know what business you are in, you cannot know what customers you are trying to serve and what competition you are facing. *However, underlying this question is the fundamental problem that still faces most organisations, how to compete in today's markets with the handicap of a product or technology focus. The literature and the business press is full of examples of organisations that have failed to reach their full potential simply because they were unable to place their customers' needs and wants before internal product/technology imperatives.The strategic checklist for your organisation is:*	

1 What business are we in?	*What are we currently selling? How do we define what we are and what we do?*
2 What business do we want to be in or should we be in?	*How might this be expressed in market terms?*
3 How does this define the market/customer needs we should be satisfying?	*What solutions are the target customers seeking?*
4 Where/how should we be growing the business?	*What solutions should we be addressing next?*
5 What are the strategic opportunities and threats?	*What are the market and environmental factors?*
6 What competition are we facing?	*Who is offering alternative solutions?*
7 What are the boundaries for effort?	*What should we be doing more of/less of?*

12b	**Our Customers**	
	Lest we forget, the customer is the name of the game.	

	Customers produce all the organisation's revenues and profits and are the only reason for an organisation's continued existence. At the very least the organisation intent on survival will need to know who its customers are and what they want. *The organisation intent on achieving success rather than simple survival will need to much more if it is to compete successfully in rapidly internationalising markets. Although 'knowing' may itself be a tall order – often customers do not really 'know' what they want, they just want – and need.* *What is the current analysis of the customer base?* *Do we know where the target customers are?* *What are their most important (driving) needs and wants?* *The strategic checklist for your organisation is:*	

1 Who are they?	*What do we really know about our customers?*
2 What do they currently buying from us/our competitors and why?	*Remember that customers buy benefits, not 'features!*
3 What are their problems/needs/wants?	*Customers will normally pay for solutions to existing problems – they do not need additional problems.*
4 What do they want from us now/will they want in the future?	*Anticipation of future needs and wants is the key to revenue and profit growth.*
5 What barriers are getting in the way?	*Are the barriers external or are there internal barriers that we create?*
6 What will make them come to us?	*And the answer is unlikely to be 'price'*
7 Where do customers interface (connect) with our organisation?	*Check all the points of contact – and make sure they are joined up*

12c	**Market Segmentation and Targeting**	
	Market Segmentation or customer profiling is one of the basics of good marketing strategy. The 'mass market' is long dead and today one size no longer fits all! To compete effectively, segmentation is not a 'like-to-have' for marketers it is a 'must-have' tool.	

	It has been said that if the organisation is not talking segments, it is not talking markets (Levitt). Without an understanding of the different groupings of needs and wants in the marketplace no organisation can hope to have the clarity and depth of customer focus required to stay relevant. *There is no 'one way' of segmenting markets, it always depends on the sophistication of the market, the degree of competition and the ability of the organisation to market to more than one segment.* *The strategic checklist for your organisation is:*	
	1 What is the current state of segmentation in the organisation?	*No matter what it is called, how is the market 'broken up' currently?*
	2 What do we want segmentation to do for our organisation?	*Don't get involved until you know what you want from the investment*
	3 What segments exist in our target market?	*How are they different? Can you explain it simply?*
	4 How durable are the segments identified?	*Why invest in them unless you know they will repay on the investment?*
	5 How can we prioritise the segments for approach?	*Which order should we approach the segments? Everything at the same time is unlikely to succeed.*
	6 Which segments should we target?	*Which segments should we ignore/ avoid? There are always some customers that we will never make a profit from.*
	7 How can we market to different segments?	*Without confusing the whole market with offers that just do not make sense to them (in that segment)*
12d	**Positioning and Branding**	
	Whether you believe in market positions or brands rather depends on whether you and your organisation believe in differentiation or 'slugging it out' in commodity markets of your own creation. *Customers do not want the cheapest nor do they want the same offer from all suppliers – research shows this in every market. In this scenario, the brand really is the ultimate vehicle for wealth creation.*	

	Commodity markets really do not exist unless commodity marketers are intent on creating them. Being the cheapest and benchmarking the closest competitor to create the ultimate 'standard' offer is not strategy. Marketing strategy is about being different, not about being the same. *The strategic checklist for your organisation is:*	
	1 Differentiation or 'Commodity' marketing?	*Positioning is about uniqueness, which is about VALUE in your customers' eyes – it is not about being the same as all the others.*
	2 Which market positions exist?	*What positions do the competition hold? What positions are 'credible' from the customers' perspective?*
	3 What market position do we own, or do we want to own?	*How can we be first?*
	4 How are we going to be different from the competition?	*Does your organisation believe in Brands or Commodities? If the former, are you clear what you are creating?*
	5 What is a brand? What are its unique 'values' and 'personality?'	*The brand is the ultimate vehicle for wealth creation but it cannot be done without the support of the whole marketing mix*
	6 What are the costs and benefits of building a brand?	*A brand is more than just a name, it makes unique promises, and is trusted to keep them, that takes time and money*
	7 How do we invest in the brand and a differentiated market position?	*Brands are about strategy, not just tactics!*
12e	**Retention Strategies**	
	The value of customer retention has been researched, written about, conferenced and discussed – but rarely applied. The systems and structures of most organisations make it difficult to do much more than talk about 'lifetime value' or 'relationships' although, over time and with increased competition, this will change. *Also changing are accepted ideas about strategy. Generally, the older (1980s) ideas are being replaced by new thinking. Today's markets are too fast moving to allow any of us to stand back from the competitive battle long enough to draw elaborate plans and 'emergent strategy' is staring to make an impact.*	

	However, speed of response should not be confused with customer focus, nor should the search for increased value imply that the mantra 'Cheaper-Faster-Smaller' is all there is to retention. Recent adoptees of some of the CRM systems currently being sold will soon appreciate that there is more to creating and maintaining relationships than cutting costs among front-line staff! *The strategic checklist for your organisation is:*	

1 How important is 'Retention' in our market?	*Do the numbers, you will convince nobody otherwise*
2 How big is the 'problem' and the potential gains?	*Exactly how much money will you get back from improved retention?*
3 Is retention just about customer satisfaction?	*No. Its about commitment.*
4 Do accounting and reporting systems impede retention activities?	*Yes. How can you get round them?*
5 How good is our Marketing Information Systems (MkIS)?	*How do you hope to get more customers to stay longer without understanding what they want more of?*
6 What is the strategic role of Customer Relationships?	*If it does not fit into strategy it will not be done*
7 How are we planning to invest in our primary asset?	*Your customers are your primary asset and under threat from competition every day.*

12f	**Organisation: Processes and Culture**	
	Although not traditionally a part of marketing, no amount of careful planning or accurate research will pay off unless the organisation is able to deliver on its customers' needs. The systems, structures and culture of any organisation tend to be created for the benefit of the people working in the organisation rather than for the customers of the organisation. This is not mischievous – it just is. Nevertheless, organisation systems need to be in line with customer needs and expectations if the business is to survive – they will need to be actively supportive of customer needs if the organisation is to grow.	

	Culture is most often defined as 'the way we do things round here.' The hidden element that can create (and destroy) customer relationships can be changed but the task should not be underestimated. *The strategic checklist for your organisation is:*	

1 Is the organisation focused on internal or external issues?	*We know the answer – how can you make the organisation customer friendly?*
2 What is the organisation really good at – and does it matter?	*You will need core competences to be different*
3 What is going on with Culture?	*Culture can kill – if it's not the right one*
4 Is the organisation joined up?	*Does anyone manage the organisation and line it up to face the customer?*
5 Is the organisation driven by the right information?	*Customer, not product/service information is required*
6 Which metrics are used to manage and drive the organisation?	*What get measured gets done – measure the bright things*
7 Change management – what is that?	*The organisation must change – to keep up with its customers*

12g	**Offerings**	
	Offerings are about much more than just the products or services that the organisation presents to the market and managing the offerings is a strategic task *We need to really understand our target customers' needs and wants and how these are likely to change and modify in the future. Nothing is static and value in the marketplace will migrate over time – if we do not follow (or better, anticipate) such migration we will lose sales and eventually be overtaken by competition.* *The Value Proposition is a difficult task but essential if marketing is to create consistent offers and messaging to meet market needs. The Value Proposition also crystallises the unique properties of the offer and so safeguards or profits over the longer term* *The strategic checklist for your organisation is:*	

<table>
<tr><td></td><td colspan="2">
<table>
<tr><td>1 Where is the Customer Value?</td><td>The customer's search for Value must drive all that we do – what do they see?</td></tr>
<tr><td>2 What is the Value Proposition?</td><td>The CVP should drive ALL activities – spend time on it – get it right</td></tr>
<tr><td>3 What is the most appropriate business design?</td><td>So that it can deliver maximum customer value and extract maximum financial value from the market</td></tr>
<tr><td>4 Where are the new offerings?</td><td>Value migrates – how are we managing the flow of new ideas to offerings?</td></tr>
<tr><td>5 How do we assess the Risk?</td><td>Business is about risk – but risk should be identified and managed</td></tr>
<tr><td>6 Are we managing the life cycle?</td><td>The life cycle is not written in stone, do we manage it or are we driven by it?</td></tr>
<tr><td>7 How do we take the Offerings to market?</td><td>Routes to market and the use of partners/intermediaries/co-opertition is crucial and strategic</td></tr>
</table>
</td></tr>
<tr><td>13</td><td>IMPLEMENTATION</td><td></td></tr>
<tr><td></td><td>Transforming the strategy into action:</td><td></td></tr>
<tr><td>13a</td><td>The Marketing Mix:</td><td></td></tr>
<tr><td></td><td>The marketing mix shows all the different elements involved in successfully getting a service to market, and the key relationships between these different elements.</td><td></td></tr>
<tr><td>13b</td><td>Product Policy</td><td></td></tr>
<tr><td></td><td>The product 'portfolio' that will meet the described customer needs and will establish a differentiated position/brand in the marketplace.</td><td></td></tr>
<tr><td></td><td colspan="2">
<table>
<tr><td>To be developed</td><td>To be improved</td><td>To be discontinued</td></tr>
<tr><td>■
■</td><td>■
■</td><td>■
■</td></tr>
</table>
</td></tr>
<tr><td>13c</td><td>Pricing Policy</td><td></td></tr>
<tr><td></td><td>What pricing (including discounts and intermediary pricing (if relevant)) to support the strategy?</td><td></td></tr>
<tr><td>13d</td><td>Distribution Policy</td><td></td></tr>
<tr><td></td><td>Routes to Market are essential at this point</td><td></td></tr>
</table>

13e	**People Policy**	
	Who are the people (including customer service) to support the strategy and position/brand?	
13f	**Physical Evidence Policy**	
	How do we make the intangible service more tangible therefore easier to understand?	
13g	**Processes Policy**	
	How do we integrate the customer into the delivery process?	
13h	**Promotion Policy**	
	How do we communicate the unique values and attributes of the service to the target market so that they will test and buy? *The four questions are:*	
	1 Who is the one person you want to talk to?	
	2 What is the one thing you want to say to them?	
	3 Why should they believe you?	
	4 How do you want them to feel as a result?	
13g	**Timing:** *A detailed plan for the first year in detail and the second year in outline – with all inputs (marketing) and outputs (for example, finance) included.*	
14	**BUSINESS DEVELOPMENT**	
	Definition:	
	Business Development is the activity of initiating and brokering strategic partnerships and affiliate deals with the aim of building the business commercially, strategically and globally.	
14a	**Business Development Objective:**	'To … '
14b	**Business Development Strategy:**	'To … '
14c	**Business Development Areas:**	'To … '
14d	**Business Development Tactics:**	'To … '
15	**SALES PROGRAMMES**	
	How do the sales (theoretically part of marketing communications but normally listed separately) link into the overall plan? *Include detailed timings of sales campaigns and expected sales revenues*	

16	**RESOURCE PLANNING**	
	What resources are required for the plan to be implemented?	
16a	**People**	
16b	**Money**	
17	**TIMING**	
	Detailed timings of all activities – may include pre and post launch of various activities	
18	**GLOSSARY**	
	To explain any terms that may not be commonly understood in the organisation	

4 Linking market strategy with market research

To be truly market-based, the strategy needs to be securely rooted in information collected from the marketplace. Independent data is always best, it avoids any chance of internal bias and it may help to persuade staff and senior managers of the need for change.

Step one: Identify the key steps in the process of developing the market strategy

Step two: Identify the key steps in the process of developing the market research programme:

Market strategy	and	Market research
What business? *(Industry or Market?)*	↓	Desk research
Business objective		Industry background, discover the already researched
Business strategy		Qualitative research
Market objective(s)		Test 'What Business' hypothesis
Market strategy **(SCORPIO)**		Identify the critical market issues
Customer needs		Pre-Quantitative market assessment
Segmentation and targeting		Quantitative research
Positioning and branding		Assess most important market issues
Retention		Customer needs, wants and perceptions
Organisation structure and culture		Segmentation
Offerings		Competition
Market tactics		Analysis
Product, Price. Place, Promotion		Segmentation
Market plans		Prioritisation of company focus
Implementation		Metrics and controls
Control systems		Presentation

Step three: Link the market strategy process with the market research process to create a total development process

Step four: Draw out the combined activities into a detailed activity plan

Market strategy	and	Market research
What business? *(Industry or Market?)*		Desk research
Business objective		Industry background, discover the already researched
Business strategy		Qualitative research
Market objective(s)		Test 'What Business'hypothesis
Market strategy (SCORPIO)		Identify the critical market issues
Customer needs		Pre-Quantitative market assessment
Segmentation and targeting		Quantitative research
Positioning and branding		Assess most important market issues
Retention		Customer needs, wants and perceptions
Organisation structure and culture		Segmentation
Offerings		Competition
Market tactics		Analysis
Product, Price. Place, Promotion		Segmentation
Market plans		Prioritisation of company focus
Implementation		Metrics and controls
Control systems		Presentation

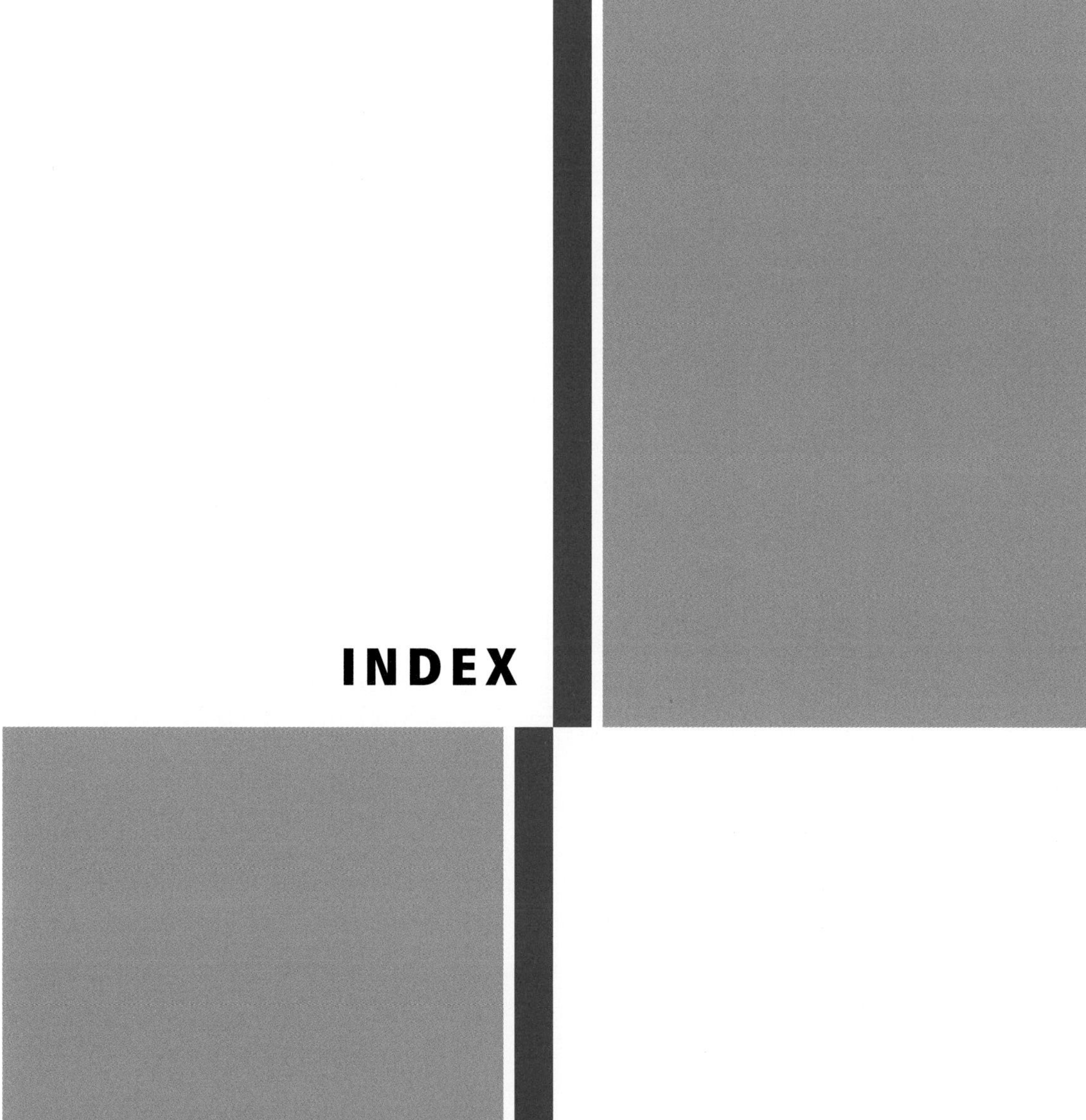

INDEX